The Political Economy of Financial Crises
Volume I

The International Library of Writings on the New Global Economy

Series Editor: Helen V. Milner
B.C. Forbes Professor of Politics and International Affairs
Princeton University, USA

1. Environment in the New Global Economy (Volumes I and II)
    Peter M. Haas

2. Foreign Aid in the New Global Economy
    Peter Burnell and Oliver Morrissey

3. International Monetary Relations in the New Global Economy (Volumes I and II)
    Benjamin J. Cohen

4. International Conflict and the Global Economy
    Edward D. Mansfield

5. The Political Economy of Financial Crises (Volumes I and II)
    Roy E. Allen

Future titles will include:

International Institutions in the New Global Economy
Lisa L. Martin

Wherever possible, the articles in these volumes have been reproduced as originally published using facsimile reproduction, inclusive of footnotes and pagination to facilitate ease of reference.

For a list of all Edward Elgar published titles visit our site on the World Wide Web at
www.e-elgar.com

The Political Economy of Financial Crises
Volume I

Edited by

Roy E. Allen

*Professor of Economics
and Dean, School of Economics and Business Administration
Saint Mary's College of California, USA*

THE INTERNATIONAL LIBRARY OF WRITINGS ON THE NEW GLOBAL ECONOMY

An Elgar Reference Collection
Cheltenham, UK • Northampton, MA, USA

Published by
Edward Elgar Publishing Limited
Glensanda House
Montpellier Parade
Cheltenham
Glos GL50 1UA
UK

Edward Elgar Publishing, Inc.
136 West Street
Suite 202
Northampton
Massachusetts 01060
USA

A catalogue record for this book is available from the British Library.

Library of Congress Cataloguing in Publication Data

The political economy of financial crises / edited by Roy E. Allen.
     p. cm. — (The international library of writings on the new global economy ; 5) (An Elgar reference collection)
   Includes bibliographical references and index.
   1. Financial crises. I. Allen, Roy E., 1957- II. Series. III. Series: An Elgar reference collection

HB3722.P654 2004
338.5'42—dc22   2004053039

ISBN   1 84376 106 8 (2 volume set)

Printed and bound in Great Britain by MPG Books Ltd, Bodmin, Cornwall

Contents

Acknowledgements

The editor and publishers wish to thank the authors and the following publishers who have kindly given permission for the use of copyright material.

American Economic Association for article: Graciela L. Kaminsky and Carmen M. Reinhart (1999), 'The Twin Crises: The Causes of Banking and Balance-of-Payments Problems', *American Economic Review*, **89** (3), June, 473–500.

Blackwell Publishing Ltd for articles: Rod Cross and Douglas Strachan (1997), 'On George Soros and Economic Analysis', *Kyklos*, **50** (4), 561–74; Riccardo De Bonis, Alessandro Giustiniani and Giorgio Gomel (1999), 'Crises and Bail-Outs of Banks and Countries: Linkages, Analogies, and Differences', *World Economy*, **22** (1), January, 55–86; Roberto Marchionatti (1999), 'On Keynes' Animal Spirits', *Kyklos*, **52** (3), 415–38; Brigitte Granville (1999), 'Bingo or Fiasco? The Global Financial Situation is not Guaranteed', *International Affairs*, **75** (4), October, 713–28; Jesper Rangvid (2001), 'Second Generation Models of Currency Crises', *Journal of Economic Surveys*, **15** (5), 613–46; Graham Bird and Ramkishen S. Rajan (2001), 'Banks, Financial Liberalisation and Financial Crises in Emerging Markets', *World Economy*, **24** (7), July, 889–910; Prema-chandra Athukorala and Peter G. Warr (2002), 'Vulnerability to a Currency Crisis: Lessons from the Asian Experience', *World Economy*, **25** (1), January, 33–57; Taimur Baig and Ilan Goldfajn (2002), 'Monetary Policy in the Aftermath of Currency Crises: The Case of Asia', *Review of International Economics*, **10** (1), February, 92–112.

Carnegie Endowment for International Peace and Copyright Clearance Center, Inc. for article: George Soros (1998–99), 'Capitalism's Last Chance?', *Foreign Policy*, **113**, Winter, 55–66.

Cato Institute for article: Alan Greenspan (1998), 'The Globalization of Finance', *Cato Journal*, **17** (3), Winter, 243–50.

Philip G. Cerny for his own excerpt: (1993), 'The Political Economy of International Finance', in Philip G. Cerny (ed.), *Finance and World Politics: Markets, Regimes and States in the Post-hegemonic Era*, Chapter 1, 3–19.

Federal Reserve Bank of Kansas City for article: Charles Morris and Klara Parrish (1997), 'Maintaining Financial Stability in a Global Economy: A Summary of the Bank's 1997 Symposium', *Federal Reserve Bank of Kansas City Economic Review*, **82** (4), Fourth Quarter, 23–35.

Kluwer Academic/Plenum Publishers for excerpt: Paul Krugman (1999), 'Balance Sheets, the Transfer Problem, and Financial Crises', in Peter Isard, Assaf Razin and Andrew K. Rose (eds), *International Finance and Financial Crises: Essays in Honor of Robert P. Flood, Jr.*, Partly reprinted from *International Tax and Public Finance*, **6** (4), (1999), 31–44, 265–68.

Manchester University Press and the University of Michigan Press for article: Susan Strange (1998), 'The New World of Debt', *New Left Review*, **230**, July–August, 91–114.

MIT Press Journals for article: Linda Y.C. Lim (1998), 'Whose "Model" Failed? Implications of the Asian Economic Crisis', *Washington Quarterly*, **21** (3), Summer, 25–36.

New Left Review for article: Robert Wade and Frank Veneroso (1998), 'The Asian Crisis: The High Debt Model Versus the Wall Street–Treasury–IMF Complex', *New Left Review*, **228**, March–April, 3–23.

Ohio State University Press for article: Paul Krugman (1979), 'A Model of Balance-of-Payments Crises', *Journal of Money, Credit, and Banking*, **11** (3), August, 311–25.

Oxford University Press for articles: Chalmers Johnson (1998), 'Economic Crisis in East Asia: The Clash of Capitalisms', *Cambridge Journal of Economics*, **22**, 653–61; Lance Taylor (1998), 'Capital Market Crises: Liberalisation, Fixed Exchange Rates and Market-driven Destabilisation', *Cambridge Journal of Economics*, **22**, 663–76; J.A. Kregel (1998), 'Derivatives and Global Capital Flows: Applications to Asia', *Cambridge Journal of Economics*, **22**, 677–92; José De Gregorio and Rodrigo O. Valdés (2001), 'Crisis Transmission: Evidence from the Debt, Tequila, and Asian Flu Crises', *World Bank Economic Review*, **15** (2), 289–314; Philip Arestis and Murray Glickman (2002), 'Financial Crisis in Southeast Asia: Dispelling Illusion the Minskyan Way', *Cambridge Journal of Economics*, **26** (2), March, 237–60.

Taylor and Francis Ltd (http://www.tandf.co.uk/journals) for articles: Eric Helleiner (1995), 'Explaining the Globalization of Financial Markets: Bringing States Back In', *Review of International Political Economy*, **2** (2), Spring, 315–41; Jonathan Nitzan (1998), 'Differential Accumulation: Towards a New Political Economy of Capital', *Review of International Political Economy*, **5** (2), Summer, 169–216.

Every effort has been made to trace all the copyright holders but if any have been inadvertently overlooked the publishers will be pleased to make the necessary arrangement at the first opportunity.

In addition the publishers wish to thank the Marshall Library of Economics, Cambridge University and the Library of Indiana University at Bloomington, USA for their assistance in obtaining these articles.

Introduction

Roy E. Allen

During recent decades, across the world, the risk of large-scale financial crisis seems to have increased. In 1996, the International Monetary Fund (IMF) indicated that approximately three-quarters of its more than 180 member countries had encountered 'significant' banking sector problems between 1980 and 1995, one-third of which warrant the definition 'crisis' (Lindgren *et al.*, 1995). Then, in 1997, unexpectedly, the East Asian financial crisis struck, which was followed by the Russian and Brazilian crises in 1998 and various others, such as the Argentine crisis in 2002.

Unlike the more traditional and well-researched banking crises that have been resolved under domestic regulations, there has been no comprehensive international law or policy that sets out the procedures for the international community to follow in these recent episodes. The *ad hoc* rescue fund provided to Mexico after its crisis at the end of 1994 was unprecedented in size – approximately $50 billion – as well as in international political scope, given the ways that it involved the IMF, the US Treasury's Exchange Stabilization Fund (normally reserved for other purposes), the Bank for International Settlements, and a variety of independent countries. Mexico's oil export revenues could even be held by the Federal Reserve Bank of New York to guarantee US loans. *Ad hoc* financial bail-outs offered to Korea and Indonesia in 1997, and Brazil in 1998, were similarly large. In Indonesia's case, the IMF insisted on a variety of unprecedented restructuring requirements that were viewed by President Suharto as a direct challenge to his leadership, including the winding-up of some domestic monopolies that were associated with his family.

Given the magnitude and devastation of these recent crises, and the size of taxpayer funds committed to their resolution, there is now a flurry of policy-making activity. Recent initiatives coming from the IMF and elsewhere seem to be working toward bankruptcy procedures for countries, which is a stark contrast from the famous, and uninformed, quote of less than three decades ago (shortly before the 1982 Latin American debt crisis) from the Chairman of CitiCorp that 'countries don't go broke'. Of course, the academic and policy-making context for an 'international financial architecture' has a rich history. The Bretton Woods conference in 1944, which established the IMF and the predecessor to the World Bank and other current institutions, was a response to the international financial anarchy that had emerged in the 1930s. The Articles of Agreement established at that time favored the US plan presented by Harry Dexter White over the more ambitious plan proposed by John Maynard Keynes and the UK. The latter proposal involved a new international currency, bancor, and an International Clearing Union to settle international debts, as opposed to the more modest international stabilization fund advocated in the US plan. To a certain degree, policy-making now moves closer to the original Keynesian vision.

Complicating efforts by the IMF, central bankers and others in the current decade – to prevent and resolve country crises and to advance a better international financial architecture – is disagreement on how recent financial crises are related to recent 'globalization' of economic activity. When I published *Financial Crises and Recession in the Global Economy* in 1994, a member of the US Federal Reserve Board concluded (in *Choice* magazine, January 1995) that the author 'grossly overstates [that financial globalization] is the principal cause and explanation of various events that Allen exaggeratedly refers to as crises'. Yet now, in light of reoccurring, severe, and persistent episodes of financial instability, including 'contagion' from country to country, more policy-makers and others admit to a relationship between economic crisis and economic globalization.

Scholarly journals have been launched in recent decades to respond to these issues. For example, in the first edition of *Review of International Political Economy*, the editors state:

> The creation of a global economic order has come to represent the defining feature of our age, as a major force shaping economies and livelihoods in all areas of the world. Globalization, of course, has many aspects ... The first of these is the emergence of a truly global financial market ... and the resulting increase in the power of finance over production. (*Review of International Political Economy*, 1(1) (1994), p. 3)

Thus, a 'political economy of financial crisis' is called for in order to give perspective to the key issues and processes that surround recent large-scale financial crises, and in order to identify procedures that will help to avoid and manage crises. Each paper in this two-volume collection, drawn from leading journals, in one way or another, responds to this challenge. The academic fields from which journals and authors are selected reveal the interdisciplinary nature of the political economy of financial crisis, and they include (the already overlapping) economics, politics, international relations, political economy (PE), and international political economy (IPE). In my view, recent literature in PE and IPE comes closest to hitting the mark. Prominent contributors to both fields, since the Great Depression of the 1930s, as identified by articles in this collection, are also prominent contributors to the study of financial crisis, such as John Maynard Keynes, Charles Kindleberger, and Susan Strange. Some technical and mathematical material is included – mainly in the section on 'Models, Common Patterns', Volume I, Part II – but, in general, the papers are chosen such that a broad interdisciplinary audience will find the material accessible and useful as a text to support classes and research.

An excellent review of PE and IPE, including the place within them for research into financial systems, can be found in another relatively new journal entitled *New Political Economy*. Also, regarding the relationship between politics, economics, and markets, this review states the following broad perspective, which is shared by most authors included in this collection: '[Recent encyclopedias on both political economy and international political economy] treat the concept of a market in an identical manner, stressing that markets are social mechanisms that facilitate the exchange of ownership (or property) rights within a context of embedded rules and procedures legitimized by some form of organized authority' (Germain, 2002, p. 304). This broad institutionalist perspective of markets, which draws attention to legal, cultural, political, and social infrastructures, applies on the international level, as well as the national level, thus showing the close analytical bonds between political economy and international political economy. Using a principle of parsimony, it thus seems better to entitle this collection simply *The Political Economy of Financial Crises* rather than *The International Political ... * . As a further justification for this choice, not all of the issues herein necessarily have international dimensions, with 'international' taken to mean 'activities taking place between nations'. For example: how is money created, transferred, and destroyed?; and how 'rational' are financial market participants?

Volume I: Part I: Issues and Concepts

Part I sets forth the scope of this project. The papers were chosen to introduce the following issues: what is a financial crisis? Can we agree on certain definitions and distinctions – banking versus balance of payments versus country crisis; insolvency versus illiquidity; etc.? Are the complex factors that lead to a 'country crisis' similar to the well-known factors that lead to a smaller-scale 'banking crisis'? For banks or countries, what is the difference between a 'liquidity crisis' and a more fundamental 'solvency crisis'? What are the early warning signs, which seemed to be so absent before the 1997 Asian crisis? What international, multinational, transnational, global, etc. political and economic systems are involved, as opposed to strictly national systems? What 'international financial architecture' will best prevent and resolve these crises? What disciplines, theories, economic and political processes, current and historical events, etc. are relevant to the political economy of financial crisis? And how do all of these issues reflect on the nature of the various capitalisms and other political economic systems that are being practiced across the world?

Authors in this collection take an eclectic view of financial crises, rather than the narrower monetarist view that emphasizes sharp declines in the money supply. As per De Bonis *et al.* (1999) in Chapter 1, they generally define 'financial crisis' to be 'a wider range of disturbances, such as sharp declines in asset prices, failures of large financial intermediaries, or disruption in foreign exchange markets'. There is a 'crisis', generally speaking, because the real economy is seriously and adversely affected, including negative impacts on employment, production and purchasing power, as well as the possibility that large numbers of households and firms or governments are fundamentally unable to meet their obligations, i.e. 'insolvency'. The effort by authors to explain linkages between financial processes and real economic activity is thus central to this collection.

When an organization is fundamentally solvent but temporarily unable to meet its financial obligations, then the notion of 'illiquidity' is often used, but, in practice, insolvency and illiquidity are difficult to distinguish. For example, a common pattern is that 'vicious circles' start from a money-liquidity crisis at a few banks, which then extends to an international crisis of investor confidence in the financial sector, which extends to a balance-of-payments problem for the country and currency devaluation, which extends to, therefore, even further liquidity and solvency crises at the banks. Early indicators of these twin crises – in banking and balance of payments – include declines in international currency reserves, excess demand for money holdings, irregular domestic and foreign interest rate movements, and a variety of other 'shocks' in trade, government budget deficits, social or political upheaval, etc. (Kaminsky and Reinhart, 1999, Chapter 2).

A liquidity crisis that might initially be avoided with better inter-bank or government reserve funding might, thus, be allowed to grow into an economy-wide solvency crisis. Recent 'financial liberalization' – i.e. deregulation and globalization of financial markets – which allows more decentralized and unconstrained relationships between international financial market participants, who are now equipped with improved communications technologies, can increase the speed and risk of these vicious circles. Thus, the following policy-response question has become increasingly important: when should a 'lender-of-last-resort' prudently intervene with fresh funding to prevent 'contagion' and the risk of systemic failure? Intervention which is too early, too often, or not ultimately necessary encourages reckless and unproductive activity, including the 'moral hazard problem' that 'the authorities will save me from the adverse consequences of my actions'. And intervention is increasingly expensive to taxpayers, as mentioned above. Many of the chapters in Part I explore these and related issues, including: whether financial liberalization has been desirable for developing countries; the role that new financial products and 'derivatives' have played in increasing the volume and risk of destabilizing international financial flows (Kregel, 1998, Chapter 3, and Granville, 1999, Chapter 4); whether better measures of 'vulnerability' to financial crisis can be developed in light of the recent Asian crisis (Athukorala and Warr, 2002, Chapter 5); etc.

Is the market capitalist system itself vulnerable to financial crisis? The long-time tendency, across the world, for crises of 'over-lending' and 'over-borrowing' to occur leads many authors to conclude that financial markets, if left mainly to themselves, will inevitably suffer crises. The trend of the last two decades toward relaxing regulations, while the international supply of lending rapidly increases, has likely over-supplied funds to borrowers beyond prudent assessments of ability to pay. As authoritatively summarized by Kindleberger in *Manias, Panics, and Crashes: A History of Financial Crises* (1989), over the long history of market capitalism, the start of an unsustainable financial boom or 'mania' is always linked to a sudden increase in money liquidity and lending. Unstable and exaggerated expectations, which are quite subjective, play a role:

> The heart of this book is that the Keynesian theory is incomplete [in explaining economic instabilities and crises], and not merely because it ignores the money supply. Monetarism is incomplete, too. A synthesis of Keynesianism and monetarism, such as the Hansen-Hicks IS-LM curves that bring together the investment-saving (IS) and liquidity-money (LM) relationships, remains incomplete, even when it brings in production and prices (as does the most up-to-date macroeconomic analysis), if it leaves out the instability of expectations, speculation, and credit and the role of leveraged speculation in various assets. (Kindleberger, 1989, p. 25)

Given the increased importance, across a larger and more dynamic global political economy, of subjective expectations, leveraged investment as supported by new electronic money forms, unregulated no-reserve-requirement offshore financial markets, etc., some current research is consistent with the innovative notion that monetary wealth, or what Marx would call 'unproductive finance capital' (as opposed to physical capital or capital goods such as machines and factories) may be a 'driver' of economic instabilities. As elaborated by Cerny (1993) in Chapter 6, the new global financial markets may even be an 'infrastructure of the infrastructure'. Cerny's initial position, elaborated in debates that began in the early 1990s, is that 'a country without efficient and profitable financial markets and institutions will suffer multiple *dis*advantages in a more open world ... [and will] attempt to *free-ride* on financial globalization through increasing market liberalization' (Cerny, 1994, p. 338). In Chapter 7, Helleiner (1995) restrains this position – of a determinist, autonomous, technology-driven financial globalization – by demonstrating that states, especially the USA and the UK, have fostered and guided the entire process.

Nevertheless, reversing the causality of Karl Marx's philosophical materialism, it may increasingly be true that autonomous, invisible financial processes can drive changes in the physical relations of production, as well as vice versa. As part of this process, central banks and other financial market participants can (haphazardly) increase or reduce wealth independently of any initial changes in the production of GDP or other 'real' economic prospects. Chairman of the US Federal Reserve Alan Greenspan allows for this possibility (1998, Chapter 8):

> Today's central banks have the capability of creating or destroying unlimited supplies of money and credit ... It is probably fair to say that the very efficiency of global financial markets, engendered by the rapid proliferation of financial products, also has the capability of transmitting mistakes at a far faster pace throughout the financial system in ways that were unknown a generation ago, and not even remotely imagined in the 19th century ... Clearly, not only has the productivity of global finance increased markedly, but so, obviously, has the ability to generate losses at a previously inconceivable rate.

Depending on the magnitudes of the transfers, re-evaluations, and creation of monetary wealth over (how much) time and space, serious real effects can be produced over time and space. These processes, traditionally not emphasized by either mainstream or Marxist economics, can nevertheless help to explain what the mainstream has historically understood as 'business cycles' or 'debt-deflation crises' (Fisher, 1933) and what Marxists have understood as crises of 'underconsumption', 'overproduction', and 'disproportionality' (Clarke, 1994).

If, although as a simplification, economics is the study of wealth, and politics is the study of power, then a key issue for this collection is the broader relationship between financial crisis and the creation, and distribution, of wealth and power. Thus, the following questions arise: what is money and wealth?; how are they created, transferred, and destroyed in the episodes that we call 'financial crises'?; and how do these crises affect the economic, political, and social power of involved parties? Some research advances the innovative notion that the subjective monetary wealth or 'capital' that is lost or transferred in financial crises might represent the first-round appropriation of broad social powers between affected parties – Nitzan (1998, Chapter 9) discusses this possibility and summarizes the ways that current neoclassical, Marxist, and other fields of thought deal with capital, wealth, and power. Similarly, finance capital might sometimes represent the first-round creation of new (rather than appropriation of fully existing) social powers – a conclusion I have arrived at recently (Allen, 1999). Of course, these re-evaluations of wealth during crisis episodes take place within a larger political-economic system, which at the moment, in the fight over capital flows, seems to favor the US and the 'Wall Street–Treasury–IMF Complex' (Wade and Veneroso, 1998, Chapter 10).

The larger political economic system, within which recent financial crises have occurred, includes a variety of competing forms of capitalism, including what authors describe as 'Anglo-American economic orthodoxy' versus 'the Asian model' and others. Johnson (1998, Chapter 11) and Lim (1998, Chapter 12) discuss the advantages and risks of these variants, especially as revealed by the recent South East Asian crisis. Soros (1998–9, Chapter 13), the consummate financial market insider, critiques Anglo-American 'free market fundamentalism' as pioneered by Ronald Reagan and Margaret Thatcher in the early 1980s. Instead, Soros suggests that newly deregulated global financial markets are inherently unstable and, in the absence of urgent reforms, they could produce ever greater crises and a powerful backlash against the global capitalist system, especially from the poorer countries on the periphery. He suggests a political-economic framework reminiscent of Keynes's position at the 1944 Bretton Woods conference, including a greater role for an international currency, international credit insurance, and other measures to reduce the natural fallibility and inequity of markets.

Susan Strange (1998, Chapter 14) provides further context for the political economy of 'the new world of debt', including an update to her 1986 assessment of 'casino capitalism', which observed: 'The sorry state of the financial system is undoubtedly aggravating the difficulties in the path of economic development for poor countries while conversely the difficulties of the deeply indebted developing countries, so long as they persist, will aggravate the instability of the banking system' (Strange, 1986, p. 181).

What to do on the policy-making side now that, since the mid-1990s, there is a consensus even in the orthodox mainstream that the risk of large-scale financial crisis has increased? Part I finishes constructing its fence around the scope of this project with a summary of a 1997 symposium that attempted to answer this question (Morris and Parrish, 1997, Chapter 15). The symposium, entitled 'Maintaining Financial Stability in a Global Economy', brought together policy-makers from the IMF, Bank for International Settlements, and various central banks, as well as various leading academics and financial market professionals, and it thus allows the reader an understanding of the major policy issues that first flowed from this new consensus of concern.

Volume I: Part II: Models, Common Patterns

The papers in Part II of this collection were chosen to answer the following questions: do the financial crises of recent decades share common patterns from start to finish, or are they fairly unique in time and space? Do taxonomies of recent crises lead to an obvious list of key crisis-related variables and important cause-and-effect relationships? What are the basic assumptions about political and economic systems that authors use to direct their scientific investigations into these issues?

Recent models of large-scale financial crises are often characterized as 'first-generation' models or 'second generation' or, in the last few years, 'third generation'. First-generation models, as pioneered by Krugman in 1979 (Chapter 16) and others, emphasize the importance of a country's foreign exchange reserves – i.e. if government budget deficits are excessive, then ultimately a government loses the ability to maintain these reserves, and a speculative attack on its currency exchange rate is inevitable. Second-generation models, as summarized by Rangvid (2001) in Chapter 17, arose during the 1990s when this cause–effect linkage no longer seemed to explain various currency crises. In particular, there now seems to be a weaker relationship between economic fundamentals, such as public sector deficits, and the timing and severity of speculative currency attacks and related instabilities. The timing of government decisions to abandon a currency regime in favor of other political-economic goals has also proved difficult to predict. Second-generation models thus tell stories of 'multiple equilibrium' values that key variables might assume, unpredictable or irrational behavior by private investors and governments, and there has been an effort to discover new 'sunspot variables' that will better explain sudden changes in markets.

Third-generation models, as per Krugman's treatment in 1999 (Chapter 18), introduce additional variables and feedback processes, especially the role of companies' and entrepreneurs' balance sheets, and the impact of international financial flows and exchange rates on those balance sheets. During and after the 1997 Asian financial crises, the financial condition of firms weakened more than was anticipated by second-generation models, which drew attention to these processes. Furthermore, until new entrepreneurs come forward, or until balance sheets return to normal, it has been difficult for economies to return to normal growth and stability.

Second- and now third-generation models have not yet fully explained sudden movements in exchange rates, interest rates, international investment flows, and other key variables related to recent financial crises. Thus, there is a revival of interest in what Keynes, in *The General Theory*, called 'animal spirits' such as 'spontaneous optimism' among entrepreneurs and others (Marchionatti, 1999, Chapter 19). Essentially, Keynes argued that people may have a limited cognitive and informational basis for fully rational decision-making, and therefore, they may rely on less rational social conventions, vague beliefs, and other psychological factors. One implication is that: 'the market will be subject to waves of optimistic and pessimistic sentiment, which are unreasoning and yet in a sense legitimate where no solid basis exists for a reasonable calculation' (Keynes, 1936, p. 154). How to build models under these circumstances? In Chapter 20, Cross and Strachan (1997) argue that a 'bounded rationality' can still yield useful predictions, and they survey this approach in the literature, especially the work of Keynes and the recent controversies generated by George Soros.

Regardless of these differences, between first-, second-, and third-generation models, between rationality and 'animal spirits' views, between endemically stable versus unstable market assumptions, etc., models developed and tested against recent experience do find common patterns, as discussed next. The remaining papers in Part II (Chapters 21–5), which use data and mostly second-generation models to explain recent large-scale crises, will not be summarized separately here. Rather, the reader will find that, collectively, they lead to these following cause–effect taxonomies.

In most recent episodes of large-scale financial crisis, a country or region initially benefits from expanded supplies of money, credit, and investment – a financial liberalization phase. The financial sector expands as it captures profit from new efficiencies and opportunities allowed by deregulation, technological change, and new international opportunities. The country or region, for a time, may be favored by international investors; thus, the banking system, including government, is well-capitalized and able to expand money-liquidity. Financial assets increase in monetary value and interest rates are low, and this wealth effect encourages consumption, borrowing, business investment, and perhaps government spending. Productive resources are more fully utilized and economic growth is well supported. There is a 'boom', as measured by increased (a) monetary wealth held by private and public sectors of an economy, such as the value of stocks, real estate, currency reserves, etc., and/or (b) the current production of merchandise and services (GDP).

Then, typically, the supply of money, credit, and/or investment contracts, and so does GDP. After this process starts, monetary policy-makers may react by rapidly expanding the money supply and issuing new debt to cover deficits – sometimes called 'sterilized intervention' – and trying to improve the environment for borrowing and investment, but this action may be too little too late. Individuals and institutions may have unpayable debts, banks may even be failing, and international confidence in the country or region may already be damaged. In this pessimistic case, which is typical in less-developed countries with weak financial systems, the desperate increase in money-liquidity may lead to hyper-inflation while GDP continues to fall. A weak financial system may be unable to maintain the circulation rate of secure currencies for productive activities, especially if people are hoarding money. Illiquidity, insolvency, and financial crisis, as defined in Part I, above, may be the result.

Keynes's 'waves of pessimism and optimism' can be seen in the liberalization and then contraction phases of crises, respectively. The initial contraction in money, credit, and/or investment may be realized when 'herd-like' national and international investors quickly move money from the country or region. A contraction in effective money supplies or withdrawal of international investment may undermine equity markets, debt markets, bank capital, or government reserves, and monetary wealth is then revalued downwards. General economic or political uncertainty worsens the situation – the resulting austerity mentality causes a contraction of spending and credit, and an increased 'risk premium' attached to business activity scares away investment. Interest rates rise, the demand for quasi-money and credit – i.e. the desire to hold and use the insecure 'monetary float' – declines and people try to convert the monetary float into more secure base money such as cash. No reserve-currency banking system is able to cover all of its monetary float with secure bank reserves if customers try to redeem all of the float at once, and thus 'runs' on banks can destroy the banks themselves. A deteriorating banking sector may be unable to honor its deposits, bad loan problems surface and a 'lender of last resort' such as the IMF may need to be found.

In the global economic system, the initial decline in money, credit, and investment in a *peripheral* country or region may be initiated by the financial *centers* or dominant reserve-currency countries in the *core* of the global system such as the USA. The base money used in the periphery, which backs its less secure quasi-moneys and credit expansion, may even be the centralized global reserve currency, typically the US dollar. For example, the 1982 debt crisis hit Latin America when the US dollar became scarce. Dollars had been loaned to Latin America in the 1970s at negative real interest rates, which provided the hard-currency monetary base for the dramatic expansion of local soft currency and credit – Latin America's financial liberalization and economic 'boom' phase. Then, because of US, UK, and other developed country monetary and fiscal policies in the early 1980s, dollar interest rates soared and dollars were both pushed and pulled out of Latin America into US deposits. Latin America lost dollar reserves, which were necessary to pay dollar-denominated debts; thus, Latin America lost its internationally recognized 'source of value', which could maintain the 'redemption value' of local moneys.

The bankruptcy of a country or region can be similar to the bankruptcy of a bank. The failure results from an insufficient supply of high-powered base money or high-quality liquid capital to honor the redemption value of the less secure monetary forms, which have been created in pyramid fashion from the secure base. Private goldsmith banks in the European Renaissance failed when they did not have enough gold to honor their gold notes; US thrifts failed in the 1980s when they ran out of hard dollar reserves to honor the soft dollar demand deposits which they had created; and Latin American economies failed when their monetary base proved insufficient to honor the monetary 'float' that had been created from that base.

Volume II: Part I: Country Studies

Country studies of the large-scale financial crises of the last two decades give breadth and depth to the basic concepts, patterns and models summarized in Volume I. For example, in

Chapters 1–6, the authors conclude that the Asian financial crises of 1997 shared most of the taxonomies identified in Volume I. First came the financial deregulation, liberalization, globalization, and 'boom' phase. The World Bank estimates that total international capital flows to 'emerging markets' increased from $50 billion in 1991 to $250 billion in 1996, with the majority going to Asia. Total capital formation (corporate, housing, and government investment) in Asia excluding Japan increased 300 per cent from 1990 to 1996, which compared with much lower increases of approximately 40 per cent in the US and Japan and 10 per cent in Europe. The important role that government interest groups, large family-owned conglomerates – *chaebols* in South Korea's case – and other organizations played in IMF-encouraged financial liberalization, in Eric Helleiner's words in Volume I, 'brings states and the political back in' the economic analysis of financial globalization. Economic deregulation and globalization becomes a more complicated and local process when various patron–client relations between official 'patrimonial' state apparatus and private interests are identified.

Perhaps Thailand was the most obvious home for international investment funds in this period. Technocrats had manipulated interest rates and currency exchange rates with a formula designed to bring in international capital – since 1987 the Thai authorities had kept their currency locked to the US dollar in a band of baht 25–6 to one dollar while maintaining domestic rates 500–600 basis points higher than US rates and keeping their borders open to capital flows. Because this Thai formula was so successful in attracting capital, it was soon copied by the central banks and finance ministers in the Philippines, Malaysia, and Indonesia. The International Monetary Fund and the World Bank praised these policies, especially the elimination of barriers between domestic and global financial markets. Newly deregulated offshore financial markets, such as the Bangkok International Banking Facility, allowed for unfettered 'waves of optimism' and excess lending into Thailand from international markets.

Then came dollar flight, monetary contraction, and crisis. Fears of inflation across the developed world were translated into contractionary monetary policies and interest rate increases of 1–2 percentage points for the 'hard' currencies of the developed countries. By mid-1997, the restrictive US dollar monetary policies, the supply–demand imbalance between the dollar and Asian currencies, and exaggerated optimism about developmental opportunities could no longer be denied. Asian monetary authorities no longer had enough reserves of US dollars to intervene (by selling them to the private markets) in support of their stable exchange rates (by buying local currencies off the private markets). The impossible rush to fully convert local quasi-moneys and credit into dollars happened, first, in Thailand with flight from the baht, and then the rush to convert was immediately copied in the Philippines, Malaysia, South Korea, Indonesia, and elsewhere. Devaluations, crashes in asset values, and capital flight were immediate, as were the resulting liquidity and solvency crises of weakened banks, companies, and governments.

The 'rush for the exit' by national and international investors, which often marks the start of a financial crisis, was especially pronounced in the 1994–5 Mexican crisis; and the Mexican case demonstrates how a country crisis can be similar to a classic bank run. In December 1994, when the Mexican government released data indicating that a currency devaluation was likely, traders rushed to get out of the peso. Furthermore, they removed their US dollar holdings out of Mexican institutions. These dollar holdings were very liquid, because debtors had issued short-term dollar bonds that promised redemption at face value. On 21 December 1994, $29 billion of dollar-denominated *tesobono* short-term liabilities were for sale, $18 billion of which were the responsibility of the Mexican government, and this news made the front page of the *Wall Street Journal*:

> Like small savers who see their neighbors lining up outside a bank and join the queue to withdraw their deposits before the bank's cash reserves are exhausted, investors in government bonds have an incentive to liquidate their holdings when others do likewise and they fear that the government's limited foreign exchange reserves will be exhausted ... the magnitude of capital flows can leave a government facing a debt run, like a bank facing a run by its depositors, no choice but to suspend payments, regardless of the damage to its creditworthiness. On the eve of the crisis, the Mexican government was responsible for more than $18 billion of dollar-denominated and dollar-indexed liabilities, roughly triple its foreign exchange reserves. Once investors began to liquidate their holdings, the authorities were at their mercy. (Eichengreen and Portes, in Federal Reserve Bank of Kansas City, 1997, p. 195)

Unlike most previous country crises, it was not possible to identify who Mexico's creditors were, much less coordinate them for a negotiated restructuring of Mexico's foreign debt. The newly deregulated, liberalized international financial environment allows for widespread and secondary ownership of country debt, unlike even the 1980s when fewer big institutional investors owned most country debt. This recent trend throughout the world has implications for policy responses to country debt crises, as discussed in Part II of Volume II.

Chapters 7 and 8 summarize and debate the possible causes of the 1994–5 Mexican crisis (Calvo and Mendoza, 1996, and Gil-Díaz and Carstens, 1996). As in Volume I, both 'first-generation models' of financial crisis and second-generation models are used. First-generation models, which would blame the crisis on unsustainable government deficits and related real phenomena, are given smaller weight than 'second-generation models' that emphasize disequilibrium, politically triggered speculative attacks against the currency, and herd-like behavior of investors. Mexico's vulnerability to speculative currency flows draws attention to its currency exchange rate regime, and whether an exchange rate can be overvalued or undervalued with respect to some equilibrium.

Brazil's crisis of 1998 shows the vulnerability of less-developed countries that have built up 'dependency' on capital inflows. Brazil's 'vicious circle' during the contraction phase – flight of foreign capital, higher interest rates and fiscal austerity to attract it back, negative impacts on domestic demand and economic growth, recession, further flight of foreign capital, etc. – provides a rich institutional context for a discussion of core–periphery issues. Namely, as elaborated in Rocha (2002, Chapter 9), 'movements on financial markets in the center are so huge that developments in the periphery are dwarfed by them. In practice, this meant that the Brazilian economy was at the mercy of international developments triggered by the opportunities or dangers facing core investors.'

These examples of financial crisis in Asia and Latin America demonstrate the vulnerability of various countries that have already, over decades, formalized many of the institutional arrangements for participation in the global economy. In contrast, the 1998 Russian financial crisis demonstrates the vulnerability of a post-communist transition state with a very short history of international financial liberalization. As argued by Robinson (1999) in Chapter 10, Russia is a perfect example of how 'interaction with the global economy can have a significant influence on the outcome of reform ... [including] how the post-communist state can be shaped by hopes for integration with the global economy and the resources that this might bring with it'.

In Chapter 11, these country financial crises are categorized further by Palma (2003), and the author aligns recent experiences in Chile and Argentina with Mexico. As this collection goes to press in early 2004, the Argentine situation continues to unfold, especially with regard to the international policy-making issues discussed in Part II of Volume II. Argentina maintained price stability and fixed currency parity with the US dollar for ten years until this currency board system failed in early 2002. The privatization, liberalization, capital inflow, and economic boom that occurred during these ten years came to a sudden end as the dollar appreciated and less international capital flowed to emerging markets like Argentina. Thus, Argentina's crisis demonstrates many of the common patterns discussed in Volume I, and it highlights the advantages and disadvantages of a currency board within this context. Argentina's ongoing negotiations with the IMF also highlights the difficult decisions and 'brinkmanship at the edge of crisis' currently required of policy-makers, which is taken up in Part II of Volume II. On 9 March 2004, Argentina's President pulled back from the brink and did not default on a $3.1 billion payment due the IMF, and the IMF promised further commitments to extend this financing, but meanwhile $88 billion-worth of private debt is not being serviced, and Horst Köhler has stepped down as head of the IMF. Thus, what next for crisis countries such as Argentina, and what next for policy-making? Part II of Volume II provides some context for these questions.

Volume II: Part II: International Adjustments and Political Responses

Supplying a growing international economy with secure currency, so that money-liquidity crises, capital flight, destabilizing currency devaluations, etc. are avoided, has long been an important concern of political economists. From World War II to the late 1960s, under the Bretton Woods system, the US dollar and gold served as the main international means of payment and source of value for the rapid expansion of international commerce. One problem with this dollar-based international monetary system, as forcefully put forward by Robert Triffin in his book *Gold and the Dollar Crisis: The Future of Convertibility* (1961), was that the US balance-of-payments deficits – which supplied the needed money to the international economy – would eventually undermine confidence in the value of the dollar and therefore the system itself. However, if the US eliminated its overall financial deficits with the rest of the world and restored world confidence in the dollar, there would not be sufficient gold or other money-liquidity to finance the growing world economy. This dilemma came to be called 'the Triffin dilemma', and it eventually led to the late 1960s break-up of the Bretton Woods system based on gold and the dollar. Attempts were made for several years to re-establish a fixed dollar–gold link and create other supportive international currencies, such as the IMF's Special Drawing Rights, but these attempts failed.

Also contributing to the break-up of the Bretton Woods system were arguments by President de Gaulle of France and others that the dollar-based system gave the USA an unfair advantage by allowing the USA to freely finance itself around the world and then settle its obligations in dollars without limit. Unilateral devaluations of the dollar, as long as the dollar remains the international currency of choice, unilaterally devalues US foreign debt – a privilege enjoyed by the USA as the only major country whose foreign debt is mostly denominated in its own currency. Currently, over 50 per cent of all international notes and bonds are denominated in dollars, 45 per cent of all cross-border bank loans are in dollars, and 60 per cent of the world's money supply is denominated in the US dollar. Thus, currently more dollars circulate outside the USA than inside.

This dominance in debt markets gives dollar-issuers, such as the US government, a 'liquidity discount' or reduced transaction costs of perhaps 25 to 50 basis points (hundredths of a percentage point). Non-US holdings of US government debt amount to $2 trillion, which means that the US government saves $5–$10 billion per year in interest expense on its debt due to the liquidity discount. Also, an additional $5–$10 billion per year may be 'earned' from other countries by the USA due to 'seigniorage', which is the profit earned by the monopoly issue of coins and notes. That is, other countries give up real goods and services to holders (and therefore issuers) of dollars in order to obtain dollars for their reserve accounts.

Monetary-wealth transfers to the US dollar core of the international monetary system need not translate into undesirable inflation. Whether inflation is affected depends on the production capacity that is available in the core, the capacity that can be added, the 'thickening' and 'commodification' of markets as new activity or non-market activity becomes part of the income–expenditure flow, the degree to which US dollars are added to non-circulating reserve accounts versus use in income–expenditure flows, etc.

Underlying (or 'overlying', depending on one's perspective) this dollar-based international monetary system are regional currency baskets and cooperative alliances that provide alternative authority and policy-making structures. Chapters 12–15 describe the regional systems that have emerged, including the European Monetary Union (EMU), the Association of Southeast Asian Nations (ASEAN), and various regional alliances in South America, including Mercosur. The EMU survived its financial crisis in 1992 despite the initial 'breakup of policy consensus in a dramatic way' (Aykens, 2002, Chapter 15). However, the future of regionalism elsewhere (Phillips, 2000, Chapter 14) does not seem to be especially propitious:

> Contrary to the apparent consensus that the [recent financial] crises will act to strengthen regionalism, developments in South America and elsewhere appear to suggest that *in the short run* possibilities for collective action are weakened and regional projects are as likely to fragment as to coalesce. However, from a longer-run perspective, it seems probable that the consequences of this process of change will favour the articulation of stronger regional identification ...

Authors agree that regionalism makes some sense in terms of currency arrangements to prevent financial crisis, and to achieve some autonomy from global authorities. However, currency boards or baskets based upon regional alliances require a variety of strict conditions, including a strong and durable financial system that has sufficient monetary reserves to withstand interest rate changes and currency selling pressures transmitted through the system (Rajan, 2002, Chapter 12). Sufficient political cooperation and institutional development can also be elusive, and recent financial crises have been detrimental to that end, as in the ASEAN group (Narine, 2002, Chapter 13).

Given the weak emergence of regionalism as a counterweight to globalization processes, various authors conclude that there have been remarkably successful labors in the core of the global economy by the US Federal Reserve Bank, the 'Wall Street–US Treasury–IMF complex', etc. (Bhagwati, 1998). Capital outflows, devaluation, and use of soft currencies in the 'periphery' of the global economy have pushed the periphery into relative poverty and pushed the dollar-haven core of the global economy into relative wealth. The role of newly deregulated offshore markets in this process has been identified by Palan (2002). The periphery has included Latin America and Africa since the early 1980s, but in the 1990s the capital-losing periphery has widened to include much of Eastern Europe and Asia. The Japanese yen has also given way to the dollar not in terms of the unit-to-unit currency exchange rate, but in terms of the share of the world's wealth that is denominated in yen, which has probably dropped 50 per cent since 1989. Japan is not covered as a major case study in Part I of Volume II, because of the drawn-out nature of both its 1970s and 1980s boom and then its 1990s and continuing contraction, which is a longer cycle than typically associated with 'financial crisis' literature. However, other than in the time dimension, the 'common patterns' and magnitude of Japan's crisis adheres to the taxonomies discussed above.

Thus, millions of private international financial market participants, along with the official international financial institutions (IFIs), have favored further 'dollarization' of the international system and an expanded role for the IMF and its affiliates as 'lender of last resort'. Freixas *et al.* (1999, Chapter 16) summarize the literature on lender-of-last-resort, which goes back to the work of Henry Thornton (1802) and Walter Bagehot (1873); and Chapter 17 by Anne Krueger (1998), written before she became, in 2001, the First Deputy Managing Director of the IMF, summarizes the more recent role and effectiveness of the IMF, World Bank, and other IFIs.

The 1997 Asian crisis drew attention to the IFIs, and it provoked various critiques of their policies. In April 1997, shortly before the crisis, US Treasury Department Secretary Robert Rubin headed a meeting by the finance ministers of the G7 largest industrial countries which issued a statement 'promoting freedom of capital flows' and the deregulation and opening of the financial markets of newly industrializing countries in Asia and elsewhere. Efforts were simultaneously made to amend the charter of the IMF, so that it could also promote 'capital account liberalization' of its member countries. However, during negotiations to resolve the crisis, financial liberalization in Asia and elsewhere was increasingly seen as a win–lose game favoring the interests of US financial firms and their multinational affiliates in foreign markets (Wade, 1998–9; *New York Times*, 1999). For example, the $57 billion restructuring bail-out of South Korea in late 1997 did not require US banks with the bad loans to put up significant new money or write off bad debts, but Citibank, J.P. Morgan, Chase Manhattan, BankAmerica, Bankers Trust, and others, were allowed two to three percentage point higher interest rates and government guarantees that passed the ongoing risk of default from their shareholders to Korean taxpayers. The main 'burden' accepted by the US banks was an extension of these risky loans for up to three years. As stated by Milton Friedman:

> The effort is hurting the countries they are lending to, and benefiting the foreigners who lent to them ... The United States does give foreign aid, but this is a different kind of foreign aid. It only goes through countries like Thailand to Bankers Trust. (*New York Times*, 15–18 February 1999)

I have called these processes 'money-mercantilism' (Allen, 1999).

Historically, 'mercantilism' is the use of restrictive trade policies and colonial empires, especially by the European *ancien régime* of the seventeenth and eighteenth centuries, in order to accumulate precious metals centrally. Various nineteenth-century German historians, especially Georg Friedrich List, gave coherence to mercantilist notions of how wealth is accumulated, and they critiqued the *laissez-faire* economics of Smith, Ricardo, and Say. The institutional advantage used by powerful and hegemonic European states to appropriate unequal win–win or even win–lose gains from international commerce was recognized by the German Historical School as an important determinant of 'the wealth of nations'. More recent defenders of the mercantilist perspective include the Caribbean School and the World System School (Hopkins and Wallerstein, 1982).

What I would add to the historical mercantilist perspective, in order to make it 'money-mercantilism', is the notion that extraction of money-wealth from the periphery, through institutional advantage, does not require GDP trade flows – instead, it only requires dominance in financial affairs. In the *ancien régime* period there was an international financial system, but it was associated more with national debts rather than with commercial finance. Hence, it was easier for France and England, and others, to extract money-species from the colonies through favorable trade and exports of goods and services rather than more directly through commercial finance. However, in the current period well-developed, international commercial financial markets allow various trade channels to be bypassed.

The current 'mercantilists', who are typically financial intermediaries, are less government affiliated, and thus mercantilism is not so intentionally associated with nationalism, but the wealth-enhancing effects obtained for the home country or its currency bloc might be the same as with the old mercantilism. The official government 'players' in this process might act as direct or indirect agents or partners for the private financial intermediaries and thus maintain much of the nationalism or core-regionalism that is historically associated with mercantilism.

At the beginning of 2004, as this Introduction is written, there is no definitive agreement within the IMF's Executive Board regarding the best way to proceed. Anne Krueger has proposed various 'Sovereign Debt Restructuring Mechanisms' (SDRM), which in some cases would require an Amendment of the IMF's Articles of Agreement in order to extend the IMF's role in resolving crises. She summarizes IMF discussions of the first SDRM proposals as follows:

> Many Directors believe that … intermediate options could help address concerns about significantly extending the Fund's powers in a statutory approach … Some Directors, however, expressed a strong preference for a contractual approach not requiring an Amendment of the Fund's Articles, and cautioned against any mechanism that would imply the creation of an international judicial body to oversee the restructuring process, either within or outside the Fund. (IMF, 2002, Chapter 20, Volume II)

At their joint meetings in spring 2003, the IMF and World Bank did decide to support contractual approaches to resolving crisis-ridden international bond deals while continuing to study the desirability of SDRM. In bond contracts, collective action clauses (CACs) are increasingly favored rather than unanimous action clauses (UACs). CACs allow a majority of holders of a bond (perhaps 75 per cent of the ownership of a sovereign bond) to vote to impose changes in the bond contract on all holders of the bond, whereas UACs require unanimous consent of all holders. Support for CACs expanded after Mexico issued a $1 billion global bond in March 2003 that contained CACs, and subsequently Korea, South Africa, Brazil, and others, have issued bonds with similar provisions.

CACs reduce the cost and stress of debt restructurings. However, by the same token, governments may not work so hard to avoid defaults if the restructuring costs are reduced – i.e. the moral hazard problem – and the risk of financial crisis may increase. The latest research into CACs begins to quantify, via interest rate effects, whether the market-place expects the moral hazard problem to dominate the benefits of lower restructuring costs, or vice versa (Federal Reserve Bank of San Francisco, 2004).

Chapters 18 and 19 (Bird, 2001, and Lee, 2002) provide further insight into these ongoing debates about the expanding role of the IMF in crisis resolution, including its systematic and problematic role in a globalizing world economy increasingly dominated by unstable private capital flows. General conclusions include a case for maintaining but reforming the IMF, a case for making its decisions and analysis more 'transparent' to improve democratic accountability, and a case for improving coordination (Lee, 2002, Chapter 19) between the IMF and the private financial sector: 'The challenge now confronting the IMF is to mobilize, as a progressive force for avoiding and resolving financial crises, the same private market actors whose propensity for volatility and contagion triggered the series of expensive bailouts which have led to the widespread discrediting of the role of the IMF in the contemporary global economy.'

Chapters 20–22 conclude this collection with a broader discussion of current efforts to reconstruct the international financial architecture. This reconstruction, called 'Keynes's revenge?' by Cartapanis and Herland (2002, Chapter 21), seems to be 'a working compromise which brings together neo-Keynesian and neo-liberal principles but which cannot fully answer the challenges of systemic risk'. The IFIs are 'rethinking' and 'groping toward' more coordinated private sector involvement (Kenen, 2002, Chapter 20), but none of the new proposals, including Krueger's, 'will banish financial crises for good' (Cooper, 2002, Chapter 22).

References

Allen, Roy E. (1994), *Financial Crises and Recession in the Global Economy*. Aldershot, and Brookfield, VT: Edward Elgar.

Allen, Roy E. (1999), *Financial Crises and Recession in the Global Economy, Second Edition*. Cheltenham, and Northampton, MA: Edward Elgar.

Bagehot, Walter (1873), *Lombard Street*. Homewood, IL: Richard D. Irwin (reprint).

Bhagwati, Jagdish (1998), 'The Capital Myth: The Difference between Trade in Widgets and Dollars', *Foreign Affairs*, **77**(3), May–June, 7–12.

Cerny, Philip G. (1994), 'The Dynamics of Financial Globalization: Technology, Market Structure, and Policy Response', *Policy Sciences*, **27**(4), 319–42.

Clarke, Simon (1994), *Marx's Theory of Crisis*. New York: St Martin's Press.

Federal Reserve Bank of Kansas City (1997), *Maintaining Financial Stability in a Global Economy: Symposium Proceedings*, Jackson Hole, Wyoming, 28–9 August.

Federal Reserve Bank of San Francisco (2004), 'Resolving Sovereign Debt Crises with Collective Action Clauses', *FRSB Economic Letter* (No. 2004-06), 20 February.

Fisher, Irving (1933), 'The Debt-Deflation Theory of Great Depressions', *Econometrica*, **1**, 337–57.

Germain, Randall G. (2002), 'Feature Review', *New Political Economy*, **7**(2), 299–307.

International Monetary Fund (2002), *IMF Board Holds Informal Seminar on Sovereign Debt Restructuring* (Public Information Notice 02/38). Washington, DC: IMF.

Keynes, John Maynard (1936), *The General Theory of Employment, Interest and Money*. London: Macmillan.

Kindleberger, Charles P. (1989), *Manias, Panics, and Crashes: A History of Financial Crises*. New York: Basic Books.

Lindgren, Carl-Johan, Billian Barcia and Matthew Seal (1995), *Bank Soundness and Macro-economic Policy*. Washington, DC: International Monetary Fund.

New York Times (1999), 'Global Contagion, a Narrative', 15–18 February, p. 1.

Palan, Ronen (2002), 'Tax Havens and the Commercialization of State Sovereignty', *International Organization*, **56**(1), 151–76.

Strange, Susan (1986), *Casino Capitalism*. Oxford and New York: Basil Blackwell.

Thornton, H. (1802), *An Enquiry into the Nature and Effects of the Paper Credit of Great Britain*, ed. with an introduction by F.A. von Hayek. New York: Rinehart, 1939.

Triffin, Robert (1961), *Gold and the Dollar Crisis: The Future of Convertibility* (rev. edn). New Haven, CT: Yale University Press.

Wade, Robert (1998–9), 'The Coming Fight Over Capital Flows', *Foreign Policy*, Winter, 41–54.

Part I
Issues and Concepts

[1]

Crises and Bail-Outs of Banks and Countries: Linkages, Analogies, and Differences

Riccardo De Bonis, Alessandro Giustiniani and Giorgio Gomel

1. INTRODUCTION

DURING the last decade or so a number of banking crises have occurred in the major industrial nations. It should suffice to mention the thrift industry in the United States, the Scandinavian banks, the Bank of Credit and Commerce International (BCCI), Banesto, Credit Lyonnais, Barings, Banco di Napoli, up to the recent difficulties of Japanese and Asian intermediaries (see Tables 1 and 2). Banking crises have been more severe in developing countries like Venezuela, Bulgaria, Mexico, Hungary, Argentina, Chile, Cote d'Ivoire. Of the 181 member countries of the IMF 131 have experienced banking problems during the past 15 years.[1]

Bank unsoundness is the focus of deep concerns for its possible interactions with macroeconomic instability. In many cases, countries' financial difficulties originated in fact from a banking crisis or were exacerbated by a banking crisis.[2] The potential size and severity of sovereign debt crises in world financial markets which have become highly integrated were highlighted by the ramifications of the Mexican crisis at the end of 1994. The amount of liquidity support mustered by the international community in that episode to bail-out the Mexican economy had no precedents. No established procedure was available to guide authorities in handling a major crisis of that kind. Subsequently, in a number of international bodies policy makers have undertaken to consider various avenues and arrangements to prevent, anticipate and resolve sovereign debt crises. In early 1997, representatives of the countries of the Group of Ten produced a report on

---

RICCARDO DE BONIS and GIORGIO GOMEL are respectively Head of Section and Director in the Research Department of the Bank of Italy. ALESSANDRO GIUSTINIANI is Advisor to the Executive Director at the International Monetary Fund.

[1] See IMF (1996b), Goldstein and Turner (1996) and BIS (1996).
[2] See Camdessus (1996).

TABLE 1
Banking Crises (1974–1995)

Country	Year	Bank	Procedure and Method to Match the Crisis	Sources of Resources
Germany	1974	*Herstatt*	Liquidation	Banks
Germany	1983	*Schroder & Co.*	Emergency aid	Banks
Italy	1981–1982	*Steinhauslin*	Special administration and afterwards take-over by bank	Banks
Italy	1982	*Banco Ambrosiano*	Liquidation and afterwards take-over by bank	Banks and Central Bank
Italy	1988–1991	*Cassa di Risparmio di Prato*	Emergency aid and afterwards take-over by bank	Deposit insurance and banks
UK	1973–1975	*Secondary banking crisis*	Emergency aid	Banks and Central Bank
UK	1985	*Johnson Matthey Bankers Ltd.*	Capital injection	Banks, Central Bank, parent company
UK	1990	*British & Common-wealth Merchant Bank*	Liquidation	Deposit insurance
UK and Luxembourg	1991	*BCCI (Bank of Credit and Comm. Internat.)*	Liquidation	Deposit insurance
USA	1980s	*Savings and loans*	Special fund (liquidation or take-over by banks)	Deposit insurance and Government
USA	1984	*Continental Illinois*	Special administration and afterwards sale	Deposit insurance, Federal Reserve, banks
USA	1985	*Bank of New York computer failure*	Emergency aid	Federal Reserve
USA	1988	*First Republic Bank*	Special administration and afterwards take-over by bank	Deposit insurance
USA	1990	*Freedom National Bank*	Liquidation	Deposit insurance
USA	1991	*Bank of New England*	Capital injection and afterwards take-over by bank	Deposit insurance, Federal Reserve
Finland	1992–1993	*Several banks*	Government Guarantee Fund	Government

Country	Years	Bank	Action	Funding
Norway	1991–1992	*Several banks*	Government Bank Insurance and Investment Funds	Deposit insurance, Government, Central Bank
Sweden	1992–1993	*Several banks*	Bank Support Authority	Government
Australia	1990	*State Bank of Victoria*	Take-over by bank	Government
Austria	1992–1993	*Bankhaus Rossler*	Rescue-package and afterwards take-over by bank	Banks and deposit insurance
Canada	1985–1986	*B. British Columbia*	Rescue-package and afterwards take-over by bank	Central Bank and deposit insurance
Denmark	1989	*DK Sparekassen*	Take-over by bank	No external funding
France	1995	*Crédit Lyonnais*	Capital injection	Government
Greece	1988	*Bank of Crete*	Special administration	Central Bank
New Zealand	1989	*DFC New Zealand L.*	Liquidation	Government
Netherlands	1981–1983	*N.V. Slavenburg*	Take-over by bank	No external funding reported
Spain	1978–1983	*54 out of the 109 banks in existence experienced financial difficulties*	Take-over by banks, liquidation, deposit insurance	Deposit insurance, banks, Government
Switzerland	1980s	*Weisscredit*	Liquidation	Banks
Switzerland	1983	*Banque Commerciale*	Liquidation	Banks
Switzerland	1991	*Spar und Leihkasse Thun*	Liquidation	Deposit insurance
Switzerland	1992	*Eko Hypothekar- und Handelsbank*	Closure, afterwards take-over by bank	No external funding
Switzerland	1992	*Bank EvK*	Take-over by bank	No external funding

Source: Goodhart and Schoenmaker (1993).

58   R. DE BONIS, A. GIUSTINIANI AND G. GOMEL

TABLE 2
The Asian Intermediaries

	Number of Banks and Finance Companies (July 1997)	Closed/ Suspended	Nationalised/ Administered by Restructuring Agency	Planning to Merge	Foreign-Bought (Majority Stake)
Thailand	108	56	4	0	4
Malaysia	60	0	0	41	0
Singapore	13	0	0	4	0
Indonesia	228	16	56	11	0
South Korea	56	16	2	0	0

Source: The *Economist* (4 April, 1998).

financial instability in emerging countries, with the aim of detecting sources of financial stress and advising on ways to promote robust financial systems.[3] The outbreak of the crisis in East Asia in the second half of 1997 in which currency devaluations were interlocked with stock market crashes and banks' bankruptcies has given further impetus to that effort. Korea was the beneficiary of the largest internationally concerted rescue package, outstripping the Mexican bail-out.

Even if a precise direction of causality is difficult to ascertain, financial instability may influence macroeconomic performance while macroeconomic developments and policies may in turn have microeconomic consequences for intermediaries. However, the effects of banks' instability are quite different in developed *vis-à-vis* developing countries. In developed nations crises have been limited to the banking sector; domino effects have been absent; intermediaries have often been bailed-out; discussion has evolved on the efficiency of bank regulation and public action. On the other hand, in emerging economies financial crises have had rather disruptive consequences on the whole economy, due to the weaker fabric of financial intermediation and of the entire institutional set-up: Albania and East Asia are the starkest examples of the interconnections between vulnerabilities of the financial sector and the deterioration of macroeconomic performance. Accordingly, one of the topics under discussion internationally is how the IMF might better incorporate banking sector issues in its surveillance activity and improve the design of programmes, the provision of technical assistance, and the co-ordination with other institutions.[4]

After a general discussion of financial crises and bank runs (Section 2), this paper is organised around some classical keywords: bail-outs and bankruptcies (Section 3); insolvency vs. illiquidity (Section 4); the difference between supervision and surveillance (Section 5); the function of the lender of last resort

---

[3] 'Financial Stability in Emerging Market Economies', Report of the Working Party on financial stability in emerging market economies (April 1997).
[4] Some indications may be found in IMF (1996a).

CRISES AND BAIL-OUTS OF BANKS AND COUNTRIES 59

(Section 6); and the problems of co-ordination and free riding (Section 7). In each section, we first discuss the prototype case of banks for which both established economic doctrine and the practical experience of policy makers and regulators offer clearer indications, even though prudential regulation is often criticised and in the process of continuous change. Further, we turn to the case of countries exploring interactions, analogies and differences between the cases of banks and countries from a number of viewpoints.

While the linkages between banks' and countries' financial difficulties are clear, the analogies between the two cases of bail-out are more blurred and should not be overstated. In both circumstances there exist similar problems of negative externalities, asymmetric information, and both market and government failures. Thus, we use the paradigm of banks' bail-outs to draw some inferences for bail-outs of countries though we are well aware that fundamental differences remain between financial intermediaries and nations and that simple-minded analogies can be misleading.

The endeavour of the paper is fraught with conceptual and empirical difficulties but we are convinced that the analysis can provide interesting insights.

2. CRISES

a. Financial Crises and Bank Runs

In finance and banking theory there is no single widely accepted definition of crisis. The meaning of a banking crisis can range from difficulties of individual banks to situations in which a large part of the credit system has collapsed. The literature on this issue is too extensive to be surveyed here, but, for the sake of simplicity, we can single out two fundamental approaches, which may be labelled, respectively, 'monetarist' and 'eclectic'.

In the 'monetarist' view, which finds its roots in the studies by Friedman and Schwartz, a financial crisis originates from a bank panic, which leads to a sharp decline in the money supply, hence to a fall in economic activity.[5] All other types of shocks, even though they can bring about a decrease in wealth, 'are not per se financial crises unless the shift from tangible or financial assets to money leads to a run on banks'.[6] This approach focuses on banks because of the unique role they play in the financial system: through the supply of deposit contracts they

---

[5] 'A financial crisis is fuelled by fears that means of payment will be unobtainable at any price and, in a fractional-reserve banking system, leads to a scramble for high-powered money. It is precipitated by actions of the public that suddenly squeeze the reserves of the banking system. In a futile attempt to restore reserves, the banks may call loans, refuse to roll over existing loans, or resort to selling assets. (...) The essence of a financial crisis is that it is short-lived, ending with a slackening of the public's demand for additional currency' (Schwartz, 1986, p. 11).

[6] Schwartz (1986, p. 24).

60   R. DE BONIS, A. GIUSTINIANI AND G. GOMEL

transform illiquid assets into liquid liabilities, which have a smoother and less uncertain pattern of returns than the illiquid assets and which are redeemable at par.

On the contrary, the 'eclectic' view, which may be traced back to Kindleberger (1989), looks at a wider range of disturbances, such as sharp declines in asset prices, failures of large financial intermediaries, or disruption in foreign exchange markets, as having potentially serious consequences for the real economy. As emphasised by Mishkin (1991, 1994 and 1996), transactions in financial markets are intrinsically subject to a problem of asymmetric information: lenders usually do not have full knowledge of borrowers' activity and investment plans. As a consequence, lenders need to solve two problems: first, to select potential borrowers in order to minimise losses due to defaults — which may give rise to an adverse selection problem — and, after the loan is made, to monitor borrowers' behaviour to avoid that it be detrimental to loan repayment — a problem of moral hazard.[7] Hence, a financial crisis is:

> a disruption to financial markets in which adverse selection and moral hazard problems become much worse, so that financial markets are unable to efficiently channel funds to those who have the most productive investment opportunities.[8]

Since the early 1980s, a wide literature on bank runs has developed although the links with the wider concept of financial crisis are not duly considered. As emphasised by Diamond and Dybvig (1983), the illiquidity of assets 'provides the rationale both for the existence of banks and for their vulnerability to runs'. The central point is that the liquidity service offered by banks through the supply of deposit contracts contains an intrinsic instability.[9] Two Nash equilibria may arise: in one the bank is able to meet its obligations with customers; in the other a bank run may develop if people think that only the first depositors will be able to get their money back. The 'first come, first serve' constraint normally followed by banks when they deal with customers may be at the origin of a co-ordination failure in which savers start to withdraw money from a healthy bank, forcing its subsequent crisis.

One conclusion of the debate which has followed the Diamond-Dybvig model is that bank runs may occur because uncertainty exists on the intermediary's profitability or on its general soundness. The literature has therefore focused on the content of information on banks' loans, whose real value is difficult to ascertain and for which a large secondary market does not exist.[10]

---

[7] For a more thorough analysis of these issues, see Davis (1992).

[8] Mishkin (1994, p. 9).

[9] The liquidity service offered by banks is central in a class of bank run models such as Diamond and Dybvig (1983), Gorton (1985), Chari and Jagannathan (1988) and Alonso (1996). Empirical analyses of contagion effects are provided by Saunders (1987) and Schoenmaker (1996).

[10] On this debate see, among others, Fama (1985) and Bhattacharya and Thakor (1993).

CRISES AND BAIL-OUTS OF BANKS AND COUNTRIES 61

Today bank runs are much less frequent than in the past because of prudential supervision and deposit insurance and the like.[11] The controversy has thus moved on to focus on the forms which regulation and public action may assume. For instance, narrow banking, i.e. demand deposits being invested entirely in short term safe assets, such as public bonds, has been frequently advocated mainly by the Chicago tradition to solve the intrinsic instability of banking. But, narrow banking 'to cope with the potential problems of banking illiquidity is analogous to reducing automobile speeds to zero'.[12] Public regulation must prevent bank runs through other means, the efficiency of which is, however, open to discussion for the risk that they might impose unbearable costs to the economy (see Section 4).

b. Countries

In the case of countries, we find it useful to start from the notion of debt crisis. Recently, countries' debt crises have been modelled in a similar way to the Diamond-Dybvig model of bank runs, showing that creditors' pessimistic expectations about the borrower's creditworthiness may become self-fulfilling, causing a liquidity crisis.[13] A debt crisis is often associated with a currency crisis. When investors lose confidence in a country's economic outlook, they will try to withdraw their investments. The resulting capital outflow, leading to a decrease of international reserves to some critical level, will force the country to let its currency depreciate. In addition, the turnaround in market sentiment will make a country unable either to issue new debt or to roll-over the outstanding stock, as happened to Mexico between the end of 1994 and the early months of 1995. A similar sequence of events was at the origin of the crisis that beset Thailand, Indonesia and in part Korea in 1997. In countries with a large share of short-term funds in their foreign debt exposure (Table 3), when international investors lost confidence in those countries' capacity to sustain low interest rates, pegged exchange rates, continuously high rates of growth and engaged in massive selling of currencies and assets, sharp devaluations and declines of equity values followed.

In order to reduce the area of ambiguity, some basic notions, such as those of '*country*' and of '*debt*', have to be clarified. The word '*country*' may have two meanings: a legal and an economic one. In the former, it is tantamount to the concept of '*sovereign state*' which is a type of legal person recognised by international law.[14] From an economic standpoint, a country is a heterogeneous entity, comprising a private and a public/government sector, each of which has

---

[11] Recently some runs have, however, affected the Japanese banks: in November 1995 a line of customers formed outside Daiwa Bank, which had been hit by big losses in its New York branch.
[12] Wallace (1996, p. 9).
[13] See Detragiache (1996).
[14] Brownlie (1987).

62   R. DE BONIS, A. GIUSTINIANI AND G. GOMEL

TABLE 3
External Debt Exposure of Selected Asian Countries
(billions of US dollars, end-June 1997)

	Towards Foreign Banks[1] (A)					*Total* (A)+(B)
	Total			*In Securities*		
		Interbank Market	*Percentage Change Between end-1995 and end-June 1997[2]*	*Percentage of Debt Maturing in 1 Year or Less*	*Held by Non-residents* (B)		*As a Percentage of GDP[3]*
South Korea	103.3	66.9	27.6	67.7	47.2	150.5	31.0
Philippines	14.1	5.5	7.2	58.7	7.7	21.8	26.0
Indonesia	58.7	12.4	16.2	59.0	7.2	65.9	29.0
Malaysia	28.8	10.5	12.0	56.4	11.7	40.5	40.8
Thailand	69.4	26.1	11.2	65.7	11.1	80.5	44.8

Notes:
[1] BIS reporting banks.
[2] Adjusted for exchange rate changes.
[3] GDP in 1996.
Sources: National Bulletins, IMF and BIS.

economic and financial links with the other one and with the rest of the world. In this paper we equate *'country'* to *'sovereign state'* and consider it in its capacity as a borrower. Hence, the notion of *'debt'* encompasses the whole stock of non-monetary interest-bearing liabilities of, or guaranteed by, the public sector.[15] This definition does not discriminate between different categories of debt holders (resident or non-resident) or between the currency in which the debt is denominated (national or foreign).

Traditionally, the literature has focused on that part of debt held by non-residents, either private or public entities, and usually denominated in foreign currency, i.e. the so-called *'external debt'*. The distinction between domestic and external liabilities of sovereign borrowers has been usually justified on two grounds. First, foreign creditors may invoke the diplomatic protection of their governments (which may be creditors themselves) whenever a country is not current in the service of its debt. Second, in an economy with administrative controls on residents' external financial transactions and with a fixed (or managed) exchange rate, shifts in foreign creditors' portfolios impinge upon the debtor country's stock of foreign exchange.[16] Although with the removal of

---

[15] International Monetary Fund (1995).
[16] In the case of fixed (or managed) exchange rates, one of the effects of a debt crisis is a run on the official reserves of the debtor country's central bank which may force the country to suspend payments on its external obligations. A similar situation may also arise in the case of flexible exchange rates because shifts in the market may indeed generate unsustainable downward pressures on the exchange rate of the debtor country.

CRISES AND BAIL-OUTS OF BANKS AND COUNTRIES   63

capital controls and the growing reliance by sovereign borrowers on the issue of liabilities in the bearer form, the distinction between domestic and external debt has been blurred, we still refer to 'debt' as 'external debt', since we are interested in the international reverberations of sovereign states' financial distress.

With these premises, a debt crisis can be defined as the incapacity or unwillingness of a sovereign borrower to meet its debt-service obligations. Since 1800, four episodes of debt crisis can be singled out: the 1820s, the 1870s, the 1930s and the 1980s (Table 4).[17] The main difference between the earlier debt crises and the recent ones lies in the form in which they manifested themselves. In the 19th century and the early part of the 20th, the worsening of debt-service

TABLE 4

Debt Crises and Major Countries in Default or Involved in Rescheduling
(estimated amounts of defaulted/rescheduled debt in millions of US dollars in parentheses)

Period	Country
1826–1830	Spain (100)[1], Greater Colombia (32), Mexico (26), Brazil (18), Greece (14), Peru (9), Argentina (5), Chile (5)
1840–1845	Spain (160)[2], nine US states (120), Mexico (54), Portugal (44)[2]
1875–1882	Ottoman Empire (1000), Spain (850), Egypt (440), Mexico (170)[3], ten southern US states (158), Peru (150), Colombia (32), Tunisia (30)[4], Honduras (26), Uruguay (15), Costa Rica (13), Bolivia (8)
1890–1900	Argentina (360), Portugal (300), Brazil (146), Greece (100), Uruguay (83), Serbia (68), Dominican Republic (32), Venezuela (22), Colombia (13)
1911–1915	Russia (8500)[5], Ottoman Empire (720), Mexico (500), Bulgaria (160)
1931–1940	Germany (2200), Brazil (1267), Romania (580), Mexico (500)[6], Greece (380), Chile (376), Austria (325), Yugoslavia (320), Poland (300), Hungary (250), Colombia (151), Turkey (140), Uruguay (130), Peru (120)
1982–1986[7]	Mexico (74000), Brazil (28000), Argentina (24000), Poland (22000), Venezuela (21000), Nigeria (11000), Turkey (11000), Yugoslavia (10200), South Africa (10000), Chile (9400), Ecuador (6800), Philippines (4200), Morocco (4000), Romania (4000), Sudan (3600), Peru (3000), Uruguay (2700), Zaire (2400)

Notes:
[1] Suspension of 1824.
[2] Suspension of 1837.
[3] Suspension of 1866.
[4] Suspension of 1867.
[5] Suspension of 1918.
[6] Suspension of 1928.
[7] Estimates for the total amount of rescheduled debt for the years 1982–1986, in the case of Turkey for the years 1979–1986.
Source: Suter (1992).

---

[17] For a thorough study of debt cycles in the world economy, see Suter (1992). For an analysis of the debt crises in the interwar period, see also Eichengreen and Portes (1987, 1988 and 1991).

64   R. DE BONIS, A. GIUSTINIANI AND G. GOMEL

difficulties induced several countries to default on their external bond obligations.[18] The situation was worsened by the difficult process of negotiation between debtor countries and bondholders (usually represented by councils). The result was the collapse of international lending. On the contrary, in the 1980s crises took the form of difficulties by countries to service their mostly bank debt. Bank lending then came to a halt, but banks and debtor countries gradually developed a co-operative strategy based on multilateral rescheduling agreements which provided debtors with immediate financial relief. The picture has changed again in the 1990s with the growing share of bond finance and non-bank financial intermediaries in world capital markets (see Section 7*b*).

3. BAIL-OUTS vs. BANKRUPTCIES

a. Definitions and Basic Principles

Bail-outs may be defined as any external intervention, driven by public authorities, in support of a troubled firm to overcome a situation of crisis without interrupting its current business. The intervention changes the ordinary distribution of risks and responsibilities among the parties involved: shareholders, managers, and creditors. Shareholders' ownership rights may be kept inoperative; creditors' expected flow of returns may be deferred; managers may be replaced.

The above definition of bail-outs captures a variety of instances: from cases where the failing firm is rescued by being acquired by others, with the old shareholders replaced by new ones and no public money involved, to other situations where public support is granted and only some claimants are shielded from losses, to other extreme instances where none of the parties involved suffer any losses.

At the other end, bankruptcy may be defined as a compulsory procedure of collective execution of a firm's estate, consisting of selling the debtor's assets and distributing the proceeds to the creditors, according to the legal priority order of claims, and to shareholders. In a bankruptcy, managers are deprived of the right to manage business; creditors' claims are met only in proportion to the firm's liquidated assets; shareholders lose their ownership other than the assets remaining after fulfilling the creditors' claims; the firm as such is dismembered and the associated costs may spill over to the economy as a whole.

Bail-outs of banks may follow a variety of procedures entailing rather different results: a payoff resolution if the bank is liquidated, a merger between the

---

[18] In the case of default, the borrowing country fails to meet its debt obligations but it recognises them; on the contrary, in the case of repudiation, the borrowing country does not recognise its debt obligations *vis-à-vis* creditors.

CRISES AND BAIL-OUTS OF BANKS AND COUNTRIES 65

unsound bank and other intermediaries, or a variety of forms of restructuring that enable the troubled bank to improve its financial position. On occasions, governments may assume the ownership of the failed banks, possibly only for a short period (as has recently happened in the Nordic countries).[19]

With regard to the forms of restructuring that have been put in place, there is a wide variety and combination of instruments. In some cases managers are replaced and new funds of a public nature are secured. In 1991 for example, 'Government Bank Insurance and Investment Funds' were introduced by law in Norway, to support the banking system, which was hit by the far-reaching crisis of the late 1980s. In other cases, the intervention of private deposit insurance may be sufficient, at a first stage, followed then by an acquisition. In other circumstances, if the financial position is really unsound, banks are liquidated, as exemplified by the large number of failures that affected the Savings and Loans industry.[20]

A cross-country survey of 100 bank failures in the 1980s and early 1990s suggests that in only 19 cases was the crisis dealt with by putting a rescue package in place, while in 29 cases the bank was liquidated; the most common way of dealing with failing banks was their take-over by other banks. As for the sources of funding, only in 24 cases was there no external funding; central banks or governments provided support in 52 instances.[21]

Bail-outs try to solve problems of market failure implied by the instability of banking, but may result in misallocations of resources and inefficiencies: some intermediaries may be rescued and others not; public funds may be allocated badly; competition may be negatively affected by public intervention. A recent example is the Crédit Lyonnais case. After having recorded large losses in 1993, this state-owned bank received state support in the following three years. The first wave of subsidies induced other French banks to apply to the European Commission to preserve competition. The outcome was that the French authorities were urged to privatise the Crédit Lyonnais as soon as the reconstructing process was completed. But the rescue has again run against difficulties; in 1997 new loan losses have been declared and in 1998 the European Commission approved another French government bail-out plan.[22]

As a general guiding principle, single banks should be allowed to fail if their failure does not destabilise the overall financial system. In spite of the special nature of banks there should be nothing automatic about the decision to grant them public support. On efficiency grounds, no protection should be extended to shareholders or top managers. But depositors — large wholesale customers,

---

[19] On the Nordic countries' banking crises see Drees and Pazarbasioglu (1995).

[20] White (1991) analyses causes and remedies of that crisis.

[21] See Goodhart and Schoenmaker (1993) and Table 1.

[22] See the *Economist* (1997) and the European Commission's decision on the Crédit Lyonnais case (Official Journal of the European Communities, December 1995).

not small retail savers — should also bear some of the burden, in order to stimulate a more careful assessment of the riskiness of individual banks. The State should intervene — using taxpayers' money — only as a residual lender, when there is a true public interest in rescuing the bank to preserve its capital and intangible assets and when comparison of the costs and benefits of the rescue convincingly shows it to be superior to alternative solutions. Scrutiny has to be particularly careful when the Government is also a shareholder — a situation in which it is difficult to draw a sharp line between recapitalisation and state aid.

Competition may be better safeguarded if privatisation is the final result following the initial bail-out. The prospect of privatisation may increase the credibility of the public action. This is the approach followed by the Italian authorities in the 1996 Banco di Napoli crisis: the acquisition of the bank's control by the State has been followed by a competitive auction. However, the goal of privatising the bank has not been reached: the Banco di Napoli's new owners are a bank owned by the Government and an insurance company which is controlled by public-sector banks. The Italian Treasury has announced the privatisation of the buyer bank which will take place in 1998.

b. Extending the Notion to Countries

Turning to the case of countries, a number of caveats are called for because of the particular nature of the borrower. In theory, sovereign states may be regarded as ordinary economic agents that tap international capital markets in order to finance the excess of their expenditures over revenues. As a consequence of exogenous events or mismanagement of domestic policies, sovereign debtors may fail to be current in servicing their foreign financial obligations.

However, the analogy with the case of firms or financial institutions may be misleading. The most striking differences between sovereign and other types of borrowers pertain to the nature and size of the debtor, and the enforcement and renegotiation mechanisms that are applicable.

One of the main corollaries of the principle of sovereignty of states is that obligations arising from customary law and treaties depend on the consent of the obligor. As a consequence, any possible remedy to overcome contingent difficulties in servicing sovereign debt has to be agreed on with the debtor country itself. Moreover, sovereign states are among the largest borrowers from the international capital markets. Therefore, the possibility that one or more sovereign borrowers declare a moratorium on their debt-service payments might affect the stability of financial markets. These peculiar features of sovereign states give them an unusual bargaining power *vis-à-vis* their creditors. In addition, without resorting to the extreme solution of coercion, there is no explicit enforcement mechanism deterring a sovereign borrower from defaulting on its

CRISES AND BAIL-OUTS OF BANKS AND COUNTRIES   67

debt.[23] There is no international law that sets out the conditions and procedures to apply in such an event. Contrary to what is usually envisaged in private commercial law, creditors cannot, for instance, rely on the possibility of seizing collateral.[24] Hence, the only compelling reasons for a country to honour its financial obligations may be the fear of punishment, i.e. of the imposition of commercial and/or financial sanctions by creditor countries, and the impairment of its reputation, hence, the subsequent inability of the defaulting country to borrow.[25] In practice, neither of these threats is fully credible because sanctions are costly also for the creditor community and historical experience has shown that past 'unclean' debt-service standing has not hindered subsequent market access.

The absence of an internationally agreed legal framework in the case of sovereign lending has important consequences. Firstly, because of the lack of an explicit enforcement mechanism as in the case of commercial law, the actions of the borrower cannot be monitored by the lender; the outcome can be the unintended encouragement of imprudent behaviour. Secondly, the responses to the debt crises have been largely *ad hoc* in nature. In particular, the approach chosen by creditor countries has been adapted to the different mechanisms and types of financial institutions through which saving has been channelled from surplus to deficit countries and hence to the different incidence of the default risk. Thirdly, the renegotiation between sovereign borrowers and their creditors is a lengthy process. This, in turn, complicates the problem of co-ordination among the parties concerned and encourages free-riding behaviour (see Section 7).

Since sovereign states cannot go bankrupt in a strict commercial sense, it is also difficult to define the concept of a bail-out. Generally speaking, any type of intervention of the international community — be it either private financial institutions or official and multilateral creditors — to financially support a state with difficulties in servicing its external debt may be regarded as an operation of bail-out.[26] However, it is possible to differentiate among 'rescue packages'

---

[23] Between the end of the 19th century and the early years of the 20th century, there were some cases of creditor countries' resort to military power against defaulting countries (Egypt in 1880, Venezuela in 1902, the Dominican Republic in 1905, Nicaragua in 1905 and again in 1911–12). On this see Lindert and Morton (1989).

[24] On the contrary, the pledge of collateral is not unusual in lending between sovereign states, e.g. in the case of the loan granted by Germany to Italy in 1976 and backed by the Bank of Italy's gold holdings or the recent loan agreement between the United States and Mexico which is guaranteed by Mexico's oil export revenues. A similar contingency is also envisaged in the Articles of Agreement of the International Monetary Fund in the case of a member country's request of waiver of the conditions governing the use of the Fund's general resources (Article V, Section 4).

[25] On this issue, see for example Eaton (1990), Gale and Hellwig (1988), Eaton, Gersovitz and Stiglitz (1986) and Rowlands (1993).

[26] If we draw an imaginary parallel between a country and a 'typical firm', we can observe that in the case of bail-outs of sovereign states the management, i.e. the government, is never forced to leave the office. In a democracy, the only potential punishment for the government, if it is deemed to be the cause of the crisis, rests in the hands of the electorate, i.e. the ultimate shareholder.

68   R. DE BONIS, A. GIUSTINIANI AND G. GOMEL

according to: (i) the nature of the debt-service crisis; and (ii) the mix between adjustment and financing, and within the latter among the different forms of financial support.

4. INSOLVENCY vs. ILLIQUIDITY

a. Banks

Insolvency is the inability of an economic agent to fulfil its obligations. In the case of illiquidity the economic agent is fundamentally solvent but is not able to meet its obligations when they fall due.

Banks' solvency is normally measured by capital adequacy, e.g. by the ratio of capital to total assets or to risk assets. Insolvency refers to the impossibility for the intermediary to use its own funds to cover credit and other losses. Illiquidity refers to an insufficient ratio of liquid assets to some indicator of business size, like total assets or total deposits. An insolvent bank is unable to face its debt and losses; an illiquid bank fails to meet current needs of funds. Permanent capital inadequacy may result in bankruptcy or a decision to bail-out the failing institution; on the contrary, illiquidity may be only a temporary problem.

In practice, the distinction between the two concepts is not easy to draw.[27] Insolvency may depend on the general state of confidence of the market, which may be measured by its degree of illiquidity. Asymmetries of information between the market and a single bank may cause liquidity difficulties to degenerate into a solvency crisis. The price mechanism may not work if the market is not able to ascertain the quality of potential borrowers, in this case banks. A form of credit rationing in the interbank market may occur and public authorities may be compelled to intervene.

Solvency is difficult to ascertain because the evaluation of bank loans is always uncertain. Banks tend in fact to underestimate the value of bad loans, first to improve their balance-sheet accounts, second to decrease the injection of new capital resources which may be required to comply with the solvency risk ratio. Such behaviour is not confined to intermediaries. On the contrary, it is also characteristic of public authorities. During the recent difficulties of their financial system, the Japanese authorities under-reported the amount of banks' non-performing loans. In recent years, non-performing loans have increased in many countries (Table 5).

Historical evidence points to the difficulties that public bodies face in distinguishing between insolvency and illiquidity. The common accusation at central banks is that they bail-out intermediaries that are insolvent, using their

---

[27] See, for a discussion, Revell (1975).

CRISES AND BAIL-OUTS OF BANKS AND COUNTRIES   69

TABLE 5
Non-performing Loans
(in per cent of total)

	1990	1994	1995
Asia			
India	n.a.	23.6	19.5
Hong Kong	n.a.	3.1	2.9
Korea	2.1	1.0	0.9
Taiwan	1.2	2.0	3.1
Indonesia	4.5	12.0	10.4
Malaysia	20.6	10.2	6.1
Thailand	9.7	7.5	7.7
Latin America			
Argentina	16.0	8.6	12.3
Brazil	4.7	3.9	7.9
Chile	2.1	1.0	1.0
Colombia	2.2	2.2	2.7
Mexico	2.3	10.5	19.1
Venezuela	3.0	24.7	10.6
United States	3.3	1.9	1.3
Japan	n.a.	3.3	3.4
Italy	5.2	8.8	10.3
Finland	8.0 (*)	4.6	3.9
Norway	9.1 (*)	5.4	4.5
Sweden	11.0 (*)	6.0	4.0

Note:
(*) Data refer to 1992.
Source: BIS (1996).

powers to create liquidity in a highly discretionary way. In 1984, for instance, the Federal Reserve provided liquidity assistance to the Continental Illinois Bank, which was suffering from a run on its wholesale deposits. The later reconstruction of the case showed that the bank was probably insolvent; its bail-out, moreover, was a bad example for the subsequent and inefficient public rescues of many Savings and Loans banks. More generally, a disturbing fact is that in many countries a high fraction of banks receiving discount window support subsequently failed. Less frequent is the opposite accusation at supervisors, i.e. that they liquidate banks which are solvent.[28]

---

[28] According to Guido Carli, Governor of the Bank of Italy in the years 1960–1974, the choice to liquidate the Banca Italiana di Sconto in 1921 was a mistake, because the intermediary was only illiquid. Cf. Carli (1987).

70   R. DE BONIS, A. GIUSTINIANI AND G. GOMEL

b. Countries

The notions of insolvency and illiquidity, when applied to the case of sovereign borrowers, need again to be adapted to the particular nature of the debtor. In this case as well as in that of banks the distinction between the two concepts is not easy to establish.

The simple definition of insolvency — negative net wealth — is hardly applicable to sovereign borrowers. In fact, countries do not usually publish a balance sheet where the assets and liabilities of the public sector are explicitly recorded as in the case of a firm.[29] In theory, one could argue that insolvency is not a real issue in the case of sovereign debtors because, in almost all instances, the outstanding debt of a state is less than the assets owned by the government or by its nationals and that the government might seize by resorting to its coercive powers.

In terms which are more relevant to the current discussion, insolvency might be defined by considering the government's budget constraint.[30] A widely accepted concept is that debt cannot accumulate indefinitely without markets questioning the borrower's ability to service it. For a sovereign borrower, like for any other economic agent, the total stock of outstanding debt (domestic plus external debt) cannot exceed the present discounted value of current and future net incomes — i.e., the difference between tax revenues and government expenditures. If this condition is not met, a sovereign borrower can be said to be insolvent. This definition, which focuses on a country's capacity to pay, misses a crucial point: a default is the result of a set of decisions rather than the mechanistic outcome of some unpleasant arithmetics.[31] A sovereign borrower's decision of being or not being current with its debt-service payments depends, at least partially, on its willingness to pay. In fact, the previous condition is derived under the hypothesis of unchanged policies. Therefore, the underlying assumption is that the government deems the economic and political costs associated with a tightening of financial policies — necessary to avoid an explosive path of the debt — excessive with respect to reputation and other costs that might be associated with the decision of defaulting on its debt. On the creditors' side, there is the decision not to extend credit any further whenever it becomes evident that a country is not pursuing sound economic policies.

If the definition of insolvency implies some latitude and discretion, more ambiguous is the concept of illiquidity. A country might be defined to be illiquid if it is denied access to financial markets even though its underlying economic fundamentals are broadly sound. This unwillingness to lend by the markets could

---

[29] An exception is New Zealand whose government is bound to publish its accounts in a similar form under the Fiscal Responsibility Act adopted in 1994.

[30] Arora (1993) and Eaton (1993).

[31] Eaton, Gersovitz and Stiglitz (1986), Eaton and Gersovitz (1981) and Summers (1996).

CRISES AND BAIL-OUTS OF BANKS AND COUNTRIES   71

be justified on the basis of an asymmetry in the available information between lenders and the borrower; or more precisely on the basis of a different perception by the markets of the sustainability of current policies to meet current debt-service obligations. The failure of capital markets to provide adequate support to an illiquid but solvent country may also be the direct consequence of a co-ordination failure, i.e. the inability of creditors to recognise that it would be in their mutual interest to continue to lend to the debtor country.[32]

In sum, the following pragmatic distinction between insolvency and illiquidity can be made. A liquidity crisis arises when the impairment of a country in servicing its debt can be overcome by a combination of debt rescheduling, new financial support, and macroeconomic adjustment (cum reforms). A solvency crisis, instead, implies that no realistic adjustment programme can restore financial stability in a reasonable period of time without the adoption of concurrent measures of debt relief.

In this different perception of the roots of the 1980s debt crisis rests the main difference between the debt strategies envisaged initially by the former US Treasury Secretary Baker and subsequently by his successor Brady. The basic philosophy was the same, i.e. to restore debtors' capacity to service their debt thus improving their creditworthiness and access to international financial markets. However, the Baker plan was structured assuming that the crisis was essentially a short-term liquidity problem.[33] Therefore, it emphasised the adoption of structural reforms and growth-oriented policies in the debtor countries supported by continued external financial assistance. On the contrary, the Brady plan, though endorsing the key elements of the previous strategy, acknowledged that the crisis was one of near insolvency and therefore placed debt and debt-service reduction at the centre of the strategy.[34]

5. SUPERVISION, SURVEILLANCE AND MORAL HAZARD

a. Supervision of Banks

Traditionally, banks have been subjected to greater regulation than industrial firms. Lately, a number of empirical and theoretical criticisms have been levelled at such an attitude. From an empirical standpoint, technological innovations have reduced the effectiveness of some regulations, because the distinctions between once different financial products and intermediaries have been blurred; moreover, regulation failures, as in the Savings and Loans experience, have reinforced the

---

[32] The underlying assumption is that the value of individual loans depends on the behaviour of the other creditors.

[33] This also explains the refusal of creditor governments to bail out commercial banks.

[34] Guitian (1992b), Cline (1994) and Dooley (1995).

72   R. DE BONIS, A. GIUSTINIANI AND G. GOMEL

arguments against the traditional justification for public intervention in banking. On the theoretical side, research and policy discussion have increasingly advocated a 'laissez faire' attitude. This has resulted from different strands of thought: the 'rational expectations revolution', with its emphasis on the structure of policy regimes; the 'public choice' theory with its sceptical view of government and regulations; the revival of 'Austrian economics', with its attention to institutional frameworks being formed spontaneously without central design; the 'regulator capture' theory, with its critique of the public interest as the origin of supervision.[35]

Changes in the forms of financial surveillance have resulted from such criticisms. Barriers to entry and geographical expansion have been relaxed. In the USA, for example, the 1994 Interstate Banking and Branching Efficiency Act relaxed several constraints to the geographic expansion of banks.[36] In many countries portfolio restrictions and forms of specialisation, preventing banks from entering some line of activities or precluding the joint supply of two or more products, have been reformed. A trend towards the 'universal bank' model seems to prevail which allows banks to offer different products or to create financial groups.[37]

Excessive credit and market risks are the classic determinants of banks' financial troubles and are influenced by macroeconomic instability, the degree of banking competition, the actual content of the separation between banking and commerce, the structure of financial conglomerates, and the effectiveness of internal and supervisory controls.

Regulatory failures contributed to the problems of Asian banks. Many countries in that area are characterised by a highly concentrated credit structure and strong interconnections between banks and firms. This was especially the case of the Korean 'chaebol', the system of relationships between the financial structure and the country's big industrial groups.

Even if credit risk is still the most important source of bank failures, the cases of Herstatt, Barings and other intermediaries heightened the attention devoted to the different forms of market risk. Regulation has designed specific tools to limit interest rate and foreign exchange risks. In 1993 the EC capital adequacy directive introduced capital requirements to face market risks. In 1995 the Basle capital ratios were amended to incorporate provisions towards market risks. Banks have a choice: either they can use their own financial models to calculate how much capital to hold against their risks or they can use the regulators' standard formula. If the first choice is adopted, each bank will calculate a 'value

---

[35] For a survey see Selgin and White (1994).
[36] See Rose (1996) and Jayaratne and Strahan (1996).
[37] The Glass-Steagall Act is under growing criticism in the USA. See Kroszner and Rajan (1994 and 1995).

at risk' for itself, i.e. the maximum amount that it might expect to lose by holding a particular position for a certain period. This 'market-friendly' regulation will probably be adopted mainly by large intermediaries; meanwhile the smaller institutions will follow the regulatory rule.

The general thrust of the recent evolution is a sharper focus on preventive measures and the efficiency of supervisory instruments. The Federal Deposit Insurance Corporation Improvement Act, approved by the US Congress in 1991, introduced forms of pre-commitment for supervisors, requiring them to take prompt action against troubled banks in order to minimise the cost for public resources.

Banking regulation has also to keep a balance between two different needs. On the one hand, it must go on relaxing barriers and unjustified limits to banks' activity, erasing bureaucratic attitudes that have often characterised public action. On the other hand, the awareness of the riskier environment in which intermediaries operate and the recent failures, might require supervisors to take a more active part in banks' strategic choices.[38]

In prudential regulation, moral hazard, i.e. the unintended encouragement by supervisors of imprudent behaviour by intermediaries, may be a limit to public action. Moral hazard derives from banks' shareholders and managers mainly handling other people's money rather than their own and from the intrinsic asymmetry of information between the intermediary and its depositors. The establishment of deposit insurance has been largely criticised on the grounds that it would induce moral hazard. According to these critiques, deposit insurance may cause more problems than it solves: managers may try to increase the riskiness of the bank's portfolio because a lower ratio between capital and assets leads to an increase in the value of the guarantee, with a gain for the owner of the bank.

However, it is not obvious that deposit insurance induces moral hazard: normally shareholders and managers of failed banks are punished for their risky behaviour; in such a way the consequences of a bankruptcy (or even of a bail-out) are distributed among the different actors. In addition, two arrangements have been envisaged to deal with the possible flaws of deposit insurance. The traditional avenue has been one of designing optimal contracts which require some sharing of risk between the parties, according to the so-called 'co-insurance principle'. deposit insurance does not cover the larger deposits; even for the smaller sums, the coverage may not be complete.[39]

---

[38] The point is discussed in Hellwig (1995). On banking regulation see Dewatripont and Tirole (1994), Goodhart (1996a and 1996b) and Quinn (1996).
[39] This approach has influenced the EU Directive on Deposit Insurance in 1993.

74   R. DE BONIS, A. GIUSTINIANI AND G. GOMEL

b. Surveillance of Countries

Even if there are substantial differences, we may draw a parallel between the supervisory function which is assigned to central banks or other public agencies and the IMF's surveillance over countries' economic policies and performances.[40] Such a function has been traditionally undercut by two factors: (i) the absence of a minimum set of widely-accepted rules which may give an operational content to the general principles outlined in the Articles of Agreement; (ii) the absence of adequate instruments of enforcement of the Fund's prescriptions, which marks one of the sharpest differences with respect to national supervisory powers.

The demise of the Bretton Woods system removed a crucial yardstick to assess the extent to which a country's domestic policies were in step with the requirements of an international 'order', i.e. the maintenance of a stable exchange rate. The move to a generalised system of floating provided scope for more discretion in the conduct of domestic policies. This might have been not an adverse consequence per se provided that the higher degree of freedom at the national level be offset by tighter scrutiny at the international one. The actual experience with the conduct of surveillance has been, however, rather mixed: the process has suffered from a basic asymmetry stemming from whether or not a member country makes use of Fund resources.

The Mexican crisis highlighted the limitations of the current institutional setting. The main challenge was to avoid the risk of contagion to other emerging economies associated with the sudden loss of confidence in one market and the attempt by investors to reshuffle the composition of their portfolios by disinvesting elsewhere in order to, at least, compensate for initial capital losses. The IMF was not only unable to foresee the crisis but also breached the conventional limits of access to its resources to provide less than a half of the rescue package.

The need for increasing resources available to the IMF to support countries in distress, however, goes hand-in-hand with the need for strengthening its surveillance activity. The efforts aimed at intensifying the exchange of information between the IMF and the authorities of member countries and improving the prompt availability and the quality of macroeconomic and financial data are all necessary steps to enhance the IMF's policy advice but do not provide the institution with suitable instruments for enforcement.[41] A rating

---

[40] On this issue, see the thorough review by Guitián (1992a).
[41] The IMF established a Special Data Dissemination Standard (SDDS) for provision of economic and financial statistics to the public by member countries. The SDDS sets the norms for IMF members that choose to participate. These are expected to be countries that participate in international capital markets or aspire to do so. In addition, the Fund opened, on the Internet, the Dissemination Standards Bulletin Board (DSBB), which describes the dissemination practices followed by 18 member countries that have, so far, subscribed to the SDDS.

CRISES AND BAIL-OUTS OF BANKS AND COUNTRIES 75

agency often has more leverage on a country than the IMF since a potential downgrading of the country's debt translates immediately into higher costs of borrowing on the international capital markets.[42] In addition, even if publicly available information were perfect, crises would still occur.

Moral hazard may arise not only in banking regulation but also in international lending to countries, because creditors are unable to ascertain the amount of disbursed credit that the sovereign borrower devotes to finance current expenditures as opposed to productive investment projects. If a high share of external financing goes to consumption, the growth prospects of the debtor country may be impaired and its debt-servicing capacity undermined. The issue becomes more sensitive when support from official sources is granted to debtor countries in cases of financial stress or to support their adjustment programmes. For example, some have argued that foreign banks had granted large loans to Asian countries with the certainty that those governments and the IMF would have covered the losses on private operations should a crisis develop. Another instance is when official support, when it assumes the form of debt forgiveness or debt reduction, discourages rather than fosters the pursuit of the necessary corrective policies. The result under those circumstances may be inappropriate financing by creditors. This can be avoided only through adequate IMF conditionality — which carries costs for the borrowing country — and the appropriate balance between adjustment and financing. These can be seen as mechanisms of 'co-insurance' with a view to avoiding such undesired consequences.

6. LENDER OF LAST RESORT

a. A Classic Story

Banks and other financial intermediaries facing temporary shortages of reserves or insufficient liquid assets can borrow funds from other institutions. Ailing banks in need of reserves may also resort to the Central bank if the interbank market is imperfect. There should be nothing automatic about the Central bank acting as a lender of last resort. The general aim should be to prevent systemic risk and safeguard the financial system as a whole, not any single institution.

The key problem lies in the difficulty of distinguishing between insolvency and illiquidity. It has been claimed that in some cases there was no time to examine the balance sheet of the bank asking for liquidity; in such cases, the lender-of-last-resort function was activated, even though the solvency of the

---

[42] For a similar argument, see Minton-Beddoes (1995).

borrower was subject to doubt, in order to avoid risks of contagion.[43] Liquidity supply for large banks may be more generous than for smaller institutions because a big intermediary has a stronger position in the interbank market, a higher number of depositors, a more important role in the financial support of industrial firms, thus a greater leverage on the overall economy. However, as the BCCI case has proved, no bank is too big to fail if its liquidation does not involve systemic risk. 'Prompt corrective action', automatic closure rules and separation between monitoring and closure responsibilities have been advocated to force supervisors to a more restrictive and efficient use of the lender-of-last-resort powers.

b. A 'Lender of Last Resort' for Countries?

Financial globalisation has made the real sector of the economy more vulnerable to upheavals in financial markets and underscored one of the key drawbacks of the current international monetary disorder — the absence of an international lender of last resort (ILLR).[44]

The debate on the need for such an institution dates back to the Bretton Woods negotiations.[45] The issue surfaced again in the 1970s when the international activity of commercial banks increased dramatically with the advent of the Eurocurrency markets and the need for recycling the sizeable surpluses of OPEC countries.

In a nutshell the issue has two dimensions. The first one is whether or not there is a need for such a function at the international level. If so, the second dimension of the problem is what institution, or group of institutions, should perform it.

In his thorough study of financial crises Kindleberger (1989) notes that the international dimension of crises makes a case for an ILLR. When a crisis is unfolding, countries may face limited access to capital markets even though they are implementing the appropriate policy corrections. The causes of this 'international' credit rationing may be traced back to either asymmetric information or policy lags. On the contrary, Schwartz (1986) and Meltzer (1986) and others reject such a proposal on two grounds: first, an ILLR would exacerbate the risk of moral hazard by sovereign borrowers as well as by international banks; second, the authority to create base money, that is the very *raison d'être* of a lender of last resort, remains within the purview of national central banks.

---

[43] On this point see Goodhart and Schoenmaker (1995, p. 549).

[44] Guttentag and Herring (1983) and Sachs (1995).

[45] The plan put forward by Keynes was centred on the establishment of an International Clearing Union, that would issue a new international money to be called *bancor*, and provide automatic financing of current account deficits. In fact, the institutional setting eventually outlined at Bretton Woods was less ambitious in nature.

CRISES AND BAIL-OUTS OF BANKS AND COUNTRIES 77

The second dimension of the problem is clearly emphasised by Kindleberger:

With no world government, no central bank, and weak international law, the question where last-resort lending comes from is a crucial one (1989, p. 201).

Historically such a role was informally performed by either the central bank or the most important financial institutions of the leading financial centres of the world: initially Britain and France, and after World War II the United States. In 1945, the institutional setting that was shaped at Bretton Woods fell short of providing a full-fledged ILLR.

The IMF was created in order to provide financial assistance to member countries to correct external imbalances without resorting to trade and payment restrictions. However, the principles governing its lending activity can hardly be reconciled with the classic Bagehot rules of: (a) lending freely to solvent borrowers; (b) against good collateral; and (c) at a penalty rate.

In the aftermath of the Mexican crisis two important results were achieved towards strengthening several aspects of the Fund's capacity to cope with abrupt and spreading crises. The first has been the setting up by the IMF of an Emergency Financing Mechanism (EFM),[46] and the doubling of the lines of credit made available to the Fund by member countries, through the General Arrangements to Borrow (GAB) and the New Arrangements to Borrow (NAB). More recently, another brick has been added with the Supplemental Reserve Facility (SRF), established by the IMF in the aftermath of the Korean crisis.[47] This facility provides an almost unlimited access to Fund resources, albeit at a penalty rate which increases over time thus providing an incentive for a speedy repayment of the loan. Such a facility should endow the IMF with an adequate instrument of intervention to deal with countries' short-term liquidity needs resulting from confidence crises or contagion and not necessarily related to their economic fundamentals.

Is the system therefore moving, though prudently, towards the establishment of an ILLR? Could the IMF perform such a function?

The answer to the first question can only be tentative. Recent experience has shown that a need exists for a mechanism to shore up market confidence and maintain orderly market conditions especially in emerging economies which lack co-operative instruments, such as co-ordinated intervention in currency markets, to meet sudden collapses of confidence or contagion effects. However, although

---

[46] The EFM is only an exceptional procedure to facilitate a rapid approval in the event a member faced a crisis.

[47] 'This facility has been put in place to provide financial assistance to member countries experiencing exceptional balance of payments difficulties due to a large short-term financing need resulting from a sudden and disruptive loss of market confidence reflected in pressure on the capital account and the member's reserves' (IMF, Press Release No. 97/59). Until now, this facility has been used only in the case of Korea: SDR 9,950 million of the Fund-supported programme (SDR 15,500 million) have been made available under the SRF.

78   R. DE BONIS, A. GIUSTINIANI AND G. GOMEL

the goal of reducing instability may require corrective public action, this public intervention can be successful only if it is consistent with the aim of maintaining market discipline.[48] Preserving the correct workings of market incentives is the only way in which the problem of moral hazard — from both the creditor and debtor perspective — may be reduced.

As far as the second question is concerned, our view is that, even if its operational setting were radically changed, the IMF's mutation into a full-fledged ILLR would be hindered by three basic facts. First, the IMF does not issue its own, globally-accepted fiat money: the SDR is a hybrid instrument and its issuance is governed by very restrictive rules. Second, the Fund's surveillance powers are of limited scope and lack enforceability. Third, the Fund still remains a co-operative institution whose activity can hardly be based on the tenets of 'pure' central banking.

7. CO-ORDINATION AND FREE-RIDING

a. Banks

Because of the possible large externalities and contagion effects associated with financial·troubles of multinational banks, international co-operation between bank regulators has a long tradition.[49] Back in 1974, following the Bankhaus Herstatt crisis in Germany, the Basle Committee was created with the goal of fostering co-operation between national supervisory bodies; in 1975, the first Basle Concordat introduced some principles of supervisory control of foreign branches and subsidiaries. Italy's Banco Ambrosiano's failure in 1982 contributed to the approval of a second version of the Concordat, which focused on consolidated supervision, specifying practical steps to assign responsibilities to national authorities with respect to multinational banking. Finally, the 1991 BCCI's case showed that the bank had deliberately confused regulators by shuffling its assets between different jurisdictions. The BCCI's failure led to the Minimum Standards Agreement, which enforces consolidated supervision, assigning responsibility to the 'home-country' authority and subordinating the international expansion of intermediaries to the availability of information and supervision.

Overall, the international co-ordination of bank supervision has made progress mainly in the area of prevention, while little has been achieved in the area of crisis management. The European directive on the reorganisation measures and winding-up procedures of credit institutions is very slow in taking off and only an informal agreement has been reached for crisis management. As far as pitfalls in

---

[48] See, for instance, Crockett (1997).
[49] This analysis is taken from Padoa-Schioppa (1994).

CRISES AND BAIL-OUTS OF BANKS AND COUNTRIES   79

supervisory co-ordination are concerned, in 1995 the Federal Reserve Bank of New York protested that Japan's Finance Ministry had failed to alert it to the problems at Daiwa's New York branch for more than a month after its $1.1 billion bond loss.

b. Countries

In the case of sovereign borrowers' debt, difficulties in devising collective action are exacerbated by the absence of an internationally agreed legal framework. As a result the international community's reactions to sovereign debt crises have been largely *ad hoc*, a reflection of the particular types of financial instruments and institutions involved, of the different historical circumstances, and the like.

In the 1930s, the bulk of foreign lending took place through the issue of bonds, a rather small share of which was held by creditor countries' commercial banks. Hence, sovereign borrowers' defaults did not represent a serious threat to the stability of their respective financial systems. Broadly speaking, the creditor countries' reaction was to let the market work. The defaults were settled through lengthy negotiations between debtor countries and bondholder councils.[50] As a consequence, most of the defaulting countries were able to regain access to financial markets only 40 years later.[51]

On the contrary, in the debt crisis of the 1980s, a similar confrontational approach might have endangered the stability of the international banking system,[52] given the dominant role played by commercial banks. This threat urged the international community to envisage a more co-operative strategy. The aim was to achieve an equitable burden sharing among the main actors involved: commercial banks, official creditors and debtor countries.[53] In this regard, the IMF played the crucial role of co-ordinator by providing the appropriate framework, that is the typical Fund-supported adjustment programme. Crucial players were also the Paris and the London Club, which represented two important fora for co-ordinated action of official and private creditors, respectively, in order to combine debt relief operations with the provision of new financial assistance in support of debtor countries' adjustment efforts. Yet international financial institutions and creditors do not provide a formal institutional framework to cope with financial crises. The process of dealing with sovereign borrowers' debt-service difficulties is still essentially voluntary in nature and exposed to the problem of free riding especially as far as private

---

[50] Usually, it took between five and ten years to reach an agreement on debt restructuring.

[51] Eichengreen and Portes (1987, 1988) and Ernandez-Ansola and Laursen (1995).

[52] When the crisis erupted, the large US banks had an exposure to developing countries amounting to 150 to 200 per cent of their capital, especially in Latin America.

[53] See for example Lipson (1986).

80   R. DE BONIS, A. GIUSTINIANI AND G. GOMEL

TABLE 6
Aggregate Net Long-term Resource Flows to Developing Countries

	1980	1990	1993	1994	1995	1996[1]
	(billions of US dollars)					
Official flows	34.3	56.3	55.0	45.7	53.0	40.8
Private flows[2]	51.7	44.4	157.1	161.3	184.2	243.8
of which:						
Commercial bank loans	21.6	3.0	−0.3	11.0	26.5	n.a.
Bonds	2.6	2.3	35.9	29.3	28.5	n.a.
Portfolio equity investment	0.0	3.2	45.0	32.7	32.1	45.7
Foreign direct investment	5.1	24.5	67.2	83.7	95.5	109.5
Aggregate net resource flows	*86.1*	*100.6*	*212.0*	*207.0*	*237.2*	*284.6*
	(in per cent of total)					
Official flows	60.1	55.9	25.9	22.1	22.3	14.3
Private flows[2]	60.1	44.1	74.1	77.9	77.7	85.7
of which:						
Commercial bank loans	25.1	3.0	−0.1	5.3	11.2	n.a.
Bonds	3.0	2.3	16.9	14.2	12.0	n.a.
Portfolio equity investment	0.0	3.2	21.2	15.8	13.5	16.1
Foreign direct investment	5.9	24.4	31.7	40.4	40.3	38.5

Notes:
[1] Projections.
[2] Includes publicly guaranteed flows.
Source: World Bank — Global Development Finance (1997).

creditors are concerned. In fact, debt rescheduling has not always been an orderly process because commercial banks have not acted as a cohesive group of lenders.

Recently, in the case of Korea the concerted effort by the Group of Seven to use 'moral suasion' on the banks to secure an orderly rollover of their short-term loans was crucial to stem the crisis. But given the present configuration of international capital markets, and in particular the growing share of bond financing and of non-bank financial intermediation (Table 6), a number of different, more complex, scenarios can be envisaged. First, the growing dispersion of creditors makes it particularly difficult to replicate the concerted strategy of the 1980s. Second, free-riding behaviour might be encouraged: in fact, dissenting bondholders might benefit from windfall capital gains if a debt reduction agreement were reached between the debtor country and part of the creditor community since this would increase bond prices on the secondary market. In the aftermath of the Mexican crisis considerable work was carried out in international fora, chiefly the Group of Ten,[54] to explore possible ways of

---

[54] *The Resolution of Sovereign Liquidity Crises* (a Report to the Ministers and Governors of the G-10, May 1996).

CRISES AND BAIL-OUTS OF BANKS AND COUNTRIES   81

dealing with this problem, but very little was done in practice to adapt existing procedures and institutions.

One solution that has been advocated would be to consider co-ordinated, temporary, standstills in servicing foreign debt. In such a context the IMF would remain at the centre of the stage, both to ensure orderly work-out procedures and to provide interim finance to countries under stress but nonetheless pursuing appropriate policies. To the latter purpose, the IMF would broaden the scope of its well-established practice of 'lending into arrears' to signal to the market its approval of those countries' policies.

In our opinion, 'lending into arrears' by the Fund should be a component of a co-operative strategy aimed at ensuring an equitable burden sharing between debtors, creditors — both official and private ones — and multilateral institutions. It would be a means through which 'working capital' is provided to the country in financial distress, not a 'bail-out' of creditors that assumed excessive risks. Furthermore, the recourse to this type of lending should be limited to exceptional circumstances in order to introduce an element of uncertainty or, as it has been called, 'constructive ambiguity'.[55] This would allow for pressure on market participants — both creditors and debtors — to act prudently, because they would not be certain of official support.

8. SUMMARY AND CONCLUSIONS

While exploring interconnections, analogies and differences between crises and bail-outs of banks and countries we have discussed a number of unsolved issues at the intersection of international finance, the economics of regulation and public policy. In drawing conclusions, we also outline a tentative list of items which should be included in an agenda for future work, for purposes of both research and policy design.

First, as far as banks are concerned, recent crises have confirmed that good internal and external governance may be insufficient to ensure full stability in banking. In fact, efficient management and proper internal oversight do not guarantee good governance of intermediaries; market discipline may fail as well if, for instance, market participants have insufficient information.[56]

The presence of market failures is a necessary condition for public action, not a sufficient one. Indeed, while the theoretical explanations of banks' instability and the recent spate of crises of intermediaries tend to reinforce the classical arguments in favour of regulation, we should carefully consider the adequacy of present regulatory arrangements, their ability to correct market failures, and the possible inefficiencies they introduce in the competitive process.

---

[55] See Crockett (1997).
[56] On these microeconomic aspects see IMF (1996c).

In particular, among the concrete tasks which regulators should focus their attention on is an effort to ensure that bail-outs do not impose excessive costs on the tax-payer. In fact, in recent years bail-outs have been largely based on public aid. While in the course of a bail-out state control may be accepted it should be followed by privatisation. Public authorities involved in managing banking crises should be accountable; bail-out procedures should be clearly designed and rigorously followed.

Second, important differences exist between nations and banks or financial institutions in general.

As we have argued in Section 3*b*, sovereign states enjoy a peculiar bargaining power *vis-à-vis* their creditors both because of their very nature and size, so that in the event of default of a large sovereign borrower the stability of financial markets world-wide might be put in jeopardy, and of the weakness of enforcement mechanisms that can deter such a sovereign borrower from defaulting on its debt obligations. On these accounts, a simple-minded analogy between countries and banks is flawed: ultimately, the decision of a sovereign state to default or suspend its debt-service payments is largely a voluntary one and the safeguards against moral hazard built into domestic bankruptcy codes cannot be applied to a state.

In other words, a sovereign debtor does not go 'bankrupt' in a strict commercial sense. As the Group of Ten report put it:

> It would be neither appropriate nor possible to replace the authorities responsible for the economic policies of a sovereign state with a new management, or to take possession of a state's non-commercial property. The need for additional protection from creditors has not in the past been a serious problem for sovereign debtors. Such debtors have few assets to seize and some of these benefit from sovereign immunities ('The Resolution of Sovereign Liquidity Crises', a Report to the Ministers and Governors of the G-10, May 1996, p. 8).

Yet, especially since the Mexican crisis and the momentum impressed by the Group of Seven leaders in Halifax in 1995, ways to prevent, manage and resolve countries' financial crises have become a paramount concern in the international community's agenda.

Such urgency has been heightened in the aftermath of the crisis in East Asia. Standard IMF lending instruments were ill-suited to cope with crises characterised by large short-term liquidity needs due to a sudden collapse of market confidence. Especially when contagion and systemic risk are involved, financial assistance is required which is at the same time sufficiently large in magnitude and quickly available, although provided at a penalty rate. In this light a major step forward has been the newly created *Supplemental Reserve Facility*, which endows the IMF with an appropriate instrument of intervention.

We do not advocate that the IMF become a full-fledged international lender of last resort. In fact, it would not be able to do so because, unlike a central bank in

CRISES AND BAIL-OUTS OF BANKS AND COUNTRIES   83

the usual domestic context, the IMF does not issue its own fiat money now it does have full powers of surveillance and enforcement.

Moreover, it is essential that the limited resources at the disposal of the IMF and more generally of the official community be used to avoid undue strains to international financial markets, not to protect lenders from the consequences of their imprudent behaviour.

To this purpose, mechanisms should be put in place to ensure an equitable burden-sharing of the cost of handling financial crises. When a relatively small number of big banks hold the bulk of a country's foreign debt, as in the Asian crises, securing that short-term foreign loans are rolled over or rescheduled in an orderly fashion is made somewhat easier. Indeed, in the case of Korea the concerted effort by the Group of Seven to use 'moral suasion' to this effect was crucial to stem the crisis. But given the growing share of bond financing and of non-bank financial intermediation, the merits of more formal work-out mechanisms should be reconsidered: among them, co-ordinated, temporary, standstills in servicing foreign debt to stem foreign exchange crises of particular gravity. Under such circumstances, the IMF's policy of 'lending into arrears' might prove a useful ingredient of a strategy aimed at an equitable burden-sharing between debtors, creditors and multilateral institutions.

Finally, since crisis prevention is such a crucial part of the story and domestic financial distress so often a key ingredient in international crises, it is essential that country surveillance better incorporate the performance of the banking system. To this end, the BIS and the IMF should endeavour jointly to establish a far more rigorous system of monitoring of prudential arrangements (capital adequacy, disclosure rules, risk ratings, deposit insurance, etc.).[57]

REFERENCES

Alonso, I. (1996), 'On Avoiding Bank Runs', *Journal of Monetary Economics*, **2**, 73–87.
Arora, V.B. (1993), 'Sovereign Debt: A Survey of Some Theoretical and Policy Issues', *IMF Working Paper* WP/93/56 (Washington).
Bank for International Settlements (1996), *Annual Report*, 66th Edition (Basle).
Brownlie, I. (1987), *Principles of Public International Law* (Oxford: Clarendon Press).
Camdessus, M. (1996), 'Promoting Safe and Sound Banking Systems. An IMF Perspective', Paper presented at the Conference on Safe and Sound Financial Systems: What Works for Latin America (Inter-American Development Bank, Washington, 28 September).
Carli, G. (1987), 'Tipicità dei dissesti bancari', in F. Belli, G. Minervini, A. Patroni Griffi and M. Porzio (eds.), *Banche in crisi, 1960–1985* (Bari-Roma: Laterza).
Chari, V.V. and R. Jagannathan (1988), 'Banking Panics, Information and Rational Expectations Equilibrium', *Journal of Finance*, **43**, 3, 749–60.
Cline, W.R. (1994), *International Economic Policy in the 1990s* (Cambridge: The MIT Press).

---

[57] On this front a first, important step has been made with the recent Basle Committee text on 'Core Principles of Effective Banking Supervision'.

84   R. DE BONIS, A. GIUSTINIANI AND G. GOMEL

Crockett, A. (1997), 'The Theory and Practice of Financial Stability', *Essays in International Finance No. 203* (Princeton).

Davis, E.P. (1992), *Debt, Financial Fragility, and Systemic Risk* (Oxford: Clarendon Press).

Detragiache, E. (1996), 'Rational Liquidity Crises in the Sovereign Debt Market: In Search of a Theory', *International Monetary Fund Staff Papers*, **43**, 3 (Washington).

Dewatripont, M. and J. Tirole (1994), *The Prudential Regulation of Banking* (Cambridge: The MIT Press).

Diamond, D.W. and P.H. Dybvig (1983), 'Bank Runs, Deposit Insurance and Liquidity', *Journal of Political Economy*, **3**, 401–19.

Dooley, M.P. (1995), 'A Retrospective on the Debt Crisis', in P.B. Kenen (ed.), *Understanding Interdependence: The Macroeconomics of the Open Economy* (Princeton: Princeton University Press).

Drees, B. and C. Pazarbasioglu (1995), 'The Nordic Banking Crises: Pitfalls in Financial Liberalization?', *IMF Working Paper*, WP/95/61 (Washington).

Eaton, J. (1990), 'Debt Relief and the International Enforcement of Loan Contracts', *Journal of Economic Perspectives*, **4**, 1, 43–56.

Eaton, J. (1993), 'Sovereign Debt: A Premier', *The World Bank Economic Review*, **7**, 2, 137–72.

Eaton, J. and M. Gersovitz (1981), 'Poor-Country Borrowing in Private Financial Markets and the Repudiation Issue', *Princeton Studies in International Finance No. 47*.

Eaton, J., M. Gersovitz and J.E. Stiglitz (1986), 'The Pure Theory of Country Risk', *European Economic Review*, **30**, 3, 481–513.

Economist The (1997), 'The Lesson of Crédit Lyonnais' (5 July).

Eichengreen, B. and R. Portes (1987), 'The Anatomy of Financial Crises', in R. Portes and A.K. Swoboda (eds.), *Threats to International Financial Stability* (Cambridge: Cambridge University Press).

Eichengreen, B. and R. Portes (1988), *Settling Defaults in the Era of Bond Finance*, CEPR Discussion Paper No. 272.

Eichengreen, B. and R. Portes (1991), 'After the Deluge: Default, Negotiation, and Readjustment During the Interwar Years', in B. Eichengreen and P.H. Lindert (eds.), *The International Debt Crisis in Historical Perspective* (Cambridge, Massachusetts: The MIT Press).

Fama, E.F. (1985), 'What's Different About Banks?', *Journal of Monetary Economics*, **1**, 29–39.

Gale, D. and M. Hellwig (1988), 'Repudiation and Renegotiation: The Case of Sovereign Debt', paper presented at a conference on The International Capital Market: Perspective and Policy Problems (University of Pennsylvania, June).

Goldstein, M. and P. Turner (1996), 'Banking Crises in Emerging Economies: Origins and Policy Options', Bank for International Settlements, *Economic Papers No. 46*.

Goodhart, C.A.E. (1996a), 'An Incentive Structure for Financial Regulation', London School of Economics Financial Markets Group, *Special Paper Series*, **88** (London).

Goodhart, C.A.E. (1996b), 'Some Regulatory Concerns', *Swiss Journal of Economics and Statistics*, Special Volume on 'Capital Adequacy Regulation as Instruments for the Regulation of Banks: Further Results', Conference (July, Basle).

Goodhart, C. and D. Schoenmaker (1993), 'Institutional Separation Between Supervisory and Monetary Agencies', London School of Economics Financial Markets Group, *Special Paper Series*, **52** (London).

Goodhart, C. and D. Schoenmaker (1995), 'Should the Functions of Monetary Policy and Banking Supervision be Separated?', *Oxford Economic Papers* (October), 539–60.

Gorton, G. (1985), 'Bank Suspension of Convertibility', *Journal of Monetary Economics*, **15**, 2, 177–93.

Group of Ten (1996), *The Resolution of Sovereign Liquidity Crises*, A Report to the Ministers and Governors Prepared Under the Auspices of the Deputies (May).

Guitián, M. (1992a), 'The Unique Nature of the Responsibilities of the International Monetary Fund', *IMF Pamphlet Series No. 46* (Washington).

Guitián, M. (1992b), 'Rules and Discretion in International Economic Policy', *IMF Occasional Paper No. 97* (Washington).

CRISES AND BAIL-OUTS OF BANKS AND COUNTRIES 85

Guttentag, J. and R. Herring (1983), 'The Lender-of-Last-Resort Function in an International Context', *Essays in International Finance No. 151* (Princeton).

Hellwig, M. (1995), 'Systemic Aspects of Risk Management in Banking and Finance', *Swiss Journal of Economics and Statistics*, **131**, 723–37.

International Monetary Fund (1996a), *Bank Soundness and Macroeconomic Policy* (February, Washington).

International Monetary Fund (1996b), *Macroeconomic Consequences and Causes of Bank Unsoundness* (February, Washington).

International Monetary Fund (1996c), *Maintaining a Sound Banking System* (February, Washington).

Jayaratne, J. and P.E. Strahan (1996), 'The Finance-Growth Nexus: Evidence from Bank Branch Deregulation', *The Quarterly Journal of Economics* (August), 639–70.

Kindleberger, C.P. (1989), *Manias, Panics and Crashes: A History of Financial Crises* (New York: Basic Books).

Kroszner, R.S. and R.G. Rajan (1994), 'Is the Glass-Steagall Act Justified? A Study of the US Experience with Universal Banking Before 1933', *American Economic Review*, **84**, 4, 810–32.

Kroszner, R.S. and R.G. Rajan (1995), *Organization Structure and Credibility: Evidence from Commercial Bank Securities Activities Before the Glass-Steagall Act* (National Bureau of Economic Research, Cambridge, MA).

Lindert, P.H. and P.J. Morton (1989), 'How Sovereign Debt Has Worked', in J.D. Sachs (ed.), *Developing Country Debt and Economic Performance*, **1** (Chicago: The University of Chicago Press).

Lipson, C. (1986), 'Bankers' Dilemmas: Private Cooperation in Rescheduling Sovereign Debts', in K.A. Oye (ed.), *Cooperation Under Anarchy* (Princeton, New Jersey: Princeton University Press).

Meltzer, A.H. (1986), 'Comment on Real and Pseudo-financial Crises', in F. Capie and G. Woods (eds.), *Financial Crises and the World Banking System* (London: Macmillan).

Minton-Beddoes, Z. (1995), 'Why the IMF Needs Reform', *Foreign Affairs*, **74**, 3, 123–33.

Mishkin, F.S. (1991), 'Asymmetric Information and Financial Crises. A Historical Perspective', in R.G. Hubbard (ed.), *Financial Markets and Financial Crises* (Chicago: University of Chicago Press).

Mishkin, F.S. (1994), 'Preventing Financial Crises: An International Perspective', NBER Working Paper No. 4636.

Mishkin, F.S. (1996), *Understanding Financial Crises: A Developing Country Perspective*, paper prepared for the World Bank Annual Conference on Development Economics (25–26 April, Washington).

Padoa-Schioppa, T. (1994), *Opening Remarks and Address to the Conference*, 8th International Conference of Banking Supervisors (12–13 October, Vienna).

Quinn, B. (1996), 'Rules vs. Discretion: the Case of Banking Supervision in the Light of the Debate on Monetary Policy', London School of Economics Financial Markets Group, Special Paper Series No. 85 (London).

Revell, J.R.S. (1975), *Solvency and Regulation of Banks* (University of Wales Press).

Rose, P.S. (1996), 'The Diversification and Cost Effects of Interstate Banking', *The Financial Review*, **31**, 2, 431–52.

Rowlands, D. (1993), 'Constitutional Rules, Reputation, and Sovereign Debt', *Journal of International Economics*, **35**, 3/4, 335–50.

Sachs, J. (1995), *Do We Need an International Lender-of-Last-Resort*, Frank D. Graham Lecture (Princeton University).

Saunders, A. (1987), 'The Interbank Market, Contagion Effects and International Financial Crises', in R. Portes and A. Swoboda (eds.), *Threats to International Financial Stability* (Cambridge University Press).

Schoenmaker, D. (1996), 'Contagion Risk in Banking', London School of Economics Financial Markets Group, Discussion paper, No. 239 (London).

86 R. DE BONIS, A. GIUSTINIANI AND G. GOMEL

Schwartz, A. (1986), 'Real and Pseudo-Financial Crises', in F. Capie and G. Woods (eds.), *Financial Crises and the World Banking System* (London: Macmillan).

Selgin, G.A. and L.H. White (1994), 'How Would the Invisible Hand Handle Money?', *Journal of Economic Literature*, **32**, 4, 1718–49.

Summers, L.H. (1996), 'Introduction', in P.B. Kenen (ed.), 'From Halifax to Lyons: What Has Been Done About Crisis Management', *Essays in International Finance No. 200* (Princeton).

Suter, C. (1992), *Debt Cycles in the World Economy: Foreign Loans, Financial Crises, and Debt Settlements, 1820–1990* (Westview Press, Boulder).

Wallace, N. (1996), 'Narrow Banking Meets the Diamond-Dybvig Model', *Federal Reserve Bank of Minneapolis Quarterly Review* (Winter).

White, L.J. (1991), *The S. & L. Debacle. Public Policy Lessons for Bank and Thrift Regulation* (Oxford University Press).

[2]

The Twin Crises: The Causes of Banking and Balance-of-Payments Problems

By Graciela L. Kaminsky and Carmen M. Reinhart*

In the wake of the Mexican and Asian currency turmoil, the subject of financial crises has come to the forefront of academic and policy discussions. This paper analyzes the links between banking and currency crises. We find that: problems in the banking sector typically precede a currency crisis—the currency crisis deepens the banking crisis, activating a vicious spiral; financial liberalization often precedes banking crises. The anatomy of these episodes suggests that crises occur as the economy enters a recession, following a prolonged boom in economic activity that was fueled by credit, capital inflows, and accompanied by an overvalued currency. (JEL F30, F41)

Pervasive currency turmoil, particularly in Latin America in the late 1970's and early 1980's, gave impetus to a flourishing literature on balance-of-payments crises. As stressed in Paul Krugman's (1979) seminal paper, in this literature, crises occur because a country finances its fiscal deficit by printing money to the extent that excessive credit growth leads to the eventual collapse of the fixed exchange-rate regime. With calmer currency markets in the mid- and late 1980's, interest in this literature languished. The collapse of the European Exchange Rate Mechanism, the Mexican peso crisis, and the wave of currency crises sweeping

through Asia have, however, rekindled interest in the topic. Yet, the focus of this recent literature has shifted. While the earlier literature emphasized the inconsistency between fiscal and monetary policies and the exchange-rate commitment, the new one stresses self-fulfilling expectations and herding behavior in international capital markets.[1] In this view, as Calvo (1995 p. 1) summarizes: "If investors deem you unworthy, no funds will be forthcoming and, thus, unworthy you will be."

Whatever the causes of currency crises, neither the old literature nor the new models of self-fulfilling crises have paid much attention to the interaction between banking and currency problems, despite the fact that many of the countries that have had currency crises have also had full-fledged domestic banking crises around the same time. Notable exceptions are: Carlos F. Díaz-Alejandro (1985), Andres Velasco (1987), Calvo (1995), Ilan Goldfajn and Rodrigo O. Valdés (1995), and Victoria Miller (1995). As to the empirical evidence on the potential links between what we dub the *twin* crises, the literature has been entirely silent. The Thai, Indonesian, and Korean crises are not the first examples of dual currency and banking woes; they are only the recent additions to a long list of casualties which includes Chile, Finland, Mexico, Norway, and Sweden.

* Kaminsky: Department of Economics, George Washington University, Washington, DC 20052; Reinhart: School of Public Affairs and Department of Economics, University of Maryland, College Park, MD 20742, and the National Bureau of Economic Research. We thank two anonymous referees for very helpful suggestions. We also thank Guillermo Calvo, Rudiger Dornbusch, Peter Montiel, Vincent Reinhart, John Rogers, Andrew Rose, and seminar participants at Banco de México, the Board of Governors of the Federal Reserve System, Florida State University, Harvard University, the International Monetary Fund, Johns Hopkins University, Massachusetts Institute of Technology, Stanford University, the State University of New York-Albany, the University of California-Berkeley, UCLA, the University of California-Santa Cruz, the University of Maryland, the University of Washington, the World Bank, and the conference on "Speculative Attacks in the Era of the Global Economy: Theory, Evidence, and Policy Implications" (Washington, DC, December 1995) for very helpful comments, and Greg Belzer, Kris Dickson, and Noah Williams for superb research assistance.

[1] See Maurice Obstfeld (1994, 1995) and Guillermo A. Calvo (1995).

In this paper, we aim to fill this void in the literature and examine currency and banking crises episodes for a number of industrial and developing countries. The former include: Denmark, Finland, Norway, Spain, and Sweden. The latter focus on: Argentina, Bolivia, Brazil, Chile, Colombia, Indonesia, Israel, Malaysia, Mexico, Peru, the Philippines, Thailand, Turkey, Uruguay, and Venezuela. The period covered spans the 1970's through 1995. This sample gives us the opportunity to study 76 currency crises and 26 banking crises. Out of sample, we examine the twin crises in Asia of 1997.

Charles Kindelberger (1978 p. 14), in studying financial crises, observes: "For historians each event is unique. Economics, however, maintains that forces in society and nature behave in repetitive ways. History is particular; economics is general." Like Kindelberger, we are interested in finding the underlying common patterns associated with financial crises. To study the nature of crises, we construct a chronology of events in the banking and external sectors. From this timetable, we draw inference about the possible causal patterns among banking and balance-of-payments problems and financial liberalization. We also examine the behavior of macroeconomic indicators that have been stressed in the theoretical literature around crisis periods, much along the lines of Barry Eichengreen et al. (1996b). Our aim is to gauge whether the two crises share a common macroeconomic background. This methodology also allows us to assess the fragility of economies around the time of the financial crises and sheds light on the extent to which the crises were predictable. Our main results can be summarized as follows.

First, with regard to the linkages among the crises, our analysis shows no apparent link between balance-of-payments and banking crises during the 1970's, when financial markets were highly regulated. In the 1980's, following the liberalization of financial markets across many parts of the world, banking and currency crises become closely entwined. Most often, the *beginning* of banking-sector problems predate the balance-of-payment crisis; indeed, knowing that a banking crisis was underway helps predict a future currency crisis. The causal link, nevertheless, is not unidirectional. Our results show that the collapse of the currency deepens the banking crisis, activating a vicious spiral. We

find that the *peak* of the banking crisis most often comes after the currency crash, suggesting that existing problems were aggravated or new ones created by the high interest rates required to defend the exchange-rate peg or the foreign-exchange exposure of banks.

Second, while banking crises often precede balance-of-payments crises, they are not necessarily the immediate cause of currency crises, even in the cases where a frail banking sector puts the nail in the coffin of what was already a defunct fixed exchange-rate system. Our results point to common causes, and whether the currency or banking problems surface first is a matter of circumstance. Both crises are preceded by recessions or, at least, below normal economic growth, in part attributed to a worsening of the terms of trade, an overvalued exchange rate, and the rising cost of credit; exports are particularly hard hit. In both types of crises, a shock to financial institutions (possibly financial liberalization and/or increased access to international capital markets) fuels the boom phase of the cycle by providing access to financing. The financial vulnerability of the economy increases as the unbacked liabilities of the banking-system climb to lofty levels.

Third, our results show that crises (external or domestic) are typically preceded by a multitude of weak and deteriorating economic fundamentals. While speculative attacks can and do occur as market sentiment shifts and, possibly, herding behavior takes over (crises tend to be bunched together), the incidence of crises where the economic fundamentals were sound are rare.

Fourth, when we compared the episodes in which currency and banking crises occurred jointly to those in which the currency or banking crisis occurred in isolation, we find that for the twin crises, economic fundamentals tended to be worse, the economies were considerably more frail, and the crises (both banking and currency) were far more severe.

The rest of the paper is organized as follows. The next section provides a chronology of the crises and their links. Section II reviews the stylized facts around the periods surrounding the crises, while Section III addresses the issues of the vulnerability of economies around the time of the crisis and the issue of predictability. The final section discusses the findings and possibilities for future research.

VOL. 89 NO. 3   KAMINSKY AND REINHART: THE TWIN CRISES   475

I. The Links Between Banking and Currency Crises

This section briefly discusses what the theoretical literature offers as explanations of the possible links between the two crises. The theoretical models also guide our choice of the financial and economic indicators used in the analysis.

A. *The Links: Theory*

A variety of theoretical models have been put forth to explain the linkages between currency and banking crises. One chain of causation, stressed in James Stoker (1994), runs from balance-of-payments problems to banking crisis. An initial external shock, such as an increase in foreign interest rates, coupled with a commitment to a fixed parity, will result in the loss of reserves. If not sterilized, this will lead to a credit crunch, increased bankruptcies, and financial crisis. Moreover, Frederic S. Mishkin (1996) argues that, if a devaluation occurs, the position of banks could be weakened further if a large share of their liabilities is denominated in a foreign currency. Models, such as Velasco (1987), point to the opposite causal direction—financial-sector problems give rise to the currency collapse. Such models stress that when central banks finance the bailout of troubled financial institutions by printing money, we return to the classical story of a currency crash prompted by excessive money creation.

A third family of models contend that currency and banking crises have common causes. An example of this may be found in the dynamics of an exchange-rate-based inflation stabilization plan, such as that of Mexico in 1987. Theory and evidence suggest that such plans have well-defined dynamics[2]: Because inflation converges to international levels only gradually, there is a marked cumulative real exchange-rate appreciation. Also, at the early stages of the plan there is a boom in imports and economic activity, financed by borrowing abroad. As the current account deficit continues to widen, financial markets become convinced that the sta-

bilization program is unsustainable, fueling an attack against the domestic currency. Since the boom is usually financed by a surge in bank credit, as banks borrow abroad, when the capital inflows become outflows and asset markets crash, the banking system caves in. Ronald I. McKinnon and Huw Pill (1996) model how financial liberalization together with microeconomic distortions—such as implicit deposit insurance—can make these boom-bust cycles even more pronounced by fueling the lending boom that leads to the eventual collapse of the banking system. Goldfajn and Valdés (1995) show how changes in international interest rates and capital inflows are amplified by the intermediating role of banks and how such swings may also produce an exaggerated business cycle that ends in bank runs and financial and currency crashes.

So, while theory does not provide an unambiguous answer as to what the causal links between currency and banking crises are, the models are clear as to what economic indicators should provide insights about the underlying causes of the twin crises. High on that list are international reserves, a measure of excess money balances, domestic and foreign interest rates, and other external shocks, such as the terms of trade. The inflation stabilization-financial liberalization models also stress the boom-bust patterns in imports, output, capital flows, bank credit, and asset prices. Some of these models also highlight overvaluation of the currency, leading to the underperformance of exports. The possibility of bank runs suggests bank deposits as an indicator of impending crises. Finally, as in Krugman (1979), currency crises can be the by-product of government budget deficits.

B. *The Links: Preliminary Evidence*

To examine these links empirically, we first need to identify the dates of currency and banking crises. In what follows, we begin by describing how our indices of financial crises are constructed.

Definitions, Dates, and Incidence of Crises.—Most often, balance-of-payments crises are resolved through a devaluation of the domestic currency or the floatation of the exchange rate.

---

[2] See Reinhart and Carlos A. Végh (1996) for a review of this literature and the empirical regularities.

476   THE AMERICAN ECONOMIC REVIEW   JUNE 1999

But central banks can and, on occasion, do resort to contractionary monetary policy and foreign-exchange market intervention to fight the speculative attack. In these latter cases, currency market turbulence will be reflected in steep increases in domestic interest rates and massive losses of foreign-exchange reserves. Hence, an index of currency crises should capture these different manifestations of speculative attacks. In the spirit of Eichengreen et al. (1996a, b), we constructed an index of currency market turbulence as a weighted average of exchange-rate changes and reserve changes.[3]

With regard to banking crises, our analysis stresses events. The main reason for following this approach has to do with the lack of high-frequency data that capture when a financial crisis is under way. If the beginning of a banking crisis is marked by bank runs and withdrawals, then changes in bank deposits could be used to date the crises. Often, the banking problems do not arise from the liability side, but from a protracted deterioration in asset quality, be it from a collapse in real-estate prices or increased bankruptcies in the nonfinancial sector. In this case, changes in asset prices or a large increase in bankruptcies or nonperforming loans could be used to mark the onset of the crisis. For some of the earlier crises in emerging markets, however, stock-market data is not available.[4] Indicators of business failures and nonperforming loans are also usually available only at low frequencies, if at all; the latter are also made less informative by banks' desire to hide their problems for as long as possible.

Given these data limitations, we mark the *beginning* of a banking crisis by two types of events: (1) bank runs that lead to the closure, merging, or takeover by the public sector of one or more financial institutions (as in Venezuela in 1993); and (2) if there are no runs, the closure, merging, takeover, or large-scale government assistance of an important financial

---

[3] The construction of the index is described in the Data Appendix. The dates of the crises appear in Appendix Table A1, and the level of the index and key events around the crises dates are reported in the working paper version of this paper (Kaminsky and Reinhart, 1996).

[4] Bank stocks could be an indicator, but in many of the developing countries an important share of the banks are not traded publicly.

institution (or group of institutions) that marks the start of a string of similar outcomes for other financial institutions (as in Thailand in 1996–1997). We rely on existing studies of banking crises and on the financial press; according to these studies the fragility of the banking sector was widespread during these periods. This approach to dating the beginning of the banking crises is not without drawbacks. It could date the crises too late, because the financial problems usually begin well before a bank is finally closed or merged; it could also date the crises too early, because the worst of crisis may come later. To address this issue we also date when the banking crisis hits its *peak,* defined as the period with the heaviest government intervention and/or bank closures.

Our sample consists of 20 countries for the period 1970–mid-1995. The countries are those listed in the introduction and Appendix Tables A1 and A2. We selected countries on the multiple criteria of being small open economies, with a fixed exchange rate, crawling peg, or band through portions of the sample; data availability also guided our choices. This period encompasses 26 banking crises and 76 currency crises.

As to the incidence of the crises (Table 1 and Figure 1), there are distinct patterns across decades. During the 1970's we observe a total of 26 currency crises, yet banking crises were rare during that period, with only three taking place. The absence of banking crises may reflect the highly regulated nature of financial markets during the bulk of the 1970's. By contrast, while the number of currency crises per year does not increase much during the 1980's and 1990's (from an average of 2.60 per annum to 3.13 per annum, Table 1, first row), the number of banking crises per year more than quadruples in the post-liberalization period. Thus, as the second row of Table 1 highlights, the *twin* crisis phenomenon is one of the 1980's and 1990's.

Figure 1 also shows that financial crises were heavily bunched in the early 1980's, when real interest rates in the United States were at their highest level since the 1930's. This may suggest that external factors, such as interest rates in the United States, matter a great deal as argued in Calvo et al. (1993). Indeed, Jeffrey Frankel and Andrew K. Rose (1996) find that foreign interest rates play a significant role in predicting

TABLE 1—FREQUENCY OF CRISES OVER TIME

| | Number of crises | | | | | |
| | 1970–1995 | | 1970–1979 | | 1980–1995 | |
Type of crisis	Total	Average per year	Total	Average per year	Total	Average per year
Balance-of-payments	76	2.92	26	2.60	50	3.13
Twin	19	0.73	1	0.10	18	1.13
Single	57	2.19	25	2.50	32	2.00
Banking	26	1.00	3	0.30	23	1.44

Note: Episodes in which the beginning of a banking crisis is followed by a balance-of-payments crisis within 48 months are classified as twin crises.

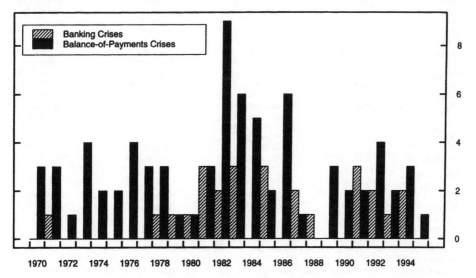

FIGURE 1. NUMBER OF CRISES PER YEAR

currency crashes. A second explanation why crises are bunched is that contagion effects may be present, creating a domino effect among those countries that have anything less than immaculate fundamentals. Sara Calvo and Reinhart (1996) present evidence of contagion in capital flows to Latin American countries while Eichengreen et al. (1996a) find evidence that knowing there is a crisis elsewhere increases the probability of a domestic currency crisis.

Table 2 provides the dates of financial liberalization, the beginning and peak of the banking crisis, and the date of the balance-of-payments

crisis that was nearest to the beginning of the banking crisis.[5] By selecting the nearest currency crisis, whether it predates or follows the beginning of the banking crisis, we allow the data to reveal what the temporal patterns are. The dates for the remaining crises are given in the Appendix tables.

The Twin Crises.—We next examine how the currency and banking crises are linked.

---

[5] If the peak month for the banking crisis is not known, we list the midpoint of that year as the date.

TABLE 2—THE TIMING OF THE TWIN CRISES AND FINANCIAL LIBERALIZATION

Country	Financial liberalization	Banking crisis		Closest balance-of-payment crisis
		Beginning	Peak	
Argentina	1977	March 1980	July 1982	February 1981
		May 1985	June 1989	September 1986
		December 1994	March 1995	February 1990
Bolivia	1985	October 1987	June 1988	September 1985
Brazil	1975	November 1985	November 1985	November 1986
		December 1994	March 1996	October 1991
Chile	1974	September 1981	March 1983	August 1982
Colombia	1980	July 1982	June 1985	March 1983
Denmark	Early 1980's	March 1987	June 1990	August 1983
Finland	1982	September 1991	June 1992	November 1991
Indonesia	1983	November 1992	November 1992	September 1986
Israel	1985	October 1983	June 1984	October 1983
Malaysia	1978	July 1985	August 1986	July 1975
Mexico	1974	September 1982	June 1984	December 1982
	1991	October 1992	March 1996	December 1994
Norway	1980	November 1988	October 1991	May 1986
Peru	1991	March 1983	April 1983	October 1987
Philippines	1980	January 1981	June 1985	October 1983
Spain	1974	November 1978	January 1983	July 1977
Sweden	1980	November 1991	September 1992	November 1992
Thailand	1989	March 1979	March 1979	November 1978
		October 1983	June 1985	November 1984
Turkey	1980	January 1991	March 1991	March 1994
Uruguay	1976–1979	March 1971	December 1971	December 1971
		March 1981	June 1985	October 1982
Venezuela	1981, 1989	October 1993	August 1994	May 1994
Memorandum item:				
Out of sample				
Indonesia		November 1992	Ongoing	August 1997
Malaysia		September 1997	Ongoing	August 1997
Philippines		July 1997	Ongoing	July 1997
Thailand		May 1996	Ongoing	July 1997

Note: Episodes in which the beginning of a banking crisis is followed by a balance-of-payment crisis within 48 months are classified as twin crises.
Sources: American Banker, various issues; Gerald Caprio, Jr. and Daniela Klingebiel (1996); *New York Times,* various issues; Sundararajan et al. (1991); *Wall Street Journal,* various issues.

We begin by calculating the unconditional probability of currency crises and banking crises in our sample. For instance, the probability that a currency crisis will occur in the next 24 months over the entire sample is simply 24 times 76 (the total number of currency crises in the sample) divided by the total number of monthly observations in the sample. These calculations yield unconditional probabilities for currency and banking crises, which are 29 percent and 10 percent, respectively (Table 3). The difference in the probabilities of the two kinds of crises highlights the relatively higher frequency of currency crises in the sample.

We next calculate a family of conditional probabilities. For instance, if knowing that there is a banking crisis within the past 24 months helps predict a currency crisis then the probability of a currency crisis, conditioned on information that a banking crisis is under way, should be higher than the unconditional probability of a balance-of-payments crisis. In other words, a banking crisis increases the probability that a country will fall prey to a currency crisis. This is precisely what the results summarized in Table 3 show. The probability of a currency crisis conditioned on the beginning of banking-sector problems is 46 percent, well above the unconditional estimate of 29 percent. Hence, it

TABLE 3—PROBABILITIES OF CRISES

Probabilities of balance-of-payment crises

Type	Value (in percent)
Unconditional	29
Conditional on the beginning of a banking crisis	46
Conditional on the peak of a banking crisis	22

Probabilities of banking crises

Type	Value (in percent)
Unconditional	10
Beginning of a banking crisis conditional on a balance-of-payments crisis	8
Beginning of a banking crisis conditional on financial liberalization	14
Peak of a banking crisis conditional on a balance-of-payments crisis	16

Notes: The balance-of-payment crisis windows are defined as the 24 months preceding the crisis. The banking crisis windows are defined as the 12 months before and the 12 months after the beginning (or peak) of the crises. The unconditional .probabilities of balance-of-payment and banking crises are calculated as the total number of months in the respective crisis windows divided by the total number of months in the sample. The balance-of-payment probabilities conditional on a banking crisis (beginning or peak) are calculated as the number of months in the balance-of-payment crisis windows that occur within 24 months of the banking crises (beginning or peak) divided by the total number of months in the banking crisis windows. The probabilities of banking crises conditional on balance-of-payment crises are calculated as the number of months in the banking crisis windows that occur within 24 months of a balance-of-payment crisis divided by the total number of months in the balance-of-payment crisis windows. The probability of a banking crisis conditional on financial liberalization is calculated as the total number of months in the banking crisis windows that occur during times of financial liberalization divided by the total number of months during which the banking sector was in a regime of financial liberalization. All probabilities were estimated using the data for the 20 countries in the 1970–mid-1995 period.

could be argued, as Díaz-Alejandro (1985) and Velasco (1987) did for the Chilean crisis in the early 1980's, that, in an important number of cases, the bailout of the banking system may have contributed to the acceleration in credit creation observed prior to the currency crises (see Herminio Blanco and Peter M. Garber, 1986; Sebastian Edwards, 1989; Eichengreen et al., 1996b; and this paper). Even in the absence of a large-scale bailout, a frail banking system is

likely to tie the hands of the central bank in defending the currency—witness Indonesia in August 1997.

If, instead, the peak of the banking crisis is used as the conditioning piece of information, no valuable information is gained; indeed, the conditional probability is 22 percent and below the unconditional. This result follows from the fact that a more common pattern (see Table 2) appears to be that the peak of the banking crisis comes after the currency crisis. For instance, knowing that there is a currency crisis does not help predict the onset of a banking crisis, this conditional probability is 8 percent; knowing that there was a currency crisis does help to predict the probability that the banking crisis will worsen, this conditional probability is 16 percent.

Taken together, these results seem to point to the existence of vicious circles. Financial-sector problems undermine the currency. Devaluations, in turn, aggravate the existing banking-sector problems and create new ones. These adverse feedback mechanisms are in line with those suggested by Mishkin (1996) and can be amplified, as we have seen in several of the recent Asian crises, by banks' inadequate hedging of foreign-exchange risk. The presence of vicious circles would imply that, a priori, the twin crises are more severe than currency or banking crises that occur in isolation.

To measure the *severity* of a currency crisis, we focus on a composite measure that averages reserve losses and the real exchange-rate depreciation.[6] For reserves, we use the six-month percent change prior to the crisis month, as reserve losses typically occur prior to the devaluation (if the attack is successful). For the real exchange rate, we use the six-month percent change following the crisis month, because large depreciations occur after, and only if, the central bank concedes by devaluing or floating the currency. This measure of severity is constructed for each currency crisis in our sample and the averages are reported in Table 4 separately for the 19 twin crises in our sample and for the others. In line with our results that the beginning of the banking crisis precedes the balance-of-payments crisis, we define the twin

---

[6] The real exchange rate is used, as high inflation countries will typically have larger nominal devaluations.

TABLE 4—THE SEVERITY OF THE CRISES

Severity measure	Banking crises		Balance-of-payments crises	
	Twin	Single	Twin	Single
Cost of bailout (Percent of GDP)	13.3	5.1*	NA	NA
Loss of reserves (Percent)	NA	NA	25.4	8.3*
Real depreciation (Percent)	NA	NA	25.7	26.6
Composite index	NA	NA	25.6	17.5

Notes: Loss of reserves is the percentage change in the level of reserves in the six months preceding the crises. Real depreciation is the percentage change in the real exchange rate (with respect to the dollar for the countries that peg to the dollar and with respect to the mark for the countries that peg to mark) in the six months following the crises. The composite index is the unweighted average of the loss of reserves and real depreciation. Episodes in which the beginning of a banking crisis is followed by a balance-of-payments crisis within 48 months are classified as twin crises.

* Denotes that the measure of severity of single-crises episodes is statistically different from the twin-crises severity at the 5-percent level. An NA denotes not applicable.

crises as those episodes in which a currency crisis follows the beginning of the banking crisis within the next 48 months. For banking crises, we use the bailout costs, as a percent of GDP, as the measure of severity. As Table 4 highlights, bailout costs are significantly larger (more than double) in the twin crises than for banking crises which were not accompanied by a currency crisis. As to balance-of-payments crises, the results are mixed. Reserve losses sustained by the central bank are significantly bigger (Table 4) but the real depreciations are of comparable orders of magnitude.

Our results also yield an insight as to the links of crises with financial liberalization (Table 3). In 18 of the 26 banking crises studied here, the financial sector had been liberalized during the preceding five years, usually less. Only in a few cases in our sample countries, such as the early liberalization efforts of Brazil in 1975 and Mexico in 1974, was the liberalization not followed by financial-sector stress. In the 1980's and 1990's most liberalization episodes have been associated with financial crises of varying severity. Only in a handful of countries (for instance, Canada, which is not in the sample) did financial-sector liberalization proceed smoothly. Indeed, the probability

of a banking crisis (beginning) conditional on financial liberalization having taken place is higher than the unconditional probability of a banking crisis. This suggests that the twin crises may have common origins in the deregulation of the financial system and the boom-bust cycles and asset bubbles that, all too often, accompany financial liberalization. The stylized evidence presented in Caprio and Klingebiel (1996) suggests that inadequate regulation and lack of supervision at the time of the liberalization may play a key role in explaining why deregulation and banking crises are so closely entwined.

II. The Macroeconomic Background of the Crises

To shed light on whether both types of crises may have common roots, we analyze the evolution of 16 macroeconomic and financial variables around the time of the crises. The variables used in the analysis were chosen in light of theoretical considerations and subject to data availability. Monthly data was used to get a clearer view (than would otherwise be revealed by lower frequency data) of developments as the crisis approaches and by the desire to evaluate to what extent these indicators were giving an early signal of impending trouble—an issue that will be taken up in the next section.

The indicators associated with *financial liberalization* are the M2 multiplier, the ratio of domestic credit to nominal GDP, the real interest rate on deposits, and the ratio of lending-to-deposit interest rates. *Other financial* indicators include: excess real M1 balances, real commercial-bank deposits, and the ratio of M2 (converted into U.S. dollars) divided by foreign-exchange reserves (in U.S. dollars).[7] The indicators linked to the *current account* include the percent deviation of the real exchange rate from trend, as a measure of misalignment, the value of exports and imports (in U.S. dollars), and the terms of trade.[8] The

---

[7] M2 to reserves captures to what extent the liabilities of the banking system are backed by international reserves. In the event of a currency crisis, individuals may rush to convert their domestic currency deposits into foreign currency, so that this ratio captures the ability of the central bank to meet those demands (Calvo and Enrique Mendoza, 1996).

[8] An increase in the real exchange-rate index denotes a depreciation.

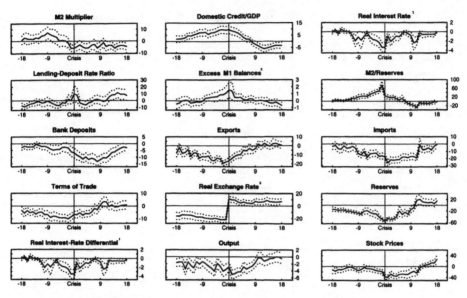

FIGURE 2. EMPIRICAL REGULARITIES DURING BALANCE-OF-PAYMENTS CRISES

Notes: The values of the variable relative to "tranquil" times are reported on the vertical axes. The horizontal axes represent the number of months before (with a negative sign) and after the crisis. The solid line represents the average for all the crises for which data was available. The dotted lines denote plus/minus one standard error around the average. Unless otherwise noted, all variables are reported as 12-month changes, in percent, relative to "tranquil" times. 1. Monthly rates, in percentage points, relative to "tranquil" times. 2. Actual less estimated money demand. Percent deviation relative to "tranquil" times. 3. Deviations from trend, in percent, relative to "tranquil" times.

indicators associated with the *capital account* are: foreign-exchange reserves (in U.S. dollars) and the domestic-foreign real interest-rate differential on deposits (monthly rates in percentage points). The indicators of the *real sector* are industrial production and an index of equity prices (in U.S. dollars).[9] Lastly, the *fiscal* variable is the overall budget deficit as a percent of GDP.

Of course, this is not an exhaustive list of potential indicators. In particular, political variables, such as the timing of an election, can also be linked to the timing of these crises. Indeed, the evidence presented in Deepak Mishra (1997), who examines a subset of the currency crises in this study, suggests that devaluations, more often than

not, follow elections. Indeed, an election raises the probability of a future devaluation, even after controlling for economic fundamentals.

Except for the interest-rate variables, the deviations of the real exchange rate from trend, our proxy for excess real M1 balances, and the lending/deposit interest-rate ratio, which are in levels, we focus on the 12-month percent changes of the remaining 10 variables. The pre- and post-crises behavior of all variables is compared to the average behavior during tranquil periods, which are all the remaining observations in our sample and serves as our control group.

Figures 2, 3, and 4 illustrate the behavior of the variables around the time of the balance-of-payments crises, banking crises, and twin crises, respectively; each panel portrays a different variable. The horizontal axis records the number of months before and after the beginning of the crises; the vertical axis

---

[9] Detailed definitions of all the variables and their sources are provided in the Data Appendix.

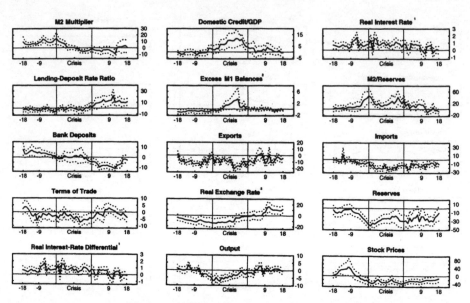

FIGURE 3. EMPIRICAL REGULARITIES DURING BANKING CRISES

Notes: The values of the variable relative to "tranquil" times are reported on the vertical axes. The horizontal axes represent the number of months before (with a negative sign) and after the crisis. The solid line represents the average for all the crises for which data was available. The dotted lines denote plus/minus one standard error around the average. Unless otherwise noted, all variables are reported as 12-month changes, in percent, relative to "tranquil" times. 1. Monthly rates, in percentage points, relative to "tranquil" times. 2. Actual less estimated money demand. Percent deviation relative to "tranquil" times. 3. Deviations from trend, in percent, relative to "tranquil" times.

records the percent difference (percentage-point difference for interest rates) between tranquil and crisis periods. In all the figures the solid line represents the average for all the crises for which data was available.[10] Hence, if no data points are missing, the solid line represents the average behavior of that indicator during the months around 76 currency crises and 26 banking crises. For Figures 2 and 3, the dotted lines denote plus/minus one standard error around the average. For example, the top center panel of Figure 2 shows that, on average, the 12-month growth in the domestic credit/GDP ratio is about 15 percent higher than in tranquil times. In Figure 4 the

solid line shows the evolution of the indicators for the twin-crises episodes while the dashed line denotes the averages for the currency crises that were not accompanied by a banking crisis.

For currency crises we focus on the 18-month period before and after the crisis. Unlike balance-of-payments crises, in which reserves are lost abruptly and currency pegs abandoned, banking crises are protracted affairs which tend to come in waves and, hence, the depth of the crisis is seldom reached at the first sign of outbreak (see Table 2). For this reason, we widen the window and focus on the 18 months before the onset of the crisis, an 18-month arbitrarily chosen crisis period, and the 18-month post-crisis period. At any rate, because most of our analysis focuses on the causes leading up to the crises, our main results will not be affected whether the crises

[10] See Appendix Tables A1 and A2 for a detailed indication of any missing data around crisis dates.

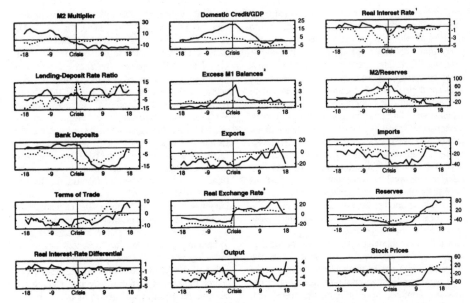

FIGURE 4. EMPIRICAL REGULARITIES DURING TWIN CRISES

Notes: The values of the variables relative to "tranquil" times are reported on the vertical axes. The horizontal axes represent the number of months before (with a negative sign) and after a crisis. The solid lines show the behavior during twin-crises episodes, and the dotted lines show the behavior during "single"-crises episodes. Unless otherwise noted, all variables are reported as 12-month changes, in percent, relative to "tranquil" times. 1. Monthly rates, in percentage points, relative to "tranquil" times. 2. Actual less estimated money demand. Percent deviation relative to "tranquil" times. 3. Deviations from trend, in percent, relative to "tranquil" times.

lasted less or more than a year. For the 19 episodes of the twin crises, we focus on the 18 months prior to the balance-of-payments crisis. Given that banking crises usually predate currency crises in our sample, this implies we are already looking at a period of heavy financial-sector stress.

A. *The Financial Sector*

Until the 1970's, most financial markets were regulated with rationed credit and, often, negative real interest rates. The late 1970's and beginning of the 1980's, however, witnessed sweeping financial reforms both in developed and emerging markets, which led to, among other things, increases in real interest rates.[11] Because financial liberalization often precedes

[11] See Vincente Galbis (1993).

banking crises—the indicators associated with financial liberalization presented in the first four panels of Figures 2, 3, and 4 (from left to right) merit scrutiny. The growth in the *M2 multiplier* rises steadily up to nine months prior to the currency crisis and the onset of the banking crisis; indeed, for banking crises the multiplier grows at above normal rate in the entire 18 months prior to the crisis. The draconian reductions in reserve requirements that often accompany financial liberalization play a role in explaining the large increases in the M2 multiplier. Yet the rise in the multiplier prior to currency crises is entirely accounted for by its evolution ahead of the twin crises, as shown in Figure 4.

The growth in *domestic credit/GDP* remains above normal as the balance-of-payments crisis nears (Figure 2) but particularly accelerating markedly as the twin crises approaches; throughout this period it remains well above the growth rates recorded for tranquil periods, consistent with a credit boom (and bust) story. This ratio also rises in the early phase of the banking crisis. It may be that, as the crisis unfolds, the central bank may be pumping money to the banks to alleviate their financial situation or the evolution of the denominator has changed. While credit is rapidly expanding 18 to 6 months before the crisis, the economy is still in a vigorous expansion phase (see below), with healthy GDP growth. The leveraging of households and business becomes evident as the economy slips into recession. The *real interest rate* evolves very differently ahead of balance-of-payments and banking crises. For currency crises, interest rates bounce around in the range of 0 to 2 percentage points per month below the average during periods of tranquility—this may reflect lax monetary policy ahead of the currency crisis or simply the fact that 26 of the currency crises are in the 1970's, when interest rates were regulated and not particularly informative. By contrast, prior to banking crises and, therefore, twin crises (which are almost exclusively in the post-liberalization part of the sample), real interest rates are 1 to 2 percentage points higher (at a monthly rate) than in tranquil times in the pre-crisis period. The above normal real interest rates may have a variety of causes: These could be the product of a recent financial liberalization; high real rates could also reflect increased risk taking by banks;[12] they could be the product of a tight monetary policy stance. Real interest rates do not return to their levels in tranquil times as the crisis deepens, perhaps reflecting that banks may respond to deposit withdrawals by keeping deposit interest rates high. The *lending-deposit rate ratio* hovers around its level in tranquil times up until about six months prior to the balance-of-payments crises and then begins to climb; by the time of the crisis it is about 10 percent higher than in tranquil times, possibly reflecting a deterioration in credit risk. For banking crises, the lending/deposit ratio remains close to normal levels in the pre-crisis period. Only at around the peak of the banking crises does the lending/deposit ratio increase above its level in tranquil times, as banks become increasingly unwilling to lend.

The next three panels show the evolution of the

monetary indicators. The middle panel in the second row of Figures 2 and 3 show the *excess M1 balances.* The periods prior to the currency and banking crises are characterized by an excess supply of real M1 balances; the excess liquidity is particularly pronounced for the twin-crises episodes, which nearly account for all the above-normal behavior ahead of currency crises. Without overinterpreting this result, given the shortcomings of money-demand estimation, the picture that emerges is consistent with the deficit financing as in the Krugman (1979) framework or the excess liquidity may be created to ease conditions for troubled financial institutions. In any case, at some point the excess liquidity becomes incompatible with maintaining the exchange-rate commitment—and a currency crisis emerges. This would suggest that the high real interest rates prior to banking crises were due to factors other than monetary policy. The next panel shows the evolution of the 12-month change in *M2/reserves* of central banks. For both currency and banking crises, this ratio grows well above its norm prior to the crises. The increases are associated with both a vigorous expansion in M2 (witness the multiplier) and a sharp decline in foreign currency reserves (discussed below). As Calvo and Mendoza (1996) do for Mexico 1994, we find that the M2/reserves ratio over the 76 currency crises indicates an abrupt decrease in the backing ratio in the months preceding the crisis. Indeed, the growth rate is 70 percent in excess of the tranquil period average, highlighting vulnerability of the system. This observation is equally descriptive of both single-currency and twin-crises episodes. The growth rate of *bank deposits* remains close to normal during the 18 months prior to the financial crises, but the loss of deposits accelerates as the crises unfold. There may be multiple reasons for this sudden decline. Past financial-crises periods have often been characterized by massive and persistent capital flight. Deposits only start to recover a year and a half after the onset of the financial crises.

B. *The External Sector*

The next four panels of Figures 2, 3, and 4 present indicators associated with the current account. The middle panel of the third row in each figure chronicles the abysmal performance of the growth of *exports* in the year and a half

---

[12] See V. Sundararajan and Tomas Baliño (1991).

preceding the currency and banking crises— exports consistently underperform (relative to normal times) during this period. By the time a balance-of-payments crisis is under way, export growth is about 20 percent below (annual rate) the average growth observed in tranquil periods. Once the appreciation is reversed, export performance improves sharply, outdoing the performance observed during tranquil periods about nine months after the crisis began. Export performance is particularly poor during the twin-crises episodes. The behavior of *import growth* is more difficult to justify on the basis of relative price developments (see below). Import growth remains close to the norm during tranquil periods up to about nine months before a currency crisis and then declines; for banking crises, we see the tail end of the import boom and the subsequent slide prior to the crisis. During this pre-crisis period, income and relative price effects are moving in opposite directions, and the observed decline in import growth may well be accounted for by the slowdown in economic activity (see below) during that time. Import growth remains below that of normal periods throughout the post-crisis period.

The next panel provides evidence on the *terms of trade*. Crises are preceded, on average, by a deterioration of the terms of trade, with an annual decline that is about 10 percent deeper than those observed in tranquil times prior to a balance-of-payments crisis. This persistent adverse performance of the terms of trade erodes purchasing power and may also account for the weakness in imports in the months preceding the crisis. This weakness is equally evident in single- and twin-crises episodes. For banking crises, up to about a year prior to the crisis, terms-of-trade shocks appear to have been positive—perhaps helping to explain the earlier boom (see below); as the crisis nears we see some evidence of adverse terms-of-trade shocks. The middle panel in the fourth row shows the evolution of *real exchange rates*. During the year before the balance-of-payments and banking crises (as stressed in Rudiger Dornbusch et al., 1996), the real exchange rate shows evidence of being overvalued, relative to its average level during tranquil times. In periods preceding the currency crash, it is appreciating relative to its trend (an overvaluation of about 20

percent relative to tranquil periods). The real exchange-rate appreciation does reverse itself rapidly with the devaluation, suggesting that productivity shocks or preference changes were unlikely to account for the initial appreciation. Exchange-rate-based inflation stabilization plans have often given rise to large cumulative real exchange-rate appreciations, as domestic inflation fails to converge to international levels. As noted in Reinhart and Végh (1996) and Kaminsky and Leonardo Leiderman (1998), many of those plans ended in a balance-of-payments crisis. Following the crash, the real exchange rate depreciates substantially (and is about 10 percent higher than in tranquil times). Over time, higher domestic inflation erodes in part the improvement in competitiveness.

In the absence of monthly data on capital flows for most of the period and most of the countries in our sample, we extract information about capital account developments by focusing on the indicators shown in the next two panels. As expected, the 12-month percentage change in foreign-exchange *reserves* of the central banks falls substantially in the months prior to both banking and balance-of-payments crises. The loss of reserves is particularly steep and longer lived following the crises for the 19 twin-crises episodes. As early as 12 months prior to the balance-of-payments crisis, reserve growth is about 20 percent below that observed during tranquil periods; although we report 12-month changes, which introduce positive serial correlation in the data, reserves do not decrease continuously. There are modest short-lived reversals in the path followed by reserves, which suggest that the central banks may have had spells in which they fought the reserve loss with contractionary monetary policy (note that there are brief spells where real interest rates rise prior to the crisis—see the third panel) before finally conceding defeat and devaluing. Following the devaluation (or flotation), foreign-exchange reserves of central banks start to increase again.

Finally, the first panel in the bottom row shows the evolution of the domestic-foreign *real interest-rate differential on deposits*. Interest differentials do not reflect increasing expectations of a devaluation as the currency crisis nears. Turning to banking crises, the picture that emerges is quite distinct from its counterpart in Figure 2; while in balance-of-payments crises interest-rate differentials were not appreciably different from tranquil periods prior to crises, differentials in the case of banking crises remain above those observed in periods of tranquility. One explanation for this difference among the two crises has to do with the bunching of the banking crises in the post-financial liberalization period.

C. *The Real Sector*

The last two panels in the figures show the evolution of *output* growth and changes in *stock prices*. The deterioration of the terms of trade, the overvaluation of the currency, and the weakening export performance are reflected in a marked slowing in economic activity and a decline in output prior to both crises. For balance-of-payments crises, the 12-month growth in output bounces in a range of 2 to 6 percent below the comparable growth rates during tranquil periods—with a tendency for the recession to deepen as the crisis nears. Interestingly, and in line with the greater severity of the twin crises, the combination of currency and banking problems appears to take a more devastating toll on the real economy as the recession is far deeper and longer than the recessions associated with currency crashes alone. At growth rates which are 8 percent below those observed in tranquil periods, the twin-crisis recession is twice as severe. As Kindelberger (1978) observes: "Financial crises are associated with the peaks in business cycles ... the financial crisis is a culmination of a period of economic expansion that leads to downturn." While in the 18 months prior to a balance-of-payments crisis there is no evidence of a residual economic boom, that is not the case in the pre-banking-crisis period. As Figure 3 shows, up to about 8 months before the banking crises the economy was recording growth rates above those observed during tranquil periods. Yet, the real exchange-rate appreciation that characterizes pre-crisis periods is often cited as a key factor behind the squeeze in profit margins that eventually leads to increased bankruptcies, a rise in nonperforming loans, a deepening in the economic contraction, and banking-sector problems.

The last panel shows the evolution of stock prices. During the 18 months prior to a balance-of-payments crisis, the equity market steadily underperforms (relative to tranquil times)—at first, not by much, but as the crisis nears, changes in stock prices (that is, stock returns [in dollars]) are about 40 percent below those observed in noncrisis periods. The weakening in equity prices is, most likely, reflecting both the deteriorating cyclical position of the economy, reduced foreign demand as capital inflows are reversed, and the worsening balance sheets of firms, as the overvaluation takes its toll. The crash is particularly severe when currency and banking crises nearly coincide (Figure 4). Unlike the onset of a banking crisis (see below), the equity market was already past it cyclical peak well before the crisis begins. On the eve of banking crises, the return on equity prices up to about nine months prior to the crises suggests a boom (relative to tranquil periods) which may (or may not) be an asset-price bubble. During the boom phase, returns exceed those of noncrises periods by about 40 percent on an annual basis. The beginning of the recession is also reflected in the stock market, which collapses the year before the crisis; this collapse is also apparent in other asset markets, most notably real estate.[13]

Finally, although not shown in the figures, the *fiscal deficit/GDP* ratio is higher in the two years prior to the currency crisis and one year prior to the banking crisis. While the bigger deficit could stem from higher government spending, the weakness in output prior to crises could lead to a shortfall in revenues.

III. The Anatomy of Crises

In what follows, we offer an alternative approach to examine the evolving nature of the

---

[13] For example, in the boom period leading up to the 1981 Argentine banking crisis, stock returns (in U.S. dollars) were as high as 813 percent during the 12 months ending May 1979; by May 1981, the 12-month capital loss was 60 percent. The crash in asset values is cited in most case studies as an important factor contributing to the problems of the banks. Also, due to either mismanagement or outright fraud, in many of the crises in our sample a substantial portion of banks and finance companies were considerably overexposed to real estate.

VOL. 89 NO. 3   KAMINSKY AND REINHART: THE TWIN CRISES   487

crises, pinpoint their origin, and gauge their probability conditioned on signals from one or more indicators. The methodology used, while not previously applied to analyze currency and banking crises, has a long history in the rich literature that evaluates the ability of macroeconomic and financial time series to predict business-cycle turning points.[14] The remainder of this section is divided into two parts, the first describes the statistical methodology used, while the second applies that methodology to the 102 currency and banking crises that make up our sample.

A. Methodology

To examine the causes of crises, gauge the vulnerability of the economy on the eve of crisis, and assess whether the crisis itself could be forecasted by anomalous economic developments, we need to make four sets of judgments: First, we must have a well-defined notion of what is classified as a crisis. Second, we must agree on a list of variables that are potential leading indicators. Third, we need to decide upon a criteria that allows us to classify the behavior of an indicator as either a *signal* of a crisis or normal (no signal). Last, if an indicator is giving a signal, we have to determine if a crisis happens within a reasonable period of time or if the signal was a *false alarm*. Hence, we also need to define what is considered to be a reasonable period of time. Section I deals with the definition and dating of banking and currency crises, while the previous section and the Data Appendix discuss the indicators. In this subsection, we describe the approach used to define what is a signal and what is a reasonable period of time.

The Interval Between Signals and Crisis: Defining a Reasonable Period of Time.—In what follows, the maximum interval of time between the signal and the crisis was decided a priori as 24 months in the case of balance-of-payments crises.[15] Hence, any signal given within the 24-month period before the beginning of the

crisis is labeled a good signal; any other signal outside that 24-month window is labeled a false alarm or noise. For banking crises, any signal given within the 12-month period before the beginning of the crisis or within 12 months following the beginning of the crisis is labeled a good signal. The two different signaling windows for currency and banking crises have to do with the different timing of the peaks of both crises, as previously discussed. In addition, the events that mark the beginning of a banking crisis are often not seen as systemic at the time and are not treated by policy makers as harbingers of a crisis. Since symptoms of a crisis are sometimes evident well before the crises erupt, the narrower windows (say, 12-month) were thought to penalize indicators (such as M2/reserves) that tend to give an early warning.

The Threshold: Defining a Signal.—In Section II we noted that the crises were preceded by marked declines in equity returns. Yet, surely, not every decline in equity returns presages a crisis. Hence, we need to select an appropriate threshold or cutoff that separates when a decline in equity returns is considered a signal of a crisis and when it is not. As is the case of selecting the size of the rejection region in hypothesis testing, choosing the optimal threshold involves a trade-off. Suppose that our null hypothesis is that we are in a tranquil state of nature and (for a particular country) we are weighing whether to arbitrarily set the threshold for annual equity returns at minus 15 percent or at minus 40 percent. Suppose further, that for this country 10 percent of the observations posted annual equity returns below minus 15 percent, but only 3 percent of the observations showed equity returns below minus 40 percent. Our aim is to use the readings for this indicator to test the null hypothesis that we are in a tranquil state of nature. If we choose the minus 15 percent threshold, the size of α (the rejection region) is 10 percent—this is the probability of rejecting the null hypothesis when it is true (Type I error). In this case, the threshold may be too lax—it is likely to catch all the crises but it is also likely to generate a lot of false alarms. Instead, we could adopt the minus 40 percent threshold, which cuts the size of α to 3 percent; this reduces the probability of Type I error at the expense of increasing the probability of Type II

---

[14] See, for instance, Francis Diebold and Glen Rudebusch (1989), James H. Stock and Mark W. Watson (1989), and Reinhart and Vincent R. Reinhart (1996).

[15] An 18- and 12-month window were also used; the results are available from the authors.

The Political Economy of Financial Crises I

error (not rejecting the null hypothesis when it is false). With this tight threshold we may miss all but the most severe of the crises—the price of reducing the number of false alarms is accurately calling a lower proportion of crises.

We select the threshold value on an indicator-by-indicator basis, by performing a fine grid search over a broad range of critical regions up to a maximum of 30 percent. For each threshold value in our grid search we compute the noise-to-signal ratio.[16] We then select the threshold value that minimizes the noise-to-signal ratio. As to the location of the rejection region, whether it is the upper or lower tail of the frequency distribution for each indicator, we rely on the theory as a guide. The threshold values for the 16 indicators, as well as the location of the rejection region and its theoretical justification, are given in Table 5. For example, for currency and banking crises large output declines signal a crisis, so a $<$ sign in Table 5 denotes that the rejection region is located at the bottom tail of the distribution.

This criterion does have drawbacks which are worth mentioning. First, if an indicator gives an early signal and policy makers heed the signal and preempt a crisis, that signal is labeled as false and the indicator is penalized with an unduly high noise-to-signal ratio. In addition, a signal within the window is treated the same irrespective of whether it was given 12 months before the crisis erupts or only the month before. Naturally, from the vantage point of the policy maker the earlier signal is the more valuable one.

B. *The Anatomy of Crises*

The methodology just described was applied to the 16 indicators and 102 crises in the sample and the four recent Asian crises out of sample.

Appendix Tables A1 and A2 show the results on a crisis-by-crisis and indicator-by-indicator basis. An NA denotes some or all the observations were missing during the pre-crisis 24-month window; a 1 denotes at least one signal was given during the 24-month window, and a zero indicates no signals were issued. Hence, for example, column (12) in Appendix Table A1 scores the performance of foreign-exchange reserves; there are four NA entries, hence we have full data for this indicator for 72 balance-of-payments crises. In 75 percent of the crises [row (1) Summary Statistics, bottom of the table] there were one or more signals during the 24 months prior to the crisis. The last column (17) lists what proportion (in percent) of the indicators were sending signals. Data availability permitting, the tables also show the evolution of the indicators out of sample for the Asian crises of 1997.

About the Origins of Crises.—Table 6 summarizes the results in Appendix Tables A1 and A2. The indicators are shown individually and are also grouped into sectors along the lines described in the previous section: financial liberalization, other financial, current account, capital account, real-side, and fiscal. For balance-of-payments crises, we also examine subsamples before financial liberalization, which encompasses the 1970's, and after financial liberalization, as well as those currency crises which occurred alongside a banking crises. The latter appear under the column labelled Twin. As nearly all banking crises fall in the post-liberalization period, no subsamples for these are reported. Table 6 presents the percentage of crises accurately called by each indicator. As to the various groups we also report the simple arithmetic average of the proportion of crises accurately called by all the indicators in that subgroup. Capital account indicators accurately called the highest proportion of balance-of-payments crises

---

[16] The definition of noise-to-signal ratio used throughout is best illustrated by considering the following two-by-two matrix:

	Crisis occurs in the following 24 months	No crisis occurs in the following 24 months
Indicator issues a signal	A	B
Indicator does not issue a signal	C	D

If a variable signals and a crisis occurs in the following 24 months (counted in cell A) the signal is considered accurate. If a variable signals and no crisis occurs in that time frame (counted in cell B), the signal is said to be a false alarm or noise. Hence, a perfect indicator would only have entries in cells A and D. More generally, the noise-to-signal ratio for any indicator is given by the number of entries in $[B/(B + D)]/[A/(A + C)]$. Hence, it is the ratio of false signals to all possible bad signals divided by the ratio of good signals to all possible good signals. An extremely noisy indicator would have few entries in A and D, many in B and C.

TABLE 5—THRESHOLD VALUES FOR SIGNALING CRISES

Indicators	Balance-of-payment crises	Banking crises	Comments
Financial sector			
Financial liberalization			
M2 multiplier	>0.86	>0.90	Both banking and currency crises have been linked to rapid growth
Domestic credit/GDP	>0.90	>0.95	(boom-bust) in credit and the monetary aggregates (see McKinnon and Pill, 1996).
Real interest rate	>0.88	>0.80	For banking crises, the choice is unambiguous since financial
Lending-deposit rate ratio	>0.80	>0.87	deregulation is associated with high interest rates (which could reflect increased risk taking [see Galbis, 1993]). A liquidity crunch (say to defend a peg) will also hurt banks. For balance-of-payments crises it is less clear-cut; higher real interest rates could reflect a higher risk premia and fears of devaluation. Yet, using the lower interest rates for signals could be justified for balance-of-payments crises on the basis of loose monetary policy. An increase in the lending/deposit ratio can capture a decline in loan quality.
Other			
Excess M1 balances	>0.94	>0.91	This is a "loose" monetary policy story (see Krugman, 1979).
M2/reserves	>0.87	>0.90	For the motivation on M2/reserves, see Calvo and Mendoza (1996).
Bank deposits	<0.10	<0.16	Capital flight and a run against the domestic banks may precede both currency and banking crises (see Goldfajn and Valdes, 1995).
External sector			
Current account			
Exports	<0.10	<0.10	Real exchange-rate overvaluations and a weak external sector are a
Terms of trade	<0.16	<0.19	part of a currency crisis. It adds vulnerability of the banking
Real exchange rate	<0.10	<0.10	sector, since a loss of competitiveness and external markets could lead to recession, business failures, and a decline in the quality of loans. Thus, large negative shocks to exports, the terms of trade, and the real exchange rate are associated with signals (see Dornbush et al., 1995).
Imports	>0.90	>0.80	Theory is ambiguous as to where we should locate the rejection region. Rapid import growth could be the sign of a buoyant economy (this would argue for a negative shock to imports); it could also be the sign of overvaluation. Hence a positive shock to imports could be a signal. Both possibilities were explored.
Capital account			
Reserves	<0.15	<0.28	See discussion under bank deposits and real interest rates.
Real interest-rate differential	<0.89	>0.81	
Real sector			
Output	<0.11	<0.14	Recessions and the burst of asset price bubbles precede financial
Stock prices	<0.11	<0.10	crises (see Gary Gorton, 1988; Charles W. Calomiris and Gorton, 1991).
Fiscal sector			
Deficit/GDP	>0.86	>0.86	Loose fiscal policy financed by credit from the central bank (see Krugman, 1979).

Note: The definitions and sources of the indicators are described in the Data Appendix.

(about 81 percent). Financial liberalization indicators were next in line, accurately signaling 74 percent of the currency crises before they occurred; for the twin crises their performance is even better. Among the capital account and financial indicators that fared the worst are bank deposits, the lending-deposit ratio, and excess M1 balances. Current account indicators followed

490 *THE AMERICAN ECONOMIC REVIEW* *JUNE 1999*

TABLE 6—THE ONSET OF FINANCIAL CRISES: EARLY SIGNALS

| | Percent of crises accurately called | | | | | |
| | Balance-of-payment crises | | | | | |
Indicators	Total	Single	Twin	Before financial liberalization	After financial liberalization	Banking crises
Financial sector	67	67	67	67	68	65
Financial liberalization	74	72	78	64	77	71
M2 multiplier	76	75	78	74	77	73
Domestic credit/GDP	61	59	67	56	65	50
Real interest rate	89	86	94	78	91	100
Lending-deposit rate ratio	71	70	73	50	73	57
Other	57	58	53	57	56	57
Excess M1 balances	37	43	22	52	26	32
M2/reserves	81	79	89	74	86	75
Bank deposits	51	52	47	44	56	67
External sector	72	71	74	72	72	82
Current account	68	67	70	70	66	75
Exports	85	83	89	78	89	88
Terms of trade	75	72	83	73	77	96
Real exchange rate	59	57	67	58	60	58
Imports	52	57	39	73	40	60
Capital account	81	80	83	74	83	96
Reserves	75	74	79	70	78	92
Real interest-rate differential	86	86	88	78	89	100
Real sector	69	69	70	61	72	85
Output	74	73	77	68	76	89
Stock prices	64	65	63	53	68	81
Fiscal sector	28	27	29	21	31	44

Notes: Episodes in which the beginning of a banking crisis is followed by a balance-of-payments crisis within 48 months are classified as twin crises. An indicator is said to have accurately called a crisis if it issues at least one signal in the crisis window on the basis of the criterion shown in Table 5. For each indicator, each cell in the table represents the number of times that indicator correctly calls a crisis as a percentage of the total number of crises. For the different sectors, each cell represents the simple average of the percentage of crises accurately called by all the individual variables in that group.

next (68 percent accurately called) but this is largely owing to the weak performance of imports in accurately calling crises; exports, the terms of trade, and the real exchange rate do much better. The fiscal variable fared the worst, accurately calling only slightly over a quarter of the currency crises.

One key difference between banking and currency crises, highlighted in Table 6, is the role of the real sector, which appears to be considerably more important for banking crises—giving early signals in 85 percent of the crises.[17] Indeed, output and stock prices signaled in 89 and 81 percent, respectively, of the banking crises for which data for these indicators

---

[17] For a discussion of the evolving nature of crises see the working paper, Kaminsky and Reinhart (1996).

was available. As much of the literature on banking crises stresses, particularly asymmetric information models (see Calomiris and Gorton, 1991), the evidence presented here suggests that the bursting of asset-price bubbles and increased bankruptcies associated with an economic downturn appear to be closely linked to domestic financial problems.

Yet another feature that is revealed in Table 6 is that the proportion of crises accurately called rises for 13 out of the 16 indicators when single-currency crises are compared to their twin counterparts. The improved performance of most of the indicators is not entirely surprising, in light of the greater severity of the twin-crises episodes.

Fragility on the Eve of Crises.—Table 7 presents strong evidence that, for both banking and currency crises, multiple economic problems

TABLE 7—ECONOMIC FRAGILITY ON THE EVE OF CRISES

| Number of indicators signaling a crisis (in percent) | Number of crises (in percent) | | | | | |
| | Balance-of-payments crises | | | | | |
	Total	Single	Twin	Before financial liberalization	After financial liberalization	Banking crises
80–100	26.7	28.6	21.1	40.0	17.8	30.8
60–79	45.3	41.1	57.9	23.3	60.0	53.8
40–59	20.0	21.4	15.8	20.0	20.0	11.5
20–39	6.7	8.9	0.0	13.3	2.2	3.9
Less than 20	1.3	0.0	5.3	3.3	0.0	0.0

Notes: This table captures the state of distress of the economy in different crisis episodes. Each cell represents the proportion of crises with a given proportion of signals. For example, 21.1 percent of the twin balance-of-payment crises had 80–100 percent of indicators signaling a crisis. Episodes in which the beginning of a banking crisis is followed by a balance-of-payments crisis within 48 months are classified as twin crises.

were simultaneously building. We construct a measure of the fragility of the economy in the 24 months preceding the crisis by tallying on a crisis-by-crisis basis what proportion of the indicators were signaling during that period.[18] Hence, if 14 of the 16 indicators are sending a signal prior to the crisis, this crisis would be counted in the first row of Table 7, labeled 80 percent to 100 percent. It appears that crises are not simply a story of an overvalued exchange rate or too rapid a monetary expansion. In about 30 percent of the currency crises, 80 percent or more of the indicators were sending signals. The economies appear to be particularly frail on the eve of twin crises, with a higher proportion of the indicators signaling. Indeed, in about 80 percent of the twin crises, at least 60 percent of the indicators were sending a signal. There were basically no banking crises with less than 20 percent of the indicators signaling. For further evidence of the diversity of the economic problems on the eve of crises on a crisis-by-crisis basis, see Appendix Tables A1 and A2. The finding that when the balance-of-payments crises occur jointly with a banking crisis (under the heading Twin, Table 7) economies appear to have more widespread problems perhaps is not entirely surprising, given the earlier results which suggest the twin crises tend to be more severe.

These results would appear to suggest that the overwhelming majority of crises, external or domestic, have a multitude of weak economic fundamentals at their core. While speculative attacks do occur as market sentiment shifts and, possibly, herding behavior takes over, such self-fulfilling crises appear to be quite rare. Indeed, in the context of the Exchange Rate Mechanism crises this issue has been the subject of much debate.[19] Not only are the signals many, but their sources are multiple, as shown in Table 7—with the financial sector external (capital account) and domestic playing a key role.

IV. Final Remarks

We have examined the empirical regularities and the sources and scope of problems in the onset of 76 currency crises and 26 banking crises. We find that banking and currency crises are closely linked in the aftermath of financial liberalization, with banking crises, in general, beginning before the currency collapse. We also find evidence of vicious cycles, in which the currency collapse further undermines an already ailing banking sector. When currency and banking crises occur jointly, they are far more severe than when they occur in isolation. In both types of crises, a financial shock, possibly financial liberalization or increased access to international capital markets, appears to activate a boom-bust cycle by providing easy access to financing. Finally, in both crises we find a

[18] These are reported for each crisis in column (17) of the Appendix tables.

[19] See Eichengreen et al. (1996a).

TABLE A1—ANATOMY OF BALANCE-OF-PAYMENTS CRISES[a]

Country	Crisis	M2 multiplier (1)	Domestic credit/GDP (2)	Real interest rate (3)	Lending-deposit rate ratio (4)	Excess M1 balances (5)	M2/ reserves (6)	Bank deposits (7)
Argentina	June 70	NA	NA	NA	NA	1	NA	NA
	June 75	0	1	NA	NA	1	1	0
	Feb. 81	1	0	1	NA	0	1	0
	July 82	1	1	1	1	0	1	0
	Sept. 86	1	NA	1	1	0	1	0
	April 89	1	NA	1	1	0	1	0
	Feb. 90	0	NA	1	1	1	1	1
Bolivia	Nov. 82	0	1	1	NA	0	1	1
	Nov. 83	0	1	1	0	0	1	1
	Sept. 85	0	0	1	1	1	1	1
Brazil	Feb. 83	0	0	NA	NA	0	1	1
	Nov. 86	1	1	1	1	1	1	0
	July 89	1	1	1	1	1	1	1
	Nov. 90	1	1	1	1	0	1	1
	Oct. 91	1	0	1	1	0	0	1
Chile	Dec. 71	1	1	NA	NA	NA	1	NA
	Aug. 72	1	1	NA	NA	1	1	NA
	Oct. 73	1	1	NA	NA	1	1	1
	Dec. 74	0	0	NA	NA	1	1	1
	Jan. 76	1	1	NA	NA	0	1	1
	Aug. 82	1	1	1	1	0	0	0
	Sept. 84	0	1	1	1	1	0	1
Colombia	March 83	1	1	1	NA	0	NA	1
	Feb. 85	1	1	1	NA	NA	1	1
Denmark	May 71	1	NA	NA	NA	1	NA	1
	June 73	1	0	NA	NA	1	0	0
	Nov. 79	1	0	NA	NA	0	0	1
	Aug. 93	1	0	1	1	1	1	0
Finland	June 73	0	0	NA	NA	1	1	0
	Oct. 82	1	0	NA	NA	0	1	0
	Nov. 91	1	0	1	0	0	1	1
	Sept. 92	1	1	1	0	0	1	1
Indonesia	Nov. 78	1	1	1	NA	0	0	1
	April 83	1	1	0	NA	1	1	1
	Sept. 86	1	1	1	1	0	0	0
Israel	Nov. 74	1	1	NA	NA	1	1	1
	Nov. 77	1	1	NA	NA	0	1	0
	Oct. 83	0	0	NA	NA	0	0	0
	July 84	0	0	NA	NA	1	0	0
Malaysia	July 75	1	0	NA	NA	0	1	1
Mexico	Sept. 76	1	1	NA	NA	0	1	0
	Feb. 82	0	0	0	0	0	0	0
	Dec. 82	0	1	0	0	1	1	1
	Dec. 94	0	1	1	1	1	1	0
Norway	June 73	1	0	NA	NA	0	0	0
	Feb. 78	1	1	NA	NA	1	1	0
	May 86	1	1	NA	NA	0	1	0
	Dec. 92	1	0	NA	1	0	1	1
Peru	June 76	1	0	NA	NA	1	1	0
	Oct. 87	1	1	NA	NA	0	1	0
Philippines	Feb. 70	NA	NA	NA	NA	NA	NA	NA
	Oct. 83	1	1	1	0	0	1	NA
	June 84	1	1	1	1	NA	1	NA

VOL. 89 NO. 3 KAMINSKY AND REINHART: THE TWIN CRISES 493

TABLE A1—*Continued*

Exports (8)	Imports (9)	Terms of trade (10)	Real exchange rate (11)	Reserves (12)	Real interest-rate differential (13)	Output (14)	Stock prices (15)	Deficit/ GDP (16)	Total number of signals[b] (17)
NA	NA	NA	NA	NA	NA	NA	NA	NA	100
1	1	1	1	1	NA	NA	NA	NA	80
1	1	0	1	0	1	NA	0	NA	54
1	1	NA	1	1	1	1	1	0	80
1	0	1	0	0	1	1	1	0	60
1	0	0	0	1	1	0	0	0	47
1	0	0	0	1	1	1	0	1	67
0	1	0	1	1	1	0	NA	NA	62
1	1	0	1	1	1	1	NA	NA	71
1	1	NA	1	1	1	0	NA	NA	77
1	0	1	0	1	NA	NA	0	0	42
1	0	1	0	1	1	NA	0	0	67
1	0	1	0	1	1	1	1	0	81
1	0	1	1	1	1	1	1	0	81
1	0	1	1	1	1	1	1	1	75
1	1	1	NA	1	NA	NA	NA	0	88
1	1	1	0	1	NA	NA	NA	0	80
1	1	0	1	1	NA	1	NA	0	83
1	1	1	1	1	NA	1	NA	0	75
1	1	1	0	1	NA	1	NA	0	75
1	1	1	1	0	1	1	1	1	75
1	0	1	0	1	1	1	1	0	69
1	1	1	1	1	NA	1	1	0	85
1	0	0	1	1	1	1	1	0	79
NA	NA	NA	NA	NA	NA	NA	1	0	80
0	1	NA	0	0	NA	0	0	1	33
0	1	1	1	0	NA	1	0	0	46
1	0	NA	0	1	1	1	1	0	67
0	0	NA	0	1	NA	0	0	NA	27
1	0	NA	0	1	NA	1	0	0	42
1	0	1	1	1	1	1	1	1	75
1	0	1	1	1	1	1	1	1	81
1	1	1	0	0	1	0	NA	0	57
1	1	NA	1	1	0	1	NA	0	77
1	0	1	1	0	1	1	NA	1	67
1	1	1	1	1	NA	1	NA	0	92
0	0	0	1	1	NA	1	NA	0	50
1	0	0	0	0	NA	1	NA	0	17
1	0	0	0	0	NA	1	1	0	31
1	1	1	0	0	NA	1	NA	0	58
1	1	0	0	0	NA	0	NA	0	42
1	1	0	1	0	0	0	1	0	25
1	1	1	1	1	0	1	1	0	69
0	0	1	1	1	1	0	0	NA	60
0	1	NA	0	0	NA	1	1	0	33
1	1	1	1	1	NA	1	1	0	85
1	1	1	0	0	NA	1	0	0	54
1	0	1	0	1	1	1	1	1	73
1	1	NA	1	1	NA	NA	NA	1	80
1	1	1	0	1	NA	0	NA	0	58
NA	NA	NA	1	NA	NA	NA	NA	NA	100
1	0	1	1	1	0	NA	0	0	50
1	0	1	1	1	0	NA	1	0	71

continued overleaf

TABLE A1—*Continued*

Country	Crisis	M2 multiplier (1)	Domestic credit/GDP (2)	Real interest rate (3)	Lending-deposit rate ratio (4)	Excess M1 balances (5)	M2/ reserves (6)	Bank deposits (7)
Spain	Feb. 86	NA	NA	1	1	NA	NA	1
	Feb. 76	1	1	NA	NA	1	1	1
	July 77	0	1	NA	NA	0	1	1
	Dec. 82	0	1	1	NA	0	1	0
	Sept. 92	1	0	1	0	0	0	0
	May 93	1	0	1	1	0	1	0
Sweden	Aug. 77	1	0	0	1	NA	1	1
	Sept. 81	1	1	0	0	NA	1	0
	Oct. 82	1	1	1	0	NA	1	0
	Nov. 92	1	0	1	1	NA	1	1
Thailand	Nov. 78	1	0	1	NA	0	0	0
	July 81	1	0	1	NA	0	1	1
	Nov. 84	1	1	1	NA	0	1	0
Turkey	Aug. 70	NA	NA	NA	NA	NA	NA	NA
	Jan. 80	0	NA	NA	NA	NA	1	1
	March 94	1	1	1	1	0	1	1
Uruguay	Dec. 71	NA	1	NA	NA	1	1	NA
	Oct. 82	1	1	1	NA	0	1	0
Venezuela	Feb. 84	1	1	NA	NA	0	1	0
	Dec. 86	1	0	1	1	1	1	0
	March 89	1	0	1	0	0	1	1
	May 94	1	1	1	1	0	1	1
	Dec. 95	1	1	1	1	0	1	1
	OUT-OF-SAMPLE CRISES							
Indonesia	Aug. 97	0	NA	1	0	0	0	0
Malaysia	Aug. 97	NA	NA	1	NA	1	1	NA
Philippines	July 97	1	1	1	1	1	0	0
Thailand	July 97	0	NA	NA	NA	0	1	1
	SUMMARY STATISTICS							
Percent of crises called[c]		76	61	89	71	37	81	51
Percent called before FL[d]		74	56	78	50	52	74	44
Percent called after FL[d]		77	65	91	73	26	86	56
Noise-to-signal ratio[e]		0.67	0.64	0.75	1.52	0.56	0.52	0.67

multitude of weak and deteriorating economic fundamentals suggesting that it would be difficult to characterize them as self-fulfilling crises.

During much of 1997 and 1998, the financial press has frequently stressed that the crises in Asia are a new breed, as they supposedly occurred against a backdrop of immaculate fiscal and economic fundamentals. Yet our analysis of earlier episodes reveals that many of the features and antecedents of the crises in Asia were common to a substantial number of crisis episodes in Latin America, Europe, and elsewhere. Consider an economy that had successfully stabilized inflation, enjoyed an economic boom,

TABLE A1—Continued

Exports (8)	Imports (9)	Terms of trade (10)	Real exchange rate (11)	Reserves (12)	Real interest-rate differential (13)	Output (14)	Stock prices (15)	Deficit/ GDP (16)	Total number of signals[b] (17)
1	0	1	1	1	1	NA	1	0	82
1	1	1	0	0	NA	1	1	1	85
1	1	1	0	1	NA	1	1	1	77
1	0	1	0	1	1	1	1	0	60
0	0	0	1	0	1	1	1	1	44
1	0	0	1	1	1	1	1	0	63
1	1	1	1	1	0	1	1	0	73
1	1	1	1	1	1	1	0	0	67
1	0	1	1	1	1	1	0	0	67
1	0	1	1	1	1	1	1	1	87
1	0	1	0	0	1	NA	NA	1	46
1	1	1	1	1	1	NA	1	1	86
1	1	1	1	1	1	NA	0	0	71
NA	NA	NA	NA	NA	NA	NA	NA	NA	NA
1	1	NA	1	0	NA	NA	NA	1	78
0	0	0	1	1	1	0	0	0	56
1	NA	NA	NA	1	NA	NA	NA	0	83
1	1	1	1	1	1	1	NA	0	79
1	0	1	1	1	NA	1	0	0	62
1	0	1	0	1	1	0	0	1	63
0	1	1	0	1	1	0	1	1	63
1	0	1	0	1	1	0	1	0	69
0	1	1	1	1	1	0	1	0	75
OUT-OF-SAMPLE CRISES									
0	0	NA	NA	0	1	1	0	NA	25
0	0	NA	1	1	1	0	0	NA	60
0	1	NA	1	0	1	NA	0	NA	62
1	0	NA	1	1	NA	1	1	NA	70
SUMMARY STATISTICS									
85	52	75	59	75	86	74	64	27	
78	73	73	58	70	78	68	54	21	
89	40	77	60	78	89	76	68	31	
0.40	1.10	0.70	0.14	0.55	0.90	0.46	0.38	0.49	

[a] A 1 indicates that there was at least one signal in the 24 months preceding a crisis. NA indicates that some or all of the data were missing for the 24-month period.

[b] Number of variables signalling a crisis as a proportion of the number of indicators for which data are available (in percent).

[c] Number of crises accurately called divided by the number of crises for which data are available for that indicator. For example, for the M2 multiplier, the indicator correctly identified crises 76 percent of the time (54 out of 71).

[d] FL: Financial liberalization.

[e] The noise-to-signal ratio is the number of bad signals as a proportion of the number of months outside the crisis window divided by the number of good signals as a proportion of the number of months in the crisis window.

and was running fiscal surpluses. However, this economy had liberalized its capital account and its domestic financial sector amidst an environment of weak regulation and poor banking supervision. Banking-sector problems emerged and intensified, eventually undermining the ability of the central bank to maintain its exchange-rate committment. While this profile fits Asia rather well, this was Díaz-Alejandro's description of the antecedents to the fierce Chilean crisis of 1982. At the roots of the meltdown of the Thai baht, Korean won, and Indonesian rupiah lay systemic banking problems. Thus, it would appear that we can only consider these

TABLE A2—ANATOMY OF BANKING CRISES[a]

Country	Crisis	M2 multiplier (1)	Domestic credit/GDP (2)	Real interest rate (3)	Lending-deposit rate ratio (4)	Excess M1 balances (5)	M2/ reserves (6)	Bank deposits (7)
Argentina	March 80	1	0	1	0	0	1	0
	May 85	1	NA	1	1	0	1	0
	Dec. 94	NA	NA	1	1	NA	NA	NA
Bolivia	Oct. 87	1	1	1	0	NA	1	0
Brazil	Nov. 85	1	1	1	1	1	1	0
	Dec. 94	NA	NA	1	1	NA	1	1
Chile	Sept. 81	1	1	1	0	1	0	0
Colombia	July 82	1	NA	1	NA	0	NA	1
Denmark	March 87	NA	1	1	0	0	1	1
Finland	Sept. 91	1	1	1	0	0	1	1
Indonesia	Nov. 92	1	0	1	1	0	0	1
Israel	Oct. 83	0	0	1	NA	1	1	1
Malaysia	July 85	1	0	1	0	0	1	1
Mexico	Sept. 82	0	1	1	NA	1	1	1
	Oct. 92	0	0	1	1	1	0	0
Norway	Nov. 88	1	1	1	NA	0	1	1
Peru	March 83	0	1	NA	NA	0	0	1
Philippines	Jan. 81	1	0	NA	NA	0	1	1
Spain	Nov. 78	0	0	NA	NA	0	0	1
Sweden	Nov. 91	1	0	1	1	NA	1	1
Thailand	March 79	0	0	1	NA	0	1	1
	Oct. 83	1	1	1	NA	0	1	0
Turkey	Jan. 91	1	0	1	1	1	0	1
Uruguay	March 71	NA	1	NA	NA	1	1	NA
	March 81	1	0	1	NA	0	1	0
Venezuela	Oct. 93	1	1	1	1	0	1	1
OUT-OF-SAMPLE CRISES								
Malaysia	Sept. 97	NA	NA	1	NA	1	NA	NA
Philippines	July 97	NA	1	1	1	1	NA	NA
Thailand	May 96	NA	NA	1	NA	1	1	1
SUMMARY STATISTICS								
Percent of crises called[c]		73	50	100	57	32	75	67
Noise-to-signal ratio[d]		0.50	0.59	0.45	1.93	0.82	0.71	1.03

crises as a new breed if we ignore the numerous lessons history offers. Thus, among the lessons that emerge from this analysis is the obvious case for strong banking regulation and supervision to allow countries to sail smoothly through the perilous waters of financial liberalization. Yet, the Asian episodes of 1997–1998, like many of their earlier Latin American counter-

parts, also remind us that capital inflows can on occasion be too much of a good thing.

The results presented in this paper are a first step in evaluating the complex linkages between currency and domestic financial crises. Analyzing how the authorities deal with the banking problems and how the problems affect exchange-rate expectations will help determine whether a bank-

TABLE A2—Continued

Exports (8)	Imports (9)	Terms of trade (10)	Real exchange rate (11)	Reserves (12)	Real interest-rate differential (13)	Output (14)	Stock prices (15)	Deficit/ GDP (16)	Total number of signals[b] (17)
1	1	1	1	1	1	NA	0	NA	64
1	0	1	0	1	1	1	1	0	67
NA	1	NA	1	1	1	1	NA	NA	100
1	1	1	0	1	1	NA	NA	1	77
1	0	1	0	1	1	NA	0	0	67
NA	1	1	1	1	1	1	1	NA	100
1	1	1	1	1	1	1	1	1	81
1	0	1	1	1	1	1	1	0	77
0	1	NA	0	1	1	1	1	1	71
1	0	1	1	1	1	1	1	1	81
1	0	1	0	1	1	1	1	1	69
1	0	0	0	1	NA	1	1	0	57
1	0	1	1	1	1	1	1	0	69
1	0	1	1	1	NA	1	1	1	86
1	1	1	1	0	1	1	0	NA	60
1	1	1	1	1	1	1	1	0	87
1	0	1	0	1	NA	1	NA	0	50
1	1	1	1	1	NA	NA	1	0	75
0	1	1	1	0	NA	0	1	0	38
1	1	1	1	1	1	1	1	1	93
0	1	1	0	1	1	NA	1	0	57
1	1	1	1	1	1	NA	0	NA	77
1	1	1	0	1	1	NA	1	1	80
1	NA	NA	0	1	NA	NA	NA	0	71
1	1	1	1	1	1	1	NA	0	71
1	0	1	0	1	1	0	1	1	75
				OUT-OF-SAMPLE CRISES					
NA	NA	NA	1	NA	1	NA	NA	NA	100
NA	NA	NA	1	NA	1	NA	NA	NA	100
1	NA	NA	1	1	NA	NA	1	NA	100
				SUMMARY STATISTICS					
88	60	96	58	92	100	89	81	43	
0.61	1.60	0.79	0.28	0.71	0.52	0.48	0.28	0.44	

[a] A 1 indicates that there was at least one signal in the 24-month window around the crisis. NA indicates that some or all of the data were missing for the 24-month period.

[b] Number of variables signalling a crisis as a proportion of the number of indicators for which data are available (in percent).

[c] Number of crises accurately called divided by the number of crises for which data are available for that indicator. For example, for the M2 multiplier, the indicator correctly identified crises 73 percent of the time (16 out of 22).

[d] The noise-to-signal ratio is the number of bad signals as a proportion of the number of months outside the crisis window divided by the number of good signals as a proportion of the number of months in the crisis window.

ing crises will lead to a balance-of-payments crisis. We have only considered macroeconomic data in our list of indicators, but data of the health of bank balance sheets would be a logical complement to the macro data. Future analysis could provide a more detailed evaluation of the univariate and multivariate signaling properties of various macroeconomic time series and composite indices along the lines of Diebold and Rudebusch (1989) and Stock and Watson (1989). Indeed, that would appear to be a logical first step in the design of an early-warning system designed to help detect when a crisis is coming.

While this paper has focused on the similarities and common patterns across crises, it would also be useful to investigate whether there is evidence of distinct regional patterns. Why is it that in some countries currency crises and banking crises are not associated with deep and protracted recessions, while in others, notably in Latin America, the aftermath is so severe? Lastly, events (such as a balance-of-payments crises in a neighboring country) may also help assess whether a crisis is brewing in the home front; hence, the role of contagion effects may warrant further scrutiny.

DATA APPENDIX

Index of Currency Market Turbulence

The index, I, is a weighted average of the rate of change of the exchange rate, Δ_e/e, and of reserves, Δ_R/R, with weights such that the two components of the index have equal sample volatilities.

$$I = \frac{\Delta_e}{e} - \frac{\sigma_e}{\sigma_R} \cdot \frac{\Delta_R}{R}$$

where σ_e is the standard deviation of the rate of change of the exchange rate and σ_R is the standard deviation of the rate of change of reserves. Since changes in the exchange rate enter with a positive weight and changes in reserves have a negative weight attached, readings of this index that were three standard deviations or more above the mean were cataloged as crises. For countries in the sample that had hyperinflation, the construction of the index was modified. While a 100-percent devaluation may be traumatic for a country with low-to-moderate inflation, a devaluation of that magnitude is commonplace during hyperinflations. A single index for the countries that had hyperinflation episodes would miss sizable devaluations and reserve losses in the moderate inflation periods, since the historic mean is distorted by the high-inflation episode. To avoid this, we divided the sample according to whether inflation in the previous six months was higher than 150 percent and then constructed an index for each subsample. Our cataloging of crises for the countries coincides fairly highly with our chronology of currency market disruptions. Eichengreen et al. (1996b) also include interest rates in this index; however, our data on market-deter-

mined interest rates on developing countries does not span the entire sample.

The Indicators

Sources: International Financial Statistics (IFS), International Monetary Fund (IMF), various issues; *Emerging Market Indicators,* International Finance Corporation (IFC), various issues; *World Development Indicators,* World Bank (WB), various issues. When data was missing from these sources, central-bank bulletins and other country-specific sources were used as supplements. Unless otherwise noted, we used 12-month percent changes.

1. *M2 multiplier:* The ratio of M2 (IFS lines 34 plus 35) to base money (IFS line 14).

2. *Domestic credit/GDP:* IFS line 52 divided by IFS line 64 to obtain domestic credit in real terms, which was then divided by IFS line 99b.p. (interpolated) to obtain the domestic credit/GDP ratio. Monthly real GDP was interpolated from annual data.

3. *Real interest rate:* Deposit rate (IFS line 60) deflated using consumer prices (IFS line 64). Monthly rates expressed in percentage points. In levels.

4. *Lending-deposit rate ratio:* IFS line 60p divided by IFS line 60 was used in lieu of differential to ameliorate the distortions caused by the large percentage point spreads observed during high inflation. In levels.

5. *Excess M1 balances:* M1 (IFS line 34) deflated by consumer prices (IFS line 64) less an estimated demand for money. The demand for real balances is determined by real GDP (interpolated IFS line 99b.p), domestic consumer price inflation, and a time trend. Domestic inflation was used in lieu of nominal interest rates, as market-determined interest rates were not available during the entire sample for a number of countries; the time trend (which can enter log-linearly, linearly, or exponentially) is motivated by its role as a proxy for financial innovation and/or currency substitution. In levels.

6. *M2/reserves:* IFS lines 34 plus 35 converted into dollars (using IFS line ae) divided by IFS line 1L.d.

7. *Bank deposits:* IFS line 24 plus 25 deflated by consumer prices (IFS line 64).

8. *Exports:* IFS line 70.

9. *Imports:* IFS line 71.

10. *Terms of trade:* The unit value of exports (IFS line 74) over the unit value of imports (IFS line 75). For those developing countries where import unit values (or import price indices) were not available, an index of prices of manufactured exports from industrial countries to developing countries was used.

11. *The real exchange rate:* The real exchange-rate index is derived from a nominal exchange-rate index, adjusted for relative consumer prices (IFS line 64). The measure is defined as the relative price of foreign goods (in domestic currency) to the price of domestic goods. The nominal exchange-rate index is a weighted average of the exchange rates of the 19 OECD countries with weights equal to the country trade shares with the OECD countries. Since not all real appreciations reflect disequilibrium phenomena, we focus on deviations of the real exchange rate from trend. The trend was specified as, alternatively, log, linear, and exponential; the best fit among these was selected on a country-by-country basis. In levels.

12. *Reserves:* IFS line 1L.d.

13. *Real interest-rate differential:* Interest rates in the domestic economy are compared with interest rates in the United States (Germany) if the domestic central bank pegs the currency to the dollar (deutsche mark). The interest-rate differential is constructed as the difference between real rates for the domestic and foreign countries. Real rates are deposit rates (IFS line 60) deflated using consumer prices (IFS line 64).

14. *Output:* For most countries, the measure of output used is industrial production (IFS line 66). However, for some countries, (the commodity exporters) an index of out-put of primary commodities is used (IFS lines 66aa) if industrial production is not available.

15. *Stock returns:* IFC global indices are used for all emerging markets; for industrial countries the quotes from the main boards are used. All stock prices are in US dollars.

16. *GDP:* Consolidated public-sector deficit as a share of GDP (*World Development Indicators*, various issues).

REFERENCES

American Banker. Various issues.

Blanco, Herminio and Garber, Peter M. "Recurrent Devaluations and Speculative Attacks on the Mexican Peso." *Journal of Political Economy*, February 1986, *94* (1), pp. 148–66.

Calomiris, Charles W. and Gorton, Gary. "The Origins of Banking Panics: Models, Facts, and Bank Regulation," in R. Glenn Hubbard, ed., *Financial markets and financial crises.* Chicago: University of Chicago Press, 1991, pp. 109–73.

Calvo, Guillermo A. "Varieties of Capital-Market Crises." Mimeo, University of Maryland, 1995.

Calvo, Guillermo A.; Leiderman, Leonardo and Reinhart, Carmen M. "Capital Inflows and Real Exchange Rate Appreciation: The Role of External Factors." *International Monetary Fund Staff Papers*, March 1993, *40* (1), pp. 108–51.

Calvo, Guillermo A. and Mendoza, Enrique. "Petty Crime and Cruel Punishment: Lessons from the Mexican Debacle." *American Economic Review*, May 1996 (*Papers and Proceedings*), *86* (2), pp. 170–75.

Calvo, Sara and Reinhart, Carmen M. "Capital Flows to Latin America: Is There Evidence of Contagion Effects?" in Guillermo A. Calvo, Morris Goldstein, and Eduard Hochreiter, eds., *Private capital flows to emerging markets.* Washington, DC: Institute for International Economics, 1996, pp. 151–71.

Caprio, Gerald, Jr. and Klingebiel, Daniela. "Bank Insolvency: Bad Luck, Bad Policy, or Bad Banking?" in Michael Bruno and Boris Pleskovic, ed., *Annual World Bank conference on development economics.* Washington, DC: World Bank, 1996, pp. 79–104.

Díaz-Alejandro, Carlos F. "Good-Bye Financial Repression, Hello Financial Crash." *Journal of Development Economics*, February 1985, *19* (1–2), pp. 1–24.

Diebold, Francis and Rudebusch, Glen. "Scoring the Leading Indicators." *Journal of Business*, July 1989, *62* (3), pp. 369–91.

Dornbusch, Rudiger; Goldfajn, Ilan and Valdés, Rodrigo O. "Currency Crises and Collapses." *Brookings Papers on Economic Activity*, June 1995, (2), pp. 219–70.

Edwards, Sebastian. "Real Exchange Rates, Devaluation, and Adjustment: Exchange Rate Policy in Developing Countries." Cambridge, MA: MIT Press, 1989.

Eichengreen, Barry; Rose, Andrew K. and Wyplosz, Charles. "Contagious Currency Crises." Centre for Economic Policy Research (London) Discussion Paper No. 1453, August 1996a.

_____ . "Exchange Market Mayhem: The Antecedents and Aftermath of Speculative Attacks." *Economic Policy*, October 1996b, *21* (21), pp. 249–312.

Emerging Market Indicators. Washington, DC: International Finance Corporation, various issues.

Frankel, Jeffrey and Rose, Andrew K. "Exchange Rate Crises in Emerging Markets." *Journal of International Economics*, November 1996, *41* (3–4), pp. 351–68.

Galbis, Vicente. "High Real Interest Rates Under Financial Liberalization: Is There a Problem?." International Monetary Fund Working Paper No. WP/93/7, January 1993.

Goldfajn, Ilan and Valdés, Rodrigo O. "Balance-of-Payments Crises and Capital Flows: The Role of Liquidity." Mimeo, Massachusetts Institute of Technology, 1995.

Gorton, Gary. "Banking Panics and Business Cycles." *Oxford Economic Papers*, December 1988, *40* (4), pp. 751–81.

International Financial Statistics. Washington, DC: International Monetary Fund, various issues.

Kaminsky, Graciela L. and Leiderman, Leonardo. "High Real Interest Rates in the Aftermath of Disinflation: Is It a Lack of Credibility?" *Journal of Development Economics*, February 1998, *55* (1), pp. 191–214.

Kaminsky, Graciela L. and Reinhart, Carmen M. "The Twin Crises: The Causes of Banking and Balance-of-Payments Problems." International Finance Discussion Paper No. 544, Board of Governors of the Federal Reserve System, March 1996.

Kindelberger, Charles. *Manias, panics, and crashes.* New York: Basic Books, 1978.

Krugman, Paul. "A Model of Balance-of-Payments Crises." *Journal of Money, Credit, and Banking*, August 1979, *11* (3), pp. 311–25.

McKinnon, Ronald I. and Pill, Huw. "Credible Liberalizations and International Capital Flows: The 'Overborrowing Syndrome', " in Takatoshi Ito and Anne O. Krueger, eds., *Financial deregulation and integration in East Asia.* Chicago: University of Chicago Press, 1996, pp. 7–42.

Miller, Victoria. "Central Bank Reactions to Banking Crises in Fixed Exchange Rate Regimes." Mimeo, Université de Québec à Montréal, 1995.

Mishkin, Frederic S. "Understanding Financial Crises: A Developing Country Perspective," in Michael Bruno and Boris Pleskovic, eds., *Annual World Bank conference on development economics.* Washington DC: World Bank, 1996, pp. 29–62.

Mishra, Deepak. "Political Determinants of Currency Crises: Theory and Evidence." Mimeo, University of Maryland, 1997.

New York Times. Various issues.

Obstfeld, Maurice. "The Logic of Currency Crises." National Bureau of Economic Research (Cambridge, MA) Working Paper No. 4640, February 1994.

_____ . "Models of Currency Crises with Self-fulfilling Features." *European Economic Review*, April 1996, *40* (1), pp. 1037–47.

Reinhart, Carmen M. and Reinhart, Vincent R. "Forecasting Turning Points in Canada." Mimeo, International Monetary Fund, 1996.

Reinhart, Carmen M. and Végh, Carlos A. "Do Exchange Rate-Based Inflation Stabilizations Sow the Seeds of Their Own Destruction?" Mimeo, International Monetary Fund, 1996.

Stock, James H. and Watson, Mark W. "New Indexes of Coincident and Leading Economic Indicators," in Olivier Jean Blanchard and Stanley Fischer, eds., *NBER macroeconomics annual.* Cambridge, MA: MIT Press, 1989, pp. 351–94.

Stoker, James. "Intermediation and the Business Cycle Under a Specie Standard: The Role of the Gold Standard in English Financial Crises, 1790–1850." Mimeo, University of Chicago, 1994.

Sundararajan, V. and Baliño, Tomas. "Issues in Recent Banking Crises," in V. Sundararajan and Tomas Baliño, eds., *Banking crises: Cases and issues.* Washington, DC: International Monetary Fund, 1991, pp. 1–57.

Velasco, Andres. "Financial Crises and Balance of Payments Crises: A Simple Model of the Southern Cone Experience." *Journal of Development Economics*, October 1987, *27* (1–2), pp. 263–83.

Wall Street Journal. Various issues.

World Development Indicators. Washington DC: World Bank, various issues.

[3]

Cambridge Journal of Economics 1998, 22, 677–692

Derivatives and global capital flows: applications to Asia

J. A. Kregel*

The role of derivatives contracts in explaining the existence of a number of puzzles associated with the Asian financial crisis is investigated. The shift to short-term commercial bank lending in a region that traditionally relied on direct investment, the allocation of resources to low return uses in an area considered to be highly profitable, lax prudential supervision in systems that had introduced financial reforms early, and the co-movement of asset prices and exchange rates, which was to have been eliminated by direct equity investments, are all linked to the characteristics of derivative contracts used to provide lending to Asia.

1. Introduction: four puzzles

There are four factors involved in the current financial crisis in Asia that have caused surprise. This paper suggests that an understanding of the role of derivatives contracts in facilitating the financial flows to Asia may provide a key to understanding them.

The Latin American debt crisis of 1982 was thought to have been aggravated by the dominance of syndicated lending by commercial banks. Developing-country borrowers were thus encouraged to increase their reliance on non-bank lending, in particular private direct investment flows. The dominance of direct investment flows to a number of Asian countries was used as an example of the greater stability of such lending. Yet, the Asian crisis appears to have been precipitated by the reversal of short-term private bank lending which had come to dominate capital flows to the region.

Second, the flows of capital to Asia have been used as an example of the benefits of free international capital markets in directing resources to the most productive uses. Yet, in the aftermath of the crisis, it appears that total returns on equity investments in Asia have in fact been lower than in most other regions throughout the 1990s.

Third, it appears that in a number of Asian countries the majority of international lending was between foreign and domestic banks. It has been suggested that the major cause of the crisis is unsafe lending practices by the Asian banks, permitted by inadequate national prudential supervision. But these economies were the most advanced on the road to market liberalisation. One of the cardinal principles of financial liberalisation, formed in the aftermath of the Chilean crisis, is that the creation of institutional structures ensuring the stability of the financial system should precede financial market liberalisation. Indeed, many of the Asian countries were following this advice. It is interesting to note that the developed-country lending banks were generally large, global banks

Manuscript received 8 April 1998.

*University of Bologna.

678   J. A. Kregel

employing highly sophisticated risk-assessment procedures. However, they appear to have continued lending well after the increased risks in the region were generally apparent. This suggests that even the most sophisticated operators in global financial markets have difficulties in assessing risk, and that their regulators were no more successful in imposing prudent limits than those in the most advanced markets.

Finally, private portfolio and direct investment flows were considered to be preferable to syndicated bank lending because they were thought to segregate the problem of foreign exchange instability from asset market instability. Syndicated lending was denominated in the currency of the lending bank, and the exchange rate risk was thus borne by the borrower. However, direct equity investors purchase foreign financial assets in foreign currency and thus bear the currency risk. It was suggested that in a crisis the foreign investor would suffer from a fall in asset prices as well as from a decline in the exchange rate, which would discourage sales of security investments, thereby reducing selling pressure in the foreign exchange market. Yet, the linkage between the collapse in exchange rates and equity markets appears to have been even closer in Asia than in other experiences of financial crisis.

One explanation of the crisis in foreign exchange markets is that a large proportion of foreign borrowing by corporates and banks was unhedged because of prevailing expectations of stable exchange rates. When these expectations were disappointed, the scramble to repay these foreign currency loans created a massive market imbalance and a collapse of the foreign exchanges. This absence of generalised hedging of foreign borrowing has been interpreted to mean that financial derivative contracts played little or no role in the crisis. This position has been reinforced by the repeated references to an IMF study which suggests that global hedge funds were not active catalysts in the Asian crisis.[1] However, the recent quarterly reports (for the 4th quarter of 1997 and 1st quarter of 1998) of US money-centre banks, reflecting the initial impact of the Asian crisis on their lending to the area, suggest that most of their initial losses have been related to derivative-based credit swap contracts. Thus, at least in the case of US banks, certain types of derivative contract appear to have played some role in the flows of funds to Asia and thus in the instability of these flows. While bank derivatives are 'tailored-to-the-client', 'over-the-counter' contracts, and as such are not generally public knowledge, the experience of such contracts in the 'Tequila' crisis earlier in this decade provides some indication of the kinds of contract that might have been involved. This short paper thus suggests ways in which bank derivative contracts may have been linked to the rise in short-term bank lending to Asia and contributed to the four puzzles noted above concerning capital flows to the region.

2. Structured derivatives: global allocation of capital, transparency and prudential supervision

Most people are now familiar with the standard derivative contracts used in hedging risk, such as forwards, futures and options. While foreign currency forwards remain the

---

[1] This frequently cited study was not available in April 1998 when this article was drafted. The summary that appears in the IMF's *World Economic Outlook* (Part II, Box 1, 1998) suggests that hedge funds mainly attack countries whose 'macroeconomic variables are far out of line with sustainable values'. Another recent study (Brown, Goetzmann and Park, 1998) suggests that hedge funds did not take major positions against Asian currencies or financial assets and did not make abnormal returns from their operations during the last half of 1997. From this one might conclude that the hedge fund managers did not detect any unsustainable policies in these countries.

Derivatives and global capital flows: applications to Asia   679

province of bank foreign exchange dealers, most basic futures and options contracts are standardised and traded in organised, regulated markets. Banks also offer derivative contracts to their clients in what is termed the 'over-the-counter' (OTC) market. But there is no market involved in these contracts, which may involve the stipulation of standard futures and options contracts outside the organised market on a bilateral basis with individual clients. However, the majority of OTC activity involves individually tailored, often highly complex, combinations of standard financial instruments, packaged together with derivative contracts designed to meet the particular needs of clients. These contract packages involve very little direct lending by banks to clients, and thus generate little net interest income. However, since they are often executed through special purpose vehicles (i.e., specialised investment firms that are independently capitalised), they have the advantage, under the Basle capital adequacy requirements, of requiring little or no capital, or of being classified as off-balance-sheet items, because they do not represent a direct risk exposure for the bank. In addition, they generate substantial fee and commission income. Rather than committing their own capital, the banks serve in these transactions as intermediaries whose services involve not only matching borrowers and lenders, but acting as market innovators to create investment vehicles that attract lenders and borrowers. Nonetheless, these activities often require banks to accept some of the risks associated with the derivatives created in order to produce packages with the characteristics desired by final borrowers and lenders. These derivative risks may or may not be hedged by the bank, depending on its own proprietary investment strategy. When hedging does occur, it can be done either by physical hedging (i.e., the actual purchase of an offsetting position in the underlying financial asset), through the purchase of derivative contracts in organised markets, or by producing a package that involves risks which offset those involved in other packages (cross hedging or risk matching across clients).

The major objective of active, global financial institutions is thus no longer the maximisation of profits by seeking the lowest cost funds and channelling them to the highest risk-adjusted return, but rather in maximising the amount of funds intermediated in order to maximise fees and commissions, thereby maximising the rate of return on bank capital. This means a shift from continuous risk assessment and risk monitoring of funded investment projects that produce recurring flows of interest payments over time to the identification of riskless 'trades' that produce large, single payments, with as much of the residual risks as possible carried by the purchasers of the package. This process has been accelerated by the introduction of risk-weighted capital requirements. As a result, banks have come to play a declining role in the process of the efficient international allocation of investment funds. Rather, they serve to facilitate this process by linking primary lenders and final borrowers. This means that the efficient allocation of funds to the highest risk-adjusted rate of return depends increasingly on assessment of risks and returns by the lender. Yet, it is the role of most derivative packages to mask the actual risk involved in an investment, and to increase the difficulty in assessing the final return on funds provided.[1] As a result, certain types of derivative may increase the difficulties faced by private capital markets in effectuating the efficient allocation of resources. By extension, if they make investment evaluation more difficult for primary lenders, they may also create difficulties for financial market regulators and supervisors.

These particular aspects can be most clearly seen by reference to structured credit

---

[1] For example, Chew (1996, p. 57) observes that '[s]tructured notes are the epitome of how investment technology helped and continues to help money managers circumvent guidelines that were framed to protect the interest of small, unsophisticated investors...'

**680		J. A. Kregel**

derivative contracts, which expanded dramatically during the 1990s. Most US institutional investors do not face unlimited investment choices. Most are limited to investments in assets with a minimum of risk as represented by an 'investment grade' credit
rating on the issue, and many are precluded from certain types of risk, such as foreign
exchange risks, or foreign credit risk (these often are simply the result of the application of
the investment grade restriction). This means that a large proportion of professionally
managed institutional investment funds cannot invest in emerging markets or in
particular asset classes such as foreign exchange. Structured derivative packages, created
by global investment banks, have often provided the means to circumvent these
restrictions.

Structured derivative contracts have been used for this purpose in two ways. In 1992
and 1993, in a falling interest rate environment, they provided a means to increase returns
for money managers and then, when rates started to rise, to provide borrowers with
below-market borrowing rates. They usually involved structured credit notes with
embedded options. 'These notes only carried a higher coupon because they contained an
embedded short position in interest rate options. In other words, often when an investor
bought a structured note, he simultaneously sold an interest rate option... There is no
doubt that some less knowledgeable investors did not realize that by buying these
securities, they were selling options or engaging in leveraged bets, because some of these
features were quite cleverly concealed' (Chew, 1996, pp. 54–5). The assumption behind
such contracts is that the price of the instrument underlying the contract would not
change sufficiently to produce a loss that completely eliminated the premium earned from
selling the option.[1]

An example closer to the present context might involve US government agency dollar-
denominated structured notes with the interest payment, or the principal value, linked to
an index representing some foreign asset.[2] The return to these notes would be higher than
US domestic rates, but the increased yield would be accompanied by the increased risk
due to foreign exchange exposure. Such an asset might be a one-year dollar-denominated
note paying a guaranteed above-market interest rate, but with the amount of repayment of

---

[1] The widely reported derivatives losses incurred by Procter and Gamble and Gibson Greeting Cards
involved contracts of precisely this type. Their borrowing costs were reduced by the amount of the option
premium gained from writing put options on interest rates with a highly levered pay-off profile. Such
contracts provided below-market borrowing costs as long as the losses on the option positions did not exceed
the premia received from selling the options contracts. However, in the winter of 1994 interest rates rose
sharply, leading to net losses. Cf., Chew, 1996.

[2] 'The Federal Home Loan Bank (FHLB), one of the largest issuers of such products in the United States,
has more than 175 indexes or index combinations against which cash flows are calculated... Structured notes
are primarily issued by government-sponsored enterprises (GSEs), such as the Federal Home Loan Bank
(FHLB), Federal National Mortgage Association (FNMA), Student Loan Marketing Association (SNMA),
and Federal Home Loan Mortgage Corporation (FHLMC). Although the credit risk of these securities is
minimal, other risks such as interest-rate risk, market (price) risk, and liquidity risk can be material.
[However,] [i]nvestment banks and the section 20 subsidiaries of banks often act to underwrite structured-
note issuances. They are often actively involved in making a market in secondary structured notes... In its
heyday, the structured-note market was a by-product of a unique period in financial history. In 1992 and
1993, Wall Street firms engineered debt that allowed borrowers to attain highly attractive below-market
funding and that rewarded investors (in large part) as long as interest rates remained low. The incredible and
at times implausible array of structure types came into being in response to the investment community's
desire for higher returns during a sustained period of low interest rates. Issuers and investment dealer firms
were more than willing to address this need, introducing investors to more attractive (and by definition
riskier) securities whose cash flows were linked to, for example, the performance of the yen; the yen's
relationship to the lira; and a host of other indexes, currencies, or benchmarks. Investors' quest for enhanced
yield caused them to adopt, in many cases, very tenuous risk-reward measures with respect to potential
investment choices.' Federal Reserve System, 1998, Section 4040.1, pp. 1, 5 ,6.

Derivatives and global capital flows: applications to Asia   681

principal linked to an index, say the Thai baht/dollar exchange rate. Since the asset is denominated in US dollars, and the interest is guaranteed and paid in US dollars, the notes carry an investment grade credit rating and would be entered on the balance sheets of investors as the equivalent of a US Treasury or Agency security, not as a foreign investment subject to foreign exchange or country risks. Yet, the above-market interest rate on the note is generated by the sale of a put option on the Thai baht at a strike price just above the current market rate that is in fact embedded in the contract. This is equivalent to the buyer having purchased the Thai currency. If the baht exchange rate remains constant, the written put is not exercised and the option premium received is retained by the writer and is used to meet the above-market guaranteed interest rate payable on the contract.

However, if the baht were to depreciate to a value below the strike price, then the buyer of the put would exercise his right given by the option to sell baht at a price that is higher than the market price. The writer of the option would thus incur a loss determined by the difference between the strike price and the market price for baht. Since the interest rate on the instrument is guaranteed, the loss cannot be reflected in a reduction in the rate of interest. However, the augmented interest payment produced by the margin over the market interest rate, and any loss on the option position, would be recovered by means of a reduction in the principal returned to the purchaser at maturity. An investor seeking to maximise yield may be attracted by the guarantee on the interest rate, and underestimate or even ignore the risk of loss in capital value. Since the writer of an option has an unlimited exposure, a large change in the exchange rate could cause a total loss of capital invested.

Alternatively, this contract could have been constructed by lending the principal (less the discounted value of the guaranteed dollar interest payment which is invested in a one-year Treasury bill) directly to a Thai bank by buying a bank acceptance. Again, the implicit assumption is that the baht/dollar exchange rate should remain constant so that the baht interest and principal repayment can be converted at maturity to a dollar value equal to the original investment of principal. If the baht devalues relative to the dollar, then the amount available to repay the principal will be lower. The buyer thus has the entire principal at risk, only the interest is guaranteed. The contract arranged in this way would provide Thai banks with below-market rate funds, provide US investors with above-market returns (US rates were in decline from 1991 to 1993) and the banks with fees and commissions for arranging the trade, but with no commitment of capital (most US banks were emerging from the experiences of the real estate crisis of the 1980s and were seeking to rebuild capital).

It is virtually impossible for the US investor to evaluate the use of the funds made by the Thai bank, and there is little incentive for the US bank to do so, since once the structured note issue is sold, the foreign credit and foreign exchange risks are borne by the US investor. The investor is not only subverting prudential controls (on its balance sheet these assets would be classified as exposure to a US entity, with investment grade credit risk), but is in all probability evaluating the return without any adjustment for the foreign exchange risk, even if that risk is recognised as such. There is thus little economic interest or possibility for the market to assess either the risk or the returns of the investment. There is thus no incentive for market agents to act so as to ensure that capital is allocated globally to those uses providing the highest risk-adjusted rates of return.

682   J. A. Kregel

3. Structured credit derivatives

Structured products have been the basis for the growing market in credit derivative contracts. These contracts usually involve credit swaps embedded in structured notes to form credit-linked notes. The objective of a credit swap is to allow counterparties to exchange the credit risks associated with an instrument, while retaining the cash-flow characteristics. Total return swaps 'enable counterparties to swap the total economic risk attached to a reference asset without actually transferring the asset itself... Under the terms of the swap, [the first counterparty] pays [the second counterparty] the cashflows generated by the reference asset, including coupon payments and any appreciations in its capital valued calculated on a periodic mark to market basis. [The second counterparty], in exchange, pays a LIBOR-linked margin plus any depreciations in the capital value of the reference asset' (Ghose, 1997, p. 3; see also the description given in Federal Reserve System, 1998, section 4350.1, pp. 1–2). A credit swap or equity swap thus transfers the credit risk, including the impact of a credit event on the capital value of the asset.

It was the creation of the Brady bond that provided the recipe for the extension of many of these structured loans to emerging markets. A collateralised Brady bond is a variety of structured derivative in which the developing country (Mexico was the first) uses foreign exchange reserves as equity capital to create an investment company (special investment vehicle). The investment company uses the equity (i.e., the foreign exchange) to buy long-term, stripped US Treasury bonds to serve as collateral. The investment company then issues its own fixed-interest liabilities in the form of long-term bonds (which came to be called Brady bonds after the US Secretary of the Treasury who held office at the time), which carry a sovereign government guarantee, in an amount equal to the maturity value of the US Treasury discount bonds. The investment company's bonds are usually only sold in exchange for the debtor country's outstanding foreign bank debt at its current market value (in Mexico's case this represented a discount to its face value of about 35%). The principal of the bonds issued by the investment vehicle (the Brady bonds) is thus guaranteed or collateralised by the Treasury bonds held, and repayment of principal in full at maturity is riskless. Additional short-term Treasury coupon strips (which provide only payment of coupon interest, without any right to principal repayment) would also be purchased by the investment vehicle to provide a guarantee for the interest payments during the first 18 or 24 months of life of the bonds. After that, interest would have to be paid from the proceeds of the underlying loans or from other government sources. The interest is thus only partially guaranteed and only riskless for the payments backed by the US Treasury strips. Banks that exchanged their participations in syndicated loans to developing countries for 'Brady bonds' could then trade those bonds in the open market, with their values determined by changes in the issuing country's sovereign credit rating and in US interest rates which affect the current value of the underlying collateral—the Treasury bonds.

Although the maturities of the Brady bonds were usually 20 or more years, in the case of a Brady bond with a two-year rolling interest guarantee, it was identical to buying a 20-year discount zero coupon bond, a 6-month zero bond, a 12-month zero, an 18-month zero, and a 2-year zero. These streams were default-free, so they could be considered as AAA. It was only the interest payments to be paid after the second year (which could be represented as 36 zero coupon bonds with maturities running from 30 months to 20 years at six-month intervals) that carried foreign exchange and sovereign credit risk. The Brady structure thus provided complicated market valuation, and it also provided an infinite

Derivatives and global capital flows: applications to Asia   **683**

number of possibilities for rearranging the various pieces of the bond into more attractive cash-flow structures.

An example would be transferring Brady bonds into a trust structure, rearranging the cash flows and swapping them from floating USD into fixed DEM with a bullet repayment. Investors are thus able to achieve a higher yield than a Latin American DEM Eurobond with essentially the same counter-party risk. The bank arranging the issue is left with a contingent default risk on the underlying Brady bonds. There can be a loss in the case of a default, as the residual value of the Brady bonds in the trust might not be sufficient to cover the bank's potential loss from unwinding the cross currency swap. (Watzinger, 1997, p. 49)

Thus, a company set up to buy Brady bonds could issue its own two-year bonds that would carry a AAA credit rating since the interest payments were backed by US Treasury securities, and another series of bonds with a 20-year guaranteed principal value at maturity and a lower credit rating reflecting the risk on the remaining interest payments. If this second series could be rated investment grade, the final result would be to transform high-risk, impaired, syndicated loans of banks to Latin American governments into low-risk investment-grade bonds that could be sold to institutional investors, with a profit from the price differences reflecting the credit-rating differential, as well as the associated fees and commissions. This is called credit enhancement, and investment banks quickly extended the Brady principle to other types of developing country debt. Since the first Brady issues were in Mexico (J. P. Morgan had produced a prototype of the Brady bond called the Aztec bond in 1988), this extension beyond syndicated bank loans also appears to have started in Mexico.

The problem facing investment bankers was to find structures that allowed improvement in credit ratings of the original issues at minimal cost. The first step in this process was the creation of a special investment vehicle in the form of an offshore trust that would buy a high interest rate domestic bond (say a Mexican government-issued security, such as Ajustabonos or Cetes, which carries an investment grade domestic credit rating), along with some zero coupon US Treasury bonds. These purchases would be financed through the issue of its own dollar-denominated bonds (no longer called Brady). The bonds could be divided into two classes: one class would have its principal collateralised by the Treasury discount bonds in Brady fashion, while the other class, backed by the domestic bonds, would carry no guarantee. The interest would be paid from the income generated by the peso asset. For the rating agencies, these were credit-enhanced peso bonds, and they were assigned a credit rating equal to the Mexican government rating on its peso issues in the domestic capital market. Since a government is always the benchmark, and thus the domestic risk-free rate, it is almost by definition investment grade in its own market. The enhanced bonds issued by the trust were thus given an investment-grade rating. But, as dollar-denominated bonds paying dollar interest rates, they could be sold to US institutional investors. What the investor was in fact buying was a peso-denominated Mexican government bond, and the exchange rate risk on the interest payments. However, on the balance sheet of the US investor, these instruments were represented as if they were US dollar investment-grade bonds. Again, the result was that US institutional investor funds were being invested in emerging market debt, earning above-market interest rates, without their balance sheets necessarily reflecting the actual risk involved. These structures were offered in various combinations, but it still remains true that neither the investor nor the bank intermediary has any direct interest in evaluating either the final use made of the funds, nor the risk-adjusted returns earned by the investments. For the intermediary there was no risk, unless the bank was required to

684   J. A. Kregel

guarantee that it could convert the interest payments into dollars, which only represented a risk if the foreign currency was to become inconvertible (this is not devaluation risk, but the risk that the currency could not be sold at any price).

This provides one possible explanation of why so much effort was made to prevent Mexico from suspending convertibility in 1994. Structures similar to these were used in Asia, as well as in Latin America. Thus the structured note and the credit-enhanced Brady structure provide simple examples of how funds were moved from developed to developing countries, despite the existence of prudential regulatory barriers, and why there was little effort expended in ensuring that the funds were moving to the highest risk-adjusted uses. The buyers were interested in enhancing yield in a low yield environment, while the intermediaries were interested in producing zero risk, zero capital-using vehicles that would maximise fee and commission income. Earnings on structured vehicles are estimated to have been in excess of 2% of principal.

The result of these packages is to change the credit-risk characteristics of the bonds by shifting the risks to different individuals. They thus allow access for investors whose activities are limited by the credit-risk classification of the assets they can buy.

Emerging market borrowers use total return swaps to get access to funding, or reduce the cost of it. The borrower sells assets to a bank and enters into a total return swap. In this swap, he receives the total return on the assets sold and pays Libor plus spread. Consequently, the borrower raises funds while at the same time still being able to benefit from a price appreciation of the asset sold... Investors use total return swaps to get access to their desired emerging market exposure. In a number of countries, severe restrictions in the cash market prevail. For instance, cumbersome settlement procedures, withholding taxes or minimum holding periods. Total return swaps can be an effective means for investors to structure a way around these restrictions. (Chew, 1996, p. 49)

4. Asset prices and foreign exchange market linkages

Linkage between foreign exchange markets and emerging asset markets may result from the use of some extensions of the structured and credit derivatives contracts discussed above. These extensions generally involve using hard currency exposure to fund a position in an emerging market asset denominated in an emerging market currency. They thus create both currency and emerging asset market price risk.

In an equity swap, the owner of an emerging market asset exchanges its return (i.e., interest or dividend income plus the change in capital value) for a fixed term (or until maturity or perpetuity) against a zero interest loan (which may be in foreign currency) of its current value (or the expected value of the future income stream) of the asset. This is, of course, equivalent to sale of the asset, but without actual transfer of ownership. Such a transaction avoids having to book a loss on the asset (an advantage to a bank in difficulty) or to book a tax event (an advantage to a rich businessman), while liquidating the value of the asset. There is currency risk represented by the receipt of the total return on the asset by the developed country bank, as well as market price risk, represented by the necessity to offset changes in capital value. Thus, both exchange rate risk and asset price risk are present in these contracts.

A variant of this structure is a form of total return swap that was common in the run-up to the 1994–95 peso crisis.[1] A total return swap can be made using any underlying asset as

[1] The use of this particular structure by a large US investment bank is described by Partnoy (1997, ch. 9). It is important to remember that even if no assets or currency are actually exchanged, the impact on the participating banks' profit and loss position is just as if the funds had actually been lent and/or invested and in the case of leveraged contracts exceed those amounts.

Derivatives and global capital flows: applications to Asia   685

the reference rate which is swapped against the benchmark rate, usually a US dollar rate plus a margin. A US bank may agree to pay the total return (in pesos) on a Mexican government security against the payment by a Mexican bank of a dollar benchmark interest rate plus a spread. The Mexican bank is effectively borrowing dollars and investing them in Mexican securities, earning the spread between dollar and peso interest rates. The advantage in this structure (as opposed to the equity swap discussed above) is that the asset does not appear on the Mexican bank's balance sheet, while it profits from what is in effect borrowing at a cost below the domestic market interest rate without adding to its risk-adjusted capital requirement.

On the other hand, the US bank is effectively lending dollars against the collateral of an emerging market asset, and paying the total peso return on the foreign asset against receipt of a dollar interest payment. The US bank profits from the spread over market interest rates, which is substantially greater than it could have charged domestic clients. As far as the developing country bank is concerned, it faces foreign exchange risk and possible interest rate or maturity risk, as well as the price risk on the asset (the borrower must compensate the lender for any depreciation in the capital value of the asset). Risk coverage for the US bank would be arranged by buying the underlying asset (this hedges the commitment to pay the interest return on the asset plus any capital appreciation), and then financing the purchase through a repurchase agreement with another US bank; thus getting the asset off its own balance sheet. But exchange rate and convertibility risk exposure still remain on the notional amount of the swap contract. This could be hedged by issuing a floating-rate note at a guaranteed above-market interest rate for the value of the principal, with a clause permitting payment in foreign currency in the event of a suspension of currency convertibility. Thus, both the US and emerging market banks incur currency mismatches, and the profitability of the contract to each depends on movements in the exchange rate as well as the relative movements of US and emerging market interest rates, and thus on asset prices in the emerging market.

Either of these two structures may thus provide an explanation of a direct linkage between exchange rates and domestic asset markets. As already mentioned, most of these instruments were set up on the presumption of stable exchange rates. Any indication that there might be a change in the way a central bank handled exchange rate policy would create the potential for substantial losses to investors. To see this, consider the foreign bank paying dollar interest and receiving total return on the domestic asset. The domestic currency costs of the dollar payments will increase with any increase in the dollar interest rate or any devaluation of the domestic currency. While a rise in domestic interest rates will increase returns, the associated depreciation in the value of the asset will normally more than offset this, so that the financing costs of the position (the cost of carry) in domestic currency terms will increase and profitability decline. When depreciation in the currency is accompanied by rising domestic interest rates, a contract with a positive carry (i.e., a profit on the interest differential paid and received) may be quickly reversed, creating an incentive to unwind the swap or to hedge the foreign exchange risk by going long dollar assets. This creates an increase in the demand for dollars in a market that is already showing excess dollar demand. If the fall in the price of the underlying asset is large, or the devaluation is large, hedging the position may be impossible, or convertibility may be suspended and there is a default.

Further, the natural response for the US bank, recognising the possibility of counter-party default, would be to hedge its dollar exposure represented by the loan against the foreign asset. This would be accomplished by unwinding the hedge of its total return commitment, i.e., unwinding the repo of the foreign asset, selling that asset in the foreign market and repatriating the proceeds at the best possible exchange rate. The net result is that both parties to the swap will react by selling emerging market financial assets and/or selling the domestic currency proceeds against dollars, providing levered downward pressure on both asset market prices and the foreign exchange market. Extensive use of these contracts would thus explain an increased correlation between exchange rates and asset prices.

Most global investment banks were cognisant of risks that exchange rate instability represented for such contracts. Given this type of exposure, it is perhaps not surprising that the investment banks selling these products continued publicly to express confidence in the prospects for exchange rate stability in countries to which they had large out-standing exposures. Even if they had performed appropriate risk assessment, it would not have been in their interests to inform market participants until they had succeeded in unwinding their derivative positions. It is thus also not surprising that funds continued to flow to countries showing a distinct risk of currency instability, for this is what was required in order for structured positions to be closed without substantial loss.

Since most of these structured products are expressly designed to hide risk exposure by providing credit enhancement, or by being classified as 'off-balance-sheet', it is not surprising that bank regulators in emerging economies had difficulty in discovering or controlling them. There is no reason why Asian regulators should be any more efficient than US regulators, who admit to difficulties in evaluating such instruments. Further, Asian banks were being encouraged, just as US thrifts were encouraged in the 1980s, to deregulate, liberalise and to attempt to grow their way out of weakness by investing in assets with higher returns. The regulators accepted this strategy for resolution of the difficulties facing US institutions; it would be difficult not to accept it in emerging markets if it was supported by both the government and the multilateral institutions.

5. Derivatives and Asian capital flows in the 1990s

Although direct information on the role of derivatives in the Asian crisis is scarce,[1] the majority of losses reported by major US money-centre banks[2] on their Asian lending has been listed as due to swaps contracts. Further, the legal suits that have been filed by J. P. Morgan and SK securities in their payments dispute, are reported to relate to total return swaps.[3] It is also the case that the issue of capital market instruments by Asian borrowers surged in 1995 and 1996. For example, Asian issuance rose from $25·2 billion in 1995 to $43·1 billion in 1996. Not only were US banks involved, but much of the success of local

---

[1] Since they are private, over-the-counter, contracts between banks and their clients, their particulars are not revealed even in reports to shareholders. They do become public if they are subject to litigation and most of the information reported here comes from this source.

[2] It is clear that German and French banks were also heavily involved in derivatives trading in the region. Andrews (1998) reports that Deutsche Bank set aside $777 million (double its loss provisions for 1996) to cover losses of as much as $100 million on derivatives trading in South Korea, Thailand, Indonesia and Malaysia. Société Générale is reported to have set aside $164 million, against a total exposure of $6·8 billion (the $4 billion lent in Korea is primarily lending to Korean companies; cf., Lavin, 1998). Commerz has $3 billion in loans (37% of equity), Dresdner 26% of equity and Deutsche 27% of equity in Asian loans..

[3] Cf., *Korea Times* (1998A), which refers to an offshore investment fund created by LG Metal and SK Hannam Investment Securities Fund: 'The $18 million fund was called "Diamond Fund", and was guaranteed by Boram Bank... JP Morgan had entered into a swap transaction with Boram in February 1997, involving an exchange of dollars for the Korean currency. [The fund lost an estimated $120 million.] Such derivatives as total return swaps were popular a year ago as they allowed investors to borrow yen at low interest rates and invest in higher-yielding currencies such as the Thai bat [sic] or Indonesian rupiah.'

Derivatives and global capital flows: applications to Asia 687

investment banks, such as Hong Kong-based Peregrine securities, was primarily in under-writing and selling debt for Asian corporations. It could only do this if it could provide reasonable guarantees for the placement for these issues. That its liquidation apparently placed a large number of Asian corporates' foreign currency hedges in jeopardy because of failure of the counterparty suggests that the investment bank Peregrine might have been a major source of the high-return Asian assets which served to form the assets of high-return, special purpose vehicles for banks in Korea and investors in the developed countries. Korean securities houses and investment banks were also apparently actively involved. The Korean Securities Supervisory Board reported that Korean institutions were operating over 100 offshore investment funds with portfolios valued at around $3 billion, two-thirds of which represented Korean assets.[1]

The lawsuits that have recently been filed by a number of Korean entities that were swap counterparties of J. P. Morgan shed some light on the nature of these transactions. For example, in one transaction Morgan engaged in a $/won currency swap with Boram Bank.[2] In a straight currency swap, the counterparties exchange principal and interest payments on the currencies, so presumably Boram gave won to Morgan in exchange for dollars, and was paying Morgan a fixed interest rate linked to the US dollar, while Morgan was paying a rate linked to won interest rates (the differential in the rates when the swap was initiated in February 1997 was about 2 to 1, suggesting a substantial profit on the interest rate differential). When the swap is unwound the principal sums are usually returned at a prearranged exchange rate, so that Boram would have had to return dollars that were worth about three times as many won as at the beginning of the swap. To cover this risk, Boram engaged in a series of swaps with SK securities, presumably passing the dollars on to SK securities which now carried the foreign exchange risks, but was borrowing at cheap dollar interest rates, against the won loans it was extending to its clients at domestic market rates. The exchange rate loss on the swap was thus borne by SK, who owed this sum to Boram, who in turn owed it to Morgan. The Morgan lawsuit places the value at $189 million. Given the changes in exchange rates, the original principal could have been less than $250 million.[3] This is a relatively straightforward derivative transaction, but it gives an idea of the potential losses involved, and why there was such pressure on the foreign exchange market to acquire funds to unwind swaps of this nature.

The other transactions relate to swaps between Morgan and Korean offshore invest-

---

[1] The Korean 'Securities Supervisory Board said that brokerage houses have more than a 10 percent stake in 66 funds. Another 23 funds were invested in by parent offshore funds of securities firms... The offshore funds were reported to have invested 68·3 percent of their money in Korean securities' (*Korea Times*, 1998B). The Board also reports that the losses that SK securities companies and investment trust companies suffered in offshore funds are estimated at 1·5 trillion won (krw)($1 = krw 1,672) as of the end of last year. 'Four investment trust companies are running 19 offshore funds, which were reported to have suffered about 400 billion won' (see AP-DJ News Service, 1998A).

[2] 'Boram had agreed to a trade of two revenue streams, giving Morgan the stream linked to the prevailing US interest rate in return for the revenue from a basket of derivatives linked to the value of South-east Asian securities and the Thai baht... A year ago, investment bankers eagerly pitched derivatives to SK companies. With benchmark Japanese rates at 0·5 percent, it made sense to sign contracts that would allow investors to borrow in yen and invest in higher-yielding Asian currencies, many of which were linked to the dollar until last year. "It's not an accident that a lot of derivatives got sold in Korea", said John Ellis, head of the Asia derivatives debt at Bank of America in Honk Kong. "It was as good as lending money"' (see *Wall Street Journal*, 1998).

[3] Although Boram was prepared to pay Morgan, SK filed a suit in a Korean court to block the payment, thus hoping to exonerate it from having to pay Boram the funds which would have ended up being paid to Morgan.

688   J. A. Kregel

ment funds operated by SK securities and Shinsegi Investment Trust.[1] It is highly likely that these transactions involved equity swaps or total return swaps. Thus bonds issued by Korean companies, underwritten by SK, were placed in an offshore, special purpose vehicle, financed by the sale of investment shares to the Korean public or other financial institutions. The offshore trusts also invested in other Asian assets. These assets could then be used by the offshore units to generate dollar loans equal to the value of the assets, plus won interest rate and capital appreciation flows, against payment of dollar interest rates. These dollars could then be used to make further loans to Korean companies, while the won payments received from Morgan would be used to pay the local investors in the offshore vehicles.

Again, the magnitude of the change in the exchange rate witnessed after the decision to float the won would have produced capital losses on the underlying assets and thus negative won inflows, which would have been transformed into larger net dollar interest payments due to Morgan. The offshore trusts would have had to borrow to meet any fixed-interest payments, while the loss on the dollar borrowing would have decimated the capital value of the investment portfolio, irrespective of changes in stock prices. The rush to hedge such exposure thus made the fall in the exchange and asset markets that much worse. The legal cases at this stage simply involve failure of the trusts to meet periodic payments on the swaps.[2] It is reported that more than 40 of the 100 or so such trusts had engaged in similar swaps with Morgan.[3] Of its total of $3·4 billion of exposure to Korea, $2 billion are linked to derivative contracts. This perhaps explains why Morgan was at the forefront of the move to convert Korean banks' short-term debt into sovereign debt.

Another way of identifying the importance of derivatives activity in the Asian crisis is with reference to the Country Exposure Lending Survey for money-centre banks published by the US Federal Financial Institutions Examination Council (FFIEC), which reports figures for total amounts lent by country of borrower, net of derivatives, and the cross-border exposure resulting from revaluation gains on foreign exchange and derivative products after adjustments for guarantees and external borrowings. These figures are given for the amounts outstanding at the end of 1997 and the end of the first quarter of 1998 (in parentheses) (see Table 1). Since derivatives exposure only results when a counterparty default places the bank under a risk of having to replace the instrument at a loss to current market conditions, the figures in the second column represent the profits for US money-centre banks on their derivatives activity plus any increases in the value of their outstanding loans due to changes in exchange rates. Since

---

[1] One of the 30 recently created investment banks, it was suspended by the Korean Government at the beginning of December and closed at the end of the year. In September it was listed as having 66 billion won in equity, 3,125 billion won in total outstanding loans, 3·66% of which were classified.

[2] Again, the legal cases are peripheral to these considerations. Housing and Commercial Bank (a government-owned bank ranked 24th in North Asia with over $1billion in equity in 1996 at 1996 exchange rates) apparently offered credit enhancement by offering to guarantee the foreign exchange payments of the offshore trusts. Morgan has filed a suit against the bank (and SK securities) for failing to make payments missed by the offshore trusts). Housing and Commercial, however, contends that their exposure was limited to a maximum of $50 million for each swap, and is therefore not responsible for the total losses of the trusts. O'Brien (1997, p. D2) suggests that the original maximum was $100 million but that the contract was changed without the knowledge of the bank to unlimited exposure. Morgan contends that an officer of the bank authorised removal of the limiting clause before closure of the contract. According to O'Brien's account, 'SK and M had a close working arrangement. SK had established offshore funds to manage the derivatives, and those funds also purchased other securities directly from Morgan.' SK was also sued as parent of the trusts. The total value of the suit is $300 million.

[3] '[T]here are about 40 other local funds that operated in similar agreements with J. P. Morgan,... J. P. Morgan has a total exposure of $3·4 billion to Korea, of which $2 billion is to derivatives products' (see Kang, 1998).

Derivatives and global capital flows: applications to Asia 689

Table 1. *Country exposure of US money-centre banks: loans and derivatives (31 December 1997) (figures for 31 March 1998 in parentheses)*

Country ($ millions)	Total amount owed by country of borrower (derivative contracts excepted)	Cross-border exposure from foreign exchange revaluation and derivative contracts
Indonesia	$3,000 (2,284)	$2,266 (1,612)
Korea	$9,791 (9,155)	$4,633 (2,890)
Malaysia	$1,543 (1,070)	$555 (266)
Philippines	$1,533 (1,357)	$40 (157)
Thailand	$1,771 (920)	$2,509 (1,145)

Source: Federal Financial Institutions Examination Council (FFIEC), 1998, *Statistical Release, e-16: Country Exposure Lending Survey/1*, Table 1, pp. 18–9, 8 April 1998 for 31 December 1997 and 8 July 1998 for 31 March 1998.

US banks' exposure is primarily in dollars, the majority of these changes should be the result of changes in the valuation of derivatives contracts rather than changes in the dollar value of outstanding direct loans.

In Thailand, for example, the profits from derivatives and currency revaluations far exceed the total amounts owed for traditional lending. This suggests that a majority of the short-term bank funds that entered Thailand were linked to derivative contracts. For Korea, the profit figures are well over half the amount of total lending, leading to a similar conclusion. In Indonesia they are roughly two-thirds. Thus, in all three countries that have had to apply for IMF support, derivatives sold by US banks to domestic institutions appear to have played as large a part as traditional financing activities.[1] While these figures do not allow a calculation of the actual amount of funds that were channelled to Asia via structured derivative products, they do support the view that derivative contracts played an integral role in the rise in short-term flows to the region. This thus helps to explain the shift in the composition of lending into the region towards short-term bank flows.

6. Conclusions

Clearly, as the crisis unfolds we shall learn more of the role of derivatives in facilitating the flow of short-term funds to the Asian economies. This note is not meant to argue that all the difficulties created by the volatility of capital flows to Asia were the result of the increased use of derivative instruments or of structured derivative packages. However, the characteristics of these contracts do provide an insight into the four puzzles that were raised in the introductory section. First, the increased use of over-the-counter derivatives contracts as the vehicle for lending to Asia explains the predominance of commercial banks as lenders, as well as the dominantly short-term nature of the flows. It also explains why the lending was so volatile. Second, the characteristics of the contracts that were most probably involved suggest that they are motivated by factors that are not directly related to the allocation of funds to their highest global returns. Rather, they are linked to attempts

[1] The Bank of Korea reported (AP-DJ, 1998B) that trading in financial derivatives by South Korean banks increased by 60·1% in 1997 to $556·5 billion. Foreign exchange forwards comprise about two-thirds of the total. It also reported that Korea's 26 banks booked losses for 1997 of 3·92 trillion won, while the 39 branches of foreign banks reported net profits of 930·48 billion won (Industrial & Commercial Bank of China and Credit Suisse First Boston were the only foreign banks reporting losses) (Park, 1998).

690   J. A. Kregel

to circumvent particular prudential regulations and to provide banks with low-risk fee and commission income, rather than to profit from assessing relative risk-adjusted returns. The incentives motivating such contracts provide little support for the common belief in the self-regulating nature of private capital markets in terms of risk assessment or of their ability to allocate capital efficiently. Third, the fact that developed country banks and regulators had difficulty in foreseeing the risks involved in the derivative positions used suggests that the crisis was not completely due to the inability of emerging markets bankers and regulators to provide acceptable risk management. Finally, the way particular swap contracts and credit derivatives combine currency risk and market price risks provides an explanation of why these markets tended to move in sympathy, creating a cumulative causation that produced unexpected declines and excessive instability in both currency and asset markets during the height of the crisis. What evidence there is of derivative contracts that were actually employed in Asia tends to support these conclusions and contradicts the commonly held position that derivative contracts played no role in the evolution of the financial crisis in Asia.

Bibliography

Andrews, E. L. 1998. Huge German bank covering risks in Asia, *New York Times*, 29 January
AP-DJ News Service 1998A. S.Korea banks sec cos from making offshore fund guarantees, 20 February
AP-DJ News Service 1998B. S. Korean banks' derivatives transactions rose 60·1% '97, 5 March
Brown, S., Goetzmann, J. and Park, J. 1998. 'Hedge Funds and the Asian Currency Crisis of 1997', NBER Working Paper 6427, Boston, MA, February
Chew, L. 1996. *Managing Derivative Risks: The Use and Abuse of Leverage*, New York, John Wiley
Federal Financial Institutions Examination Council (FFIEC) 1998. *Country Exposure Lending Survey/1*, Washington DC, 8 April
Federal Reserve System 1998. *Trading and Capital-Markets Activities Manual*, Washington DC, February
Ghose, R. 1997. What are credit derivatives?, in *Credit Derivatives: Key Issues*, British Bankers' Association
International Monetary Fund (IMF) 1998. *World Economic Outlook*, Washington DC, April
Kang, C. 1998. Korea Housing/J. P. Morgan –3: calls inaction inappropriate, AP-DJ News Service, 18 February
Korea Times 1998A. ASK Securities, JP Morgan heading for int'l court battle over derivatives, 16 February
Korea Times, 1998B. Brokerage firms incur 1·5 tril won losses from offshore funds, 19 February
Lavin, D. 1998. Profit at Société Générale up 34%; bank sees 'robust growth trend', *Wall Street Journal Interactive Edition*, 12 March
O'Brien, T. L. 1998. J. P. Morgan in Korea battle on derivatives: more US implications seen from Asian crisis, *New York Times*, 27 February, D1
Park, K. 1998. Foreign banks in S. Korea combined '97 net profit KRW930.48B, AP-DJ News Service, 13 March
Partnoy, F. 1997. *F.I.A.S.C.O. Blood in the Water on Wall Street*, New York, Norton
Wall Street Journal 1998. Review & Outlook: busting contracts, 23 February
Watzinger, H. 1997. Credit derivatives in emerging markets, in *Credit Derivatives: Key Issues*, British Bankers' Association

Appendix

Glossary of terms[16]

Bullet—a security with a payment schedule in which the fixed periodic payments are composed only of interest on principal, with no amortisation of principal, which is due in full at maturity. Used in contrast to a traditional self-amortising mortgage contract in which each payment is comprised of amortisation of principal and interest on the remaining balance.

Cost of carry, carry cost—the difference between the interest cost of borrowing funds to purchase a security and the periodic interest or dividend earned from owning the security. A positive carry position has the latter greater than the former so that the owner profits from the position without commiting any capital and irrespective of any change in the price of the asset.

Coupon payments—the fixed periodic payments of interest paid to the owner of a bond until maturity.

Coupon strips—the right to the periodic coupon interest payments that have been removed from the stripped or zero coupon bond; strips pay only periodic interest and no principal at maturity.

Credit derivatives are off-balance-sheet financial instruments that permit one party (the beneficiary) to transfer the credit risk of a reference asset, which it typically owns, to another party (the guarantor) without actually selling the asset. In other words, credit derivatives allow users to 'unbundle' credit risk from financial instruments and trade it separately.

Credit event—a change in the conditions of the issuer of an asset affecting its ability to meet its contractual obligations, leading to a change in the credit quality of the asset and usually reflected in a change in the rating assigned by a credit agency.

Credit-enhanced bonds are issued by a special purpose vehicle and have a higher credit rating than the primary assets held by the vehicle because of the inclusion of some higher quality assets or because the primary assets have a higher nominal value than the bonds issued. Brady bonds are credit-enhanced bonds.

Discount bonds—bonds that pay no coupon interest; their return is determined by the difference between their purchase price and maturity value.

Mark to market valuation—value of an asset calculated on the basis of prices recorded for recent transactions in the asset, or on the basis of firm offers to buy the asset, in difference from the price paid to aquire the asset (historic cost) or the maturity or redemption value.

Options contracts transfer the right but not the obligation to buy or sell an underlying asset, instrument, or index on or before the option's exercise date at a specified price (the strike price). A call option gives the option purchaser the right, but not the obligation, to purchase a specific quantity of the underlying asset (from the call option seller) on or before the option's exercise date at the strike price. Conversely, a put option gives the option purchaser the right, but not the obligation, to sell a specific quantity of the underlying asset (to the put option seller) on or before the option's exercise date at the strike price.

Reference asset—a derivative instrument derives its value from movements in the value of an underlying or reference security or security index.

Repurchase agreement or repo involves the sale of a security to a counterparty with an agreement to repurchase it at a fixed price on an established future date. At initiation of the transaction, the buyer pays the principal amount to the seller, and the security is transferred to the possession of the buyer. At expiration of the repo, the principal amount is returned to the initial buyer (or lender) and possession of the security reverts to the initial seller (or borrower). The security serves as collateral against the obligation of the borrower and does not actually become the property of the lender.

Stripped bonds (STRIPS) are zero-coupon securities created by the US Treasury by physically separating the principal and interest cash flows. This process of separating cash flows from standard fixed-rate Treasury securities is referred to as coupon stripping. The bonds are sold without the right to receive the periodic payment of coupon interest, thus they have 'zero' interest-rate coupons. They are equivalent to discount securities with their return determined by the difference between their purchase price and (higher) maturity value.

Structured notes are hybrid securities, possessing characteristics of straight debt instruments and derivative instruments. Rather than paying a straight fixed or floating coupon, the interest payments of these instruments are linked to the performance of a reference asset's price or interest rate or

[16] This glossary provides definitions of some of the terms employed above. The interested reader is invited to consult Federal Reserve System, 1998, for a more complete listing of terms and instruments.

692   J. A. Kregel

index. The derivative contracts are embedded in the security, and may not be presented explicitly as such. They pay a higher interest rate than a straight debt instrument with this differential determined by the value of the embedded option.

Total-rate-of-return swaps are credit derivative contracts in which one counterparty (Bank A) agrees to pay the total return on an underlying reference asset to its counterparty (Bank B) in exchange for a dollar interest rate plus a spread. Most often, the reference asset is a corporate or sovereign bond or a traded commercial loan.

[4]

Bingo or fiasco? The global financial situation

is not guaranteed

BRIGITTE GRANVILLE

Introduction

Global finance has changed beyond recognition over the last fifteen years and national capital markets have become interlinked across the globe. The rapid growth of markets for all sorts of securities has been encouraged by financial liberalization, both at the level of foreign exchange controls, which led to capital crossing borders, and at the level of domestic financial markets, which led to increased competition within the financial system. Competition between banks and non-banks encouraged financial innovation and the expansion of off-balance sheet activities which fell outside regulatory frameworks.[1] In turn, off-balance sheet activities such as derivative products and repurchase agreements (repos) have encouraged flows of capital across borders.

The unparalleled growth of derivative instruments started following the high inflation and breakdown of the Bretton Woods system in the 1970s. They aimed at transferring or reducing risks associated with various instruments from which they are derived, such as currency and interest rate risks (following the introduction of flexible exchange rates). Their development accelerated in the 1990s with the spectacular progress of information technology.

The 1999 Bank for International Settlements (BIS) survey of securities market participants indicated that the notional value of over-the-counter (OTC) derivative products outstanding was $72 trillion at the end of June 1998 (67% in interest rate instruments and 31% in foreign exchange instruments), compared to $47.5 trillion (61% in interest rate instruments and 37% in foreign exchange instruments) at the end of March 1995. Adjusting for differences in exchange rates and the change to consolidated reporting, this represented an increase of about 130% since end March 1995.[2] This compares with an equity

---

[1] Peter Warburton, *Debt and delusion: central bank follies that threaten economic disaster* (Allen Lane/Penguin, 1999), p. 271: 'examples of bank assets which do not have to appear on their balance sheet are those acquired by leasing or hire purchase, project finance, letters of credit, financial derivatives and loan assets that have been securitised.'

[2] Bank for International Settlement (BIS), *Central bank survey of foreign exchange and derivatives market activity, 1998* (Basle, May 1999), p. 4. These figures are indicative only: the derivatives market is continuously

Brigitte Granville

market capitalization of about $13 trillion, some 40% of the $33.5 trillion total
bonds and equities in 1995.

The bond market for its part grew from $2 trillion in 1980 to about $25
trillion at the end of 1997.[3] The 1980s demand for funds was stimulated by
burgeoning budget deficits in the advanced industrial countries. These peaked
in 1992–3. The financing of budget deficits—through bond issues and the sale
of public enterprises—led to a dramatic increase in the debt-to-GDP ratio as
well as the expansion of capital markets.

All these developments were punctuated by several wide-ranging financial
crises: in Europe (the 1992–3 turmoil around the Exchange Rate Mechanism);
in Latin America (the 1994–5 'tequila effect'); and in many emerging markets in
1997–8 following the Asian crisis, which combined bank, financial market and
exchange rate elements. Academics and policy-oriented experts have advanced
a wide range of causes for these upheavals, suggesting that none of them alone
provides a full explanation. In fact, causes and effects are not easily disentangled.[4]

As long as a country is solvent, there should be someone willing to buy its debt
at some price. That assumption foundered when for weeks at a time the
obligations of some countries could not be sold at any price. As Calvo wrote,
'When all the international investors are trying to pull out together, there is no
way the emerging country is able to pay its debt. Even if the debt is relatively small
you may find yourself in a situation where it is impossible to roll it over'.[5] This
assessment was echoed by Fratzscher, who noted that the lesson of the financial
crises is that it may be beyond the power of governments to prevent a crisis affecting
their countries, even when economic fundamentals in those countries are sound.[6]

But what exactly are the 'economic fundamentals'? Experience from many
countries, especially in Latin America, has shown that inadequate macro-economic
policies, especially fixed exchange rate regimes mixed with poor regulation of commercial banks, are common harbingers of currency crises.[7] Therefore, in measuring
economic fundamentals, one should focus not only on current account balances
and government finances, but also on expected future government expenditures,
including off-budget items. Examples might include a major bank bail out, such
as that of Credit Lyonnais which took place from 1994 to 1996 in France;[8] and

---

growing and because the activities take place off balance sheets, no reliable information is available. A
complete picture would require knowledge of all market participants' positions which are not easily
disclosed.

[3] Warburton, *Debt and delusion*, p. 144.

[4] As raised by various authors; see A. Kirman, 'The contagion effect', paper presented to the conference on
'Financial crises' organized by the Centre for Advanced International Studies, the Institute for Economies
in Transition, the Royal Institute of International Affairs and the Social Market Foundation, Moscow,
April 1999.

[5] G. Calvo, *The Wall Street Journal Europe*, 29 April 1999, p. 12.

[6] Marcel Fratzscher, 'Why are currency crises contagious?', *Review of World Economics* 134, 1995, pp. 664–91
(Kiele University: Institute of World Economics).

[7] I. Otker and C. Pazarbasioglu, 'Speculative attacks and currency crises: the Mexican experience', *IMF
Working Paper* 112, November 1995, Washington DC.

[8] Credit Lyonnais, a state-owned French bank, hit trouble after a reckless spending spree in the early 1990s.
The bank's downfall has been one of the costliest financial fiascos at all time. Three successive bail-outs
were necessary: in 1994 and 1995, the government bailed out the bank to the tune of FFr 21.4billion

Bingo or fiasco?

deficits in the state pension fund or the fiscal and monetary effects of German unification after 1990. Calomiris, for instance, notes that banking collapses can cost up to 20% of GDP.[9]

In the financial markets, the systemic weaknesses of emerging markets, in terms of government management and banking systems, were well known long before the crises began. Indeed, the resulting risks, and higher potential returns, constitute the rationale for emerging market securities as an asset class in the first place. Acceptance of the risk is often based on authoritative sources of knowledge and expertise. Investors constantly refer to the IMF, to the Institute of International Finance or to the BIS reports. Most investment banks spend a substantial amount of money on their own research departments which are in constant communication with their investing customers. But the reassurance sought by many investors from such products is often unsound. The BIS noted in its 1998 annual report that, in both the Mexican and Asian crises, money continued to flow in, even though widely available statistics made it clear that the stock of *tesobonos* and other short-term debt in the former instance, and the level of short-term international bank lending in the latter, had risen dramatically. These data were generally ignored, although in the Asian case there is also some evidence that non-bank financial institutions did withdraw funds before the crisis struck. These observations lead the BIS to call urgently for further studies aimed at understanding the mechanisms which led banks to increase their exposure to countries already subject to warning signals, including in some cases warnings emanating from within the banks themselves.[10]

The same lack of understanding is acknowledged by the IMF in December 1998, following the collapse of the Russian financial system: 'The features of the international financial system revealed by the turbulence in the period mid-August through mid-October 1998 suggest that neither private market participants nor the institutions in charge of prudential supervision and market surveillance have a full understanding of the ever changing international financial institutions and markets'.[11] It should be emphasized that this includes the IMF itself. And the US Federal Reserve Board Chairman Alan Greenspan commented: 'We do not as yet fully understand the new systems' dynamics. We are learning fast, and need to update and modify our institutions and practices to reduce the risks inherent in the new regime'.[12]

($4.1bn). *The Economist* reported on 17 August 1996, p. 14, that the ultimate bail-out in 1996 was about FFr 100 billion, or FFr 6,700 per French tax-payer—enough for a week at Club Med.

[9] C. Calomiris, notes that, 'the negative net worth of failed banks in the US for the years 1931–3 was roughly 4% of GDP. Nearly a hundred crises with losses of this or higher magnitude have occurred over the past two decades. Twenty of these crises have resulted in losses in excess of 10% of GDP, and ten have produced losses in excess of 20% of GDP': 'Blueprints for a new global financial architecture', paper presented to the conference on 'Asia: an analysis of financial crises', Chicago, 10 October 1998, p. 3.

[10] BIS, *68th Annual Report, 1st April 1997–31st March 1998* (Basle: 8 June 1998), p. 169.

[11] International Monetary Fund (IMF), *World Economic Outlook and International Capital Markets: Interim Assessment*, December 1998, p. 81.

[12] A. Greenspan, 'Risk management in the global financial system', paper presented to the annual financial markets conference of the Federal Reserve Bank of Atlanta, Miami, Florida, 27 February 1998.

Brigitte Granville

These comments are cause for concern, because misunderstandings can lead to wrong diagnoses, which in turn will lead to the wrong policy being implemented. In the mean time, the world goes round from bingo to fiasco but without any guarantee by governments or international institutions that the future of the financial global situation is well under control.

This article reflects on these issues in the following order. The next section describes the relation between budget deficits, debts and the dramatic expansion of the bond market, and its consequences for emerging markets. The following section analyses the rationale for pegging the exchange rate in the light of capital flows. The fourth section looks more specifically at strategies for hedging against currency risks, while the fifth looks at the Russian case as an illustration and ponders how 'little' Russia managed to make Wall Street tremble. By way of conclusion, some possible lessons from these issues and experiences are drawn for the future of the global financial situation.

Budget deficits, debt and capital flows

In the 1980s, tight credit policy aimed at lowering inflation rates (Table 1) mixed with relatively loose budget policy (Table 2) replaced the roughly balanced budgets of the 1960s.

In the OECD countries budget deficits, virtually unknown in the 1960s, rose to about 3% of nominal GDP between 1982 and 1989 and further to 3.3% between 1990 and 1995.[13] As government budget deficits have been financed in the capital markets rather than monetized through the commercial banking system, this has allowed low inflation rates to prevail and contributed to the development of the bond market, but has also substantially increased the debt-to-GDP ratio.

Table 1: Inflation (percentage changes in consumer prices, year on year)[a]

	1970–9[b]	1980–9[b]	1990–5[b]	1996	1997	1998
United States	7.2	5.6	3.5	2.9	2.3	1.6
Japan	9.1	2.5	1.7	0.1	1.7	0.6
European Union	10.1	7.1	4.0	2.4	1.9	1.6
Total OECD	9.2	8.8	5.6	5.2	4.5	3.8

[a]Aggregates are computed using weights based on 1997 consumer expenditure expressed in private consumption purchasing power parities.
[b]Average over the period.
Source: OECD, *Economic Outlook* 65, June 1999, Annex, Table 16, p. 242.

[13] Organization for Economic Cooperation and Development (OECD), *Economic Outlook* 65, June 1999, Annex, Table 30, p. 254.

Bingo or fiasco?

Table 2: General government financial balances: surplus (+) or deficit (-) as % of nominal GDP

	1960–9	1970–9	1980–9	1990–5	1996	1997	1998
United States	-0.1	-1.0	-2.5	-3.0	-0.9	0.4	1.7
Japan[a]	1	-1.7	-1.5	0	-4.2	-3.4	-6.0
European Union			-4.3	-4.8	-4.1	-2.5	-2.1
Total OECD	0	-1.6	-2.9	-3.3	-2.6	-1.2	-0.9

[a]The 1998 outlays would have risen by 5.4 percentage points of GDP if account were taken of the assumption by the central government of the debt of the Japan Railway Settlement Corporation and the National Forest Special account.

[b] Average over period.

Sources: OECD, *Economic Outlook*, various issues, quoted in Peter Warburton, *Debt and delusion, central bank follies that threaten economic disaster* (London: Allen Lane/Penguin, 1999); OECD, *Economic Outlook 65*, June 1999, Annex, Table 30, p. 254.

Equation (1) helps to understand both the development of the debt-to-GDP ratio and the behaviour of the bond market. In this equation, the single-period budget constraint is written in terms of GDP as:

(1) $\Delta b = (r - n)b + d - s$

where

b = debt/GDP ratio
r = real rate of interest on government bonds
n = rate of real GDP growth
d = primary surplus as a share of GDP; a primary deficit imples $d>0$ and a primary surplus $d<0$
s = seigniorage = rate of high-powered money growth as a share of GDP

The change in the debt-to-GDP ratio is determined by the primary balance, the rate of money creation, the GDP growth and the built-in momentum of the debt-to-GDP ratio represented by the real rate of interest. When this rate exceeds the GDP growth rate, the debt ratio feeds on itself since interest payments add more to pubic debt than growth adds to GDP, unless d–s is kept negative.

Bond financing of the deficit with a real interest rate that exceeds the growth rate of output, leads to rising debt ratios, in the absence of any deficit correction. Rising debt in turn increases the deficit and hence leads to over increasing debt and debt ratios. Bond deficit financing reaches its limit when interest rates are too high or when market participants refuse to roll over the debt; at that point the authorities have either to default on their debt or to call

Brigitte Granville

on monetary financing. Large debts are therefore a risk to the integrity of monetary policy.[14]

Despite the fiscal consolidation achieved either from higher taxation (as in Italy) or a mixture of higher taxes and lower expenditures (as in the United States), net interest payments on public debt have remained high. Net debt interest payments for the OECD countries rose from an average of 2.1 % of GDP in 1982 to 3.1% in 1995 and stood at 2.6% in 1998. In the EU the increase was from 2.8% to 5% and stood at 4.2% in 1998.[15] (Table 3)

Table 3: General government net debt interest payments as % of nominal GDP

	1982–9[a]	1990–5[a]	1996	1997	1998
United States	2.0	2.2	2.1	1.9	1.7
Japan[b]	1.6	0.6	0.7	1.0	1.2
European Union	3.6	4.7	5.0	4.6	4.2
Total OECD	2.6	2.9	3.0	2.8	2.6

[a]Average.
[b]Where net interest payments are not available, net property income paid is used as proxy.
Source: OECD, *Economic Outlook* 65, June 1999, Annex, Table 33, p. 257.

Fischer emphasized that one explanation for the crises was the search by international investors for 'attractive domestic investment opportunities', given the weak growth of Japan and Europe.[16] The decline in world interest rates in the early 1990s (Table 4) contributed to redirect international finance towards high-yield assets in emerging markets.[17] By late 1997 bond yields in continental Europe and Japan were the lowest for 30 years while in the United States they were within range of the levels reached in 1993.[18]

The financial crisis which began in Asia in 1997 is distinct from the debt crisis of the 1980s, centred on Latin America, for being dominated by the private sector not merely as provider but as user of capital. While short-term inter-bank lending to emerging countries reached a peak of $240 billion in 1996 with Asia the main beneficiary,[19] this sum diverted from mature to emerging markets is of

---

[14] R. Dornbusch, 'Debt and monetary policy: the policy issues', in G. Calvo and M. King, *The debt burden and its consequences for monetary policy* (Basingstoke: Macmillan, 1998), pp. 3–22; see also T. Sargent and N. Wallace, 'Some unpleasant monetarist arithmetic', *Quarterly Review*, Federal Reserve Bank of Minneapolis, 1981, pp. 1–17.
[15] OECD, *Economic Outlook* 65, 1999, Annex, Table 33, p. 257.
[16] S. Fischer, 'The Asian crisis: a view from the IMF', speech deliverered at the IMF, Washington DC, 22 January 1998. 1998.
[17] G. Calvo, L. Leiderman and C. Reinhart, 'Inflows of capital to developing countries in the 1990s', *Journal of Economic Perspectives* 10, Spring 1996, pp. 123–9.
[18] BIS, *68th Annual Report*, p. 80.
[19] IMF, *World Economic Outlook and International Capital Markets*, December 1998, p. 40.

Bingo or fiasco?

Table 4: Short-term interest rates (%)

	1981–9[a]	1990–5[a]	1996	1997	1998
United States	8.5	4.9	5.0	5.1	4.8
Japan	6.0	4.3	0.6	0.6	0.7
European Union	10.5	9.0	4.7	4.2	3.9
Korea[b]	n.a.	15[c]	12.7	13.4	15.2
Mexico	61.1	24.9	32.9	21.3	26.1

[a] Average.
[b] The average for Korea is between 1991–5.
Source: OECD, *Economic Outlook 65*, June 1999, Annex, Table 36, p. 260.

marginal importance relative to the global capital market: 'A hypothetical shift of 1% of equity holdings by institutional investors in the G7 countries away from domestic equities would represent slightly more than a 1% share of total market capitalization in 1995. The same funds would be equivalent to a 27% share of market capitalization in emerging Asian economies, and a share of over 66% of Latin American equity markets'.[20]

Exchange rate, interest rate and debt

Like most policy debates, the debate over exchange-rate policy stemmed in part from conflicts of interest and in part from legitimate disagreements over empirical parameters.

A particular question concerns the choice between an exchange-rate-based stabilization and a money-based programme as the means of promoting a functioning stable price system. Exchange-rate-based stabilization uses simpler tools than a money-based programme. For instance, the unreliability of money demand and velocity characteristic of an emerging market economy do not affect the exchange-based programme. A fixed exchange rate establishes an immediate focal point for coordinating price expectations and price setting.

An exchange-rate peg, as emphasized by Mishkin, provides a constraint on policy which prevents the pursuit of discretionary policies to achieve short-run objectives.[21] A fixed exchange rate implies that the monetary authorities are then committed to a certain parity, while credit expansion is restricted by the availability of international reserves and the capacity to borrow internationally. If the authorities do not control the expansion of credit—including, necessarily, the way the budget deficit is financed—they will eventually have to devalue and so lose credibility possibly compromising the whole stabilization attempt.

[20] BIS, *68th Annual Report*, p. 90.
[21] F. Mishkin, 'The dangers of exchange rate pegging in emerging markets countries', *International Finance* 1: 1, October 1998, pp. 81–99 at p. 83.

Brigitte Granville

A supplementary argument in favour of an exchange-rate-based stabilization programme is that during high inflation virtually all prices are indexed to the dollar or quoted in dollars (or another inflation-free foreign currency); hence holding the exchange rate is tantamount to achieving price stability. The decision to peg the exchange rate is often linked to capital inflows. These facilitate government and private borrowing and both the budget constraint and the constraint on restructuring the banking system are, therefore, softened. Governments and banks tend to see capital inflows as an opportunity to borrow more rather than an opportunity to tighten and restructure the fiscal deficit or the banking system.

Capital inflows also encourage exchange-rate appreciation. If the central bank reacts by accumulating foreign reserves thus expanding the monetary base, this is liable to aggravate inflation and/or inflationary expectations. On the other hand, if the demand for cash balances also increases, inflation is not aggravated. Conversely, capital outflows may put pressure on the exchange rate to depreciate. By selling foreign reserves to support the rate, the central bank reduces the monetary base. Interest rates then tend to rise. This endangers the fiscal situation by raising debt service costs. The central bank may therefore intervene in the secondary securities market to re-expand the monetary base and push interest rates down. In doing so it is liable to renew the threat to exchange rate parity. Ultimately, the central bank has to let either the interest rate or the exchange rate go: if the exchange rate is to be maintained within the band or on the peg, interest rates have to be allowed to move to whatever level is necessary to achieve this. The strategy of pegging the exchange rate therefore has its weaknesses.

Most of the countries hit by the Asian financial crisis were on a pegged exchange rate. Credit policy was not loose; fiscal policy was in Russia,[22] but most other countries had a balanced budget or nearly so.[23] The huge drain on international reserves was caused not by expansionary monetary policy but through capital outflows triggered by the fear of financial loss including devaluation. Basing their analysis on balance of payments data, the monetary authorities tried to stop the depletion of foreign reserves by raising short-term interest rates sharply. However, the success of this medicine depends, as pointed out by Furman and Stiglitz,[24] on a number of factors: the composition of the debt, whether it is owned by residents or non-residents; the maturity structure of the debt; and whether the banking system is strong and well regulated. In the event, increases in interest rates lead to two perverse effects which helps to explain why the medicine proved inefficient.

---

[22] B. Granville. 'The problem of monetary stabilisation', in B. Granville and P. Oppenheimer, eds, *Russia's post-communist economy* (Oxford: Oxford University Press, forthcoming).

[23] As shown for Mexico by J. Sachs, A. Tornell and A. Velasco, 'Financial crisis in emerging markets: the lessons from 1995', *Brookings Papers on Economic Activity* 1, 1996, pp. 147–215, and for Asia by S. Radelet and J. Sachs, 'The east Asian financial crisis: diagnosis, remedies, prospects', *Brookings Papers on Economic Activity* 1, 1998, pp. 1–90.

[24] J. Furman and J. Stiglitz, 'Economic crises: evidence and insights from east Asia', *Brookings Papers on Economic Activity* 2, 1998.

Bingo or fiasco?

Table 5: Foreign reserves as per cent of short-term foreign debt[a]

	End 1990	Mid-1994	End 1996	End 1997	Mid-1998
Indonesia	55	58	53	47	65
Korea	73	62	50	142	123
Malaysia	475	397	241	34	176
Thailand	151	101	83	67	93
Russia	n.a.	n.a.	43	40	32

[a]Foreign reserves equal total reserves minus gold; short-term debt is defined as claims of all BIS reporting banks *vis-à-vis* these countries, at maturities up to and including one year.
Source: Bank for International Settlements/IMF, quoted in OECD, *Economic Outlook 65*, June 1999, Table VI.3, p.189.

First, these high real interest rates intensified investor worries towards sovereign insolvency: increased real interest rates and relatively low seigniorage worsened the debt problem. While monetary policy is restrictive, the ratios of debt service and domestic debt-to-GDP ratio grow rapidly (see equation 1). Increasing debt levels whether public induced (large budget deficit) as in Russia or private induced (borrowing from the banking system but state guaranteed) as in Asia[25] triggers investors' fears that governments will default on their debt or solve their debt problem by an inflationary monetary policy. Table 5 shows that in all crisis stricken countries the ratio of foreign reserves to short-term foreign debt declined dramatically. Moreover, expectations of growth expectation were dashed: in Russia by high interest rates and the fall in oil prices; in Asia, by the drop in export prices, after years of not a single year of zero or low growth (the last year in which real GDP growth was significantly less than 5% in Indonesia was 1985; in Malaysia 1986; in Korea, 1980 and in Thailand 1972).[26] High real interest rates in the presence of low expectation growth rates intensified investor worries, and the government's creditworthiness gradually crumbled.

Second, this policy underestimated the degree of openness and financial liberalization achieved by these countries. Financial liberalization led to large short-term borrowings in foreign currencies encouraged by the stability of the exchange rate regime. Local commodity exporters, real estate companies and domestic commercial banks borrowed in dollars or yens, avoiding high domestic interest rates, and invested the proceeds converted into local currencies, either on the domestic bond market where yields were high, as in Russia, or in local short-term loans profiting from the high interest rates, as in

[25] See J. Corbett and D. Vines, 'The Asian crisis: lessons from the collapse of financial systems, exchange rates, and macroeconomic policy', in R. Agenor, M. Miller, D. Vines and A. Weber, eds, *The Asian financial crisis: causes, contagion and consequences* (Cambridge: Cambridge University Press, forthcoming).
[26] BIS, *68th Annual Report*, p. 119.

Brigitte Granville

the Asian countries where bank credit increased by more than 10% a year in real terms during the 1990s.[27] When the capital flows began to reverse, central banks sold foreign exchange in defence of the exchange rate. This ensured that foreign exchange remained cheap for long enough to be bought by holders of loans denominated in foreign currency as a hedge against their exposure. But by taking out these hedges, they put more pressure on the central banks' defence, and contributed to the abandonment of the peg.

Financial crises: and the derivatives market

The efficacy of the interest rate in defending the exchange rate parity is affected by volume and sensitivity of hedging transactions on the part of banks, corporations and other institutions active in the foreign exchange market. Speculative attack generally takes place on the forward exchange market. Hedgers and speculators lock in a price—that is, they commit themselves to buy foreign currency from a bank at some future date (30 days for instance) at a predetermined rate of exchange. In turn, the bank which buys the domestic currency will rebalance its net currency position by selling the currency on the spot market.

To resist the speculative attack, the central bank sells foreign exchange and thereby reduces the monetary base. But at the same time, the central bank has to refinance the banks, which need to sell currency in order to match their forward and spot foreign exchange positions, through the discount window. In doing so, the central bank is effectively financing the attack on its own reserves. As the level of foreign exchange reserves drops, the central bank counteracts this trend by raising the discount rate, thereby increasing the cost of speculating against the currency by borrowing from the central bank. If large short positions are due for settlement, holders of short positions sell foreign exchange to the central bank rather than face the high interest costs of rolling over overnight loans in the weak currency.

All this has been familiar for much of the twentieth century. What is different about the 1990s is the sheer relative volume of hedging and speculative transactions, plus the growing use of so-called dynamic hedging techniques, which replace human judgement with computerized decision-taking analogous to stop-loss orders on the stock exchange.

Garber and Spencer explain how the widespread use of dynamic hedging strategies, and the rapidity of their implementation, interfere with the central bank policy's defence of the exchange rate:

In an exchange rate attack, a large defensive rise in the interest rates aimed at imposing a squeeze on speculators will instantaneously trigger hedging programmes to order sales of the weak currency... The existence of such programmes in the market undermines the use of an interest rate defence of a weak currency—the moment that a central raises

[27] Ibid., p. 118.

Bingo or fiasco?

interest rates, it might face an avalanche of sales of its currency rather than the purchases of the squeezed shorts that it had anticipated. In effect he hedging programmes make the hedgers insensitive to the added costs of funding their weak currency sales.[28]

The interest rate defence by the central bank will fail or succeed depending on whether or not the volume of hedging operation exceeds the amount of the weak currency demanded by those short of liquidity and on the timing of hedging sales. If there is a time lag between selling programmes and the buying operations to cover short positions, the central bank may be forced to devalue before the expected buyers of its currency appear.

The Russian case

The adverse shift in attitude to the Russian market by mid-1998 was attributable mainly to external shocks, rather than to further deterioration in the funda-mental macroeconomic-related risk factors in the Russian economy itself. Given the difficulty of attracting Russian domestic savings into government debt instruments on a sufficient scale either directly or through the banking system, the budget deficit was being funded to a significant extent by foreign buying of domestic treasury bills. When Asian banks suffered losses on lending at home, they sold their holdings of Russian high-yielding bonds to improve their liquidity position putting pressure on the rouble and on the bond market.

The focal point for the tension between exchange rate and monetary policy became the domestic market in domestic currency-denominated government debt. The market became the main mechanism by which confidence in the exchange-rate peg affected interest rates. By allowing yields to rise, the authorities aimed to demonstrate their commitment to holding the exchange rate band, thus attracting new inflows and hence securing a decline in interest rates. The calculation was that inflows would be attracted by the huge real returns available from the combination of high nominal yields on rouble-denominated debt and the promise of a stable exchange rate.

As things turned out, however, investors were less attracted by this prospect than they were deterred by the present reality of ever higher interest rates in face of low or zero growth prospects, which created doubts that the govern-ment could afford the consequent rising debt service costs: hence the perception of increasing default risk. This perception in turn increased the risk of devaluation: having let interest rates rise to defend the exchange rate, the government might be forced into letting the exchange rate go to prevent insolvency. The problem was exacerbated by a fall in oil prices and a rise in imports which lead to the first current account deficit since 1993.

---

[28] P. Garber and M. Spencer, 'Foreign exchange hedging and the interest rate defence', *IMF Staff papers* 42: 3, September 1995, pp. 490–15 at p. 513. See also IMF, *World Economic Outlook and International Capital Markets: Interim Assessment*, December 1998.

Brigitte Granville

The long-term source of the Russian crisis was the consistent failure to tighten fiscal policy sufficiently. The timing of the financial débâcle, on the other hand, was set by the banking system. Pressure on the rouble exchange rate had been intensified by a particular effect of the financial market crises on leading Russian banks. Unable at any stage to attract large-scale retail deposits, the banks had funded themselves by using their portfolios of dollar-denominated Russian government securities for repurchase ('repo') operations with foreign counterparties. The progressive collapse in mid-1998 of investor confidence in all types of Russian government debt triggered margin calls on those 'repos'. To meet these margin calls, the banks raised liquidity by selling their holdings of rouble-denominated treasury bills (GKOs) and other assets, and buying the necessary foreign exchange with the proceeds. Completing the vicious circle, the central bank responded by tightening money market lending in order to keep the rouble in its target band. And commercial banks reacted by cutting limits to each other and selling bonds and stocks to sustain liquidity.

In this environment, all demand, domestic and foreign, for new issues of rouble treasury bills disappeared. That meant that the government could no longer pay debt with debt. Redemption of weekly maturities averaging about Rbs 9bn ($1bn) had to be financed out of general taxation (plus emergency eurobond issues, which glutted the last segment of the debt market). Given the impossibility of sufficiently drastic cuts in non-debt-service expenditure, at least temporary government default became unavoidable, leading to the decision of 17 August.[29] The devaluation for its part exposed the insolvency of the banks by leaving them with dollar obligations on forward contracts many times greater than their capital. But the banks' earlier struggle against insolvency had itself precipitated that devaluation.

At the time, it was difficult to foresee the impact of the Russian financial crisis on financial markets of both emerging and matures markets: GDP was about $440bn (or 1.5% of world GDP), and the Russian presence in international trade (1.2% of world trade) and financial markets was small (Table 6). The external debt on the eve of the August débâcle amounted to about $160bn, equivalent to one-third of the combined external debts at the end of 1996 of the five Asian countries and just 8% of emerging markets' total external debts. Russia accounted for little more than 3% of the total international loan commitments and issuance of international bonds and equities by emerging markets in the period from 1992 to the end of June 1998.[30]

And yet, when the Russian market collapsed, the financial world was badly shaken: 'Yield premia for emerging market bonds rose sharply to an average of

---

[29] The decisions of 17 August included the de facto devaluation of the rouble: the rouble target band was widened. The band was to range from 6 Rbs to the dollar to 9.5 for a mean of 7.75 Rbs. The internal day-to-day band of 1.5% was abandoned; a forced extension of the treasury bills (GKO) maturities; a 90-day moratorium on debt servicing of private foreign credits of over 180 days maturity, as well as margin calls and currency contracts. See Granville, 'The problem of monetary stabilisation', in Granville and Oppenheimer, eds, *Russia's post-communist economy*.

[30] IMF, *World Economic Outlook and International Capital Markets*, December 1998, p. 28.

Bingo or fiasco?

Table 6: Russia in international capital markets (US$bn)

	Total external debt[1] (end 1996)	International bank lending[2] (end 1997)	Total gross financing[3] (1992– June 1998)	Stock market capitali- zation[4] (June 1998)
Emerging markets	2095	897	1037	1922
Russia	125	72	33	53
Asia–5	459	259	251	175
Indonesia	129	58	51	13
Korea	158	94	92	44
Malaysia	40	28	33	67
Philippines	41	20	22	29
Thailand	91	59	53	22

Sources: Quoted in IMF, *World Economic Outlook and International Capital Markets: Interim Assessment,* December 1998, p. 29.

1 World Bank, *Global Development Finance,* Washington DC.

2 Bank for International Settlements, *The Maturity, Sectoral and National Distribution of International Bank Lending,* Basle.

3 Bonds, Equities and Loans database and Developing Country Bonds, Equities and Loans database.

4 International Finance Corporation, *Emerging Markets Database* (Washington DC). The figure for emerging markets includes only the group of countries covered by IFC.

1,700 basis points in early September from below 600 basis points in most of 1997 and early 1998. Equity prices fell sharply in both emerging and mature markets.'[31] This immediate impact on mature market shows that a significant holdings of rouble-denominated treasury bills were financed in the mature markets. Some investors bought the Russian bonds on margin, through investment banks. These investment banks secured the deal with short-term repurchase agreements in US markets. Other Russian securities purchases have been funded in Japan and swapped into local currencies or dollars.[32]

When the Russian crisis struck, investors suffered huge losses as a result of the drop of bond prices; this in turn gave rise to margin calls, forcing investors to raise liquidity by selling first their Russian securities and then, when the demand for these dried up, any other high-yield asset they could dump. Numbers of hedge funds with holdings of Russian securities suffered large losses because many investors attempted simultaneously to close out positions and reduce

[31] Ibid., p. 2.

[32] Ibid., p. 27: 'repurchase agreement are essentially a short-term loan to the seller, with securities used as collateral. As the value of a security falls, margin calls are triggered.'

Brigitte Granville

leverage in the wake of the global market turmoil which followed the collapse of the Russian market.

One can only commend the ex-post assessment of the IMF, albeit too late:

> The paucity of off-balance-sheet data makes it difficult to assess overall exposures and vulnerabilities, although in some instances these exposures may be relatively large. For example, one estimate suggests that total credit exposure (including off-balance-sheet positions) of foreign banks to Russia may have been 40 to 65 percent higher than on-balance sheet exposure. In addition, as the recent period of turbulence amply demonstrated, when emerging market financing and leveraged derivatives positions are unwound, the mature markets that finance these positions are also affected. Even if the off-balance-sheet exposures of mature banking systems to emerging markets are relatively limited, therefore, they may still have significant consequences for the mature derivatives markets.[33]

Dynamic hedging encouraged mechanistic selling of securities perceived as risky and in doing so dried up international liquidity, putting at risks mature markets such as the United States or members of the European Union. Indeed, 'little' Russia gave international finance a severe fright. Only actions by the Federal Reserve and other central banks to ease monetary conditions prevented the crises from spreading deeper and further.

Conclusion

We have seen that the financing of high budget deficits in mature economies gave rise to substantial development of the bond markets. This occurred in parallel with financial liberalization and deregulation which removed most impediments for the movement of savings across borders and to the internationalization of investment portfolios. Competition among banks and non-banks pushed financial institutions towards emerging markets in search of high returns, and encouraged them to invest in portfolio insurance and/or derivatives to reduce their risks. The trend was accelerated by progress in information technology.

While the sums invested in emerging economies are small compared to the overall global size of the financial market, they are large for the recipient countries. When vulnerable economies are hit by financial crises, the extent and nature of hedging techniques mean that contagion effects can be quickly observed in both emerging and mature markets. Financial engineering, such as dynamic hedging techniques tends to drive market participants to buy assets when prices have risen and sell when they have fallen. Such behaviour amplifies price movements.

The rapid expansion of financial products is not going to slow down. Despite fiscal consolidation in the last four years in mature markets, no major growth in

---

[33] Ibid., p. 62.

Bingo or fiasco?

physical savings has been observed, implying that rising wealth is concentrated on the securities markets. The supply of inflation-proof government paper has declined, and the same is true of net new equity issues as a result of the wave of mergers and acquisitions. There is therefore an imbalance between the supply of securities and the demand for them.

The search for high-return, highly leveraged instruments may partly explain why financial crises in the 1990s were frequent, rapid and violent. It also explains why capital flows have proved so resilient. After the Mexican crisis of 1994–5, 'the total flow to emerging markets rebounded as early as 1995 when it increased by 20 percent'.[34] The same applied to the Asian countries in 1999 and to some extent to Russia as well. By contrast, after the 1982 Latin American crisis, capital flows took almost ten years to return, and did so then largely thanks to the Brady plan involving write-downs of existing debt.

The global financial turbulence following the Russian default raised uncertainties about the guarantee that sound economic fundamentals provide and about the extent of penalties that the global financial market impose on emerging economies whatever their macro economic outlook. The Russian default challenged the view that the international community was able and willing to bail out countries in difficulty. That Russia has been allowed to default led to a broad repricing of risks in emerging economies, whether warranted by economic fundamentals or not. No country from now on was seen as 'too big to fail'. The rapid closing of positions which followed penalized excessively emerging economies struggling to integrate the global economy.

The development of the global capital markets in both size and sophistication has therefore led to considerable concern. This concern is twofold. First, the linkages between credit expansion and the money supply, and between credit expansion and price levels have been weakened by the expansion of financial markets and the proliferation of domestic credit channels outside the monetary system. The relevance of the interest rate has been called into question. Peter Waburton notes in his recent book that, 'While financial commentators are apt to attribute a falling US treasury bond yield to a lowering of inflation expectations or a new credibility that the Federal Budget will be balanced, the true explanation may lie in progressive gearing'.[35] Derivatives and other capital-market initiatives continue on a daily basis, spreading to all branches of activities. The BIS reports, for instance, that investments such as leveraged buyouts funds, international private equity and venture capital have made their way into institutional investor portfolios, with commitments standing at about $70 billion for US and Canadian pension funds.[36] Derivatives are off-balance-sheet instruments, while most analysis of capital flows reversals are based on on-balance-sheet data. Derivative products make balance sheet information of little

---

[34] C. Giannini, 'Enemy of no one but a common friend of all? An international perspective on the lender of last resort function'. *IMF Working Paper 99/10*, January 1999, p. 27.
[35] Warburton, *Debt and delusion*, p. 120.
[36] BIS, *68th Annual Report*, p. 96.

Brigitte Granville

use, if not seriously misleading. Garber shows, by giving examples of specific derivative products such as currency swaps, equity swaps and repos, that since the transactions are taking place off-balance-sheet they will not be recorded in the balance of payments data for what they are: loans. Bond or equity swaps, for instance, will appear as if foreign lenders are buying domestic debt in the form offered, or as a gross inflow of equity purchases for portfolio investment or perhaps foreign direct investment, while in fact foreign lenders are making short-term dollar loans to the government or to private institutions.[37] The derivatives market has both positive and negative influence, but whatever its pros and cons, the reality is that it exists and therefore it may be time, preferably before the next crisis, to take its existence into account.

The second concern is to design a circuit break, in other words how to stop financial crises spreading once they have started. This reopens discussion on the global financial 'architecture' covering issues such as regulation, the introduction of an international bankruptcy court and the role of the IMF as lender of last resort. The series of recent financial crises has illustrated how badly equipped the IMF is to handle liquidity crises. Assistance is too slow in coming, because agreement has to be reached, and too small in volume, because the amounts granted are usually spread over several months. An intense debate has therefore developed on the question of the role of the IMF and the lender of last resort. For instance, Calomiris and Sachs argue that the IMF should be transformed into a fully fledged lender of last resort, providing unconditional liquidity under certain ex ante criteria, while Schwartz see no further role for the IMF and is in favour of letting the market do the job. This discussion is especially complicated because of the question of moral hazard. It goes beyond the sole issue of the IMF and extends to central banks in general, and to the question of how to protect a country or institution from bankruptcy and at the same time make sure that the rescue is not going to encourage either further risk-taking from investors or even more badly managed economic policies from emerging market economies.[38]

The moral hazard question, coupled with the sheer size of private capital flows, has led monetary authorities and international institutions such as the BIS to consider involving the private sector in solving financial crises. Private investors could be asked, for instance, to share some of the responsibility for the continuing provision of credit to customers to whom they had previously lent. Some better means of burden-sharing will be required, such as developing contingent liquidity facilities in which the private sector would take an important stake, as well as improved arrangements in the case of moratoria on foreign debt. Such provisions could force lenders to be more careful in appraising loans, because they would be hit harder financially if a crisis did occur.

---

[37] P. Garber and M. Spencer, 'Foreign exchange hedging and the interest rate defence'. p. 12.
[38] See Giannini, 'Enemy of no one but a common friend of all?', for an extensive account of both the literature and the questions raised by this debate.

[5]

Vulnerability to a Currency Crisis: Lessons from the Asian Experience

Prema-chandra Athukorala and Peter G. Warr

1. INTRODUCTION

CURRENCY crises are rapid outflows of financial capital in anticipation of a possible currency depreciation, inducing depletion of reserves, financial instability and subsequent economic contraction.[1] In recent years, increasing numbers of countries have fallen victim to such crises.[2] Recent examples include the Mexican crisis of 1994 and the Asian crises of 1997–98. These events and the global reverberations which followed them have added new impetus to debate on their causes. The present paper attempts to contribute to this debate.

The already-sizeable literature on the Asian crisis[3] contains two rival depictions of the underlying causes of currency crises. The two are not mutually exclusive, but differ crucially in their emphasis. The most common is what we shall call the *self-fulfilling panic* theory. It sees a currency crisis as an unforeseeable financial panic reflecting inherent instabilities in international capital markets. The basic notion is that the crisis was primarily prompted by what Keynes called 'animal spirits' and contagion, striking guilty and innocent countries alike. According to this view, domestic policies are to be blamed only in relation to *ad hoc* financial market opening in crisis countries, which combined

PREMA-CHANDRA ATHUKORALA and PETER WARR are from the Division of Economics, Research School of Pacific and Asian Studies, Australian National University. They are grateful to the two anonymous referees of this journal for very helpful comments.

[1] In his introduction to a recent collection on 'currency crises', Krugman writes: 'There is no generally accepted formal definition of a currency crisis, but we know them when we see them. The key element is a sort of circular logic, in which investors flee a currency because they fear that it might be devalued, and in which much (though not necessarily all) of the pressure for such a devaluation comes precisely from that capital flight' (2000, p. 1).

[2] The authoritative world history of currency (and other forms of financial) crises up to 1990 is Kindleberger (1996). For details on the world experience during the post-Bretton Woods era up to the Asian crisis see Federal Reserve Bank of Kansas City (1997).

[3] For useful overviews with extensive referencing to the relevant literature see Goldstein (1998), Corden (1999) and Garnaut (1998).

with bountiful global liquidity conditions to provide the pre-conditions for the crisis. Proponents of this view include some leading mainstream economists.[4]

An alternative view is the *vulnerability* theory. According to this, the Asian currency crisis reflected an unsustainable deterioration in macroeconomic conditions within the affected countries (e.g. Goldstein, 1998; Fischer, 1998; and Corsetti et al., 1999). This view accepts that market over-reaction, triggered by 'manias and panics' (as in Kindleberger, 1996), may have made the subsequent financial instability and economic collapse more severe than was warranted by the macroeconomic circumstances of the country at the time of the crisis; but it sees the genesis of the crisis primarily as in terms of errors in the country's economic policies. This is the view behind the policy advocacy of the IMF and the US Treasury for the crisis countries in Asia.

Accepting one view over the other has implications for the choice of policies for preventing and/or managing future crises. The panic theory draws on the analogy with a viral infection, a 'contagion', which spreads through the air unpredictably. At the national level there is no defence other than limiting short-term capital build-up through capital controls in order to deter speculation. At the international level there is an emphasis on reforming the 'international financial infrastructure' with a view to policing international capital flows and providing 'no-questions-asked' drawing rights at levels commensurate with the growth of the world economy and more especially the growth of mobile 'hot' money. On the other hand, the vulnerability school of thought emphasises the role of domestic policies aimed at keeping the macroeconomic house in order. This view is also consistent with the conventional wisdom on the appropriate sequencing of economic reforms – that the opening of the capital account should be done gradually and in a way that avoids 'unnecessary' real exchange rate appreciation (Krueger, 1984; and Michaely et al., 1991, Chapter 10).

The two views described above are not mutually exclusive in that the true causes of currency crises could well be a combination of these two extreme forms. But where the truth lies in the spectrum between the two polar cases is very important for policy purposes. So far, the debate has not provided clear policy guidance in one direction or the other. In some instances, the arguments

---

[4] For instance, Bhagwati (1998) observes that 'none of the Asian economies that were hit [by the crisis] had any serious fundamental problems that justified the panic that set in to reverse the entire huge capital inflows [and] ... [T]he only explanation that accounts for the massive net [capital] outflows is panic and herd behaviour'. According to Tobin (1998, p. 353) the recent Asian example shows that 'countries can suffer liquidity crises through no fault of their own'. Radelet and Sachs (1998) infer that 'the crisis was triggered by dramatic swings in creditors' expectations about the behaviour of other creditors, thereby creating a self-fulfilling – although possibly individually rational – financial panic' (p. 43). Interestingly, economists belonging to the 'statist' school of thought on East Asian development have also been attracted to this panic theory in their attempts to justify state-engineered 'guided lending' in some countries (particularly in Korea) during the period leading up to the crisis (see, for instance, Wade, 1998; and Chang et al., 1998).

VULNERABILITY TO A CURRENCY CRISIS   35

presented have been mere commentaries resting on leaps of faith rather than inferences based on hard evidence coming from comparative analysis. Proponents of both extreme schools of thought tend to select variables from a seemingly boundless list, without specifying their relevance for the occurrence or non-occurrence of a currency crisis.

In this paper, we take a fresh look at the genesis of the Asian currency crisis with a view to informing the ongoing policy debate. The East Asian crisis first developed in Thailand and was subsequently experienced in several other East Asian countries, but by no means all. Two central questions are therefore why Thailand's crisis occurred and why some Asian countries were apparently more susceptible than others to the 'contagion' arising in its wake.

We shall examine data for ten Asian countries. The five *crisis countries*, identified on the basis of the initial shock and the subsequent economic contraction are Thailand, Indonesia, South Korea, Malaysia and the Philippines. The five comparator *non-crisis countries*[5] are China, Taiwan, Singapore, India and Sri Lanka, identified on the basis of the absence of either a severe currency shock or economic contraction and the availability of data adequate for this study.[6] According to the country classification adopted by the International Financial Corporation (IFC), all ten countries belong to the group of 'emerging market economies' which have been exposed to international capital flows (though to varying degrees) in the 1990s. In the lead-up to the crisis, all of them were adopting adjustable (quasi) peg exchange rate systems, with the United States dollar as the key intervention currency.

The paper proceeds in two steps. First, at a theoretical level, we identify a set of early warning indicators for identifying the vulnerability of a given country to a 'currency crisis'. Second, at an empirical level, we ask whether the crisis countries differed systematically from the 'non-crisis' countries in terms of these indicators. The analysis uses data covering the period 1988 to mid-1997, which includes the entire boom-bust cycle of the recent East Asian economic expansion.[7] Given the small country sample, formal statistical tests are not performed – the analysis instead focuses on the common patterns in the chosen

---

[5] For convenience, we shall use the term 'country' throughout, even though Taiwan is often considered a part of China and thus not a 'country'.

[6] Hong Kong is not covered in the study primarily because its unique experience in the context of the Asian crisis emanated from the long commitment to a currency board mechanism. The Hong Kong dollar was able to withstand the initial round of speculative outflow in mid-1997. The subsequent financial and economic collapse in Hong Kong is widely attributed to miscalculated policy initiatives taken by the Hong Kong Monetary Authority to tame speculators with a view to defending the currency board mechanism (Miller, 1998). Thus it is difficult to classify Hong Kong clearly either as a crisis or non-crisis country in terms of the definition of currency crisis used in this study. In any case, data on a number of key variables used in the analysis of this paper are not available for Hong Kong.

[7] For detailed discussion of the development of vulnerability in terms of these three indicators in the context of Thailand and Korea, respectively, see Warr (1999 and 2000).

variables during the period leading up to the crisis. The paper is not about *predicting the timing* of a currency crisis. Rather, it is an attempt to identify the economic variables that make a country more or less vulnerable to such a crisis.[8]

An alternative approach would have been to test econometrically the predictive power of alternative vulnerability indicators using a larger country sample of emerging market economies (as in Radelet and Sachs, 1998; Sachs et al., 1996; Goldstein and Reinhart, 1998; and Kaminsky et al., 1997). We do not adopt this approach for two reasons. First, we do not believe that all emerging market crises can be lumped into a single model. In particular, working with a larger sample of countries spanning the entire developing world generally involves mixing pure currency crises with traditional balance of payments crises. This approach is also subject to an element of arbitrariness resulting from overlooking the historically observed 'regionalisation' element of the contagion effect of a financial crisis (Kindleberger, 1996). Asian countries are different from those in Latin America in terms of history and reputation in maintaining financial stability and these differences are presumably important in the search for determinants or predictors of currency crises (Cooper, 1996, p. 205). Second, focusing on a small sample enables us to give greater attention to relevant country-specific factors, avoiding overdrawing conclusions.

The remainder of the paper is structured as follows. Section 2 addresses the conditions that make an economy more or less vulnerable to a crisis. Section 3 discusses the indicators of vulnerability that are implied by this analysis. Section 4 undertakes a comparative analysis of the Asian economies in terms of these indicators. It asks whether the vulnerability account fits with the experiences of the five crisis countries of East Asia, compared with the experiences of the five non-crisis countries. Section 5 concludes.

2. THE CONCEPT OF VULNERABILITY

The Asian crisis erupted as a *currency crisis*, although it was quickly transformed into a full-blown financial and economic crisis. A currency crisis occurs when market participants lose confidence in the currency of a particular country and seek to escape assets denominated in that currency. They may also attempt to flee other assets whose value might be affected by policy responses induced by a run on the currency. Because investors try to avoid short-term capital losses, they exit from countries where they expect that a large nominal exchange rate depreciation will soon take place. Thus, the fundamental concerns governing their action are the likelihood that the currency would depreciate

---

[8] Examination of the determinants (policy-related or non-policy-related) of these variables is beyond the scope of this paper.

VULNERABILITY TO A CURRENCY CRISIS 37

should capital inflows reverse, and the possible magnitude of that depreciation. Under what conditions might asset owners make a radical upward revision in their assessment of the probability of a large currency depreciation?[9]

a. Vulnerability vs. Trigger

Vulnerability means susceptibility to a currency crisis. The concept must be understood in relation to the concept of a *trigger*. As Dornbusch (1997, p. 21) notes, '[V]ulnerability means that *if* something goes wrong, then suddenly a lot goes wrong' (emphasis added). A state of vulnerability by itself does not give rise to a currency crisis. There needs to be a certain disturbance (a trigger) that will push a vulnerable situation into an actual collapse. Some likely disturbances are policy errors such as a minor devaluation in the context of a significant and persistent overvaluation of the real exchange rate, failure to implement a promised crucial policy reform, or simply a contagion[10] – investor panic spreading from events in a neighbouring crisis country. Since an actual currency crisis requires both vulnerability and a trigger, analysis of vulnerability alone could not be expected to enable one to predict the timing of a currency crisis.

It is possible that a currency may come under the pressure of speculative capital outflow, by which we mean simply capital outflow in anticipation of a currency depreciation, regardless of the country's domestic economic circumstances. It could occur because of wrong market calculations on the part of speculators or other unpredictable events causing a shift in expectations. However, a country would be able to shrug off such events if it was not in a state of vulnerability, provided serious policy errors were not induced by the panic resulting from the unexpected outflow. International currency crises, by their very nature, are rarely anticipated. But by putting appropriate policies and structures in

---

[9] Throughout the following discussion we assume that the country under consideration is in an adjustable (quasi) peg exchange rate regime – a characterisation that is valid, during the period leading up to the crisis, for all ten countries covered in this study.

[10] The forces of contagion can be divided into two categories – organic or economic effects (real contagion) and the 'wake-up call effect' on the financial market participants (pure or financial contagion) (Cooper, 1999, pp. 21–22). Real contagion arises from direct trade linkages – for instance, as a country's import falls, the exports of its trading partner falls. Financial contagion, the concept we refer to here, concerns the response of financial markets. When things suddenly go badly with a country which until then was considered a favourable investment location, investors swiftly re-examine equity and bank portfolios in other countries (notably those in the neighbourhood) which were treated as belonging to the same economic category. It is important to reiterate that according to this characterisation, financial contagion acts only as a trigger; it cannot 'cause' a crisis. Only the countries that have developed vulnerability will succumb to the contagion. Real contagion is presumably of little relevance for explaining crises in emerging market economies because there is very little direct trade among them; most of their trade is oriented toward the major markets of Japan, the United States and Europe.

38   PREMA-CHANDRA ATHUKORALA AND PETER G. WARR

place, a country can make it more likely that crises will be avoided. Therein lies the policy relevance of identifying indicators of vulnerability.

b. Determinants of Vulnerability

Suppose that a country is maintaining a pegged exchange rate and that a substantial and unexpected outflow of capital suddenly occurs – due to some trigger causing a loss of confidence in the capacity of the central bank to maintain the exchange rate. Can the peg be defended? First, we note the accounting identity $\Delta R = B_{KA} + B_{CA}$: the change in the level of reserves (a flow) is equal to the net balance on capital account plus the net balance on current account (both flows). Suppose, for simplicity, that the current account was initially in deficit, the capital account was initially in surplus and that the two magnitudes were approximately equal, implying that the net change in the level of reserves was zero. Starting from this position, a capital outflow now implies a lower level of the net balance on capital account. If nothing else changes, the level of reserves must fall.

Three responses are now possible. First, the authorities could defend the currency and permit the level of reserves to decline until confidence is restored. Whether this is possible depends on the adequacy of the level of reserves in relation to the possible size of the capital outflow. In particular, the smaller the level of reserves (a stock) relative to the volume of short-term foreign liabilities (also a stock), the lower is the credibility of this policy response. If reserves are inadequate to meet a sudden outflow caused by an investor panic and the government still wishes to maintain the exchange rate peg, then it is necessary to ameliorate the loss of reserves by containing the right-hand side of the above identity – the negative value of the net balance on capital account plus the net balance on current account.

The second possible response is an increase in the interest rate. This may be expected to ameliorate the downward pressure on the level of reserves in two ways. First, it helps maintain relative expected returns to investment in the given country by compensating for the potential loss of return due to (the expected) exchange rate depreciation. This reduces, and possibly reverses, the net deficit on capital account which resulted from the investor panic. Second, it may bring about a reduction in domestic absorption (private consumption and investment) which in turn reduces the negative value of the net balance on current account.

But the feasibility of using interest rate policy in the event of a speculative outflow depends on the health of the domestic financial institutions. If these institutions have been operating with unsound (fragile) asset portfolios characterised by high non-performing loans, low levels of capital adequacy and other related weaknesses, an interest rate increase is likely to engineer a domestic credit squeeze, bank failure and business bankruptcies leading to economic collapse. Therefore, the more fragile the banking system, the less scope exists for

VULNERABILITY TO A CURRENCY CRISIS   39

the government to use interest rate policy to defend the currency and the less credible is the policy option of raising interest rates to defend the currency.

If the solution of increasing interest rates cannot be adopted, then the required adjustment has to come through the third possible response – a depreciation of the real exchange rate, by which we mean an increase in the domestic prices of tradables relative to non-tradables. Real exchange rate depreciation facilitates a domestic expenditure switch against tradables and towards non-tradables, and thus accommodates a reduction in the current account deficit. Maintaining the existing exchange rate peg means that the nominal prices of tradables will remain roughly constant. A real depreciation therefore requires a decline in the nominal prices of non-tradables and this will require a monetary and/or fiscal contraction, and presumably a recession, depending on the downward flexibility of non-tradables prices. The required degree of real depreciation and thus the required magnitude of this recession will be greater the more appreciated is the real exchange rate relative to the level compatible with lower capital inflows.

It is important to emphasise that a steady, systematic appreciation of the real exchange rate that occurs in line with changes in underlying economic circumstances is not problematic. If a country borrows to invest and/or attracts significant foreign direct investment, the resulting capital inflow naturally strengthens the real exchange rate – which is the expected effect of an inward transfer. An appreciation can also be a reflection of deep reforms that open up large and lasting opportunities for economic expansion. The 'Balassa-Samuelson' effect – long-term improvement in productivity that normally has a greater price lowering effect on tradables than on non-tradables – can be another factor. Provided these events are permanent rather than temporary, real appreciation arising from them should not cause concern about the macroeconomic health of the economy.

A persistent, excessive appreciation (exchange rate misalignment), that is, an appreciation caused by temporary, reversible events, is what bothers investors and may induce a run on the currency. Such an appreciation implies that the authorities may be unable to defend the currency successfully in the event of a speculative capital outflow because the required real depreciation consistent with lower capital inflows may be too large. In sum, the relevant question is not the actual *level* of the real exchange rate, but its *sustainability*. There is no unique benchmark against which to judge the current level of the real exchange rate. On the other hand, a real exchange rate that is far higher than ever before and which continues to appreciate is suspicious even when past major reforms and access to capital markets have justified some real appreciation.

The discussion so far points to three key indicators that may help in assessing a country's vulnerability to a currency crisis:[11]

---

[11] Previous empirical analyses of the causes of currency crises have used a plethora of other indicators (including the current account deficit, the size of capital inflows, total public debt,

40   PREMA-CHANDRA ATHUKORALA AND PETER G. WARR

- adequacy of reserves relative to the stock of volatile (mobile) capital,
- financial sector fragility, and
- real exchange rate misalignment.

A state of *vulnerability* – a situation where there is reason to doubt the ability of the country to defend the currency in the event of a sudden loss of confidence on the part of the holders of internationally mobile financial assets – can be created by one or a combination of these factors. There is no unique way of implementing these measures empirically. Further discussion is thus needed on the procedures adopted in this study.

3. THE MEASUREMENT OF VULNERABILITY

a. Reserve Adequacy

In the literature on balance of payments issues involving countries with fixed or adjustable peg exchange rates, the conventional yardstick of reserve adequacy is the import-month equivalent of reserves (the ratio of reserves to one month's worth of imports).[12] This measure is not appropriate for the present analysis because 'a run against a currency is rarely associated with an import spree' (Calvo, 1995). What is required is to assess reserve levels in relation to the volume of 'hot money' or 'mobile capital' that may be presented, in the short run, against these reserves. In other words, the appropriate level of reserves depends on the volume of all short-term external liabilities, including portfolio capital inflow.

Some recent studies (e.g. Radelet and Sachs, 1998; and Goldstein, 1998) have defined mobile capital to cover only short-term bank credit, as reported by the Bank of International Settlements (BIS) based on the balance sheets of banks reporting to the BIS. This definition, while obviously more appropriate than the conventional import-month yardstick, tends to understate significantly the volume of mobile capital, particularly because in recent years emerging market economies have experienced large increases in portfolio equity inflows. A country which has accumulated substantial portfolio investments held by non-

government spending (all measured as a percentage of GDP), export growth rates, and so forth) without clearly spelling out the theoretical reasoning behind the anticipated causality. In reality, in the context of a currency crisis, most of these variables can be treated as 'leading' indicators whose influences are appropriately captured by one or more of the three vulnerability indicators that we have specified. Some variables are relevant only for various other forms of financial crises.

[12] An old rule of thumb is that official foreign exchange reserves should be equivalent to at least three months' worth of imports. This rule originated under the Bretton Woods system when, given the combination of fixed exchange rates and controls on flow of capital, the worst situation that could be imagined relating to balance of payments management was that a country would lose its trade credit, worth roughly three months of imports (Huhne, 1998, p. 63).

VULNERABILITY TO A CURRENCY CRISIS 41

residents needs high reserves, particularly because those shares are held by open-ended funds which may be forced to liquidate their holdings quickly in response to adverse shifts of sentiment. In this study we employ a broad definition of mobile (volatile) capital that covers (i) short-term bank credit of all banks, not only BIS-reported banks, (ii) accumulated portfolio investment, and (iii) balances on non-resident bank accounts and trade credits.[13] The data series on the sum of these three variables, reported below, was constructed by carefully accumulating the relevant items in annual balance of payments records.[14]

When capital inflows are reversed, holders of liquid domestic liabilities may also try to convert them into foreign exchange and flee the country. On these grounds, some analysts have opted to measure reserve adequacy by relating foreign reserves to M2, or a broad measure of liquidity money assets (e.g. Calvo, 1995; Sachs et al., 1996; Kaminsky et al., 1997; and Corsetti et al., 1999). In our view, M2 is too broad a measure for this analytical purpose because it includes too much that is not highly mobile. In most emerging market economies domestic financial markets are not fully integrated with world financial markets and in practice conversion of money balances into foreign currency is not an option available to (or considered by) the majority of such asset holders. M2 in the domestic economy, other than foreign currency deposits of resident sectors,[15] is presumably largely independent of speculative factors.

Another indicator often used to measure the ability of a country to withstand speculative capital outflow is the maturity structure of outstanding foreign debt (e.g. Calvo, 1995; Huhne, 1998; and Eichengreen, 1999). The underlying reasoning is that, since short-term foreign debt needs to be rolled over regularly, a country, which has accumulated a large stock of short-term debt, faces difficulty in defending the currency in the event of a speculative outflow. By contrast, so the argument goes, a debt structure characterised by low short-term debt gives a country extra breathing space to turn its policy around. Such a country does not need continuous large-scale access to the market to service its debt. This indicator, however, suffers from two major limitations. Firstly, official data on the maturity structure of foreign debt, by their very nature, do not capture accumulated portfolio inflows, which in some countries can be an important item of volatile capital. Secondly, in analysing vulnerability what is relevant is the volume of short-term capital in relation to the stock of foreign exchange reserves. A country with a large stock of total foreign debt could well have a small share of short-term debt, yet the magnitude of the latter may be large in relation to the

---

[13] As far as we are aware this is the first attempt in the literature on financial crisis to measure reserve adequacy by taking into account all these three components of mobile capital.

[14] For all countries the starting year used in this compilation is 1980. However, it was found that the results were highly insensitive to the choice of starting year.

[15] This component of M2 (and of course deposits held by foreign residents in the domestic banking system) is covered by our definition of mobile capital.

42   PREMA-CHANDRA ATHUKORALA AND PETER G. WARR

stock of national reserves. For these reasons, this indicator could provide misleading signals as to the state of a country's vulnerability.

b. Financial Sector Fragility

The standard indicators of the health of the banking system are the non-performing credit ratio and the capital adequacy ratio. These measures suffer from serious limitations, however, both conceptual and in relation to data quality. First, both are backward looking and in a context of rapid credit growth any such historical summary measure is unlikely to be an adequate indicator of future performance. During an ongoing credit boom creditors normally have the option of arranging credit rollover through their banks (a process known as *evergreening*). Second, not only in developing countries but also in developed countries with more efficient bank supervisory mechanisms, these measures are subject to large measurement errors, primarily because of ambiguities of definitions. Usually, in the face of trouble, banks tend to give themselves the benefit of the doubt, thus making the indicators even more dubious in the context of a crisis (Mishkin, 1997).

Reflecting these considerations, a widely used indicator of the soundness of the banking system is total outstanding institutional credit to the private sector as a ratio of GDP (private sector leverage ratio) (Radelet and Sachs, 1998; Sachs et al., 1996; Mishkin, 1996; and Backstrom, 1997). The underlying hypothesis, which has been amply supported in the context of financial crises in many countries, is that countries with rapid build-up in bank credit would have more fragile banking systems, a greater quantity of bad loans, and therefore greater vulnerability to a crisis. Also, rapid build-up of credit in a short period may imply a growing share of lending to less credit-worthy borrowers, and therefore a sign of weakening of the banking system. This is the measure of financial sector fragility used in this study.

c. Real Exchange Rate

The real exchange rate is the relative price of traded to non-traded goods. In the absence of readily available indices of tradable and non-tradable prices, the real exchange rate has to be proxied by available domestic and world price indices and nominal exchange rates. There is no unique way of constructing a proxy measure, but all commonly used measures compute the ratio $RER = EP^*/P$, where E denotes the nominal exchange rate, P^* is an index of foreign prices and P is an index of domestic prices. E and P^* are weighted averages computed across trading partner countries. The country weights may be based on export shares, import shares or, most commonly, shares based on the sum of exports and imports, although the latter has no apparent theoretical foundation.

VULNERABILITY TO A CURRENCY CRISIS 43

We shall describe three proxy measures of this general kind, which differ according to the measures used for P^* and P. Our preferred proxy measure, subsequently denoted RER_1, uses foreign producer (wholesale) prices for P^*, domestic consumer prices for P and uses country weights based on export shares for E and P. In intuitive terms, RER_1 is simply producer prices in export partner countries relative to domestic consumer prices, both measured in a common currency (domestic currency). By construction, the producer price index is dominated by the prices of tradables much more than the consumer price index. The index RER_1 may thus serve as a rough proxy for the theoretical concept of the real exchange rate – the relative prices of tradable to non-tradable goods.[16] At least, it seems a better proxy than the two, more widely used indicators discussed below.

Previous studies have typically used either of two other indicators, although the theoretical reasoning behind the particular measurement choice is seldom made explicit. One (which we denote RER_2) is the J.P. Morgan index, which uses non-food producer prices in trading partners for P^* and wholesale (producer prices) in the given country for domestic prices, P. Wholesale price indices are made up predominantly from traded goods, the prices of which generally adjust to exchange rate changes.[17] This measure may thus be viewed as an indicator of the international competitiveness of traded goods produced in the given country. It is not a measure of *internal competitiveness* (the relative profitability of domestic production of tradables compared with non-traded goods and services), the concept of real exchange rate which is theoretically more appropriate for identifying the ability of the given country to defend the currency successfully in the event of a speculative outflow.

The third index (RER_3), is perhaps the most widely used, particularly in publications of the IMF and the World Bank. It uses a trade-weighted index of consumer prices in trading partner countries for P^* and an index of consumer prices in the given country for P. The use of this indicator as a proxy for the theoretical concept of a real exchange rate is usually justified on the premise (Edwards, 1989) that under the low inflation conditions that prevail in developed countries (which are generally the major trading partners), producer prices and consumer prices tend to move together. According to this reasoning, the choice of one proxy over the other is important only in developing countries, which generally tend to experience relatively higher rates of inflation.

---

[16] For an analysis of the accuracy of this approximation, see Warr (1986).

[17] For an interesting exposition of this limitation of international price comparison based on wholesale price indices (made in the context of the debate on UK's return to the gold standard at a seemingly appreciated gold parity compared to the pre-war level) see Keynes (1925, p. 249).

44   PREMA-CHANDRA ATHUKORALA AND PETER G. WARR

4. RESULTS

a. Reserve Adequacy

Table 1 compares the crisis countries with the non-crisis countries in terms of the reserve adequacy ratio – the total foreign exchange reserve relative to the stock of volatile (mobile) capital, R/V. In the run-up to the crisis, R/V declined significantly in each of the five crisis countries, but not in any of the non-crisis countries. Among the crisis countries, the decline in the ratio is most striking for Thailand and Korea. By the end of June 1997, Korea's foreign reserves provided cover for only 18 per cent of total accumulated mobile capital in the country. The comparable figure for Thailand was 45 per cent. There are reasons to believe that the decline would have been even sharper if *net* rather than gross international reserves were used in the calculation.

Immediately before the crisis the Bank of Thailand was involved heavily in the forward exchange market to defend its fixed exchange rate. Although the Bank of Thailand could show on its books that it still had some $37 billion, on the eve of abandoning the peg, in effect it had committed substantial amounts of reserves[18] in long positions in the (weakening) forward market (Miller, 1998, p. 356). The Korean central bank had also lent a substantial (as yet unknown) portion of its foreign exchange reserves to troubled commercial banks (Goldstein, 1998; and Ito, 2000). Reserve positions in Indonesia, Malaysia and the Philippines were relatively higher compared with Korea and Thailand, when measured in the above manner, but in all these cases there was a persistent deterioration in the degree of reserve cover provided for mobile capital compared with the first half of the 1990s.

The non-crisis countries as a group are clearly distinguishable from their crisis counterparts in terms of the strength of their reserve positions. Taiwan had virtually no accumulated mobile capital in the country and China had ample reserves to back up such capital. The relatively low R/V ratio for Singapore compared with China and Taiwan reflects its role as an international banker.[19] By mid-1997, Singapore's total foreign reserves amounted to US$80 billion, the second highest level of national reserves among the countries under study after Taiwan (US$88 billion). In Sri Lanka there was little 'hot' money left in the country by the time of the Asian crisis; most of the funds accumulated in the first half of the 1990s had left the country in response to political instability (regime shift) and worsening civil unrest. India's R/V ratio continued to remain below 100 reflecting the massive inflow of funds to foreign currency accounts in Indian banks held by non-resident Indians

---

[18] The amount committed was over $30 billion, according to some press reports (*Far Eastern Economic Review*, 13 September, 1998).
[19] According to the IMF guidelines for balance of payments classification adopted by all IMF member countries, balances in non-resident bank deposits are classified as short-term debt.

TABLE 1

Reserve Adequacy (R/V): Foreign Exchange Reserves (R) as a Percentage of Stock of Mobile Capital (V)

	1988	1989	1990	1991	1992	1993	1994	1995	1996	1997[1]
Crisis countries										
Indonesia	434.8	285.7	125.0	156.3	144.9	106.4	76.9	68.5	70.4	70.5
Korea	126.6	153.8	116.3	71.9	60.2	49.0	43.7	37.7	29.4	17.8
Malaysia	142.9	153.8	158.7	171.3	148.8	124.3	93.7	80.4	72.5	56.2
Philippines[2]	476.2	434.8	416.7	243.9	270.3	208.3	147.1	125.0	93.5	39.5
	(714.3)	(714.3)	(667.7)	(370.4)	(769.2)	(333.3)	(222.2)	(178.6)	(149.3)	(64.1)
Thailand	133.3	161.3	175.4	227.3	169.5	105.3	70.4	61.3	54.1	45.0
Non-crisis countries										
China	135.1	181.8	555.6	625.0	666.7	476.2	1111.1	3333.3	1000.0	769.2
India	54.3	35.5	12.8	22.6	31.7	48.3	72.5	59.9	45.9	48.3
	(2500.0)	**	**	**	(1428.6)	(256.4)	(181.8)	(140.8)	(133.5)	(155.3)
Singapore	52.9	45.0	66.7	93.5	81.3	104.2	126.6	153.8	158.7	101.0
Sri Lanka	17.7	18.1	27.2	40.5	46.5	77.5	87.7	92.6	87.0	79.4
	(114.9)	(222.2)	(416.7)	(263.2)	(476.2)	**	**	**	**	**
Taiwan	1111.1	3333.3	**	**	3333.3	2500.0	1666.7	2000.0	**	**

Notes:
[1] Data for 1997 relate to the first half of the year only, preceding the Thai crisis in July of that year.
[2] Data in parentheses give the R/V ratio estimated after excluding accumulated balances on non-resident foreign currency accounts in commercial banks.
** Stock of mobile capital is negative (cumulative outflow was greater than cumulative inflow).

Sources: Compiled from IMF, *International Financial Statistics* (CD-ROM) supplemented with, Republic of China: Council for Economic Planning and Development, *Taiwan Statistical Data Book 1998* (all data for Taiwan) and Bank Negara Malaysia, *Monthly Statistical Bulletin*.

46   PREMA-CHANDRA ATHUKORALA AND PETER G. WARR

(balances of which are treated as short-term liabilities for balance of payments accounting purposes) following the liberalisation reforms initiated in 1991 (Joshi and Little, 1997). The reserve position was sufficient to provide adequate cushion against potential hot money movements.

Alternative indicators of reserve adequacy can give very different perspectives. Three such indicators are summarised in Table A1 in the Appendix. The time patterns of import-month equivalent of reserves do not correspond at all with the growing mismatch of volatile capital and reserves discussed above for the crisis countries. For all crisis countries, the former indicator remained either virtually unchanged or increased considerably during the immediate pre-crisis years. The implication of this comparison is that within the context of a continuous increase in short-term capital inflows, a persistent deterioration in the country's ability to back-up such mobile capital (in the event of a crisis) can coexist with a deceptively healthy foreign exchange position as measured by the conventional, but misleading, yardstick of the number of months of import coverage. It can also co-exist with the situation where the absolute level of reserves is steadily increasing, because the stock of mobile capital can be increasing even faster.

Differences between the two groups of countries in terms of the reserve-M2 ratio correspond to that revealed by our preferred indicator of reserve adequacy. However, within the two groups there is some overlap among countries in terms of the former indicator, presumably because this measure is significantly influenced by other factors such as differences in the degree of financial development.

In terms of short-term debt build-up there is some difference between the non-crisis and crisis countries, but there is no such difference in relation to the level of the short-term debt share. Within the crisis group, inter-country differences are not consistent with what we observe in terms of R/V. In the lead-up to the crisis, Indonesia and Malaysia had much lower short-term debt shares than Korea and Thailand. These differences seem to reflect both differences in the relative foreign exchange reserve levels and in the importance of portfolio inflows, which are appropriately captured in R/V.

b. Financial Fragility

All crisis countries experienced credit booms in the lead-up to the crisis (Table 2). In Malaysia, the degree of private sector leverage, as measured by the ratio of total institutional credit to GDP was the highest of all the ten countries, from 1992 until the crisis.[20] The ratio continued to remain relatively low in Indonesia

---

[20] In his highly-publicised interchange with the Malaysian Prime Minister Dr Mahathir, the financier George Soros pointed to massive private sector credit accumulation as the main source of vulnerability of the Malaysia economy (Athukorala, 1998, p. 927).

TABLE 2
Ratio of Private Sector Credit to GDP, 1988–97

	1988	1989	1990	1991	1992	1993	1994	1995	1996	1997[1]	Per Cent Change from the Average for 1989–95	
											1996	1997[1]
Crisis countries												
Indonesia	27.1	33.3	46.9	46.2	45.5	48.9	51.9	53.5	55.4	61.1	25.4	34.8
Korea	72.7	84.3	87.5	87.9	95.3	105.2	112.5	117.5	126.5	141.4	32.7	48.3
Malaysia	114.3	118.0	123.0	128.9	135.4	147.4	153.1	166.0	175.9	192.5	29.6	42.8
Philippines	18.8	20.4	22.3	20.8	25.0	32.0	35.9	45.1	54.2	61.6	96.8	127.3
Thailand	51.1	56.3	64.5	67.7	72.2	80.0	91.0	97.6	101.9	116.3	45.5	60.3
Non-crisis countries												
China	74.3	78.4	86.6	89.3	88.8	95.5	87.1	85.8	91.7	101.1	7.0	17.9
India	33.2	33.7	31.1	29.3	29.9	28.6	27.6	26.3	27.4	27.8	–8.6	–7.2
Singapore	91.9	96.0	95.4	95.7	97.7	96.8	98.4	104.9	110.4	112.9	13.7	16.3
Sri Lanka	21.8	20.2	19.6	20.6	22.1	22.7	24.3	26.3	25.1	24.0	13.1	8.1
Taiwan	84.7	54.5	100.5	109.1	126.4	136.8	146.9	148.9	144.1	145.2	21.6	22.6

Note:
[1] Data for 1997 relate to the first half of the year only, preceding the Thai crisis in July of that year.

Sources: Compiled from IMF, *International Financial Statistics* (CD-ROM) supplemented with, Republic of China: Council for Economic Planning and Development, *Taiwan Statistical Data Book 1998* (all data for Taiwan).

48   PREMA-CHANDRA ATHUKORALA AND PETER G. WARR

and the Philippines, but in the lead-up to the crisis the rate of growth was higher in each of the crisis countries than in any non-crisis country.

Both the level and the rate of growth in the credit to GDP ratio was uniformly lower in non-crisis countries. India is unique among these countries in that the growth of total credit lagged behind GDP growth throughout the 1990s. This pattern reflected credit restraints imposed under structural adjustment *cum* stabilisation reforms during this period. Sri Lanka had the second lowest rate of credit growth after India. In other non-crisis countries, credit growth was generally rapid throughout the period under consideration (reflecting financial deepening as part of rapid growth), but none of these countries showed an abrupt rise in the rate of credit growth in the lead-up to the crisis.

The above evidence, when interpreted in the light of the theoretical reasoning given in the previous section, suggests that the crisis countries had experienced a continuous weakening in the health of their financial systems in the years prior to the crisis. The non-crisis countries did not. To recapitulate, rapid credit expansion relative to growth of the overall economy within a short period is likely to be accompanied by an accumulation of bad debts and an increase in the proportion of loans to less productive investments and to non-tradable activities, including real estate. This view is supported by direct evidence (both qualitative and quantitative) on the financial sector performance coming from recent case studies of the crisis countries (Athukorala, 2001, Chapter 4; Chang et al., 1998; Nidhiaprabha, 1999; and Goldstein, 1998).

c. Real Exchange Rate Appreciation

Real exchange rate behaviour is shown in Table 3, in terms of our preferred indicator (RER_1). For comparison, the alternative measures of RER_2 and RER_3 are reported in the Appendix, Table A2.[21] The estimates in Table 4 point to a continuous appreciation of the real exchange rate in the crisis countries as a group from about 1992, with the rate of appreciation accelerating in the run-up to the crisis. By June 1997 the real value of the Thai baht stood about 17 per cent above its average level for the period 1988–96; the corresponding figures for the Indonesian rupiah, the Malaysian ringgit, the Philippine peso and the Korean won were 15.7 per cent, 19.1 per cent, 19 per cent and 7.5 per cent. Thus, contrary to claims by some authors (e.g. Kregal, 1998; McKinnon, 1998; and Goldstein, 1998), our estimates suggest that the crisis-5 were experiencing significant real exchange rate appreciation in the lead-up to the crisis.

Unlike the clear contrast observed in terms of the preceding two vulnerability indicators, there is some overlap between the two groups of countries in relation to the patterns of real exchange rate behaviour. Within the non-crisis group of countries,

---

[21]The original J.P. Morgan index has been inverted to make it comparable with the other two indices.

TABLE 3

Real Exchange Rate: Preferred Index (RER_1),[1] 1988–97 (1988 = 100)

	1989	1990	1991	1992	1993	1994	1995	1996	1997[2]	Per Cent Change from the Average for 1988–95	
										1996	1997[2]
Crisis countries											
Indonesia	101.8	101	97.5	93.6	86.3	81.7	78.3	76.4	76.5	−17.4	−17.3
Korea	90.7	90.8	86.3	86.5	84.7	79.7	74.7	75.8	80.8	−12.5	−11.3
Malaysia	103.7	103.7	100	87.5	85.3	82	76.6	75.2	73.2	−18.5	−20.7
Philippines	93.2	97.1	87.6	88	82.9	80.7	74.7	75.4	70.2	−14.3	−20.2
Thailand	100	96.5	90.8	86.4	82.9	78	74.4	72.4	72.1	−18.3	−18.6
Non-crisis countries											
China	89.2	112.3	120.6	117.2	106.1	127.3	106.8	99.4	97.0	−9.6	−10.8
India	114.1	116.6	134.2	137.3	152.6	143.3	137.9	139.9	135.2	8.0	4.4
Singapore	98.7	91.4	85.2	79.2	77.1	70.8	66.4	66.3	66.9	−20.6	−20.0
Sri Lanka	106.3	100	93.2	89.5	89	84.5	84	79.5	78.7	−14.8	−15.7
Taiwan	92.4	95.6	86.1	81.7	83	80.4	81.8	87.9	95.3	0.3	8.8

Notes:
[1] An increase (decrease) in the index indicates a depreciation (appreciation).
[2] Data for 1997 relate to the first half of the year only, preceding the Thai crisis in July of that year.

Sources: Compiled from IMF, *International Financial Statistics* and *Direction of World Trade* data tapes supplemented with, Republic of China: Council for Economic Planning and Development, *Taiwan Statistical Data Book 1998* (all data for Taiwan).

50   PREMA-CHANDRA ATHUKORALA AND PETER G. WARR

TABLE 4
Determinants of Vulnerability to a Currency Crisis: Summary Results

	Vulnerability Indicators		
	(1) Sustained Decline in Foreign Exchange Reserves Relative to Mobile Capital Stock	*(2)* Private Sector Credit Boom	*(3)* Real Exchange Rate Appreciation
Crisis countries			
Indonesia	Yes	Yes	Yes
Korea	Yes	Yes	Yes
Malaysia	Yes	Yes	Yes
Philippines	Yes	Yes	Yes
Thailand	Yes	Yes	Yes
Non-crisis countries			
China	No	No	Yes
India	No	No	No
Singapore	No	No	Yes
Sri Lanka	No	No	Yes
Taiwan	No	No	No

Sources: Tables 1 to 3.

Taiwan and India managed to avoid real exchange rate appreciation throughout the period. However, the degree of real exchange rate appreciation experienced by Sri Lanka and Singapore in the lead-up to the Asian crisis was similar in magnitude to that of the crises countries. Clearly, the significant depreciation of the yen against the US dollar during this period induced real exchange rate appreciation across those countries in the region which continued to use the US$ as the dominant intervention currency in their pegged exchange rate systems.

The Chinese experience calls for some elaboration. In early 1994 China decisively reformed its exchange rate mechanism resulting in a real depreciation of the yuan by 17 per cent over the previous year (Table 3).[22] The resultant export upswing helped China to build up massive foreign exchange reserves, placing the country in a position of strength to withstand a speculative outflow. The degree of appreciation recorded by the estimates for 1996 and 1997 must therefore be viewed in the context of this successful, early exchange rate adjustment.

Are the results sensitive to the uses of RER_1 instead of RER_2 or RER_3 (Appendix, Table A2)? Yes. One clear example is the behaviour of RER_2 for

---

[22] For details on China's exchange rate reform in 1994 and its implications for the country's competitiveness see Lardy (1998), Naughton (1996), Noland et al. (1998), and Wei and Zeckhauser 1998 and the work cited therein. Reflecting differences in methodology, the degree of depreciation reported in these studies varies in the range of 12 per cent to 20 per cent, with the majority of estimates clustering at the upper end.

Korea, which records real exchange rate depreciation prior to the crisis. We hypothesise that this finding reflects price-lowering effects on traded goods of continuing trade liberalisation in that country. For other countries the degree of real appreciation measured by both RER_2 and RER_3 is generally smaller than that recorded by our preferred index (RER_1). The choice of real exchange rate proxy index clearly matters, which is why the theoretical basis of these measures, as discussed above, is important.

Finally, Table 4 summarises the evidence presented above in this section on the relevance of the three potential indicators for identifying a country's vulnerability to a currency crisis. Two of the three indicators of vulnerability unambiguously discriminate between the crisis and non-crisis countries. In the years preceding the crisis, all crisis countries exhibited a significant decline in the ratio of international reserves to the stock of mobile capital and a significant increase in the ratio of private sector credit to GDP. None of the non-crisis countries showed either of these features. In addition, all crisis countries showed significant real exchange rate appreciations, provided a theoretically consistent proxy measure of the real exchange rate is used for this purpose. However, real exchange rate appreciation also occurred in some non-crisis countries. This result confirms that a substantial real exchange rate appreciation is not in itself a sufficient condition for a country to be vulnerable to a financial crisis. Nevertheless, it may be a contributing factor if other predisposing conditions for crisis vulnerability, such as reserve inadequacy and financial sector fragility, are also present.

5. CONCLUSION

There is strong evidence that in the lead-up to the 1997–98 crisis, the macroeconomic circumstances of all the five crisis countries were characterised by (i) rapid accumulation of mobile capital, (ii) domestic lending booms and (iii) overvalued exchange rates. None of the non-crisis countries exhibited either of the first two characteristics and only two of them exhibited the third. In sum, the results of this study point to the importance of monitoring indicators of vulnerability on a more systematic basis than occurred prior to the crisis. Attributing the crisis solely, or even primarily, to irrational market behaviour misses this central point. Thus there is a strong case for considering carefully the policy errors that caused some countries to become vulnerable to a crisis while others did not.

Does the inference that accumulation of mobile capital made these countries vulnerable to currency crisis necessarily imply that capital account opening was a fundamental culprit in causing the crisis?[23] Capital account opening no doubt

---

[23]Among many others, Bhagwati (2001, p. 56) argues that '[T]he chief underlying cause of the Asian crisis starting mid-1997 was to be found in the hasty opening to freer capital flows under

52   PREMA-CHANDRA ATHUKORALA AND PETER G. WARR

facilitated the foreign borrowing and short-term debt build up that contributed to the vulnerability that we have identified. But our results do not necessarily suggest that the liberalisation of the capital account was the central problem. Macroeconomic policy slippage that led to an appreciation of the real exchange rate and financial fragility caused by massive credit build-up at the same time as the capital account was being liberalised were also important.

For example, among the crisis countries, Malaysia's short-term credit build up was below average, but it experienced the most dramatic lending boom among these ten countries. Capital account regimes in Thailand and Korea were not more liberal than those in Indonesia and Malaysia, yet the former countries recorded the most rapid decline in the ratio of reserves to volatile capital stocks. Taiwan introduced significant financial liberalisation reforms from the mid-1980s, even though they were arguably not as dramatic as in Korea, yet domestic credit expansion in that country was much more orderly throughout the period reviewed in this study.[24] Singapore, despite its wide open capital account, was able to weather the crisis with only minor bruises, given its strong reserve position, orderly domestic credit expansion and robust banking system.

To our knowledge, this paper contains the first attempt to examine causes of the Asian financial crisis through a systematic comparison of crisis and non-crisis countries in Asia using a theoretically-based, common set of vulnerability indicators. Earlier studies have predominantly relied on intertermporal comparisons within individual crisis countries and/or identification of common patterns among the crisis countries alone. However, in broader terms, our inference that the explanation for the Asian crisis lies in unstable deteriorations in macroeconomic conditions, rather than irrational financial markets, is consistent with that of Goldstein (1998), Corsetti (1998) and Rajan 2001.

---

pressure from. .... the 'Wall Street-Treasury complex'. See also Williamson (1999), Furman and Stiglitz (1998) and Radelet and Sachs (1998).
[24] See also Radelet and Sachs (1998, p. 46).

APPENDIX

TABLE A1

Reserves to M2 ratio (Per Cent), Import-Month Equivalence of Reserves, Short-term Debt as a Share of Total Foreign Debt (Per Cent)[1]

	1988	1989	1990	1991	1992	1993	1994	1995	1996	1997[2]
Crisis countries										
Indonesia										
R/M2	25.4	20.7	19.4	19.8	20.5	18.4	16.9	15.4	16.4	17.0
Import months	5.7	5.0	4.9	4.7	5.3	5.4	5.0	4.4	5.5	6.3
Short-term debt	12.4	13.4	15.9	18.3	20.5	20.2	18.1	20.9	25.1	32.2
Korea										
R/M2	24.0	21.9	18.5	14.7	16.6	16.8	20.0	17.6	16.5	11.7
Import months	3.7	3.7	3.1	2.5	3.0	3.4	3.3	3.1	2.9	4.0
Short-term debt	27.3	29.9	30.9	28.2	27.0	25.8	41.3	47.5	49.1	49.4
Malaysia										
R/M2	32.2	32.2	33.0	26.5	26.1	32.1	36.0	26.6	20.6	16.9
Import months	5.6	4.4	3.8	2.8	3.7	5.0	4.5	3.3	3.1	3.5
Short-term debt	7.9	12.7	10.5	12.6	23.5	25.0	19.3	19.1	25.7	25.3
Philippines										
R/M2	80.0	81.3	87.0	82.0	80.6	82.6	76.9	75.8	75.8	36.4
Import months	1.4	1.5	0.9	3.0	3.4	3.0	3.2	2.7	3.5	3.7
Short-term debt	13.3	13.9	14.6	15.3	15.9	14.0	14.3	13.3	19.3	22.3
Thailand										
R/M2	16.7	23.5	22.9	25.8	25.9	25.8	26.2	28.0	26.7	31.0
Import months	3.7	5.2	5.0	5.9	6.4	6.7	6.5	6.3	6.9	6.6
Short-term debt	22.2	26.1	29.5	33.1	35.2	43.0	44.5	49.4	41.4	46.2

continued overleaf

TABLE A1
(Continued)

	1988	1989	1990	1991	1992	1993	1994	1995	1996	1997[2]
Non-crisis countries										
China										
R/M2	5.1	4.2	7.9	11.0	8.2	6.3	12.6	12.5	13.4	14.3
Import months	2.9	2.6	5.5	7.2	5.4	4.4	7.1	8.5	10.6	13.4
Short-term debt	20.7	15.4	16.8	17.9	19.0	17.8	17.4	18.9	19.7	—ᶜ
India										
R/M2	3.7	3.0	1.1	2.9	4.4	7.9	1.4	11.1	11.5	13.2
Import months	2.9	2.1	0.8	2.1	3.0	5.1	8.0	5.7	5.6	2.3
Short-term debt	10.5	10.0	10.2	8.2	7.0	3.8	4.1	5.3	7.5	—ᶜ
Singapore										
R/M2	81.3	76.9	81.3	84.7	86.2	95.2	94.3	95.2	97.1	97.1
Import months	2.3	2.5	3.0	3.6	4.1	4.2	4.5	4.7	5.0	10.4
Sri Lanka										
R/M2	10.1	11.6	18.5	25.2	31.1	48.8	52.6	46.7	42.7	42.9
Import months	1.3	1.4	2.2	2.9	3.7	5.5	5.7	5.2	4.8	4.4
Short-term debt	11.1	7.7	6.9	6.2	3.9	3.9	6.8	6.5	7.9	7.2
Taiwan										
R/M2	70.9	51.0	41.2	36.6	30.2	28.0	25.2	22.1	20.7	22.6
Import months	16.8	15.8	14.3	14.3	12.7	12.1	11.6	9.1	9.3	8.3

Notes:
[1] Singapore and Taiwan are net creditor countries with no (or negligible) foreign debt.
[2] Data for 1997 relate to the first half of the year only, preceding the Thai crisis in July of that year.
[3] — Data not available.

Sources: Data on foreign debt are from World Bank, *World Development Indicators* data tapes. Sources for other data as indicated in Table 1.

TABLE A2

Real Exchange Rate: Alternative Indices (RER_2 and RER_3),[1] 1988–97 (1988 = 100)

		1989	1990	1991	1992	1993	1994	1995	1996	1997[2]	Per Cent Change from the Average for 1988–95	
											1996	1997[2]
Crisis countries												
Indonesia	RER_2	99.1	101.8	100.8	102.2	100.2	101.5	103.1	98.4	94.6	−2.7	−6.4
	RER_3	101.6	102.2	102.3	101.2	96.7	93.8	90.3	88.2	88.7	−10.5	−10.0
Korea	RER_2	89.4	96.3	99.4	108.8	112.2	114.6	112.5	108.7	110.6	4.4	6.2
	RER_3	90.7	92.2	90.7	93.4	93.8	90	84.3	85.9	92.4	−6.5	0.6
Malaysia	RER_2	102.5	106	107.3	99.5	96.7	99.7	99.9	95.3	89.9	−6.1	−11.4
	RER_3	103.7	105.3	106.5	96.6	96.9	95.7	89.8	88.6	87.4	−10.8	−12.0
Philippines	RER_2	93.9	99.6	102.7	94.2	102.3	95.4	96.2	86.8	83.9	−11.5	−14.4
	RER_3	97.9	98.9	97.5	85.8	85.6	79.3	76.3	69.3	64.8	−23.1	−28.1
Thailand	RER_2	97.1	97.4	95.1	98.7	97.2	97.9	99.7	92.2	89.1	−5.8	−9.0
	RER_3	96.9	86.6	84.4	76.2	64.1	60.9	67.6	64.3	56.1	−19.2	−29.5
Non-crisis countries												
China[3]	RER_3	89.1	113.7	126.2	126.1	117.7	144.4	121.3	113.2	111.1	−3.5	−5.3
India	RER_2	105.7	115.5	135.1	146.4	153.3	148.5	153.4	154.6	142.4	16.9	7.9
	RER_3	114.3	118.7	140.8	147.5	167.3	160	153.7	156.7	152.7	13.7	10.8
Singapore	RER_2	94.3	90	87.8	85.5	84.8	82.4	81.7	78.3	75.7	−11.3	−14.3
	RER_3	98.8	92.9	89.1	84.7	84.1	78.6	73.5	73.7	75.1	−16.2	−14.3
Sri Lanka	RER_2	108.9	101.7	97.4	95.8	99	97	95.4	86.9	88	−12.6	−11.5
	RER_3	106.5	101.9	97.8	96.1	97.2	93.8	92.8	88.4	88.5	−10.0	−9.9
Taiwan	RER_2	93.8	101	104	106.7	110.2	111.7	110.7	113.9	111.5	8.7	6.4
	RER_3	92.7	97.1	91.8	88.8	92.5	90.2	91.5	91.6	110.5	−1.6	18.7

Notes:
[1] An increase (decrease) in the index indicates a depreciation (appreciation).
[2] Data for 1997 relate to the first half of the year only, preceding the Thai crisis in July of that year.
[3] RER_2 is not estimable because of the unavailability of a domestic wholesale price index.

Sources: As for Table 1.

56   PREMA-CHANDRA ATHUKORALA AND PETER G. WARR

REFERENCES

Athukorala, P. (1998), 'Malaysia', in R. H. McLeod and R. Garnaut (eds.), *East Asia in Crisis* (London: Routledge), 85–91.

Athukorala, P. (2001), *Crisis and Recovery in Malaysia: The Role of Capital Controls* (Cheltenham: Edward Elgar).

Backstrom, U. (1997), 'What Lessons can be Learned from Recent Financial Crises? The Swedish Experience', in Federal Reserve Bank of Kansas City, *Maintaining Financial Stability in a Global Economy* (Wyoming: Jackson Hole), 55–96.

Bhagwati, J. (1998), 'Asian Financial Crisis Debate: Why? How Severe?', Paper presented at the international conference *Managing the Asian Financial Crisis: Lessons and Challenges*, Asian Strategic Leadership Institute and Rating Agency Malaysia (2–3 November, Kuala Lumpur).

Bhagwati, J. (2001), 'The Asian Economic Crisis: What Do We Know Now?', Chapter 5 in his *The Winds of the Hundred Days: How Washington Mismanaged Globalization* (Cambridge, Mass.: MIT Press), 51–60.

Calvo, G. A. (1995), 'Varieties of Capital-market Crises', Center for International Economics Working Paper No. 15 (College Park, MD: University of Maryland).

Chang, H-J., H. J. Park and C. G. Yoo (1998), 'Interpreting the Korean Crisis: Financial Liberalisation, Industrial Policy and Corporate Governance', *Cambridge Journal of Economics*, **22**, 4, 735–46.

Cooper, R. N. (1996), 'Comments on Sachs, Tornell and Velasco (1996)', *Brookings Papers on Economic Activity*, **1**, 203–08.

Cooper, R. N. (1999), 'The Asian Crisis: Causes and Consequences', in A. Hardwood, R. E. Litan and M. Pomerleano (eds.), *Financial Markets & Development: The Crisis in Emerging Markets* (Washington, DC.: Brookings Institution Press), 17–28.

Corden, W. M. (1999), *The Asian Crisis: Is There a Way Out?* (Singapore: Institute of Southeast Asian Studies).

Corsetti, G. (1998), 'Interpreting the Asian Financial Crisis: Open Issues in Theory and Policy', *Asian Development Review*, **16**, 2, 1–45.

Corsetti, G., P. Pesenti and N. Roubini (1999), 'What Caused the Asian Currency and Financial Crisis?', *Japan and the World Economy*, **11**, 2, 305–73.

Dornbusch, R. (1997), 'A Thai-Mexico Primer: Lessons for Outmaneuvering a Financial Meltdown', *The International Economy* (September/October), 20–23 and 55.

Edwards, S. (1989), *Real Exchange Rates, Devaluation and Adjustment: Exchange Rate Policies in Developing Countries* (Cambridge, Mass.: MIT Press).

Eichengreen, B. (1999), *Towards a New International Financial Architecture* (Washington, DC: Institute for International Economics).

Federal Reserve Bank of Kansas City (1997), *Maintaining Financial Stability in a Global Economy: A Symposium* (Kansas City: Federal Reserve Bank of Kansas City).

Fischer, S. (1998), 'Lessons from a Crisis', *The Economist* (3 October), 19–23.

Furman, J. and J. Stiglitz (1998), 'Economic Crises: Evidence and Insights from East Asia', *Brookings Papers on Economic Activity*, **2**, 1–136.

Garnaut, R. (1998), 'The Financial Crisis: A Watershed in Economic Thought About East Asia', *Asian Pacific Economic Literature*, **12**, 1–11.

Goldstein, M. (1998), *The Asian Financial Crisis: Causes, Cures, and Systemic Implications* (Washington, DC: Institute for International Economics).

Goldstein, M. and C. Reinhart (1998), *Forecasting Financial Crises: Early Warning Signals for Emerging Markets* (Washington, DC: Institute for International Economics).

Huhne, C. (1998), 'How the Rating Agencies Blew it on Korea: An Industry Insider's Honest Admission', *International Economy* (May/June), 46–49.

IMF (International Monetary Fund) (1997), *Exchange Rate Arrangements and Exchange Rate Restrictions – Annual Report* (Washington, DC: IMF).

Ito, T. (2000), 'Capital Flows to East Asia', in M. Feldstein (ed.), *International Capital Flows* (Chicago: University of Chicago Press), 111–32.

VULNERABILITY TO A CURRENCY CRISIS 57

Joshi, V. and I. M. D. Little (1997), *India's Economic Reforms 1991–2001* (Oxford and Delhi: Oxford University Press).

Kaminsky, G., S. Lizondo and C. M. Reinhart (1997), 'Leading Indicators of Currency Crises', IMF Working Paper WP/97/79 (Washington, DC: IMF).

Keynes, J. M. (1925) [1963], 'The Economic Consequences of Mr. Churchill', in his *Essays in Persuasion* (New York: W. W. Norton), 244–70.

Kindleberger, C. P. (1996), *Manias, Panics, and Crashes: A History of Financial Crises* (3rd Edition, New York: John Wiley & Sons).

Kregal, J. A. (1998), 'East Asia is not Mexico: The Difference between Balance of Payments Crises and Debt Deflation', in K. S. Jomo (ed.), *Tigers in Trouble: Financial Governance, Liberalization, and Crisis in East Asia* (London: Zed Books), 44–62.

Krueger, A. O. (1984), 'Problems of Liberalization', in A. C. Harberger (ed.), *World Economic Growth* (San Francisco, Cal.: ICS Press).

Krugman, P. (1991), 'International Aspects of Financial Crises', in M. Feldstein (ed.), *The Risk of Economic Crisis* (Chicago: University of Chicago Press), 85–109.

Krugman, P. (ed.) (2000), *Currency Crises* (Chicago: University of Chicago Press).

Lardy, N. R. (1998), *China's Unfinished Economic Reforms* (Washington, DC: Brookings Institution).

McKinnon, R. I. (1998), 'Exchange Rate Coordination for Surmounting the East Asian Crisis', *Asian Economic Journal*, 12, 317–29.

Michaely, M., D. Papageorgiou and A. M. Choksi (1991), *Liberalizing Foreign Trade: Lessons of Experience in the Developing World* (Oxford: Basil Blackwell).

Miller, M. (1998), 'Asian Financial Crisis', *Japan and the World Economy*, 10, 355–58.

Mishkin, F. S. (1996), 'Understanding Financial Crises: A Developing Country Perspective', *Annual World Bank Conference on Development Economics*, 29–61.

Mishkin, F. S. (1997), 'The Causes and Propagation of Financial Instability: Lessons for Policy Makers', in Federal Reserve Bank of Kansas City, *Maintaining Financial Stability in a Global Economy* (Wyoming: Jackson Hole), 55–96.

Nidhiprabha, B. (1999), 'Economic Crises and the Debt Deflation Episode in Thailand', *ASEAN Economic Bulletin*, 15, 309–18.

Naughton, B. (1996), 'China's Emergence and Prospects as a Trading Nation', *Brookings Papers on Economic Activity*, 2, 293–344.

Noland, M., L-G. Liu, S. Robinson and Z. Wang (1998), *Global Economic Effects of the Asian Currency Devaluation* (Washington, DC: Institute of International Economics).

Radelet, S. and J. Sachs (1998), 'The East Asian Financial Crisis: Diagnosis, Remedies, Prospects', *Brookings Papers on Economic Activity*, 2, 1–89.

Rajan, R. S. (2001), '(Ir)relevance of Currency-Crisis Theory to the Devaluation and Collapse of the Thai Baht', *Princeton Studies in International Economics No. 58* (Princeton, NJ: International Economics Section, Department of Economics, Princeton University).

Sachs, J. D., A. Tornell and A. Velasco (1996), 'Financial Crises in Emerging Markets: The Lessons from 1995', *Brookings Papers on Economic Activity*, 1, 147–215.

Tobin, J. (1998), 'Asian Financial Crisis', *Japan and the World Economy*, 10, 351–53.

Wade, R. (1998), 'From "Miracle" to Cronyism: Explaining the Great Asian Slump', *Cambridge Journal of Economics*, 22, 4, 693–706.

Warr, P. G. (1986), 'Indonesia's Other Dutch Disease: Economic Effects of the Petroleum Boom', in J. P. Neary and S. van Wijnbergen (eds.), *Natural Resources and the Macroeconomy* (Oxford: Basil Blackwell), 288–320.

Warr, P. G. (1999), 'What Happened to Thailand?', *The World Economy*, 22, 7, 631–50.

Warr, P. G. (2000), 'Macroeconomic Origins of the Korean Crisis', in H. Smith (ed.), *Looking Forward: Korea After the Economic Crisis* (Asia Pacific Press, Canberra), 23–40.

Wei, S-J. and R. J. Zeckhauser (1998), 'Two Crises and Two Chinas', *Japan and the World Economy*, 10, 359–69.

Williamson, J. (1999) 'Development of the Financial System in Post-Crisis Asia', Paper presented at the High-Level Dialogue on Development Paradigms (10 December, Tokyo: Asian Development Bank Institute).

[6]

The political economy of international finance

Philip G. Cerny

Human relationships are principally made up of three elements. The first consists of relationships of power or force, of systematic patterns of conflict, domination and submission. The second consists of relationships of exchange, of 'truck and barter', as Adam Smith put it, which enable groups of people to accomplish things together through a division of labour which they could not do as solitary individuals. The third consists of relationships of affect, identity and culture, of social bonds with a special group of others who share kinship, common values, or mere close acquaintance – relationships of 'justice' and 'friendship', as Aristotle described them. Politics – sometimes seen as a fourth element – is the particular amalgam or compound of these different kinds of relationships, a conscious human construction which builds into an overarching, ongoing pattern of control of the process of mixing the other three elements. Institutionalized political systems are those patterns which reproduce themselves over time. The institutionalized political systems which we call 'states' are the complex structures which have evolved or have been established in the modern era in order to systematize and manage the blending of these three kinds of relationships.

In the course of modern history – over the past 500 years or so which have seen the emergence, consolidation and spread of the nation-state as the dominant organizational unit of world politics – feelings of affect, identity and citizenship have for the most part been appropriated by the nation-state through the development (and often the proactive inculcation) of national cultures. Despite the spread of such 20th century ideologies as Western capitalism and Soviet communism, nationalism has been the main cultural legacy of this period, as we have seen even more clearly since the fall of the Berlin Wall in 1989 as well as in the politics of the Third World. Institutionalized political systems, too, have increasingly taken the form of nation-states; international law and international regimes are the products of the politics of states and depend upon the continuing consent of governments.

The international system, by contrast, has primarily been the arena of the politics of military power, on the one hand, and of political economy, on the other. The first of these, the politics of military power (or 'security'), has been mainly characterized by the projection of the resources and goals of

3

4 Finance and world politics

domestically organized nation-states into the international arena. 'Collective security' at the international level is by definition fragile at best in a Hobbesian world of independent, self-regarding nation-states, and stabilization usually requires the presence of a balance of power among states seen as unitary agents.

Political economy is only contained with-difficulty within the national cage, and is only controlled with difficulty by a hierarchical state. Truck and barter between and across national boundaries existed long before nation-states emerged; they have constrained the way that states have developed; and they have been less and less amenable to state control, especially since the Second World War and the growth of a more open international economy. At the same time, markets have bypassed national regulations, command economies have collapsed and governments have seen Keynesian fine-tuning and the national welfare state undermined by import penetration and financial flows. Recently these changes have led state actors (bureaucrats and politicians) to try to transform political institutions and policy-making processes themselves into agents of internationalization, mainly in order to promote competitiveness.

In this context, international political economists have for the most part tended to focus on trade politics and the politics of production (the 'real economy') in explaining the dynamics of the international political economy – taking the American emphasis on free trade in the postwar period as the touchstone of its developing structure. In contrast, the authors in this book look to the political economy of international finance. We believe that there are certain characteristics of money and finance, and of the markets and other structures through which they flow, which give finance a critical role in shaping world politics. This is especially true of the late 20th century, when the main conflicts between powerful nation-states, conflicts rooted in the Cold War, have quite suddenly dissolved. But it has also been true of critical eras in the past.

I Money and world order
Money and finance today constitute an increasingly abstract representation of the process of exchange of goods and of values between human beings. Money has always represented an attempt to assess the *relative* value of things and ideas exchanged between people and groups of people, but until recently it also had an alternative life as a commodity itself – from simple coinage to its most advanced commodity form, the gold standard, by which the economic life of the 19th century in particular was organized and measured. Even then, however, lines in a bookkeeper's ledger were more important for a general understanding of the social, political and economic role of money than physical gold. At the end of the 20th century, money consists

primarily of electronic impulses stored in computer memories and transmitted instantaneously world-wide 24 hours a day – from the ubiquitous credit or debit cards of the ordinary consumer to massive minute-by-minute transfers in the international currency markets.[1] Money is not merely an economic phenomenon; like ideology, it is also a cultural phenomenon. Finance thus constitutes an intellectual challenge different in kind from most other structural issue areas in international relations.

The modest aim of this book is to provide an introduction to some of the problems and consequences which derive from the changing role of money in the world, and the way that that role interacts with other dimensions of society, politics and economics. A major theme of the book, taken up in different ways by all of the authors, is the way that developments in international and transnational finance – given that finance within countries is increasingly inseparable from finance between and cutting across countries – interact with changing relationships and structures of power in the international arena, in particular the question of *hegemony*. We live in a 'post-hegemonic' era, a period when it is no longer possible for any one hegemonic state (such as Britain in the late 19th century or the United States in the mid-20th) to provide the 'public goods' of political and economic stability to the world capitalist order (and to do so because it thinks it to be in its own interests). This situation has come about to a great extent because of the way that nation-states themselves, and therefore hegemony itself, are inextricably intertwined with the structure of international finance. Therefore we are not dealing just with money. Money 'dematerializes' other relationships, creating a 'structured field of action' within which they are linked together. Just as financial issues were at the core of the phenomenon (and also the theory) of hegemony, so they are also at the core of the problematic of 'post-hegemony' – what a post-hegemonic world order will be like.

In setting out the issues and perspectives represented in this volume, our approach is quite straightforward. In Part I, Chapters 1 and 2, we look at some of the background necessary for understanding, first, the academic and intellectual significance of finance in the wider arena of international relations (and political science) and, second, the problems and tensions built into the preceding epoch of international financial relations, the post-Second World War international financial system which was established at the Bretton Woods Conference in New Hampshire in 1944. In Part II, Chapters 3, 4 and 5, we examine some of the structural changes to international finance itself over a more recent period, the late 1980s and early 1990s. These changes all represent ongoing issues: the way that the internationalization of finance is intertwined with changes in systems and practices of financial regulation (deregulation and re-regulation) across different countries; the development of international cooperation between the main financial powers (the Group

6 Finance and world politics

of Seven, or G7); and the most significant attempt to establish a set of international rules for more open 'trade' in financial services which forms part of the Uruguay Round of the General Agreement on Tariffs and Trade (still unfinished at the time of writing). In Part III, Chapters 6, 7 and 8, the focus shifts to the main declining and rising financial powers themselves, the United States, Europe and Japan, looking both at the way their domestic financial systems interact with international finance and at what their changing fortunes may mean for the emerging global financial order – and for the international system in general.

The main theme shared by all of the authors is that the *control* of the way that finance flows around, through and between countries is at the core of the structure of the international system itself. So long as this systemic control – not so much power over particular market outcomes, but what Peter Vipond in Chapter 7 calls the capacity of the state to 'design' the structure of financial markets and systems – is in the hands of a particular state, especially a hegemonic state, then the government of that state has an unrivalled capacity to provide *stability* to the world economy. However, when that capacity is not only spread across several states, but also cross-cut and challenged by more autonomous transnational financial markets and linked financial structures, both hegemony and stabilization raise new questions and problems, concerns which are at the core of the issues addressed in this book.

Stability is probably the most important of all public goods for an international order without a supranational government. Of course military supremacy is an important part of the international stability equation, but it ultimately depends upon the threat of the direct application of force by the hegemonic state or by a group of states. Design control over the international financial system, however, as with other markets, simply establishes a set of rules for the interaction of myriad individuals, and day-to-day decision-making is decentralized to a wide range of market actors. Therefore while military force is clearly a 'top down' form of power, part of what Marx called the 'superstructure' of society, stable markets are inherently the sinews of the 'base' (or 'substructure' or 'infrastructure'), holding society together through myriad individual exchanges which feed back into the system itself and reinforce it.

There is thus a subtle relationship between the 'design capacity' of the state, which is undoubtedly part of the superstructure, and the stability of the base. On the one hand, design capacity needs to be exercised in a way which is stabilizing and not destabilizing; that is, it must be compatible with the development and intensification of decentralized market decision-making while maintaining allocative efficiency. But on the other hand, if market decision-making is in turn to be efficient and self-sustaining, it must itself be stable and not undermined, for example, by corrupt, market-distorting or monopolistic practices which feed back in destablizing ways into the system. Furthermore designing an international financial system is inherently problematic in the absence of an international 'state'. Although international 'regimes' such as the Bretton Woods system can develop a certain amount of legitimacy and authority, their autonomy can be fragile under systematic pressure.

II   Political economy, finance and international relations

Several features of this problematic relationship between finance and world order are addressed by the authors in this volume. The first is the relationship of the abstract financial economy to the economy of material production, 'making things', often called the 'real economy'. Economists and economic historians are divided over this issue. Some see a 'free' and open financial system as the ultimate guarantee of allocative efficiency throughout the economic system, as money will spontaneously flow into its most productive and profitable uses. Others see such an open financial economy as a potential drag on the productive economy, because money can be made so easily from the trading of money; thus a 'free' financial market system may crowd a significant amount of money out of less profitable but more productive uses (meeting real demands and needs in society) and into what is called *rentier* capital. The frequent charges of 'short-termism' levelled against open financial markets, as well as the accusation of 'churning', where brokers keep buying and selling the same financial instruments and take a profit each time, are characteristic of the latter view. If financial capital is indeed parasitic in this way, then the design capacity of the system must be highly interventionist in such a way as to channel money into more materially productive uses.

But the issue of the 'financial economy' versus the 'real economy' goes much further, indeed to the heart of the world order. For it leads into the fundamental question of how power and order are established and maintained in the first place, and how they decay. As we have already mentioned, it is commonplace nowadays to agree that international relations are played out on two analytically distinct and structurally contrasting kinds of arenas, 'playing fields' or 'structured fields of action'. The first is that constituted by military power and political *Realpolitik*; the second comprises the international political economy.[2] In the first arena, the currency of control – power, influence and system stability – is physical force. Of course the amount, usability and effectiveness of physical force derive from a more complex set of factors, including size, geopolitical location, economic resources, a cultural sense of the 'national interest' and the autonomous political will of 'state actors' (bureaucrats and politicians). But the fundamental organizing

8   Finance and world politics

unit is the nation-state. The international system is one of Hobbesian 'anarchy', although based on anarchy among states rather than anarchy among individuals. This has several behavioural consequences.[3]

This world of force and power, usually referred to in academic international relations as the question of 'security', therefore most clearly reflects the division of the planet into nation-states. Without an overarching state-like structure of collective security at supranational level to hold an *international* 'monopoly of legitimate violence', the preeminent unitary actor has indeed been the most institutionalized form of political system, the nation-state. Defending the national territory is usually seen as the primary and indeed overriding duty, responsibility or function of the state itself, that is, of the institutions of the state and of the various office holders ('state actors') who occupy positions of authority within those institutions. The concept of the 'national interest' is the overriding criterion for decision-making in this sphere. Furthermore, given that domestically the state claims the 'monopoly of legitimate violence' within the territory (to use Max Weber's famous term), this means that structures of force established by the domestic state – essentially the armed forces – are organized in a very hierarchical fashion. Indeed the military is normally by far the most hierarchical bureaucratic structure within the state.

Therefore the structure of international security is predominantly one of conflict and cooperation between states, states which are first and foremost self-interested and self-regarding. In this context, security relationships have a high potential for instability. Alliances are by definition conditional (even if they can in some circumstances lead to more complex and long-term bonds); in effect, 'the enemy of my enemy is my friend'. Ensuring national security often seems to require an increase in armaments and military preparedness, but this can actually reduce national security if other nation-states do it too. In such a case it may lead either to destabilization or to outright conflict. This is what is called the 'security dilemma', and is characterized by arms racing. Different manifestations of the security dilemma are often seen, for example, as the main cause of the First World War and at the core of the politics of nuclear weapons in the Cold War.

The structure of international security itself is usually seen to derive from the interaction of two dimensions of power: hierarchy and polarity. The first of these, the hierarchy of international power – the pecking order of nation-states in the security arena – is based primarily on the possession of military and related strategic resources. The better endowed states will usually have disproportionate influence over outcomes in the system, although the elements of national interest (with its part of domestic input) and of national will (with its national culture component) are also significant features. Where the more powerful states can effectively impose their will on the less power-

ful, a certain stabilization will occur. However a sufficient disparity in resources to establish effective dominance in and of itself is unlikely to occur,
given the existence of a multiplicity of states with different levels of power
resources. Alliances, technological developments and changes in the conception of the national interest can also occur which may upset any precarious stability based solely on the hierarchy of military power.

Within the resource givens of this hierarchy, however, the second dimension of power and security comes into play. Certain configurations of powerful states can crystallize into relatively stable 'balances of power', in effect
system equilibria. The way that a *bipolar* balance of power works – its
dynamics – will be familiar not only from the recent Cold War but also from
Thucydides's classical treatment of the Peloponnesian Wars between Athens
and Sparta. The dynamics of multipolar balances of power (for there are
several variations) are most familiar from the period from the end of the
Napoleonic Wars until the First World War, when relative stability gradually
deteriorated into general war, and from the period between the two world
wars, when a more extreme form of multipolarity undermined all attempts to
balance the system.

Ultimately, then, the stabilization of power relations in a system based on
independent nation-states depends upon the emergence of a configuration of
power in which the dimensions of hierarchy and polarity fuse into a working
balance of power. When that balance decays, or when the actors reach a
point when dynamics inherent in the balance itself lead to destabilization –
as with the outbreak of the First World War, or with a perceived need in a
crisis to end a cycle of arms racing by actually using the weapons previously
acquired – then military conflict is the ultimate sanction. Military conflict
itself is also a balancing mechanism, of course; wars are often seen as the
main historical cauldrons in which new systemic balances can emerge. Despite the tendency to conflict inherent in a system of independent nation-
states, however, states themselves desire first and foremost to survive. Therefore, although they may wish to abandon a particular balance of power when
circumstances suggest that a certain configuration is (or has become) inimi-
cal to the national interest, in fact they will usually be constrained by the
danger of self-destruction from going too far.

III Structural dynamics of international finance

The structural dynamics of the international political economy are usually
seen to be quite different from those of the security order. But the question
is, how different? As we will see later in the book, some analysts borrow
quite heavily from security-based conceptions of world politics, and argue
that the international political economy is also primarily organized around
the need for cooperative or equilibrium outcomes among states, states which

10   Finance and world politics

are primarily self-regarding in economic terms in a way that is analogous to their behaviour in the security arena. Others, including those in this book, argue that international economic relations are increasingly difficult to shoe-horn into the nation-state mould – that they are neither domestically hierarchical nor capable of being insulated from the outside world, and that they in fact increasingly cut across and even ignore national boundaries. Although modern capitalism is the product of the emergence of the nation-state, as competing national elites (starting in Europe and spreading throughout the world) sought to increase their wealth as well as their military power, dramatic increases in transnational economic interpenetration and interdependence, especially in the 19th century and again after the hiatus of the Great Depression and the Second World War, have led to a vast expansion of international markets, multinational corporations, foreign direct investment, continually growing trade, and an international financial system of unrivalled scope and complexity.[4]

In this context, the authors in this volume are fundamentally in agreement that the most international, the most transnationalized and the most constraining structure in the international political economy is international finance. Finance is the 'infrastructure of the infrastructure', the most integrated 'playing field' in the world order. This is not to say that finance is wholly international or cosmopolitan. It is merely to say that it is the *most* integrated aspect, relatively speaking, of the international system. Two interrelated problematics, then, arise from this unique position of finance for our understanding the relationship between finance and the world order: in the first place, there is an ongoing tug-of-war between national governments and transnationalized markets for control of the design of the international financial system (and therefore of the domestic systems which are inextricably intertwined with it); and in the second place, the relationship outlined earlier between the financial economy and the real economy is a long way from being resolved.

The authors in this book, to a greater or lesser extent and with some differences of emphasis, argue that the transnationalization of finance has not only become an *autonomous* process – in Margaret Thatcher's words, that 'You can't buck the markets' – but also that in a range of highly significant ways it is actually *in the ascendancy over the real economy*. In this sense, then, the development of the transnational financial structure is setting growing constraints on both state and private actors, increasingly subordinating both government intervention and industrial decision-making to specifically financial criteria and norms. Indeed some authors here go so far as to suggest that the transnationalization of finance is at the heart of the booms, slumps and austerity policies of the 1980s and 1990s.

These changes in the salience and impact of international finance lead to the issue of whether (and how) financial systems are actually constituted at the international level. Given that there is no broadly supranational state at the global level, about the only way to set up, maintain and adapt such systems might seem to be through the interaction of the most powerful nation-states, however episodic or incomplete. The classical answers of 'realist' and 'neo-realist' international relations theorists would involve some form of cooperation between a concert of leading states with common interests in the economic expansion of the international capitalist system and the enforced acquiescence of the rest. However history and the application of a form of collective action theory derived from the seminal work of Mancur Olson[5] have suggested that this form of collective action is difficult to maintain and enforce because of the unwillingness of at least some of the actors involved to pay their share of the costs of cooperation.[6]

Instead several prominent writers (following Olson) have argued that the most likely way that cooperation could be sustained would be in cases where one actor was both (a) disproportionately endowed with resources so as to be *able* to pay the costs by itself and (b) *willing* to provide the requisite 'public goods' by itself alone because it judges the benefits to itself to sufficiently outweigh the costs. This, in terms of international relations theory, is what is meant by neo-realist writers when they speak of 'hegemony'. As we shall see later in the book, 'hegemonic stability theory' (HST), also called the 'theory of hegemonic stability' (THS), has been adopted by many analysts in recent years as a seemingly powerful tool in attempting to explain how the international financial system has been designed and maintained during key periods of modern history.

IV   The critique of hegemonic stability and the transnationalization of finance

The writers in this book, however, are broadly critical of hegemonic stability theory. They adduce a number of arguments for this stance. In the first place, they suggest that, although British hegemony in the 19th century and American hegemony in the 20th were real and significant phenomena, they represented not the automatic translation of material power resources into financial control, but rather a specific conjunction of social, economic and political forces during particular historical epochs. These social forces comprised not only state actors and domestic interests but also international markets and other transnational economic structures.

Indeed, the economic historian Karl Polanyi, writing in his seminal work, *The Great Transformation*, in 1944 (cited in different ways by several of the writers in this volume), argued that in the late 19th century, the period often labelled as one of 'British hegemony' was actually controlled not by Britain

12   Finance and world politics

or by the British state *per se*, but by a market-like network or structure of powerful financial market actors which may have been centred in London but which stretched around the financial world. Britain of course played a key role in making the system work, but this wider network, which Polanyi called *haute finance*, was essentially a transnational one, cutting across British, French and other financial systems and tying them into a set of international norms and practices, underpinned by the gold standard. In this book, too, Eric Helleiner (Chapter 2) shows how such a more complex analysis provides a much fuller and more accurate picture of the period which saw the emergence of 'American hegemony' after the Second World War. Thus the wider international 'power' of Britain and America respectively, while a significant part of the equation, was certainly not the whole of the picture and was in many ways as much effect as cause.

In the second place, they argue that system change over the past 25 years or so has resulted not from a decline of America or American hegemony *per se*; rather the equation of cause and effect has been the other way around. American decline has been the consequence of changes in the transnational market structure. Of course these changes have themselves resulted from the very success of the sorts of policies pursued by the United States during the postwar period, when the United States was by far the predominant economic and financial power in the world, and therefore American hegemony (it is agreed) did broadly exist in the international economic and financial system. In these circumstances, the 'economic war aims' and postwar goals of the United States were permeated with three sorts of belief about the role of economics and finance in the world order. There was first a consciousness which came to the fore through the group which called themselves 'internationalists' within the Roosevelt Administration in the 1930s that a successful and peaceful international order had to be based on an open international trading system which would permit capitalism to expand and would avoid the closing of economic borders characteristic of the Great Depression, of fascism and of Stalinism.[7] Furthermore there was a belief that such a system needed to be *institutionalized at an international level*, that is, that it was not sufficient for a hegemonic power like 19th-century Britain to provide informal guarantees, because mercantilist rivals would be too powerful (as shown by the experience of the First World War and the interwar period). Finally there was an elite awareness that the United States had to use its disproportionate economic and political power in the aftermath of the Second World War to establish and to guarantee such a system, at least until it was up and running by itself.

American hegemony, therefore, along with the new hegemony within the United States of anti-isolationists or internationalists in both of the major American political parties (bipartisanship) as well as within the Administration, was indeed essential for the establishment and guaranteeing of the new international economic system. At the same time, however, that system itself was supposed to work at arm's length. As it increasingly did so, with the recovery of Europe and Japan and a boom in world trade, the United States became more and more ambivalent about some of the consequences of the system it had set up. The key to the structure was the system of fixed exchange rates, based on the United States' willingness to guarantee the value of the dollar in gold. But as the dollar itself came under increasing pressure from other countries in the late 1960s to be devalued – for reasons dealt with in more detail by the authors in this volume – the United States unilaterally abrogated the Bretton Woods system.[8]

The subsequent move, after 1971, to a system of floating exchange rates, which had the support of the newly fashionable monetarist economists in the early 1970s, essentially created a totally new situation for the international economic and financial systems. Although in the short run, in the 1970s, it led to an outbreak of 'neo-mercantilism' and attempts to impose new forms of protectionism, its most important consequence was the freeing of *financial* exchanges from the disciplines of the fixed exchange rate system. The shift to floating exchange rates thus led to an explosion of financial flows, the deregulation of domestic financial systems, experiments in international financial crisis management and a variety of attempts to develop new partial and global regimes (for example, the European Monetary System and the General Agreement on Trade in Services, respectively) for the regulation of international finance.

The key to change, therefore, was not the decline in US hegemony as such, but the crystallization and consolidation of genuinely *transnational* and increasingly autonomous financial markets. These came to be more and more important with regard to financial transactions in general, both in terms of volume of transactions and in terms of the structure of the financial marketplace itself. These changes were not so much the results of decisions by states, but rather, as Susan Strange has argued, the consequence of a series of *non-decisions*; the real agent of change was the transnationalization of markets themselves.[9] Furthermore, interstate cooperation in the changing of market structures was a marginal factor; the failure in 1971–3 to agree on a workable system of managed exchange rates to replace the Bretton Woods arrangements undermined serious cooperation in these matters for nearly 15 years (and, as Stephen Gill shows in Chapter 4, such cooperation is still highly circumscribed and fragile).

The neo-realist logic of collective action was thus turned on its head in the financial arena, and unilateral deregulatory decisions led to a widening circle of deregulation across countries, regions and the globe. In this structural sense, then, the authors in this volume argue that the very concept of he-

14   Finance and world politics

gemony must be reassessed. To say that American hegemony was (and perhaps could only be) of the 'arms-length' variety in the postwar period is not to deny that the American role in setting up and guaranteeing the Bretton Woods system was perhaps the key *conjunctural* factor in its early success, but merely to argue that the key *structural* factor in its success was rather different. This structural durability lay in the way that the system was capable of being transformed over time into, and ultimately replaced by, a more and more transnationalized financial system based on an increasingly autonomous international financial market-place.

V   The transnationalization of finance and the power of the state

The final criticism of hegemonic stability theory in the book is much simpler, and derives from the first two. This is the view that in future the hegemony, not merely of any one nation-state, but of any nation-states *per se*, is increasingly unlikely. Any future national control would be limited, indirect and constrained to conform to the imperatives of the transnational financial markets. Within this context, the United States, despite its market power and the role of its deficit financing in setting the pace for certain markets, is too internally fragmented in terms of its political institutions, regulatory system and interest group structure to exercise much influence on the transnational financial structure. The European Community, similarly, despite the coming of the European Financial Area and the Single Market, certainly seems to lack hegemonic potential, as Peter Vipond shows. The EC not only suffers in terms of political authority from continuing divisions between the member states and Brussels, but has also found that the goal of monetary union has so far been both a bone of contention (with Britain's 'opt-out' enshrined in the Maastricht Agreement, now itself in doubt) and a fragile reed (with the withdrawal of sterling from the Exchange Rate Mechanism). Japan may still be gaining in financial power relatively speaking, as Eric Helleiner argues in Chapter 8, but its future influence is problematic and is likely to be exercised in such a way as to reinforce, rather than undermine or alter, the wider international financial structure.

At the same time that the influence of particular states is waning, furthermore, processes of transnationalization are proceeding apace. These processes are not, however, developing primarily through the establishment of international regimes to coordinate cooperation. Although a General Agreement on Trade in Services, as Geoffrey Underhill argues, would ratify changes already in progress and further level the playing field somewhat, it would not represent a qualitative leap forward. The G7, as Stephen Gill shows, may develop an increasing role in crisis management, but is not coherent enough to be the focus for a new round of international cooperation which would lead to the emergence of an effective regime in the financial field. However he does think that the influence of transnational financial capital is growing, and may increasingly affect G7 through both private and public elite networks in the future. Finally, of course, such existing groups as the Bank for International Settlements (BIS), despite the relative success of the 1988 Basle international capital adequacy standards for banks, and the International Organization of Securities Commissions (IOSCO) lack the autonomous political authority to act effectively.

Indeed, the main motor force of change, as the present writer argues in Chapter 3, is the increasing transnational integration and competitive deregulation/re-regulation of financial markets themselves. As currency and securities are more and more traded internationally, as multinational firms seek increasingly to speculate and hedge their financial resources, as foreign direct investment continues to expand, and as banking systems diversify and banks have to compete on an ever-widening international scale, the cycle of deregulation – reluctantly supported and sometimes even promoted by the state – will continue to widen. Governments, international regimes and regulatory authorities within governments will increasingly come to be 'whipsawed' between different sectors and firms in the financial services industry seeking the most amenable regulators and the most permissive rules – what is called 'regulatory arbitrage' or 'competition in laxity'. Governments will be internally split and different 'state actors' linked into different policy communities will increasingly operate within *transnational networks*, with securities regulators establishing networks with securities regulators abroad as well as with (often multinational) securities firms, competing with similar networks among banking regulators or insurance regulators and their pressure group constituencies and so on.[10] In addition deregulation may complicate these networks further as markets are further decompartmentalized. And even where the state does try to make authoritative economic policy (under the pressure of growing democratic demands) that policy will be circumscribed by ever-tighter financial considerations in the quest to boost international financial competitiveness – anti-inflationary policies, tax cuts and incentives, spending cuts and generally trying to 'get more out of less'.

Polanyi argued that markets are created by states in order to promote the general creation of wealth; that the self-regulating markets which states have attempted to design are liable to distortions, failures and widespread social injustices; and that states, in turn, must always attempt to find new ways to control markets to limit those distortions, failures and injustices. In effect, the Keynesian welfare state which grew out of the experiences of the 1930s and 1940s was the product of governments' attempts to do just that in order to counteract the potential dangers of a new world slump. But in a world of transnationalized finance, a world in which 'competition states' have lost the power to use a range of financial controls and policy instruments to shape

16   *Finance and world politics*

and promote economic development, who is to counteract the failures of the
new *haute finance*?

VI   Financial transnationalization and the future of government policy

There are somewhat different stances on this vital question taken by the
authors of this book, although all agree that it looks like a labour of Sisyphus.
Broadly speaking, some authors are more optimistic, some more pessimistic.
Among them, Stephen Gill is broadly pessimistic, but even so suggests that
perhaps the elites of the new transnational financial structure will in the end
influence governments to cooperate in a strengthened G7. Eric Helleiner
suggests that Japan, although not a fully-fledged hegemon in the neo-realist
sense, will increasingly exert a stabilizing influence on the system. Geoffrey
Underhill and Peter Vipond are fairly agnostic, seeing an ongoing politics of
negotiation both within and across borders. The present writer sees states
themselves as increasingly fragmented and constrained by the imperatives of
international financial competition.

What is interesting in this environment is the way that politicians, bureaucrats and policy analysts are beginning to look for approaches which will
enable them to cope more effectively with the new financial constraints.
Probably the most interesting aspect of the campaign and economic ideas of
President Bill Clinton in the United States is his focus on reducing and
streamlining the size and operation of government bureaucracies while actually *strengthening* processes of 'governance' or 'steering' through recurrent
contracting and systematic monitoring of the performance of highly flexible
bureaucracies.[11] This is the result of an attempt by a range of policy analysts
to assimilate into policy-making and policy implementation theory the lessons of 'flexible manufacturing systems' in industry.[12] At the same time,
following the approach outlined by his advisor Robert Reich, Clinton is
suggesting that government policy should also focus on state promotion of
'immobile factors of capital' – essentially infrastructure and 'human capital'
such as education and training (especially those oriented towards the high
value-added end of the Third Industrial Revolution) – rather than trying
directly to influence more mobile factors such as the direct promotion of
finance and industry.[13] In other countries, however, attempts to cope with the
new financial constraints have either been seen as part of the wider free-
market approach of Reaganomics and Thatcherism characteristic of the 1980s,
or have been grafted onto neo-corporatist structures, as in Scandinavia. At
the international level, too, we are beginning to hear growing calls from
politicians, bureaucrats, journalists and academics for the creation and/or
strengthening of international regulatory regimes, including the BIS.

But whether or not any of these approaches is successful in dealing with the transnational financial structure remains to be seen. In the shorter term, government policy is likely to consist at best of various forms of muddling through, partial experimentation and reactive rather than proactive attempts to deal with the new constraints in practice. Unlike the 1920s, however, and in spite of a strong belief to the contrary in the 1980s embodied in the views of Ronald Reagan and Margaret Thatcher, there seems to be a widespread recognition today of the importance of the state's role in the design of markets and the maintenance of stability. In contrast to the early 1930s, too, there is a widespread awareness that neo-mercantilism and protectionism are increasingly counterproductive. What is most different from the Keynesian welfare state pattern, however, is a sense that the state itself is not somehow set apart from the market, that there is not a rigid distinction between 'market' and 'hierarchy', but rather a range of mixes between the two which includes the state itself.[14] The private sector is not always characterized by efficient competitive behaviour (indeed it is often the vehicle of greed and monopoly) and the state is not merely a vehicle for protective cartels and special interests. Indeed, in recent years, probably the most significant trend is the 'commodification' or 'marketization' of the state apparatus itself in the pursuit of international competitiveness – what has elsewhere been called the 'competition state'.[15] This means that the state has become an agent of its own transformation. But it is perhaps in the arena of finance that the state has been most fully 'marketized': in its regulatory systems, in its economic policy and in its very organizational structure.

VII   Conclusions: finance and world politics

Finance, we argue in this book, constitutes the 'infrastructure of the infrastructure' – the structural bottom line or most significant common denominator (although certainly not the lowest) within the international political economy. The control of finance has always been one of the major functions of national state apparatuses, and the transnationalization of finance has led – in the mid-to-late 19th century, in the 1920s and today – to severe problems for the maintenance of political stability and economic growth. In the 19th century, these problems were for a time solved by a system which was partially held together through British hegemony, but the growth of more mercantilist forms of competition and the beginnings of Britain's long economic decline led to the failure of the system in the First World War and to futile attempts to reconstruct it afterwards. In the 1920s, these problems were not solved but indeed made worse, as the 1929 Wall Street Crash demonstrated; the 1930s were subsequently characterized by a vicious circle of destabilization and slump, only partly relieved by corporatist and Keynesian experiments prior to the Second World War. In the late 1980s and early

18   Finance and world politics

1990s, too, a tenacious recession and the volatility of financial flows have provided a contrast both to the bubble boom of the mid-1980s and to the long boom from the end of the 1940s to the early 1970s.

The transnationalization of finance, however, has taken on a more wide-spread and structurally complex form in the late 20th century. National security considerations have diminished in importance over several decades, and the end of the Cold War has underlined just how far this process has gone. In political economy, governments have promoted the transnationalization of finance, while ongoing processes of deregulatory competition since the collapse of Bretton Woods have expanded international financial markets in myriad directions and circumscribed the scope and power of the state not just in financial regulation but in economic policy more generally. Furthermore economic linkages have been increasingly shaped by financial imperatives, as the financial economy calls the tune for the real economy, whether in terms of short-term financial flows, patterns of investment, the restructuring of industries and markets, or the contours of state economic intervention. Finally, in the international political economy, whether in terms of markets, regimes or states, the transnationalization of finance has developed its own autonomous structural dynamic, a dynamic with regard to which international politics has yet to find a workable consensus on objectives or a feasible method of control. Indeed one might say, echoing Cordell Hull, that the world order follows the financial order.

Notes

1. Susan Strange, 'Finance, Information and Power', *Review of International Studies*, **16**, (3), (July 1990), pp. 259–74.
2. See James N. Rosenau, *Turbulence in World Politics: A Theory of Change and Continuity*, Princeton, NJ: Princeton University Press, 1990.
3. Cf. Hedley Bull, *The Anarchical Society: A Study of Order in World Politics*, London: Macmillan, 1977 and Kenneth Waltz, *Theory of International Politics*, Reading, MA: Addison-Wesley, 1979.
4. For an exploration of this transnationalization process and a development of the concept of 'transnational structures', see Susan Strange, *States and Markets: An Introduction to International Political Economy*, London: Pinter, 1988.
5. Mancur Olson, *The Logic of Collective Action*, Cambridge, MA: Harvard University Press, 1971.
6. For a recent exploration of these issues which argues that the possibilities of collective action in a multipolar system are perhaps greater than other analysts would suggest, see Robert O. Keohane, *After Hegemony: Cooperation and Discord in the World Political Economy*, Princeton, NJ: Princeton University Press, 1984.
7. See Lloyd C. Gardner, *Economic Aspects of New Deal Diplomacy*, Boston, MA: Beacon Press, 1971.
8. See Fred L. Block, *The Origins of International Economic Disorder: A Study of United States Monetary Policy from World War II to the Present*, Berkeley and Los Angeles: University of California Press, 1977.
9. Susan Strange, *Casino Capitalism*, Oxford and New York: Basil Blackwell, 1986.
10. Analogous tendencies have been observed in a range of issue areas, including high technology and the chemicals industry.

11. See David Osborne and Ted Gaebler, *Reinventing Government: How the Entrepre-neurial Spirit is Transforming the Public Sector, from Schoolhouse to Statehouse, City Hall to the Pentagon*, Reading, MA: Addison-Wesley, 1992.

12. See Michael J. Piore and Charles F. Sabel, *The Second Industrial Divide: Possibilities for Prosperity*, New York: Basic Books, 1984.

13. See Robert Reich, *The Work of Nations: Preparing Ourselves for 21st-Century Capital-ism*, New York: Alfred A. Knopf, 1991.

14. As well as, for example, 'networks'; see Grahame Thompson, Jennifer Frances, Rosalind Levačic and Jeremy Mitchell (eds), *Markets, Hierarchies and Networks: The Coordina-tion of Social Life*, London and Newbury Park, CA: Sage Publications, 1991. I would argue, however, that networks are only one of a wide range of structures which blend and fuse the analytically polar ideal types of 'market' and 'hierarchy'.

15. P.G. Cerny, *The Changing Architecture of Politics: Structure, Agency and the Future of the State*, London and Newbury Park, CA: Sage Publications, 1990, especially Ch. 8.

[7]

Review of International Political Economy 2:2 Spring 1995: 315–41

Explaining the globalization of financial markets: bringing states back in

Eric Helleiner

Department of Political Studies, Trent University

ABSTRACT

Many accounts of the globalization of financial markets over the past three decades explain it as a product of unstoppable technological and market forces. This article emphasizes that the behaviour of states was also of central importance in encouraging and permitting the process. States are shown to have supported financial globalization in three ways: (1) granting freedom to market actors through liberalization initiatives; (2) preventing major international financial crises; and (3) choosing not to implement more effective controls on financial movements. These roles are illustrated historically through a description of five sets of episodes since the late 1950s. States are found to have increasingly embraced the globalization trend because of: a competitive deregulation dynamic, political difficulties associated with the implementation of more effective capital controls, the 'hegemonic' interests of the US and Britain, the growing domestic prominence of neoliberal advocates and internationally-oriented corporate interests, and the unusually cooperative nature of central bank interaction.

KEYWORDS

Finance; globalization; states; money; liberalization; capital.

The globalization of financial markets over the past three decades has been one of the most spectacular developments in the postwar global political economy. Since the 1960s, cross-border movements of private capital have grown from almost nothing to a volume where they now dwarf international trade flows. This development has been all the more striking when it is recalled that the 'constitution' of the postwar international monetary and financial order – the Bretton Woods Agreement – strongly endorsed the use of capital controls. The Bretton Woods architects had explicitly sought to prevent global financial markets from reassuming the dominant role they had held in the global political

ARTICLES

economy in the decades before the 1931 international financial collapse (Helleiner 1993).

Discussions of the globalization of financial markets often explain it as a product of unstoppable technological and market forces. In the words of Walter Wriston:

> we are witnessing a galloping new system of international finance. Our new international financial regime differs radically from its precursors in that it was not built by politicians, economists, central bankers or finance ministers ... It was built by technology ... [by] men and women who interconnected the planet with telecommunications and computers.
>
> (Wriston 1988: 71)

Although technological and market forces were important, this dismissal of the role of political choices and state behaviour seems simplistic to a student of international political economy (IPE). At the very least, as Morgan Guaranty's vice-president, Rimmer De Vries reminded the US Congress in the early 1970s, it is clear that 'every participant in the [international financial] market ... is a resident of some country and thus falls under the control or potential controls or supervision of its monetary authorities' (US Congress 1971: 4).

In recent years, a growing number of IPE scholars have begun to demonstrate the specific roles played by states in the globalization of finance. To date, however, there has been no synthetic 'political' history of the globalization of financial markets that explains exactly how and why states were important to the overall process. After briefly explaining why little private international financial activity existed in the period between the 1930s and late 1950s, I sketch the outlines of such a history in this article.[1] I argue that states can be seen to have played three key roles in the globalization process: (1) granting freedom to market actors through liberalization initiatives; (2) preventing major international financial crises; and (3) choosing not to implement more effective controls on financial movements. These three roles are illustrated through a brief description of five sets of historical episodes over the last three decades. The article concludes by summarizing the factors that explain the growing enthusiasm of states for the financial globalization process: a competitive deregulation dynamic, political difficulties associated with the implementation of more effective capital controls, the 'hegemonic' interests of the US and Britain, the growing domestic prominence of neoliberal advocates and internationally-oriented corporate interests, and the unusually cooperative nature of central bank interaction.

GLOBALIZATION OF FINANCIAL MARKETS

THE MID-CENTURY ORDER: A WORLD WITHOUT PRIVATE GLOBAL FINANCE

It is important to note that from a long historical perspective there is nothing unusual about the existence of international financial markets. Bankers in eighteenth century Amsterdam or nineteenth century London, for example, moved enormous sums of private financial capital around the world with a level of expertise similar in many ways to their present-day counterparts. Indeed, the financial sector has traditionally been the most internationalized sector of economic life. What was unusual, however, was a period – one might call it the 'mid-century order' – lasting from the 1930s until the late 1950s when there was little private global financial activity. To understand the politics involved in the re-emergence of global finance, it is necessary first to look at why private global financial activity was so limited in these mid-century years.

One explanation concerns the behaviour of market actors. In the wake of the international financial crisis of 1931, private financial operators lost confidence in the safety and profitability of international financial activity. The economic and political upheavals of the next two decades then did little to restore it. The emergence of cartelized domestic financial structures across the advanced industrial world in the 1930s also bred a kind of inward-looking financial conservatism that discouraged interest in international financial activity among market actors.

State behaviour was equally important in inhibiting international private financial activity in the mid-century years. In the decades before the 1930s, a largely liberal order had existed with respect to the international movements of private finance. When capital controls had been used, they had always been employed in a limited and temporary fashion and generally for the strategic purpose of preventing unfriendly states from borrowing in domestic capital markets. In the wake of the 1931 international financial collapse, and particularly after the outbreak of the Second World War, this liberal regime collapsed. States began to experiment with increasingly *comprehensive* systems of capital controls, and such controls came to be seen as a *permanent* feature of their foreign economic policies. The new financial interventionism was then confirmed by the 1944 Bretton Woods Agreement which granted countries the explicit 'right' to use capital controls. Following this lead, almost all advanced industrial states employed extensive capital controls throughout the early postwar years. Even US policymakers, who did not employ capital controls in the 1940s and 1950s, were remarkably accepting of the use of capital controls abroad. They made little effort in these years to encourage financial liberalization in Japan and Western Europe. Moreover, when European governments finally restored the

317

ARTICLES

convertibility of their currencies in 1958, the US also fully supported their decisions to restrict this convertibility to the current account.[2]

Why were states across the advanced industrial world so sceptical of the virtues of a liberal international financial order in this period? The widespread enthusiasm for capital controls was largely a product of a kind of structural break in financial affairs which took place in the wake of the financial crises of the early 1930s. Discredited by the crises, the private and central bankers who had dominated financial politics before the 1930s were increasingly replaced at the levers of financial power by a new class of professional economists and state managers whose social base was among labour and national industrial leaders. In place of the bankers' *laissez-faire* ideology, these new social groups favoured more interventionist policies that would make finance the 'servant' and not the 'master' of political and economic life (Helleiner 1993).

The chief negotiators at Bretton Woods, John Maynard Keynes and Harry Dexter White, both representatives of this new class, explained particularly well the two central reasons why controls on international capital movements were now seen as necessary. First, as Keynes put it, 'massive sweeping and highly capricious transfers of short-term funds . . . constituted a major source of damage to the international monetary system' (quoted in Bloomfield 1946: 687–8). Such capital flows would need to be controlled if a stable set of exchange rates was to be maintained. Second, capital controls were needed to prevent speculative international financial movements from disrupting the policy autonomy of the new Keynesian welfare state. Keynes, for example, noted that: 'the whole management of the domestic economy depends on being free to have the appropriate rate of interest without reference to the rate prevailing elsewhere in the world. Capital control is a corollary to this' (Keynes 1980: 148–9). Similarly, White argued that capital flight motivated by political reasons or by the desire to escape the 'burdens of social legislation' had to be prevented from operating 'against what the government deemed to be the interests of any country' (Horsefield 1969: 31–2, 67). Although both acknowledged that capital controls would interfere with desirable 'productive' and 'equilibrating' capital movements, this was seen as the necessary cost of protecting stable exchange rates and especially the welfare state from speculative and 'disequilibrating' flows. In this sense, 'embedded liberalism' (Ruggie 1982) in the financial sphere was tilted heavily in the 'embedded' direction.

HOW DID WE GET FROM THERE TO HERE? FIVE SETS OF EPISODES

Many explanations of the re-emergence of global finance from this restrictive mid-century order stress the role played by technological and

GLOBALIZATION OF FINANCIAL MARKETS

market factors.[3] Technological developments, especially the growth of global telecommunications networks, are shown to have dramatically reduced the costs and difficulties involved in transferring funds globally. Important market developments are said to include: the restoration of private confidence in international financial transactions in the late 1950s; the growth of multinational corporations from the 1960s onwards; the response of market actors in the 1970s to the introduction of the floating exchange rate system and the 1973 oil price rise; and finally the competitive pressures emerging out of the unravelling of domestic cartelized financial structures across the advanced industrial world in the 1970s and 1980s.

According to these accounts, states have played a marginal role in the overall globalization process. They are said to have been forced to accept these technological and market pressures because of the enormous difficulties involved in controlling international movements of finance, difficulties that stem from the fact that finance is the most easily disguised and inexpensive of commodities to transport. Technological developments and increased economic integration in recent years are said to have only multiplied the channels for evasion for market operators. It has, thus, become common to argue that the endorsement of capital controls in the Bretton Woods Agreement was largely useless in that it misjudged the ability of states to control financial movements.

In this section, I argue that this attempt to diminish the importance of states needs to be challenged. I suggest that states can be seen to have played three central roles in the globalization process. First, they gave market actors much more freedom to operate than they would otherwise have had by liberalizing and removing barriers to the international movement of private financial capital. Second, through international lender-of-last-resort activities and international prudential regulation and supervision, states played a crucial role in containing and preventing international financial crises, crises which might otherwise have brought down the emerging global financial order. Third and most controversially, I argue that states might have tried to control capital movements more effectively than they did. This last point requires a brief elaboration. Although it is true that there are many difficulties in controlling financial movements, it is worth noting that Keynes and White argued that these could have been overcome in one of two ways: (1) through the use of *comprehensive exchange controls* in which all international transactions were monitored for illegal financial flows or (2) through cooperative measures in which all states agreed to *cooperate in enforcing each other's capital controls*. Both of these mechanisms, albeit in a somewhat watered down form, found their way into the final Bretton Woods Agreements (Helleiner 1993), and an explanation must be found for why

ARTICLES

states chose to employ them in an effort to render their capital controls more effective.[4]

The three roles that states played in supporting the globalization process can be highlighted by outlining five sets of episodes in the last three decades.

1 Early support for the Euromarket from the US and Britain

The first – an episode in which market actors were granted an extra degree of freedom – involved the support provided by certain states for the emergence of the Euromarket in the 1960s. Since the history of the market has been explained in detail elsewhere, it is necessary only to recall briefly several central points. Created in London in the late 1950s, the market acted as the key locus for international financial transactions in the 1960s largely because, in a world of widespread capital controls, it represented the one location where international financial operations could be conducted relatively freely. Transactions could be made in non-local currencies, especially the dollar, completely free from state regulations. Although this 'offshore' activity remained strictly segmented from national financial systems, it still represented the most liberal international financial environment that market actors had experienced in several decades and they quickly took advantage of it.

Despite frequent claims to the contrary, the Euromarket was not a 'stateless' market. Rather, its existence was heavily dependent from the outset on state support, particularly from the US and Britain. The importance of the British state was that it refrained from imposing regulations on Euromarket activity in London. In fact, it actively encouraged the market's growth on British soil through various regulatory and tax changes (Kelly 1976). The support of the British state had its roots in that country's hegemonic past. Although Britain's international financial position had declined dramatically since its days as a financial hegemon in the nineteenth century, British financial authorities remained wedded – in a kind of hegemonic 'lag' – to the notion that London should act as a global financial centre after the Second World War.[5] With capital controls needed on sterling to defend Britain's weak balance of payments position and its postwar commitment to Keynesian macroeconomic policies, London's role was initially limited to acting as a financial centre for the sterling bloc. By the late 1950s, however, as it became clear that the controls would stay in place, London bankers began to deal in dollars in order to capture international business without being constrained by sterling controls. The Bank of England quickly gave this new Euromarket activity its full support through a number of regulatory initiatives, seeing it as a way to combine London's international role with Britain's diminished economic position.

320

GLOBALIZATION OF FINANCIAL MARKETS

The support of the US state was equally important because of the dominant role of American banks and corporations in the market in the 1960s. Although it had the power, the US state chose not to prevent them from participating in the market. By the mid-1960s, US officials were in fact actively encouraging US banks and corporations to move their operations to the offshore London market. There were two distinct reasons for the US support of the Euromarket. The first stemmed from a desire of US officials to preserve their policy autonomy in the face of growing US external deficits. From the early 1960s, US officials had tried to postpone the need for adjustment to the external deficits by persuading foreigners to finance them through dollar holdings. Although US officials introduced various incentives to increase the attractiveness of dollar holdings, in the end it was the appearance of the eurodollar market which proved particularly helpful. The market encouraged investors to hold dollars because it was freer and more liquid that most other financial markets of the time and because the unregulated interest rates on dollar holdings offered in the Euromarket proved much more attractive to foreigners than those available in the regulated US financial system. The importance of the Euromarket in increasing the attractiveness of foreign dollar holdings was recognized early on by US officials, and it became an important basis for US support of the market's growth in the 1960s (De Cecco 1987: 187; Strange 1971: 209).

The second reason for US support for the Euromarket emerged after 1963 when the US government chose to introduce a capital controls programme as a means of reducing the deficit. Although the US had supported the use of capital controls abroad in the 1940s and 1950s, the programme marked the first attempt by the US government to introduce such controls at home in the postwar period and it provoked strong opposition from US banking and multinational industrial leaders whose international operations were constrained under the programme. Although they had little success repealing the controls during the 1960s, these businesses were able to find in the Euromarket some temporary relief from their problems. New York bankers could retain their dominant place in international finance by moving their dollar operations to London. American industrial multi-nationals could finance their overseas operations in the London market unencumbered by the US regulations. By the mid-1960s, the Johnson administration, as well as US Congress, were actively supporting this move offshore, seeing it as a way by which 'national interest and corporate interest could be reconciled' (Strange 1981: 698).

2. A failed cooperative control initiative in the early 1970s

Whereas the key role of states in the 1960s was that of providing market actors with a greater degree of freedom, the second important political

321

ARTICLES

development involved their failure to implement cooperative capital controls of the kind outlined at Bretton Woods. The creation of the Euromarket, in addition to technological developments and increased economic interdependence, led to a rapid growth in international financial movements in the 1960s. Just as Keynes and White had predicted, the growth of private international financial activity brought with it large speculative financial flows that proved disruptive of the Bretton Woods fixed exchange rate system. By the late 1960s, in face of growing speculative flows, West European governments and Japan made clear their preference for maintaining the stable exchange rate system through the means of returning to a more controlled financial order. At first, in the late 1960s, and particularly following the suspension of dollar convertibility in August 1971, they focused on strengthening their domestic capital controls to preserve existing exchange rate values. It quickly became apparent that limited unilateral capital controls would not be sufficient. Evasion through leads and lags in current account payments could likely be curtailed unilaterally only with very draconian exchange controls of a kind which they were not willing to employ in the increasingly interdependent world economy of that period. Moreover, speculation in the offshore Euromarket could be prevented only with the help of other states.

When enormous speculative pressures forced the Europeans and Japanese to float their currencies in early 1973, they began to press for the second mechanism outlined by Keynes and White at Bretton Woods to effectively control finance: *cooperative* controls. While much has been written about the international monetary reform talks in this period, little attention has been paid to these proposals despite the importance given to them by participants at the time. In the crucial 1973 discussions in the Committee of Deputies of the Committee of Twenty, for example, European and Japanese officials actively pushed for the powers of the IMF to be extended in order to allow it to force states to cooperate in controlling financial movements. Such cooperation would involve not just the sending and receiving countries, but also 'throughflow' countries where Euromarket activity was located (IMF 1974: 85; Helleiner 1994: 102–11). The proposals also found strong support among the IMF staff who felt 'that disruptive capital movements were the single most important cause of the collapse of the Bretton Woods system' (quoted in De Vries 1985: 192).

The proposals for cooperative action were, however, blocked by US opposition. Although the US was completely isolated during the reform talks on the question of capital controls – an isolation that one internal US government memo at the time admitted 'makes us appear irresponsible' (quoted in Helleiner 1994: 109) – the proposals could not succeed without US approval because of the importance of US financial markets

GLOBALIZATION OF FINANCIAL MARKETS

and financial institutions in international financial activity. The US stance reflected a new liberal approach toward international financial movements in American foreign economic policy. In addition to opposing the European and Japanese proposals, the US in fact tried to use the reform talks to insist that foreign countries begin to dismantle their capital controls in order that a fully liberal international order be created. The new US financial liberalism was also demonstrated in two other important ways in this period. First, at the height of the currency crisis in early 1973, it announced that its own capital controls programme would be abolished the following year. Second, in the wake of the oil price rise, the US strongly opposed proposals from West European governments and the IMF that recycling of OPEC petro-dollars take place through IMF channels. The US position ensured that petrodollars would be recycled through the international private banking system rather than through public international institutions. In the words of the British Chancellor of the Exchequer Dennis Healey, 'the Americans were bitterly opposed [to the proposals] because it would have meant interfering with the freedom of the financial markets' (Healey 1989: 423).

There were two reasons for the new financial liberalism in US foreign economic policy in this period, each of which can be seen to have had their roots in US support for the Euromarket in the 1960s. First, US officials realized that the emerging open, liberal international financial system would help preserve US policy autonomy. Speculative international financial movements were central to the strategy of 'talking down the dollar' as a means of indirectly forcing Europe and Japan to bear the burden of adjusting to US external deficits. Market pressures would achieve what direct negotiations could not: a revaluation of European and Japanese currencies (Odell 1982: 191–9; Conybeare 1988: 248–9). Over the longer run, US officials also recognized that a more liberal international financial system would preserve the privileged global financial position of the US at a time when the Japanese and Europeans hoped to negotiate a more 'symmetrical' regulated international financial order. This was because New York financial markets and the eurodollar market remained by far the most attractive markets for private investors around the world. If market actors were given the freedom to invest globally, their investment choices would secure the dollar's central international role and help the US to continue to fund external and internal deficits with foreign funds (Helleiner 1994: 113–15). Indeed, the pattern of OPEC investment after 1973 confirmed these predictions (Mattione 1985). In this way, the basis of American hegemony was being shifted from one of direct power over other states to a more market-based or 'structural' form of power.[6]

The new liberal stance toward capital movements in US policy was also related to a domestic political shift within the US. During the

Nixon and Ford administrations, prominence was given in international financial policy to figures who strongly rejected on ideological grounds the restrictive embedded liberal approach to financial movements that had inspired the Bretton Woods order.[7] These 'neoliberals' – inspired by Friedrich Hayek[8] and Milton Friedman – praised the role of market forces in promoting an efficient allocation of capital not only internationally but also within domestic financial systems. They also opposed capital controls on the grounds that such controls represented a use of coercive 'police power' by the state that was incompatible with a 'free' form of government and individuals' freedom to move their money where they pleased.[9] Moreover, neoliberals took issue with the two reasons outlined at Bretton Woods as justifying capital controls. First, they rejected the postwar concern that speculative financial flows would disrupt stable exchange rate arrangements by arguing strongly in favour of a floating exchange rate system. Second, they did not sympathize with the commitment of Keynes and White to national Keynesianism and the autonomy of the welfare state. Instead, they applauded the way international financial markets would discipline government policy and force states to adopt more conservative, 'sound' fiscal and monetary programmes.

The sudden prominence of neoliberal thinkers in US international financial policy-making circles in the early 1970s was partly related to the way that their views on the desirability of a liberal financial order dovetailed perfectly with the 'national interest' concerns outlined above. Equally important, however, was the broad unravelling of the coalition within US politics which had supported the earlier embedded liberal approach. In particular, industrial leaders who had been sympathetic to capital controls in the early postwar period had become frustrated in the 1960s with the way US and foreign capital controls increasingly infringed on their growing multinational activities. As early as the mid-1960s, they were beginning to support neoliberal thinkers and financial interests who had been promoting a more favourable view of financial liberalism throughout the postwar period. By the early 1970s, they had become strong proponents of the neoliberal message and their voices found considerable influence in the Nixon and Ford administrations.

3 Three failed regulatory initiatives in the late 1970s/early 1980s

The failure of the European and Japanese initiative to move back towards a more closed financial order marked the collapse of the first principle established at Bretton Woods: that financial movements should be controlled in the interests of preserving a stable international exchange rate system. It had been hoped by many that the floating exchange rate system would grant states considerable policy autonomy from external market pressures. The increasing flows of speculative capital, however,

GLOBALIZATION OF FINANCIAL MARKETS

ensured that the system of floating exchange rates, far from insulating the domestic economy, often subjected it to new pressures. Not only did the same problems of trying to retain monetary control in an open global financial system remain, but also 'vicious circles' of disequilibrium afflicted countries pursuing expansionary policies in which the depreciation of the country's currency would reinforce domestic inflationary pressures, thus further undermining confidence. These pressures forced policymakers to a second choice: whether or not to give up the second principle of the Bretton Woods order, the commitment to policy autonomy.

In the late 1970s/early 1980s, there were three key turning points when state officials gave serious thought to trying to restore more effective controls over capital movements in the interest of preserving policy autonomy. These involved the UK in 1976, France in 1983, and the US in 1979–80. In each case, initiatives to move back to a more controlled international financial order failed. Had they succeeded, however, the globalization trend might have been considerably set back. Although the episodes are well known to international financial specialists, their importance as crucial 'non-decisions' is often neglected in histories of the globalization process.[10]

The first major turning point involved Britain in 1976 (Fay and Young 1978; Burke and Cairncross 1992). After borrowing extensively in international financial markets in 1974–75 to finance a domestic economic expansion, British authorities suddenly found the markets speculating heavily against sterling in 1976. A vicious circle of disequilibrium quickly emerged in which sterling's depreciating value reinforced domestic inflationary pressures that in turn only further undermined confidence in sterling. The currency crisis forced the Labour government to a difficult choice. On the one hand, winning back the confidence of the international markets would require giving up its domestic expansion and accepting an austerity programme being advocated by the IMF and the international financial markets. On the other hand, preserving policy autonomy would require insulating the domestic economy from external financial market pressures with the kind of draconian exchange controls outlined by Keynes and White at Bretton Woods.

Faced with these choices, a serious split emerged within the government. Initially, there was considerable support for the latter option. At the Labour Party conference in September, for example, this 'Alternative Economic Strategy' was passed as party policy and a resolution was approved calling for an investigation into 'ways in which the buying and selling of sterling and foreign exchange can be taken out of the hands of private firms in the City of London' (Labour Party 1976: 308). Two factors, however, led the Cabinet to reject this strategy and adopt the IMF's austerity package in December. First, it was thought that the costs associated with a regime of rigid exchange controls would be very high. Given Britain's extensive international economic linkages, there would be enormous domestic economic disruption. Prime Minister James Callaghan (1987: 441) also noted that there would be 'serious implications for our relations with the GATT, the European Community and NATO, as well as the US'. Second, the stagflationary environment of the 1970s had encouraged an increasing disillusionment with Keynesianism and 'embedded liberal' frameworks of thought among key members of the government. Chancellor Healey, in particular, had given up on Keynesianism and had became a strong advocate of austerity (Healey 1989: 378–9). Many of his key advisors in the Treasury and Bank of England, in addition to influential private bankers in the London markets, had also embraced neoliberal frameworks of thought, often under the influence of US-based neoliberals such as Friedman as well as institutions such as the Institute of Economic Affairs which had been founded under Hayek's leadership in the 1950s (Healey 1989: 412–3, 426–7, 430, 434; Fay and Young 1978: 10, 14, 22, 24).

The decision to accept the discipline of international financial markets was a central one for British politics. As Joel Krieger (1986: 58) notes, it 'signified the end of Keynesian society in Britain. Thatcherism was soon to follow'. It was also a key turning point for the global financial system as a whole. Britain had played a vital role in promoting the reemergence of an open global financial system, and it would continue to do so in the 1980s. Had the British Cabinet chosen to close down London's position as an international financial centre, the embryonic global financial system would have been dealt a strong blow. As the US Secretary of State at the time noted: 'it was a choice between Britain remaining in the liberal financial system of the West as opposed to a radical change of course . . . I think, if that had happened the whole system would come apart . . . So we tended to see it in cosmic terms' (quoted in Fay and Young 1978: 5).

The French experience of 1981–83 provided the second important turning point (Bauchard 1986). Elected in May 1981, the new Mitterrand government was strongly committed to a national Keynesian expansion to bring France out of its recession. From the outset, however, it found itself constrained by speculative activity against the franc in international financial markets. After two devaluations within the European Monetary System (EMS) failed to stem speculation, the Mitterrand government split in early 1983 along the same lines as Britain's Labour government had in 1976. One group of senior advisors advocated leaving the EMS and introducing tight exchange controls in order to maintain the expansion. Opposed to them was a group led by Finance Minister Jacques Delors who had become advocates of a more neoliberal solution to France's economic woes involving monetary discipline and market liberalization. Although Mitterrand initially sided with the former group

GLOBALIZATION OF FINANCIAL MARKETS

after a disastrous municipal election in early March, thereby plunging the government into chaos, he quickly became persuaded of the enormous political and economic costs – both domestically and internationally – that would be associated with a 'seige' economy. By mid-March, the government had chosen the deflationary course, abandoning its earlier Keynesian programme and accepting the discipline of the markets.

The dramatic 'U-turn' of the Mitterrand government was an important moment for the globalization process in several ways. Within France, the embedded liberal framework of thought with which the Mitterrand government had come into office was rejected overnight in favour of a more neoliberal approach. Market liberalization, especially in the financial sector, and monetary discipline became key policy goals (Loriaux 1991; Cerny 1989). The French experience also resonated beyond its borders. France soon became an important advocate of the pan-European neoliberal project that was led by Delors in his new capacity as European Commission President. Equally important, for many on the left around the world who had closely followed the Mitterrand experiment, the French experience signalled the enormous difficulties involved in preserving the 'old world' of embedded liberalism in the new global financial environment.

The third significant turning point in the late 1970s/early 1980s involved the failure of an initiative by the US Federal Reserve to regulate the Euromarket in 1979–80 (Hawley 1987: ch. 7). Whereas the British and French governments had sought to defend expansionary Keynesian policies from international financial discipline, the US Federal Reserve was concerned in this period about the way US banks and corporations were evading its restrictive monetary policy by borrowing dollars in the offshore Euromarket, a market that had grown to be as large in size as 10 percent of the US M-3 money supply by 1980. To deal with this growing threat to its policy autonomy, the US Federal Reserve decided to try to reduce the market's size by introducing reserve requirements on Euromarket activity. These regulations would, it was hoped, both reduce the market's attractiveness and bring its regulatory structure in line with bank regulation in the US.

To be effective, however, this initiative required the cooperation of other central banks. A unilateral imposition of reserve requirements on US financial institutions operating offshore would only have had the effect of driving Euromarket activity into foreign bank hands. Consequently, the Federal Reserve began to press other G-10 central banks in 1979–80 to consider a proposal whereby each central bank would impose reserve requirements on their own bank's Euromarket activities. The proposal was defeated, however, by opposition from Britain and Switzerland at a May 1980 meeting. As Euromarket centres,

ARTICLES

these states had the most to lose from any effort to reduce the attractiveness of the market. The proposal had also met with considerable opposition at home from the US banking community who were demanding instead a deregulation of US banking laws to meet the lax rules in the Euromarket. Indeed, their demands were largely met not only with the passage of the 1980 and 1982 bank deregulation packages, but more importantly with the introduction on US soil of regulation-free International Banking Facilities (IBFs) in December 1981. After the defeat of their reregulatory initiative, the Federal Reserve had agreed to the introduction of IBFs simply in order 'to make the best of a bad Euro-currency situation' (Hawley 1987: 139). Although they would further disrupt the management of domestic monetary policy, the IBFs would after all bring Euromarket business to the US, thereby raising 'the share of American banks in international finance' (Dale 1984: 30).

The failure of the Federal Reserve's initiative was important in several ways. To begin with, had the initiative succeeded it could have considerably slowed the momentum that grew in the 1980s in favour of the deregulation and liberalization of financial markets across the advanced industrial world. Competitive pressures from the Euromarket, as well as from the deregulating US financial system, would play a major role in promoting financial reform elsewhere in the 1980s. Second, it confirmed a lesson learned in the early 1970s that the cooperative mechanisms of restoring control over international financial markets advocated by Keynes and White at Bretton Woods were easily scuttled by the opposition of states who derived benefits from financial openness. Finally, it demonstrated that the desire to preserve policy autonomy from financial openness was not restricted to those pursuing expansionary Keynesian policies. Central bankers too had emerged from the mid-century order committed to macroeconomic management, albeit of a more conservative type, making them also somewhat wary of financial openness.

4 Liberalization decisions in the 1980s

These three failed initiatives to reregulate global financial markets set the stage for the fourth key political development in the globalization process: a flurry of liberalization moves in the 1980s. During the 1980s, governments across the advanced industrial world abolished external capital controls which had been in place for half a century giving market actors a degree of freedom unparalleled since the 1920s. Indeed, by the end of the decade, an almost fully liberal order had emerged across the OECD region. The restrictive Bretton Woods financial order outlined by Keynes and White had been effectively abandoned.

The US and Britain were the leaders of this trend to dismantle restric-

328

GLOBALIZATION OF FINANCIAL MARKETS

tions on the international movement of private financial capital. As we have seen, the US had already abolished its capital controls in 1974. After the events of 1979–80, however, US policymakers became even more active proponents of financial liberalization. In addition to introducing IBFs in 1981, they abolished the withholding tax on foreign holdings of US bonds in 1984 and issued special Treasury bonds directly into the Euromarket for the first time in the same year. Moreover, US Treasury officials also began to press foreign states to liberalize their capital controls after 1983. They played a particularly significant role, for example, in encouraging Japanese policymakers to begin to liberalize their regime of capital controls during the 1980s, a regime that had been among the most comprehensive in the OECD region throughout the postwar period. As Destler and Henning (1989: 29–30) note, US enthusiasm for financial openness after the early 1980s stemmed largely from the realization that, as in the 1960s and early 1970s, a more open and liberal global financial order could play a major role in financing the large US budget and current account deficits that emerged after 1982. US officials predicted accurately that internationally mobile funds would be attracted by the unique depth of US financial markets and the international role of the dollar, as well as by the high US interest rates which emerged out of the combination of tight monetary policy and loose fiscal policy in the Reagan years.

Britain's leading role in the financial liberalization trend stemmed from two decisions (Moran 1991: ch. 3). The first was the dramatic abolition of Britain's forty-year old exchange controls by Margaret Thatcher's new government in October 1979. Although the ground had been laid for this move by the Labour government's handling of the 1976 crisis, it was the neoliberal orientation of the new Thatcher government which was central to this decision. Capital controls were viewed by the new government as both an unnecessary form of state intervention and a 'substantial restriction on ... individual liberty'.[11] The abolition of exchange controls was also pressed by figures within the City of London who argued that full financial freedom was necessary for London to compete effectively with New York for international financial business. The latter concern was even more central in explaining the decision in 1986 to liberalize the London Stock Exchange and open it to foreign institutions. In an era when international financial activity was shifting away from banking to securities, this 'Big Bang' was seen as vital by British financial authorities for the London Stock Exchange to compete with the New York Stock Exchange which had been deregulated back in 1975.

The liberalization decisions in the US and Britain, as well as the broader deregulatory trends within their respective financial systems, played a major role in encouraging similar liberalization moves elsewhere in the

ARTICLES

OECD region in the 1980s (Moran 1991; Enkyo 1989; Strange 1990). Unless they matched the liberal and deregulated nature of the British and US financial systems, foreign financial authorities could not hope to attract new financial business and capital from abroad or even maintain the financial business and capital of their own multinational corporations or international banks. These competitive pressures encouraged the idea that the financial sector required an 'industrial policy' like any other sector to retain its competitiveness. In the financial sector, such a policy consisted of liberalization and deregulation decisions designed to appeal to and attract footloose international financial market operators. These competitive concerns were important, for example, in encouraging financial liberalization decisions across the European continent after the mid-1980s (Cerny 1989; Hamilton 1986), decisions that in turn laid the ground for the 1988 decision by the European Community as a whole to abolish all capital controls by mid-1990 (with a slightly later deadline given to Greece, Portugal, Spain and Ireland).[12] Competitive pressures from the US and Britain also played an important role in prompting liberalization and deregulation in the Japanese financial system throughout the 1980s (Strange 1990; Rosenbluth 1989: ch. 5, 224) as well as the announcements in 1989–90 by the Scandinavian countries that they would eliminate their capital controls (Helleiner 1994: 165–6).

Countries across the OECD region were responding not just to external competitive pressures in liberalizing their capital controls in the 1980s, but also to new domestic political pressures. One of these was the growing domestic political prominence of advocates of neoliberal economic thinking during the 1980s (Helleiner 1994: ch. 7). Whereas capital controls had previously been a central element in national Keynesian and corporatist planning strategies, neoliberals were increasingly successful in convincing policymakers in the 1980s that such controls were defending outdated interventionist economic policies. New emphasis was placed across the advanced industrial world on the role that financial liberalization and deregulation could play in providing freedom for savers and investors as well as in enhancing the efficiency of the financial intermediation process both domestically and internationally.

The new political prominence of neoliberal advocates was partly a product of the broad disillusionment with 'embedded liberal' economic policies in the context of the economic troubles of the 1970s and 1980s. Equally important, neoliberal arguments in favour of financial liberalization were supported by financial firms as well as by multinational businesses in this period, both of whom saw capital controls as a cumbersome interference in their increasingly internationally-oriented activities (Frieden 1991; Goodman and Pauly 1993; Moran 1991: 12, 130–1). As had been true in the US in the early 1970s and Britain in the late 1970s, this

GLOBALIZATION OF FINANCIAL MARKETS

alliance of neoliberal advocates and internationally-oriented corporate interests played a key role in prompting financial liberalization decisions across continental Europe, Scandinavia as well as the decisions of Australia and New Zealand to abolish overnight their extensive postwar capital controls in 1984–85. Financial and industrial firms with growing international ambitions in Japan were also important in encouraging financial liberalization in that country during the 1980s.[13]

5 Preventing international financial crises

In the four sets of political developments that have been outlined so far to explain this reemergence of global finance, the key role of states was that of either liberalizing capital controls or refraining from tightening them. A 'political' history of this reemergence of global finance would not be complete without outlining one further role of states in the process: that of preventing financial crises. Financial markets are especially prone to experience periodic panics because of imperfect information and the mobile nature of finance. At the international level, such panics can quickly shatter the confidence of market operators in the safety of cross-border transactions and destroy international financial markets. In particular, during international financial crises, private financial operators tend to retreat to the safety of domestic markets because of the lesser familiarity of foreign markets, the currency risks involved in international investment, and uncertainties regarding the issue of how states will treat foreign assets. The international financial crisis of the early 1930s provided a vivid example of this phenomenon.

It is widely recognized, however, that states can play a central role in preventing international financial panics, and thus preserving an open financial order, through lender-of-last-resort activity and through prudential regulation and supervision of financial markets. In Charles Kindleberger's (1978: 4) words, states can provide 'the public good of stability that the private market is unable to provide for itself'. At Bretton Woods, little attention was given to the need for these activities at the international level as few expected global financial markets to reappear. The growth of international banking in the 1960s and 1970s, however, raised the question of who would act to prevent a banking crisis from spreading rapidly through the nascent international markets.

The first major test came in 1974 with the collapse of the Herstatt and Franklin National Banks (Spero 1980). Because both banks had many outstanding foreign exchange contracts and held large deposits from other banks, their collapse threatened to trigger a serious panic in international banking markets. A financial panic was prevented for two reasons. First, the US Federal Reserve acted swiftly to assume the role of international lender of last resort in the crisis. It was particularly

ARTICLES

concerned that the crisis might undermine confidence in the dollar and
the US financial system (Spero 1980: 113–14), a confidence that was
important to maintain given America's centrality within the emerging
global financial order and its increasing reliance on international financial support to fund its economic imbalances. The Federal Reserve was
also greatly aided in this lender-of-last-resort role by cooperation from
G-10 central bankers who shared a common desire to prevent instability
in international financial markets. This cooperation was made particularly easy because of close links that had been established between
G-10 central bankers within the Bank for International Settlements (BIS).
The BIS had been created in 1929–30 with the goal of creating a forum
in which international financial stability could be pursued in a pragmatic and depoliticized fashion (Costigiola 1972). Although it had failed
to prevent the 1931 international financial collapse, the BIS had found
new life in the 1960s as an institution where G-10 central bankers could
meet and try to handle to the growing currency turmoil of that decade.
Its monthly meetings in this period helped rekindle a kind of 'internationalism of central bankers' dedicated to the task of preserving
international financial stability. This sentiment had been largely dormant
since the prewar period and the relationships between central bankers
that developed during the 1960s proved helpful in handling the 1974
banking crisis (Spero 1980: 153).

The BIS also served as the forum in which discussions began in the
wake of the 1974 crisis to create more formal arrangements aimed at
preventing future crises. In September 1974, for example, a communique
was issued by G-10 central bankers declaring that 'means are available'
for lender-of-last-resort activities in international banking markets.
Although it was unclear the extent to which lender-of-last-resort responsibilities had been formally defined, Jack Guttentag and Richard Herring
(1985: 31) note that this statement did much to restore confidence in the
international markets. Moreover, at the Bank of England's instigation, a
committee was created within the BIS in 1974 to study how more permanent arrangements could be established to reduce the risk of future
banking crises. In 1975, the committee announced the Basle Concordat,
a set of jurisdictional rules governing regulatory and supervisory
activities in international banking markets.

The 1982 international debt crisis, triggered by Mexico's declaration
of default, was the second major crisis to strike the international financial system (Kraft 1984). More serious than the 1974 crisis, Mexico's
default threatened to bring down the entire international banking system
at one stroke. Once again, the immediate crisis was avoided by a combination of US and BIS action. From the US, large credits were quickly
extended to Mexico partly in the form of an advance on oil payments
from the Department of Energy and partly as a loan from the Commodity

GLOBALIZATION OF FINANCIAL MARKETS

Credit Corporation for the purchase of US agricultural products. Once again, the US action was driven by its stake in the crisis: the bulk of Mexican debt was held by American banks and the crisis threatened their stability as well as that of the dollar. The US funds were also supplemented by a $1.85 billion bridging loan from the BIS to the Bank of Mexico, of which the US Federal Reserve contributed approximately half. In the subsequent Brazilian and Argentine crises, the BIS central bankers acted decisively again to provide bridging loans needed to overcome temporary liquidity crises in these countries.

With the short-term crises handled, complex negotiations were initiated between all the major debtors and the international banking community to prevent further defaults. Although it is not possible to summarize this process in this article, the US Federal Reserve, the US Treasury and US bank regulators continued to play a central role facilitating the rescheduling agreements. Moreover, like the 1974 crisis, the international debt crisis acted as a catalyst for further strengthening supervisory and regulatory cooperation in international banking. In particular, it focused the attention of bank regulators on the need for healthy capital–asset ratios in international banking. The US Federal Reserve and the Bank of England took a particular leadership role in encouraging their central bank colleagues within the BIS to consider the introduction of a common capital adequacy standard for all banks under their jurisdiction. By 1988, an agreement had been reached which set 1992 as the deadline by which that standard would be introduced (Kapstein 1992). Even before its implementation, this agreement is said to have played a key role in 'forcing more discipline into the banking markets.'[14]

Although less serious than the 1982 crisis, the 1987 international stock crash also shook confidence in international financial markets. Whereas the 1974 and 1982 crises had affected banking markets, this crisis struck the growing international securities markets. In this episode, global markets were stabilized primarily through concerted BIS central bank intervention in the markets (Helleiner 1994: 184–5). As with the two previous crises, the crash served to focus attention on the need to extend supervisory, regulatory, and lender-of-last-resort cooperation to securities markets. The BIS played a major role in pressing for action in cooperation with the newly formed International Organization of Securities Commissions (IOSCO). By early 1992, there was agreement in principle between the BIS and IOSCO on a common worldwide framework for international capital rules for securities companies to match that existing in the banking field. As in the banking field, regulators from the US and Britain played a lead role in the negotiations (Porter 1993).

Without the decisive actions of states acting as lenders-of-last-resort to restore stability in the emerging global financial markets during each of these three crises, the globalization trend might well have lost much of its momentum. Indeed, even with the lender-of-last-resort action by the US, Britain and the BIS central banks, there was a considerable retreat from international financial markets by private operators in the wake of each crisis as they withdrew to the greater safety and familiarity of domestic markets. States also played an important role in seeking to minimize further instability in international financial markets through the various norms, rules and decision-making procedures they devised to facilitate their regulation and supervision of those markets. These can be seen as representing the emergence of an increasingly sophisticated 'regime' designed to preserve international financial stability of the kind that the Bretton Wood conference failed to set up.

CONCLUSION

The re-emergence of global finance over the past three decades was not a product solely of market and technological developments. Rather, as has been demonstrated in these five sets of episodes, state behaviour and political choices have also played an important role in the process. Why have states increasingly embraced and encouraged the globalization trend in the last three decades? In this conclusion, it is worth briefly summarizing the reasons.

First, states were partly encouraged to liberalize their existing capital controls because of a competitive deregulation dynamic. Through financial liberalization and domestic deregulation, governments sought to lure to their markets footloose financial business and capital which could provide such important benefits as employment, foreign exchange earnings and funding for current account and fiscal deficits. Financial liberalization and deregulation were the chosen policy tools to attract financial business and capital because states recognized that the mobility and fungibility of money made financial market operators display what Richard Dale (1984: 40) calls 'unusual sensitivity to regulatory differentials between financial centres'. This competitive dynamic in the financial sector ensured that a closed financial regime such as that existing in the early postwar years was likely to unravel over time. Once a major state or group of states initiated the liberalization and deregulation of their financial markets, others would feel obliged to follow in order to avoid losing financial business and capital to them. In the postwar situation, the US and Britain played the key role in encouraging this competitive liberalization and deregulation process first through their support for the liberal, deregulated Euromarket in the 1960s, and then through their broader liberalization and domestic deregulation programmes in the 1970s and 1980s.

Second, states also increasingly accepted and embraced the globaliza-

GLOBALIZATION OF FINANCIAL MARKETS

tion trend because the two mechanisms outlined at Bretton Woods for more effectively controlling capital movements proved politically difficult to implement. As became clear in the 1970s and early 1980s, states were unlikely to introduce unilateral comprehensive exchange controls because of the enormous economic and political costs associated with them in an increasingly interdependent world economy. More effective *cooperative* strategies for controlling finance were also difficult to implement because they could be easily scuttled by individual states exercising a veto, as the US showed in the early 1970s and Britain and Switzerland demonstrated in 1980. Indeed, it could be said that cooperative control initiatives were hampered by a classic collective action problem in that states were tempted to derive the benefits from a more closed international financial system (such as greater policy autonomy and more stable exchange rates), while 'free-riding' on that system by unilaterally liberalizing their markets in order to capture financial business and capital for their national financial system. The difficulties in preventing such behaviour provided a further reason why it was likely that the restrictive Bretton Woods financial order would unravel over time.

Third, the particularly strong support shown by the US and Britain for financial globalization was in large part a product of their unique 'hegemonic' interests in international finance. In the case of the US, we have seen how it explicitly encouraged the creation of more open, liberal international financial order as a means of exploiting its hegemonic position with that order, a position that resulted from the centrality of the dollar, US financial institutions, and US markets in the emerging open global financial order. This strategy began with the promotion of the Euromarket in the 1960s, followed through its stance in the reform talks in the early 1970s and culminated in its enthusiasm for financial liberalism during the Reagan years. In each instance, the US saw that its hegemonic position in the emerging open global financial order could be used to help finance its growing current account and fiscal deficits. In this sense, the US role in promoting financial globalization since the 1960s fits predictions of the 'hegemonic stability theory' that a state with a hegemonic position will seek to create and maintain an open and liberal order from which it benefits.[15]

The key British role in promoting the globalization trend can also be understood using a slightly modified 'hegemonic' model. The British support for the Euromarket, its enthusiasm for financial liberalization in the 1980s, as well as its role in promoting financial stability are best seen as products of a kind of hegemonic 'lag' in behaviour in which the British state remained 'locked in' to a commitment to financial leadership stemming from its days as a financial power in the nineteenth century. The 'lag' in finance endured after 1945 primarily because of the power of what Geoffrey Ingham (1984) calls a 'Bank of England–

ARTICLES

Treasury–City' nexus within British politics which favoured the promotion of London's internationalism. It was also encouraged because of the way in which the Euromarket provided London with a mechanism by which to rebuild its leading position in finance.

Although 'hegemonic interests' may account for some of the reasons why the US and Britain showed a special willingness to promote financial globalization, these two states were also influenced during the 1970s and 1980s by the growing domestic political prominence of neoliberal advocates in the financial sector. A similar domestic development also was important in explaining the sudden commitment of other states across the advanced industrial world to financial liberalization during the 1980s. This new prominence of neoliberal advocates across the advanced industrial world partly reflected the growing disillusionment with 'embedded liberal' policies in the stagflationary environment of the 1970s and 1980s. Equally important, the neoliberal advocacy of financial liberalization was also supported by financial and industrial interests whose interests had become increasingly internationalized during this period. The growing domestic influence of coalitions of neoliberal advocates and internationally-oriented corporate interests across the advanced industrial world constitutes the fourth explanation of state support for the financial globalization process.

The fifth and final explanation concerns the role that G-10 central banks played in preventing international financial crises. In part, financial crises were prevented by the leadership behaviour of the US and to a lesser extent Britain, behaviour which stemmed in large part from their respective 'hegemonic' interests in financial openness. Equally important in preventing financial crises, however, was the behaviour of G-10 central bankers who demonstrated a keen interest in cooperating to preserve international financial stability. Ethan Kapstein (1992) has argued that their common belief in the need to stabilize global financial markets through lender-of-last-resort activities and international regulation and supervision as well as their strong commitment to cooperation suggests that G-10 central bankers shared some of the characteristics of what Peter Haas (1992) has termed 'transnational epistemic communities'.[16] In their pursuit of common policy projects to prevent financial crises, it is important also to note that the G-10 central banks were aided particularly by the existence of the BIS. Ironically, this was an institution which the Bretton Woods participants attempted to abolish in 1944 largely because of its association with the pre-1931 world of 'haute finance' that they sought to eliminate (Eckes 1975: 152–3). The resolution that called for the BIS's elimination 'at the earliest possible moment' was, however, never enforced and the institution survived to play a major role in helping to preserve exactly the kind of private global financial order that the Bretton Woods architects opposed.

GLOBALIZATION OF FINANCIAL MARKETS

Although I have emphasized the need to 'bring states back in' to histories of the globalization of finance in this article, two of the five factors explaining state behaviour highlight the need not to draw too large a distinction between 'political' accounts of financial globalization, such as that offered here, and those emphasizing technological and market factors. I have argued, for example, that a key reason why states in the 1970s and early 1980s chose not to introduce the kind of comprehensive exchange controls outlined by Keynes and White was that they perceived the costs associated with such controls to be too high in an increasingly interdependent world economy. Since growing interdependence was partly a function of technological and market developments, such developments have clearly encouraged financial globalization not only directly (by prompting private actors to engage in global financial operations) but also indirectly by encouraging state behaviour that further supported the globalization process.[17] Similarly, I have suggested that a central factor explaining the decision of states to liberalize their capital controls in the 1970s and 1980s was domestic pressure from corporate interests whose operations had become increasingly internationalized. Once again, the internationalization of corporate activity was linked partly to technological and market changes, changes that can thus be seen to be encouraging financial globalization indirectly by creating domestic political constituencies that lobbied states to remove capital controls. In these ways, it is clear that state behaviour, market developments and technological change have interacted in complicated ways to encourage the financial globalization trend. In emphasizing the role played by states in this article, I have sought not to downplay the importance of market and technological factors but rather simply to stress one cause of the globalization of financial markets which has hitherto received less attention than it deserves.

NOTES

I would like to thank the Social Sciences and Humanities Research Council of Canada for providing financial support for the research underlying this article. I am also grateful to the following for their helpful comments on various aspects of the argument: Phil Cerny, Jennifer Clapp, Robert Cox, Nilesh Dattani, Stephen Gill, Michael Loriaux, Lou Pauly, Gautam Sen, Susan Strange, Geoffrey Underhill and three anonymous referees.

1 For a more detailed discussion, see Helleiner (1994). Some of the other more comprehensive recent IPE works in this area include Frieden (1986), Pauly (1988), Porter (1993), Strange (1986), Underhill (1991) and Moran (1991). See also Kapstein's (1994) more general argument calling for more state-centred approaches to the study of financial globalization.
2 See Helleiner (1994: 51–77). Only the Federal Republic of Germany also restored convertibility on the capital account in 1958.

ARTICLES

3　See for example Wriston (1988), McKenzie and Lee (1991), O'Brien (1992).
4　The obvious criticism of this third argument is that there is no clear proof that these mechanisms would necessarily have been able to control financial movements. It is certainly true, for example, that experiences of draconian total exchange controls – such as those in place in Germany in the 1930s – suggest that they are not able to prevent all capital movements. The potential effectiveness of a regime of extensive cooperative controls is also unclear given that it has never been put in place. Still, as supporters of such proposals argue, the objective is not to stop *every* international financial transfer but rather to limit the bulk of them (see for example Glyn 1986 or Tobin 1978). Indeed, the point I am making is simply that the globalization trend would certainly not be nearly as extensive nor would it have proceeded so rapidly if a regime of either cooperative controls (which included control of Euromarket activity) or tight unilateral exchange controls had been in place during the previous three decades.
5　See, for example, Strange (1971), Ingham (1984). The notion of hegemonic 'lags' is taken from Krasner (1976: 341–3).
6　The notion of 'structural power' is developed by Strange (1988). For a similar interpretation of the changing nature of US financial power in this period, see Walter (1991).
7　Such figures included George Shultz (Treasury secretary after mid-1972), William Simon (who succeeded Shultz as Treasury secretary), Gottfried Haberler (an advisor to President Nixon on international financial issues), and Paul Volcker (in the Treasury department). For a more detailed discussion of the themes in this and the following paragraph, see Helleiner (1994: 115–21).
8　For the influence of Hayek and other European neoliberals on the revival of the US conservative movement, see Nash (1976: ch. 1).
9　The quotations are from Machlup (1968: 108), a prominent US neoliberal at the time.
10　Strange (1986: 31) emphasizes the importance of 'non-decisions' in the financial globalization process, although she refers to different episodes.
11　This quotation comes from a 1979 pamphlet issued by the Institute for Economic Affairs which was very close to the new government (Miller and Wood 1979: 68).
12　See for example Underhill (1991), Vipond (1991). The 1988 decision was also linked closely to the drive towards economic and monetary union (EMU). The European Commission hoped that financial liberalization would accelerate the move to EMU both by increasing British and German support for the process and by forcing European governments to recognize the need for closer monetary cooperation in the new open financial environment.
13　Japan's emergence as a major creditor after 1981 was also important in encouraging liberalization in that country because it eliminated the external balance of payments constraint that had previously provided a major justification for controls.
14　Quotation from the IMF's 1992 edition of *International Capital Markets*, reprinted in *IMF Survey*, 9 November 1992, pp. 345–6.
15　For advocates of this theory, see for example Krasner (1976) and Gilpin (1987).
16　Kapstein is wary, however, of endorsing Haas' analytical framework entirely, given the important role played by the US and Britain in encouraging central bank cooperation.
17　Goodman and Pauly (1993) develop a similar case with respect to the liberalization of capital controls in the 1980s, arguing that states were prompted

GLOBALIZATION OF FINANCIAL MARKETS

to remove controls because the globalization of production and emergence of international financial markets had raised the costs associated with their maintenance.

REFERENCES

Bauchard, Pierre (1986) *La Guerre des deux roses: du rêve à la réalité 1981–5*, Paris: Grasset.

Bloomfield, Arthur (1946) 'The postwar control of international capital movements', *American Economic Review*, 36: 687–709.

Burke, Kathleen and Cairncross, Alec (1992) *'Goodbye, Great Britain': 1976 IMF Crisis*, New Haven, CT: Yale University Press.

Callaghan, James (1987) *Time and Change*, London: Collins.

Cerny, Phil (1989) 'The Little Big Bang in Paris: financial market deregulation in a dirigiste system', *European Journal of Political Research*, 17: 169–92.

Conybeare, John (1988) *US Foreign Economic Policy and the International Capital Markets: The Case of Capital Export Controls 1963–74*, New York: Garland Publishing Co.

Costigliola, Frank (1972) 'The other side of isolationism: the establishment of the first World Bank 1929–30', *Journal of American History*, 59: 602–20.

Dale, Richard (1984) *The Regulation of International Banking*, Cambridge: Woodhead-Faulkner.

De Cecco, Marcello (1987) 'Inflation and structural change in the Eurodollar market' M. De Cecco and J.P. Fitoussi (eds) *Monetary Theory and Economic Institutions*, London: Macmillan.

De Vries, Margaret (1985) *The International Monetary Fund 1972–8: Volume 1*, Washington, DC: International Monetary Fund.

Destler, I. and Henning, C. Randall (1989) *Dollar Politics: Exchange Rate Policymaking in the US*, Washington, DC: Institute for International Economics.

Eckes, Alfred (1975) *A Search for Solvency: Bretton Woods and the International Monetary System 1941–71*, London: University of Texas Press.

Enkyo, Yoichi (1989) 'Financial innovation and international safeguards: causes and consequences of "structural innovation" in the US and global financial system: 1973–86', Ph.D. dissertation, London School of Economics.

Fay, Stephen and Young, Hugo (1978) *The Day the Pound Nearly Died*, London: Sunday Times.

Frieden, Jeffry (1987) *Banking on the World*, London: Hutchison Radius.

——— (1991) 'Invested interests: the politics of national economic policies in a world of global finance', *International Organization*, 45: 425–52.

Gilpin, Robert (1987) *The Political Economy of International Relations*, Princeton, NJ: Princeton University Press.

Glyn, Andrew (1986) 'Capital flight and exchange controls', *New Left Review*, 155: 37–49.

Goodman, John and Pauly, Louis (1993) 'The obsolescence of capital controls? Economic management in an age of global markets', *World Politics*, 46: 50–82.

Guttentag, Jack and Herring, Richard (1985) 'Funding risk in the international interbank market', in *International Financial Markets and Capital Movements; A Symposium in Honor of Arthur Bloomfield*, Essays in International Finance no. 157, Princeton, NJ: Princeton University.

Haas, Peter (1992) 'Introduction: epistemic communities and international policy coordination', *International Organization*, 46: 1–35.

ARTICLES

Hamilton, Adrian (1986) *The Financial Revolution*, New York: Free Press.
Hawley, James (1987) *Dollars and Borders: US Government Attempts to Restrain Capital Flows 1960–80*, London: M.E. Sharpe.
Healey, Denis (1989) *The Time of My Life*, London: Michael Joseph.
Helleiner, Eric (1993) 'When finance was the servant: international capital movements in the Bretton Woods order', in Phil Cerny (ed.) *Finance and World Politics: Markets, Regimes and States in the Post-Hegemonic Era*, Aldershot: Elgar.
—— (1994) *States and the Reemergence of Global Finance: From Bretton Woods to the 1990s*, Ithaca, NY: Cornell University Press.
Horsefield, John (1969) *International Monetary Fund 1945–65: Volume 3*, Washington, DC: International Monetary Fund.
Ingham, Geoffrey (1984) *Capitalism Divided: The City and Industry in British Social Development*, London: Macmillan.
International Monetary Fund (1974) *International Monetary Reform: Documents of the Committee of Twenty*, Washington, DC: International Monetary Fund.
Kapstein, Ethan (1992) 'Between power and purpose: central bankers and the politics of regulatory convergence', *International Organization*, 46: 265–87.
—— (1994) 'Governing global finance', *Washington Quarterly*, 17: 77–87.
Kelly, Janet (1976) *Bankers and Borders: The Case of American Banks in Britain*, Cambridge, MA: Ballinger.
Keynes, John Maynard (1980) *The Collected Writings of J.M. Keynes: Vol.25– Activities 1940–44: Shaping the Postwar World, The Clearing Union* edited by D. Moggridge. London: Cambridge University Press.
Kindleberger, Charles (1978) *Manias, Panics and Crashes: A History of Financial Crises*, London: Macmillan.
Kraft, Joseph (1984) *The Mexican Rescue*, New York: Group of Thirty.
Krasner, Stephen (1976) 'State power and the structure of international trade', *World Politics*, 28: 317–47.
Krieger, Joel (1986) *Reagan, Thatcher, and the Politics of Decline*, Cambridge: Polity Press.
Labour Party (1976) *Report of the Seventy Fifth Annual Conference of the Labour Party*, Blackpool: Labour Party.
Loriaux, Michael (1991) *France After Hegemony: International Change and Financial Reform*, Ithaca, NY: Cornell University Press.
Machlup, Fritz (1968) *Remaking the International Monetary System: The Rio Agreement and Beyond*, Baltimore, MD: Johns Hopkins Press.
McKenzie, Richard and Lee, Dwight (1991) *Quicksilver Capital*, New York: Free Press.
Mattione, Richard (1985) *OPEC's Investments and the International Financial System*, Washington, DC: Brookings Institution.
Miller, Robert and Wood, John (1979) *Exchange Control For Ever?*, London: Institute for Economic Affairs.
Moran, Michael (1991) *The Politics of the Financial Services Revolution: The USA, UK and Japan*, London: Macmillan.
Nash, George (1976) *The Conservative Intellectual Movement in America Since 1945*, New York: Basic Books.
O'Brien, Richard (1992) *Global Financial Integration: The End of Geography?*, London: Pinter.
Odell, John (1982) *US International Monetary Policy: Markets, Power and Ideas as Sources of Change*, Princeton, NJ: Princeton University Press.
Pauly, Louis (1988) *Opening Financial Markets: Banking Politics on the Pacific Rim*, Ithaca, NY: Cornell University Press.

GLOBALIZATION OF FINANCIAL MARKETS

Porter, Tony (1993) *States, Markets and Regimes in Global Finance*, London: Macmillan.

Rosenbluth, Frances M. (1989) *Financial Politics in Contemporary Japan*, Ithaca, NY: Cornell University Press.

Ruggie, John (1982) 'International regimes, transactions and change: embedded liberalism in the postwar economic order', *International Organization*, 36: 379–415.

Spero, Joan (1980) *The Failure of the Franklin National Bank: Challenge to the International Banking System*, New York: Columbia University Press.

Strange, Susan (1971) *Sterling and British Policy*, London: Oxford University Press.

—— (1981) 'The world's money: expanding the agenda for research', *International Journal*, 36 (4): 691–712.

—— (1986) *Casino Capitalism*, Oxford: Blackwell.

—— (1988) *States and Markets*, London: Pinter Publishers.

—— (1990) 'Finance, information and power', *Review of International Studies*, 16: 259–74.

Tobin, James (1978) 'A proposal for international monetary reform', *The Eastern Economic Journal*, 4: 153–9.

Underhill, Geoffrey (1991) 'Markets beyond politics?: the state and the internationalization of financial markets', *European Journal of Political Research*, 19: 197–225.

United States Congress (1971) *Hearings Before Subcommittee on International Exchange and Payments, Joint Economic Committee, June 22, 1971*, Washington, DC: United States Government Printing Office.

Vipond, Peter (1991) 'The liberalisation of capital movements and financial services in the European Single Market: a case study in regulation', *European Journal of Political Research*, 19: 227–44.

Walter, Andrew (1991) *World Power and World Money: The Role of Hegemony and International Monetary Order*, London: Harvester Wheatsheaf.

Wriston, Walter (1988) 'Technology and sovereignty', *Foreign Affairs*, 67: 63–75.

[8]

THE GLOBALIZATION OF FINANCE
Alan Greenspan

As a result of very rapid increases in telecommunications and computer-based technologies and products, a dramatic expansion in cross-border financial flows and within countries has emerged. The pace has become truly remarkable. These technology-based developments have so expanded the breadth and depth of markets that governments, even reluctant ones, increasingly have felt they have had little alternative but to deregulate and free up internal credit and financial markets.

In recent years global economic integration has accelerated on a multitude of fronts. While trade liberalization, which has been ongoing for a longer period, has continued, more dramatic changes have occurred in the financial sphere.

World financial markets undoubtedly are far more efficient today than ever before. Changes in communications and information technology, and the new instruments and risk-management techniques they have made possible, enable an ever wider range of financial and nonfinancial firms today to manage their financial risks more effectively. As a consequence, they can now concentrate on managing the economic risks associated with their primary businesses.

The solid profitability of new financial products in the face of their huge proliferation attests to the increasing effectiveness of financial markets in facilitating the flow of trade and direct investment, which are so patently contributing to ever higher standards of living around the world. Complex financial instruments—derivative instruments, in one form or another—are being developed to take advantage of the gains in communications and information technology. Such instruments would not have flourished as they have without the technological advances of the past several decades. They could not be priced properly, the markets they involve could not be arbitraged properly, and

Cato Journal, Vol. 17, No. 3 (Winter 1998). Copyright © Cato Institute. All rights reserved.
Alan Greenspan is Chairman of the Federal Reserve Board. This paper is an edited version of his keynote address at the Cato Institute's 15th Annual Monetary Conference, October 14, 1997.

the risks they give rise to could not be managed at all, to say nothing of properly, without high-powered data processing and communications capabilities.

New Challenges

Still, for central bankers with responsibilities for financial market stability, the new technologies and new instruments have presented new challenges. Some argue that market dynamics have been altered in ways that increase the likelihood of significant market disruptions. Whatever the merits of this argument, there is a clear sense that the new technologies, and the financial instruments and techniques they have made possible, have strengthened interdependencies between markets and market participants, both within and across national boundaries. As a result, a disturbance in one market segment or one country is likely to be transmitted far more rapidly throughout the world economy than was evident in previous eras.

In earlier generations information moved slowly, constrained by the primitive state of communications. Financial crises in the early 19th century, for example, particularly those associated with the Napoleonic Wars, were often related to military and other events in faraway places. An investor's speculative position could be wiped out by a military setback, and he might not even know about it for days or even weeks, which, from the perspective of central banking today, might be considered bliss.

As the 19th century unfolded, communications speeded up. By the turn of the century, events moved more rapidly, but their speed was at most a crawl by the standard of today's financial markets. The environment now facing the world's central banks—and, of course, private participants in financial markets as well—is characterized by instant communication.

It is worthwhile to trace the roots of this extraordinary expansion of global finance, to assess its benefits and risks, and to suggest some avenues that can usefully be explored in order to contain some of its potentially adverse consequences.

The Roots of Globalization

A global financial system, of course, is not an end in itself. It is the institutional structure that has been developed over the centuries to facilitate the production of goods and services. Accordingly, we can better understand the evolution of today's burgeoning global financial markets by parsing the extraordinary changes that have emerged, in the past century or more, in what we conventionally call the real side of economies: the production of goods and services. The same technological forces currently driving finance were first evident in the production process and have had a profound effect on what we produce, how we produce it, and how it is financed. Technological change or, more generally, ideas have significantly altered the nature of output so that it has become increasingly conceptual and less physical. A much smaller proportion of the measured real gross domestic product constitutes physical bulk today than in past generations.

The increasing substitution of concepts for physical effort in the creation of economic value also has affected how we produce; computer-assisted design systems, machine tools, and inventory control systems provide examples. Offices are now routinely outfitted with high-speed information-processing technology. Because the accretion of knowledge is, with rare exceptions, irreversible, this trend almost surely will continue into the next century and beyond. Value creation at the turn of the 21st century will surely involve the transmission of information and ideas, generally over complex telecommunication networks. That development will create considerably greater flexibility of where services are produced and where employees do their work. A century earlier, transportation of goods to their most value-creating locations served the same purpose for an economy whose value creation still rested heavily on physical, bulky output.

Not unexpectedly, as goods and services have moved across borders, the necessity to finance them has increased dramatically. But what is particularly startling is how large the expansion in cross-border finance has become, relative to the trade it finances. To be sure, much cross-border finance supports investment portfolios, doubtless some largely speculative. But, at bottom, even they are part of the support systems for efficient international movement of goods and services.

The rapid expansion in cross-border banking and finance should not be surprising given the extent to which low-cost information processing and communications technology have improved the ability of customers in one part of the world to avail themselves of borrowing, depositing, or risk-management opportunities offered anywhere in the world on a real-time basis.

Benefits and Risks of Global Finance

These developments enhance the process whereby an excess of saving over investment in one country finds an appropriate outlet in another. In short, they facilitate the drive to equate risk-adjusted rates of return on investments worldwide. They thereby improve the worldwide allocation of scarce capital and, in the process, engender a huge increase in risk dispersion and hedging opportunities.

But there is still evidence of less than full arbitrage of risk-adjusted rates of return on a worldwide basis. This suggests the potential for a far larger world financial system than currently exists. If we can resist protectionist pressures in our societies in the financial arena as well as in the interchange of goods and services, we can look forward to the benefits of the international division of labor on a much larger scale in the 21st century.

What we do not know for sure, but strongly suspect, is that the accelerating expansion of global finance may be indispensable to the continued rapid growth in world trade in goods and services. It is becoming increasingly evident that many layers of financial intermediation will be required if we are to capture the full benefits of our advances in finance. Certainly, the emergence of a highly liquid foreign exchange market has facilitated basic forex transactions, and the availability of more complex hedging strategies enables producers and investors to achieve their desired risk positions. This owes largely to the ability of modern financial products to unbundle complex risks in ways that enable each counterparty to choose the combination of risks necessary to advance its business strategy, and to eschew those that do not. This process enhances cross-border trade in goods and services, facilitates cross-border portfolio investment strategies, enhances the lower-cost financing of real capital formation on a worldwide basis, and, hence, leads to an expansion of international trade and rising standards of living.

But achieving those benefits surely will require the maintenance of a stable macroeconomic environment. An environment conducive to stable product prices and to maintaining sustainable economic growth has become a prime responsibility of governments and, of course, central banks. It was not always thus. In the last comparable period of open international trade a century ago, the gold standard prevailed. The roles of central banks, where they existed (remember the United States did not have one), were then quite different from today.

International stabilization was implemented by more or less automatic gold flows from those financial markets where conditions were lax to those where liquidity was in short supply. To some, myself included, the system appears to have worked rather well. To others, the gold standard was perceived as too rigid or unstable, and in any event the inability to finance discretionary policy, both monetary and fiscal, led first to a further compromise of the gold standard system after World War I, and by the 1930s it had been essentially abandoned.

THE GLOBALIZATION OF FINANCE

The fiat money systems that emerged have given considerable power and responsibility to central banks to manage the sovereign credit of nations. Under a gold standard, money creation was at the limit tied to changes in gold reserves. The discretionary range of monetary policy was relatively narrow. Today's central banks have the capability of creating or destroying unlimited supplies of money and credit.

Clearly, how well we take our responsibilities in this modern world has profound implications for participants in financial markets. We provide the backdrop against which participants make their decisions. As a consequence, it is incumbent upon us to endeavor to produce the same noninflationary environment as existed a century ago, if we seek maximum sustainable growth. In this regard, doubtless, the most important development that has occurred in recent years has been the shift from an environment of inflationary expectations built into both business planning and financial contracts toward an environment of lower inflation. It is important that that progress continue and that we maintain a credible long-run commitment to price stability.

While there can be little doubt that the extraordinary changes in global finance on balance have been beneficial in facilitating significant improvements in economic structures and living standards throughout the world, they also have the potential for some negative consequences. In fact, while the speed of transmission of positive economic events has been an important plus for the world economy in recent years, it is becoming increasingly obvious, as evidenced by recent events in Thailand and its neighbors and several years ago in Mexico, that significant macroeconomic policy mistakes also reverberate around the world at a prodigious pace. In any event, technological progress is not reversible. We must learn to live with it.

In the context of rapid changes affecting financial markets, disruptions are inevitable. The turmoil in the European Exchange Rate mechanism in 1992, the plunge in the exchange value of the Mexican peso at the end of 1994 and early 1995, and the recent sharp exchange rate adjustments in a number of Asian economies have shown how the new world of financial trading can punish policy misalignments, actual or perceived, with amazing alacrity. This is new. Even as recently as 15 or 20 years ago, the size of the international financial system was a fraction of what it is today. Contagion effects were more limited, and, thus, breakdowns carried fewer negative consequences. In both new and old environments, the economic consequences of disruptions are minimized if they are not further compounded by financial instability associated with underlying inflation trends.

Maintaining Financial Stability

The recent financial turmoil in some Asian financial markets, and similar events elsewhere previously, confirm that in a world of increasing capital mobility there is a premium on governments maintaining sound macroeconomic policies and allowing exchange rates to provide appropriate signals for the broader pricing structure of the economy.

These countries became vulnerable as markets became increasingly aware of a buildup of excesses, including overvalued exchange rates, bulging current account deficits, and sharp increases in asset values. In many cases, these were the consequence of poor investment judgments in seeking to employ huge increases in portfolios for investment. In some cases, these excesses were fed by unsound real estate and other lending activity by various financial institutions in these countries, which, in turn, undermined the soundness of these countries' financial systems. As a consequence, these countries lost the confidence of both domestic and international investors, with resulting disturbances in their financial markets.

The resort to capital controls to deal with financial market disturbances of the sort a number of emerging economies have experienced would be a step backwards from the trend toward financial market liberalization, and in the end would not be effective. The maintenance of financial stability in an environment of global capital markets, therefore, calls for greater attention by governments to the soundness of public policy.

Governments are beginning to recognize that the release of timely and accurate economic and financial data is a critical element to the maintenance of financial stability. We do not know what the appropriate amount of disclosure is, but it is pretty clear from the Mexican experience in 1994 and the recent Thai experience that the level of disclosure was too little. More comprehensive public information on the financial condition of a country, including current data on commitments by governments to buy or sell currencies in the future and on nonperforming loans of a country's financial institutions, would allow investors—both domestic and international—to make more rational investment decisions. Such disclosure would help to avoid sudden and sharp reversals in the investment positions of investors once they become aware of the true status of a country's and a banking system's financial health. More timely and more comprehensive disclosure of financial data also would help sensitize the principal economic policymakers of a country to the potential emerging threats to its financial stability.

Thus, as international financial markets continue to expand, central banks have twin objectives: achieving macroeconomic stability and a safe and sound financial system that can take advantage of stability while exploiting the inevitable new technological advances.

The changing dynamics of modern global financial systems also require that central banks address the inevitable increase of systemic risk. It is probably fair to say that the very efficiency of global financial markets, engendered by the rapid proliferation of financial products, also has the capability of transmitting mistakes at a far faster pace throughout the financial system in ways that were unknown a generation ago, and not even remotely imagined in the 19th century.

Today's technology enables single individuals to initiate massive transactions with very rapid execution. Clearly, not only has the productivity of global finance increased markedly, but so, obviously, has the ability to generate losses at a previously inconceivable rate.

Moreover, increasing global financial efficiency, by creating the mechanisms for mistakes to ricochet throughout the global financial system, has patently increased the potential for systemic risk. Why not then, one might ask, bar or contain the expansion of global finance by capital controls, transaction taxes, or other market-inhibiting initiatives? Why not return to the less hectic and seemingly less threatening markets of, say, the 1950s?

Endeavoring to thwart technological advance and new knowledge and innovation through the erection of barriers to the spread of knowledge would, as history amply demonstrates, have large, often adverse, unintended consequences. Suppressed markets in one location would be rapidly displaced by others outside the reach of government controls and taxes. Of greater importance, risk taking, so indispensable to the creation of wealth, would undoubtedly be curbed, to the detriment of rising living standards. We cannot turn back the clock on technology—and we should not try to do so.

Rather, we should recognize that, if it is technology that has imparted the current stress to markets, technology can be employed to contain it. Enhancements to financial institutions' internal risk-management systems arguably constitute the most effective countermeasure to the increased potential instability of the global financial system. Improving the efficiency of the world's payment systems is clearly another.

The availability of new technology and new derivative financial instruments clearly has facilitated new, more rigorous approaches to the conceptualization, measurement, and management of risk for such systems. There are, however, limitations to the statistical models used in such systems owing to the necessity of overly simplifying assumptions. Hence, human judgments, based on analytically looser but far more realistic evaluations of what the future may hold, are of critical importance in risk management. Although a sophisticated understanding of statistical modeling techniques is important to risk management, an intimate knowledge of the markets in which an institution trades and of the customers it serves is turning out to be far more important.

In these and other ways, we must assure that our rapidly changing global financial system retains the capacity to contain market shocks. This is a never-ending process that requires never-ending vigilance.

[9]

Review of International Political Economy 5:2 Summer 1998: 169–216

Differential accumulation: towards a new political economy of capital

Jonathan Nitzan

Department of Social Science and Commerce, Marianopolis College, Montreal, Quebec

ABSTRACT

Existing theories of capital, neo-classical as well as Marxist, are anchored in the material sphere of production and consumption. This article offers a new analytical framework for capital as a crystallization of power. The relative nature of power requires accumulation to be measured in differential, not absolute, terms. For absentee owners, the main goal is not to maximize profits, but rather to 'beat the average' and exceed the 'normal rate of return'. The theoretical framework builds on Thorstein Veblen's separation of industry from business and on Lewis Mumford's dichotomy between democratic and authoritarian techniques. Extending their contributions, we argue that capital is a business, not an industrial category, a human mega-machine rather than a material artefact. Indeed, it is the *social* essence of capital which makes accumulation possible in the first place. Capital measures the present value of future business earnings, and these depend not on the productivity of industry as such, but on the ability of absentee owners strategically to limit such productivity to their own differential ends. Introducing the twin concepts of the 'differential power of capital' (*DPK*) and the rate of 'differential accumulation' (*DA*), we examine the non-linear and possibly negative link between industrial growth and accumulation in the USA.

KEYWORDS

Capital; power; technology; institutional economics; Veblen; Mumford.

1 INTRODUCTION: THE UNSETTLED QUESTION OF CAPITAL

Political economy, understood as the search for the 'anatomy of civil society' (Marx, 1859b: 20), studies the pursuit of plenty as much as the quest for power. When focusing on capitalist society, however, it suffers from a serious structural drawback: one of its major building blocks – capital – remains elusive and seriously biased.

The reason is twofold. First, with the growing bureaucratization of academia, the study of political economy was gradually segmented into separate 'departments'. Capital was monopolized by 'economists'. 'Political scientists', 'sociologists' and 'anthropologists' were more or less forced to accept whatever definition the dismal science of economics came up with. And given the growing materialistic bent of the latter, the result was to leave power pretty much out of the picture. Thus, as political economy lost its original cohesion, the intellectual journey of capital began limping on one leg. And as if to make a bad situation worse, this leg itself was not in such good shape. Indeed, the second problem is that economists could not agree on the proper definition of capital. Capital was monetary wealth. That was clear enough. Figuring out what made it grow, however, was much harder. 'What a mass of confused, futile, and downright silly controversy it would have saved us', wrote Schumpeter (1954: 323), 'if economists had had the sense to stick to those monetary and accounting meanings of the term instead of trying to "deepen" them!' Of course, the problem was not the desire to 'deepen', but the direction in which the economists went digging. And the difficulty persists precisely because economists insist it is exclusively theirs. According to Bliss (1975: vii), once economists agree on the theory of capital, 'they will shortly reach agreement on everything else'. But then how could they agree on it, if capital, by its very essence, involves power which they view as lying largely outside their domain?

Historically, the principal contention among economists stemmed from trying to marry two different perceptions of capital: one as an income-generating fund, or 'financial wealth', the other as a stock of physical contrivances, or 'capital goods'. The central question has been whether and in what way 'capital goods' are productive, and how their productivity affects their overall magnitude as 'capital'. Mainstream economics has generally tried to show that capital goods were indeed productive, and that this 'positive' attribute is what made capital as a 'fund' valuable.

The marriage did not work well, partly due to a large age difference. The older partner, capital, comes from the Latin *caput*, a word whose origin goes back to Babylon. In both Rome and Mesopotamia capital had a similar, unambiguous economic meaning: it was a pecuniary magnitude. There was no relation to produced 'means of production'. Indeed, *caput* meant 'head', which fits well with another Babylonian invention, the human 'work day' (Bickerman, 1972: 58, 63; Schumpeter, 1954: 322-3). The younger partner, 'capital goods', was born millennia later, roughly together with capitalism, and it was only since the physiocrats that economists began associating 'capital' with roundabout production processes.

For most economists this association is common sense. But then the fact that 'capital' predates 'capital goods' by a few thousand years suggests

DIFFERENTIAL ACCUMULATION

that their overlap is not that self-evident. 'Capital' is best viewed as a *shell*, an abstract form in need of contents. The shell is a readily observable monetary magnitude, and is largely beyond dispute; its contents, on the other hand, are not at all apparent, and must hence be reasoned theoretically. Over the past few hundred years, perhaps due to the highly productive thrust of capitalism, most writers have chosen to look for 'materialistic' contents. But this need not be the only route. In fact, by focusing on 'material' considerations alone, much of the 'social' contents of capital, including that which is not unique to capitalism, has been left out of the picture. This neglect has proven costly, leaving capital theory, as well as many of its derivatives, mired in controversy.

For the neo-classicists, the basic problem stemmed from trying to quantify 'capital goods' so that they can be aggregated into 'capital'. The 'formal' problem, identified already by Wicksell (1935: 149), was that unlike labour and land, capital goods were *heterogeneous*, and therefore could not be added in terms of their own technical units. The only way to do so was by using money values, but the value of capital goods depended on the rate of return, which already incorporated the quantity of capital in its denominator. The result was a circular definition in which the quantity of capital depended on the . . . quantity of capital! A more substantive, 'social' challenge came from Veblen (1908a, 1908b, 1908c, 1908d, 1909), but it was only half a century later that the criticism began to echo. Following Sraffa (1960) and the ensuing Cambridge Controversy, it was shown that the 'quantity of capital' was a fiction, and that productive contributions could not be measured without prior knowledge of prices and distribution. Sraffa's famous 'reswitching' examples demonstrated that, contrary to neo-classical theory, 'capital intensity' need not have a unique, inverse relationship with the rate of interest. In other words, the fact that a capitalist uses a less 'mechanized' process (fewer 'capital goods'?) does not necessarily mean she is using less 'capital'.

The neo-classicists conceded there was a problem, offering to treat Clark's quantitative definition of capital not literally, but as a 'parable' (Samuelson, 1962). Some, like Ferguson (1969), even went so far as admitting that neo-classical theory was a 'matter of faith'. But then parables and faith were hardly enough. With the 'quantity of capital' undefined, there is no production function, no supply function and no equilibrium. And with these gone, economics fails its two celebrated tasks of explaining prices and quantities. The material footing of capital therefore had to be retained. The first and most common tactic was to gloss the problem over, or ignore it altogether. So far this seems to be working, as Robinson (1971) predicted and Hodgson (1997) confirmed. Indeed, with the exception of 'specialists', most economists rarely lose sleep over capital theory. A more subtle line of defence was to argue that the problem, however serious in principle, was of limited importance in

ARTICLES

practice (Ferguson, 1969). Given the abstract nature of neo-classical theory, however, resting its defence on relevance is hardly persuasive. The third and probably most significant response was to embrace disaggregate general equilibrium models, in which there was no 'capital' and no general 'rate of interest', only individual inputs and individual input prices. But then this was hardly a solution at all. While the shell called 'capital' may or may not consist of individual physical inputs, its existence and pivotal social significance are hardly in doubt. By ignoring capital, general equilibrium has augmented its other weaknesses, turning itself into a hollow formality.

The Marxist treatment of capital, though different in goals, has run into similar problems. Throughout *Das Kapital* there is no 'analytical' definition of capital, perhaps for a good reason. Marx saw capital not as a 'thing', but as a comprehensive social context whose description was intertwined with its explanation (Marx, 1894: 947–8). The context of capital included the production process, the division of labour, technological progress and, above all, the institutional and power arrangements shaping the collective consciousness. According to Wright (1977: 198), the notion that capital accumulation involves merely the tangible augmentation of machinery, buildings, raw materials and the like is alien to Marxist thinking. Instead, he maintains, 'capital accumulation must be understood as the reproduction of capitalist social relations on an ever-expanding scale through the conversion of surplus value into new constant and variable capital.' Emphasizing this aspect of Marx's writing, Shaikh (1990: 73) similarly reiterates that 'capital is not a thing, but rather a definite set of social relations', and that in order to understand it, 'one must therefore decipher its character as a social relation'.

But then when it came to *measuring* capital, Marxist theory has never really managed to transcend the 'materialistic' boundaries of labour time. Marx (1867: 114) insightfully emphasized the *societal* essence of valuation, making the value of a commodity an expression of the 'portion of the total labour-time of society required to produce it'. His troubles began when he tried to build this total from the bottom up – that is, on the basis of quantifiable labour inputs. In so doing, Marx not only assumed that production contained the code of distribution and accumulation (which the post-Sraffa controversy put into question), but also that the production process, including that of 'labour power', could – at least in principle – be *objectively* identified in functional, quantitative terms.

Indeed, by concentrating on the role of production, Marxist value theory tends to ignore the impact on measurement of power institutions such as monopoly and oligopoly, dual labour markets and redistribution by government, to name only a few (Howard and King, 1992: 282; Sweezy, 1942: 270–4). In the absence of price-taking, freely mobile capitalists and

DIFFERENTIAL ACCUMULATION

workers, labour values become practically useless for the study of prices
and accumulation. In fact, under non-competitive conditions, with the
wage rate deviating from the worker's 'socially necessary' cost of reproduction, the value of labour power itself – the basic input in all production
processes – is already 'contaminated' by power relations.

The problem of all production-based theories of accumulation – be
they neo-classicist or Marxist – is well reflected in their inability to define
clearly *what is being accumulated*. The implicit assumption is that accumulation could somehow be measured in *material* terms. In the
neo-classical world, where the goal is 'well-being', capital is presumably
reducible to some units of pleasure, or 'utils' as the neo-classicists like
to call them. Marxists see capitalists as driven by the circular goal of
accumulation for the sake of accumulation, a principle best understood
in terms of power. Their analytical category of capital, however, is
measured in terms of 'labour time', and therefore remains entangled in
the material intricacies of production.

The purpose of this article is to offer an alternative approach to the
study of capital, seeking to break it loose from the overly 'materialistic'
grip of economists and put it back where it belongs – in the broader
field of political economy.[1] Drawing on the institutional frameworks of
Veblen and Mumford, our principal contribution is to *integrate power
into the definition of capital*. Briefly, the value of capital represents
discounted expected earnings. Some of these earnings could be associated with the productivity (or exploitation) of the owned industrial
apparatus, but this is only part of the story. As capitalism grows in
complexity, the earnings of any given business concern come to depend
less on its own industrial undertakings and more on the *community's
overall productivity*. In this sense, the value of capital represents a *distributional* claim. This claim is manifested partly through ownership, but
more broadly through the *whole spectrum of social power*. Moreover,
power is not only a means of accumulation, but also its most fundamental end. For the absentee owner, the purpose is not to 'maximize'
profits but to 'beat the average'. The ultimate goal of business is not
hedonic pleasure, but *differential* gain. In our view, this differential aspect
of accumulation offers a promising avenue for putting power into the
definition of capital.

The literature on social power is extensive and the relationship
between power and accumulation has recently attracted considerable
attention from Marxist and institutionalist writers. However, as far as
we know, power has never been incorporated into the *definition* of accumulation. If this can be done successfully, the theoretical consequences
for political economy will be significant. In particular, it will help clear
logical road-blocks in existing capital theory, making political economy
more theoretically coherent.

ARTICLES

Following this introduction, Section 2 uses Veblen's separation between business and industry to examine the non-linear links between power and production. Section 3 builds on Mumford's emphasis of symbolic drives, arguing that accumulation is possible only because capital is not a tangible artefact, but a social mega-machine. Bringing these two issues together, Section 4 offers a tentative operational definition for differential accumulation, examines its development in the USA, and assesses some preliminary implications. The last section touches on the significance of power for the future of capitalism and beyond.

2 TOWARDS A NEW THEORY OF CAPITAL

Our starting point is that accumulation is not an offshoot of production, but rather an *interaction between productivity and power*. The concept of power is problematic, no less than that of capital. Without getting too deeply into its complexities, our own emphasis is on asymmetric power, or 'power over'. Following Lukes, we see power in capitalism as held and exercised by groups of individuals, whose action or inaction significantly affects the actions and thoughts of others. This power is applied within structural constraints, though the agency–structure distinction is itself potentially ambivalent and theory-dependent. For instance, the power of one group is often imposed as structure on another, power could be solidified into structure and then melted back into power, structure could be altered by power, or it could have its own internal dynamics (for a critical treatment, see Lukes, 1974, 1977, 1978).

The link between power and accumulation is evident from Marx's two forms of circulation: simple circulation ($C \to M \to C$), where the purpose is use value, and expanded circulation ($M \to C \to M'$), where the end is *more* money. The difference is fundamental. In the first case, typical of the worker's life cycle, the goal is material; in the second case, representing the capitalist drive, the aim is symbolic. Capitalists of course tend to consume more than workers, but that is beside the point. 'Accumulate, Accumulate! That is Moses and the Prophets!' writes Marx. 'Accumulation for accumulation's sake, production for production's sake' (1867: 652). The capitalist seeks higher profit, not in order to buy *more goods and services*, but in order to assert his or her *differential power*. Unfortunately, Marx's insight into the power drive of accumulation has never been integrated into his analytical framework. The parallel dynamics of simple and expanded circulation captured the duality of productivity and power, but the vehicle of accumulation, C, remained arrested in a one-dimensional material framework of 'labour content'.

The first step in reinstating the duality of productivity and power is to remove the superficial separation between 'economics' and 'politics'. Capitalism is not an 'economic system', but a whole social order, and

DIFFERENTIAL ACCUMULATION

its principal category of capital must therefore have an 'encompassing' definition. As we see it, capital should be understood in terms of ideology, religion and the basic instincts of violence and sex, as well as in terms of production, creativity, consumption and well-being. In short, an attempt to define capital – if that is at all possible – should begin with a broad institutionalist view of society.

Perhaps the first attempt to develop an institutionalist theory of capital along such lines was offered at the turn of the century by Thorstein Veblen. Later, his student and colleague Lewis Mumford expanded some of Veblen's themes into a broad theory of power civilization. The frameworks of both writers build on the primal social interaction between creativity and power: Veblen associated this interaction with a distinction between industry and business, whereas for Mumford it was part of a conflict between democratic and totalitarian technologies. Their profound insights, unduly neglected by political economists, deserve close scrutiny and we turn to them now.

Industry and business

Neo-classical economists see hedonic pleasure and the pursuit of material well-being as the ultimate goal of human beings, and the drive to equilibrium as the governing mechanism (or at least the underlying ideal) of all societies. Veblen, on the other hand, started by identifying the *conflict between creativity and power* as the prime mover of human history. In the modern capitalist order, he argued, this duality is reflected in a fundamental distinction between *industry* and *business*.

For Veblen, industry and business are two separate spheres of human activity. Industry constitutes the material context of capitalism, although it is not unique to it. When considered in isolation from contemporary business institutions, the principal goal of industry, its *raison d'être* according to Veblen, is the efficient production of quality goods and services. The hallmark of industry is the so-called 'machine process', which Veblen equated not merely with the use of machines, but more broadly with the systematic organization of production and the reasoned application of knowledge. Above all, Veblen accentuated the holistic nature of industry. The neo-classical emphasis on individualism and its Robinson Crusoe analogies of the innovative 'entrepreneur' and single 'consumer' were misleading myths. The machine process was essentially a *communal* activity, whose productivity derived first and foremost from *cooperation* and *integration*. The reasons were both historical and spatial.

First, modern industrial production is contingent on the 'technological heritage' of society, the general body of 'community knowledge' grounded in the 'accumulated wisdom of the past' (Veblen, 1908b: 326–9). Second, over time the gradual accumulation of knowledge makes

ARTICLES

production more spatially interdependent. 'Evidently', writes Veblen, 'the state of industrial arts is of the nature of a joint stock, worked out, held, carried forward, and made use of by those who live within the sweep of the industrial community. In this bearing the industrial community is a joint going-concern' (1923: 64). Following Sombart, he emphasized the *comprehensive* nature of industry, in that it 'draws into its scope and turns to account all branches of knowledge that have to do with the material sciences, and the whole makes a more or less delicately balanced complex of sub-processes' (Veblen, 1904: 7–8). Given this growing dependency of both knowledge and processes, says Veblen, the efficiency of industrial production increasingly hinges on synchronization and standardization of both production and wants (an issue resurrected half a century later by Galbraith (1967) with his 'revised sequence' and attack on 'consumer sovereignty'). As a highly integrated system, industry is strongly disposed towards elaborate planning and close cooperation. Ultimately, it calls for 'solidarity in the administration of any group of related industries' and, more generally, 'for solidarity in the management of the entire industrial traffic of the community' (Veblen, 1904: 17).

Although Veblen's emphasis of integration and synchronization seems hardly earth shaking, mainstream economists have managed to ignore systematically two of its key implications. One is that distribution cannot possibly be based on factor productivity. The other is that distribution should therefore be sought in the realm of power.

According to Veblen, business differs from industry in both methods and goals. Business enterprise means investment for profit. It proceeds through purchase and sale towards the ulterior end of accumulated pecuniary wealth. While industry is carried by the 'instinct of workmanship', business is a matter of ownership and power; whereas the former requires integration, cooperation and planning throughout society, the latter spells conflict and antagonism among owners, and a cleavage running between businessmen and the underlying population of working consumers.

These profound differences have crystallized into two different 'languages'. Unlike industrial activity with its tangible, material categories, business traffic and achievements are counted in strictly pecuniary terms. Economists insist on reducing business magnitudes to 'real' utilitarian units, though that merely attests their pre-capitalist habit of thinking. Under the price system,

> men have come to the conviction that *money-values are more real and substantial than any of the material facts in this transitory world.* So much so that the final purpose of any businesslike undertaking is always a sale, by which the seller comes in for the price of his

DIFFERENTIAL ACCUMULATION

goods; and when a person has sold his goods, and so becomes in effect a creditor by that much, he is said to have 'realized' his wealth, or to have 'realized' his holdings. *In the business world the price of things is a more substantial fact than the things themselves.*

(1923: 88–9; italics added)

The pecuniary nature of business terminology is not a mere accounting convention; it is the very essence of business enterprise.

At first sight, Veblen's separation between industry and business seems to resemble Marx's distinction between simple and expanded circulation. There is a crucial difference, however. Unlike Marx, who used a single material unit (labour) to measure both processes, Veblen began at the outset with two distinct categories – material for industry, pecuniary for business. This duality enabled him to avoid the Marxist 'Transformation Problem' altogether: prices and accumulation were business magnitudes, and hence their determination cannot be attributed, at least not in any straightforward way, to the complex and largely intractable sphere of industrial interactions.

According to Veblen, capitalist industry was subordinated to business ends; its aim was not serviceability and livelihood, but profit. Simple as it seems, this hierarchy inverts conventional economic reasoning. Being a quest for profit, argues Veblen, business enterprise is essentially a *claim* on earnings. It is wholly and only an act of *distribution*. Commodities against which profits constitute an effective claim are created elsewhere, in the industrial sphere. Yet, given that industry is carried on for the sake of business, it follows that the primary line of causality runs not from production to distribution, but from distribution to production. And if causality is a guide for analysis, the study of capitalism should begin with business, not industry.

Indeed, on its own, industry provides no insight into distribution. Anticipating the Cambridge Controversy more than half a century before it arose, Veblen pointed out quite bluntly that Clark's marginal productivity theory (1899) was wishful thinking. In order to explain distribution by productivity, we must first identify the productivity of each individual factor of production. Yet this, he said, could not be done since economic inputs did not possess any individual productivity to begin with.

As already noted, Veblen viewed industrial activity as an integrated community process centred on the 'technological heritage' of society. On the surface, this may look similar to prevailing convictions, popular since Galbraith (1958, 1967), which emphasize the growing significance of technology vis-à-vis the traditional factors of production, land, labour and capital. That is not what Veblen had in mind, however. In his opinion, technology, or the 'immaterial equipment' of society as he liked

ARTICLES

to call it, was not just another 'factor of production', however important. Instead, it was the *vital* cultural substance which made raw materials, machines and physical human labour useful in the first place: 'To say that these minerals, plants and animals are meaningful – in other words, that they are economic goods – means that they have been brought within the sweep of the community's knowledge of ways and means' (1908b: 329). Without this 'immaterial equipment', the physical factors of production were *economically* meaningless objects.

For instance, the usefulness of any given computer depends crucially on the current 'state of technology'. With the arrival of new software, it quickly ends up in the junk heap; the new technology makes it economically obsolete, and although it may have lost none of its operational features, it is no longer a 'capital good'. Or, to roll history in reverse, a modern factory producing semiconductors would have been a worthless (indeed, meaningless) collection of physical objects during Veblen's time – first, because it could not have been operated and, second, because its output would have had no perceptible use. In this and every other case, the transformation of a physical object into an economically useful capital good can neither lead nor lag the existing 'state of industrial arts'. The same logic applies to labour power and raw materials: a jungle tribesman would be lost in a modern factory much as a bank clerk would be in the Sahara desert, while ancient stone utensils are as useless today as was petroleum before the invention of modern engines.

Labour, land and capital goods are obviously essential for production, but only because they are part of a comprehensive social and cultural process. Hence it 'seems bootless to ask', argued Veblen, although few neo-classicists were listening, 'how much of the products of industry or of its productivity is to be imputed to these brute forces, human and non human, as contrasted with the specifically human factors that make technological efficiency' (1908b: 349–50). In short, as the industrial system grows in complexity, the productivity theory of distribution becomes an oxymoron.

The increasingly 'holistic' nature of modern industry was well understood by Marx (1859a: 592f.), who prophetically anticipated its devastating consequences for his own labour theory of value, and hopefully for capitalism itself:

> As large-scale industry advances, the creation of real wealth depends less on the labour time and quantity of labour expended than on the power of the instrumentalities set in motion during the labour time. . . . Human labour then no longer appears enclosed in the process of production – man rather relates himself to the process of production as supervisor and regulator. . . . He stands

DIFFERENTIAL ACCUMULATION

outside of the process of production instead of being the principal agent in the process of production. In this transformation, the great pillar of production and wealth is no longer the immediate labour performed by man himself, nor his labour time, but the appropriation of his own universal productivity, i.e., *his knowledge and his mastery of nature through his societal existence* – in one word, the development of the *societal individual*. . . . As soon as human labour, in its immediate form, has ceased to be the great source of wealth, labour time will cease, and must of necessity cease to be the measure of wealth, and the exchange value must of necessity cease to be the measure of use value. . . . The mode of production which rests on the exchange value thus collapses.

(cited and translated by Marcuse, 1964: 35–6; italics added)

Although this last prediction is yet to materialize, the *societal* nature of productivity, on which Marx hung his hopes, seems beyond dispute.

To illustrate, consider the automobile industry. Its research and development process incorporates knowledge from fields as diverse as mathematics, physics, chemistry, biology, metallurgy, economics, demography, sociology and politics. Its production relies on coordinating the interaction of raw materials, labour, assembly facilities, infrastructure, transportation and distribution systems in numerous countries. Finally, both development and production are path-dependent. For example, the emergence of large-scale petroleum refining, suburbanization and the highway system accelerated automobile production in the twentieth century, while congestion and environmental concerns may hinder it in the next. In this highly complex context, where technology is cumulative, spatially interdependent and intermingled with politics, it is practically impossible as well as theoretically inconceivable even to identify all inputs, let alone determine their individual productive contributions. As Wicksell put it when he decided to ignore Marshall's notion of 'organization' as a fourth agent of production (1920, Book IV), the whole thing 'lacks *quantitative precision*' (1935: 107; original italics).

Following Veblen (and the reluctant Marx), we can hence argue that the conventional input/output ideology is a misleading simplification: it focuses on first-order interactions between observed (or quasi-observable) quantities, while ignoring the invisible but far more important multi-layer cultural/political/technological interactions, without which physical objects cannot become 'inputs'. Although most economists refuse to admit it, this neglect has seriously undermined their empirical research. Neoclassical production functions are notoriously weak when it comes to predicting output on the basis of physical inputs, typically leaving a wide margin of unexplained variation. The usual defence is to attribute this failure to inadequate measurement of 'technology', dubbing the residual

179

a 'measure of our ignorance'. This language is highly deceptive, however, since it implies that eventually the problem *will* be overcome. But then how could it when production becomes *ever more* intractable?

Of course, none of this implies that distribution is unrelated to production. According to Veblen, the two are very much related, but their link is alien to the 'productivity doctrine'. Contrary to the common view of distribution as a corollary of creativity, Veblen maintained it was a consequence of 'sabotage'. Most generally, the income of an owner is proportionate not to the specific productive contribution of his or her input, but rather to *the overall damage the owner can inflict on the industrial process at large*. It is this 'negative' relationship to which we now turn to explore.

Absolute ownership and the strategic limitation of industry

Over the long term, argued Veblen, output depended mostly on population and technical knowledge; 'tangible assets' were relatively insignificant. Throughout history, the occasional destruction of material equipment and resources was usually a relatively minor inconvenience. Indeed, even in the twentieth century, when physical accumulation reached unprecedented levels, it took war-stricken Germany and Japan only a few years to launch their 'economic miracles'. The significance of tangible equipment arises mainly in the *short term*, and this according to Veblen is where ownership comes into the picture:

> For the transient time being, therefore, any person who has the legal right to withhold any part of the necessary industrial apparatus or materials from current use will be in a position to impose terms and exact obedience, on pain of rendering the community's joint stock of technology inoperative for that extent. Ownership of industrial equipment and natural resources confers such a right legally to enforce unemployment, and so to make the community's workmanship useless to that extent. *This is the Natural Right of Investment.*
>
> (1923: 65–6; italics added)

Hence, the causal link runs not from the creation of earnings to the right of ownership, but from the right of ownership to the appropriation of earnings. 'Capital goods' yield profit not because of their individual productivity, but because they are *privately owned* to begin with. Business enterprise thrives on the implicit threat or explicit exercise of economic power embedded in ownership, with capitalist income being the 'ransom' for allowing industry to function. As Veblen saw it, the Natural Right of Ownership was synonymous with the vested power to incapacitate:

DIFFERENTIAL ACCUMULATION

Plainly, ownership would be nothing better than an idle gesture without this legal right of sabotage. Without the power of discretionary idleness, without the right to keep the work out of the hands of the workmen and the product out of the market, *investment and business enterprise would cease*. This is the larger meaning of the Security of Property.

(1923: 66–7; italics added)

Of course, the role of power is hardly unique to capitalism. According to Veblen, all forms of ownership were based on the same principle of coercive appropriation, which in his view dated back to the early stages of barbarism and the initial emergence of predatory social customs (1898, 1899). The differentiating factor was technological: the institutionalization of forceful seizure was intimately linked to the nature of tangible implements and to their relative significance in production. In the earlier stages of social development, forced appropriation was limited if only because there was little to appropriate and most objects were easily replaceable. But as the 'immaterial assets' of society started to accumulated, so did the benefit from controlling its key 'material assets'.

The first form of property rights according to Veblen (1898, 1899) was the ownership of people, particularly women (the English word 'husband' and the Hebrew word 'baal' both share the double meaning of ownership and marriage, and in the latter case also sexual exploit). The focus of ownership has subsequently shifted (although not necessarily linearly) from slaves, to animals, to land, depending on the nature of technological development, and it was only recently that it moved primarily to produced means of production. Of course, neither slave ownership nor landed wealth was ever justified on grounds of productive contributions; both were institutionalized as a 'right' – by virtue of divine will or sheer force, but never as a consequence of creativity. Since the mere ownership of capital is no more productive than the ownership of slaves or land, why do economists insist it is? The answer, according to Veblen, is that economic theory had been unduly affected by the transitory institutions of handicraft existing during the transformation from feudalism to capitalism. Common sense suggested that craftsmen, working for themselves with their own material appliances, had a 'natural right' to own what they had made; it also implied they could dispense with their product as they saw fit – that is, sell it for an income. Handicraft and petty trade thus helped institutionalize pecuniary earnings as a natural extension of ownership-by-creativity. With exchange seen as a 'natural right of ownership', the very earning of income became a proof of productivity.

But this common sense is misleading. First, even at the handicraft stage, production was already a societal process. Thus, despite the myth

ARTICLES

of 'individualism', private ownership was at least partly dependent on the dynamics of power (with the monopoly practices of guilds offering a conspicuous illustration). Second and more significantly, the institutions of handicraft were short-lived. As Veblen pointed out, technical change ushered in by the onset of the Industrial Revolution meant that production had to be conducted on a *large scale*, which in turn implied the progressive *separation of ownership from production*.

During the earlier stages of capitalism, production and business were still partly interwoven. Indeed, even as late as the nineteenth century, US 'captains of industry', such as Cornelius Vanderbilt and Andrew Carnegie, were seen as creative factors, acting as master workmen as well as astute businessmen (Josephson, 1934). This did not last for long, however, and as business became increasingly separate from industry, the implication was no less than profound. Gradually, capitalism came to mean not merely the amassment of 'capital goods' under *private* ownership but, more profoundly, a division between business and industry effected through the rise of *absentee* ownership.

The institution of absentee ownership has altered the very nature and meaning of 'capital'. Modern capitalists have become investors of 'funds', absentee owners of pecuniary wealth with no industrial dealings; their investment is a business transaction in which they acquire a claim over a future stream of money income; and accumulation involves no longer the augmentation of physical means of production, but of financial values. Under absentee ownership, capital is stripped of any tangible characteristic, assuming the universal face of money value. (Marx was of course aware of the 'financial' appearance of capital, but because this conflicted with his value analysis of constant capital, he took the easy way out, defining it away as 'fictitious capital'. See Perlman, 1990.)

Whereas most economists continue to view capital as an amalgamation of machines, structures and semi-finished commodities, for the businessman capital has long signified something totally different. In the eyes of a modern investor, capital means a *capitalized earning capacity*. It consists not of the owned factories, mines, aeroplanes or retail establishments, but of the present value of profits expected to be earned by force of such ownership.

True, neo-classicists never had a quarrel with capital as a present value of future earnings: in the long run, demand and supply made this equal to the cost of producing that capital (assuming competitive markets, perfect foresight and all the rest). But as Veblen (1908b) acutely observed long before the Cambridge Controversy, things were not that simple. If capital and capital goods were indeed the same 'thing', how could capital move from one industry to another, while capital goods, the 'abiding entity' of capital, remained locked in their original position?

DIFFERENTIAL ACCUMULATION

Similarly, how could a business crisis diminish the value of capital when, as a material productive substance, the underlying capital goods remained unaltered? Or, how could existing capital be denominated in terms of its productivity, when technological progress seemed to destroy its pecuniary value?

For Veblen, the answer was straightforward: capital was simply not a double-sided entity. It was a pecuniary magnitude and *only* a pecuniary magnitude. The value of capital depends on pecuniary earnings, which in the final analysis depend not on the *productive* contribution of the owned capital goods and not even on the overall productivity of the company's industrial apparatus. Instead, they hinge on the *institutional* ability of the individual firm, operating as a business undertaking (rather than as an industrial unit), to appropriate part of the community's technological efficiency. What is being capitalized is not the *ability to produce*, but the *power to appropriate*.

The contention surrounding the link between profit and power persisted partly because the historical consolidation of property rights slowly substituted manipulation and authority for brute force and open coercion. With profit becoming a legal norm, power has solidified into 'structure' – at least for those subjected to it. Although force and violence remain a latent threat, earning power is now institutionalized through the conventional subordination of industry to business. For the absentee owner, industrial control is designed to generate the largest differential gain, which generally requires the *strategic limitation* of productive activity. In the normal course of business enterprise, this strategic limitation – or 'sabotage' as Veblen liked to call it – becomes the central manifestation of capitalist power.

But then what 'sabotage'? Is it not true that in order to profit, business enterprise needs to *promote* industrial creativity? The answer is *up to a point and only under certain conditions*. Earnings do depend on output, but in a non-linear way, and in following Veblen, that is why we use the notion of *strategic* limitation.

Seen as an entire social order, business enterprise has surely been far more productive than any earlier mode of social organization. Yet, in Veblen's opinion, its immense productive vitality was essentially an industrial, not a business, phenomenon. Business enterprise is possible only in conjunction with large-scale industry, though the reverse is not true. The practices of business – exchange and its surrounding institutions – are of course related to industry, but only in point of control, never in terms of production and creativity. From this a priori vantage point, business *cannot* 'boost' industry. Even companies in possession of cutting-edge technology do not promote industrial creativity; instead, they merely relax some of the constraints which otherwise limit creativity.

ARTICLES

A business enterprise will certainly seek to incorporate new methods or products, *but only in so far as they confer an adequate differential advantage*. The R&D departments of Sony and Intel, for example, have generated more and better innovations than those actually used for profitable ends. The production of digital audio tapes (DAT) in the early 1990s, for instance, has been postponed (to the point of making the technology outdated) because several large firms could not reach a consensus regarding its effect on recording profits, a saga which has since been replayed with respect to digital versatile discs (DVD). Similarly, there is usually a substantial lag between the development and introduction of a new Intel microprocessor, depending on the balance between the success of existing models and competitive threats. Moreover, the very development of new technologies and products is often conditioned by their potential effect on existing profit and capitalization. Thus, the petroleum companies, for example, would be interested in new drilling technology but opposed to the development of alternative sources of energy; or the automobile companies would favour the development of manufacturing robots, but object to innovations which could facilitate efficient public transport (as they did earlier in the century by buying and dismantling 100 electric railway systems in forty-five US cities; see Barnet, 1980: ch. 2). The common thread here is simple: business enterprise can and does benefit from the 'state of industrial arts', but only by *restricting it to its own ends*.

Why is it so essential for business to restrict industry? The simple reason is that otherwise profit will collapse to zero. Consider again the automobile business. If the large car companies decided to produce as much as possible rather than as much as the 'traffic can bear', output could probably double at short notice. And this potential is hardly unique to automobiles. Almost every modern industry – from petroleum, through electronics, to clothing, machine tools, telecommunications, construction, food processing and film, to name only a few – is operating far below its full *technological* capacity (not to be confused with full business capacity).[2] If all industrial undertakings were to follow the reckless example of automobiles, the relentless pressure of oncoming goods would undermine tacit agreements and open cooperation, trigger massive downward price spirals, and sooner or later end in a great depression and a threat of political disintegration. Speculating in similar terms, Veblen (1923: 373) concluded it was therefore hardly surprising that 'such a free run of production has not been had nor aimed at; nor is it all expedient, as a business proposition, that anything of the kind should be allowed.' Profits are inconceivable without production, but they are also impossible under a 'free run' of production. For profits to exist, business enterprise must *partially restrict human creativity and livelihood below their full potential capacity*.

DIFFERENTIAL ACCUMULATION

Industrial limitation and the normal rate of return

Extending Veblen, we can distinguish between two types of industrial limitations: (a) *universal*, 'business-as-usual' practices carried out routinely and uniformly by all firms; and (b) *differential* practices carried out by only a single company or group of companies.

To the uninitiated, universal practices of industrial limitations are practically invisible; indeed, in relentlessly trying to raise sales, business firms seem to be doing precisely the opposite. But there is more here than meets the eye. Note that the standard practice in most modern firms, documented extensively since the 1930s, is first to set the price and then to sell as much as needed to satisfy demand. What remains concealed is that the price already incorporated a predetermined profit target, which in turn implies that output must fall short of full potential. Thus, in the normal course of business enterprise, industrial sabotage is brought in, albeit indirectly, simply by 'charging what the traffic will bear' at a predetermined profit target.

This link between pricing policies and profit leads straight to the question of power. The notion that production is restricted by the ability of firms to *set* profitable prices implies that such firms possess a certain monopolistic power to begin with. Indeed, Veblen was probably the first to emphasize that even without open business cooperation, modern business competition was usually 'imperfect', and that monopoly and oligopoly were the rule rather than the exception. Moreover, even in those isolated cases where free competition is said to reign, the 'power to incapacitate' is not at all absent.

Consider a neo-classical 'perfectly competitive' firm, but instead of focusing on what it does, think of what it is unwilling to do. To illustrate, take the case of mining, where prices are presumably set by global supply and demand. Could we not argue that at least in such cases the existence of 'market prices' removes the spectre of business sabotage? The answer is no. Mining output, much like any other output, is controlled by business. The actual production of a single firm, as well as the number of firms in operation, are therefore bounded not by the state of industrial arts, but by what could be sold at a 'reasonable' profit. In fact, this is exactly what standard neo-classical theory tells the owner of a perfectly competitive firm: in the long run, have your company produce only if you expect to earn at least the 'normal' rate of return. Otherwise, shut down.

For neo-classicists who make normal returns equal to the marginal revenue product of capital, this simply assures efficient resource allocation. On the other hand, from a Veblenian standpoint which delinks earnings from production, the unwillingness to produce for less than some conventional rate of return is the very manifestation of industrial

ARTICLES

sabotage. Thus, although perfectly competitive firms do not determine prices, their productive activity – individually and in the aggregate – is nevertheless limited by the imperative of earning the 'normal' rate of return.

The normal rate of return is of course a fuzzy magnitude, a convention which varies among business owners and over time. The important point, however, is that it exists in the first place. With the gradual penetration of capitalist institutions, businessmen have come to believe that the flow of profit is a *natural, orderly phenomenon with a more or less predetermined pace*. According to Veblen, this is hardly trivial. Until a few hundred years ago, profit was seen more as a coincidence than as a regular feature of ownership. The main goal was to *retain* property, and owners of land, slaves or gold rarely expected their assets to 'grow on their own'. But under capitalism, where the business limitation of industry grows increasingly universal, the consequent profit is regarded as 'natural' and its rate of expansion as 'normal'. In this way, the strategic limitation of any given industry can prevail even in the absence of explicit binding arrangements.

The normality of profit has been so thoroughly accepted that the industrial limitation from which it derives is no longer self-evident. For instance, over the past 100 years, the US unemployment rate has averaged 7 per cent (5.7 per cent without the 1930s). However, since this rate has been associated with 'business as usual', most economists now take it to represent 'the natural rate of unemployment'. In an unconscious Orwellian bent, modern textbooks casually talk about the 'full employment unemployment rate', 'unemployment equilibrium' and 'over-full employment' – generally without quotation marks (see for example: Branson, 1989: 188; Parkin and Bade, 1986: 282–3).

Where does the 'normal rate of return' come from? Paradoxically, the *universality* of profit and the regularity of its expansion are based on *specific* institutions of differential sabotage. Indeed, a normal rate of return can exist only because businessmen are never satisfied with it. What businessmen believe they are entitled to under normal circumstances is not what they seek in practice. The primal drive of business enterprise is not to meet but '*beat* the average'. Business performance is denominated in relative, not absolute, terms, and it is 'getting ahead of the competition' which constitutes the final aim of all business undertakings. This compelling desire to earn more, grow larger and expand faster *than others* is perhaps the most fundamental drive of business, and in that sense, even members of the tightest oligopolistic coalition are fiercely competitive. The *differential* essence of accumulation lies at the heart of our theory of capital, and we return to it below. For the moment, though, our focus is on how the differential limitation of industry forms the basis for the normal rate of return.

DIFFERENTIAL ACCUMULATION

Differential returns mean above-average profit growth. This usually required raising one's *own* profit growth, though that in itself is rarely feasible without also limiting the *average* growth of profit. The problem is simple. Profit is a product of sales and the profit share of sales. Individual firms can try to raise their sales faster than the average, though that alone would not guarantee differential profit growth since sales and the profit share are not independent. If all firms push their sales up, the consequence is an overall loss of business control over industry and a resulting drop in the overall profit share of income. The conclusion – well known since antiquity but broadly institutionalized only since the late nineteenth century – is the *imperative of restricted access*: for the profits of one owner (or a coalition of owners) to beat the average, others must be prevented from accessing the same source of earnings.

The means of achieving this end are numerous, transcending both business and politics, and spanning the societal spectrum from the individual to the global. Without attempting a fuller analysis, we can mention direct 'business-like' limitations, such as predatory pricing, formal and informal collusion, advertisement and exclusive contracts. 'Political' examples include patent and copyright laws, industrial and labour policy, legal monopolies, preferential tax treatment, trade and investment pacts and barriers, as well as the occasional use of force, including military, for differential business ends (for various case studies, see: Nitzan, 1992; Bichler and Nitzan 1996a, 1996b; Nitzan and Bichler, 1995, 1996, 1997).

The negative industrial impact here is often indirect. For the beneficiary owner, the differential gain accrues because the necessary industrial limitation is borne by *other owners*. For instance, the large petroleum companies have gained from expanding world demand at least partly because they were politically able to keep smaller 'independent' companies largely out of the loop (Blair, 1976). On the other hand, when exclusion cannot be ensured, as in the case of microchips in the past few years, soaring production often ends up 'overshooting' into 'excess capacity' and falling profits. In general, then, the negative impact of business on industry is both indirect and non-linear: *while profits usually correlate positively with one's own production, beyond a certain point this correlation is maintained only in so far as production by others is contained.*

In sum, business profits are possible because absentee owners can strategically limit industry to their own ends. Such control is carried out routinely, either by pricing products towards earning a 'target rate of return' at some 'standard capacity', or by making industrial activity conditional on earning a 'normal rate of return'. Underlying these *universal* business principles are numerous *differential* practices, with individual or groups of owners trying to redistribute income via institutional change. The aim of most (though not all) differential tactics is

ARTICLES

to restrict the industrial activity of existing or potential rivals. Their aggregate effect is to undermine the industrial community at large, which in turn gives rise to a 'normal' rate of return.

The link between differential and universal industrial sabotage is closely related to the twin cleavages pervading business enterprise – one between absentee owners and the industrial community (Marx's 'class struggle'), the other between absentee owners themselves ('competition'). On a disaggregate level, the distribution of profit among absentee owners is roughly related to the balance of *business* damage they inflict on each other. On an aggregate level, their total profit depends (although not in any linear way) on the overall *industrial* damage arising from their business warfare. In other words, business goals revolve around the distribution of profit, while business methods assure that such profit is made available in the first place.

Capital and the corporation

One reason why Veblen's analysis never became too popular is that it effectively made business capital a *negative* industrial magnitude. This conclusion is alien to both neo-classical and Marxian thinking. For the former, with its emphasis on harmony and equilibrium, the 'positive' social value of capital is hardly questionable. Marx accentuated the antagonistic social basis of capital, linking accumulation to exploitation. In parallel, however, he also stressed the relentless pressure to improve productivity – pressure which derived not from the lure of monopoly, but from the discipline of competition. And so despite the antagonism – or perhaps because of it – capitalists must use their capital in the most productive way.

Even British contributors to the Cambridge Controversy were still ambiguous on the industrial footing of capital. Sraffa (1960) broke the 'conspiracy of silence' by destroying the presumption that the profit rate measured the contribution of investment to national income, let alone to human welfare. This called into question the positive connotation of both accumulation and growth, and refocused attention on distribution (Robinson, 1971: 20). Yet, the Veblenian link between distributive power and industrial limitation remained largely unexplored, even after Robinson realized Veblen had anticipated much of her critique (Robinson, 1979: 60; 1980: 115–16). Indeed, while the Cambridge Controversy raised the possibility that capital *could* be unproductive, Veblen contended that, from an industrial point of view, it was *necessarily* counterproductive. Without the business right for a 'conscious withdrawal of efficiency', he maintained, there was no profit and thus no investment and no capital. Capitalization was determined not only by what was produced, but also by what was *not* produced. The institution of capital, by its very essence, was therefore a fetter on industrial progress.

DIFFERENTIAL ACCUMULATION

It is essential to reiterate the a priori nature of this position. Veblen's starting point – the distinction between 'business' and 'industry' – meant that *any* extra-industrial system of distribution could operate only by limiting productive activity. Contrary to Knight (1921: 188–9), for whom 'productivity is a matter of limitation', that is, a direct *consequence* of property rights, for Veblen, the 'technological heritage' was rooted solely in the 'instinct of workmanship'. Institutions of social power and subordination could never enhance that instinct, only limit it to a greater or lesser extent. And so, even if business enterprise were shown to be the least industrially harmful of all potential modes of distribution, that still would not make capital 'productive': because business was separate from industry, profits could arise only from the former limiting the latter.

The emergence of capital as a business limitation of industry was intimately linked to the rise of the modern corporation, and to the larger use of credit as a means of ownership. The popular view, supported by mainstream economic thinking, is that the corporation is an outgrowth of technology. The corporation, we are told, is the most efficient mode of business organization, and it is this organization which enables society to reap the benefits of large-scale production. Samuelson *et al.* (1988: 453) are a typical example. 'Large-scale production', they say, 'is technically efficient, and a large corporation is an advantageous way for investors to pool the irreducible risks of business life. Without limited liability and the corporation, a market economy simply could not reap the benefit that comes when large supplies of capital need to be attracted to efficient-sized corporations.' This view is well reflected in contemporary business jargon which commonly explains the high profitability of corporate giants by equating their business size with technological 'competitiveness'.

From a Veblenian standpoint, however, this logic makes no sense. The corporation is a business institution, not an industrial unit, and so the reason for its emergence and continuous success must go beyond economies of scale. Large-scale production is a sound business practice only if it serves to raise profits, and contrary to popular conviction the link between them is not self-evident. Since the 1890s, the modern corporation has outgrown its largest industrial unit, suggesting that economies of scale are no longer the paramount determinant of business size (Edwards, 1979: 217–18; Scherer *et al.*, 1975: 334–6). A typical modern firm now owns numerous, in some cases thousands of, industrial establishments, often in unrelated industries. Moreover, while the corporation continues to grow in size, its industrial units do not. The fact that industrial size is not a necessity for business success has been brought home forcefully with the growing significance of 'outsourcing'. Many of today's corporate giants have successfully reinstated the 'putting out' system of the Industrial Revolution, the result being rising profit coupled with a *falling* payroll.

ARTICLES

The rise of the corporation is of course related to the emergence of large-scale industry, but causality may well run opposite to what mainstream economics argues. The corporation emerged not to *enable* large-scale industry, but rather to *prevent* it from becoming 'excessively' productive.

In the case of the USA, this is well illustrated by the two principal processes charted in Figure 1. Between 1790 and the Civil War, population growth averaged 3 per cent annually. With the conquering of the western 'frontier', this fell to 2.2 per cent between the Civil War and the turn of the twentieth century, and further down to 1.6 per cent between the turn of the century and the onset of the Great Depression. The second significant development occurring in the latter half of the nineteenth century was rapid productivity growth. In manufacturing, the growth of output per employee rose from less than 0.5 per cent in the 1860s, to over 3 per cent by the turn of the century.

The crucial intersection of these two opposing trends occurred during the last decade of the nineteenth century. Until then, with population

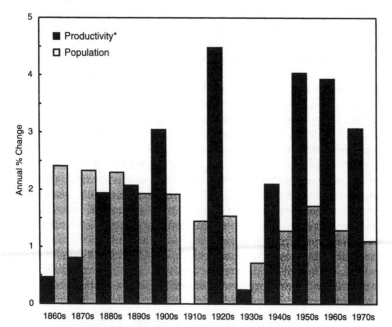

Figure 1 The productivity threat

Source: US Department of Commerce.
Note: * Labour productivity in US manufacturing, based on Edwin Frickey's Federal Reserve Board index of manufacturing production continued by the index of manufacturing production and divided by the number of manufacturing production workers.

190

DIFFERENTIAL ACCUMULATION

expanding faster than productive capacity, the main concern for individual firms was how to satisfy soaring demand. Sales could hence grow at maximum potential without threatening mark-ups and profitability. This was the golden age of 'free competition'. But then things began to change. After the Civil War, the 'state of the industrial arts' benefited from an unprecedented increase in the use of new raw materials, the development and assimilation of innovations, new production techniques and growing product diversity. The net result was a marked acceleration in capacity growth. Given that this coincided with slowing population growth, the threat was that sooner or later the industrial system would become 'inordinately productive'. If the earlier pattern of competitive production were to continue, industry would tend to generate much more output than could be sold at *profitable* prices, bringing business enterprise to a halt.

It was at that point that the modern corporation as we know it was born. Until then, business combination largely took the form of 'pools' and 'trusts'. Their primary purpose was to constrain aggregate output to 'what the traffic could bear' at profitable prices. Yet as Olson (1965, 1982) convincingly argues, collaboration is usually difficult and often impossible for large groups, and an excessive number of firms was indeed a primary reason for the relative fragility of these early combinations (Chandler, 1977: 317–18; Cochran and Miller, 1961: 140–6). There was hence a pressing need to reduce the number of firms, and the most effective method was merger.

Mergers, however, were not only structural transformations but also financial transactions. They involved *buying and selling capital* which meant that *firms had to have a pecuniary value*. In short, capital itself had to become 'vendible'. The developments that followed were quick and swift. During the 1890s, the USA saw the widespread incorporation of business firms, the rapid growth of stock and bond markets and the expanding use of credit. It was in that period that the separation of business from industry was finally complete. Firms were turned into corporations and investors into absentee owners. From then on, the predicament of excess capacity remained a more or less permanent feature of US capitalism. As Figure 1 shows, productivity growth continued to run ahead of population growth. Industrial limitation therefore remained a business necessity, carried out by progressive corporate concentration and by relentless restructuring of political and business institutions.

Material wealth and corporate finance

With the corporation seen as a means of *limiting* industrial activity for business gain, accumulation can no longer be understood in terms of the underlying physical apparatus of the firm. The reason is twofold. First, accumulation is forward-looking. Being a financial portfolio,

ARTICLES

capital denotes the present value of *expected future earnings*. In other words, accumulation normally occurs *before* the profit is earned and usually before any material equipment is created. Second and more importantly, capacity growth is an industrial activity, which, as noted earlier, could be good as well as bad for business.

The 'twisted' link between accumulation and production becomes evident from a closer examination of equity and debt. For the archaic 'captain of industry', capital meant equity; debt did not provide the direct control necessary to run industry. As capitalist ownership gradually shifted into absentee footing, however, the difference started to blur. With the show now being run by modern 'captains of solvency', equity and debt have become undifferentiated, self-expanding claims on the asset side of the balance sheet. For the absentee owner, they are both capital, qualified only by their risk/reward profiles.

Although entries on the liabilities side of the balance sheet do not stand against specific entries on the assets side, it is generally accepted that equity capitalizes the corporation's 'immaterial assets' and debt its 'material assets'. The conventional wisdom is that both 'assets' are valuable because of their productivity. The former represent the company's *unique* knowledge, client loyalty and other aspects of its supposed industrial superiority; the latter its *undifferentiated* plant and equipment.

Consider first the 'immaterial assets'. Contrary to popular perceptions, these are only marginally related, and commonly totally unrelated, to the productivity of the firm's *own* industrial apparatus. Take innovations. There is no denial that these are productive. The company books, however, capitalize not the innovation, but the patent or copyright protecting it. (Think of what would happen to the profits of Bayer or Microsoft without these legal shields.) Knowledge can generate *differential* profit only if others are *prevented* from using it. Common knowledge therefore can never be capitalized as an 'immaterial asset'. Moreover, from a broader communal perspective, the company's own contribution to knowledge is marginal at best. Any invention, even the most revolutionary, is only one step at the end of a long 'historical thought process' which is largely unprotected by property rights. Microsoft's software, for instance, could not have been developed without computer languages, the 'chip', the discovery of semiconductivity, binary logic, mathematical functions or, for that matter, human language. Such knowledge owes its existence to society at large, and was available to Microsoft free of charge. Had Microsoft followed the productivity doctrine of distribution to the letter, paying royalties on the use of such knowledge, it would have gone bankrupt in no time. Of course, some of Microsoft's principal owners have contributed to human knowledge, though it is hard to believe their contributions were in any way proportionate to their profit and capitalization. The difference is wholly attributed to power.

DIFFERENTIAL ACCUMULATION

Moving from specific, legally sanctioned items to general unsanctioned ones, the alleged productivity of 'immaterial assets' becomes even more dubious. Corporate mergers, for instance, commonly lead to a higher combined capitalization. The effect on productive potential, however, is at best marginal and often negative, particularly when the new amalgamation is 'downsized' to shed excess capacity. The source of added capitalization must therefore be traced to the additional market or political power generated by the merger, though that is rarely admitted in public. Instead, it is minted on the balance sheet as fresh 'goodwill'. (This happened regularly during the US 'buy-and-rationalize' takeover boom of the 1980s, when 'junk bonds' were issued against higher earning expectations of the merged companies.) Indeed, the meaning of 'goodwill' has deviated considerably from its original connotation of customer loyalty based on intimate knowledge in a small community. Instead, it is now used (or abused) as a catch-all term for the power to limit industry strategically for differential business gains.

The conclusion is simple: equity accumulation capitalizes not *differential productivity* but *differential power*. In this sense, *any* institutional arrangement leading to higher profit expectations – whether it is favourable political rearrangements, the creation of new consumer 'wants', the reorganization of collusion or the weakening of competitors – will sooner or later lead to higher equity values backed by new 'goodwill'.

But then what about debt? Is it not true that, unlike equity, this is commonly backed by a material apparatus whose productive essence can hardly be denied? Does this not suggest that capital income is at least partly a function of productivity? The answer again is negative. Plant and equipment are productive in the context of industry 'at large'. It is only because of that broader context that the ownership of machines yields a right to appropriate part of the societal output. Only under these circumstances can machines be 'capitalized'.

For instance, consider a supertanker vessel. Its ability to transfer crude petroleum changes very gradually and predictably over time. Its value as 'capital', on the other hand, could vary dramatically with oil prices. The latter are affected by very broad social circumstances, such as the relative cohesion of OPEC and the large petroleum companies, Middle East wars, global growth and energy conservation. If these lead to higher oil prices, a larger share of the overall societal output will probably go to supertanker owners. The value of their tangible asset will have appreciated while its productivity did not. And there is nothing unique about oil tankers. Indeed, the same principle applies to aircraft, factories, office space and every other piece of 'capital equipment'. Their capitalized value depends not on their intrinsic productivity, but rather on the general institutional, political and business circumstances within which they are operated.

ARTICLES

Now, on the company books, physical assets are recorded not at current market value, but at cost. Consciously or not, there is an attempt to separate the portion attributable to market power (which should hence be capitalized as goodwill), from the so-called 'true' value of the asset as measured by its historical cost. However, even that latter portion has little relationship to the productivity of the underlying equipment.

The reason is that at any point in time, the very 'cost' of producing plant and equipment is itself a function of institutional circumstances. First, if ownership of supertankers confers large profits, some of these will be appropriated by the companies producing them (as well as their workers, if they have enough bargaining power). The redistributional mechanism works through a higher selling price, recorded as higher cost by the acquiring shipping line. Second and more importantly, even under so-called normal circumstances with no differential earning capacity, the price of tangible equipment already embodies the conventional 'normal rate of return'. And as noted earlier, the latter reflects the *average* limitation of industry by business.

To sum, the distinction between stocks and bonds is rooted in institutional, not industrial, circumstances. Both forms of capital rest on power, though the nature of power is different in each case. Equity capitalizes the firm's *differential* ability to restrict industry for its own benefit; whereas debt capitalizes the *average* ability of all owners to limit industry at large.

For this reason, long-term swings in the ratio of interest to profit could be interpreted as a proxy for the 'maturity' of capitalism. Our notion of maturity here does not imply a linear or even an upward progression, but merely the strength and solidity of business institutions. Viewed in this light, the 'maturity' of capitalism is intimately linked to the nature of earning expectations and their associated forms of capitalization. Frankel (1977, 1980) sees the basic difference between equity and debt as a question of trust: the former represents an *expected return*, the latter a *promise of return* (1980: 20). But then, under business enterprise, the progression of trust among owners depends on the 'normalization' of their power. For this reason, we can expect that as capitalism matures and industrial control is increasingly petrified into accepted institutions, perceptions of 'risk' should decline, 'trust' should rise and debt should become an increasingly acceptable form of accumulation. Conversely, when changing circumstances work to loosen the previous grip of existing conventions and understandings (and in that sense 'invigorate' capitalism), debt should become relatively more difficult to issue, and the more 'risky' equity investment should again be used as the primary vehicle of capitalization.

Following this logic, we expect the maturity of capitalism, approximated by the share of interest in total capital income, to be positively

DIFFERENTIAL ACCUMULATION

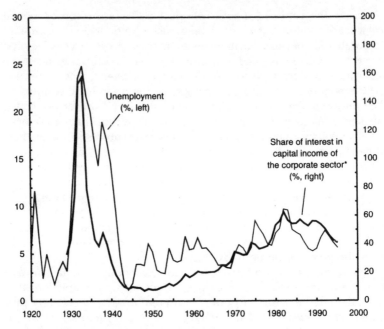

Figure 2   Business trust and industrial sabotage

Source: US Department of Commerce; *Economic Report of the President.*
Note: * Capital income comprises pre-tax corporate profit (with capital consumption allowance and inventory valuation adjustment) and net interest.

correlated with 'industrial sabotage'. And, indeed, this seems to be the case in the USA, as illustrated in Figure 2. Since the early 1930s, this index of maturity has been closely correlated with the unemployment rate, a readily available (albeit imperfect) proxy for industrial limitation. At first sight, the relationship seems intuitive and not particularly significant. After all, economic fluctuations affect profit more than interest, so when unemployment rises so should the ratio of interest to overall capital income. However, this triviality holds only in the shot term. In the longer haul, interest payments are much more flexible, so there is no *technical* reason for their share in total capital income to correlate positively with unemployment. That such correlation exists is therefore significant.

The 1930s and 1940s were marked by great turbulence, with business control over industry first growing 'excessive' and then, with the war-induced boom, turning 'too loose'. The 1950–80 period was much more stable. Business has slowly regained control over industry, boosting confidence in the regular flow of capital income and 'trust' among lenders and borrowers. The consequence was a gradual rise in unemployment on the one hand and a shift from profit to fixed income on the other. Since the mid-1980s, the increasing globalization of business enterprise and the progressive opening of the US economy have reversed or at least counteracted this trend. Existing business institutions have come under assault and the ability to control industry for business ends has been somewhat compromised. The result has been falling unemployment, coupled with a drop in the ratio of interest to capital income, as the 'promise' of return weakened relative to the mere 'expectation' of return.

3   CAPITAL AS POWER: THE MEGA-MACHINE

The essence of accumulation is an interaction between production and power. So far, we have dealt with power as a *means* of accumulation. Now we shall argue that power is also the *final end* of accumulation. From this latter perspective, material measurements of capital, regardless of their feasibility, are irrelevant. As a quest for power, capital is inherently *relative* and must therefore be measured *differentially*. Capital represents an abstract distributional claim. Its essence as power, however, goes beyond the overall distribution of 'rewards', as suggested by Parkin (1971: 46) for example. The reason is that what workers stand to 'lose' is *qualitatively different* from what capitalists seek to 'gain': the former are giving up *goods and services*, the latter win *control over social production itself*. In other words, it is only for the capitalist that distribution means power; for the worker it is largely a matter of well-being. In dealing with the power drive, therefore, our focus, at least as a first approximation, is not on society in general, but on those who dominate it.

Material and symbolic drives

One of the most comprehensive attempts to understand the interaction between technology and power was offered by Lewis Mumford (1934, 1961, and primarily 1967, 1970). Mumford challenged the conventional emphasis on material technology, arguing instead that techniques were integral to man's higher culture. The final aim of technology, he maintained, was society rather than nature. Indeed, the most complex machines were not tangible but social.

Thus, whereas Veblen emphasized the progressive separation between the positive aspects of material technology and negative features of social power, Mumford (who was greatly influenced by Veblen) suggested a different dichotomy between democratic and authoritarian technologies. Democratic technology centred on *human progress*; authoritarian technology focused on *human control*. Rather than following Veblen's notion of

DIFFERENTIAL ACCUMULATION

power as a fetter on technology, Mumford began by viewing power itself as a form of technology.

Contrary to the conventional wisdom, Mumford emphasized the *symbolic* aspects of human development. Limited by the material bias of their profession, he argued, archaeologists were naturally disposed towards judging human progress on the basis of physical objects. 'Man the maker', however, was a fairly late arrival, preceded by other, less visible but equally important mental activities. Moreover, the growth of material production has hardly diminished the primacy of symbolic drives.

According to Mumford, perhaps the most important human technology – invisible to archaeology until the invention of writing – is language. Material technology of the palaeolithic and neolithic cultures (and in some sense even of our own age) remained infinitely inferior to the complexity, flexibility, uniformity, efficiency and growth of their spoken language. It is unclear how long language took to develop, but according to Mumford little of what followed could have been achieved without the prior construction of this wholly symbolic technology. Moreover, it is unlikely that the development of language was driven by the everyday imperatives of survival – the hunting pack was dependent on short commands and had little use for the subtlety of language common even among the most primitive tribes still living today. According to Mumford, the principal drive was self-discovery.

Mumford argues that the latent function of language – much like the earlier appearance of ritual and taboo and the subsequent evolution of science and technology – was *to control, for better or worse, man's own mental and emotional energies*. In many ancient cultures, words were considered the most potent force: God is commonly believed to have created the world with his words, a feat of power which humans have since striven to emulate. Both in goal and structure, language was a precursor for all later technological developments.

Mumford differentiated between two qualitatively distinct technologies: one associated with the democratic outlook of neolithic culture, the other with the power bias of 'civilized' society. In his opinion, their distinct paths stem from a different reaction to death: neolithic technology takes the 'biological' route, seeking to enhance life, while accepting the inevitability of death. Power technology, on the other hand, uses 'mechanical' force and violence in the vain hope of achieving immortality.

Neolithic culture does not see work as alienating labour, but rather as a communal process intertwined with the broader ecological system. Work is often back-breaking, but physical toil is compensated by companionship, cooperation, song and rhyme, and aesthetic achievements are valued no less than abundance of yield. Indeed, many early feats of domestication – such as fertilization, the sacrifice of food for future growth, the harnessing of cattle and the use of a plough – were probably practised first as religious rituals. Feminine traits abound – from the lunar cycle linking cultivation to menstruation and sexuality, through the primary role of containers (pot, jar, house, village), to the careful cultivation of gardens and the patient rearing of children. Festivities, ceremonies and rituals revolve around the family, neighbours and community. Eating, drinking and sexual activity occupy a central place. There is no lifetime division of labour. Knowledge is rarely monopolized, and most types of work could be performed by all members of the community. Systemic gender inequality is uncommon. There are no social classes and authority stems from age. Violence is limited and dictatorial power rarely tolerated.

Neolithic culture established the merit of morality, self-discipline, cooperation and social order. It has shown the value of public goods and forethought. Most importantly, it has proved the most resilient social organization, always outlasting the far more energetic yet vulnerable power civilization. These aspects of neolithic culture, Mumford argues, did not disappear with the archaic village. As a form of social technology, they persist within modern society – sometimes visibly as in villages, communal organizations and even business companies, and at other times invisibly as resistance to the dictates of mechanical civilization.

Mumford makes no attempt to romanticize. Neolithic culture, he points out, has significant shortcomings. The exclusive nature of small associations restricts human interaction, the horizons are limited, and pettiness and suspicion prevent broader cooperation. After an initial burst of discoveries and inventions, neolithic innovation died down and stagnation set in.

Against this backdrop of a peaceful if limited form of democratic organization, rose the spectre of power civilization under the authoritarian rule of divine kingship. The first of these social amalgamations evolved in the great river deltas – from Egypt, through Mesopotamia, to the Indus Valley and China. According to Mumford, their unifying hallmark was *absolute power*. The need for such power was partly rooted in material circumstances. Economic surplus and the consequent amalgamation of wealth had for the first time created the possibility of 'total loss'. A large and growing population, subdivided by advancing division of labour, was becoming increasingly interdependent. Under these conditions, flooding, drought and later total war could have easily spelled catastrophe, perhaps complete annihilation. Whereas neolithic culture could flexibly respond to the first two and rarely faced the third, in the urban amalgamates of the deltas these had to be counteracted resolutely and ruthlessly. And given the large scale of activity, that could be achieved only through the sanction of absolute authority.

DIFFERENTIAL ACCUMULATION

But as Mumford argues, material considerations tell only part of the story; the more important part was symbolic. The rise of power civilization was accompanied by the appearance of the *sky gods*. Neolithic earth gods, attuned to the 'micro' biological cycle of fertility and operating on a human scale, were no longer sufficient for the task at hand. For the kings, risk of disaster made failure increasingly unacceptable, thus amplifying the ever-present fear of death. Neolithic culture, humbled by its limited potential, had to accept mortality, but kings were no longer bounded by neolithic horizons. Control over a growing economic surplus and larger populations suggested to them, admittedly with some justification, that the 'skies were the limit'. Expanding insight into writing, mathematics and astronomy gave their task cosmic proportions. But rationality grew hand in hand with irrationality, and the king, dazzled by his own achievements and fears, was driven towards the ultimate feat of becoming an immortal sun god himself.

Power civilization appeared after rising agricultural productivity had for the first time enabled a systematic generation of surplus. According to Mumford, it was probably at this point that hunting chiefs who earlier entertained symbiotic relationships with neolithic settlements, first discovered the promise of redistribution. Weapons, which previously were used primarily against animals, were increasingly applied against people, and total war had become a permanent institutional feature. (Neolithic excavations offer little or no evidence of fortification or weaponry. The first fortifications are associated with urban centres, while heaps of cracked skulls – early evidence of organized murder – do not appear until kingship.) From then on, civilization has been on a power trip to control nature and, most importantly, humans.

The mega-machine

According to Mumford, the first power machine was social. In attempting to emulate the perfect cosmic order so as to annul their own mortality, kings have turned to design, assemble and operate a human *mega-machine*. Absolute control of this mega-machine served as evidence of supernatural power, and its most fantastic output – megalomaniacal graves – was supposed to open the gate to immortality.

The mega-machine constructed by early kingships, says Mumford, typically comprised three principal components: a *labour machine* of peasant conscripts toiling in the erection of public works; a *military machine* needed to impose internal discipline and later to engage in war; and a *bureaucratic machine* to keep the accounts. Control was in the hands of a coalition comprising the royal court and the high priesthood – the former maintaining a monopoly over physical force, the latter over knowledge and ideology. Division of labour and advanced specialization

ARTICLES

(Egyptian mining expeditions, for instance, had up to *fifty* different job descriptions), strict regimentation, uncompromising discipline and tough punishment have reduced the workers, soldiers and officials in these organizations to a state of near-mechanical components. Initiative was all but forbidden and flexibility disallowed. Taken as whole, these organizations formed 'a combination of resistant parts, each specialised in function, operating under human control, to utilize energy and to perform work'. In short, they fulfilled all the requirements of Franz Reuleaux's classic definition of a machine (Mumford, 1967: 191).

The fusion of rational insight and highly irrational aspirations resulted in a massive explosion of what we today call 'productivity'. Seen from a material standpoint, the technological achievements of the early mega-machine – particularly the construction of the pyramids – remained unparalleled until our own epoch. But the more significant contribution, according to Mumford, was the construction of the human mega-machine itself. It was here that the three basic principles of mechanization – complex coordination, dehumanization and remote control – were first applied. The original object of mechanization was *society itself*. Indeed, Mumford argues that just as the cosmic world view was a necessary prerequisite for the adoption of universal weights, coins, the calendar and clockwork, so was the human mega-machine the ultimate model for subsequent non-human mechanization.

The mega-machine enabled human beings to transcend for the first time some of their own biological limitations. The principles of universality, order and predictability opened the door to a continuous expansion of knowledge. Urban amalgamations created by the first mega-machines opened new horizons for human interactions, triggering a flurry of creativity difficult to achieve in small disjoined neolithic settlements.

But the unleashing of such positive forces was neither the prime purpose nor the most important consequence of the mega-machine. According to Mumford, the ultimate goal of human organization on a large scale was and remained the *exertion of social power*. The use of brute force was more than a means of exacting obedience; it was the very manifestation of a power civilization. Human sacrifice, though predating kingship, has become a growing preoccupation and slowly institutionalized, if only unconsciously, in the form of war. In its extreme incarnation, argued Mumford (1967: 184), kingship was a 'man eating device', and the cannibalistic lust of earlier kings has repeatedly resurfaced in subsequent appearances of social mega-machines. Even today, wealth (capital) and the death penalty (capital punishment) remain linked to the same root, *caput*.

In sum, Mumford puts the power orientation of the mega-machine model in sharp contrast to the democratic features of neolithic society. With the rise of the mega-machine, neolithic dispersion had been replaced

DIFFERENTIAL ACCUMULATION

by power concentration, ecological production by mechanization, lack of specialization by lifelong division of labour, limited local violence by the institutionalization of total war, cooperation by exploitation, forced labour and slavery, and egalitarianism by a class structure.

The resurrection of the mega-machine: the normal rate of return

Eventually, the mega-machines of the great deltas crumbled under their own weight. For all their external might, they were internally vulnerable: dehumanization and obedience stifled initiative, and the preoccupation with power and death was bound to undermine legitimacy. And when the 'myth of the machine' died – that is, when the power structure no longer fulfilled the Pharaoh's promise of 'life, prosperity and wealth' – the social pyramid was liable to falter.

But according to Mumford, the 'myth of the machine', much like neolithic culture before it, has outlived its first historical incarnation. In the sixteenth century, after more than two millennia of relatively small-scale social organization, power returned to centre-stage. The most significant sign was the resurrection of the sky gods and the growing assimilation of Galileo's mechanical world picture. Within only a few centuries, mechanization has once again taken command – so much so that in 1933 the entrance to the World's Fair at Chicago could proudly boast: 'Science explores: Technology executes: Man conforms.' This, together with the title of the fair – 'The Century of Progress' – attest to the extent to which the 'myth of the machine' has been restored (Mumford, 1970: 213).

Extending Mumford, we argue that the new mega-machine was in fact much more powerful then the old. In his writing, Mumford focused mainly on the newly resurrected institution of kingship and on its successor, the sovereign state. But lurking under the surface and soon rising to prominence was another, perhaps more potent, power structure which Mumford did not emphasize: *capital*. In our view, capital fulfils all the characteristics of a mega-machine. Based on a fundamental belief in the 'normal rate of return', it is a symbolic crystallization of power, exercised over a large-scale human organization, typically by a small group of people – the large absentee owners. As a symbolic shell, capital wraps within it not production for the sake of welfare, but production as a means of power. The quantitative nature of accumulation therefore involves the mechanization not of industry, but of social relations in general.

The renewed mechanization of social structures has led many to believe that capital – which they erroneously equated with machines – was on the decline. One of these was Galbraith (1967, 1983), who mistakenly interpreted the return of the mega-machine as a new social organization, the 'technostructure'. Beginning by assuming that property was distinct from organization, he went on to argue that capitalists became dependent on knowledge and hence lost their primacy to the technocrats. Galbraith himself provided no real evidence that this was indeed the case, although following *The Modern Corporation and Private Property* by Berle and Means (1932), and *The Managerial Revolution* by Burnham (1941), he was not alone in inferring that ownership was becoming increasingly separate from control.

Despite their popularity, however, the 'separation thesis' and the consequent belief that capital was on the decline were founded on pretty shaky grounds. As Zeitlin (1974) convincingly shows, the direct evidence, including Berle and Means's own study, was dubious from the very start, and the separation of ownership from control was largely a 'pseudofact' (neither the earlier data nor those furnished by subsequent attempts have been able to show that such separation has actually taken place). Zeitlin's critique is corroborated indirectly though no less forcefully by the data in Figure 3. If capital was indeed on the descent, the earnings of its owners should have diminished in significance. The evidence, however, shows the exact opposite. In the USA, where systematic historical data are available, the combined share of pre-tax profit and interest in national income has in fact shown an *upward* trend since the 1920s (recall that we treat both interest and profit as capital income). Not surprisingly, the idea of the technostructure proved a passing fad (at least outside academia). Knowledge of production techniques is not a prerequisite for exacting obedience. In the final analysis, it is the owners, not the engineers, who are in the driver's seat, and their ultimate goal is not 'continuity', 'security' or 'sales growth' as Galbraith would have us believe, but accumulation.

The underlying driving force of large-scale business organizations is not fundamentally different from that which propelled early kingships and the sovereign state. As power structures, all seek to control nature and, ultimately, human beings. Business enterprise does this through the differential appropriation of profit. In the process, it unleashes the community's industrial knowledge, but only partially. Because profits are contingent on the strategic limitation of industry, it follows that the final purpose is not the *growth* of industry, but the *control* of industry.

And it is here that the new mega-machine is potentially more powerful than the old. The basic reason is that unlike kingship and the sovereign state, capital is vendible. This has several related implications. First, *power can be bought and sold* and, as a result, *can be augmented on an ever-increasing scale*. Unlike the old mega-machines, whose expansion was inherently limited by their ability to amass physical symbols of prowess such as pyramids, canals, public works and large standing armies, the growth of capital is *potentially boundless*. Capitalists increase

DIFFERENTIAL ACCUMULATION

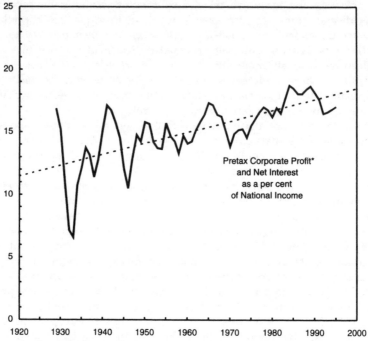

Figure 3 Capital's share of income in the USA

Source: US Department of Commerce.
Note: * Including capital consumption allowance and inventory valuation adjustment.

their power by accumulating ownership titles over the entire social production process, and the only limit on such ownership is an all-encompassing, global monopoly. Second, contrary to earlier forms of power which expanded largely by force, capital can do so peacefully as well. Instead of exerting punishment, it expands mainly by extending reward (although its differential limitation of industry is itself a form of 'punishment'). Third, compared with previous mega-machines whose power symbols were often culture-specific, capital is far more universal. Regardless of its underlying contents, its shell is always the same: *a pecuniary growth of money values*. By the late twentieth century, the universality of capital has reached the point where its symbols have been reduced to electronic flickers, bits and bytes parked in computer storage or racing the information highways.

By virtue of its limitlessness, versatility and universality, capital has become much more *flexible* than earlier mega-machines. Whereas kingship and the sovereign state are relatively rigid social structures, capital is highly malleable. When destroyed through loss or bankruptcy, large-scale capital commonly resurrects itself through merger and realignment. Indeed, *this flexibility is what makes 'capital accumulation' possible in the first place*. The significance of such pliability can hardly be overstated. If orthodox economics was right, and capital was indeed a physical amalgamation of 'machines' or 'production lines', its immobility would have made accumulation impossible. On the other hand, if we treat capital as a human mega-machine, a structure of *social* control, capitalization and recapitalization become possible as business organizations adapt to a changing reality. Literally, capital can be accumulated only because it is *not* a physical entity.

Extending Mumford, we can therefore argue that the 'myth of the machine' has progressed in a series of increasing abstractions: from kingship, through the sovereign state, to capital. The acceptance of mechanization as a social mode of organization is now reflected in the 'normal rate of return', the belief that the expansion of power is the 'natural' order of things. And since the quest for power should be treated symbolically, capital, by virtue of being the most abstract form of power, is in that sense also the highest form of power. The first step towards a power-based theory of capital, therefore, is to integrate power into the *definition* of accumulation.

4   DIFFERENTIAL ACCUMULATION

Mainstream as well as Marxian economics view profit and accumulation as related though distinct concepts. Profit is seen as a potential source of accumulation, but accumulation is said to take place only if the profit is 'invested' in newly produced plant and equipment, and in more roundabout production processes. We reject this interpretation. As a crystallization of power, accumulation has little to do with so-called 'real investment' *per se*. As noted earlier, capitalization is a forward-looking process. What is being accumulated are claims on the future flow of profit. The pace of accumulation therefore depends on two factors: (a) the institutional arrangements affecting profit expectations; and (b) the normal rate of return used to discount them into their present value. The effect of rising industrial capacity on these factors is not only highly complex and possibly non-linear, but its direction can be positive as well as negative.

But then if capital is not 'tangible', how should its accumulation be measured? Surely, the mere augmentation of money values tells us little about power, particularly in the presence of inflation or deflation. The answer is rooted in the *relative* nature of power. The power of the absentee owner is the power to control part of the social process, and that becomes meaningful primarily against the power of other owners.

The relative nature of power is not unique to capitalism, of course.

DIFFERENTIAL ACCUMULATION

Kings have gauged their power against other kings, states against other states. But in these earlier mega-machines, comparisons were still largely subjective and their social significance more limited. It is only under capitalism, where power could be 'objectively' quantified through the pecuniary units of capital accumulation, that the relative essence of power rises to centre-stage.

Absentee owners exercise power over society in general, though their reference point is usually much more focused. *The power of capitalists – at least in their own minds – is gauged relative to other capitalists.* Some Marxian economists, for example Bowles *et al.* (1986, 1990), have offered to weigh capitalist power more widely – relative to workers, foreign suppliers and the country's citizenry, among others (see also Kotz, 1994, for a review). These proxies of power differ from ours in two respects. First, they tell us little on the distribution of power among capitalists. Second, they do not bear directly on the *measurement* of accumulation. They treat power and accumulation as separate categories, whereas for us *power is the very essence of accumulation*.

For the individual absentee owner, the rate of accumulation is relevant primarily in comparison to some benchmark. Economists tend to use a price index as such a benchmark, ostensibly in order to express accumulation in 'real' terms. Consciously or not, this procedure makes hedonic pleasure the ultimate purpose of profit. Capitalists, we are told, are never satiated, and regardless of how much they consume (or save for future consumption), they are relentlessly driven to 'maximize' their profits in order to augment their utility further and further. The problem with this logic is twofold. First, capitalists are of course concerned with consumption, but beyond a certain level of wealth, it is only marginally affected by their rate of accumulation. Moreover, profit-induced consumption is usually conspicuous – that is, aimed at establishing a *differential* status. This is highly important, because once we move into the realm of conspicuous consumption, the notion of 'real profit' assumes an entirely different meaning: higher prices, which from a utilitarian perspective imply a lower real income, for the conspicuous consumer often mean the exact opposite, since they bestow a higher differential status. The second difficulty is that, despite endless academic debates, the precise meaning of 'profit maximization' is still unclear. Capitalists may of course wish to earn 'as much as possible', but since the maximum attainable profit is for ever unknown, the principle seems irrelevant in practice.

In reality, accumulation is benchmarked not against a price index, but against its own average. Capitalists focus on *differential* accumulation. Rather than subject themselves to the absolutism of 'profit maximization', they commonly seek something much simpler: to 'beat the average'. Indeed, for the absentee owner there seems to be no greater

ARTICLES

disgrace than falling consistently below the 'normal rate of return'. Unlike the elusive 'maximum', reference to the 'normal' and 'average' is everywhere. Large companies gauge their performance relative to listings published by periodicals such as *Fortune, Business Week, Far Eastern Economic Review, Euromoney* or *Forbes*; fund managers are hired and fired according to whether they exceed or fall short of their relevant benchmark; and stock performance is meaningless unless compared to market or industry indices. In fact, the notion of normality as a benchmark for competitive achievements has been so thoroughly accepted in capitalist society that it now dominates numerous non-business spheres, such as education, sports, the arts and even foreign relations, where GDP per capita, growth rates and the like are constantly contrasted with regional or global averages.

Our general aim is to define capital as a *differential power claim over the social process*. The issue is of course highly complex and cannot be fully explored here, but the following tentative suggestions may offer a useful starting point.

1 The 'differential power of capital' (*DPK*) possessed by a particular group of owners should be measured relatively, by comparing the group's combined capitalization to that of the average capital unit. If this average is $5 million, capital worth $5 billion represents a *DPK* of 1,000. It means that as a group, the owners of that capital are 1,000 times more powerful than the owners of an average capital.

2 With this definition, the pace of 'differential accumulation' (*DA*) is given by the rate of change of *DPK*. Positive, zero or negative rates of *DA* imply rising, unchanging or falling differential power, respectively.

3 Strictly speaking, only capitalists with a positive *DA* are said to 'accumulate'. The study of accumulation should therefore have them at its centre.

Within this simple framework, the next question concerns the proper unit of analysis. Note that our focus here is not on the individual owner, but on a group of owners. The reason is that the vendability of capital creates centrifugal as well as centripetal forces, thus limiting the power of any single capitalist. In counteracting the centrifugal forces, the elementary solution is the corporation itself. But the need for business to control industry means that collective action usually requires corporate coalitions (overt or tacit). As a first approximation, therefore, our emphasis is on a corporate cluster of '*dominant capital*' – a concept which we tentatively use to denote the most powerful/profitable corporations at the centre of the economy.

Operationally, we define differential accumulation as the rate at which the capitalized income of 'dominant capital' expands relative to the

DIFFERENTIAL ACCUMULATION

economy's average. Because capital income includes both profit and interest, the proper aggregate is that of total assets (rather than owners' equity). Given the forward-looking nature of capital, this could be measured by the market value of all outstanding equity and debt. However, this measure is often 'contaminated' by investor 'hype' – that is, by swings of optimism and pessimism which respond more to the prospects of capital gain and loss than to a cool-headed assessment of future earnings and the likely course of the 'normal rate of return' (Nitzan, 1995, 1996). The alternative is to use 'book value' as reported in the financial statements. This is a somewhat 'lagging' indicator for capitalization, reflecting earning expectations prevailing when the assets were first recorded. However, given that differential accumulation is concerned with relative rather than absolute values, the benefit of relative stability may well offset the drawback of inaccuracy, particularly over the longer term.

Applying this definition to the US case, Figure 4a provides capitalization indicators for a 'typical' corporation of the 'dominant capital' group, as well as for the average corporation in the economy. 'Dominant capital' is provisionally defined here as equivalent to the 500 largest US-based industrial companies, listed annually since 1954 by *Fortune*. This group is limited to publicly traded companies with 50 per cent or more of their sales coming from manufacturing and/or mining. Diversified companies, those relying more heavily on other lines of activity, and private firms are excluded. (Since 1994, the *Fortune* 500 coverage has been expanded to the entire universe of publicly traded companies. For consistency, our series ends in 1993.) Based on these data, the average capitalized income of 'dominant capital' is given by the total assets of the *Fortune* list divided by 500. Two proxies for the economy's average are given by dividing total corporate assets by the number of corporate tax returns – first for the economy as a whole, and then for the combined mining and manufacturing sector, both using data from the US Internal Revenue Service. (For comparison, all series are rebased with 1954 = 100.)

Figure 4b charts two alternative measures for the differential power of capital (DPK) possessed by an average *Fortune* 500 company, one based on comparison with the average US corporation, the other on comparison with the manufacturing and mining average. With a logarithmic scale, the slopes of the two DPK series indicate the difference between the rate of accumulation of a typical company in the 'dominant capital' group, and the average rate of accumulation in the broader corporate universe. These slopes therefore provide proxies for the rate of differential accumulation (DA) by US 'dominant capital'.

What do the figures tell us? Most generally, they suggest that US differential accumulation has proceeded more or less uninterruptedly

ARTICLES

for the past four decades, and possibly longer. Relative to the manufacturing and mining average, differential accumulation by US
'dominant capital' has averaged 2 per cent annually (the slope of the
trend line). The broader comparison against the economy's average
suggests a far faster rate, averaging 3.8 per cent. In fact, even this higher
rate may well understate the pace of differential accumulation. There
are two reasons for this. First, our *Fortune* 500 proxy for 'dominant
capital' is heavily biased towards manufacturing and mining which have
tended to decline vis-à-vis the tertiary sector. As a result, the generally
faster-growing service-oriented companies are excluded from our
'dominant capital' proxy but included in the economy's average. Also,
over the years, some of the *Fortune* 500 became 'too' diversified and
were dropped from the list, although conceptually they remained an
integral part of 'dominant capital'. For these reasons, an alternative
proxy for 'dominant capital', based solely on size, is likely to show an
even faster rate of differential accumulation.

Seen as a *power* process, US accumulation appears to have been on a
sustainable keel throughout much of the postwar era. This conclusion
is hardly intuitive. Indeed, according to the analysis of the regulation
and social structure of accumulation (SSA) schools, the USA has experienced an accumulation *crisis* during that very period, particularly since

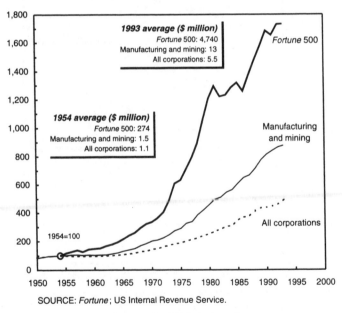

Figure 4a Total assets per firm in the USA (rebased)
Sources: Fortune; US Internal Revenue Service.

208

DIFFERENTIAL ACCUMULATION

the late 1960s. How is this difference possible? In our view, the reason is rooted in the troubled definition of capital. The conventional wisdom which focuses on profit (rather than capital income as a whole) indeed suggests a crisis. Figure 5a shows that net profit as a share of national income has been on a downward trend; and given that profit is seen both as the principal source of investment finance as well as its major inspiration, it is then only natural that accumulation (measured in material rather than power terms) should follow a similar downward path, as the figure patently confirms.

This notion of accumulation crisis lies in sharp contrast to the evidence based on differential accumulation. As illustrated in Figure 5b, unlike profit, *total* capital income has in fact shown an upward trend since the end of the Second World War, reaching a record high during the 1980s. These data show no sign of crisis; if anything, they indicate that capital income has grown *increasingly abundant*.

From a conventional viewpoint, this evidence presents a serious theoretical inconsistency: if capital income has indeed risen, why did it not

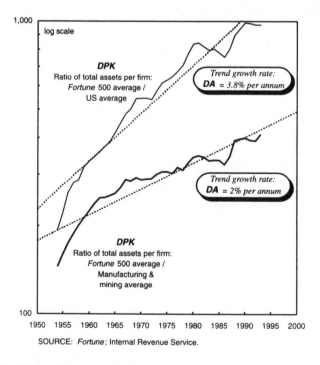

SOURCE: *Fortune*; Internal Revenue Service.

Figure 4b   Differential accumulation in the USA

Sources: Fortune; US Internal Revenue Service.

209

ARTICLES

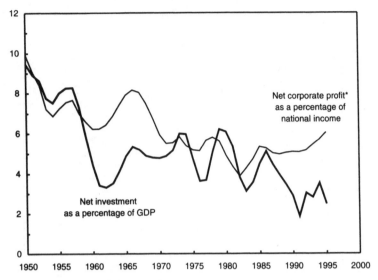

Figure 5a An accumulation crisis? . . .

Source: US Department of Commerce.

Notes: Series shown as three-year moving averages.

* Including capital consumption allowance and inventory valuation adjustment.

fuel a 'real' investment boom? From a Veblenian viewpoint, on the other hand, the two developments are consistent: capital income depends not on the *growth* of industry, but on the strategic *control* of industry. Had industry been given a 'free rein' to raise its productive capacity, the likely result would have been *excess* capacity and possibly a *fall* in capital's share. From this perspective, it is entirely possible that the upward trend of the income share of capital occurred precisely because 'real' investment declined.

To close the circle, note that the postwar upward trend in the income share of capital coincided with the positive path of differential accumulation by 'dominant capital' (Figure 5b). This relationship is hardly trivial, at least from the viewpoint of economic orthodoxy. Neo-classical analysis, for one, suggests that because of diminishing returns, accumulation (defined as rising capital goods per head) should be associated with lower rates of returns and hence downward pressure on the income share for capital. Marxist analysis is more ambivalent on the issue, accepting on the one hand that distribution could depend on power, but remaining hostage to the labour theory of value in which a rising organic composition of capital is a depressant of surplus.

DIFFERENTIAL ACCUMULATION

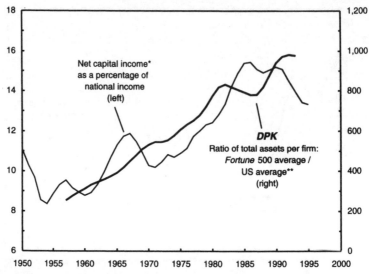

Figure 5b   ... Or a differential accumulation boom?

Sources: US Department of Commerce; US Internal Revenue Service; *Fortune.*
Notes: Series shown as three-year moving averages.
* Net capital income is the sum of after-tax corporate profit (with capital consumption allowance and inventory valuation adjustment) and net interest.
** US average comprises all corporations.

From a Veblenian viewpoint, however, the positive association between accumulation and capital's income share is exactly what one would expect. Accumulation is a power process, not a material one. Defined in differential terms, it involves the growing relative power of the economy's leading business concerns, which in turn helps sustain or expand the overall income share of capital. This is consistent with our analysis in the second section, where we suggested that the distribution of capital income among absentee owners (and hence the differential rate of accumulation) is roughly related to the balance of *business* damage they inflict on each other, whereas the income share of all absentee owners depends (although non-linearly) on the overall *industrial* damage arising from the business warfare raging among them.

These observations lead us to the following tentative proposition about the general nature of modern capitalism. A *sustainable regime of capital accumulation* is defined by two related long-term conditions:

1 A non-negative rate of differential accumulation by the 'dominant capital' group, which suggests that the relative power of the largest

ARTICLES

absentee owners is either stable or growing. This condition reflects both the power drive of accumulation as well as the necessity to exercise power in order to bring industry under effective business control.

2　A steady or rising capital share of income. Although this is partly an indirect result of the first condition, it also reflects the overall balance of power between capitalists and other societal groups. Unless this condition is fulfilled, the very 'capitalist' nature of the system could be put into question.

Within this context, the violation of one or both criteria brings the threat of a *major capitalist crisis*.

5　A LAST NOTE ON POWER

The issues discussed in this article go to the heart of political economy. It is therefore natural, indeed desirable, that they should raise more questions than they answer. Although such questions can be neither enumerated nor dealt with here, one in particular is worth mentioning since it could well present the greatest challenge: is power inherent to human society, and if so, what are the implications for the future of capitalism and beyond?

The general neglect of the whole issue is well reflected in Keynes's famous article 'The economic possibilities for our grandchildren' (1930). In calculating the prospects for humankind a century ahead, Keynes presented accumulation merely as a *means*, a historical 'trick' for eliminating the 'economic problem'. Once scarcity was no more, he argued, the 'money motive' would be recognized for what it was, 'a somewhat disgusting morbidity, one of those semi-criminal, semi-pathological propensities which one hands over with a shudder to the specialist in mental disease', something which 'we shall then be free, at last, to discard' (1930: 329). But then dispensing with accumulation seems easy only because Keynes assumes it has little to do with power. Unfortunately, capital has everything to do with power. Discarding it therefore requires either an alternative form of power, or the elimination of social power altogether. This fundamental dilemma has been succinctly summarized by Koestler (1946), in his discussion of the kibbutz. Even there, under small-scale communism, he argued, 'The instinct to dominate had not been abolished, merely tamed and harnessed.' But then, he added, that 'was as much as anybody could hope for' (1946: 340–1). Perhaps this 'harnessing' will be the main task if capitalism is to give way to a better society.

DIFFERENTIAL ACCUMULATION

NOTES

Research for this article was partly supported by a grant from the Social Sciences and Humanities Research Council of Canada.

1   This approach was introduced in Nitzan (1992), and further developed in Nitzan and Bichler (1995, 1996, 1997) and Bichler and Nitzan (1996a, 1996b).
2   The difference is fundamental. Conventional capacity measures consider what is feasible *under the existing social order of business enterprise and production for profit*, and usually estimate normal utilization to be in the 70–90 per cent range. Alternative measures based on a *material/technological* limit, however, are likely to suggest far lower capacity utilization. Veblen, for one, estimated this to fall short of 25 per cent (1919: 81), a figure not much different from later estimates reported in Blair (1972: 474) and Foster (1986: ch. 5). Interestingly though not surprisingly, US military contractors, engaged in the most destructive form of business enterprise, sometimes operate at as little as 10 per cent of their capacity, while earning superior rates of return (US Congress, Office of Technology Assessment, 1991: 38).

REFERENCES

Barnet, R. J. (1980) *The Lean Years. Politics in the Age of Scarcity*, New York: Simon & Schuster.

Berle, A. A. and Means, G. C. [1932] (1967) *The Modern Corporation and Private Property*, rev. edn, New York: Harcourt, Brace & World.

Bichler, S. and Nitzan, J. (1996a) 'Military spending and differential accumulation: a new approach to the political economy of armament – the case of Israel', *Review of Radical Political Economics* 28(1): 52–97.

—— (1996b) 'Putting the state in its place: US foreign policy and differential accumulation in Middle East "energy conflicts"', *Review of International Political Economy* 3(4): 608–61.

Bickerman, E. J. (1972) 'Mesopotamia', in J. A. Garraty and P. Gay (eds) *The Columbia History of the World*, New York: Harper & Row.

Blair, J. M. (1972) *Economic Concentration. Structure, Behavior and Public Policy*, New York: Harcourt Brace Jovanovich.

—— (1976) *The Control of Oil*, New York: Vintage Books.

Bliss, C. J. (1975) *Capital Theory and the Distribution of Income*, Amsterdam and Oxford: North-Holland.

Bowles, S., Gordon, D. and Weisskopf, T. (1986) 'Power and profits: the social structure of accumulation and the profitability of the postwar U.S. economy', *Review of Radical Political Economics* 18(1&2): 132–67.

—— (1990) *After the Waste Land. A Democratic Economics for the Year 2000*, Armonk, NY: M. E. Sharpe.

Branson, W. H. (1989) *Macroeconomic Theory and Policy*, 3rd edn, New York: Harper & Row.

Burnham, J. (1941) *The Managerial Revolution*, Harmondsworth: Penguin Books.

Chandler, A. D. Jr. (1977) *The Visible Hand. The Managerial Revolution in American Business*, Cambridge, Mass.: Harvard University Press.

Clark, J. B. [1899] (1965) *The Distribution of Wealth*, New York: Augustus M. Kelley.

Cochran, T. C. and Miller, W. (1961) *The Age of Enterprise. A Social History of Industrial America*, rev. edn, New York: Harper & Row.

Edwards, R. (1979) *Contested Terrain. The Transformation of the Workplace in the Twentieth Century*, New York: Basic Books.

ARTICLES

Ferguson, C. E. (1969) *The Neoclassical Theory of Production and Distribution*, Cambridge: Cambridge University Press.

Foster, J. B. (1986) *The Theory of Monopoly Capitalism. An Elaboration of Marxian Political Economy*, New York: Monthly Review Press.

Frankel, S. H. (1977) *Money: Two Philosophies. The Conflict of Trust and Authority*, Oxford: Blackwell.

—— (1980) *Money and Liberty*, Washington, DC: American Enterprise Institute for Public Policy Research, in Hebrew trans. from the English by A. Sand, Tel Aviv: Hakibbutz Hameuchad.

Galbraith, J. K. (1958) *The Affluent Society*, Boston, Mass.: Houghton Mifflin.

—— (1967) *The New Industrial State*, London: Hamish Hamilton.

—— (1983) *The Anatomy of Power*, Boston, Mass.: Houghton Mifflin.

Hodgson, G. M. (1997) 'The fate of the Cambridge Capital Controversy', in P. Arestis, G. Palma and M. Sawyer (eds) *Capital Controversy, Post-Keynesian Economics and the History of Economic Thought, Essays in Honour of Geoff Harcourt*, Vol. 1, London and New York: Routledge.

Howard, M. C. and King, J. E. (1992) *A History of Marxian Economics*, Vol. II: *1929–1990*, Princeton, NJ: Princeton University Press.

Josephson, M. (1934) *The Robber Barons. The Great American Capitalists, 1861–1901*, New York: Harcourt Brace.

Keynes, J. M. [1930] (1970) 'The economic possibilities for our grandchildren', in *The Collected Writings of John Maynard Keynes*, Vol. IX: *Essays in Persuasion*, Cambridge: Macmillan and St Martin's Press.

Knight, F. H. (1921) *Risk, Uncertainty and Profit*, New York: Harper Torchbooks.

Koestler, A. (1946) *Thieves in the Night. Chronicle of an Experiment*, London: Macmillan.

Kotz, D. M. (1994) 'The regulation theory and the social structure of accumulation approach', in D. M. Kotz, T. McDonough and M. Reich (eds) *Social Structure of Accumulation. The Political Economy of Growth and Crisis*, Cambridge: Cambridge University Press.

Lukes, S. (1974) *Power: A Radical Analysis*, London and Basingstoke: Macmillan.

—— (1977) 'Power and structure', in *Essays in Social Theory*, London and Basingstoke: Macmillan.

—— (1978) 'Power and authority', in T. Bottomore and R. Nisbet (eds) *A History of Sociological Analysis*, New York: Basic Books.

Marcuse, H. (1964) *One Dimensional Man. Studies in the Ideology of Advanced Industrial Society*, Boston, Mass.: Beacon Press.

Marshall, A. [1920] (1952) *Principles of Economics. An Introductory Volume*, 8th edn, London: Macmillan.

Marx, K. [1859a] (1953) *Grundrisse der Kritik der politischen Oekonomie*, Berlin: Dietz Verlag.

—— [1859b] (1971) *A Contribution to the Critique of Political Economy*, Introduction by M. Dobb, London: Lawrence & Wishart.

—— [1867] (1906) *Capital. A Critique of Political Economy*, Vol. 1: *The Process of Capitalist Production*, Chicago: Charles H. Kerr.

—— [1894] (1909) *Capital. A Critique of Political Economy*, Vol. 3: *The Process of Capital Production as a Whole*, Chicago: Charles H. Kerr.

Mumford, L. (1934) *Techniques and Civilization*, New York: Harcourt, Brace & World.

—— (1961) *The City in History. Its Origin, Its Transformation and Its Prospects*, New York: Harcourt, Brace & World.

—— (1967) *The Myth of the Machine. Techniques and Human Development*, New York: Harcourt, Brace & World.

DIFFERENTIAL ACCUMULATION

—— (1970) *The Myth of the Machine. The Pentagon of Power*, New York: Harcourt, Brace, Jovanovich.

Nitzan, J. (1992) 'Inflation as restructuring. A theoretical and empirical account of the U.S. experience', unpublished Ph.D. Dissertation, Department of Economics, McGill University, Montreal.

—— (1995) 'The *EMA* "Phoenix": soaring on market "hype"', *Emerging Markets Analyst*, 4(6): 10–17.

—— (1996) 'The EMA *Phoenix*: shorting on market "hype"', *Emerging Markets Analyst* 5(6): 14–25.

Nitzan, J. and Bichler, S. (1995) 'Bringing capital accumulation back in: the Weapondollar–Petrodollar coalition – military contractors, oil companies and Middle East "energy conflicts"', *Review of International Political Economy* 2(3): 446–515.

—— (1996) 'From war profits to peace dividends – the new political economy of Israel', *Capital & Class* 60: 61–94.

—— (1997) 'From breadth to depth in differential accumulation: the great U-turn in South Africa and Israel', paper presented at the International Studies Association meeting, Toronto, March.

Olson, M. (1965) *The Logic of Collective Action. Public Goods and the Theory of Groups*, Cambridge, Mass.: Harvard University Press.

—— (1982) *The Rise and Decline of Nations. Economic Growth, Stagflation and Social Rigidities*, New Haven, Conn., and London: Yale University Press.

Parkin, F. (1971) *Class Inequality and Political Order. Social Stratification in Capitalist and Communist Countries*, London: MacGibbon & Kee.

Parkin, M. and Bade, R. (1986) *Modern Macroeconomics*, 2nd edn, Scarborough, Ontario: Prentice-Hall, Canada.

Perlman, M. (1990) 'The phenomenology of constant capital and fictitious capital', *Review of Radical Political Economics* 22(2&3): 66–91.

Robinson, J. (1971) 'The relevance of economic theory', repr. in J. Schwartz (ed.) (1977) *The Subtle Anatomy of Capitalism*, Santa Monika: Goodyear.

—— (1979) 'Thinking about thinking', repr. in J. Robinson (1980) *What Are the Questions? and Other Essays. Further Contributions to Modern Economics*, Armonk, NY: M. E. Sharpe.

—— (1980) 'Survey: 1960s', in J. Robinson, *What are the Questions? and Other Essays. Further Contributions to Modern Economics*, Armonk, NY: M. E. Sharpe.

Samuelson, P. (1962) 'Parable and realism in capital theory: the surrogate production function', *Review of Economic Studies* 29(3): 193–206.

Samuelson, P. A., Nordhaus, W. D. and McCallum, J. (1988) *Economics*, 6th Canadian edn, Toronto: McGraw-Hill Ryerson.

Scherer, F. M., Beckenstein, A., Kaufer, E. and Murphy, R. D. (1975) *The Economics of Multi-Plant Operation: An International Comparisons Study*, Cambridge, Mass.: Harvard University Press.

Schumpeter, J. A. (1954) *History of Economic Analysis*, ed. E. B. Schumpeter, New York: Oxford University Press.

Shaikh, A. (1990) 'Capital as a social relation', in J. Eatwell, M. Millgate and P. Newman (eds) *The New Palgrave. Marxian Economics*, New York and London: W. W. Norton.

Sraffa, P. (1960) *Production of Commodities by Means of Commodities. Prelude to a Critique of Economic Theory*, Cambridge: Cambridge University Press.

Sweezy, P. M. [1942] (1970) *The Theory of Capitalist Development. Principles of Marxian Political Economy*, New York and London: Modern Reader Paperbacks.

US Congress, Office of Technology Assessment (1991) *Global Arms Trade*, OTA-ISC-460, June, Washington, DC: US GPO.

ARTICLES

Veblen, T. (1898) 'The beginning of ownership', repr. in T. Veblen (1934) *Essays in Our Changing Order*, ed. L. Ardzrooni, New York: The Viking Press.
—— (1899) 'The barbarian status of women', repr. in T. Veblen (1934) *Essays in Our Changing Order*, ed. L. Ardzrooni, New York: The Viking Press.
—— [1904] (1975) *The Theory of Business Enterprise*, Clifton, NJ: Augustus M. Kelley, Reprints of Economics Classics.
—— (1908a) 'Fisher's capital and income', repr. in T. Veblen (1934) *Essays in Our Changing Order*, ed. L. Ardzrooni, New York: The Viking Press.
—— (1908b) 'On the nature of capital. I: The productivity of capital goods', repr. in T. Veblen (1919) *The Place of Science in Modern Civilisation and Other Essays*, New York: Russell & Russell.
—— (1908c) 'On the nature of capital. II: Investment, intangible assets, and the pecuniary magnate', repr. in T. Veblen (1919) *The Place of Science in Modern Civilisation and Other Essays*, New York: Russell & Russell.
—— (1908d) 'Professor Clark's economics', repr. in T. Veblen (1919) *The Place of Science in Modern Civilisation and Other Essays*, New York: Russell & Russell.
—— (1909) 'Fisher's rate of interest', repr. in T. Veblen (1934) *Essays in Our Changing Order*, ed. L. Ardzrooni, New York: The Viking Press.
—— [1919] (1964) *The Vested Interest and the State of Industrial Arts*, New York: B. W. Huebsch.
—— [1923] (1967) *Absentee Ownership and Business Enterprise in Recent Times. The Case of America*, Introduction by Robert Leckachman, Boston, Mass.: Beacon Press.
Wicksell, K. (1935) *Lectures on Political Economy*, Vol. 1: *General Theory*, 2nd edn, trans. from the Swedish by E. Classen and edited and with an introduction by L. Robbins, London: George Routledge & Sons.
Wright, E. O. (1977) 'Alternative perspectives in Marxist theory of accumulation and crisis', in J. Schwartz (ed.) *The Subtle Anatomy of Capitalism*, Santa Monika: Goodyear.
Zeitlin, M. (1974) 'Corporate ownership and control: the large corporation and the capitalist class', *American Journal of Sociology* 79(5) (March): 1073–119.

[10]

Robert Wade and Frank Veneroso

The Asian Crisis: The High Debt Model Versus the Wall Street-Treasury-IMF Complex

How could the widely acknowledged real estate problems of Thailand's banks in 1996 and 1997 have triggered such a far-reaching debt-and-development crisis?[1] The devaluation of the Thai baht in July 1997 was followed by currency crises or financial instability in Indonesia, Malaysia, the Philippines, Taiwan, Hong Kong, Korea, Estonia, Russia, Brazil, Australia and New Zealand. Commodity producers around the world have suffered. Yet there were few signs of impending crisis, such as rising interest rates in the G-7 countries or a sudden suspension of capital flows to developing countries after the baht devaluation. On the contrary, bank lending to Asia actually rose to a record level in the third quarter of 1997. The Japanese government's de facto credit rating agency, the Japan Center for International Finance, gave Korea one of its highest credit ratings for any developing country in June 1997. The IMF and the World Bank lavished praise upon the governments of the region through 1997, including on the Korean authorities as recently as September 1997.

What began as a debt crisis has become a fully fledged development crisis. Throughout this most successful of developing regions living standards are falling as unemployment rises and the effects of huge devaluations work through into higher import prices. Many millions of poor people are at risk, and many millions of people who were confident of middle-class status feel robbed of their lifetime savings and security. It is not a humanitarian tragedy on the scale of North Korea, but the loss of security and productivity is a tragedy nonetheless, almost as cruel as war.

Financial crises—speculative bubbles followed by collapse—have recurred throughout the history of capitalism. In the early 1980s Latin America, another fast-growing developing region, suddenly went into debt-and-development crisis and stopped rising up the world economic hierarchy. The Latin American crisis was due, according to the consensus of analysts, to the combination of bad macroeconomic policies and foreign borrowing by governments. That borrowing was wasteful and corrupt because done by *governments* rather than by private firms operating in competitive markets. But the Asian crisis has occurred in the opposite conditions. In East and Southeast Asia today most debt is *private* debt. And prior to the crisis, the macroeconomic 'fundamentals' looked fine. The countries in question have had low inflation, budget surpluses or only small deficits, and until recently stable or rising foreign exchange reserves. They have been growing fast. East and Southeast Asia accounted for a quarter of world output, but fully half of world growth over the 1990s and almost two-thirds of world capital spending. Firms throughout the region make products that sell in the most demanding markets—if the exchange rate is right.

There is little agreement on why the magnitude of the crisis has been so large, what can be done to get out of it, who will gain and who will loose, and what changes need to be made in international regimes to reduce the likelihood of repeats. These matters should be the subject of an international debate as important as the Bretton Woods conference at the end of the Second World War.

The New Wisdom

According to the IMF, the solution entails domestic austerity programs to restore the capacity to repay foreign debt, and radical institutional change, including further liberalization of the financial sector. Many analysts have come forward to disagree. Indeed, a new 'conventional wisdom' among the IMF's critics has emerged, which goes like this:[2] The cri-

---

[1] Thanks to Paul Streeten, Martin Wolf, Adrian Wood, Peter Evans, J.D. Von Pischke, Francis Daniels, Devesh Kapur, Manfred Bienefeld, Bruce Scott, Richard Doner, Albert Fishlow, Robert Brenner, Thomas Biersteker, David Hale, David Seckler, Ronald Dore and Robert K. Merton for their comments, which do not implicate them at all in the result.

[2] For example, Jeffrey Sachs, 'The Wrong Medicine for Asia', *New York Times*, 3 November 1997; Alice Amsden and Yoon-Dae Euh, 'Behind Korea's Plunge', *New York Times*, 29 November 1997, p. A39; Joseph Stiglitz, 'How to Fix the Asian Economies', *New York Times*, 31 October 1997; Stiglitz, 'More Instruments and Broader Goals: Moving Toward the Post-Washington Consensus', The 1998 WIDER Annual Lecture, Helsinki, Finland. Stiglitz is chief economist at the World Bank. He has not concealed his disagreements with the IMF's austerity push. 'You don't want to push these countries into severe

sis is a crisis of liquidity more than solvency.[3] Creditors have 'run' on the currency and on domestic assets, leaving the borrowers unable to continue to finance their loans. It happened partly because of excessive financial *deregulation*, including, above all, allowing firms to borrow abroad without any government control or coordination. The crisis has then built upon itself as each lender tries to call in loans and firms try to cut operating costs and sell assets, causing unemployment to rise and asset values to crash.

'Instead of dousing the fire, the IMF in effect screamed fire in the theatre', says Jeffrey Sachs.[4] Its insistence on shuttering many banks despite the absence of deposit insurance caused panicky depositors to withdraw their deposits in return for cash. Its insistence on cutting demand and liquidity has caused the bankruptcy or radical devaluation of the value of firms that were efficient and profitable, as well as those that were not. Its push for institutional liberalization in finance, corporate goverance and labour markets convinced creditors that the economics were structurally unsound.

The immediate goal must be to restore confidence, which requires overcoming the collective action problem in which no lender wants to re-finance for fear that others will not. Demand and liquidity must be increased, not reduced, in order to keep firms turning over. The IMF should be concentrating its attention on organizing debt rescheduling negotiations and then in helping to erect the structure of financial regulation, especially at the border, that will help to minimize the risks of such a melt-down occurring again.

We agree with this line of argument, as far as it goes. We go further, however, arguing that the long-term damage to Asian economies of the IMF's prescriptions is likely to be even greater than the critics have recognized. The reason has to do with a neglected dimension of the crisis—the financial structure of East and Southeast Asian economies, that differs from the kind of case the IMF usually deals with. Because of this difference, a unit of IMF 'austerity' and 'financial liberalization' will have higher costs and smaller benefits in Asia than elsewhere. The slowness of the IMF's packages for Thailand, Indonesia and Korea to revive confidence, despite being the biggest in the organization's history, reflects both their imposition of impossibly far-reaching institutional liberalization and their inappropriateness for Asian financial structures.

---

recession. One ought to focus...on things that caused the crisis, not on things that make it more difficult to deal with', he is quoted in a *Wall Street Journal* story as saying. The article continues, 'Mr Stiglitz's critique is a departure from the usual closed-door disagreements between the two institutions...An exchange of views "Isn't unhealthy", says IMF Treasurer David Williams, "but we shouldn't have closely related institutions coming out with different macroeconomic analyses".' ('World Bank Questions IMF Plan: Austerity in Asia may Worsen Crisis', *Wall Street Journal*, 8 January 1998). Stiglitz's views, however, are not the same as those of the operational part of the Bank dealing with Korea, which are closer to the IMF's.
[3] On a continuum from illiquidity to insolvency, Korea is towards the illiquidity-with-fringe-of-insolvency end, Indonesia towards the insolvency end.
[4] Jeffrey Sachs, 'The IMF and the Asian Flu', *The American Prospect*, March-April 1998, pp. 16-21, citation at p. 17.

The Asian High Debt Model

In a Western, including Latin American, financial system companies normally carry an amount of debt that is no bigger than and generally less than the value of their equity capital; and banks will not, or should not according to standard prudential limits, lend to companies with higher levels of debt. In East and Southeast Asia, and especially in Japan and Korea, corporate debt/equity ratios of the bigger firms are commonly two to one or more.[5]

Why are corporate debt/equity ratios so much higher than in Western systems? First, because savings are much higher. Gross domestic savings to GDP ratios in Asia are one third of GDP or more, compared to 15-20 per cent in Western systems. The savings are done in large part by households.[6] Households hold their savings mostly in bank deposits, bank deposits being much less risky than equities. Banks have to lend.[7] When neither households nor government are significant net borrowers, the system is biased towards borrowing by firms. (Lending or investing abroad is only a very partial alternative, given the amount of savings to be absorbed.)[8]

---

[5] Reliable comparative data on corporate debt/equity ratios are hard to find, and we are still searching.

[6] We shall not pursue the question of why household savings are high, except to say that the reasons are not well understood.

[7] We are puzzled by World Bank and IMF data that suggests that Korea's bank credit/ liabilities to GDP is relatively low, less than the developing East and Southeast Asian average, and are seeking further information on the figures. See for example, Stijn Claessens and Thomas Glaessner, 'Are Financial Sector Weaknesses Undermining the East Asian Miracle?', *Directions in Development*, World Bank, September 1997, figure 1.

[9] Our argument differs in emphasis from the UNCTAD *Trade and Development Report* 1997. The report claims to find evidence that 'the exceptional savings-investment performance of East Asian economies has been due not so much to household as to corporate savings' (p. 169), and that East Asia is marked out by a high share of corporate retained earnings that are then reinvested. The report therefore downplays the process of bank intermediation from households to firms and highlights reinvestment from retained earnings. We stress, first, that the statistics on savings and profits in developing countries are especially unreliable. Companies hide profits, inflation is difficult to take account of, savings are calculated as a residual, the profits of the informal sector may be counted as household savings, and East Asian *household* savings are a function of bonus payments that are directly related to *corporate* profits. Is it remotely plausible that Peru in 1980-84 had the second highest rate of household savings of the seventeen developing countries plus Japan in the UNCTAD sample (table 44). Second, the UNCTAD data is very old, from the first half of the 1980s or earlier. Third, UNCTAD's own data suggests that in East and Southeast Asia corporate investment exceeds corporate savings by a margin that roughly corresponds to the excess of household savings over household investment (table 44), consistent with the idea of large-scale bank intermediation from households to firms. Fourth, if corporate savings are unusually high in East and Southeast Asia, as the UNCTAD report says, this is not necessarily inconsistent with unusually high corporate debt/equity ratios and unusually large bank intermediation from households to firms. High corporate savings, high bank intermediation from households to firms, and high corporate debt/equity ratios can all occur together when corporate investment (and 'animal spirits') are high. Take Japan in the 1960s where the corporate sector invested about 23 per cent of GDP while corporate savings were about 15 per cent of GDP. Corporate savings financed less than two-thirds of corporate investment, the rest being financed by household (and/or public or external savings). Compare this with the US where corporate savings (8.5 per cent of GDP) financed over 90 per cent of corporate investment (of 9 per cent of GDP). Both debt/equity leverage and corporate savings are higher in Japan. We thank UNCTAD's Yilmaz Akyuz for discussions on these issues.

6

Second, firms that aim to make an assault on major world industries—as especially in Japan, Korea, Taiwan—must get their hands on very large amounts of resources, which they can do only by borrowing. Neither equity markets nor corporate retained earnings are feasible alternatives for mobilizing resources on the scale required to compete in these export markets and continually upgrade.

High ratios of bank deposits and loan intermediation to GDP, and of corporate debt to equity, make the financial structure vulnerable to shocks that depress cash flows or the supply of bank or portfolio capital. The deeper the intermediation of debt (that is, the higher the ratio of bank deposits to GDP and the higher the ratio of corporate debt to equity), the more likely that any depressive shock will cause illiquidity, default, and bankruptcy. Debt-intensive strategies should be labelled, 'This product can be harmful to your wealth'.

Such a financial structure requires cooperation between banks and firms, and considerable government support. The trick is to buffer firms' cash flow and supply of capital against 'systemic' shocks, while not protecting firms from the consequences of bad judgement or malfeasance. Restrictions on the freedom of firms and banks to borrow abroad, and coordination of foreign borrowing by government, are a necessary part of this system.

Crony Capitalism?

Western commentators often dismiss the system as 'crony capitalism', seeing only its corruption and favouritism. They miss the financial rationale for cooperative, long-term, reciprocal relations between firms, banks and government in a system which intermediates high savings into high corporate debt/equity ratios.[9] (They also miss the cronyism of US capitalism, generated by the electoral finance regime.)

The need for state support allows the state to influence the decisions of banks and firms in line with a national industrial strategy, by withholding support from banks and firms that operate against the strategy. The whole system can be disciplined by making investment incentives conditional on export performance or on reductions in the gap between the firm's prices and international prices for the same products.

High household savings, plus high corporate debt/equity ratios, plus bank-firm-state collaboration, plus national industrial strategy, plus investment incentives conditional on international competitiveness, equals the 'developmental state'.[10] For all the white elephants and

---

[9] Legal contracts between Korean and foreign firms engaged in infrastructure projects commonly use language that implies backing by Korean government agencies or by the Overseas Contractors Association of Korea. In practice the taking and enforcing of collateral assets is largely irrelevant; what matters is the implicit government support. Much the same applies elsewhere in East Asia.

[10] See Robert Wade, *Governing the Market: Economic Theory and the Role of Government in East Asian Industrialization*, Princeton 1990; Chalmers Johnson, *MITI and the Japanese Miracle: The Growth of Industrial Policy, 1925-1975*, Stanford University Press, 1982; Stephan Haggard, *Pathways from the Periphery: The Politics of Growth in the Newly Industrializing Countries*, Cornell University Press, 1990; Linda Weiss and John Hobson, *States and Economic Development*, Cambridge 1995.

corruption—inevitable when a third of national income is being inter-mediated—the system that allows firms to borrow multiples of their equity has yielded a quantum leap up the world hierarchy in technology and scale, and rates of improvement in living conditions that surpass virtually all other countries.

Notice the parallels with Keynesian theory, which identifies savings rates in excess of investment rates as a cause of depressions and insecurity and even higher savings rates. Keynesian theory, however, posits govern-ment deficit spending as the solution. We see in East Asia a model of pri-vate debt based on high corporate debt/equity ratios, which give rise to the need for government protection against periodic slippages that would otherwise lead to widespread bankruptcy.

The Impact of Shocks

The other side of the equation, however, is very high levels of corporate debt. It is likely that Korea's corporate debt/GDP ratio is of the order of 30 to 50 per cent higher than the corresponding ratio in the US. This rep-resents a debt mountain that sits at the heart of the Korean problem. The mountain may be less high in other Asian countries, but it remains much higher than is normal in Western systems.

To see the dangers of debt, compare systems with low and high corporate debt/equity ratios. Low corporate debt/equity systems, as are found in Latin America and North America, are not able to invest as heavily as the others but are also less vulnerable to shocks. They can sustain a sharp rise in real interest rates for some time. Corporate gross profits before interest and taxes are more likely to be high enough relative to the higher interest charges that some degree of debt repayment out of cash flow remains possi-ble. Therefore the tendency for real debt to grow as a result of higher real interest charges is less than when debt/equity ratios are high. If the interest rate rises to the point where the firm cannot repay any of the extra cost out of cash flow or reserves and therefore must recapitalize it (that is, add it to its stock of debt), the balance sheet still has room for a higher debt/equity ratio without threatening the firm's viability by wiping out its equity.

The risk that an interest rate above the rate of gross profit has disastrous consequences increases with the debt/equity ratio. In higher debt/equity systems firms have to use more of their gross profits on interest charges. A significant rise in interest costs may not be able to be met out of prof-its, in which case it has to be recapitalized into debt. But the balance sheet may not have room for more debt without threatening the firm's viability. A rise from 10 to 20 per cent lifts a debt/equity ratio of 80:20 (or 4:1) to 88:12 in the first year—if the interest due is all recapitalized and if the corporation is just breaking even at the start. Replicated across many firms, the country's overall debt to GDP ratio rises. If, in addition, the high real interest rate policy also depresses aggregate demand, it will further depress cash flow relative to interest charges, accelerating the indebtedness of the corporate sector. And all the worse if, as is true in Asia, a substantial share of the debt is foreign debt and the domestic cur-rency is devalued, raising the fixed interest payments on the foreign debt in domestic currency.

8

A higher debt/equity ratio not only makes for higher borrower's risk; the lender's risk equally rises with the ratio, unless the IMF bails them out. 'Shocks and Debt' (the box at the end of this article) illustrates the contrast between high and low debt/equity systems with a simple example. It shows how a 'Latin American' firm with low debt to equity is able to survive a devaluation, interest rate hike and austerity programme much more easily than an 'Asian' high debt to equity firm.

The Crisis of 1997-98

What made for the high-growth performance of Asian systems in the past has led to or at least amplified the present crisis. Over the 1990s Western and Japanese banks and investment houses lent heavily to Asian companies. They assumed, contrary to all historical knowledge about growth rates, that fast growth (four times the OECD average) would continue, and consequently that exchange rates would remain stable.[11] They also each ignored their own prudential limits on lending to companies with high debt/equity ratios, because everyone else was ignoring the limits and they each wanted to win business. International bankers have a powerful incentive to follow the herd, because the banker who does not make money where others are making it risks being seen as incompetent but does not suffer by making losses when everyone else is making losses too.

Meanwhile, Asian governments undertook radical financial deregulation, encouraged by the IMF, the OECD, and by Western governments, banks and firms. They removed or loosened controls on companies' foreign borrowings, abandoned coordination of borrowings and investments, and failed to strengthen bank supervision. By doing so, they violated one of the stability conditions of the Asian high debt model, helping to set the crisis in train.[12] It is particularly puzzling that the Korean government acted in this way, counter to the whole thrust of Korean development policy for decades past. Anecdotal evidence suggests that key people were bribed by Japanese and Western financial institutions. Bribery aside, the government placed great emphasis on joining the OECD, and the OECD made financial openness a condition of membership. As part of the same set of reforms, the government abolished the Economic Planning Board, the main body for making eco-

---

[11] There were, indeed, serious internal obstacles to the continued fast growth and industrial and service sector upgrading of the South East Asian economies. The economies have continued to engage in the world industrial economy largely as sub-contractors, largely for Japanese firms. They have experienced relatively little technology spill-over from the export-oriented sub-contractors to the rest of the economy, so much so that their industrialization has been characterized as 'technology-less', in the sense that even adaptive technology continues to come from abroad. Shortages of skilled people have grown 'from a crisis to a critical emergency', according to a Thai analyst. Thailand's gross enrolment ratio at secondary school level languished at only 37 per cent in 1992, less than half of Taiwan's in 1978 when Taiwan had the same per capita income as Thailand in 1992. In Malaysia, too, the skills shortage has become so acute that some prominent foreign companies long operating in the country have moved production elsewhere, mainly to China and Indonesia. Throughout the region infrastructure is chronically congested, attested to by electricity blackouts, traffic paralysis and the rising cost of water. In short, serious problems in the 'real' economy have been building up, even if they are problems of success. But the calamity unleashed on the region is hugely disproportional to the severity of the problems in the real economy.

[12] See Wade, *Governing the Markets*, p. 367.

nomic strategy since the early 1960s, making the Finance Ministry the economic supremo. In Thailand the central bank undertook capital liberalization just as it and its regulatory agencies were being overwhelmed with other complex issues and political strife.

Domestic corporate borrowers discovered that they could borrow abroad half as cheaply as they could at home. Foreign debt escalated, most of it private and short-term—maturing in twelve months or less. In Korea, foreign debt incurred by its banks and the companies that borrowed from them exploded from very little in the early 1990s to roughly $160 billion by late 1997.

China's devaluations of 1990 and 1994, together with its lower inflation and faster productivity growth, made the yuan the most undervalued major currency in the world, worsening the export competitiveness of other East and Southeast Asian economies. The US dollar appreciated against the yen after 1995—the result of an agreement between the US Treasury and the Japanese Finance Ministry to help Japan export its way out of trouble and use the resulting surpluses to buy US Treasury bills, thereby allowing US interest rates to be kept at politically desirable levels and assisting the re-election of President Clinton.[13] This worsened the East and Southeast Asian economies' competitiveness still further, because their own currencies were pegged to the dollar and rose with it. Thailand in 1996 experienced zero growth of exports, the slowest rate of growth of GDP in a decade, and a ballooning current account deficit. The Thai stock market lost a fifth of its value in the first nine months of 1996, and growth of direct foreign investment fell sharply. In Korea, manufacturing production started to fall in 1996, the current account went strongly negative in the same year, and industrial bankruptcies occurred.

When, later, foreign lenders began to worry about currency falls, they 'discovered' their heavy exposure to companies with debt/equity ratios far above their prudential limits. More exactly, they discovered the possibility that others might make a similar 'discovery', the aggregation of which would precipitate falls in the exchange rate—multiplying the loan burden and the risks of default. Hence they have tried in every way to call in their loans and not make new ones. The Japanese banks that lent heavily to firms in East and Southeast Asia have been especially anxious to call in these loans as their domestic position deteriorated with the falls in the stock market and the yen.

This is why the run has been so surprisingly big. International banks have slashed credit lines to all borrowers, including the export-oriented firms that should be benefitting from currency depreciation. Even the big Korean chaebol, with world-wide brand names, are finding it difficult to get even *trade* credit—letters of credit to cover the import of inputs into export production. In Latin America during the 1980s, where companies had much lower debt/equity ratios, foreign lenders found that *companies* continued to meet their test of prudence, even if

[13] Klaus Engelen, 'How Bill Clinton Really Won', *The European*, 14-20 November 1996; and Chalmers Johnson, 'Cold War Economics Melt Asia', *The Nation*, 23 February 1998, pp. 16-19.
10

countries did not. Latin American companies therefore did not suffer such a withdrawal of bank credit, though the Latin American countries were far less credit-worthy. As of this time of writing, the IMF, the United Nations and other international forecasters continue to chase the whole world economy downhill, at least for 1998.[14]

The IMF to the Rescue?

The IMF is designed to provide bridging finance while a country gets its balance of payments in order. IMF programmes normally seek to reduce current account deficits, keep inflation in check, and keep domestic demand constrained. Such objectives are set out in the opening lines of the IMF stand-by agreement with South Korea, dated December 5, 1997:[15]

> *1. Objectives The program is intended to narrow the external current account deficit to below 1 per cent of GDP in 1998 and 1999, contain inflation at or below 5 per cent, and—hoping for an early return to confidence—limit the deceleration in real GDP growth to about 3 per cent in 1998, followed by a recovery toward potential in 1999.*

From this point on the IMF programme for Korea goes well beyond standard IMF programmes, calling for structural and institutional reform, even though they are not needed to resolve the current crisis. It requires major financial restructuring to make the financial system operate like a Western one, though without actually saying so. It includes closing down or recapitalizing troubled financial institutions; letting foreign financial institutions freely buy up domestic ones; requiring banks to

---

[14] Every step in our argument should be treated as hypothesis in need of testing, especially against regional variation. The high debt-developmental state model applies more in East than in South East Asia; within the latter, it applies more to Malaysia than to Thailand, and least to Indonesia. In the current crisis, some countries have suffered more of a financial shock than others, and the same sized shock has caused a bigger deterioration in economic performance in some than in others. Our argument emphasizes the debt/equity ratio as an important factor in both the size of the shock and the effect on economic performance. But the effect on performance is also a function of the degree of latent social conflict in the society and the robustness of institutions for conflict management, among other things. Taiwan has been relatively little affected, its currency falling only about 13 per cent in the latter part of 1997 and 20 per cent between the start of 1997 and early 1998, while growth has remained fairly steady at 6 per cent and inflation around 1 per cent. Why? Taiwan has towering foreign exchange reserves, and a very low ratio of short term foreign bank debt to foreign exchange reserves; it has moved counter-cyclically, its property and stock market bubble bursing in the early 1990s and most of the consequences for bank balance sheets having been absorbed by 1997; it has lower savings debt/equity ratio. It is also linguistically and ethnically relatively homogenous, with relatively robust institutions for conflict management. Singapore and Hong Kong provide more regional variation, though we find it hard to treat these city states as equivalent to nation states, as so much of their dynamics comes from their role as regional hubs. Chile is an interesting comparison outside the region: it saves at near East Asian rates (29 per cent of GDP in 1995), its corporate debt/equity ratios are close to 'Western' norms, it has discouraged surges of capital inflows by in effect taxing them, and it has enjoyed fast growth over the past decade. It has been affected by Asian contagion through trade, with pressure on the exchange rate and the current account due to falls in exports and copper prices, but has experienced little financial instability.

[15] The IMF requirements are summarized in 'Republic of Korea: IMF Stand-by Arrangement: Summary of the Economic Program, December 5, 1997'.

follow Western ('Basle') prudential standards; requiring 'international' (read 'Western') accounting standards to be followed and international accounting firms to be used for the auditing of financial institutions. It requires the government to undertake not to intervene in the lending decisions of commercial banks, and to eliminate all government-directed lending; and to give up measures to assist individual corporations avoid bankruptcy, including subsidized credit and tax privileges.

The Fund also requires wider opening of Korea's capital account, to enable even freer inflow and outflow of capital. All restrictions on foreign borrowings by corporations are to be eliminated. The trade regime, too, will be further liberalized, to remove trade-related subsidies and restrictive import licensing. Labour market institutions and legislation will be reformed 'to facilitate redeployment of labour'.

The IMF programs for the other Asian cases differ from case to case, but they also push for capital account opening and financial sector deregulation, as well as high real interest rates and other measures to restrict domestic demand.

Conflicting Objectives

In terms of the first set of objectives—to remove the current account deficits and achieve macro-economic balance—we are already seeing, at current heavily depreciated exchange rates, big trade *surpluses* from several Asian countries. Korea ran a giant current account surplus of $3.7 billion dollars in December 1997, equivalent to something like 15 per cent of Korean GDP when annualized at the post-devaluation exchange rate of 1,600 won to the US dollar. Thailand ran a current account surplus for the last several months of 1997. So did Malaysia. So far the surplus is due more to falls in imports than to rises in exports. But the majority of imports are capital goods and industrial materials and fuel rather than consumer goods, and their cutback hurts exports. Only truly heroic improvements in the trade balance could garner enough foreign exchange to cover interest payments falling due in the next several years.

The difficulties of doing so are compounded by the costs associated with the Fund's second set of objectives, those to do with liberalizing the financial sector both domestically and externally. Movement in this direction will face very large 'transitional' costs; and in any case, even if a 'Western' look-alike system is established it would not be stable given the high flow of savings. It would also sacrifice the developmental advantages of a high debt system.

The transitional difficulties relate to the implications of the existing debt. Before Western prudential limits can be viable, before the financial system can be made to work like a Western one, the debt mountain must be brought down. The IMF seems not to have thought through the consequences of doing this.

Historically, debt mountains have been reduced in one of four market-based ways. The first is through inflation: the debt is vaporized by means of a domestic inflation that causes real interest rates to turn *negative*. The

12

second is bankruptcy: existing creditors lose some of the value of their assets as the debt is written down, the new creditors reorganize the assets and (hopefully) make the company viable again at the lower level of debt. The third is repayment of the debt out of cash flow. The fourth is by debt-to-equity swaps. The government can also absorb the debt and finance its repayment out of taxation. But this is not a market-based response.

All of these have social costs, but some more than others. A country that goes along the bankruptcy route will suffer major social disruption and loss of output while 'resources' (including people) are reallocated. The principal lenders are banks, which are always highly leveraged—have high debt/equity. When banks write down the debt of the companies to whom they have lent, they lower their own asset base, and jeopardize their own ability to meet their principal and interest payment obligations on deposits. They may have to stop refinancing sound companies that then become insolvent, in turn transmitting insolvency pressures to their customers and suppliers. Asset prices may begin to collapse as fore-closing creditors sell at firesale prices, causing further problems for hold-ers of existing assets who see their value knocked down. Fears of bank deposit failures increase the demand for currency relative to bank deposits. The banking system may undergo a multiple contraction of deposits and loans. Layoffs proliferate. Consumers cut back. The disinfla-tionary impetus is reinforced.

The bankruptcy route has been an integral part of all great depressions. Irving Fisher observed that the central propagating mechanism of the Great Depression of the 1930s was the rising real value of dollar liabili-ties—a rising real interest rate. As the price level fell, the real value of the principal of the debt rose. Firms found themselves facing higher and higher levels of indebtedness and repayment obligations, and banks called their loans and refused to lend. The resulting bankruptcies deep-ened and propagated the deflationary dynamic just described.

The repayment-out-of-cash flow route is likely to be protracted—if the existing levels of debt and interest rates are not too high for it to be workable from the start. As firms use most of their return on assets to repay principal and interest, their investment falls. This route is associ-ated with prolonged stagnation. It takes many years to pay down the debt to the point where Western prudential standards can be met. Japan has tried to follow this route during the 1990s. We can see its costs in the very slow growth of the Japanese economy since the stock market and property market bubbles burst in 1990.

The inflation route also has social costs, but historically the costs have tended to be lower than those associated with the others. Provided the inflation is kept at 40 per cent or less the social costs are small.[16] This approach requires the price level to be rising fast enough to make real

---

[16] See for example Michael Bruno and William Easterly, 'Inflation Crises and Long-Run Growth', *Journal of Monetary Economics*, February 1998. They put the threshold above which countries fall into a high inflation/low growth trap at between 30 and 50 per cent per year. Below the threshold, the social costs can be fairly easily mitigated by means of indexing.

interest rates low or negative, and it requires a semi-closed capital account in order to check capital flight.

The IMF prescriptions preclude the inflation route. They call for *high* real interest rates—in order not only to curb demand but also to encourage a reversal of the capital outflow. And they emphatically call for the capital account to be opened wide.

The Second Opium War

Debt-to-equity swaps were used to help reduce the Latin American debt crisis of the 1980s. In the Asian context, where debt to equity ratios are much higher, it is not clear that they could be used on a scale sufficient to make a big difference. In any case, given the lack of equity resources now held by post-crisis Asian nationals, a significant reduction of debt by this method implies massive foreign ownership positions in Asian firms and banks. Vast swathes of the corporate sector would end up in foreign hands. Already we are seeing Japanese and American companies jumping from minority to majority owners of Southeast Asian firms in return for a writing down of the debt. And debt-to-equity swaps aside, the devaluations enable foreign companies to pick up Asian companies at fire-sale prices—or in the current Korean phrase, 'IMF cold wave prices'. We are already seeing a political backlash against the sudden jump in foreign ownership. Korean and Southeast Asian editorialists have started to write about 'The Second Opium War' and US/IMF imperialism.

If the debt claims were swapped for equity claims held by domestic banks, the banks would end up as huge equity holders, something that banks are not supposed to be. If the debt claims were transferred to the state, and the state in return acquired a voting interest in the company, this would amount to nationalization—not something the IMF or the US Treasury wish to encourage. Morgan Bank has suggested government guarantees for private foreign borrowing, in the hope that this would allow foreign lenders to resume lending to highly indebted firms on the grounds that the guarantee makes the debt look like sovereign debt. But the debt mountain would remain.

If the IMF prescriptions for reshaping Asian financial systems into something more like the Western model require, as a condition of viability, a running down of corporate debt, and if the inflation route is ruled out, then the social costs are likely to be huge and long-lasting—especially because of the sheer amount of corporate debt relative to GDP that has to be shrunk to Western levels. Inflation is the only way to reduce such a debt mountain without years of stagnation, nationalist backlash, or chaos.

The Fund's much higher real interest rates will tip many high debt/equity firms into bankruptcy—and the resulting financial instability and unrest may cause net capital *outflow* instead of the inflow that the Fund expects. Meeting Western standards for the adequacy of banks' capital requires a rapid fall in banks' debt/equity ratios, and a sharp cut in their lending, causing more company bankruptcies. Opening up the financial sector to foreign banks will result in a large-scale take-over, because after the bankruptcies and liquidations foreign banks and

14

companies will be the only ones with the capital for recapitalizing the domestic ones. But foreign banks may not lend to high debt/equity local companies, and may not participate in the kind of alliances between government, the banks, and companies that a high debt/equity financial structure requires. If Citibank buys up Korean banks and applies its normal prudential limits (by which lending to a company with a debt/equity ratio of 1:1 is getting risky), it will not lend to Daewoo with a debt/equity ratio of 5:1. The amount of restructuring of Daewoo before its debt/equity ratio comes close to 1:1 is hard to imagine.

It seems particularly unwise for the IMF to insist that companies receive even more freedom than before to borrow on international capital markets on their own account, without government coordination, when it was their uncoordinated borrowing that set up the crisis in the first place. This will make the country more, not less, vulnerable to capital flight.

In short, the IMF approach is likely to generate large social costs long before there is any significant amount of debt reduction, all because of a short-term and unforeseeable run by mobile capital. It aims to dismantle the high debt system, its developmental advantages notwithstanding. And it wants to see a Western-type financial system in its place that can only work with a huge reduction in levels of corporate debt. The Fund has not properly weighed the economic and social costs of such actions. Eventually Asian economies will start to grow again, for their 'fundamentals' are strong—but by then their fundamentals will not be as strong. There will be an inner source of instability created by the attempt to integrate the massive flow of household deposit savings with a financial structure based on Western norms of prudent debt/equity ratios. And by then they will have a rather different pattern of ownership, with foreign firms and banks—in particular, US firms and banks—having much more control than before and receiving much more of the profits. They will have given up the developmental advantages of a high debt system based on government-bank-firm collaboration in return for somewhat lower risks of financial crashes.

Once the crisis is passed, some reneging on IMF agreements may occur. But by that time foreign banks and other financial institutions may be well established, making the high debt/equity system difficult to rebuild.

An Alternative Path

The high savings of Asian households impart a bias towards high levels of corporate debt. Household saving rates may come down over the next several decades. But saving rates much higher than in the West are likely to be a feature of these economies for many years to come, and the current crisis will only intensify households' wish to save.

Households' risk aversion precludes transfer of more than a small part of the savings through equity markets. Equity markets will of course develop over time as the infrastructure for a well-working stock market is gradually built up. But even in the most highly developed equity markets only a few percentage points of GDP or less are transferred. In the

United States, where the equity market is a celebrated national institution, net savings transferred to the corporate sector through the equity channel have averaged less than 1 per cent of GDP, and have often been negative over the past decade. Such small flows may be meaningful in a country like the US where household savings are only 4 per cent of GDP, but are trivial where household savings are more like 12 per cent of GDP. Moreover the current crisis has caused huge losses for most of the Asian households that have recently begun to participate in national stock markets. This makes it all the more likely that sizeable development of equity markets is a dead issue in Asia for another decade at least. The Japanese experience is cautionary. Since the crash of 1990, over 90 per cent of the mutual fund holdings accumulated over the 1980s have been redeemed.

If Asia continues to save at anything close to current levels, there is an inescapable problem of how to invest the savings productively. It is a fine irony, since Asia's high savings have been instrumental in its fast growth and the envy of the rest of the world.

We argue that high savings and high corporate debt yield powerful advantages in terms of national development. The high levels of debt can be sustained under normal conditions provided that banks and firms have mutual understandings about the refinancing of the debt, and provided the government supports them. This in turn requires, above all, closing or semi-closing the capital account, so that mobile capital cannot go freely in and out.[17] In such high saving societies, foreign savings are not needed; it is already difficult enough to allocate domestic savings to efficient investments at the margin. These arrangements may stop well short of a developmental state on the model of Japan, Korea and Taiwan, but they are well along in that direction, and far from the IMF's model of a desirable financial system.

To resolve the crisis, inflation is the least costly way to reduce debt. Real interest rates have to be kept negative or at least very low, which would also reduce the pressure for bankruptcies and financial instability more generally. Household savers have been content with the low rates they have been getting, so there is no reason to raise the rate above the level of inflation. The government would let the exchange rate float, removing the impetus to raise interest rates in order to keep the currency stable. The IMF assumes that low real interest rates will lead to net capital flight and greater refinancing difficulties. It is not obvious that *high* real interest rates will not have an even worse effect on capital flight, because of the magnitude of bankruptcies and financial instability caused by high rates in the context of high debt/equity ratios. At the least, the trade-off has to be raised as an issue, as the IMF, reading from the script prepared for low debt/equity situations, has not.

---

[17] Jagdish Bhagwati, professor of economics at Columbia University, agrees. '[Capital markets] are very volatile. Suddenly expectations can turn around. You may be very healthy but sudden you can catch pneumonia. And then you may have to do unspeakable things to your economy just to regain that confidence because you are now hooked into the system. Markets may do something when you've done nothing wrong and you may have to do something wrong in order to convince the markets that you are doing something right! I would put off [capital account convertibility] for quite a while' (interview in *Times of India*, 31 December 1997).

The government should push weak banks to merge with strong domestic ones. It should use its own strong balance sheet to support existing banks, not close them down or let them be bought by foreign banks. Many of these banks are insolvent only by Western standards and under transitory crisis conditions, not according to the rules of the developmental state in conditions of reasonably fast growth.[18]

Hence the government should step in to reintroduce controls on capital movements, to create credit in order to cover the extra costs of foreign debt incurred by the devaluation—injecting equity into banks, directly buying loans from foreign creditors, and so on—thereby setting off a controlled inflation which will spread the ultimate costs among the whole population of savers and the consumers of imports.

The Advantages of Bankruptcy

Why should not Korea, for one, not just declare a debt moratorium and set about exporting its way out of trouble, using internal financing drawn from its high domestic savings? The vast increase in the servicing and repayment costs of foreign loans due to the devaluation is a national disaster, the costs of which should be borne collectively. Let belts be tightened, to the extent of refusing any new reliance on external finance. In any case it would not take long for a Korea to be able to borrow again. The government might even put aside its anxiety to remain in the good books of the OECD and focus more on the *region* for a change, taking the lead in bringing in China and in organizing a debtors' cartel with Thailand and Suharto's successor in Indonesia to bargain for better terms from the Fund and Western banks. After all, default is perfectly consistent with certain American values. Personal bankruptcies in the US rose last year from $30 billion to $40 billion. One can find in any newspaper advertisements reading 'Personal bankruptcy may be a way out of your problems, call now: 212-BANKRUPT'.

The Japanese government, which for a time seemed to be moving towards the IMF approach—particularly in allowing the bankruptcy of even large banks and security houses—appears now to be changing course. The vice minister for international finance emphasized on national television recently that, 'We should make clear to the public that we will not allow banks to fail. We should not let securities companies of considerable size fail either. The United States and the United Kingdom have not done it either. This is the global standard.'[19] He went on to say that it is up to politicians and bureaucrats to save the banks from failing and it is up to banks to prevent companies from failing. The Ministry of Finance has announced a $98 billion fund for bailing out the

---

[18] Our argument needs to be tested against answers to the following questions: would a low real interest rate hinder a rise in the exchange rate? What would be the impact on firms of continuing to carry the higher principal of foreign debt? Would the costs of more bankruptcies among firms with large dollar debts exceed the costs of the more extensive bankruptcies caused by high real interest rates that hurt all domestic companies? How much would the low real interest rate discourage personal savings? Could domestic demand be sustained by fiscal stimulus (a government deficit) coupled with relatively high real interest rates?

[19] Eisuke Sakakibara, quoted by Reuters, 28 December 1997.

Japanese financial sector. With this fund the government will inject capital into the banks, which are now paralyzed as they try to meet Western capital adequacy standards in the face of declining asset values. The government may also use the fund to boost the stock market, which will raise asset values. It is dramatically expanding the monetary base, to increase economic growth and corporate returns to assets as well as to generate an inflationary reduction in debt. It may also ask financial institutions to buy domestic bonds, and perhaps to sell some foreign bonds. One hopes it will become active in creating an organization of the most affected countries to coordinate their bargaining strategies, and involve China.

Capital Opening and the Wall Street-Treasury-IMF Complex

Why is the Fund saying what it is saying? It has gone far beyond its traditional concern with balance-of-payments adjustments partly because it had already crossed the line in dealing with the former Soviet Union and Eastern Europe, and legitimized its expanded agenda in that context. Those countries needed advice about the creation of basic market institutions, and the Fund was able to get its advice accepted because it brought vital financial rewards. In its next great intervention, in Asia, the Fund has continued to operate over this much wider jurisdiction, seeking to impose on Thailand, Indonesia and Korea institutional free-market reforms as comprehensive as those imposed on Russia—even though such reforms in the Asian case are not necessary to restart the flow of funds.[20]

The legitimizing precedents of the former Soviet Union and eastern Europe is one thing. But the deeper answer involves the interests of the owners and managers of international capital. The reforms sought by the Fund are connected in one way or another with further opening up Asian economies to international capital. Why is the Fund insisting on capital account opening in countries that are awash with domestic savings? Why has the Fund done so little by way of organizing debt *rescheduling* negotiations, preferring to administer bail out funds *in return for structural and institutional reforms*? James Tobin, the Novel laureate in economics, observes that, 'South Koreans and other Asian countries—like Mexico in 1994-95—are...victims of a flawed international exchange rate system that, under US leadership, *gives the mobility of capital priority over all other considerations.*'[21] Jagdish Bhagwati, professor of economics at Columbia University and champion of free trade, takes the argument further. Asked why the IMF was seeking to open financial markets everywhere he replied,

> Wall Street has become a very powerful influence in terms of seeking markets everywhere. Morgan Stanley and all these gigantic firms want to be able to get into other markets and essentially see capital account convertibility as what will enable them to operate everywhere. Just like in the old days there was this 'military-industrial complex', nowadays there is a Wall St.-Treasury complex' because Secretaries of State like Rubin come from Wall Street...So today,

---

[20] Martin Feldstein, 'Refocusing the IMF', *Foreign Affairs*, March/April 1998, pp. 20-33.
[21] James Tobin, 'Why We Need Sand in the Market's Gears', *Washington Post*, 21 December 1997.

18

Wall Street views are very dominant in terms of the kind of world you want to see. They want the ability to take capital in and out freely. It also ties in to the IMF's own desires, which is to act as a lender of last resort. They see themselves as the apex body which will manage this whole system. So the IMF finally gets a role for itself, which is under-pinned by maintaining complete freedom on the capital account.

Bhagwati goes on to observe that many countries have grown well without capital account convertibility, including China today and Japan and Western Europe earlier. 'In my judgement it is a lot of ideological humbug to say that without free portfolio capital mobility, somehow the world cannot function and growth rates will collapse.'[22]

What Bhagwati calls the 'Wall St-Treasury complex' has helped over the past year to push the process of amending the IMF's articles of agreement to *require* member governments to remove capital controls and adopt full capital account convertibility.[23] The extended Wall St-Treasury-IMF complex has likewise worked to promote the World Trade organization's agreement on liberalizing financial services being hammered out in 1996-97. Many developing country governments, including promi-nently several Asian ones, opposed the WTO's efforts to liberalize financial services. In response, 'Executives of groups including Barclays, Germany's Dresdner Bank, Société Générale of France and Chubb Insurance, Citicorp, and Ford Financial Services of the US... agreed dis-creetly to impress on finance ministers around the world the benefits of a WTO deal'.[24] Then came the financial crisis that ricocheted around the region from one country to another. By December 1997 the Asian leaders agreed to drop their objections, and on 12 December, more than seventy countries signed the agreement that commits them to open banking, insurance and securities markets to foreign firms. By then the Asian holdouts—including Thailand and Malaysia—saw no choice: either they signed or their receipt of IMF bail-out funds would be com-plicated. Meanwhile the OECD has been pushing ahead quickly with the negotiation of the Multilateral Agreement on Investment, that liberalizes all direct foreign investment restrictions, requiring signatory governments to grant equal treatment to foreign as to domestic compa-nies. It will preclude many of the policies of the developmental state.

The Winners

These events—the revision of the IMF's articles of agreement, the WTO's financial services agreement, and the OECD's Multilateral Agreement on Investment—are the expression of a Big Push from international organi-zations, backed by governments and corporations in the rich countries, to institute a world-wide regime of capital mobility that allows easy

---

[22] Interview in *Times of India*, 31 December 1997.
[23] The process of modifying the articles of agreement to require countries to adopt capital account convertibility has been under way for about a year. At the Hong Kong Annual Meetings of the Fund and Bank in September 1997, the Interim Committee agreed in principle that the Fund should adopt an aggressive policy to encourage countries to insti-tute full convertibility.
[24] Guy de Jonquières, 'Vision of a Global Market: WTO Members are Hoping to Deregulate Financial Services', *The Financial Times*, 10 April, 1997, p. 28.

entry and exit everywhere. If the agreements are ratified and enforced, they will ratchet up the power and legitimacy of the owners and managers of capital in the world at large. Yet, for all their implications for sovereignty, democracy, and social stability, they are being negotiated with scarcely any public debate. They have been protected from public concern partly because the champions of the wider movement towards free capital movement and lifting of government regulations have managed to harness to their cause the most self-justifying of slogans, 'stopping corruption'. Capital freedom, we are invited to believe, checks corruption (Asia's 'crony capitalism'), and is therefore self-evidently a good thing. The next step will be an international agreement to deregulate labour markets, intended to make them more 'flexible' while stopping short of open migration. This would further consolidate the global governance of capital.

There is always a fine line to be trod between an interest-based theory and a conspiracy theory—for all that everyone accepts the former and hardly anyone accepts the latter. It is difficult to know to what extent and at what point some events in the Asian crisis were deliberately encouraged by those who stood to gain from the sudden loss of resources by Asian governments and from the opportunities to gain control of Asian companies at knock-down prices. Certainly the role of the US Treasury in stiffening the IMF's insistence on radical financial opening in Korea is documented. The Treasury made it clear that Korean financial opening was a condition of US contributions to the bail-out, on the understanding that financial opening would benefit US firms that would in turn give political support for US contributions.[25]

Financial crises have always caused transfers of ownership and power to those who keep their own assets intact and who are in a position to create credit, and the Asian crisis is no exception. Whatever their degree of intentionality and their methods of concerting strategy, there is no doubt that Western and Japanese corporations are the big winners. The transfer to foreign owners has begun in a spirit of euphoria captured in the remark of the head of a UK-based investment bank, 'If something was worth $1 billion yesterday, and now it's only worth $50m, it's quite exciting'.[26] The combination of massive devaluations, IMF-pushed financial liberalization, and IMF-facilitated recovery may even precipitate the biggest peacetime transfer of assets from domestic to foreign owners in the past fifty years anywhere in the world, dwarfing the transfers from domestic to US owners that occurred Latin America in the 1980s or in

---

[25] See Paul Blustein and Clay Chandler, 'Behind the S. Korean Bailout: Speed, Stealth, Consensus', *The Washington Post*, 28 December 1998, p. 1. The US Treasury likewise managed to bury Japan's attempt at long-promised but never delivered international leadership, in the form of a summer 1997 proposal to create an Asia fund with which to redeem some of their fellow Asians' debts. Not wanting the Japanese to send their capital to Asia rather than to the US, and not wanting Japan to emerge as the Asian bail-out leader, the Treasury (Deputy Secretary Lawrence Summers, most emphatically) insisted that the cleanup be entrusted to the IMF. The Japanese agreed to desist in a November 1997 meeting in Manila. See Johnson, 'Cold War Economics Melt Asia'.
[26] Clay Harris and John Ridding, 'Asia Provides Golden Buying Opportunities', *Financial Times*, 26 February 1998, p. 16. See also 'South Korea: Bargains Galore', *The Economist*, 7 February 1998, pp. 67-8.

Mexico after 1994. One recalls the statement attributed to Andrew Mellon, 'In a depression, assets return to their rightful owners'.

The crisis has also been good for the multilateral economic institutions, including the IMF, the World Bank, and the WTO. The ability of the IMF and the Bank to provide refinancing and to link refinancing to governmental acceptance of WTO rules gives all three organizations leverage with which to cajole Asian governments to reshape their domestic economies in line with Western models. For them the crisis is a short-run blessing not even in disguise. But both they and the incoming foreign firms may eventually suffer from the mounting political backlash. As Henry Kissinger recently warned, 'Even [Asian] friends whom I respect for their moderate views argue that Asia is confronting an American campaign to stifle Asian competition'. 'It is critical that at the end of this crisis', he went on to say, 'when Asia will re-emerge as a dynamic part of the world, America be perceived as a friend that gave constructive advice and assistance in the common interest, not as a bully determined to impose bitter social and economic medicine to serve largely American interests'.[27]

How long will it be before the affected countries regain 1996 levels of output and wealth? Korea escaped the debt trap of the early 1980s in a couple of years, unlike the Latin American countries, partly because it was able to resume fast export growth. But it was able to do so partly because the Latin Americans were out of the market. Today, every Asian country is seeking to export its way out of trouble at the same time. How long the crisis lasts depends partly on how successful they are, which depends on the growth of the Japanese, US and European markets and their access to them. It also depends on the extent to which international lenders co-operate among themselves and the borrowers to reschedule the loans. This in turn depends on whether the IMF concentrates on helping them to co-operate, and softens its demand for fundamental restructuring. If Asia resumes fast growth within the next two years and if in the meantime the US goes into recession as the stock market and currency bubbles burst, we may again look to Asian models, as in the 1980s, for lessons on how to improve the parlous performance of American capitalism.

Restricting the Free Movement of Capital

The great lesson of the Asian crisis is that the desirability of free movements of short-term capital has to be put in question. We have tended to lump together trade liberalization with capital liberalization, and discuss them as though what applies to one also applies, more or less, to the other. Bhagwati's point is their effects are fundamentally different. He argues for trade liberalization without capital account liberalization. Significantly, Martin Wolf of the *Financial Times* largely agrees. The question that arises from the Asian crisis, he says

> is what to do about capital account liberalization, which the IMF is strongly promoting in all its programmes... The evidence now

---

[27] Henry Kissinger, 'The Asian Collapse: One Fix does not Fit all Economies', *The Washington Post*, 9 February 1998, Op-Ed, p. A19.

seems clear that any substantial net draft on foreign savings creates huge risks…almost any large-scale international borrowing, even by non-banks, threatens economic stability if it becomes big enough to threaten the currency…At the least, there is an overwhelming case for permanent prudential regulation of foreign borrowing, particularly short-term borrowing, by commercial banks…Unregulated flows of short-term international capital are a licence to rack up losses at the expense of taxpayers.'[28]

And a senior economic advisor at the World Bank, Pieter Bottelier, argues that 'The world needs to understand more fully what the consequences are of unlimited international freedom of capital movements between countries that have vastly unequal levels of economic development and vastly different standards for monitoring their financial systems.' He raises the question of whether to equip the World Bank and the IMF with better monitoring tools or perhaps even the power to impose sanctions to protect the system.[29] When influential voices at the World Bank and the *Financial Times*, joined by academic champions of free trade, begin to question the benefits of capital opening, the idea of a new Bretton Woods conference is not quite as far-fetched as at first it seems.

In the end we come back to the mysteries of finance and financiers. In good times we tend to think of them as being like engine oil, necessary to make the engine work but neither part of the engine nor its fuel. The analogy is misleading, however, because the structures of financial intermediation are as much part of the 'engine' as the stocks of human resources, capital, technology and organizations. The contrast between the development performance of Latin America and East and Southeast Asia shows how some financial structures can help the economy to grow faster than others. The contrast in their debt crises shows how the same Asian high-performance financial structures can respond to shocks in ways that make the economy not just grind to a halt, but go haywire. As the Cambridge economist A.C. Pigou said with the Great Depression in mind, finance, far from being merely 'the garment draped around the body of economic life', can take on the appearance of 'an active and evil genius'.[30] For just this reason John Maynard Keynes famously proposed, 'Ideas, knowledge, art, hospitality, travel—these are things which should of their nature be international. But let goods be homespun whenever it is reasonably and conveniently possible; and above all, let finance be primarily national.'[31] But we now have in place a powerful phalanx of international organizations and multinational corporations devoted to maximizing the freedom of financial capital around the world. The question is what institutional muscle can be brought to bear by those convinced that such untrammelled freedom is even more dangerous for human welfare today than it has been in the past.

[28] Martin Wolf, 'Caging the Bankers' *The Financial Times*, 20 January 1998.
[29] Pieter Bottelier, speaking at World Bank conference on the Asian financial crisis, cited by Reuters, Paris, 2 Febuary 1998.
[30] A.C. Pigou, *The Veil of Money*, London 1949.
[31] John Maynard Keynes, *Collected Writings of John Maynard Keynes*, vol. XXI [1933]: *Activities 1931-39*, edited by Donald Moggeridge, London 1982, p. 237

SHOCKS AND DEBT

Compare the balance sheets of a 'Latin American' firm and an 'Asian' firm, the former representing the kind of economy that the IMF is used to dealing with. The Latin American firm has, on the liabilities side, equity of 80 pesos and debt (in the form of bank loans, etc.) of 20 pesos, giving it a debt/equity ratio of 1/4.[1] Its assets are equal to the sum of its equity and its debt, or 100 pesos. Assume the rate of interest on its debt is 10 per cent. Assume the gross return on its assets is 12 per cent. Its gross profit is then 12 pesos (12 per cent of assets of 100 pesos).

Suppose that one quarter of its debt is borrowed from abroad, in US dollars. Its dollar debt is then equivalent to 5 pesos, its domestic debt is 15 pesos. Suppose now that the currency is devalued by half (from 800 pesos to the US dollar to 1,600). The firm's dollar debt doubles, to 10 pesos, raising its total debt to 25 pesos. On this debt it must pay 2.5 pesos by way of interest charges. It can easily pay this out of its gross return on assets of 12.[2]

Suppose further that, in line with an IMF programme, the rate of interest on the firm's peso debt doubles from 10 per cent to 20 per cent. The interest cost of the peso debt rises from 1.5 pesos to 3 pesos (20 per cent of 15 pesos). The interest cost on the dollar debt continues to be 0.5 pesos. The total interest cost is now 3.5. This too can be covered out of the gross return on assets of 12 pesos. Suppose also that because of the IMF austerity programme the return on assets falls from 12 per cent to 8 per cent, or 8 pesos. Again, the firm can still easily cover its interest charges.

In short, in the face of a 100 per cent devaluation, a doubling of interest rates on domestic debt, and a 50 per cent fall in the rate of return on assets the 'Latin American' firm, with its low debt/equity ratio, remains viable. It continues to be able to meet the fixed payment obligations represented by its interest charges out of its return on assets.

Consider now the 'Asian' firm. The key difference lies in its debt/equity ratio. Big firms in Korea normally have debt/equity ratios of 4/1 or more. Let us assume that our Asian firm has 20 won of equity and 80 won of debt, giving a debt/equity ratio of 4/1. Assume an interest rate of 10 per cent; so the firm has interest costs of 8 won. Assume a return on assets of 12 per cent, or 12 won.

Suppose, as in the Latin American case, one quarter of the debt is foreign, amounting to the dollar equivalent of 20 won, with 60 won in domestic debt. If the currency is devalued by half, the won value of the foreign debt doubles to 40 won. Total debt (domestic plus foreign) is now 100 won. The devaluation thus wipes out the firm's equity—the difference between its assets and its debts. Using Western prudential standards the firm is in crisis. It is either thrown into bankruptcy, or the lenders agree to restructure the firm's balance sheet, involving writing down the firm's debt—such as accepting an interest rate well below the market rate—by sufficient to restore some positive equity.

If, also, thanks to an IMF programme, the interest rate on the domestic debt rises from 10 per cent to 20 per cent the firm's interest charges on its domestic debt rise from 6 won to 12 won. Together with the interest charge on foreign debt (equal to 10 per cent of 40 won), total interest charges now amount to 16 won, compared to pre-interest profits of 12. The firm is even more unviable, its gross returns are even less than its interest charges. If also the return on assets falls—because of an austerity programme—from 12 per cent to 8 per cent the situation is worse. Gross profit is now 8, interest costs are 16. The deficit is minus 8. The firm has no equity and runs at a big loss. The loss must be recapitalized: that is, the interest payments due but unpayable must be added to the principle of the loan, raising the company's debt/equity ratio still further, compounding its vulnerabilities.

When this happens across many firms, the debt/GDP ratio of the corporate sector rises and the country's refinancing difficulties multiply.

---

[1] Equity in this simple model is valued at the difference between the value of assets and the debt. It includes shares in the company, retained earnings, and other things.
[2] Assume that the firm's assets are employed in business tied to the domestic economy, not the foreign economy. If the assets were used for export production, the devaluation would raise their value by raising the prospects for export sales and the calculation would be more complicated.

[11]

Cambridge Journal of Economics 1998, **22**, 653–661

Economic crisis in East Asia: the clash of capitalisms

Chalmers Johnson*

The Asian economic model does not exist uniformly in East Asia and is itself only a model, not the complex economic reality of a huge and diverse area. 'Crony capitalism' is an inadequate explanation for what has happened in East Asia. And in the debate between Anglo-American economic orthodoxy and revisionism, the meltdown has tended to confirm the results of revisionist research. There are three main contenders among explanations for the meltdown—all three of which may prove to be true. These are the liquidity-crunch explanation, the overcapacity explanation, and the end-of-the-Cold-War-in-East-Asia explanation.

For the past six months Americans have been told repeatedly that the Asian economic model is obsolete and that the meltdown in East Asia will not affect them, their jobs, or the American stockmarket. Even the 1997 US trade deficit with Asia of well over $100 billion is considered good news because cheap imports will keep down inflation. But what is at risk in East Asia is the real possibility of a global collapse of demand and another Great Depression. Even if that does not happen, America's system of rich satellites serving as hosts to an expeditionary force of some 100,000 US troops is virtually certain to come to an end.

Something very serious has happened in East Asia. But the causes are so complex and so few agree on them that any prudent observer should be very careful about making overly quick judgements. There are at least three caveats that must precede any discussion of the details of the so-called meltdown.

First, the Asian model does not apply evenly across East Asia. For the sake of discussion and simplification, I think of the East Asian model as consisting of Asian values on subjects such as the nature of government, priority given to the community over the individual, and government guidance of a nonetheless privately owned and managed market economy, with economic growth tied above all to exports. This contrasts with the Anglo-American emphasis on what Westerners claim are (or should be) universal values: individualism and *laissez-faire*, with economic growth tied above all to domestic demand. In terms of the countries affected by the meltdown, the Asian model really only applies to Japan and South Korea. It never existed in Thailand or Indonesia—that is one reason why they were the first to crash under the speculative pressures against their currencies. It is only incipiently relevant to mainland China or Vietnam. And although the Malaysians

Manuscript received 3 March 1998; final version received 17 June 1998.

*Japan Policy Research Institute, Cardiff, CA, USA.

654   C. Johnson

talk a great deal about Asian values, they violated the tenets of the Asian economic model by allowing Japanese, European, and American banks to export their own versions of the bubble economy to Malaysia. The Asian economic model is alive and flourishing in Taiwan, the Hong Kong Special Administrative Region of the People's Republic of China, and Singapore, and it seems about to take hold, now that the Americans have finally left, in the Philippines. In the minds of most Asians, particularly the Chinese, the meltdown has, if anything, reinforced the need for the Asian model of development rather than repudiating it. Linda Weiss, in her new book *The Myth of the Powerless State* (1998) offers the best analysis of the differences between the North-east Asian transformative states and the South-east Asian pilotless states.

The second caveat is that an explanation of the meltdown in terms of 'crony capitalism' is wildly overdrawn. I take crony capitalism to mean corruption, nepotism, excessive bureaucratic rigidity, and other forms of trust violation that can occur whenever a state tries to manipulate incentives or, in other ways, alter market outcomes. The system of tax deductions for household mortgages in the US is a standard example of this form of state guidance of the market.

Crony capitalism is said to promote many sins, including the overbuilding of real estate throughout the region and the excessive importing of consumer goods, such as luxury cars—that is, the kinds of things the Mexicans did a few years ago when foreign financial institutions poured money into their country. But foreign loans to South Korea did not go into real-estate investment, and what has been wrong in Thailand and Indonesia was precisely the lack of a pilot agency, such as Japan's Ministry of International Trade and Industry, to keep such practices under control. The most glaring instance of nepotism affecting an economy in East Asia has been under General Suharto in Indonesia, who is, we hope, the last of the Marcos-style Asian dictators that the Americans have always preferred and supported. The ultimate in crony capitalism is actually the US-dominated International Monetary Fund (the IMF) and its bailing out of Thailand, Indonesia, and South Korea; the IMF's money does not go to the people of those countries. It goes to the foreign banks that made too many shaky and imprudent loans to Thai, Indonesian, and South Korean banks and businesses in the first place.

In 1994 South Korea, in an attempt to follow the nagging of its patron, the United States, abolished the Economic Planning Board, Korea's main body for making economic policy since the early 1960s, and loosened virtually all controls over financial institutions. In return for these self-inflicted wounds, Korea was admitted to the club of rich nations, the Organization for Economic Cooperation and Development (OECD), with its head-quarters in Paris. As a direct result of these 'reforms', the government failed to monitor properly the foreign borrowing activities of inexperienced merchant banks. But the situation in Korea differs greatly from that in South-east Asia. With the election of a new, anti-establishment president in South Korea, Kim Dae Jung, the country is using the meltdown as a cover for ruthlessly killing off its weak conglomerates while strengthening and rationalising the big ones. Because of his credentials with the trade unions, President-elect Kim will probably manage to restrain labour by promising it a leaner, meaner Korean industry in the future. South Korea's re-emergence as an economic powerhouse will also smooth the way for unification with the North, without interference from the US, China or Japan.

Throughout the region, the current crisis was caused much more by under-regulation than by corruption or any other side effects of an overly close relationship between businesses and the government. What all these places need is neither more nor less regu-

Economic crisis in East Asia: the clash of capitalisms   655

lation but effective, expert guidance of the sort Japan and South Korea exercised during their periods of high-speed economic growth.

Only Japan truly fits the crony capitalism description. Ever since Japan's bubble economy started to deflate in 1989 and 1990, Japan has complacently continued to protect its structurally corrupt and sometimes gangster-ridden firms and has made only gestures toward holding anyone responsible. Virtually all of its public funds to stimulate the domestic economy have gone to the politically powerful but environmentally disastrous construction industry. Japan has been able to get away with palliatives largely because of the perpetuation of Japan's cosy Cold War relationship with the United States. This means that Japan is not being forced to make the painful choices that adjusting to a global economy would require. Japan remains today essentially a protectorate of the United States, not fully in charge of its own government or destiny. When that changes, Japan will change.

In the meantime, it is well to remember that crony capitalism was not the intent but a by-product of the structural characteristics of the Asian-type economies. These structures include cartelisation of the *keiretsu–chaebol* variety, bank-based systems of capital supply, mercantilism and protectionism *vis-à-vis* external economies, and rule by bureaucratic elites despite a pretence of democracy. The intent of these structures was to enrich the nations of East Asia, not to meet consumer demand, global efficiency, individual choice, or any of the other motives posited by neoclassical economics. That they succeeded so spectacularly during the historical era known as the Cold War altered the world balance of power.

Over time crony capitalism has become a serious side effect of Japanese-type economies, but its economic costs can easily be exaggerated. The United States's strong economic performance during the 1990s coincided with the biggest outbreak of American crony capitalism since the arrival on the scene of the military-industrial complex during the 1950s. Yet no one is proposing a total restructuring of the American economy because the Lippo Bank of Jakarta tried to buy influence in Washington, or despite evidence of the sale of ambassadorships and burial plots in Arlington National Cemetery, or military budgets bigger than all the United States's allies and potential enemies combined. John Carlin in *The Independent* (24 May 1998) describes the United States as 'the most legally corrupt political system in the world'. If crony capitalism brought down East Asia, why has it not similarly affected the United States, where it seems to be endemic?

The third caveat about the Asian meltdown concerns the widespread criticism that foreign analysts of East Asian capitalism failed to predict it or even to perceive the shadowy side of the East Asian model. This criticism is directed particularly against the so-called 'revisionists' and their books on the Japanese economy (including writers such as James Fallows, Clyde Prestowitz, Karel van Wolferen, and myself). These writers are now routinely lumped together with the Chrysanthemum Club of Japan apologists and accused of wishful thinking about Asia. For the editorial boards of the *Wall Street Journal* and the London *Economist*, together with virtually the whole tenurocracy of professors of economics in the English-speaking countries, the news of the East Asian meltdown has come as a gift from heaven. They see it as a massive vindication of their neoclassical economic orthodoxy. But has revisionism been repudiated? I think not.

It was the so-called revisionist writers who first outlined the differences between East Asian and American capitalism. During the early 1980s, when Japan's trade surpluses with the United States set new records every month and came close to destroying vital parts of the manufacturing base of the American economy, the revisionists warned that this situation was not the result of 'invisible hands' guiding market outcomes but of 'capitalist developmental states' engineering high-speed economic growth. The revisionists advocated using the full market power of the United States—which was and still is the main market for all the East Asian economies—to force them to make international trade mutually beneficial by opening their markets.

During the Reagan, Bush, and Clinton administrations, American elites listened to the revisionists' message, but they did something else. In the Reagan era, they had become too dependent on Japan's savings to finance their combination of tax cuts and rearmament to confront Japan directly. Therefore they set out to cut the trade imbalances by manipulating the exchange rates of the US dollar and the Japanese yen. This was good neoclassical economics but abominable Japanese area studies. In order for a cheap dollar and an expensive yen to make a difference, the primary problem between the two countries would have had to have been competition on prices. But the real issue was that Japan's markets were closed to foreign investors and retailers, as well as cartels, lack of enforcement of trade agreements, sham antitrust laws, and a host of other practices that Japan had perfected over the previous 40 years.

The results of the United States pursuing an exchange-rate approach to the problem of trade with Japan were profound. They made no difference to the trade imbalance, but they stimulated Japan to undertake countermeasures to the high yen, which led to Japan's bubble economy, then to the collapse of the bubble economy, then to Japan's export of its bubble economy to South-east Asia, and finally to the economic meltdown that confronts us today. What Japan needed was to develop an economy that relied more on domestic demand than on exports. But Japan's answer to the high yen was wild overinvestment to enlarge productive capacity in order to continue exporting to any and all markets.

This is, of course, not what the revisionists advocated. A stronger case could be made that the current economic crisis threatening the entire world—it is certainly the worst such crisis since the OPEC oil price hikes of 1973—came about because too many rich nations knew next to nothing about the nations of East Asia. The Anglo-American economies refused to heed in a timely fashion the extraordinary imbalances, dependencies, and irresponsibilities that the East Asian capitalist developmental states were creating. Western economists, unable to explain Japan's growth or, for that matter, even to read a Japanese newspaper, rejected so-called revisionism because its findings were incompatible with orthodox neoclassical economic theory. The disaster of 1997 did not refute revisionism but rather confirmed the essence of the revisionists' message—there are differences among capitalist systems that are not trivial and that under certain circumstances can blow the system apart.

But the revisionists did not get the whole story right. Above all, they did not analyse correctly the Cold War context of East Asia's enrichment. They knew that the United States's chief contribution to this enrichment had not been its wars, its military deployments or its diplomacy, but rather its markets. The Americans bought the high-quality, low-cost manufactured goods of East Asia in greater quantities than any other external market. The revisionists understood that Asia's rigged economies depended to a critical extent on access to the American market and that they would all be in trouble if and when the US ceased to play the role of market of last resort. But they did not understand how the collapse of the Soviet Union, the end of bipolarity, and the tendencies toward globalisation of finance and manufacturing would expose the contradictions in the American–East Asian relationship. The revisionists, like virtually all Western analysts, were intellectually captives of the separation of economics and politics, of trade and defence,

Economic crisis in East Asia: the clash of capitalisms   657

that has for so many years dominated all thinking about the role of the United States in East Asia.

The events of 1997 were the first developments that would force an end to the artificial distinction between trade and defence and cause Asians and Americans alike to begin to look with clarity at the political, military and economic relations that lie behind the Asian meltdown. Thus far in the crisis, the United States has been willing to tolerate growing trade deficits as the stricken economies of East Asia try to export their way out of their troubles. But as Japan's refusal to help by opening its own markets, and even its competing with the stricken economies in exporting to the US, become common knowledge, the pressures to protect the US market will become intense. A concomitant will be a rethinking of American military strategy in East Asia, possibly beginning to bring to an end Japan's status as the most privileged satellite of the US in the area.

The Asian economic model does not exist uniformly in East Asia and is itself only a model, not the complex economic reality of a huge and diverse area. Crony capitalism is an inadequate explanation for what has happened in East Asia. And in the debate between Anglo-American economic orthodoxy and revisionism, the meltdown has tended to confirm the results of revisionist research. Like the caveats, there are also three main contenders among explanations—all three of which may prove to be true. I call these differing views the liquidity-crunch explanation, the overcapacity explanation, and the end-of-the-Cold-War-in-East-Asia explanation.

The liquidity-crunch explanation asserts that the current East Asian crisis is essentially a financial problem rather than a crisis of the 'real economy'. Given a globalised financial system overloaded with money and a lack of elementary prudence on the part of borrowers in Thailand, Indonesia, Malaysia, and South Korea, these countries, starting in about 1994, borrowed hundreds of billions of dollars from foreign lenders. They invested these funds in sometimes foolish projects, such as fancy apartment and office buildings, or in export industries that were soon crippled by overcapacity. They believed, without truly analysing the matter, that their export industries would continue to grow and remain in their countries indefinitely, even though jogging shoes—to name one example—were once made in South Korea, then Indonesia, and now China and Vietnam. Businessmen in these countries also believed that, in the context of a continuously growing economy, their governments would help out any particular bank or conglomerate that found itself running out of money to pay back the loans.

But in July 1997, starting first with Thailand, foreign lenders began to realise that some of their Asian clients could not repay their loans. This caused other foreign investors to start withdrawing huge amounts of money from both poorly managed and completely healthy enterprises. Given globalised financial markets, the instantaneous transmission of data to anyone who wants it, and a lack of effective safety-valves, the crisis rapidly spread all over Asia. It raised the possibility of runs on banks even in the world's second largest economy, which is also the richest in per capita terms and the major source of long-term capital for the world—namely, Japan. The foreign lenders, big banks such as Citicorp and J. P. Morgan, had made the loans because the four international bail-outs of Mexico since 1976 taught them that, so long as they lent money to countries that were part of the informal American empire, they could expect the American government or some surrogate of it such as the IMF to step in and make good on their so-called non-performing assets.

The crisis was exacerbated not just by gullible borrowers and complacent lenders but also by some developments among the great powers that have been largely overlooked. In the last ten years China's share of East Asia's exports to the US market has grown from 6% to 26%. Even more important, in 1994 China devalued its currency by 35%, thereby making its exports hypercompetitive with those of South Korea and South-east Asia.

Something similar to the emergence of China as a competitor occurred elsewhere in the summer of 1995. The American Treasury and the Japanese Ministry of Finance agreed on a deal intended to help re-elect President Clinton the following year and to allow Japan to grow its way out of its own, post-bubble banking crisis via the usual export drive. Robert Rubin for the Americans and Eisuke Sakakibara for the Japanese decided between themselves that they would depreciate the yen against the dollar, thereby greatly increasing Japan's export competitiveness, in return for which Japan would continue to supply capital to the United States, thereby keeping American interest rates at politically desirable low levels. The American government also agreed to end its plan to put duties on imported luxury cars from Japan, keep quiet about America's billion-dollar-a-week trade deficit with Japan, and shift the focus of the Japanese–American alliance away from economic relations and back to security issues, even though there were no threats to security in the region.

Between April 1995 and April 1997, the yen fell 60% against the dollar. That alone priced most economies of South-east Asia out of the market. Thailand still tied the exchange rate of its own currency to the now seriously overvalued dollar and was ruined as a result. Given the overcapacities that too much investment generated and the competitive challenges from China and Japan, export growth in South Korea and in the ASEAN countries fell from 30% in early 1995 to zero by mid-1996. A balance-of-payments crisis was inevitable.

When the loans started to come due in the summer of 1997, the logical, economic-textbook response of the borrowers should have been to default and declare bankruptcy. That would have seriously pained the lenders, teaching them what markets are supposed to teach—that one is responsible for the risks one assumes. The foreign bankers would have had to renegotiate their loans to the East Asian countries, spreading them out over time and also adding a few profitable points to their interest rates. The Western and Japanese banks would probably never have got all their money back. However, under this scenario, the people who lost financially would have been the investors in the G-7 democracies, not the people of Asia; and reform of the East Asian economies would have been forthcoming because of market forces, not orders from Washington. Many Asian and American bankers and politicians would have been sacked, but the people of East Asia would have accepted the need for long overdue reforms and would have implemented them much more willingly.

What was actually done turned a liquidity crisis into a full-blown economic disaster. At first the Japanese stepped forward and said that they would provide at least some of the money in order to redeem their fellow Asian's debts. They proposed a new multinational financial institution led by Japan and restricted to making loans to Asian countries. The Americans instantly objected. They correctly sensed that Japan was about to try its hand at long promised but never delivered international leadership. If the Japanese had succeeded, they would have slipped the leash of the American Cold War system. Moreover, they would have started using their surplus capital to help countries in Asia rather than continuing to send it to the world's number one debtor nation, the United States. If the Americans ever have to finance their own stupendous debts rather than depend on Japanese savers, American interest rates will soar to double-digit levels. At the 19 November 1997 meeting in Manila where the newly proposed Japanese institution was

Economic crisis in East Asia: the clash of capitalisms   659

quietly put to sleep, the Americans' point-man, Deputy Treasury Secretary Lawrence Summers, declared himself pleased that the clean-up was to be entrusted to the IMF. Japan's vice-minister of international finance, Eisuke Sakakibara, commented *sotto voce* that he and others still believed the IMF was not up to the task. He turned out to be right.

The IMF is an old Bretton Woods institution set up in 1944 to service the system of fixed exchange rates that lasted until the 'Nixon Shocks' of 1971. It survived its loss of mission to become, in Robert Kuttner's words, 'the premier instrument of deflation, as well as the most powerful unaccountable institution in the world' (*Boston Globe*, 4 January 1998). It is also an instrument of American power, one that allows the United States to collect money from its allies and to spend the amassed funds on various international economic operations that serve American national interests.

The IMF roared into Asia and promised to supply $17 billion to Bangkok, $40 billion to Jakarta, and $57 billion to Seoul. In return it demanded austerity budgets, high interest rates, and sales of local businesses to foreign bargain-hunters. It claimed that these measures would restore economic health to the 'Asian tigers' and turn them into orthodox Anglo-American-type capitalist economies.

There was almost no chance that the IMF's one-size-fits-all remedies would succeed. Its economic ideologues not only know nothing about East Asia, they believe there is no *need* for them to know anything. Totally devoid of concepts of culture or of cultural differences, the IMF did not know that it was undercutting Korean housewives' investment co-ops with their millions of untaxable funds, or that the Indonesian government's subsidies go towards food and fuel, not just to cronies of Suharto. Not surprisingly, Asian editorial writers started to write essays with titles like 'The Second Opium War' and to mutter about American imperialism. Meanwhile, the social chaos that Western advisers produced in post-communist Russia seems just around the corner in Asia.

The second explanation of the meltdown, that it was caused by overcapacity, follows directly from the first but has much more ominous implications. The difference is that the first explanation stresses Asia's short-term indebtedness problems, whereas the second explanation says that, regardless of the rather obvious financial problems, the Asian economies do not rest on good fundamentals. The Asians may save a lot, keep their children in school longer than anybody else, and recruit smarter state bureaucrats than Washington does, but they are catastrophically overinvested in the wrong industries—principally cars, shipbuilding, steel, petrochemicals, and semiconductors. This explanation also explicitly includes Japan as part of the Asian problem.

Because Japanese, European, and American multinational corporations have also moved so much of their manufacturing to places where skilled workers are paid very little, these new workers cannot possibly consume what they produce. But the consumers back in the G-7 democracies also cannot buy much more because either their economies are stagnant or they have just lost their jobs. The financial difficulties that the IMF is trying to deal with are only a symptom of a more serious disease. The underlying danger is a structural collapse of demand leading to recession and ultimately to something like the Great Depression. As William Greider has put it in his *One World, Ready or Not*, 'Shipping high-wage jobs to low-wage economies has obvious, immediate economic benefits. But, roughly speaking, it also replaces high-wage consumers with low-wage ones. That exchange is debilitating for the entire system' (1997, p. 221).

It is one thing to have IMF bungling cause a recession in East Asia; it is quite another to have a huge overcapacity to manufacture things that no one wants or can afford causing a recession. If the meltdown of 1997 represents manufacturing capacity that can never

660   C. Johnson

recover its costs, then the world requires the direct opposite of the policies the IMF is pursuing today in East Asia. It requires the creation of new demand, not the deflation of the demand that exists at the present time.

The third explanation—the end of the Cold War in East Asia—relates to the second in that it starts by asking how so much overcapacity came to be built in East Asia in the first place. One answer is that the economies of Japan and South Korea have been rigged since early in the Cold War in order to serve the grand strategy of the United States against communism in Asia and to ensure that they did not toy with neutralism or socialism. Many other places in East Asia, including Taiwan, Hong Kong, Singapore, Thailand and the Philippines, were outposts of American capitalism, protectorates, or recently closed bases of operation for America's wars. The Cold War deal the Americans offered to keep these satellites in line was unrestricted access to the American market, toleration of their mercantilism and protectionism, and technology transfers at often concessionary prices in return for public anti-communism and basing rights. (There are still 100,000 American troops based in Japan and South Korea and the US Seventh Fleet patrols the waters of East Asia.)

The Cold War ended in Europe in 1989 when the Soviet Union allowed the people of Berlin to tear down the wall that divided their city. It is possible that what happened to the Soviet Empire in Eastern Europe in 1989 started to happen to the American empire in East Asia in 1997. The difference is that in Eastern Europe the Soviet Union's satellites wanted to end their deal with the Russians, whereas in East Asia the American satellites still want to remain in their deal with the US. As far as Japan and South Korea are concerned, they have kept their side of the bargain—the American bases are still on their soil and they are still paying for them more generously than any other American allies around the world. (In Japan's case, the bases are on Okinawan soil that the US and Japan collaborate in keeping dependent.) What the two systems of satellites have in common is that neither the Russians nor the Americans can afford them any longer. Even if he might later have regretted it, in 1989 Gorbachev decided that he could no longer afford to keep the Red Army based in East Germany, Poland and the former Czechoslovakia. The Americans have not yet acknowledged that they cannot afford their satellites in East Asia. But either because of fiscal constraints or because their currency has depreciated so badly, the Japanese and the South Koreans cannot continue to pay for the upkeep of American troops on their soil or buy the panoply of American weapons that the Pentagon wants to sell them. Already the Thai government has had to cancel its purchase of eight American-made F/A-18 fighter jets, and South Korea does not have the money to pay for the power reactors promised to North Korea. The more the Americans succeed in forcing the Asians to revamp their economies, the more independent the Asians will become of American influence.

What is to be done? That depends on which explanation you accept. If it is the first, then the answers are fairly straightforward. Stop the IMF before it turns a problem into a disaster and implement some elementary controls on capital movements. The idea is to end the volatility of hot money. A tax on short-term loans of 2%–3% would have the same effect. Government regulations could also favour direct foreign investment over purchases of shares of stock. An appropriate regulatory regime would be one that inhibits short-term investments and discourages local businesses from accumulating big debts in foreign currencies. It is absolutely certain that China, so far relatively insulated from the meltdown by the lack of convertibility of its currency, will be experimenting with these types of control over the coming years.

Economic crisis in East Asia: the clash of capitalisms   661

If one accepts the overcapacity explanation, then the US should start using the full power of the American market to raise the wages of workers in places where multinational companies are investing, so they can purchase new products more or less on a par with employed American workers. The collapse of demand that caused the Great Depression was ultimately overcome only by war production for the Second World War. The better way is to stimulate demand among poor people by increasing their incomes.

If one accepts the third explanation, then the Americans must finally let the Cold War end. This will have the effect in East Asia of forcing economically powerful countries such as Japan and South Korea to start coming to grips with the real challenges of the next century—the unification of Korea, adjustment to the emergence of China, avoidance of ethnic and religious violence in South and South-east Asia, and mitigating environmental degradation. Failure of the United States to adjust to its status as an ordinary country will only expose it further to imperial overstretch and Soviet-style decline. Certainly, the US should continue to push for economic reform in countries like South Korea and political reform in countries like Indonesia. But these will make no difference without reform and greater independence in Japan. And no amount of foreign money or pressure will cause Japan to reform. Only cutting its apron strings to the US will energise the Japanese political system. If that happens, we are likely to see a renewed burst of growth and prosperity throughout the region. If not, global recession is a serious possibility.

Bibliography

Fallows, J. 1994. *Looking at the Sun: The Rise of the New East Asian Economic and Political System*, New York, Pantheon

Greider, W. 1997. *One World, Ready or Not: The Manic Logic of Global Capitalism*, New York, Simon & Schuster

Johnson, C. 1982. *MITI and the Japanese Miracle: The Rise of Industrial Policy, 1925–1975*, Stanford, CA, Stanford University Press

Prestowitz, C. 1988. *Trading Places: How We Allowed Japan to Take the Lead*, New York, Basic Books

Weiss, L. 1998. *The Myth of the Powerless State: Governing the Economy in a Global Era*, Cambridge, Polity Press, and Ithaca, New York, Cornell University Press

Wolferen, K. van. 1989. *The Enigma of Japanese Power*, New York, Knopf

[12]

Linda Y.C. Lim

Whose 'Model' Failed?
Implications of
the Asian Economic Crisis

The Asian economic crisis is cause for rethinking the long-estab-
lished consensus among mostly Western and Western-trained economists
about the causes of the region's "miracle" economic growth and industrial
development. Most recently restated in the Asian Development Bank's
1997 study *Emerging Asia: Changes and Challenges*, essentially an update of
the World Bank's 1993 study *The East Asian Miracle*, this consensus interpretation among mainstream economists goes as follows:

Asian economic success is the product simply of the application of orthodox Western textbook economic principles—external "openness" to trade and
foreign investment on the one hand, and domestic "good government" with
small, balanced, or surplus government budgets and conservative monetary
policy leading to low inflation and high savings rates, on the other. For these
reasons, Asian countries typically rank relatively high on the "economic freedom" indices annually produced by think tanks such as the Fraser Institute in
Canada[1] and the Heritage Foundation in Washington, D.C.[2] Of the countries
currently in crisis, South Korea has been less open than the various countries
of Southeast Asia, but nonetheless has subjected its firms to the discipline of
the international marketplace through export manufacturing.

But mainstream economists are not the only Western or Western-trained
scholars who have sought to dissect the Asian economic miracle through
the lens of their particular discipline. Political scientists and political economists have also had their play with the subject, usually concluding that the
"developmental state"—focused on promoting economic development in
the national interest—and statist industrial policy—government protection

Linda Y. C. Lim, an economist from Singapore, is Associate Professor of International
Business and Director of the Southeast Asia Business Program at the University of
Michigan Business School.

Copyright © 1998 by The Center for Strategic and International Studies and the
Massachusetts Institute of Technology
The Washington Quarterly • 21:3 pp. 25–36.

| Linda Y. C. Lim

and subsidies targeted at developing specific "strategic" industrial sectors—have been essential to the rapid industrialization of the East Asian newly industrialized economies.[3] South Korea is the classic case, but it is harder to identify "developmental states" and successful statist industrial policy in Southeast Asia outside of Malaysia and Singapore. Rather, state development policy in Thailand, Indonesia, and the Philippines is more likely to be viewed as having been captured by crony capitalists with close personal relations with governments, thereby violating the developmental state principle of state autonomy from special interests.[4]

Notwithstanding this, and despite the contradiction between the economist and the political scientist/political economist views, the Southeast Asian countries are always included as part of the so-called Asian economic miracle or "Asian model" that has been promoted by advocates of free-market economics. These include both conservative Western think tanks like the Heritage Foundation and more liberal multilateral institutions like the World Bank and the International Monetary Fund, whose Washington consensus of liberal economic policies has been foisted on emerging economies around the world.

> **Culture has been neglected or dismissed.**

Although economists like these generally did not care for the industrial policies and microeconomic state interventions pursued by Asian governments, they did praise the latter's practice of conventional macroeconomic policy embracing both openness and fiscal and monetary conservatism. It is not an exaggeration to say that the Asian economies became showcases for the success of a policy prescription that is being peddled to other newly liberalizing emerging economies in Latin America, East Central Europe, Central Asia, and Africa.

When the Philippines, Taiwan, South Korea, and Thailand became politically democratic as well in the late 1980s, this completed the picture of triumph for the Western liberal model of free-markets-with-democracy that Francis Fukuyama proclaimed ushered in *The End of History*[5] or the end of the ideological political-economic conflict between East and West that defined the Cold War. In Asia, for example, it was proclaimed that the United States "lost the Vietnam war (against communism) but won the peace," as reflected in the economic prosperity and political stability enjoyed by its capitalist allies in the region, and the subsequent embarkation of their socialist neighbors, particularly China and Vietnam, on the path of market-oriented economic reform.[6]

Culture as an element in the Asian economic miracle has largely been neglected or dismissed by both Western economists and political scientists, although the former might occasionally acknowledge that the highly entre-preneurial, economically responsive populations in the region, themselves the product of market forces, might have spurred the development of pri-vate-enterprise economies. The latter sometimes note that Confucian cul-tures may have lent moral authority and political legitimacy to interventionist developmental states. Western and some Asian anthropolo-gists and sociologists, on the other hand, have identified kin and ethnic net-works, or "culturally embedded network capitalisms," as locally efficient means of mobilizing capital and industrial growth in the Asian miracle economies.[7]

Culture has also played a much larger role in explaining the Asian miracle by Asian intellectuals who hail mostly from the political establish-ment in patriarchal-authoritarian and semi-authoritarian states like Singapore, Malaysia, China, and Indonesia. They argue that "Asian val-ues"—emphasizing the primacy of order over freedom, family and commu-nity interests over individual choice, and economic progress over political expression, together with thrift, ambition and hard work—were largely re-sponsible for the fortunate public sector policies and private sector actions that resulted in the Asian miracle.

Whose Model Failed?

The "Asian values" school was unpopular among many Western commenta-tors for suggesting, among other things, that capitalism and democracy need not go hand-in-hand. So it was predictable that when the Asian economic crisis hit during a period of unprecedented economic strength in the United States and economic recovery in Western Europe, opponents of the "Asian values" school were out in full swing (chiefly in the editorial pages of the *Wall Street Journal*), crowing over its assumed demise and the concomitant assumed triumph of the "American way."

The Asian miracle was particularly attacked for its reliance on industrial policy and cronyism, or relationships between big business and government, both of which contributed to moral hazard in the inefficient financial sector and the resultant over-investment in a classic asset bubble. Paul Krugman, the MIT economist who had some years earlier pronounced the Asian miracle a "myth" based on low total factor productivity growth,[8] is one of those who fa-vor the moral hazard argument that "crony capitalism" or Asian reliance on *guanxi* (relationships) is what caused the crisis, which in this view is essen-tially a crisis of bad investments in both the public and private sectors.[9] This

| *Linda Y. C. Lim*

line of argument directly challenges both the praise of statist industrial policy by mostly Western political scientists and of "culturally embedded networks" favored by mostly Western anthropologists and sociologists.

There is no question that crony capitalism did play a role in the over-inflation and subsequent deflation of economic growth and asset prices in Asia. But this is far from the only or most plausible interpretation for the crisis and it is certainly not the whole story. Indeed, in the affected Asian countries and other emerging economies around the world, another interpretation is taking hold, one that is much less favorable to the liberal orthodoxy favored by Western economists. In this view, it is the Western model of free-markets-with-democracy that has failed along with the collapse of its prime success stories in Asia—or a case of "the West won the Cold War, only to lose the peace."

The Perils of Openness

First, if openness was an essential ingredient of the Asian economic miracle, too much openness too fast was responsible for its downfall. In particular, rapid and sweeping (although not yet complete) capital market liberalization that began in the late 1980s led to a massive influx of foreign capital, especially short-term loan and equity capital, which contributed to the boom economy and over-investment bubble of the 1990s. Without this influx of foreign funds—which in some cases amounted to as much as 75 percent of the equity capital on local stock markets—domestic crony capitalism alone could not have fed a boom and bubble of such proportions. Even without crony capitalism, high growth and the expectation of continued uninterrupted high growth, fed in large part by foreign capital, might have led to excessive risk-taking and overleveraging of local businesses believing that their economies were immune from the business cycle.

High domestic growth and investment in turn contributed to ballooning current account deficits, with imports (mostly of machinery and equipment required by the flood of new investments) constantly exceeding exports by a wide margin. This was further fueled by overvalued exchange rates, the result both of more or less fixed exchange-rate regimes, established to attract foreign capital by removing currency risk, and of large inflows of capital. Open capital markets and capital-account convertibility also increased these economies' vulnerability to currency speculation that could, at the appropriate moment, trigger a sudden massive exit of foreign funds as easily as these funds had previously entered.

Financial market liberalization in Asia also occurred before there were appropriate state or collective institutions to monitor and regulate financial institutions or local expertise to manage them. The region's much-vaunted entrepreneurialism led to the establishment of a horde of new banks and finance companies—Indonesia alone had more than 200 banks—within a short span of time and with inadequate experience in money management. Even without crony capitalism, excess capacity in the financial sector and intense competition to lend and invest among these neophyte institutions would have led to a fair proportion of "bad investments." It was aggravated by the easy availability of cheap capital from abroad, in many cases pressed on local borrowers by overeager foreign lenders who should have known better, but faced intense competition among themselves and were attracted by the returns presented by higher interest rates and by rosy projections of continued rapid growth.

> **B**oth the Western economists' and the political scientists' models have failed.

With or without the moral hazard presented by local crony capitalism, the resultant excess supply of capital was bound to lead to some bad investments as capital started flowing to more and more marginal projects. Unlike their local borrowers, foreign lenders and investors from Western countries and Japan possessed the requisite expertise in risk assessment and credit evaluation. But they apparently chose not to apply this knowledge, yielding instead to herd instinct[10] and, as Alan Greenspan characterized the sentiments toward the booming U.S. stockmarket, "irrational exuberance." This exuberance contributed first to the overvaluation of assets, then reversed course and with "irrational pessimism"[11] led to the current undervaluation, as the following quotes indicate.

> All banks are under certain competitive pressure. If the market is attractive, you go with the herd. Even if you have doubts, you don't stop lending.[12] —*Ernst-Mortiz Lipp, member of the board of managing directors of Dresdner Bank AG*

> There was a huge euphoria about Asia and Southeast Asia. It was the place to be.[13] —*Dennis Phillips, Spokesman for Commerzbank*

> All the banks would be standing in line—J.P. Morgan, Deutsche Bank, Dresdner. We were all standing in line trying to help these countries borrow money. We would all see each other at the same places. We all knew each other.[14] —*Klaus Friedrich, chief economist, Dresdner Bank AG*

> There are problems in Asia now because investors and bankers were overly optimistic about the Asian economies, and then they panicked.[15] —*Anonymous American banker*

Openness and the dominance of private enterprise in the Asian economies also severely limited their governments' ability to intervene to control these flows. Given domestic excess demand and external imbalance (huge current account deficits), governments should have allowed their currencies to depreciate or raised taxes and interest rates and cut government spending to reduce domestic demand and correct the imbalance. But in very open economies such as these, with high import shares of GDP, currency depreciation would increase costs, including offshore loan servicing costs, and cause inflation from higher import prices, while higher domestic interest rates would be ineffective so long as businesses could resort to cheaper borrowing in accessible offshore markets—that is, they may as well have *increased* rather than reduced external borrowing.

> We could have borrowed locally, something like 14 percent per annum, or borrowed overseas, where we could get (dollar) loans for 8 percent or 9 percent. If I had borrowed locally, the analysts would be saying that we were being foolish for not taking advantage of lower rates overseas... We could have bought insurance, but that would only be adding to the cost. Our government, our bankers, economists, even foreigners were telling us that the baht was stable... We never imagined that the baht would be devalued.[16] —*Chumpol Nalamlieng, CEO of Siam Cement, a blue-chip Thai company on their $4.2 billion dollar debt*

At the same time, public sectors were small and mostly in balance, and governments had little control over overborrowing in the private sector. This reduced the effectiveness of raising taxes and cutting expenditures as is typically required, for example, in IMF programs in countries that have large fiscal deficits and loose money policies. In short, the dominance of private enterprise reduced the influence that governments had over the macroeconomy.

The Perils of Democracy

The nascent democracies that since the late 1980s had taken hold in Korea, Thailand, and the Philippines also caused a loss of government control over the macroeconomy. Whereas previous authoritarian regimes could impose higher interest and taxation costs on local business communities almost at will, and had done so to maintain currency stability for decades prior, this became difficult with the increased political influence of businesses over elected legislatures whose members were either business persons themselves, or required business support to get elected.

As *Wall Street Journal* reporter George Melloan commented on the American political process,

> Practicing politics costs money, and all politicians, unless they are fabulously wealthy, depend on campaign contributions. The more generous donors usually would like a favor or two. Quid pro quo, dating back at

least to the steps of the Roman Forum, is alive and well in the U.S., as in most other corners of the world.[17]

Thailand's short-lived coalition governments (five in six years), frequent general elections, and extensive vote-buying ($1.1 billion in the November 1996 general election alone) made it particularly vulnerable to vested interest opposition to the fiscal and monetary contraction necessary to correct an external imbalance—as suggested by the parade of four finance ministers and three central bank governors in the year before the July 2, 1997, devaluation of the baht. Democracy has also contributed to the expansion of crony capitalism, as exemplified by the favoring of businesses with ruling political party connections in Malaysia's joint public-private sector infrastructure projects, who naturally would oppose both interest rate increases and cuts in public expenditures from which they benefit.

By contrast, Hong Kong—which does not have an elected government—and Singapore—which has a single-party-dominated parliament—have done relatively well through the economic crisis. Like the authoritarian governments of the past in Korea and Thailand, both administrations maintain strong central economic control and can impose economic hardship on their populations or take politically unpopular measures when necessary for economic stabilization. Thus the Singapore government cooled off the domestic property market when it was still booming in 1996, and the Hong Kong authorities were able to ignore domestic business leaders' complaints about the currency peg hurting their businesses and were able to raise local interest rates to beat back an attack by currency speculators in 1997. In the terminology of political scientists, both states have an autonomy from business interests that their newly democratic neighbors do not have.

In Defense of the Western Model

Proponents of the Western liberal model do not, of course, see things this way. Instead, they assert that open markets and democracy have worked and that instead it is the "Asian" parts of the Asian economic model that have failed—particularly statist industrial policy in Korea (beloved though it is of some Western political scientists); crony capitalism in Thailand, Malaysia, and Indonesia (a reflection of both statist industrial policy and culturally embedded networks); and political mismanagement everywhere—from the virtual absence of government in Thailand, to persistent authoritarianism in Indonesia, and an idiosyncratic strong leader in Malaysia. They further argue that the excessive lending and investment by domestic and foreign financial institutions resulted from information gaps caused by inadequate local government regulation, monitoring, and disclosure requirements, not

| Linda Y. C. Lim

from mistakes made by financial markets. They believe that financial restructuring along Western lines and the takeover of troubled local financial institutions by more experienced and expert foreign counterparts would increase efficiency in the channeling of local savings to investments, reduce the risk of bad investments, and forestall a recurrence of the present crisis.

The IMF occupies a peculiar position in the Western economic policy canon. On the one hand, the multilateral agency is seen and has operated as an instrument of Western policy orthodoxy that advocates free trade and capital flows together with fiscal austerity and monetary conservatism. The IMF typically requires policy deregulation and liberal economic reforms, including financial sector liberalization and restructuring, in exchange for low-interest emergency loans of foreign exchange for client countries facing balance of payments difficulties and inability to meet their external liabilities. At the same time, it is recognized that the availability of IMF "bailouts" creates another moral hazard problem, by encouraging governments and private borrowers, lenders and investors to take excessive risks in emerging markets, secure in the knowledge that their risk is minimized by the likelihood of an IMF rescue should things go really bad. The result is periodic overinvestment and overlending bubbles such as characterized Mexico in 1994 and Southeast Asia and Korea in 1997.

The Asian Response

For Asians, disillusionment with market openness has set in. At worst, they see themselves as the victims of a massive conspiracy of Western governments, the IMF, financial markets, and industrial corporations to first deliberately inflate and then deflate the asset values of Asian banks and corporations, and then to subsequently take control of them at post-crisis fire sale prices under forced liberalization by the IMF.[18] At best, Asians view the current crisis as a case of massive market failure, particularly on the part of globally unregulated foreign financial market actors who, despite their greater expertise and global experience, still indulge in excess lending and investment to Asian markets and so cannot be trusted to better manage the local financial institutions that they may take over.

One of Thailand's most respected economists, Ammar Siamwalla, former president of the Thailand Development Research Institute, has been very critical of his own government's errors that led to the crisis, but still expresses extreme doubts about the policy of financial liberalization.

> The currency market is really crazy...we are receiving all the punishment because we have opened our currency markets to the forces of globalization (which) in retrospect has been far too rapid.[19]

Others share his views:

> The West has pushed us to open our markets, but what are we getting in return? Through globalization we have created a monster.[20] —*Park Yung Chul, President of Korea Institute of Finance*

Already, China and Vietnam have postponed capital market liberalization that would expose their currencies to speculation, and there have been calls for regional and global cooperation in the monitoring and possibly regulation of international capital flows. This idea was first raised by Malaysian prime minister Mahathir and supported by his nemesis, currency trader George Soros, who has said:

> Financial markets are inherently unstable, and international financial markets are especially so. International capital movements are notorious for their boom-bust pattern...The recent turmoil in Asian markets raises difficult questions about currency pegs, asset bubbles, inadequate banking supervision, and the lack of financial information which cannot be ignored. Markets cannot be left to correct their own mistakes, because they are likely to overreact and to behave in an indiscriminate fashion.[21]

Today, even the World Bank has lent its support to some forms of capital controls for small open economies that can be severely disrupted by massive inflows and outflows of foreign capital. There is a growing consensus that, at a minimum, some international monitoring and perhaps risk-insuring agency is necessary to oversee these currently largely unregulated flows.

At the same time, some Asians may also lose their enthusiasm for the chaos, corruption, and weak and unstable government that political democracy has ushered in to different degrees, in countries like Korea, Thailand, and the Philippines, which contributed to the crisis both by weakening government macroeconomic control in some cases and by increasing financial markets' perception and punishment of political risk in these countries.

Conclusion

Clearly, both the Western economists' and Western political scientists' competing open and statist models have, in some sense, failed with the crisis in their showcase economies in Asia. On the one hand, market openness without the requisite institutional infrastructure and expertise—including political infrastructure and managerial expertise—to manage it can be a recipe for economic disaster. Even the normal workings of global financial markets themselves can be disruptive to small open economies. On the other hand, statist industrial policy can lead to crony capitalism, excess capacity, overleverage, and bad investments (as can Western sociologists' "culturally embedded networks" of ethnic business relationships or *guanxi*). Both openness and statism have contributed not only to the Asian miracle, but also to the Asian meltdown.

What about "Asian values"? At first glance, the indictment of openness and democracy in the crisis, and the evident need for more state-led institution building, state monitoring if not control of private sector financial transactions, and state autonomy from private interests in the political sphere, might seem to be a confirmation of the wisdom of the Asian values school. Too much freedom too fast in both markets and politics can lead to downfall, suggesting a continued need for a strong, benevolent, central state authority.

> The Asian crisis exposes the futility of simplistic ideological models.

But at the same time, Asian government involvement in industrial policy and Asian cultural networks may also be indicted for fostering the crony capitalism that led to overinvestment in bad projects—ranging from Indonesia's Timor "national car" project[22] (of President Suharto's son), to Malaysia's privatization of huge public infrastructure projects favoring politically well-connected businesses and individuals, and the overextension of credit by overseas Chinese-owned banks to overseas Chinese industrial conglomerates with the presumed security of "relationships" substituting for modern risk assessment. The fact that the authoritarian regime and Indonesia's policy errors have compounded both the economic crisis and its adverse social and political consequences also undermines the belief of some Asian values advocates that authoritarianism might be superior to democracy in economic policy management. The Indonesian case contrasts vividly with the market confidence inspired, at time of writing, by the policy statements and actions of newly elected President Kim Dae Jung of Korea.

In short, the Asian economic crisis does not provide unqualified support for *either* the Western open-markets-and-democracy model *or* the Asian strong-government-and-cultural-values model. Both need some adjustment for global and national capitalisms to work smoothly. Certainly, the paths to capital market liberalization and democracy should be carefully planned, and perhaps staged to occur only in line with the concomitant development of supportive state and civil institutions. At the same time, governments need to resist the pressures of would-be crony capitalists to interfere with their fiscal, monetary, and regulatory autonomy, while private sector business networks need to be adjusted to adequately account for risk and to reduce purely rent-seeking behavior.

The Asian crisis does expose the futility of applying simplistic and essentially ideological models to the messy practical business of public and private sector economic management in developing countries whose political, economic, and business systems are not only diverse and complexly intertwined, but also still evolving. Far from yet another presaging of the end of history—in this case the presumed triumph of "Western" over "Asian" models—the crisis suggests that it is time to *return* to history, that is, to each country's particular configuration of economic, political, social, and cultural forces, to discern both the complex, multifaceted causes of the crisis and its eventual solutions. This is a task too important to allow to be jeopardized by those who would approach it only through the limited lenses of partial, monocausal theories and models of one or the other cultural-ideological predilection.

Notes

1. James Gwartney, Robert Lawson, and Walter Block, *Economic Freedom of the World 1975–1995* (Canada: Fraser Institute, 1996).

2. Bryan T. Johnson, Kim R. Holmes, and Melanie Kirkpatrick, eds., *1998 Index of Economic Freedom* (Washington, D.C.: Heritage Foundation and the Wall Street Journal, 1998).

3. Frederic C. Deyo, *The Political Economy of the New Asian Industrialism* (Ithaca, NY: Cornell University Press, 1987); Alice Amsden, *Asia's Next Giant: South Korea and Late Industrialization* (New York: Oxford University Press, 1989); Stephan Haggard, *Pathways from the Periphery: The Politics of Growth in Newly Industrialized Countries* (Ithaca: Cornell University Press, 1990); Robert Wade, *Governing the Market: Economic Theory and the Role of Government in East Asian Industrialization* (Princeton, N.J.: Princeton University Press, 1990); Karl Fields, "Strong States and Business Organization in Korea and Taiwan," in Sylvia Maxfield and Ben Ross Schneider, eds., *Business and the State in Developing Countries*, (Ithaca, N.Y.: Cornell University Press, 1997), pp. 122–151.

4. Andrew MacIntyre, ed., *Business and Government in Industrializing Asia* (Ithaca: Cornell University Press, 1994); K. S. Jomo, ed. *Southeast Asia's Misunderstood Miracle* (Boulder, Colo.: Westview Press, 1997).

5. Francis Fukuyama, *The End of History and the Last Man* (New York: The Free Press, 1992).

6. About the only sour note in this triumph was sounded by Samuel Huntington's *Clash of Civilizations*, which warned that the cessation of the Cold War's ideological conflicts would usher in an era of mounting cultural conflict between the West on one side and the competing civilizations of Islam and Confucianism on the other. See Samuel Huntington, *The Clash of Civilizations* (New York: Simon and Schuster, 1996).

7. S. Gordon Redding, *The Spirit of Chinese Capitalism* (Berlin: Walter de Gruyter, 1990); Gary G. Hamilton, ed. *Business Networks and Economic Development in East and Southeast Asia* (Hong Kong: Center of Asian Studies, University of Hong Kong, 1991); Robert W. Hefner, *Market Cultures: Society and Morality in the New Asian*

| Linda Y. C. Lim

Capitalisms (Boulder, Colo.: Westview, 1998). Richard Whitley, *Business Systems in East Asia: Firms, Markets and Societies* (London: Sage Publications, 1992); World Bank, *The East Asian Miracle: Economic Growth and Public Policy* (New York: Oxford University Press, 1993).

8. Paul Krugman, "The Myth of Asia's Miracle," *Foreign Affairs* 73 (November/December 1994), pp. 62–78.

9. Paul Krugman, "What Happened to Asia?" (mimeo, January 1998).

10. Jeffrey A. Frankel, "How Well Do Foreign Exchange Markets Function?" in Mahbub ul-Haq, Inge Kaul, and Isabelle Grunberg, eds., *The Tobin Tax: Coping with Financial Volatility*, (New York: Oxford University Press, 1996), pp. 41–81.

11. "Irrational pessimism" is how Japanese finance ministry official Eisuke Sakakibara's characterized sentiment toward the depressed Japanese stockmarket.

12. Nayan Chanda, "Rebuilding Asia," *Far Eastern Economic Review*, February 12, 1998, pp. 46–50.

13. Timothy O'Brien, "Covering Asia With Cash, Banks Poured Money Into Region Despite Warning Signs," *New York Times*, January 28, 1998, p. D1.

14. Ibid.

15. Ibid.

16. Assif Shameen, "Biting the Bullet: Siam Sement Tackles its Debts," *Asiaweek*, October 24, 1997, p. 62.

17. George Melloan, "Influence Peddlers Have a Growing Global Clientele," *Wall Street Journal*, February 17, 1998, p. A23.

18. I have analyzed and dismissed such "conspiracy theory" in Linda Lim, "Economic Crisis and Conspiracy Theory in Asia" (mimeo, February 1998).

19. Paul Scherer, "Distrust of Western Economics Grows in Thailand Amid Crisis," *Wall Street Journal*, January 20, 1998, p. A14.

20. Brian Bremmer, Pete Engardio, et al., "What to Do about Asia," *Business Week*, January 26, 1998, pp. 26–30.

21. George Soros, "Toward a Global Open Society," *Atlantic Monthly*, January 1998, pp. 20–24.

22. This project gave special tariff privileges to a new car company started by Tommy Suharto in a joint venture with Kia Motors of Korea, enabling their product, the Timor, to be sold on the local market for a price far below that of established competitors (mainly Japanese) and aspiring new entrants (from U.S. and European carmakers).

[13]
Capitalism's Last Chance?

by George Soros

The world is in the grip of an acute financial and political crisis. This crisis, if left unchecked, will lead to the disintegration of the global capitalist system. It is a crisis that will permanently transform the world's attitude toward capitalism and free markets. It has already overturned some of the world's longest established, and seemingly immovable, political regimes. Its effects on the relationships between advanced and developing nations are likely to be permanent and profound.

This situation came about unexpectedly, almost out of a clear blue sky. Even the people who expected an Asian crisis—and my firm, Soros Fund Management, was the first to anticipate the inevitability of the 1997 devaluation of the Thai baht that started the global chain reaction—had no idea of its extent or its destructive power.

What makes this crisis so politically unsettling and so dangerous for the global capitalist system is that the system itself is its main cause. More precisely, the origin of this crisis is to be found in the mechanism that defines the essence of a globalized capitalist system: the free, competitive capital markets that keep private capital moving unceasingly around the globe in a search for the highest profits and, supposedly, the most efficient allocation of the world's investment and savings.

The Asian crisis was originally attributed to various contingent weaknesses in specific countries and markets. Most economists focused initially

GEORGE SOROS *is chairman of Soros Fund Management and author of* The Crisis of Global Capitalism *(New York: PublicAffairs, 1998).*

on policy misjudgments that resulted in overvalued currencies and excessive reliance on foreign-currency borrowing. As the crisis spread, it became clear that such economic misjudgments were symptomatic of deeper sociopolitical problems. Political commentators have put the blame on the nexus of sociopolitical arrangements now described pejoratively as "crony capitalism" but previously extolled as "Confucian capitalism" or "the Asian model." There is some truth to these claims. Most Asian governments did make serious policy misjudgments, in some cases encouraged by international investors and the International Monetary Fund (IMF). They allowed investment and property booms to go unchecked and kept their currencies tied to the dollar for too long. In general, the Asian model was a highly distorted and immature form of the capitalist regime.

However, as the crisis has continued to develop, it has become apparent that its spread cannot be attributed simply to macroeconomic errors or specifically Asian characteristics. Why, after all, is the contagion now striking Eastern Europe, Latin America, and Russia, and even beginning to affect the advanced economies and efficient financial markets of Europe and the United States?

FINANCIAL PENDULUM OR WRECKING BALL?

The inescapable conclusion is that the crisis is a symptom of pathologies inherent in the global system. International financial markets have served as more than just a passive transmission mechanism for the global contagion; they have themselves been the main cause of the economic epidemic.

If it is true that the operation of free financial markets was in and of itself the fundamental cause of the present crisis, then a radical reconsideration of the dominant role that deregulated financial markets play in the world is inevitable. In the absence of urgent reforms, this rethinking could produce a powerful backlash against the global capitalist system, particularly in the developing countries on its periphery.

The essential point is that the global capitalist system is characterized not just by global free trade but more specifically by the free movement of capital. The system can be envisaged as a gigantic circulatory system, sucking capital into the financial markets and institutions at the center and then pumping it out to the periphery, either directly in the form of credits and portfolio investments or indirectly through multinational corporations.

Until the Thai crisis, the center was vigorously sucking in and pumping out money, financial markets were growing in size and importance, and countries on the periphery were obtaining an ample supply of capital from the center by opening up their capital markets. There was a global boom in which the emerging markets fared especially well. At one point in 1994, more than half the total inflow of capital to U.S. mutual funds went into emerging-market funds. The Asian crisis reversed the direction of the flow. Capital started fleeing emerging markets such as Korea and Russia. At first, the reversal benefited the financial markets at the center. But since the Russian meltdown in August 1998, the banking and financial systems at the center have also been adversely affected. As a result, the entire world economy is now under threat.

> *Today's crisis cannot be attributed simply to macroeconomic errors or specifically Asian characteristics.*

With the growing realization that the underlying cause of this threat is the inherent instability of deregulated financial markets, the ideology of world capitalism faces a historic challenge. The financial markets are playing a role very different from the one assigned to them by economic theory and the prevailing doctrine of free market capitalism. According to the ideology of free market fundamentalism, which has swept the world since it was pioneered in the early 1980s by Ronald Reagan and Margaret Thatcher, competitive markets are always right—or at least they produce results that cannot be improved on through the intervention of nonmarket institutions and politicians. The financial markets, in particular, are supposed to bring prosperity and stability—the more so, if they are completely free from government interference in their operations and unrestricted in their global reach.

The current crisis has shown this market fundamentalist ideology to be irredeemably flawed. Free market ideology asserts that fluctuations in stock markets and credit flows are transient aberrations that can have no permanent impact on economic fundamentals. If left to their own devices, financial markets are supposed to act in the long run like a pendulum, always swinging back toward equilibrium. Yet it can be demonstrated that the very notion of equilibrium is false. Financial markets are inherently unstable and always will be. They are given to excesses, and when a boom/bust sequence progresses beyond a certain point, it inevitably transforms the economic fundamentals, which in turn can never revert to where they began. Instead of acting like a pendulum, financial markets can act like a wrecking ball, swinging from country to country and destroying everything that stands in their way.

The current crisis presents policymakers with what may be a final opportunity to recognize that financial markets are inherently unstable before the wrecking ball takes aim at the foundations of the global capitalist system itself. What, then, needs to be done?

SAVING CAPITALISM FROM ITSELF

Many of the widely discussed solutions to today's crisis are designed to improve the efficiency of financial markets and impose more market discipline through such means as deregulation, privatization, transparency, and so on. But imposing market discipline means imposing instability. Financial markets are discounting a future that is contingent on the bias that prevails in markets, and the reflexive interplay between expectations and outcomes yields unstable results. Market discipline is desirable, but it needs to be supplemented by another kind of discipline: Public-policy measures are needed to stabilize the flows of international finance required by the global capitalist system and to keep the inherent instability of financial markets under control.

Within the main capitalist countries, strong frameworks of state intervention already exist to protect against financial instability. The United States has the Federal Reserve Board and other financial authorities whose mandates are to prevent a breakdown in its domestic financial markets and, if necessary, act as lenders of last resort. They have been quite successful. I am confident that they are capable of fulfilling their responsibilities. Indeed, now, in the second phase of the current crisis, as the problems of the periphery have begun to spill over into the center and threaten serious financial instability in U.S. markets, stabilizing mechanisms have been brought powerfully into play. The Federal Reserve has urgently eased monetary policy and made clear that it will continue to print money if that is what financial stability requires. More controversially, the Fed has pressured the private sector into organizing a lifeboat for Long Term Capital Management, a hedge fund that the Fed itself declared to be too big to fail.

The trouble is that international mechanisms for crisis management

Soros

Stop us before we kill again.

are grossly inadequate. Most policymakers in Europe and the United
States worry today whether their countries can be protected from the
global financial contagion. But the issue at the global level is much
broader and more historically important. Even if the Western economies
and banking systems do survive the present crisis without too much
harm, those on the periphery have been significantly damaged.

The choice confronting the world today is whether to regulate
global financial markets internationally to ensure that they carry out
their function as a global circulatory system or leave it to each individual state to protect its own interests. The latter course will surely
lead to the eventual breakdown of global capitalism. Sovereign states
act as valves within the system. They may not resist the inflow of capital,
but they will surely resist the outflow, once they consider it permanent. Malaysia has shown the way. A rapid spread of foreign-exchange
controls will inevitably be accompanied by the drying up of international investment and a return to inward-looking economic strategies
on the periphery. Economic withdrawal from world markets is likely
to be accompanied by political disengagement and domestic repression. (Again, Malaysia stands out as an example.) In short, the global
capitalist system will disintegrate.

What can be done to stop this process of disintegration? It is necessary to look beyond transparency, regulation, and other mechanisms that simply improve the efficiency of free markets. The flow of capital—and most importantly of private capital— from the center to the periphery must be revived and stabilized.

In seeking solutions to today's crisis, two common fallacies must be avoided. The first is the mistake of shutting the stable door after the horse has bolted. Reforms designed to improve the global financial architecture in the long term may be desirable, but they will do nothing to help the afflicted economies of today. In fact, the opposite may be true: Greater transparency and tougher prudential requirements are likely to discourage capital flows in the short term, just as the austere financial policies imposed by the IMF to restore the long-term soundness of stricken economies tend to make matters worse in the short term. The second fallacy is to embrace the delusion of market fundamentalism: that if markets can be made more transparent, more competitive, and generally more "perfect," their problems will be automatically solved. Today's crisis cannot be solved by market forces alone.

Emergency efforts to stabilize the world economy must focus on two goals: arresting the reverse flow of capital from the periphery of the global capitalist system to the center and ensuring the political allegiance of the peripheral countries to that system.

President Bill Clinton and Treasury Secretary Robert Rubin spoke in September 1998 about the need to establish a fund that would enable peripheral countries following sound economic poli- cies to regain access to international capital markets. Although the two men did not say so publicly, I believe that they had in mind financing it with a new issue of Special Drawing Rights (SDRs), an international reserve asset created by the IMF to supplement mem- bers' existing assets.

Although their proposal did not receive much support at the annual meeting of the IMF in October 1998, I believe that it is exactly what is needed. Loans could be made available to countries such as Brazil, Korea, and Thailand that would have an immediate calming effect on interna- tional financial markets. Furthermore, such a mechanism would send a powerful signal because it would reward countries doing their utmost to play by the rules of the global capitalist system rather than succumbing, like Malaysia, to the temptation to cut themselves off. The IMF programs in countries such as Korea and Thailand have failed to produce the desired results because they do not include any scheme for reviving the flow of private capital to these countries or reducing their foreign debt. A debt reduction scheme could clear the decks and allow their domestic economies to recover, but it would force international creditors to accept and write off losses. The problem is that creditors would be unwilling and unable to make new loans, making it impossible to finance recovery in these countries without finding an alternate source of international credit. That is where an international credit guarantee scheme would come into play. It would significantly reduce the cost of borrowing and enable the countries concerned to finance a higher level of domestic activity. By doing so, such a mechanism would help revive not only the countries concerned but also the world economy. It would reward countries for playing by the rules of the global capitalist system and discourage defections along Malaysian lines.

> *Reforms designed to improve the global financial architecture in the long term will do nothing to help today's affected economies.*

At present, the Clinton proposal is not being seriously pursued because European central banks are adamantly opposed to the issue of SDRs. Their opposition stems from doctrinaire considerations: Any kind of money creation is supposed to fuel inflation. But in using SDRs as guarantees, there would be no new money created; the guarantees would kick in only in case of default.

After the German elections, left-of-center governments are now in power in most of Europe. These governments are likely to prove more amenable to a loan guarantee scheme than their central banks, especially when the recovery of important export markets hinges on it. Japan too is likely to support such a scheme as long as it covers Asia as well as Latin America.

NEEDED: INTERNATIONAL CREDIT INSURANCE

Although I strongly endorse the Clinton proposal, I would go even further. Earlier in 1998, I proposed establishing an International Credit Insurance Corporation. My proposal, however, was premature, as the reverse flow of capital had not yet become a firmly established trend. Moreover, the Korean liquidity crisis in late 1997 was followed

Capitalism's Last Chance?

by a temporary market recovery that lasted until April 1998. My proposal fell flat then, but its time has now come.

A credit insurance mechanism managed by the IMF could provide the cornerstone for the "new architecture" that policymakers and pundits are talking about these days. The new institution, which could become a permanent part of the IMF, would explicitly guarantee, up to defined limits, the loans that private lenders make to countries. If a country defaults, the IMF would pay the international creditors and then work out a repayment process with the debtor country. The borrowing countries would be obliged to provide data on all borrowings, public or private, insured or not. This information would enable the authority to set a ceiling on the amounts it would be willing to insure. Up to those amounts, the countries concerned would be able to access international capital markets at prime rates plus a modest fee. Beyond these limits, the creditors would be at risk. Ceilings would be set taking into account the macroeconomic policies pursued by individual countries, as well as other overall economic conditions in each country and throughout the world. The new institution would function, in effect, as a kind of international central bank. It would seek to avoid excesses in either direction, and it would have a powerful tool in hand.

The thorniest problem raised by this proposal is how the credit guarantees allocated to an individual country would be distributed among that country's borrowers. To allow the state to make this decision would be an invitation for abuse. Guarantees ought to be channeled through authorized banks that would compete with each other. The banks would have to be closely supervised and prohibited from engaging in other lines of business that could give rise to unsound credits and conflicts of interest. In short, international banks would have to be as closely regulated as U.S. banks were after the breakdown of the American banking system in 1933. It would take time to reorganize the global banking system and introduce the appropriate regulations, but the mere announcement of such a scheme would calm financial markets and allow time for a more thorough elaboration of the details.

The credit insurance plan would obviously help the peripheral countries and the Western banking system to weather the immediate crisis. By providing some inducements for lenders scarred by recent and impending losses, it would help restart the flow of funds from the financial markets toward the peripheral countries. But credit insurance would also strengthen the entire global financial architecture

The Big Fix

The global financial crisis has spawned countless proposals on what to do with the International Monetary Fund (IMF). Herewith some examples:

Tear it down: "Let the IMF be abolished," says economics giant **Milton Friedman** in a November 1998 interview with *Forbes*. "Distribute the assets to each country and let the markets take care of the fallout." His fellow Hoover Institution scholar and former secretary of state **George Shultz** agrees. Instead of throwing money at the IMF, remarks Schultz, Congress should boost the global economy by cutting U.S. taxes by 10 percent across the board.

Clip its wings: The IMF can play a constructive role in crisis management if it avoids finger wagging and excessive interference in a nation's fiscal and monetary policies, says Harvard economics professor and former chairman of the President's Council of Economic Advisers **Martin Feldstein**. He urges the fund to focus on coordinating the rescheduling of international obligations for creditors and debtors and to create a collateralized credit facility to lend to governments that are illiquid but able to repay foreign debts through future export surpluses. The Columbia Business School's **Charles Calomiris** says that instead of doling out cash, the IMF should simply offer advice and encouragement and closely monitor government attempts at macroeconomic reform.

Make it bigger and better: Fleshing out proposals made by President Bill Clinton and British prime minister Tony Blair, the **Group of Seven** (G-7) announced in October 1998 a plan for the fund to extend short-term credit lines to any government that implements IMF–approved reforms, drawing from the recently approved $90 billion increase in the IMF's lendable resources. The G-7 ministers also called for increased collaboration between private-sector creditors and national authorities and the adoption by IMF member nations of a code of financial transparency enforced by annual IMF audits.

Create a new institution: Forget the IMF and World Bank, says **Jeffrey Garten**, dean of the Yale School of Management. Instead, create a global central bank that could provide liquidity to ailing nations by purchasing bonds from national central banks; encourage spending and investment by acquiring national debts at discounted prices; and set uniform standards for lending and provide markets with detailed, credible information on the world's banks.

—FP

Capitalism's Last Chance?

and improve financial stability in the long term. At present, the IMF does not have much influence in the internal affairs of its member countries except in times of crisis when a member country turns to the IMF for assistance. The fund may send its staff to visit and consult with country leaders, but it has neither the mandate nor the tools to shape economic policy in normal times. Its mission is crisis management, not prevention. By giving the new agency a permanent role in the surveillance of participating countries, the credit insurance scheme would help avoid both feast and famine in international capital flows.

Credit insurance would also help counteract the IMF's perverse role in the unsound expansion of international credit. IMF programs have served to bail out lenders, which encourages them to act irresponsibly, thereby creating a major source of instability in the international financial system. This defect of the current architecture is often described as "moral hazard." Moral hazard is caused by the asymmetry in the way that the IMF treats lenders and borrowers. It imposes conditions on borrowers (countries) but not on lenders (financial institutions); the money it lends enables debtor countries to meet their obligations, indirectly assisting the banks to recover their unsound loans. This asymmetry developed during the international crisis of the 1980s and became blatant in the Mexican crisis of 1995. In that case, foreign lenders to Mexico came out whole, even though the interest rates that the Mexican government paid them before the crisis clearly implied a high degree of risk. When Mexico could not pay, the U.S. Treasury and the IMF stepped in and took investors off the hook. The asymmetry and the moral hazard in IMF operations could be corrected by loan guarantees. Instead of bailing out foreign lenders to Mexico in 1995, the IMF would have guaranteed investors up to insured levels and then allowed uninsured debt to be converted into long-term bonds and written off. Had this happened, lenders and investors (myself included) would have been much more cautious about investing in Russia or Ukraine.

THE WILL TO STABILITY?

Some will wonder whether it would be possible for the IMF, let alone any new institution, to carry out the complex tasks I propose. Would it establish the right limits on sound international borrowing and be able to supervise the global circulatory system? A new institution would be bound to make mistakes, but the markets would provide valuable feedback and the mistakes could be corrected. After all, that is how all central banks operate and on the whole they do a pretty good job. It is much more questionable whether such a scheme is politically feasible. There is already a lot of opposition to the IMF from market fundamentalists who are against any kind of market intervention, especially by an international organization. If the banks and financial-market participants that currently benefit from moral hazard and asymmetry cease to support the IMF, it is unlikely to survive even in its present inadequate form.

Constructive reform will require governments, parliaments, and market participants to recognize that they have a stake in the survival of the system—and that this stake is far more valuable than any short-term gains that they may make from exploiting the flaws in the existing deregulated system. The question is whether this change of mentality will occur before or after the global capitalist system has fallen apart.

WANT TO KNOW MORE?

The flaws of the global financial system have been the focus of much analysis and debate. Karl Polanyi, in **The Great Transformation** (New York: Rinehart & Co., 1944), argues that capitalism is an anomaly since it embodies a system wherein social relations are defined by economic relations. In previous economic systems, he observes, economic interactions followed from social relations. Robert Kuttner's **Everything for Sale: The Virtues and Limits of Markets** (New York: Alfred A. Knopf, 1997) makes a case for the market's insufficiency in many fields and argues for intelligent intervention to produce better outcomes. In **Has Globalization Gone too Far?** (Washington: Institute for International Economics, 1997), Dani Rodrik posits that the world's leaders must ensure that international economic integration does not further domestic social disintegration.

For more analysis of the link between social relations and economic arrangements, see George Soros' **"The Capitalist Threat"** (*Atlantic Monthly*, February 1997), which argues that the free market undermines efforts to achieve open and democratic societies. Other works by Soros include: **"Toward Open Societies"** (FOREIGN POLICY, Spring 1995) in which he proposes that the creation of open societies should be a primary foreign-policy objective; **"After Black**

Capitalism's Last Chance?

Monday" (FOREIGN POLICY, Spring 1988), which advocates a reform of the international currency system; and *The Alchemy of Finance* (New York: John Wiley & Sons, 1987), which describes the "theory of reflexivity" that guides his investment strategies.

Other excellent recent articles include **"The Crisis of Global Capitalism"** (*The Economist*, September 12–18, 1998) in which Jeffrey Sachs argues that world leaders should focus on a "development agenda" and suggests a Group of Sixteen summit—the Group of Eight countries plus eight developing nations—to tackle international financial reform, specifically, the international assistance process. Ricardo Hausmann's article, **"Will Volatility Kill Market Democracy?"** (FOREIGN POLICY, Fall 1997) describes alternatives to the common solutions for stabilizing the intense boom-and-bust cycles that characterize today's markets.

Speeches by Treasury Secretary Robert Rubin over the last six months track the evolution of the official U.S. position on reforming the global financial system. Especially useful are his **"Statement at the Special Meeting of Finance Ministers and Central Bank Governors"** on April 16, 1998, the transcript of the **"Post–Group of Seven Press Conference"** on April 15, 1998, the **"Statement at the 58th Annual Development Committee of the World Bank and the International Monetary Fund"** of October 5, 1998, and the **"Statement to the IMF Interim Committee"** on October 4, 1998.

For links to the texts of these speeches and relevant Web sites, as well as a comprehensive index of related FOREIGN POLICY articles, access **www.foreignpolicy.com**.

[14]

Susan Strange

The New World of Debt

The debtors and how best to deal with them is surely one of the continuing but unresolved issues for the international financial system.[1] Here I will argue that the evolution of that system has changed the nature of the debt problem, but that neither governments nor markets are any nearer a final solution to the question of how to manage transnational debt than they were in the 1980s. Indeed, the evidence suggests that they may be even further away from a sustainable solution. If so, this is a conclusion that throws serious doubt on many optimistic incrementalist assumptions about the progressive improvement of 'global governance' through the increased role of international organizations— assumptions often cherished by some academics—and, of course, in bureaucratic circles.

By transnational debt, I do not mean only the financial credits extended by governments to other governments. They are but a small part of the story. The term covers all the forms of debt across state frontiers: all the liabilities incurred, and claims established, between institutions or individuals under one political jurisdiction, and institutions or individuals under another political jurisdiction. It would thus include assets claimed by foreign shareholders in enterprises in another country, interbank loans across frontiers, bonds issued to non-nationals both by governments and other institutions and firms, as well as credits or guarantees extended by states or multilateral organisations like the IMF or World Bank or the regional development banks in Asia, the western hemisphere or Africa.

The purpose here is not to give a comprehensive survey of all the recent developments in the international financial system. That would be a vast undertaking. Even to survey all the developments in the treatment of transnational debt would be a massive task. Rather, my aim is the more limited purpose of analyzing—and if possible explaining—how the system has changed in recent years, and with what consequences for social classes, for creditors and debtors, and for institutions, including firms as well as national governments. The main purpose is neither descriptive nor prescriptive, but analytical and interpretative. It can be boiled down to finding the answers to three rather straightforward questions.

The first, obviously, is what has changed since the 1980s, and what is the same—and why. The next is who, in the 1990s, has been involved in transnational lending and borrowing—which players, new and old, political and financial, have to be taken into account when it comes either to state or intergovernmental policy-making or, for that matter, corporate strategy. The third question is whether transnational debt is in any sense a threat or potential danger to the international financial system. It certainly was believed to be so in the early 1980s. By the late 1990s, it is not so clear whether and when it is, or is not, threatening the financial foundations of the world market economy.

One basic point in political economy has to be remembered. The phenomenon of borrowing—getting money today in exchange for money tomorrow—is economic. But how such transactions are managed is political. To political economists, it is clear that how national societies manage debt within the borders of state authority differs fundamentally from how the collectivity of national governments manage transnational debts. Within national market economies, it became clear even in the nineteenth century that the national economic interest was not well served by a legal system that relied on deterrence, by punishing debtors when they failed to meet their obligations to creditors. Prison was no solution. Some other arrangements had to be evolved: either ways had to be found to rehabilitate the indebted enterprise or individual, usually by agreement with the creditors to accept only part repayment; or else ways had to be devised that would allow others to take control in exchange for assuming the debtor's liabilities in whole or in part. Either arrangement had to have the legitimacy of an enforceable legal contract. Bankruptcy therefore, whether temporary or permanent, could be imposed on debtors—and their creditors—only with the authority of the state.

---

[1] The following is an extract from Susan Strange's book *Mad Money*, forthcoming from Manchester University Press.

That is much more difficult when the debt is transnational, involving two or more state authorities and legal systems.[2] It has been particularly difficult when one of the parties to the borrowing was itself a supposedly sovereign state. The international political system had developed no general rules for the treatment of bankrupt states. Such states there had been, in the nineteenth century as in the twentieth century.[3] Each had been dealt with in an ad hoc manner. In rare cases, like Egypt in the 1880s, or Central American banana republics in the early 1900s, creditor states intervened and acted as receivers, temporarily taking over the country's financial management from the indebted government. A kind of delegated collective form of receivership was developed in an ad hoc way in the 1920s for the administration of countries getting loans from the League of Nations—although in fact the funds were subscribed by the British and French. More commonly, creditors' governments either ignored their nationals' losses as bad luck, or practised the exclusionary strategy of simply closing off their credit systems to the government and nationals of the defaulting state. This was the Western response to the Soviet Union's renunciation of Tsarist foreign debts in the 1920s.

Palmerston, Kautsky, Lenin

The preference for uncertainty and ad hoc solutions goes back a long way. It was Lord Palmerston in 1848 who first devised the smart policy of leaving open and undecided whether, in any particular case of bad transnational debt, the British government would or would not intervene, possibly with naval force, to recover unsettled claims by British investors. This uncertainty addressed the problem of moral hazard at both ends. It discouraged rash investors—usually bondholders at the time—from thinking that their government would always be ready with military or naval force to come to their aid. At the same time, it left the debtors in some doubt as to whether their country might suffer the humiliation and disruption of military intervention if they failed to honour their foreign debts.

Pragmatically, creditor governments since 1945 have followed the same strategy of leaving undecided what punitive measures would or would not be applied against foreign defaulters on transnational obligations.[4] They have not, until recently, contemplated developing a systematic legal process for the treatment and possible rehabilitation of bankrupts. Only in a partial fashion, as we shall see, have they come close to doing so by the device of negotiating Multi-Year Rescheduling Agreements (MYRAs) with Less Developed Countries' (LDCs') governments and by

---

[2] See Strange, *Mad Money*, ch. 9.
[3] H. Feis, *Europe the World's Banker, 1870–1914*, New York 1964.
[4] On this, see C. Prout, 'Finance for Developing Countries: An Essay' in S. Strange, ed., *International Economic Relations of the Western World, 1959-1971*, Vol. II, *International Monetary Relations*, Oxford 1976. Prout (now Sir Christopher and a former leader of British Conservatives in the European Parliament) commented on the totally different attitude of nations when they cease to become lenders and become creditors. 'As lenders [they] were behaving like highly speculative fringe bankers devoted entirely to profit considerations and mindless of asset security...As creditors they establish elaborate procedures to salvage a financial disaster which need never have happened if even a fraction of the cooperation they demonstrated *ex post* the insolvency had been demonstrated *ex ante* the insolvency' (p. 389).

offering Structural Adjustment Loans (SALs) as the way out for indebted governments. Both are negotiated in a more or less ad hoc fashion. This is as close as the creditor governments have dared come to the sort of collective colonialism feared and predicted by Kautsky in his famous disagreement with Lenin in 1915. Where Lenin predicted the inevitable clash of national capitalist-imperialist states, Kautsky argued that their common interest in maintaining a stable but open world economic order would lead the imperialist powers to collective intervention in what were then, still, colonies. On the whole, Lenin has been proved wrong, and Kautsky—and the late Ernest Mandel—right.[5]

Compared with the treatment of transnational debt in the 1980s and before, the treatment in the 1990s has not substantially changed. It has not changed because the logic of the international political system of states does not easily permit international agreement on the terms and conditions of a legally enforceable system of bankruptcy. So, while some—mainly Asian—countries have escaped the debt trap, the problem of how to deal with debtors—and especially poor African countries and former Soviet states and allies—remains, and, in a long-term perspective, it is rather worse than it was a decade earlier. Such a conclusion would go far to explain the paradox of official support for an enhanced role for the IMF and the World Bank. The IMF in particular lost its chief raison d'être when the United States decided in the 1970s to abandon the fixed exchange rate regime it was set up to oversee and enforce. Finding an alternative role in the surveillance of developing countries brought it by stages into partnership with the World Bank, whose image in Latin America and Africa was somewhat more benign. Then, in the 1990s, when technological and financial innovations allowed the integration of new financial centres in Asia and other emerging markets into the financial system, the problem arose of how these were to be supervised and regulated. Hence, perhaps, the popularity in official government and central bank circles of bringing the IMF into the picture.

So if this is new, what is still much the same? In *Casino Capitalism* I observed,

> The sorry state of the financial system is undoubtedly aggravating the difficulties in the path of economic development for poor countries while conversely the difficulties of the deeply indebted developing countries, so long as they persist, will aggravate the instability of the banking system.[6]

This judgement is still valid even though some of the poor developing countries since the mid-1980s have managed, despite the financial system—or even with help from it—to achieve very rapid economic growth, and even though not all the sources of instability in the banking system can be laid at the door of indebted LDCs. In short, there is still a complex interaction between the system by means of which credit is created and allocated and the prospects and opportunities opened to countries seeking greater wealth and economic development. But there

---

[5] The debate is summarised in S. Strange, *Casino Capitalism*, Oxford 1986, pp. 92–5.
[6] Ibid., p. 181.

are important respects in which this complex interaction has changed, producing new winners and new losers.

The Mexican Story

As it happens, there was one country, Mexico, which experienced two acute crises arising from its foreign debts, one in 1982 and the other in 1994-95. By comparing the two, we can observe both some similarities in the two incidents and some important differences. From this empirical experience, we should be able to draw at least some wider conclusions about what was the same and what was different as between the 1980s and the 1990s. Fortunately there is a large and exhaustive literature, in English and Spanish, on both crises, so that the salient points can be picked out without going into too much tedious detail.[7]

Responsibility for bringing about the 1982 peso crisis must be shared between creditors and debtors. Foreign banks lent unwisely and too much in Mexico, and the leaders of the Mexican ruling party, the Partido Revolucionario Institucional (PRI), allowed a fatal flight of capital out of the country which eventually made it impossible for the government to service—let alone repay—its foreign debts. For years, the PRI as a party and its successive leaders had profited from a bizarre constitution which gave each president a once-in-a-lifetime opportunity to amass a personal fortune by means of fraud, patronage and protection. Presidents could only ever serve one six-year term and, in earlier times, the fortunes they made were mostly invested in land, property or businesses within Mexico. Political power was used regressively to redistribute wealth within the country, but the balance of payments and the value of the currency were not affected.

But by the 1970s and 1980s, the financial innovations and the integration of financial markets almost invited Mexican presidents to stash their loot where it was safer from successive peso devaluations. President Portillo (1976-82) and his friends and relations led a fatal flight of capital out of Mexico, mostly to the United States and into real estate and financial assets. Foreign exchange to service the debt was borrowed at shorter and shorter terms. The probability of eventual default was obvious—but ignored until it was too late.

The second Mexican debt crisis, in 1994-95, did not involve foreign banks as creditors. They had learnt a lesson the hard way since the rescue operation mounted by President Reagan in 1983 used the threat of total loss eventually to coerce the major creditor banks—US and foreign—into contributing to an emergency rescue package. They were later pressured into accepting a Brady Plan deal, launched in 1989 and first negotiated with Mexico. This succeeded where the earlier Baker Plan, launched in

---

[7] Some important contributions to this literature were S. Maxfield, *Governing Capital: International Finance and Mexican Politics*, Ithaca 1990; R. Bouzas, 'The Mexican Peso Crisis and Argentina's Convertibility Plan: Monetary Virtue or Monetary Impotence?', in R. Roett, ed., *The Mexican Peso Crisis: International Perspectives*, Boulder 1996; L. Thurow, *The Future of Capitalism: How Today's Economic Forces Shape Tomorrow's World*, London 1996; W. Greider, *One World, Ready or Not: The Manic Logic of Global Capitalism*, New York 1997; and a series of articles on the 1994–95 crisis in *The Economist*.

1985, had failed. It effectively persuaded the banks to cut their losses, by writing off about a third of the interest they would have been paid.[8] In return they acquired Brady bonds backed by the US government, the World Bank and the IMF—each contributing $12 billion—and the Japan Export-Import Bank, which added another $10 billion. Over the next seven years, twenty-six countries signed up for Brady deals. On balance, the banks had been helped out with public money. This had triggered a recovery in the value of secondary-market debt, making the banks substantially better off than they were at the start in 1989.

One long-term result was that the international financial institutions—the World Bank and the IMF—averted de facto default by lending out, year after year, more than they were owed.[9] Another was that the banks belatedly recognised that past performance by debtor countries was not necessarily a safe or reliable guide to present and future performance. Once bitten, they were twice shy of risking their own money on LDC loans. But the alternative strategy, of acting as a conduit for OPM (other people's money), could be profitable as well as less risky. The Mexican experience also gave a fillip to political risk analysis, a new service industry born out of the political upsets—as in Iran—and expropriations of the 1970s, which now found new clients in investing circles.

The Second Peso Crisis

In the second peso crisis, as in the first, responsibility was not all on one side. Mistakes were made by both the Mexican debtors and the foreign creditors. The PRI and its leaders, first Salinas and then Zedillo were certainly responsible for clinging too long and too hard to an unrealistic exchange rate which grossly overvalued the peso; and then for adding to the danger by issuing *tesobonos*—Mexican government securities denominated in US dollars. Before the collapse in December 1994, it had issued no less than $30 billion *tesobonos*. These constituted about a half of the whole foreign debt, of $60 billion.[10] As Martin Mayer commented, 'When Mexico blew again in late 1994, it was almost a non-event to the banks which had suffered so in 1982. They had brokered customers' money into Mexican securities at the customers' own risks, but had made few direct new loans to Mexican borrowers'.[11]

If the banks had learnt the hard way to be cautious, why were other creditors quite so ready to invest in Mexican securities? Like the banks before them, these new investors were led to do so by the prospect of profit. There was a divergence between the interest rates to be earned in the United States and those to be earned in Mexico. Thus, it was possible in 1994 to borrow money in New York at 5 or 6 per cent, and invest it in Mexico at 12 to 14 per cent. This game is called arbitrage. In a sense, it is not new. Even in the nineteenth century, there were opportunities to

---

[8] M. Bowe and J.W. Dean, *Has the Market Solved the Sovereign Debt Crisis?*, Princeton Studies in International Finance, Princeton 1997, p. 13.
[9] Ibid., p. 53.
[10] M. Aglietta, *Financial Market Failures and Systemic Risk*, Centre d'Etudes Prospectives et d'Information Internationales Working Paper 96–101, Paris 1996, p. 13.
[11] M. Mayer, *The Bankers: The Next Generation*, New York 1997, p. 446.

borrow money at home, in London for example, and invest it more prof-itably abroad—but at a higher level of risk. What was new was the ease with which large funds could be employed in this way and the rapidity with which they could be moved.

And Mexico was not the only country to experience this shift, although it did get more than its share. In the 1990s, the managers of British and American insurance and pension funds led a wave of portfolio invest-ment into the emerging markets of Asia and Latin America, especially to Mexico, Brazil and Argentina. Between 1990 and 1993, Mexico received $91 billion, which was one-fifth of all net capital inflows to developing countries. Two-thirds of this was portfolio investment and most of that was invested in the Mexican stock market, setting off a boom in share prices. The market rose 436 per cent in dollar terms in that three-year period.[12]

But it was not only Mexicans who were blowing hot air into this danger-ous bubble. As William Grieder has commented, politicians, the media and market dealers outside Mexico played a large part in encouraging the false optimism that allowed the issue of the *tesobonos*.[13] President Clinton especially had a political axe to grind in promoting popular belief in the myth of a newly modernised Mexico as partner to the United States and Canada in NAFTA. In his election campaign in 1992 he had ridiculed the objections of Ross Perot and others to the NAFTA strategy, discounting the risks not only to Mexico but also to the United States. Politically, NAFTA and the enlarged market it represented gave Americans a new and more powerful weapon when it came to bargaining over trade terms with both the Japanese and the Europeans.

Grieder also pointed out that a more proximate factor behind the burst-ing of the bubble in December 1994 could be found in the monetary policies of the US Federal Reserve. As the US economy started to grow again, the Federal Reserve Board, fearing inflation, began to raise inter-est rates. The spread between returns in the United States and Mexico would have narrowed, but to keep the flow going and to sustain confi-dence in the peso, Mexico raised its own interest rates and began to spend its monetary reserves to boost demand for pesos. The alternative strategy of putting some controls on capital inflows and outflows was suggested to President Zedillo but rejected.[14] Grieder suggests this was for ideo-logical reasons although, given the size of the foreign debt, there were also practical difficulties.[15] Mexican reserves started to run out rather fast even before the 1994 elections; the Chiapas revolt and the assassination of presidential candidate Luis Colosio shook confidence. The unravel-ling, when it came, was much faster than in 1982. There were just three days between 19 December 1994 when Zedillo lowered the guaranteed

---

[12] J. D'Arista, *The Evolution of US Finance*, Vol. II. *Restructuring Institutions and Markets*, New York 1994, p. 16.
[13] Grieder, *One World, Ready or Not*, p. 259.
[14] Ibid., p. 263.
[15] There is an interesting comparison to be made here with Taiwan, whose central bank, in 1987, imposed ceilings on banks' foreign liabilities after a surge of hot money flooded into Taiwan from abroad. These were successively eased and finally abolished ten years later, see *Free China Journal*, 30 May 1997.

dollar rate for *tesobonos* and 22 December when he gave up supporting the exchange rate and let the currency fall. The country faced a shortfall between assets and liabilities of some $55 billion. By the first week of February 1995, the United States was ready with a rescue package even larger than the one arranged, also under US leadership, in 1982. This time, it was the IMF and the BIS, not the banks, who were persuaded to contribute. The US put up $20 billion by raiding the Exchange Stabilization Fund and the two international bodies contributed $32 billion.[16] (Clinton had first proposed a unilateral US $40 billion bailout but the Congress had baulked at this so he had had to go to the IMF and BIS for help).[17]

On both occasions, therefore, the peso had been forcibly devalued; the government had had to give in to the market. Both times, the United States had arranged a rescue package. Both times it was the Mexican economy and Mexican people that suffered most.

International System on the Brink

But there were significant differences. From the point of view both of the rescuer as well as the rescued, the second crisis was costlier and more dangerous than the first. For the United States, the whole NAFTA enterprise—and beyond it the dream of an even bigger single market, covering the whole of the western hemisphere—was at risk. More than that, as the distinguished French economist Michel Aglietta has argued, the stability of the entire international financial system was at stake. He pointed out that the financing gap facing Mexico in the first half of 1995 was huge—$55 billion—with no prospect of raising money from the markets. Ninenty per cent of the debt was owed to non-official investors, including the holders of *tesobonos*, foreign fund managers and non-banks. If the international monetary authorities had stood by and done nothing, the subsequent economic slump would have been even worse. The Mexican government would have had no other choice but to pay back *tesobonos* in pesos. The currency would have become worthless. Banks and other firms would have gone bankrupt in their hundreds, bringing the open economy predicated by the NAFTA agreements to an abrupt end.[18]

In the aftermath, the US administration had committed a substantial part of the monetary reserves over which it had direct authority. These were funds that could be mobilized without the need to seek permission of the Congress. Fortunately, the Mexican rescue brought a much more rapid recovery than expected, so that the United States was able to get most of its money back. If it had not, a second raid on the Exchange Stabilization Fund would have been impossible. The result was twofold.

---

[16] The Exchange Stabilization Fund was the result of a 1936 tripartite agreement between the United States, Britain and France to give mutual support to each other's currencies. Though not wholly successful, it is seen by historians as the forerunner of the Bretton Woods fixed exchange rate system. See S. Clarke, *The Reconstruction of the International Monetary System: The Attempts of 1922 and 1933*, Princeton Studies in International Finance, no. 33, Princeton 1973.

[17] P. Erdman, *Tug of War: Today's Global Currency Crisis*, New York 1996, p. 13; L. Pauly, *Who Elected the Bankers? Surveillance and Control in the World Economy*, Ithaca 1997, p. 124.

[18] Aglietta, *Financial Market Failures*, pp. 12–14.

In the spring of 1997, the US Treasury contemplated seeking agreement
from the other rich countries to a New Arrangement to Borrow, much
larger than the 1962 General Arrangement to Borrow.[19] But then, by the
summer, when turmoil hit the Asian markets and their currencies, the US
strategy shifted even more from the unilateral to the multilateral. That is
to say, the United States decided to be the leader of the rescue parties,
but to make sure that other governments and the IMF, the World Bank
and the Asian Development Bank between them put up most of the
funds. It was a sort of replay on the monetary front of US strategy during
the Gulf War on the military front. Thus the chain of events which
started with apparently local events in Mexico like the Chiapas uprising,
and with the rise in US interest rates, ended by saddling the United
States with a new kind of dependency—the need to negotiate with the
other G7 governments and with major international banks the provision
of funds in defence of the international financial system.

But while American opinion rejoiced in the Mexican 'recovery', that
recovery related only to a restoration of confidence in financial markets.
It did not mean that life in Mexico was the same in 1997 as it had been in
1994. For the Mexican people, the consequences of the 1995 crisis were
even worse than those of the earlier crisis. Badly hit were small banks and
small and medium-sized businesses—some 8,000 firms were closed.
Worst affected were poor people. Official figures spoke of cuts in real
wages of 25-30 per cent. A parish priest I spoke to in the prosperous
northern town of Monterrey, assured me his poor parishioners had had
family incomes cut by half. What this meant in reality was no meat to
eat, only the eternal beans and tortillas, no new clothes or shoes to
wear—only second-hand or makeovers for the children. Even the bus
fares to get to work had to be borrowed from friends or relations. And
even better-off people often lost their mortgaged houses or cars if the
debt had been financed in dollars. Respect for ruling elites—and especially the PRI—will not easily recover. A spontaneous protest movement
grew rapidly. It called itself El Barzon, referring to the strap that held an
ox under the yoke—as Mexicans felt themselves held in the yoke of foreign debt.

As Grieder comments:

> The case of Mexico illustrates, in the most horrendous terms, that
> developing nations make a kind of deal with the devil when they
> open themselves to the animal spirits of global capital. As liquidity
> sloshes about in the global financial system, seeking the highest
> returns, a nation may find itself inundated with 'hot money' from
> abroad that can ignite a giddy boom—or abruptly starved for credit
> when the foreign money decides, for whatever reason, to leave.[20]

The players in the drama, too, were different. Instead of the big transnational banking interests, the chief players in the 1990s were the more
mobile, less vulnerable insurance and pension fund managers and other

---

[19] See S. Strange, 'International Monetary Relations', in A. Shonfield, ed., *International
Economic Relations in the Western World, 1959–1971*, Vol. II, Oxford 1976, pp. 105–16.
[20] Grieder, *One World, Ready Or Not*, p. 263.

portfolio investors. Although by 1995 there may have been some losses, on the whole these can be counted as winners from the arbitrage game, in that they made money while the brokerage game lasted but did not have to pay up afterwards, as the banks had done.

The Contagion Question

In the longer perspective and in the light of the 1997–98 Asian crises, the other question for the system as a whole was how far the contagion of lost confidence was apt to spread. A big difference between the two Mexican crises was the effect on other indebted countries in the international financial system. Why was there this difference and why later did contagion spread so rapidly in Asia?

In 1982, the Mexican collapse and devaluation had had an immediate—and much resented—effect on the Brazilian economy. Where in 1981 and up until August 1982 Brazil had been easily able to finance its borrowing with Eurodollar loans from the banks, after September this source of credit had completely dried up. Hungary had experienced the same financial drought when Poland was unable to service its foreign loans, mainly from German banks. In 1995, this contagion effect seemed at first to be the same. Portfolio investment flows into Latin America, especially into Brazil and Argentina, dried up and began to withdraw. Because Mexico was seen to be the cause, it became known as the Tequila effect. But as it turned out, the contagion, though sharply felt, was relatively short lived. That is to say, it did not spread fast and fatally to the whole financial system. To the extent it did spread, the damage was done to the debtors, not to the creditors, and was long term.

In Brazil, for instance, the central bank began to lose its $40 billion reserves as capital outflows added to a growing current account deficit. Too rapid, unsustainable domestic expansion was caught unawares by the Tequila effect on foreign capital markets. A Brazilian economist commented that the Mexican crisis set off a small capital flight out of Brazil. Debts maturing early in 1995 could not be rolled over. And the unavailability of external financing dashed hopes of domestic monetary stabilization based on a fixed exchange rate. The Brazilian real was devalued and President Cardoso found it necessary to raise interest rates and restrict credit. This effectively checked economic growth and opened new opportunities for arbitrage between US and Brazilian interest rates.[21]

In Argentina, similarly, from 1991 to 1994, the government had managed dramatically to bring down inflation rates, build up reserves and start the economy growing. An Argentine economist commented that this expansion was brought to a halt by the combination of rising US interest rates and the Tequila effect.[22] Impending elections compounded the effect of a quite modest capital flight and a run on bank deposits. Sticking faithfully to its anti-inflationary currency board

---

[21] Martone, 'Recent Economic Policy in Brazil Before and After the Mexican Peso Crisis' in Roett, ed., *The Mexican Peso Crisis*, p. 61.
[22] Bouzas, 'The Mexican Peso Crisis and Argentina's Convertibility Plan', p. 71.

strategy, the Menem government with the help of the IMF stopped the rot with a restrictive fiscal programme. But the harsh medicine also hurt the patient. The economy stagnated through 1995 and 1996. Real investment and output fell. Unemployment rose—though neither the stagnation nor the unemployment was as bad as in Mexico. The conclusion seemed to be, first, that the government had no option but to follow deflationary policies, given the pressures of the ultra-sensitive world financial system. But how quickly growth and relative prosperity would return after the contagion had eased depended not on Argentine responses so much as on the mood of global capital markets. Should they fail to supply external financing at reasonable cost, the automatic adjustment mechanisms of Menem's Convertibility Plan would keep the economy in recession or even take it into deflation for some time to come.

The Brazilian Experience

Before we consider the Asian situation, an earlier study of contagion is worth noting. Some research based on the experience of the 1980s by Sylvia Maxfield compared the policy responses of Brazil with those of Mexico in the 1982 debt crisis.[23] Her conclusion was that policy makers in debtor (and other) countries do not all react in the same way. Nor do they always just passively respond to market signals. Rather, national policies and national monetary institutions reflected different balances of power between economic interests. In Brazil, coffee and sugar exporters and later manufacturing interests dominated over financial interests, so that economic policies were marked by frequent devaluations backed up by capital controls. In Mexico, financial interests were strong and concentrated and favoured orthodox liberal policies of free exchange convertibility. Brazil therefore responded to the 1980s crisis and to the 1990s one with heterodox intervention, while Mexico from the 1920s to the 1990s reflected the strength of the bankers' alliance behind the central bank and opted repeatedly for orthodox neo-liberal responses to external pressures and crises. Maxfield's conclusion is in sharp contrast to IMF orthodoxy: 'unorthodox, capital-controlling policies can have benefits that may for newly industrializing countries in a rapidly internationalized world, outweigh their social welfare costs'.[24]

Her analysis was consistent with the explanation given by Jeff Frieden of the clash of interests in Mexico between those with liquid assets—for example, US bonds or shares—and those with illiquid assets—such as fixed capital assets in Mexican land, factories and real estate. The latter would have preferred a more interventionist, even protectionist, economic strategy, while those with liquid assets wanted convertibility into dollars and tight deflationary policies at home in order to pacify foreign creditors. Class structures, in a word, and the nature of wealth, explained the differential definitions of national interest and the divergent preferences of policy makers faced with a credit crisis.[25]

---

[23] Maxfield, *Governing Capital*.
[24] Ibid., p. 192.
[25] J. Frieden, 'Invested Interests: The Politics of National Economic Policies in a World of Global Finance', *International Organization*, vol. 45, no. 4, 1991, pp. 425–51.

The Asian Scene

If one instructive comparison can be made between the Mexican debt crises of 1982 and 1994–95, another might be made between the latter and the crisis in Thailand and other East Asian countries two and a half years later. The bottom-line question in both cases for many observers was whether either crisis threatened the stability of the global financial system or jeopardized the prosperity of its core countries. For most of the winter of 1997–98, the financial press and the academic pundits worried away at the question, like a dog with a bone. As on other questions, there was no consensus. Some argued that although Japan, as the major exporter to and investor in East Asia, might suffer, America and Europe would feel an unpleasant draught, but one that would not blow their economies off course. Others, foreseeing a scramble for export market shares by the stricken Asian industries, and cancellation of their orders for foreign aircraft, arms and construction projects, saw signs of slower but still inexorable contagion spreading across the Pacific and indeed the Atlantic oceans.

Once again, comparisons can help, if only by identifying, and separating, the common and the divergent factors. How did the crisis originate? What kinds of foreign capital were involved? Did the authorities in America, Japan and Europe react quickly enough, and similarly, or not? What, then, sets the limits of the contagion effects of national financial crises on the wider system?

One obvious common factor was the surge of foreign capital going into the country in the months before the crisis. That, in both cases, had more to do with external factors than with internal ones—specifically, the hungry search by international fund and pension managers for profitable places to put their money. At first, this seems to pay off because the inflow itself tends to create a boom in asset values. Share market indices rise, encouraging yet more inflow.

Jeffrey Sachs's 1996 Brookings study drew what he called 'some basic economic lessons' from the experience of emerging markets.[26] One lesson was that players were deluded by the optical illusion that the strong currency that follows economic liberalization was due to the liberalization and not to the capital inflows chasing high rates of return. The effect of these inflows is to start a bubble in real estate prices and in non-traded goods and services. When the bubble bursts and share prices start falling, the currency starts to lose value in the markets. The other optical illusion was that the freedom given to local banks by deregulation was risk-free, whereas the reality is that borrowing abroad and investing in the local bubble economy is vulnerable to the local currency's exchange rate. That rate is apt at first to be overvalued. Using a rough index based on the ratio of domestic price increases from 1900 to 1996 compared with price rises in a weighted basket of the countries' main trading partners, Sachs found the Malaysian ringgit, the Singapore dollar and the Thai baht had appreciated by 10 per cent, the Indonesian currency by 20

---

[26] See also an updated summary in his article, 'Lessons from the Thais', *The Financial Times*, 30 July 1997.

per cent, and the Philippines' by 30 per cent. These figures should have given warning of future vulnerability. So should the fact that Thailand's foreign interest payments at 1 per cent of GNP were three times as big as Mexico's in 1994.

There was also the slowdown in the Asian tigers' export growth. In dollar terms the average in 1995 was almost 23 per cent; in 1996 it was only 5.6 per cent. That again was due more to external than to local factors. European and Japanese markets were sluggish and competition from low-cost exports from China was beginning to bite. The dollar, too, was part of the problem. In Mexico it was the higher interest rates chosen by the Fed. In Thailand, it was the strong dollar which made the fixed link less sustainable.

The Sachs model of emerging markets vulnerable to new external risks and internal mismanagement naturally emphasizes the common factors. But there were also some important differences. Mexico's political system actually encouraged capital flight. But the economy was less deeply in foreign debt than the tigers' and moreover had its oil output and potential as an underlying source of strength. These factors helped markets to bounce back comparatively quickly. Geopolitics also mattered. Mexico in NAFTA meant the United States could not afford to stand aside. The Japanese government was slower to realise that its banks and multinationals had such a strong interest in stopping the contagion from Thailand and Malaysia spreading to Indonesia, the Philippines, Hong Kong and South Korea. Yet the key deal was eventually struck in Tokyo under Japanese leadership. In both cases, the rescue was a collective one. And in both the IMF was given the thankless task of pulling political chestnuts out of the economic fire—notably for the corrupt Suharto regime in Indonesia and the *chaebol*-dominated system in South Korea.

Why the Warnings were Ignored

Why were the warning signs ignored both in Mexico and in East Asia? Western comment tended to put the blame on the Mexican and then the Thai and other Asian governments. Certainly the Bangkok government waited too long before acting and mismanaged the floating of the baht in early July. But, as with the Mexican government in 1994, the money managers, focusing on dollar exchange rates, had wrongly dissuaded the Thai government from devaluing sooner. Also too little and too late in the Thai case was the collective action by regional central banks. Meeting in late July, their declaration of mutual support failed to impress the markets. So did individual market intervention on behalf of the baht and the rupiah. The big guns—Japan, China, the United States—were silent for too long, so much so that there were many Asians who firmly believed their troubles had been deliberately engineered by the Americans.

The result was that when finally, in August, the IMF had to be called in, the terms of the first $16 billion collective bailout were tough. The foreign debt would be rolled over with funds from the IMF itself, the Asian Development Bank and smaller contributions from Australia, Hong Kong, Malaysia, Singapore, South Korea and Indonesia, possibly backed up with a roll-over deal with Japanese banks. In Thailand, General Chavalit's government would have to stop putting public money into bad banks and the IMF would also try to force political reform on the corrupt administration and an electoral system based—like that of the United States or Japan—on bought votes.

Before the end of 1997, it had become clear that the size of the funds needed to prevent total economic collapse of these Asian currencies had been seriously underestimated. All told, something like $100 billion was going to be needed—possibly even more. And that might not be enough to stop a political backlash. Mahathir was not alone in pointing at Soros and the foreign speculators as the prime cause of Asian troubles. Thailand, so proud of its non-colonial past, would not take kindly to IMF interference in local politics. A weak government in South Korea was certain to hinder the IMF and the creditors in their effort to get political as well as economic reform. Meanwhile, there was the risk of fallout on the US strategy in the WTO of forcing on Asian governments an agreement on liberalizing markets in financial services. Their resistance would, in turn, widen the existing differences between Washington and Beijing.

As for the contagion question, the responses to the Mexican and Asian debt crises suggest that the fear of contagion spreading from debtors to the entire system certainly exists. Otherwise, why negotiate lavish collective rescue packages to prevent outright default? Sometimes, as with the Tequila effect in 1995, the risks of contagion proved exaggerated and the effects short-lived. The rescue packages do work as antidotes to the virus that could attack the global financial system. They do not necessarily cure the carrier of the virus—the indebted country. The IMF empire expands but the inhabitants do not necessarily like or benefit from its technocratic intervention in their affairs.

The 1990s have certainly seen a general trend towards orthodoxy and conformity with the policy prescriptions given by the IMF. The tightening hold of liberal economics on political and professional opinion all over the world was surely one of the underlying changes marking that decade from the one before. The wisdom of the IMF's deflationary recipe, developed in the 1970s and early 1980s for Latin America, came under question only from economists like Sachs and Paul Krugman towards the end of 1997. India's experience with the IMF, for example, was typical of the shift in economic orthodoxy. From the 1940s on, India had chosen the import-substitution strategy for development, reinforced by protection of the domestic market and discouragement of foreign investors likely to compete with Indian firms in the domestic market. This strategy was turned around rather sharply in the early 1990s when an unforeseen balance of payments crisis threw it on the mercy of the IMF. But, in face of the weak political system and the size of the country, the IMF could only nag. Six years later, the Indian government was still being scolded and lectured by the IMF. Executive Director Camdessus told newspapers in March 1997 that 'further fiscal consolidation'—in other words, higher taxes—was needed to lower the public sector deficit, that more state enterprises should be privatized and more trade liberalized.[27] But who is to say

---

[27] IMF press summary, 6 March 1997.

104

whether, if all this had been done, the predicament of India would have been significantly better? It may even have been worse. The slow pace of 'reform'—that is, liberalization—meant that foreign funds did not rate India highly as an emerging market. Little came in, so there was little to flood out, as happened in Malaysia and the other East Asian cases.

The Taiwanese Exception

The other notable escape from Asian contagion was Taiwan. True, its reserves of foreign exchange were second only to China's in size. But that is hardly a sufficient explanation, for Hong Kong too had large reserves but did not escape the contagion. Its savings rates were high—but lower than Korea's—and not that much higher than in other Asian societies. But on top of these factors, Taiwan was an exporter of capital—mainly to China—yet it restricted capital inflows. It had also suffered a stock market crash in the early 1990s, so that there was no 'bubble' in share prices such as that in Thailand or Indonesia.

China also escaped the contagion. Not only did it still have exchange controls so that its currency was not fully convertible, but it had a big trade surplus and massive reserves, of over $100 billion. It had avoided dependence on short-term foreign borrowing to finance a deficit. That had been the common factor in Indonesia, Malaysia, Thailand, the Philippines and South Korea.[28] Ten years before, in the late 1980s, all of them had had substantial surpluses, but in 1997 all were hit by currency markets. The only weak point in China's preventive armour was in the psychology of its traders. If the belief spread that a devaluation of the yuan, to maintain a competitive edge in export pricing, was a possibility, the traders could weaken confidence in the currency by delaying the repatriation of their earnings abroad and paying promptly for imports. Years ago, Italy, for instance, and Britain suffered from traders playing this 'leads and lags' game.

All the evidence briefly rehearsed here goes to underline the immense complexity of the phenomenon of international debt. Internal factors sometimes combine with external ones—and sometimes work the other way. It is evident that the lifeboats sent out to rescue the debtors are only an emergency service, not a permanent solution. And while the IMF's empire may be growing, it would be wise as an institution to beware the hubris of its own experts.

In this connection, it would be salutary to recall a 1996 IMF study comparing episodes of current account imbalances in three Asian countries (Korea, Malaysia and Thailand) with three Latin American ones (Chile, Colombia and Mexico) during both debt crisis periods. Its authors found that only three episodes out of ten resulted in a currency crisis with the outside world.[29] They concluded that this 'depends in large part on key microeconomic and structural features of the economy—in particular the level of savings and investment, the degree of openness, the level and

---

[28] Korea's trade deficit in 1997 was the highest at $19 billion, Thailand's next at $10 billion, followed by Indonesia at $8 billion.
[29] *IMF Survey*, 24 March 1997.

flexibility of the exchange rate and the health of the financial system'.[30] Predictably, the study emphasized the shortcomings of national financial systems and economies rather than any shortcomings or weaknesses in the international system. IMF researchers evidently are not encouraged to bite the hands that feed them.

What to do with the Poorest Debtors?

Generalization about transnational indebtedness in the 1980s, moreover, has often obscured important differences in the experience of specific countries.[31] It is even less defensible in the late 1990s, especially when it comes to generalizing about the poorest debtors as compared with the rest. These go by the acronym of HIPCs (highly indebted poor countries), or SILICs (severely indebted low-income countries), as distinguished from SIMICs (severely indebted middle-income countries). For African HIPCs, the cost of servicing debts to the multilateral organisations that are their main creditors is now greater than what they have to spend on health, education and basic nutrition.[32] It is now generally acknowledged by economists that the 'debt trap' for these poorest of debtors has been getting deeper; that it will continue to get worse if nothing more is done; and that this is in part because of their treatment by the multilateral organisations who are their chief creditors.[33] Yet despite much publicity, efforts to find a solution have so far got nowhere. At best, the proposals put forward by the IMF and the World Bank can be described as tinkering with the problem.[34]

The facts are that transnational debt owed by HIPCs to multilateral organisations has grown faster since the first debt crisis than any other type of debt. It was $98 billion in 1982. By 1992, it was $304 billion. The cost of servicing this debt was $7 billion in 1980. By 1992, it was $36 billion. While the creditor states—led by the US Secretary of the Treasury—managed to agree on the Brady initiative to allow SIMICs to reschedule their foreign debt, agreement on a comparable way out of the vicious circle of poor country debt has been possible only in principle. A joint IMF/World Bank initiative launched in 1996 by the World Bank's president, Wolfensohn, and given lavish publicity by both sponsors, apparently encountered three insuperable difficulties when it came to

[30] G. Milesi-Ferretti and A. Razin, *Current Account Sustainability: Selected East Asian and Latin American Experiences*, IMF Working Paper 96/110, Washington, DC 1997.

[31] J. Stopford and S. Strange, *Rival States, Rival Firms*, Cambridge 1991, pp. 45-7.

[32] Oxfam, *Multilateral Debt: The Human Costs*, Oxford 1996.

[33] International Monetary Fund, *International Capital Markets: Developments, Prospects, and Key Policy Issues*, Washington, DC 1996; T. Killick, *IMF Programmes in Developing Countries: Design and Impact*, London 1995; P. Mistry, *Resolving Africa's Multilateral Debt Problem: A Response to the IMF*, The Hague 1996.

[34] The phrase 'debt trap' was first coined by Cheryl Payer, a radical American critic who wrote a rather hysterical book with that name in the mid-1970s (C. Payer, *The Debt Trap: The IMF and the Third World*, New York 1974). Payer argued fervently that 'The IMF has been the chosen instrument for imposing imperialist financial discipline upon poor countries under a facade of multilateralism and technical competence.' Substitute 'system-preserving' for 'imperialist' and the charge is more sustainable. See also D. Delamaide, *Debt Shock*, London 1984; and for the argument that the IMF was partly to blame, see S. George, *A Fate Worse Than Debt: A Radical New Analysis of the Third World Debt Crisis*, London 1988.

translating principles into a practical scheme of debt relief. The first difficulty was definitional—how to define a 'poor' (therefore eligible) HIPC,
and how much short of 100 per cent to wipe out. The second was distributional—how was the burden of 'forgiveness' to be shared out? Thirdly,
how should it be financed? None of these questions was technical; all
were political. True, some unilateral arrangements to wipe out debts of
poor African and Caribbean states had already been taken by the British
and French governments on their own account. Getting agreement
among a collective of creditors was bound to prove much more difficult.

To make the escape sustainable, the economists calculated, it was not
enough to wipe out the agreed 67 per cent of the total. It had to be 80 per
cent or the cost of servicing the remaining 20 per cent would continue to
overburden export earning and capital inflow (if any), so that growth
would be halted. Growth in these HIPCs had already slowed from an average 2 per cent per year over 1985–90 to an average 1 per cent over
1990–95. The World Bank argued that if the agreed enhanced Toronto
terms for the relief of HIPC debt were implemented, incentives for foreign investment would improve, raising the chance of exporting to
world markets and, with it, people's living standards.

Fear of Forgiveness

But—as already pointed out—implementation meant political agreement on the definitional, tactical and distributional issues. British and
French governments had their favourite candidates—Ivory Coast for
France, Uganda for Britain. The Ivory Coast had comparatively strong
exports, in relation to its debt, but its government revenues were low
and the economy small. According to the Bank and the IMF, however, it
did not qualify. By comparison, Uganda's export earnings—mainly from
coffee—were substantial, yet vulnerable to price falls in the volatile
world market. So the British wanted the escape route opened for Uganda
earlier than the Bank and IMF had suggested. France objected.

The obvious fact is that every one of the twenty-one SILICs on the Toronto
list can be included or excluded on one ground or another. And at least
the same number could find reasons for being added to the list, many on
the grounds that the fiscal burden of the debt on state revenues is unsup-
portable. If they were to be added, however, this would put up the cost of
the whole scheme to the Bank and IMF to the point where the IMF would
think it necessary to part with some of its gold reserves. This is bitterly
opposed by Germany, supported by Japan and Italy.[35] Indeed, almost all
the G10 governments share an unspoken fear that if the debts of the
HIPCs were cancelled, it would be increasingly difficult to resist requests
for similar treatment by other poor countries for whom debt servicing
was a perpetual handicap in achieving higher economic growth.

There is the further fear—perhaps not even articulated—that forgiving
debt is no guarantee that the problem of unsustainable debt is not going
to be repeated. The nineteenth century was full of examples of debtors
being rescued, only to need a second or third rescue in a few years' time.

---

[35] 'Not Much Sign of Relief, *The Financial Times*, 16 April 1997.

Portugal before the fall of the monarchy in 1911 was a prime case; the reason for the repeated rescues was political not economic—its special relationship to Britain, rather like Mexico's special relationship with the United States almost a century later. While it is neither very costly for France or Britain unilaterally to cancel loans to their respective African ex-colonies, a multilateral plan for doing the same thing to a whole group of countries opens a Pandora's box that the G10 governments would really rather keep tight shut. Hence the disagreements serve a deeper but unspoken purpose.

However, according to Percy Mistry, himself a former World Bank official, these disagreements not only delay the whole project, making the debt trap ever harder to escape, but the trap itself is of the creditors' own making. That is to say, the Bank and the Fund actually created a debt trap even worse than the one they purported to remedy. What happened was that the multilateral organisations in the after-math of the debt crises of the 1980s lent debtor governments new money to pay off or reschedule private or bilateral debts. But the terms on which this money was lent were much harsher and the sanctions against non-payment much stricter than for the debts they took over. Then, between 1986 and 1988, the IMF started withdrawing funds from debtor countries, exacerbating the effect of commercial with-drawals. Similarly, the World Bank started taking more money from the debtors than it lent them for new or old projects. As with money-lenders of old, the unpaid interest, added to the capital, actually increased the amount of debt.

> The pyramiding of multilateral debt has hurt not just the develop-ing countries. Its reciprocal but less visible effect has been to erode and compromise the financial strength and asset portfolio quality of key multilateral institutions which are central pillars of the official international financial system.[36]

The reason why he says this is that both institutions are constitutionally accountable to their members, who are guarantors of their solvency—the World Bank through the capital markets from which it has to borrow the money it lends, the Fund through the collective guarantee of the avail-ability of drawing rights (special and original) to its members. Together, the Fund and Bank have been jointly backed up with whatever funds may be available through the New Arrangement to Borrow, the nearest thing that the international financial system has to a lender of last resort in case one may be needed at any time in the future. But the whole point of the role of lender of last resort is that a national central bank can refuse its help, enforce very tough terms for it or even sack the managers and bring about bankruptcy and closure. Until the Asian crises in 1997, the IMF had not dared to play the role in full. When a state is indebted, the Fund cannot and will not go as far as bankrupting the country. With banks, the IMF is not experienced enough to take on the role everywhere. The role is difficult enough at all times, since each decision to support or to allow a bank to go under is circumstantial rather than subject to ratio-nal or preordained principles or guidelines. When it is compounded by

---

[36] P. Mistry, *Multilateral Debt: An Emerging Crisis*, The Hague 1994, p. 15.

political partialities reflected in basically political conflicts over the choice of different technical criteria, the prospects for progress look poor indeed.

On another occasion, Mistry suggested that thinking about reform of the Bretton Woods organisations—of which there has in the 1990s been a great deal—tends to start from the wrong end.[37] It is based, he said, on a stale view of the institutional framework inherited from the past rather than starting from the pragmatic question of what to do about HIPCs—in particular, about the multilateral indebtedness of the African states, which make up the largest number.[38] These remarks were made in response to a much-discussed paper by the eminent Princeton economist Peter Kenen, commissioned by the independent Dutch Forum on Debt and Development (Fondad), on international monetary reform and the developing countries. Both Mistry and the veteran Canadian development economist Gerald Helleiner criticised Kenen for being too cautious and conservative in his approach; both thought that 'tinkering' with the multilateral organisations was not enough and that the excuse that there was no interest among politicians and officials was one no independent academic should accept. Helleiner commented in verse:

> The poor complain.
> They always do.
> But that's just idle chatter
> Our system brings rewards to all,
> at least to all that matter.

But this is just the point. The assumption is that Africa does not matter because no important economic interests are greatly affected. Who cares, it implies, if Liberia is in chronic turmoil, if Hutus and Tutsis are killing each other in tens of thousands? Who cares about Algerian massacres or if one-party governments and their autocratic rulers keep people in subjection and backwardness? Probably, in the short term, none of the rich or the powerful. In the longer term, however, perhaps they should be concerned, in their own long-term interest. Historically, the rich and powerful in all pre-revolutionary periods have been complacent and unmoved by the suffering of the poor. Remember Marie Antoinette's cynical 'Let the people eat cake!'. Remember the myopia of the ruling class in Tsarist Russia.

The difference is that, today, discontent leading to violence in Africa has repercussions outside the continent. Not only do aid workers, UN blue berets and foreigners trying to do business get caught in the crossfire and cannot always escape in time. Moreover, even before trouble states, African revolutionaries and malcontents do not stay at home. They emigrate, and tinkering with the IMF and the World Bank is not going to stop them.

---

[37] B. Fischer and H. Reisen, eds., *Financial Opening: Policy Issues and Experiences in Developing Countries*, Paris 1993; J. Williamson, *The Failure of World Monetary Reform, 1971–74*, Sunbury-on-Thames 1977.
[38] Mistry, *Multilateral Debt*, p. 48.

Failure of the African Development Bank

Mistry's suggested solution was a devolution of responsibility from the
IMF and the World Bank to the regional development banks, the African
Development Bank, the Asian Development Bank, the Inter-American
Development Bank, and the EBRD.[39] This, he thought, might make
sense at a time when everywhere governments were busy building
regional associations with their neighbours for preferential trade and
other reasons. Neighbours, moreover, were more likely to understand
and make allowances for cultural and social factors, and to empathize
with the needs of very poor countries for the infrastructural investment
in health and education, and in transport and communications, without
which private capital was unlikely to play a part in long-term economic
growth.

Perhaps these considerations led him to write a detailed and informed
study of these institutions.[40] Although it is clear that he would like the
regional development banks to open up an escape route for HIPCs in
Africa and elsewhere, his honest account of their evolution is not
encouraging. It shows how the African Development Bank, since its
establishment in 1965, has staggered from one self-serving expedient to
another without ever either achieving long-term viability for itself or
contributing anything substantially to the prospects for African people.
Since 1983, its administrative costs—what the bank spends on its
staff—have doubled. By the mid-1990s, the staff was about twice as
large as it needed to be. It had allowed governments to get into a mire of
arrears in their contributions. Its poor financial structure exposed it to
serious currency risk—by borrowing funds denominated in dollars or
yen, for example. And the response to that is to engage in sophisticated
dealing in derivatives, which serves only to obscure, not to solve, its real
problems.

The administration of the African Development Bank, in short, is no
better than that of the Fund or the World Bank. In both, as Mistry has
pointed out, over the years there has been a shift of decision-making
power from the executive directors appointed by governments to the
senior officials of the organisation. He notes correctly that this has been
achieved by the 'mushroom theory of management', that is, a strategy of
keeping the Executive Board in the dark and burying them in horse
manure—actually, loads of mostly useless documentation. He argues
that there are in fact a wide range of options and possible solutions but
that their consideration by governments is hampered by the resistance of
the bureaucracies. These bureaucrats need, he concludes, to become 'less
defensive, less complacent, more open-minded and more concerned
about finding a way out of the present situation with its attendant dangers—and less prone to tediously repeating self-serving justifications
and rationalisations'.[41] Mistry may be right about what should be done.
But the record he gives of what has been done—or left undone—either

---

[39] Ibid., and Mistry, *Resolving Africa's Multilateral Debt Problem*.
[40] P. Mistry, *Multilateral Development Banks: An Assessment of their Financial Structures,
Policies and Practices*, The Hague 1995.
[41] Mistry, *Resolving Africa's Multilateral Debt Problem*, p. 71.

in Washington or in the African Development Bank holds out precious little hope for positive change.

Central and Eastern Europe

If one of the big failures of the 1990s was the treatment of African debt, the other has surely been the treatment—or neglect—of the financial needs of post-socialist countries of East and Central Europe, including Russia. Already in the early 1980s, both Hungary and Poland had been involved as debtors with the international financial system. Central banker Fekete, visiting the Council on Foreign Relations in New York in the aftermath of the 1982 Mexican and Polish debt crises, had complained bitterly that the markets had unjustly punished Hungary for Poland's over-exuberant borrowing just as Brazil complained about being judged by Mexico's near default. Before the end of the decade and the fall of the Berlin Wall, both countries had nevertheless increased their involvement, commercial and financial, with the western market economy. Then, with the end of the Cold War, the shadow of Moscow and the Politburo over Central and Eastern Europe was gone. New opportunities beckoned to escape the stultifying hand of state economic planning and to take whatever help might be offered by the West.

The situation was not unlike that which existed after the end of World War II in Western Europe. Economies long subject to state controls and the demands of government for armaments were suddenly in sore need of help with a difficult transition. Their own resources were slender and would soon be exhausted. In June 1947, Secretary of State Marshall had thrown away the speech he had written for Harvard University's commencement celebrations and called instead for a new initiative to put Western Europe back on its economic feet with massive help from the United States. The Marshall Plan was born, welcomed in Britain, spurned by Moscow, and eventually passed through the US Congress as a necessary investment in keeping Europe—France and Italy especially—out of the hands of the communists.

That, of course, was the big difference. In 1990, there was no other superpower threatening to overrun eastern Europe if its 'post-war' transition stumbled. Otherwise, the experience of the European Recovery Program (ERP) between 1948 and 1952 was a classic demonstration of Keynesian logic and the effectiveness of a large programme of foreign aid in boosting confidence and setting in motion the processes of economic reform. The Marshall Plan gave $13 billion in credit to Western Europe, asking no repayment in dollars but only the agreed investment of counterpart funds in local currency. Other key features of the plan were that Western European governments had to agree among themselves as to who should get how much of this largesse—or no one got anything. Secondly, they were each monitored by an Economic Cooperation Agency mission which offered free help from American industrialists on improving productivity. These missions also used their political leverage to force governments to liberalize trade relations with their neighbours and to privatize them by taking trade away from state officials and returning it to private enterprises. Most revolutionary of all the provisions of the Plan was the licence given to Western Europe to save its scarce dollars for essentials by keeping controls over foreign exchange and by allowing the Europeans—contrary to liberal most favoured nation principles enshrined in the GATT—to discriminate in trade against tobacco and other commodities and manufactures exported from the United States. Revisionist historians have since argued that European economic recovery by the time Marshall spoke at Harvard was going well and that US aid was not needed.[42] They conveniently forget that, by then, Europe's reserves of hard currency were running desperately short and that, without US credits, there would have been severe shortages of food and raw materials, not to mention the capital goods to re-equip industry and the economic infrastructure that only North America could still supply

Why then, with such a detailed political and economic blueprint on how to manage a post-war economic reconstruction so readily at hand, did the western governments in 1990 not simply look back at the historical record and do for Eastern Europe what the United States had done forty years before for Western Europe? Here, surely, was a golden opportunity to prime the pump in a group of economies well endowed with an educated, skilled workforce, with leaders and people desperately keen to 'come home' and to become accepted in a community of European states that was building a single common market for anything they could produce. For it was not only post-war Europe which had benefited from the Marshall Plan. As left-wing critics later pointed out, the United States also gained.[43] Where Henry Wallace had predicted and feared a post-war recession in America, it never happened. The ERP had opened up new business for US firms in Europe, both as exporters and as foreign investors in offshore production.

But instead of a Marshall Plan for Eastern Europe, the ex-socialist countries were given the EBRD, a pathetically small, self-serving regional development bank with its potentially helping hands tied tight behind its back. Instead of the 1990s equivalent of the $13 billion 1940s dollars—probably about $130 billion—the EBRD ended up merely with some $3.4 billion to lend or guarantee, or 30 per cent of its agreed capital base of $11.5 billion. Peanuts indeed. Instead of a flexible system of counterpart funds that could be used for public infrastructure like roads, bridges and ports, or to finance industrial re-equipment of municipal housing, the EBRD was bound, under orders from the United States, to dedicate 60 per cent of its loans to the private sector, leaving only 40 per cent for publicly funded infrastructure. Here was a development bank pretending that what was needed was a profit-making merchant bank.

The Missing Marshall Plan

Why the missed chance for an initiative? It would have not only accelerated the transition for the ex-socialist countries but would also have given a kick-start to Western Europe's sluggish slow-growth economy by providing it with eager new consumers with purchasing power—just as the ERP had done for American industry in the post-war years. It was

---

[42] A.S. Milward, *The Reconstruction of Western Europe, 1945-51*, London 1984.
[43] F. Block, *The Origins of International Economic Disorder*, Berkeley 1977.

not because no one thought it a good idea. Max Kohnstam, an early founder of the EEC, several economists and economic commentators made the suggestion. A conference of East and West academics and journalists in Florence in February 1990 endorsed it. Why then was the chance missed?

Everyone shares the blame. Germany, whose economy stood most to gain from it, was self-absorbed in the problems and dilemmas of German unification; its short-sighted politicians showed little interest in helping their eastern and southern neighbours. The United States, led by President Bush, put up only 10 per cent of the money but adamantly insisted on the 60-40 rule. The British, who had benefited so much from Marshall aid and should have known better, went tamely along with the Americans and were determined only that the EBRD be set up in London. Mitterrand, for France, insisted that if that was to be so, the head of the bank must be French—and then appointed Jacques Attali, whose ignorance of development economics was equalled only by his administrative extravagance. The 'glistening bank' became a byword for wanton luxury and mismanagement. By the end of 1993, it had lent or guaranteed only $2 billion and concentrated its energies on getting income for itself by investing more than this in the markets—profits soon eaten up by its soaring administrative costs—and by charging fat front-end and wind-up fees to its debtors.

Conclusion

To sum up this long survey, unlike the 1980s, there was no general 'debt crisis' in the 1990s.[44] There were various kinds of debtors, each with rather different problems and prospects. There were the Mexicans, the other Latin Americans and there were the East Asians. There were also the HIPCs in Africa and the ex-socialist countries of Central and Eastern Europe, whose problems were not so much that they had debts that they could not repay as that they had not been given the right sort of credit in sufficient amounts for their needs.

For all of these debtors, and for many would-be debtors, the system seemed even further away from finding a long-term solution than it had been a decade earlier. In a market economy you could not stop—did not want to stop—the use of credit, the right to borrow. But when almost all the market economies were open to the world economy, and the system allowed debts to be incurred in any currency, private debts were easily translated into public ones. The collapse of share prices for private debtors became the collapse of the national currency, for which the government was responsible. The very size of the rescues necessary in 1998 compared with the 1980s showed how the problem had escalated. And meanwhile disagreement was growing about the two big questions.

---

[44] If could be argued that, even in the 1980s, 'the debt crisis' was an over-simplification. There were debtors who had borrowed heavily, like South Korea, but whose chief creditor had saved them from the clutches of the IMF or the Paris Club. There were debtors who had borrowed, but with moderation and prudence, like Malaysia whose export earnings coming from commodities and manufacturers gave confidence to foreign investors, who kept up an inflow of capital from abroad. And there were others like India, whose debts in relation to their current balances had not yet become a problem.

Who is to blame? What is to be done? On the one hand, the IMF, backed
by conservative economists, was still insisting, 'Take the IMF medicine
and you will soon mend'.[45] On the other, a growing number of economists, many from leading business schools, was protesting that the IMF
was fighting yesterday's war, that deflation was the major risk and that
either one big shock or a series of smaller shocks were very likely to end
in a world depression. In short, not only were the prime causes contested,
there was deep dispute over the gravity of the debt problems and the
optimum response to them.

---

[45] The title of an upbeat article by Michael Mussa and Graham Hacche, the IMF's Chief
Economist and its Assistant Director of Economic Studies, respectively (*International
Herald Tribune*, 17–18 January 1998). Paul Krugman, Lester Thurow and others pro-
foundly disagreed (ibid.). Thurow likened the situation to the risk of earthquakes on
California's San Andreas geological fault line; there was no doubt that catastrophe would
strike. The only question was when—and where.

[15]

Maintaining Financial Stability in a Global Economy: A Summary of the Bank's 1997 Symposium

By Charles Morris and Klara Parrish

World financial markets have experienced tremendous growth in recent years. New financial instruments have been developed, the volume of transactions within individual markets has skyrocketed, and capital flows across countries have risen dramatically. While these developments have made financial markets more efficient, they have also increased the risk that events at one institution or in one market will have immediate and wide-ranging effects on the entire global financial system. In developing policies to respond to these changes, policymakers must balance the need for financial stability with the desire for an innovative and efficient financial system.

To better understand how to design policies to keep a financial system safe, efficient, and stable, and how to respond to financial crises when they occur, the Federal Reserve Bank of Kansas City sponsored a symposium entitled "Maintaining Financial Stability in a Global Economy." The symposium, held at Jackson Hole, Wyoming on August 28-30, 1997, brought

Charles Morris is a vice president and economist at the Federal Reserve Bank of Kansas City. Klara Parrish is a research associate at the bank.

together a distinguished group of central bankers, academics, and financial market representatives from around the world.

The participants generally agreed that, to maintain financial stability, regulation of financial institutions is important and that financial regulators should focus on making regulation more consistent with market forces. In addition, financial stability requires a sound macroeconomic environment—particularly price stability and, for most countries, an exchange rate regime that does not attempt to permanently fix exchange rates. Finally, participants agreed that both domestic and international safety nets should be used cautiously in financial crises to avoid the destabilizing effects of moral hazard.

I. WHY DOES FINANCIAL INSTABILITY MATTER?

Symposium participants agreed that policymakers care about financial instability because a financial sector crisis often causes a severe reduction in real economic activity. Recent examples include banking crises in Scandinavia and Japan, the 1995 peso crisis in Mexico, and the current exchange rate and banking problems in the emerging market economies of Southeast Asia. While there is little doubt that financial instability can harm an economy, there is less agreement about how a financial crisis is defined and under what circumstances governments or other official bodies should intervene.

How is instability defined?

In defining financial instability, Andrew Crockett distinguished between instability in institutions and in markets. According to Crockett, institutional instability exists when the failure of one or a few institutions spreads and causes more widespread economic damage. In fact, as Alan Greenspan noted in his opening comments, occasional failures are an important and normal part of the market process because they promote market discipline, provided of course that the failures do not lead to more systemic consequences. Historically, policymakers have focused on commercial banks because their failure can have systemic consequences. Crockett argued that while banks are still "special" in this regard, policymakers also need to be more watchful for problems at nonbank financial institutions because the distinctions among financial institutions have become blurred.

Crockett defined market instability in terms of the wider impact that volatility in asset prices and flows can have on the economy. By this definition, large changes in asset prices themselves do not necessarily indicate financial instability because they may reflect fundamental changes in the economy, such as changes in expected income flows or in discount factors. Indeed, markets work only if prices are allowed to respond to changes in demand and supply conditions. The difficulty for policymakers, Crockett pointed out, lies in identifying whether a given change in prices is justified by changes in fundamentals.

When is intervention appropriate?

Crockett noted that even though financial stability in terms of institutions and markets is important, government intervention to help maintain stability may not be appropriate. In general, government intervention is appropriate if there are market failures or externalities. Crockett argued that in the case of financial institutions—particularly banks—there are external costs and systemic problems associated with runs on individual institutions and the potential contagion effects. As a result, economists generally agree that official intervention is necessary to maintain the stability of financial institutions.

In contrast, Crockett argued that there is general agreement that official intervention should rarely be used to maintain stability in asset prices and flows because there are few market failures or externalities. As a result, the free market generally leads to prices that reflect economic fundamentals. In addition, he maintained that even when prices seem to deviate from fundamentals, it is difficult to "say with confidence that the prices are indeed wrong." He also noted, however, that government has a role in promoting policies that limit market imperfections, such as policies that promote disclosure and reduce information asymmetries.

In commenting on Crockett's paper, Stanley Fischer discussed how the International Monetary Fund promotes information disclosure in international markets. First, the IMF staff prepares comprehensive analytical and descriptive reports on economic developments in its member countries for its Executive Board and for all member governments. Second, the IMF produces regular statistical publications. Third, since the 1995 Mexican peso crisis, the IMF has posted market-relevant data on the Internet through its Special Data Dissemination Standard and its associated Dissemination Standards Bulletin Board.

II. THE CAUSES AND PROPAGATION OF FINANCIAL INSTABILITY

The first step in developing policies to maintain financial stability is to determine what causes financial instability. Frederic Mishkin provided a conceptual framework for the causes and the propagation of instability, focusing on the different effects economic shocks have on both emerging market economies and industrialized countries. Morris Goldstein then discussed an empirical early warning model of financial crises, after which officials from countries that have gone through financial crises described their countries' experiences.

Conceptual framework

According to Mishkin, a key feature of financial markets that can lead to instability is asymmetric information among market participants. Asymmetric information exists because parties on either side of a transaction have different information and choose to disclose only what suits their strategy best. An important problem caused by asymmetric information is moral hazard. Moral hazard refers to the tendency for individuals to take on extra risks when they do not bear the full cost of their activities. For example, banks may make excessively risky loans if they believe a lender of last resort will bail them out if they are about to fail.

Mishkin identified four types of shocks that can destabilize the financial system by worsening asymmetric information: exogenous increases in real interest rates, increases in uncertainty, asset market effects on balance sheets, and problems in the banking sector. While all four types of shocks can lead to financial instability, Mishkin made a distinction between how the instability propagates in emerging market economies and in industrialized countries. The

difference, he noted, may not always be clear cut, but some general distinctions can be made.

In emerging market countries, Mishkin argued that a key factor in the propagation of instability is the country's inflation history. Emerging market countries often have a record of high and variable inflation, making long-term debt contracts risky. As a result, a large share of government and private debt in emerging market countries tends to be of short duration and denominated in the currency of a foreign country with a record of relatively low and stable inflation. Suppose an economic shock causes a large depreciation of the currency. In this case, the domestic currency value of interest payments on debt owed in foreign currency will rise sharply. In addition, if the devaluation causes expected inflation to rise, domestic interest rates will rise, which will lead to higher interest payments on short-term debt when it is rolled over. The sudden increase in interest payments makes it more difficult for households and firms to service their debt, leading to a deterioration of loan quality and bank portfolios. Furthermore, banks may become illiquid due to the short-term nature of their liabilities and the long-term nature of their assets. Thus, what started as an exchange rate crisis turns into a banking crisis. In addition, it is difficult for a central bank to defend the currency by raising interest rates because doing so causes bank costs to rise, further weakening the banking system.

The propagation of instability in industrialized countries, Mishkin argued, generally follows a different path. Because industrialized countries typically have a history of relatively stable prices, debt contracts are usually of long duration and denominated in domestic currency. Under these circumstances, a negative shock does not propagate instability through a depreciation of the currency. The shock, however, still causes a decline in economic activity, which diminishes cash flows. As a result, households and firms have difficulty in paying back their debt, asset values diminish, and banks incur losses just as in emerging market countries. Additional problems arise if the decline of the economy substantially changes the expected path of inflation. The problems arise because the interest rates on long-term debt reflect inflation expectations that turn out to be substantially wrong. If inflation is lower than expected, real interest rates turn out to be higher than anticipated, which raises the real debt burden of firms. This "debt deflation" hinders the recovery process and further propagates instability.[1] In addition, the sharp decrease in net worth can increase moral hazard because it gives firms an incentive to hide information and to engage in risky transactions in order to boost their value.

After Mishkin's theoretical discussion, Morris Goldstein presented an empirical model of leading indicators of financial crises. Differentiating between banking and currency crises in 25 emerging market economies and small industrialized countries, Goldstein concluded that there are four leading indicators common to both types of crises and two indicators specific to each type of crisis. The four indicators useful in predicting both types of crises are a real exchange rate appreciation, a stock market decline, a recession, and a decline in exports. Additional indicators for banking crises are a rise in the money multiplier and the real interest rate. For currency crises, the additional indicators are the presence of a banking crisis and a rising ratio of broad money balances to international reserves.

Recent financial crises

Using Japan's recent experience, Yoshio Suzuki showed how declining asset values can lead to a financial crisis in industrialized countries. In the late 1980s, interest rates in Japan

were kept artificially low to support the U.S. dollar. This resulted in asset price bubbles and an abundance of new loans in the highly protected banking sector. When the asset price bubble burst, collateral values fell and balance sheets deteriorated, which led to large losses at banks and a full-scale banking crisis. The problem was exacerbated by an increase in deposit insurance fees and by government intervention to protect depositors of failed banks at the cost of the efficient financial institutions. Suzuki argued that Japan should change its policies in two ways to solve its financial problems. The first change, which the government has largely adopted, is to remove some of the financial regulations so that Japanese financial institutions are on a more equal footing with their competitors in other countries. Second, the government should promptly resolve the bad loan problem, making sure that the safety net is adequately funded to deal with any fallout from deregulation and from the resolution of the banking system's problem loans.

Urban Bäckström of Sweden discussed how his country dealt with its banking crisis in the early 1990s. Realizing that restoring the banking system's liquidity was the key to avoiding further propagation of the crisis and to restoring financial stability, the government and opposition jointly announced a general guarantee for the whole banking system. This broad political consensus facilitated the prompt handling of problems and made the guarantee more credible. In order to limit moral hazard, tough negotiations were held with the banks that needed support and shareholders were forced to absorb losses before any other group of creditors. In addition, an independent Swedish Bank Support Authority was created to administer the bank guarantee and to manage problem banks. This new banking authority valued the assets of the banks that applied for the guarantee, divided them into categories according to the severity of their problems, *fully* disclosed expected loan losses and asset values to the public, and managed the problem banks. Thanks to the prompt and transparent handling of the banking crisis, confidence was reestablished. Thus, debt deflation, further propagation of the instability, and a collapse of the whole economy were avoided.

Pedro Pou gave insight into moral hazard issues and their consequences by describing Argentina's experience with the propagation of instability in the 1982 banking crisis and the 1989-90 hyperinflation. In 1982, Argentina experienced a banking crisis, propagated to a large extent by moral hazard. The moral hazard stemmed from several aspects of the institutional setup of the banking system: full unlimited deposit insurance, free entry into the market, and weak supervision. With this institutional setup, banks had no incentive to limit the riskiness of their activities, resulting in many bank failures. The subsequent bailout of banks by the government resulted in a large increase in the public debt, which was financed through the banks. In the following years, the debt caused persistent fiscal problems, and its monetization was a key factor in the 1989-90 hyperinflation. Since the banks' main assets were government debt, the solvency of the banking system was soon questioned, and a run on government debt caused the financial system to collapse. Argentina responded to the crisis through extensive reforms. Market forces were reinforced by the deregulation and privatization of banks. In addition, the credibility of the monetary authority was enhanced by establishing a currency board that tied the Argentinean peso to the U.S. dollar on a one-to-one basis. The currency board arrangement essentially freed the central bank from having to finance government debt.

Barry Eichengreen discussed the financial crisis in Thailand, arguing that the Thai authorities made two critical mistakes.[2] First, they pegged the exchange rate within a narrow band, allowing it to become overvalued. The peg also encouraged domestic banks and firms to borrow funds in foreign currency without consideration of exchange rate risks. Second, management of the financial system was lax. When combined with large capital inflows, the lax management led to excessive lending and ultimately to a significant amount of bad loans. The Thai baht came under pressure, and when it was finally allowed to float, the sharp depreciation of the currency weakened already fragile balance sheets even further. Eichengreen's description of the causes and propagation of the Thai crisis closely paralleled Mishkin's description of a typical financial crisis in an emerging market economy.

In the luncheon address, Václav Klaus reported on the Czech Republic's transition to a market economy, its struggle to achieve an external equilibrium, and its recent exchange rate problems. According to Klaus, the flood of imports that followed the unprotected opening of the economy led to a current account deficit. Much of the inflow of foreign capital under the fixed exchange rate was not used to finance "productive" investment. Klaus argued that productive investment would have increased international competitiveness and eased the pressures on the current account. Moreover, the banking system was fragile due to bank portfolios of questionable quality and inadequate transparency and disclosure procedures. In addition, regulators in the new environment could not catch up with the fast growth of the financial system. As problems became apparent, the currency came under attack, forcing an unintended depreciation. Ultimately, policymakers decided to let the currency float. Thus, the Czech instability was partly due to a dependence on foreign funds, an immature regulatory and law enforcement infrastructure, and a weak banking system.

III. INTERNATIONAL RESPONSES TO CRISES

For many years, the International Monetary Fund and high-income countries have provided aid to countries experiencing financial crises. Symposium participants generally agreed this practice would have to continue. But with the globalization of financial markets and the increased speed with which problems can spread from one country to another, participants also agreed that the support mechanisms have to change. In addition, to minimize the moral hazard problems associated with safety nets, support should be offered on a case-by-case basis and not be automatic.

In a paper written with Richard Portes, Barry Eichengreen argued that changes in the foreign debt of emerging market countries have made it necessary to change the international mechanism used to provide financial support to countries in financial crisis. A key difference between recent emerging market crises and earlier crises is the way countries have obtained international financing. In the 1980s, banks were the primary international financiers of emerging-market sovereign debt. While the lending groups generally consisted of several hundred banks, the lending was typically concentrated in a handful of the world's largest banks. Given this lending structure, it was fairly easy for the banks to form an advisory committee to reschedule the debt if a default seemed imminent. In addition, because banks had a strong incentive to refinance to prevent large losses, the IMF could wait with adjustment loans until most of the commercial banks had arranged new financing and restructured their debt.

During the 1995 Mexican crisis, it became apparent that the source of international financing had shifted from a few hundred banks to thousands of investors holding government-issued bonds. This shift from bank loan to bond financing has two major implications for the way in which the international community must respond to financial crises in emerging markets. First, international officials must be able to respond faster because the shift in financing has increased the speed at which a crisis might develop. The speed has increased because investors holding securities can liquidate their holdings and will do so when they see others selling. As a result, when a country's securitized debt is large and investors decide to run, the government has no choice but to suspend payments. The second implication is that the IMF can no longer wait for countries to restructure their debt or to arrange for alternative private financing before providing adjustment loans. The IMF cannot wait, not only because the Fund must respond faster, but also because restructuring debt or arranging new financing is more difficult and takes longer. Bonded debt is difficult to restructure because it is virtually impossible to achieve the required unanimous consent of the thousands of small bondholders, many of whom are hard to find due to secondary markets. Moreover, the difficulty in restructuring is aggravated since small creditors have an incentive to hold out in the hope that a larger creditor will buy them out at full value. Finally, this climate of uncertainty causes potential lenders of additional liquidity to hold back, making it difficult for the country to fund even productive domestic investments.

Eichengreen described how the international community responded to the need for it to change the way it supports emerging market countries in crisis. At the 1995 Halifax summit, the Group of Seven governments recommended that the IMF develop a mechanism for providing faster access to IMF credit and larger amounts of money in crisis situations. In response, the IMF established an emergency-financing mechanism through which funds can be disbursed to countries in as little as three weeks, compared with the several months required under normal procedures. In addition, the IMF improved its surveillance of national policies and its data publication and dissemination.

At the Halifax summit, the Group of Seven governments also chartered a Group of Ten committee under the chairmanship of Jean-Jacques Rey to reassess the crisis response mechanisms. The Rey Committee found that substantial institutional changes, such as the creation of an international bankruptcy court, were not needed. However, they made several recommendations to improve the international community's ability to respond to financial crises. One set of suggestions was aimed at modifying loan contracts to facilitate the orderly restructuring of defaulted sovereign debt. In addition, the report made specific suggestions for providing countries in crisis faster access to IMF funds.

While Eichengreen and Portes applauded the changes to debt contracts proposed by the Rey Committee, they thought it unlikely that the markets would quickly incorporate the provisions into debt contracts. As a result, they argued, "Management of future crises, even more than crises past, will rest with the IMF." In commenting on the Eichengreen and Portes paper, Jeffrey Sachs voiced concern that giving the IMF so much power over countries in financial crisis without appropriate checks and balances and without a place to appeal decisions is an inappropriate and dangerous policy.

Did the new procedures work for Thailand? According to Eichengreen and Portes, there was no immediate danger of default on securitized public debt in Thailand, so the orderly workout procedures were not needed. The IMF's faster emergency-financing mechanism, however, was used to provide Thailand with $3.9 billion in standby credit over a 34-month period, of

which $1.6 billion was available immediately to support the government's economic program and to mitigate problems and contagion.[3]

There was some discussion about whether the intervention in Thailand was appropriate. Jeffrey Sachs claimed that the government had been warned about the overvaluation of its pegged currency but did not take corrective measures. International support under such circumstances, he implied, fails to teach a lesson and is not necessary. In addition, he questioned whether the devaluation that ultimately took place was a crisis, arguing that it was just a large decline in value over a short time period that created large losses for some market participants. Indeed, he noted, the percentage depreciation of the baht was about the same as that of many Western European currencies over the past year, but the European depreciations are not considered crises because they occurred more slowly.

Other participants disagreed with Sachs' views that Thailand was not experiencing a crisis and that an intervention was inappropriate. Mishkin argued that the Thai and Western European devaluations were fundamentally different because Thailand is an emerging market with large amounts of short-term debt denominated in dollars. In his view, Thailand's difficulties exemplified how a crisis can result from the combination of a weak banking system, short-term debt contracts denominated in foreign currency, and misaligned exchange rates. Stanley Fischer thought the intervention in Thailand was appropriate because, even though punishing the government might seem tempting, the international community is obliged to mitigate the consequences of sharp adjustments to help the people of the country in crisis and to avoid contagion to other countries.[4]

Finally, in his discussion of Argentina's problems during the 1995 Mexican peso crisis, Pedro

Pou had raised the issue of the international community providing a country in crisis with automatic access to liquidity. Pou argued that despite sound economic policy in Argentina, contagion from the Mexican crisis precipitated a run on the Argentinean currency. Because Argentina had a currency board, the currency run automatically caused a severe contraction in monetary policy. Pou argued that the contraction of monetary policy and the associated costs to the economy were unnecessary and could have been avoided if Argentina had automatic access to international liquidity. He suggested that the IMF was one possible lender of last resort, replacing the private international banks that currently provide liquidity to Argentina's central bank.

Most participants did not share Pou's view about an automated lending mechanism or an unconditional line of credit. Fischer and other participants argued that a lender of last resort should be used only in exceptional cases because any automatization would worsen moral hazard. The moral hazard problem was stressed by Jean-Jacques Rey, who argued that a central concern in responding to financial crises is to avoid moral hazard so that debtors and creditors do not underestimate the risks of their positions or transactions. Thus, while intervention is often ultimately necessary, conditionality of that intervention is also necessary to maintain the correct incentives.

IV. POLICIES FOR MAINTAINING FINANCIAL STABILITY

Design of policies for maintaining financial stability was the final topic of the symposium. In general, the discussions focused on regulatory policies for maintaining the stability of financial institutions and on how macroeconomic policy—particularly inflation and exchange rate policies—can contribute to maintaining overall financial stability.

Maintaining the stability of depository institutions

Consistent with Andrew Crockett's discussion of the need for regulation of financial institutions but not asset markets, Robert Litan discussed how the regulation of financial institutions should change to reduce the risk of financial crises. He argued that the regulation of banks and other depository institutions (hereafter collectively referred to as banks) should shift from what he called a *prevention-safety net* paradigm to a more market-oriented *competition-containment* paradigm. The prevention-safety net paradigm, which according to Litan has characterized U.S. bank regulation since the Great Depression, is a regulatory system that attempts to prevent individual banks from failing and, when banks do fail, relies on an extensive safety net to protect depositors from loss. The underlying idea is that if individual institutions do not fail or cause problems for individual depositors, problems at individual banks will not lead to a wider financial crisis.

Litan argued that the prevention-safety net paradigm began to break down in the 1980s, making it necessary to switch to a competition-containment paradigm to maintain the stability of depository institutions. Philosophically, this approach differs from the traditional approach in that policies focus less on protecting individual institutions and more on protecting the overall financial system. Under this approach, competition and market forces would play a more important role in limiting bank risk taking, while policies would be focused on containment—making sure that when problems at individual institutions do occur, they do not threaten the entire financial system. Litan emphasized that under this approach supervision would not be abandoned. To the contrary, he argued, in order for market forces to contain risk taking by individual institutions, supervision would be necessary to make sure the market had accurate and timely information about individual institutions. In addition, he noted that prevention would not be discarded but aimed at preventing systemic crises instead of preventing failures of individual institutions.

Litan listed three ways market forces could be used to provide individual institutions with incentives for avoiding excessive risks, while ensuring that the effects of failures do not spread to other institutions. First, he welcomed the steps already taken to allow large banks to use their own models for estimating risk. In particular, he liked the Federal Reserve Board's proposed "pre-commitment" approach, which allows banks to use internal models to specify the maximum losses they might accumulate over a specific time period and then pay a penalty if losses exceed that amount. Second, he argued there is a useful role for self regulation, such as the voluntary risk management guidelines recommended in a recent Group of Thirty report. Litan's third suggestion for harnessing market forces was to require certain banks to back a limited portion of their assets with uninsured, subordinated debt. The purchasers of subordinated debt could not run like depositors, but would have to wait until their debt instruments matured. Since these debt holders would only have downside risk, they would discourage risk taking by requiring riskier banks to pay a higher interest rate on their subordinated debt. Litan also proposed that regulators report overall bank exam ratings to the public to improve the information that debt holders have about banks.

On this last point, however, some participants disagreed, arguing that premature disclosure can sometimes be destabilizing. In the discussion, for example, Gerald Corrigan noted that if such a disclosure policy had been used in the late 1980s and early 1990s, it would have given a false signal to the market and probably would

have led to more serious problems than actually occurred. Earlier in the symposium, Stanley Fischer made a similar point in an international context, arguing that if the IMF discloses information that turns out to be a false signal, it could actually lead to the crisis the Fund is trying to prevent.

In addition to making better use of market forces, another key element of Litan's containment policy is to improve the safety of clearing and settlement systems by moving toward real time gross settlement (RTGS). Introducing real time settlement would lower the risk of one party having insufficient funds at settlement time. Litan noted that moving toward shorter settlement times is important not only for domestic interbank payments, but also for foreign exchange and securities transactions. There was widespread agreement among symposium participants that moving toward shorter settlement times in all markets would make an important contribution to financial stability.

In discussing Litan's paper, Randall Kroszner placed an even greater emphasis on the role of market forces in promoting the stability of global banking and financial markets. Kroszner thought the key lesson for policymakers is that government regulation should not be allowed to "crowd out" private regulation. He argued that the private sector, through innovations in organizational design and governance for financial institutions, has been an efficient regulator when a public regulator was not active. As an example of private strategic responses to concern over financial stability, Kroszner noted the historical importance of "members-only clubs" with high membership standards for institutions that wanted to deal in financial transactions. Examples of such "clubs" are the clearing systems used by the free-banking system in eighteenth and nineteenth century Scotland, the Suffolk System in New England in the early 1800s, and the clearinghouse associations of the Chicago Board of Trade and Chicago Mercantile Exchange. While the recent growth in international markets has occurred outside such clubs, the market has responded through the growth of independent rating agencies, covenants in financial contracts, and new organizational forms—such as special purposes vehicles—to isolate risks from the rest of the organization.

Although symposium participants viewed the trend toward a greater emphasis on market forces as moving in the correct direction, most thought that Kroszner's "laissez-faire" approach went too far and that some rules are necessary to make up for market inefficiencies. In the discussion, for example, Donald Brash said he favored greater use of market forces to increase efficiency and reduce risk, especially with the movement toward RTGS systems. Brash argued, however, that because there is a very strong public belief in most countries that depositors will be protected by some type of safety net, some public sector involvement in banking is necessary. He noted that even New Zealand, whose regulatory structure is "very light," has a lender of last resort, abides by the Basel minimum capital ratios, has limits on connected lending, and mandates bank disclosure.

Throughout the symposium, there was an obvious tension in many participants' minds between the benefits and costs of safety nets. Clearly, most felt that some form of a safety net is necessary so that policymakers can step in to stop a contagion problem when necessary. Andrew Crockett also noted that "any *ex ante* announcement by governments not to support the financial system lacks credibility" because it would be "very hard for elected authorities to refuse assistance to institutions whose depositors have powerful electoral influence." At the same time, participants were clearly uncomfortable with the moral hazard implications of

safety nets. Much of the discussion focused on how the moral hazard of safety nets could be reduced. With respect to deposit insurance, several participants noted that, unlike today's FDIC in the United States, deposit insurance must be set up to comprise sharing and appropriate pricing of risks. In his opening remarks, Alan Greenspan argued that central banks have necessarily become the lenders of last resort because of their unlimited power to create money. To reduce the moral hazard problem, however, Greenspan argued that central banks should use these powers only to provide what amounts to "catastrophic financial insurance" and that such public subsidies "should be reserved for only the rarest of disasters." Similarly, Crockett argued for a policy of *constructive ambiguity*—a term made popular by Gerald Corrigan. Constructive ambiguity is a policy in which central banks intervene to preserve financial stability without giving explicit or implicit assurances to individual institutions.

Macroeconomic policies for maintaining financial stability

While none of the symposium presentations focused on macroeconomic policies, several speakers discussed the importance of solid macroeconomic policies for maintaining financial stability. In particular, price stability was viewed as crucially important for financial stability. In addition, the consensus view was that while fixed exchange rates are useful for reducing inflation in some countries, keeping them fixed for too long can ultimately threaten financial stability.

Frederic Mishkin argued that price stability and financial stability are mutually reinforcing goals. In Mishkin's discussion of the propagation of crises in industrialized and emerging market countries, the differences between the two types of countries hinged on the behavior of inflation. As discussed earlier, nonfinancial firms and banks in countries with high and variable inflation tend to be vulnerable to economic shocks because their debt tends to be of short duration and denominated in foreign currencies. A low, steady rate of inflation, on the other hand, allows countries to avoid these problems because debt tends to be structured with longer durations and denominated in domestic currency. Mishkin also noted that highly variable inflation reduces the credibility of policymakers, making it more difficult for them to promote recovery from a financial crisis. For example, expansionary monetary policy or lender-of-last-resort actions are less effective for shoring up weakened balance sheets because they can lead to increases in expected inflation, which in turn, cause interest rates to rise and balance sheets to weaken further.

Mishkin also argued that price stability means not only that inflation is low, but also that price deflations are avoided. As was noted earlier in the discussion of financial crises in industrialized countries, when debt contracts tend to have a long duration with fixed interest rates, a large unanticipated decline in inflation can prolong a financial crisis by increasing the real burden of indebtedness.

Andrew Crockett took the point a step further by discussing the implications for regulatory structure. Crockett noted distinctions have been made in recent years between the government institutions responsible for maintaining price stability and the stability of the financial system. While those responsible for monetary and financial stability are distinct concepts, the close linkages between them imply collaboration among the institutions responsible for maintaining both. As a result, he concluded, those who desire to separate the functions need to think carefully about the costs of doing so.

In many cases, discussions about price stability could not be separated from discussions about exchange rate regimes. In particular, Mishkin noted that a common method used by smaller countries to reduce inflation and keep it low is to peg their exchange rate to that of a large, low-inflation country. Mishkin argued, however, that while fixed exchange rates may be a successful antiinflation strategy, it can be a dangerous one, particularly if the banking system is weak, debt has short duration, and substantial amounts of debt are denominated in foreign currency. In this case, a shock that makes it necessary to substantially devalue the currency can precipitate a full-scale financial crisis. Jeffrey Sachs agreed, concluding that strictly pegged exchange rates should only be used in special circumstances.

Finally, Jacob Frenkel emphasized the importance of making fixed exchange rate regimes temporary phenomena, drawing a distinction between the first and subsequent phases of a price stabilization strategy. In the first phase, he argued, it makes sense to fix exchange rates for a while to break the inertia of high inflation. But, he warned, the strategy must include an exit policy to make the transition to a more flexible exchange rate regime.

V. CONCLUSIONS

The conclusions of the symposium were summarized by three overview panelists, Martin Feldstein, Edward George, and Jean-Claude Trichet. The panelists commented on four main issues—the regulation of financial institutions, the role of international support in times of crisis, intervention in asset markets, and macroeconomic policies for maintaining financial stability.

The majority view of the symposium participants was that regulation of financial institutions is needed but that it must be consistent with market forces. Trichet argued that while market participants should be measuring risks and adjusting to those risks, central bankers must retain the right for setting capital requirements because they are responsible for assessing systemic risks and preventing systemic crises. In addition, he noted that policymakers can mitigate the problems associated with information asymmetries by assuring transparency and full disclosure of information. Feldstein called for deposit insurance reform to provide better incentives to avoid excessive risks, such as by lowering the limit on insured deposits or by allowing high insured deposit limits in combination with copayments (as a percent of insured deposits) if a bank should fail. He also favored basing regulatory capital requirements on the risk of failures and the resulting systemic risk. As a final point on banking supervision, Feldstein thought that supervisors should not be concerned about banks with small problems but instead should focus their attention on banks whose failure could lead to systemic problems.

George and Trichet both commented on the regulatory implications of financial globalization and innovation. First, in light of globalization and the associated surge of financial transactions, they both endorsed Litan's view that moving to quicker settlement of payments is key for reducing the risk of financial instability. In George's words, we need to think about moving toward "real-time gross everything." Trichet added that with the globalization of financial markets, a well functioning payments and settlement system is needed not only in the United States and the other G-10 countries, but also in the rest of the world. Second, they both agreed that international banking regulators need to coordinate their activities, not just among themselves, but also with securities and insurance regulators. George also called for some form of consolidated or umbrella oversight to make sure that regulators have a continuous view of the overall risks faced by international financial firms. He argued, "The absence of arrangements

of this sort in relation to multinational, multifunctional firms in particular seems to me to be one of the major weaknesses in current international regulatory arrangements."

As for international responses to financial crises, George believed it is generally accepted that there are situations when official international support is appropriate, particularly when a banking system is in turmoil. He cautioned, however, that to avoid the moral hazard problems typically associated with national lenders of last resort, borrowing countries and creditors should expect that international intervention will be the exception and not the rule. He reiterated that the trick is maintaining an appropriate balance between the potentially conflicting objectives of financial stability and the distorting effects of moral hazard.

Symposium participants agreed that intervention in asset markets generally is not desirable. Feldstein commented that asset prices should be left to the market because it is never clear ahead of time what the "correct" price should be. Jean-Claude Trichet agreed, saying that he did not know who should be the judge for determining when market prices are in line with fundamentals. He noted, however, that while it is difficult to determine if prices are correct, it is "absolutely clear" that a crisis exists and that policymakers must step in when markets are illiquid. Feldstein also cautioned that while asset prices should not be targets for monetary policy, it does not mean monetary authorities should ignore prices such as exchange rates and stock prices. To the contrary, asset prices can be good indicators of future economic activity.

In the area of macroeconomic policies, Feldstein argued that large current account deficits cannot be sustained in the long run. He agreed with other participants that a common denominator of the 1995 Mexican peso crisis and the current problems in Thailand was a large current account deficit, amounting to about 8 percent of GDP in both cases. He concluded that countries that try to have sustained current account deficits and capital inflows, and that base their domestic policies on the assumption that such flows will persist, are putting their exchange rates and their domestic financial markets at risk.

Finally, the three panelists and the symposium participants agreed that price stability is one of the most important ways policymakers can support financial stability. Martin Feldstein argued that the U.S. banking problems in the 1980s show how even relatively moderate rates of inflation can lead to financial problems. More generally, Edward George argued that destabilizing influences, such as weak policy or real shocks, typically flow from the macroeconomy to the financial sector rather than the other way around, and that macroeconomic risks are possibly the major risks affecting the stability of financial intermediaries. Thus, a stable macro situation is necessary for financial stability, and a good way for authorities to prevent financial instability is by providing consistent and transparent macroeconomic policies.

ENDNOTES

[1] "Debt deflation" is the term Irving Fisher used for the propagation of instability due to an unanticipated decline in inflation combined with long-term debt contracts with fixed nominal interest rates in his article, "The Debt-Deflation Theory of the Great Depression," *Econometrica*, 1933, vol. 1, pp. 337-57.

[2] Eichengreen actually made his comments in his presentation on the second day of the symposium.

[3] International Monetary Fund. 1997. Press release no. 97/37 (*http://www.imf.org/external/np\sec\pr\1997\pr9737.htm*), August 20.

[4] Fischer's comments on Thailand were made in his discussion of Crockett's paper and in the discussion afterwards on the first day of the symposium.

Part II
Models, Common Patterns

[16]

PAUL KRUGMAN

A Model of Balance-of-Payments Crises

INTRODUCTION

A GOVERNMENT CAN PEG the exchange value of its currency in a variety of ways. In a country with highly developed financial markets it can use open-market operations, intervention in the forward exchange market, and direct operations in foreign assets to defend an exchange parity (see [2] for an analysis of central bank operations and their effects on the exchange rate); the list could be extended to include such other instruments as changes in bank reserve requirements. But all of these policy instruments are subject to limits. A government attempting to keep its currency from depreciating may find its foreign reserves exhausted and its borrowing approaching a limit. A government attempting to prevent its currency from appreciating may find the cost in domestic inflation unacceptable. When the government is no longer able to defend a fixed parity because of the constraints on its actions, there is a "crisis" in the balance of payments.

This paper is concerned with the analysis of such crises. Although balance-of-payments crises have not received much theoretical attention, there are obviously features common to many crises, and the empirical regularities suggest that a common process must be at work. A "standard" crisis occurs in something like the following manner. A country will have a pegged exchange rate; for simplicity, assume that pegging is done solely through direct intervention in the foreign exchange market. At that exchange rate the government's reserves gradually decline. Then at some point, generally well before the gradual depletion of reserves would have exhausted them, there is a sudden speculative attack that rapidly

PAUL KRUGMAN *is assistant professor of economics, Yale University.*

0022-2879/79/0879-0311$00.50/0   ©1979 Ohio State University Press
JOURNAL OF MONEY, CREDIT, AND BANKING, vol. 11, no. 3 (August 1979)

eliminates the last of the reserves. The government then becomes unable to defend the exchange rate any longer.

It sometimes happens, however, that the government is able to weather the crisis by calling on some kind of secondary reserve: it draws on its gold tranche or negotiates an emergency loan. At this point there is a dramatic reversal—the capital that has just flowed out returns, and the government's reserves recover. The reprieve may only be temporary, though. Another crisis may occur, which will oblige the government to call on still further reserves. There may be a whole sequence of temporary speculative attacks and recoveries of confidence before the attempt to maintain the exchange rate is finally abandoned.

One might question whether dramatic events of this sort, depending so heavily on the psychology of speculators, can be captured by a formal model. An analogy with another area of economics suggests, however, that sudden crises in the balance of payments may not be so hard to model after all. In the theory of exhaustible resources it has been shown that schemes in which the government uses a stockpile of an exhaustible resource to stabilize its price—an obvious parallel to using foreign reserves to peg an exchange rate—eventually end in a speculative attack in which private investors suddenly acquire the entire remaining government stock.[1] The increase in private stocks is justified, ex post, by the increased yield on holding stocks; for when the price stabilization policy breaks down, the price of the resource begins rising, providing a capital gain that makes the holding of stocks more attractive.

In this paper I will show that a similar argument can be used to explain balance-of-payments crises. A speculative attack on a government's reserves can be viewed as a process by which investors change the composition of their portfolios, reducing the proportion of domestic currency and raising the proportion of foreign currency. This change in composition is then justified by a change in relative yields, for when the government is no longer able to defend the exchange rate the currency begins depreciating.

Perhaps more surprising is that the pattern of alternating speculative attacks and revivals of confidence is also a natural event when the market is uncertain about how much of its potential reserves the government is willing to use. The reason is that speculators are faced with a "one-way option"; they do not lose by speculating against the currency even if fears of abandonment of fixed rates prove unjustified.

This paper, then, develops a theory of crises in the balance of payments. It is organized in six sections. Section 1 develops the macroeconomic model within which the analysis is conducted: a simple one-good, two-asset model originally expounded by Kouri [3]. In sections 2 and 3 the working of the model, and the evolution of the economy over time, are analyzed for flexible and fixed exchange rates respectively. Section 4 contains the central analysis of the paper, an analysis of the circumstances under which government pegging of the exchange rate suddenly collapses. This basic analysis is extended in section 5 to the case when government

---

[1]This result was brought to my attention by Stephen Salant. A brief discussion of speculative attacks on government resource stocks is contained in [4].

policy is uncertain, producing the possibility of alternating crises and recoveries of confidence. Finally, section 6 discusses the significance and limitations of the analysis.

1. A MACROECONOMIC MODEL

In order to study balance-of-payments crises we must have a model with two characteristics: (1) the demand for domestic currency depends on the exchange rate; (2) the exchange rate that clears the domestic money market changes over time. An elegant and tractable model with these characteristics was developed by Kouri [3], and I will use a slightly modified version of his model to provide the underpinnings for the discussion. The model involves many special assumptions, and no claims are made for its realism. But it should become clear later that the main points of the analysis would go through in a variety of models.

We will assume, then, that we are dealing with a small country producing a single composite tradable good. The price of the good will be set on world markets, so that purchasing power parity will hold. That is to say,

$$P = sP^*, \tag{1}$$

where P is the domestic price level, s is the exchange rate of domestic currency for foreign, and P^* is the foreign price level. I will assume P^* fixed, so we can choose units to set $P^* = 1$. We can then identify the exchange rate with the price level.

The economy will be assumed to have fully flexible prices and wages, assuring that output is always at its full employment level Y. The balance of trade, which will also turn out in the model to be the balance of payments on current account, will be determined by the difference between output and spending:

$$B = Y - G - C(Y - T, W) \qquad C_1, C_2 > 0, \tag{2}$$

where B is the real trade balance, G is real government spending, T is real taxation, and W is real private wealth (to be defined).

Turning now to the asset markets, investors are assumed to have available a choice between only two assets; domestic and foreign money. Both currencies bear zero nominal interest.[2] The total real wealth of domestic residents is the sum of the real value of their holdings of domestic money M and their holdings of foreign money F:

$$W = M/P + F. \tag{3}$$

As a final simplifying assumption we suppose that foreigners do not hold

[2]The reason for making this assumption is that it rules out international interest payments, allowing us to identify the current account with the trade balance.

domestic money. Then M is also the outstanding stock of domestic money and in equilibrium domestic residents must be just willing to hold that stock. Since I assume that the desired holdings of domestic money are proportional to wealth, the condition for portfolio equilibrium is

$$M/P = L(\pi) \cdot W \qquad L_1 < 0, \qquad (4)$$

where π is the expected rate of inflation. In this model π is also the expected rate of depreciation of the currency.

The determination of π is of crucial importance for the analysis, but it can more usefully be discussed in the context of a full dynamic analysis. For the moment I will treat π as exogenous.

In this paper two exchange rate regimes will be considered. First will be a freely floating exchange rate, with the government abstaining from either buying or selling foreign money. Second will be a fixed exchange rate: the government holds a reserve of foreign money and stands ready to exchange foreign for domestic money at a fixed price. The short-run behavior of the economy under the two systems can be analyzed using Figure 1, in which the upward-sloping schedule LL represents the condition for portfolio balance (4); an increase in holdings of foreign money will be accompanied by an increase in real domestic money for a given π. The downward-sloping schedule WW represents the wealth constraint (3). To acquire foreign money at any instant, domestic residents must reduce their real holdings of domestic money.[3]

Under a flexible rate regime, since neither the government nor foreigners will trade domestic money for foreign, there is no way for domestic residents to alter the composition of their aggregate portfolio. If they attempt to alter portfolio composition the effect will be to change the price level (exchange rate) instead. Suppose, for instance, that π rises. This will make domestic money less attractive,

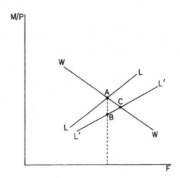

Fig. 1.   Effects of a Change in π with Fixed and Floating Rates

[3]Note that I am making a clear distinction between stocks and flows; in any instant asset holdings are not affected by current saving.

lowering LL to $L'L'$. Since F cannot change, P rises, moving the equilibrium from A to B.

Matters are different if the government has a reserve of foreign money R, and stands ready to exchange foreign for domestic money at a fixed price. Domestic residents can now trade freely up and down their wealth constraint, WW. An increase in π that leads to a downward shift in LL to $L'L'$ now leads to a shift in the portfolio of domestic residents, with the equilibrium moving from A to C. There is a compensating change in the government's reserve position as the government supplies the desired foreign money; the changes in asset holdings are related by

$$\Delta R = -\Delta F = \Delta M/P.$$

Thus, under flexible rates, changes in expectations are reflected in the short run in changes in the exchange rate; whereas under fixed rates they are reflected in changes in the government's reserves. The next step is to examine the determination of expectations; this must be done in the context of an analysis of the economy's dynamics.

2. DYNAMIC BEHAVIOR WITH A FLEXIBLE EXCHANGE RATE

If the government does not peg the exchange rate, the exchange rate can change for any of three reasons: a change in the quantity of domestic money outstanding, a change in private holdings of foreign assets, or a change in the expected rate of inflation. We will analyze each of these in turn, then combine them to describe the evolution of the economy over time.

I will assume that creation of money is dictated by the needs of government finance. Money will be created only through the government deficit; conversely, the government deficit will be financed entirely by printing money. Then the growth of money stock will be determined by

$$\dot{M}/P = G - T. \tag{5}$$

A convenient, if somewhat artificial, assumption is that the government adjusts its expenditure so as to keep the deficit a constant fraction of the money supply. If we let $M/P = m$, this means that G is adjusted to make $G - T = gm$, where g is constant. This in turn makes the rate of change of real balances depend only on the rate of inflation, for

$$\dot{m} = \dot{M}/P - (M/P)(\dot{P}/P)$$

$$= (g - \dot{P}/P)m. \tag{6}$$

Turning next to holdings of foreign money, recall that such holdings represent claims on the rest of the world. They can only be increased by exchanging goods in return. So the rate of accumulation of foreign money must equal the current account balance.

$$\dot{F} = B = Y - G - C(Y - T, W). \tag{7}$$

Finally, we arrive at the question of expectations of inflation. This is a subject of considerable dispute. For the purposes of this paper it is essential to recognize that speculators are actively attempting to forecast the future in a sophisticated manner. This sort of sophisticated forward-looking behavior is best captured by the assumption of *perfect foresight*,[4]

$$\pi = \dot{P}/P. \tag{8}$$

To analyze the system as a whole, we begin by eliminating $\dot{P}/P$. Recall the portfolio balance condition (4). Combined with perfect foresight, this function implies a relationship between real balances, foreign money holdings, and inflation, of the form

$$\dot{P}/P = \pi(m/F), \qquad \pi_1 < 0. \tag{9}$$

The partial derivative in (9) follows from the fact that domestic residents will only be willing to increase the proportion of domestic money in their portfolio if they are offered a higher yield in the form of reduced inflation.

Substituting back, we get a dynamic system in the state variables m, F:

$$\dot{m} = [g - \pi(m/F)]m$$
$$\dot{F} = Y - G - C(Y - T, m + F). \tag{10}$$

This system is shown in Figure 2, with arrows indicating representative paths.

There are two points that should be noted about the dynamic system. First, even if we know the asset holdings of domestic residents, the exchange rate is indeterminate. For any arbitrary initial price level, given M and F, we have an initial position (m,F) and an implied path for the economy. The second point is that the system exhibits knife-edge instability. There is only one path converging to a steady state: if the initial exchange rate is not chosen so as to put the system on that path, the system will diverge ever further from the steady state.

A natural solution to both these difficulties is to assume that investors do not believe in the possibility of endless speculative bubbles, and that the initial exchange rate must therefore be one that implies eventual convergence to the steady state. Some theoretical justification for this assumption has been given by Brock [1];

---

[4]A more general assumption would be "rational expectations," allowing for the existence of uncertainty. The special case of perfect foresight is easier to work with, however, and sufficient for present purposes.

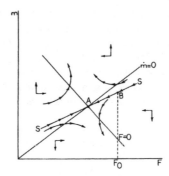

Fig. 2. Dynamic Behavior with a Floating Exchange Rate

the best argument for the assumption, however, is that it 'gives economically sensible results.

In Figure 2, then, the economy is assumed to always be on the stable arm *SABS*. If the initial holdings of foreign money are F_0, the price level will adjust so as to make the real domestic money supply be m_0, with the initial position of the economy being at point *B*. The system then converges gradually to *A*.

Notice that the real money supply depends positively on the stock of foreign money and is independent of the nominal stock of domestic money. Other things equal, then, the price level is proportional to the money supply and negatively related to *F*. We can write

$$P = M \cdot G(F) \qquad G_1 < 0, \tag{11}$$

where (11) is the equation of the stable path *SABS*.

3. DYNAMIC BEHAVIOR WITH A FIXED EXCHANGE RATE

Suppose, now, that the government possesses a stock of foreign money R and uses it to stabilize the exchange rate. This is, of course, equivalent to stabilizing the price level at some level $\bar{P}$. How does the economy evolve over time?

The easiest way to proceed is by examining the budget constraints of the private sector and the government in turn. The private sector can acquire assets only by spending less than its income. Let us define *private savings* as the excess of private income over spending,

$$S = Y - T - C(Y - T, W). \tag{12}$$

Then from the budget constraint and the fact that the price level is pegged we immediately know that

$$\dot{W} = \dot{M}/\bar{P} + \dot{F} = S. \tag{13}$$

But private savings is in turn a function of private wealth, with $\partial S/\partial W = -C_2$ < 0. So (13) is a differential equation in W, and since $\partial S/\partial W$ is negative it is stable.

How is saving allocated between domestic and foreign money? This is determined by the portfolio balance condition (4). As long as investors believe that the government will continue to peg the price level, π will be zero and there will be a stable relationship between wealth and money holdings. Of a change in wealth, a proportion L will be allocated to domestic money and $1 - L$ to foreign money, so we have

$$\dot{M}/\overline{P} = LS$$

$$\dot{F} = (1 - L)S. \tag{14}$$

The government can pay for its deficit $G - T$ either by issuing new domestic money or by drawing on its reserves of foreign money R. The government budget constraint can then be written

$$\dot{M}/P + \dot{R} = G - T = g \cdot (M/P). \tag{15}$$

As long as the government is committed to pegging the exchange rate, it has no control over how its deficit is financed. If the government issues more domestic money than the private sector is willing to hold, private investors can always withdraw the excess money from circulation by trading it for foreign money at the exchange window. As a result, the extent to which the government finances its deficit by running down its foreign currency reserves is determined by the private sector's willingness to acquire additional domestic money:

$$\dot{R} = -(G - T) + LS. \tag{16}$$

An interesting point to note is that the rate of reserve loss does not stand in any one-to-one relationship with the trade balance. It can easily be shown that (16) implies the relationship

$$\dot{R} = LB - (1 - L)(G - T), \tag{17}$$

which can be either greater or less than B.

Over time, then, both private wealth and government reserves will change. I illustrate the behavior of the two stocks in Figure 3. When the government runs a deficit it will lose reserves even if private saving is zero. As the paths illustrated by arrows show, pegging the rate ultimately becomes impossible if the budget is in deficit, no matter how large the initial reserves. If the budget were balanced, the lines $\dot{R} = 0$ and $\dot{W} = 0$ would coincide, and it would be possible for the economy to reach an equilibrium at the given exchange rate if initial reserves were large enough.

If the economy reaches an equilibrium with some reserves left, the model

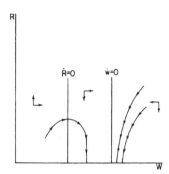

Fig. 3. Dynamic Behavior with a Fixed Exchange Rate

developed above is just a particular case of the price-specie flow mechanism. When it is not possible to peg the exchange rate forever, the pegging effort will at some point collapse in a sudden balance-of-payments crisis. In the next section I analyze the nature and timing of such crises.

4. THE ANATOMY OF A BALANCE-OF-PAYMENTS CRISIS

In the last section I examined the behavior of an economy with a balance-of-payments "problem"; that is, of an economy gradually losing reserves. There comes a point when the problem becomes a "crisis": speculators, anticipating an abandonment of the fixed exchange rate, seek to acquire the government's reserves of foreign money. This crisis always comes before the government would have run out of reserves in the absence of speculation.

To see why this must be so, consider what would happen if investors did not anticipate the end of pegging. As long as the government has reserves left, the domestic money supply will be determined by the portfolio preferences of domestic residents $M/\overline{P} = L(\pi)W$, where $\pi = 0$. At the instant at which reserves are exhausted, portfolio balance begins to determine the price level instead of the money supply. The price level will immediately begin rising, for either or both of two reasons. Domestic residents may still be dissaving, and will try to reduce their holdings of domestic as well as foreign money; and, if the government is running a deficit, the nominal money supply must begin rising.

But when the price level begins rising, this will be reflected immediately in π, by the assumption of perfect foresight. When π increases, the demand for domestic money falls and the price level jumps instantly by a discrete amount. The way this would happen is shown in Figure 4, which superimposes on the dynamic system of Figure 2 the position of the economy under fixed exchange rates. The ray OX is the expansion path of portfolios under fixed rates as private wealth changes; it is steeper than $\dot{m} = 0$ because a higher proportion of domestic money is held in the portfolio when $\pi = 0$ than when $\pi = g$ (as it does along $m = 0$). When reserves run out the

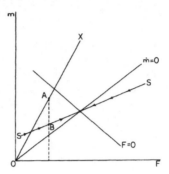

Fig. 4.   Windfall Capital Gains from the Transition to a Floating Rate

system is at a point such as A. We know that when pegging ends and the exchange rate is allowed to float, real balances jump so as to put the system on the stable path SS. So the economy moves suddenly from A to B. Because the nominal money supply is fixed at any instant, this occurs through a jump in the price level.

The argument I have just made depends on the assumption that when reserves run out the economy's position is to the right of the intersection of the expansion path OX with the stable path SS. Otherwise, the exchange rate would fall instead of rising when reserves run out. But it is easily shown that at the moment of exhaustion of reserves private wealth must be large enough to put the economy in the assumed position.[5] So if there is no speculation against the currency, the exhaustion of reserves will always produce a discrete jump in the price level, causing a windfall capital loss.

But investors cannot have expected such a capital loss to happen, because they would have avoided it. In particular, by exchanging domestic for foreign money an instant before reserves are exhausted, a speculator could earn an infinite rate of return. If everyone tried to do this, of course, the government's reserves would be eliminated; the prospect of this would cause speculators to attempt to get out of domestic money still earlier, and so on.

The upshot of all this is that if investors correctly anticipate events, the reserves of the government must be eliminated by a speculative attack that enables all

[5]The proof runs as follows. Just before reserves were exhausted they must have been falling. If we can show that at the point at which OX crosses SS reserves are rising, we know that the position at the moment of exhaustion must be one at which wealth is larger and hence private saving less—i.e., that it lies to the right of the intersection. But consider the magnitude of saving where the lines cross. Under *flexible* rates, the intersection is the point at which inflation is zero, implying that investors are willing to add real balances at a rate just matching the government deficit. That is,

$$\dot{m} = G - T = L(0)S + L_1 m \cdot \dot{\pi}.$$

But $\dot{\pi} > 0$, because the share of domestic money in wealth is falling. So

$$L(0)S - (G - T) > 0.$$

But under *fixed* rates, $\dot{R} = L(0)S - (G - T)$. So, $\dot{R} > 0$ at the intersection of OX with SS.

investors to avoid windfall capital losses. Consider what such a speculative attack involves. From the government's point of view, it represents a liquidation of its reserves. From the point of view of domestic residents, however, what they are doing is altering the composition of their portfolio, exchanging domestic for foreign money. If we let M,F be the asset holdings of domestic residents just before the attack, and M',F' be holdings afterwards, we know that

$$M'/\bar{P} = M/\bar{P} - R$$

$$F' = F + R. \tag{18}$$

Immediately following the attack, the economy is on a flexible rate regime. As discussed in section 2, the immediate post-crisis price level P' can be determined from asset holdings:

$$P' = M' \ G(F') \tag{19}$$

or

$$P'/\bar{P} = (M'/\bar{P}) \ G(F')$$

$$= (M/\bar{P} - R) \ G(F + R).$$

In order that there be no windfall capital loss, the speculative attack must not lead to a discrete change in the price level—that is, we must have $P' = \bar{P}$ or $P'/\bar{P} = 1$. It is this condition that determines when a balance-of-payments crisis occurs. For both $M/\bar{P}$ and F are, under a fixed rate, functions of private wealth W. So the condition $P'/\bar{P} = 1$ can be written as an implicit function in R and W,

$$1 = [L(0)W - R] \ G[W - L(0)W + R]. \tag{20}$$

Equation (20) defines a *threshold* in W,R space. Under a pegged exchange rate W and R gradually evolve over time until they cross the threshold; then there is a sudden balance-of-payments crisis, which eliminates the remaining reserves and forces a transition to a floating exchange rate.

Figure 5 shows what happens in the crisis. Just before the speculative attack the economy is on the fixed-rate expansion path OX; just after, it is on the flexible-rate stable path SS. Suppose that, at the moment of the attack, private asset holdings are represented by point A. In the attack investors reallocate their portfolio, moving southeast along the line of constant wealth WW to point B. The increase in holdings of foreign money is achieved by acquiring the government's reserves R.

Suppose that, at the time of the crisis, private wealth had been larger—i.e., WW had been further to the right. It is then obvious from the diagram that the reserves acquired from the government must also have been larger. This establishes that the threshold at which a crisis occurs is upward sloping in W,R space.

322 : MONEY, CREDIT, AND BANKING

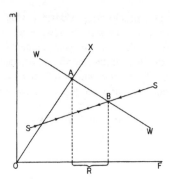

Fig. 5. The Elimination of Reserves by a Speculative Attack

The approach to the crisis is illustrated in Figure 6, where the threshold (20) is represented by TT; it is upward-sloping and cuts the horizontal axis to the left of $\dot{R} = 0$.[6] We can learn something about the factors determining the timing of a crisis by comparing some representative paths like those leading from A, B, C, and D. B differs from A, and D from C, only in there being a higher initial level of reserves. In each case we can see that when reserves are larger, the absolute value of the change in private wealth before the crisis is larger. Since $\dot{W}$ is independent of R, this means that the time until the crisis is longer. Thus we confirm the intuitively plausible result that the length of time for which a government can peg the exchange rate is an increasing function of its initial reserves.

When the government policy is certain, then, an economy with a balance-of-payments problem will pass through three stages: a period of gradually declining reserves, a sudden speculative attack, and a post-crisis period during which the currency gradually depreciates. The next step is to examine what happens if government policy is uncertain.

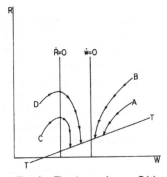

Fig. 6. The Approach to a Crisis

[6]The intersection of TT with the horizontal axis corresponds to the intersection of OX with SS in Figure 5. But as argued in note 5, that intersection takes place at a level of wealth for which $\dot{R} > 0$.

5. SPECULATION WHEN GOVERNMENT POLICY IS UNCERTAIN: THE "ONE-WAY OPTION"

Many different kinds of uncertainty could be introduced into the preceding analysis. I will deal with only one source of uncertainty: incomplete knowledge on the part of investors about how much of its reserves the government is willing to use to defend the exchange rate. This produces the possibility of alternating balance-of-payments crises and recoveries of confidence.

To consider the simplest case, suppose that the government's reserves can be divided into a primary reserve R_1, which investors know it will commit to the defense of the exchange rate, and a secondary reserve R_2, which it may or may not be willing to use. We may suppose that the market believes that R_2 will be used with probability $\alpha < 1$. I also assume that once the government has used any part of R_2 to defend the exchange rate, the market can be sure that it will use all of it.

As before, we suppose that there is an initial period during which reserves gradually decline. Eventually there comes a point at which a speculative attack would take place *if* R_1 were the only reserve; but at that point there would not yet be a crisis if the market knew that the reserves committed to defending the exchange rate were $R_1 + R_2$. What happens?

The answer is that the speculative attack takes place, as investors acquire the whole of the government's remaining primary reserve R_1. If the government then commits its secondary reserve to maintain the value of the currency, investors reverse themselves and exchange foreign for domestic money, producing a recovery of the government's reserves.

To see why this must be so, consider two points. First, in the absence of transaction costs the speculative attack is costless. Investors need only hold a higher proportion of foreign money for an infinitesimally short period until it becomes clear whether or not the secondary reserve will be used. Second, if the capital outflow did not take place, there would be a possibility of a windfall capital loss. Suppose there were no speculative attack, or the attack was not large enough to completely eliminate the primary reserve. Then if the government eventually decided not to commit the secondary reserve, when R_1 was exhausted there would be a discrete jump in the exchange rate—a capital loss that an individual wealth owner could have costlessly avoided. So there must be a speculative attack just as if there were no secondary reserve. Once the secondary reserve is committed, of course, the risk of capital loss has been eliminated and the holdings of domestic money return to their previous level.

We can obviously extend this analysis to a whole series of reserves: $R_1, \ldots, R_n$. The effect is to produce a series of balance-of-payments crises, each ended by the government's decision to commit the next reserve.

SUMMARY AND CONCLUSIONS

This paper has been concerned with the circumstances in which a balance-of-payments problem—defined as a situation in which a country is gradually losing reserves—becomes a balance-of-payments crisis, in which speculators attack the currency. I have shown that balance-of-payments crises are a natural outcome of maximizing behavior by investors. When the government's willingness to use reserves to defend the exchange rate is uncertain, there can be a series of crises in which capital flows out of the country, then returns, before the issue is finally resolved.

The analysis is subject to two major limitations. The first is that it is based on a highly simplified macroeconomic model. This makes it easier to develop the main points of the argument, but means that the analysis of the factors triggering a balance-of-payments crisis is incomplete. The second limitation is that the assumption that only two assets are available places an unrealistic constraint on the possible actions of the government, because the only way it can peg exchange rate is by selling its reserves. In a more realistic model we would have to allow for the possibility of other policies to stabilize the exchange rate, such as an open-market sales of securities or intervention in the forward market.

In spite of these limitations, however, the analysis is suggestive, and does help explain why efforts to defend fixed exchange rates so often lead to crises.

APPENDIX: THE DETERMINATION OF THE PRICE LEVEL UNDER FLEXIBLE RATES

In section 2 I derived a relationship between asset stocks and the price level under flexible rates from the requirement that the economy be on the stable path in Figure 2. An alternative algebraic derivation is the following. The dynamic system (10), linearized around the steady-state values $\bar{m}$, $\bar{F}$, can be written

$$\begin{bmatrix} \dot{m} \\ \dot{F} \end{bmatrix} = \begin{bmatrix} -\pi_1 \bar{m}/\bar{F} & \pi_1(\bar{m}/\bar{F})^2 \\ -C_2 & -C_2 \end{bmatrix} \begin{bmatrix} m - \bar{m} \\ F - \bar{F} \end{bmatrix}. \tag{A1}$$

This system has the characteristic values

$$\lambda_1 = -\tfrac{1}{2}(C_2 + \pi_1\bar{m}/\bar{F}) - \tfrac{1}{2}\sqrt{(C_2 + \pi_1\bar{m}/\bar{F})^2 - 4C_2\pi_1(\bar{m}/\bar{F})^2} < 0$$

$$\lambda_2 = -\tfrac{1}{2}(C_2 + \pi_1\bar{m}/\bar{F}) + \tfrac{1}{2}\sqrt{(C_2 + \pi_2\bar{m}/\bar{F})^2 - 4C_2\pi_1(\bar{m}/\bar{F})^2} > 0.$$

A solution must be of the form

$$\begin{bmatrix} m - \bar{m} \\ F - \bar{F} \end{bmatrix} = \begin{bmatrix} a_{11} & a_{12} \\ a_{21} & a_{22} \end{bmatrix} \begin{bmatrix} e^{\lambda_1 t} \\ e^{\lambda_2 t} \end{bmatrix}. \tag{A2}$$

If the system is to converge to a steady state the initial condition must be such that $a_{12} = a_{22} = 0$, so m and F converge exponentially to $\bar{m}$, $\bar{F}$. But then we have

$$\dot{m} = \lambda_1(m - \bar{m})$$

$$= \pi_1(\bar{m}/\bar{F})(m - \bar{m}) + \pi_1(\bar{m}/\bar{F})^2(F - \bar{F}),$$

(A3)

which defines the stable path

$$m - \bar{m} = \frac{\pi_1(\bar{m}/\bar{F})^2}{\pi_1 + \pi_1(\bar{m}/\bar{F})} (F - \bar{F}).$$

The rest of the argument in the text then follows.

LITERATURE CITED

1. Brock, William A. "A Simple Perfect Foresight Monetary Model." *Journal of Monetary Economics*, 1 (April 1975), 133–150.
2. Girton, Lance, and Dale W. Henderson. "Central Bank Operations in Foreign and Domestic Assets under Fixed and Flexible Exchange Rates." Federal Reserve Board International Finance Discussion Paper No. 83, May 1976.
3. Kouri, Pentti J. K. "The Exchange Rate and the Balance of Payments in the Short Run and in the Long Run: A Monetary Approach." *Scandinavian Journal of Economics*, 78 (1976), 280–304.
4. Salant, Stephen W., and Dale W. Henderson. "Market Anticipation of Government Policy and the Price of Gold." *Journal of Political Economy*, 86 (August 1978), 627–648.

[17]

SECOND GENERATION MODELS OF CURRENCY CRISES

Jesper Rangvid

Copenhagen Business School

Abstract. Until the beginning of the 1990s, currency crises were typically analyzed within the framework of a generation of models that *assumed* that the foreign exchange reserves of a country that was running a fixed exchange rate policy were falling (because the government was running a deficit on its budget that was financed by printing money). When the foreign exchange reserves reached a lower bound, a speculative attack on the fixed exchange rate was launched. Today, this theory is no longer the benchmark when explaining the occurrence of a currency crisis. Actually, a new generation of models that seeks to take explicitly into account the costs and benefits associated with the maintenance of a fixed exchange rate has emerged. This paper surveys these 'second generation models of currency crises'. This generation of models emphasizes that it is an *endogenous* decision if a government chooses to abandon a policy of fixed exchange rates. The survey pays special attention to the fact that the second generation of currency crises models often generates multiple equilibria for the rate of devaluation given one state of the economic fundamentals. A currency crisis can thus occur even if no secular trend in economic fundamentals can be identified, as in recent currency crises.

Keywords. Currency crises; Loss functions; Multiple equilibria

1. Introduction

Since 1992, the international monetary system has witnessed a considerable number of currency crises: the crises in the European Monetary System (EMS) during 1992–1993 (eventually leading to the de facto breakdown of the EMS, as the bilateral fluctuation bands of the EMS currencies were increased from ±2.25% to ±15%), the crises related to the fall of the Mexican Peso in December 1994 (which spread to a number of other South American countries; the so-called Tequila effect), the crises in the southern part of Asia during the autumn of 1997 (beginning with the Thai Baht crisis on July 2, 1997 and quickly spreading to a number of other countries in the region), and most recently the crises in Russia and Brasil.

Whereas the 1990s have been particularly rich on incidents of currency crises, the history of the international monetary system is replete with examples of such dramatic events putting an end to policies of fixed exchange rates.[1] From the point of view of the present paper, though, the crises of the 1990s are particularly

0950-0804/01/05 0613–34 JOURNAL OF ECONOMIC SURVEYS Vol. 15, No. 5
© Blackwell Publishers Ltd. 2001, 108 Cowley Rd., Oxford OX4 1JF, UK and 350 Main St., Malden, MA 02148, USA.

noteworthy in the sense that these crises have led to the development of new theories to explain and understand currency crises. Today, these new theories are collected under the heading of a 'second-generation literature' on speculative currency attacks. It is the aim of this paper to explain why a new generation of models has seen the light of the day, provide perspectives on the theory as it has developed since the beginning of the 1990s, and comment on the empirical evidence.

The characterization of a first and a second 'generation' of currency crises models will be maintained in the survey (as is by now a standard characterization in the literature). The first-generation models are those pioneered by Krugman (1979). Krugman (1979) predicted that if a government runs a policy of financing public expenditures by printing money and at the same time seeks to keep the nominal exchange rate fixed, a speculative attack on the exchange rate is inevitable if the central bank possesses only a limited amount of foreign exchange reserves. Basically, the government is forced to abandon the fixed exchange rate policy because the way it finances the deficit is inconsistent with its intention to keep the exchange rate fixed. This inconsistency makes all agents in the economy (including the government) aware of the fact that the realization of a speculative attack is a probability one event. The basic Krugman (1979) model has been extended in various directions and the literature has eventually developed into what is now referred to as 'first-generation models of speculative currency attacks'.[2] This literature, with its assumption of a fundamental inconsistency between the policy of a fixed exchange rate and other government policies, practically remained unchallenged as an explanation of currency crises until the crises of the 1990s.

What were the problems with this first 'generation' of models and why have new theories been developed during the 1990s? First of all, it is somewhat hard to reconcile with the way the international financial system works today that the foreign exchange reserves should play such an important role for the possibility of keeping the exchange rate fixed when, in principle, central banks can always resist a speculative attack if they are willing to pay the price (by absorbing domestic credit thereby raising interest rates to levels which make position-taking against the domestic currency a non-profitable action, see Obstfeld and Rogoff, 1995).[3] Furthermore, within the framework of the model it is difficult to understand why the government on the one hand tries to keep the exchange rate fixed and on the other hand conducts a policy which the government knows will ultimately lead to a currency crisis. Basically, this suggests that governments are 'smarter' than assumed in first-generation models as they will consider whether it is 'too expensive' to keep the exchange rate fixed as compared to the option of abandoning the policy of a fixed exchange rate. Finally, casual empirical observations (and more detailed econometric studies) have shown that it was difficult to predict many of the recent currency crises. In general, unpredictable currency crises are not in accordance with the implication of a speculative attack as a probability one (and in deterministic environments, perfectly foreseeable) event in first-generation models.

As a consequence of these deficiencies (and others described in more detail in the paper), a new 'generation' of currency crises models has seen the light of day. In particular, the second-generation models suggest new ways to understand (*i*) how a government behaves in periods leading up to currency turmoils and (*ii*) the weak relation between economic fundamentals and the timing of speculative attacks (i.e. the unpredictability of speculative attacks). In order to deal with the first issue and describe more reasonably how a representative government behaves, it is assumed that the government in every single period of time evaluates the costs and the benefits from keeping the exchange rate fixed. In order to deal with the second issue and explain why speculative attacks have been realized even in situations where no obvious inconsistencies between the goal of a fixed exchange rate and other government policies could be identified (such as those in France in 1992–1993, see Jeanne and Masson, 2000, or in Southeast Asia in 1997, see Radelet and Sachs, 1998), the models rely on the implications of multiple equilibria for the rate of devaluation. The intuition underlying a multiple equilibria story can be illustrated by recognizing that there are situations where the expectations of the private sector regarding a high rate of devaluation imply high 'costs' to be paid by the government, if the government does not actually change the exchange rate.[4] If, in this situation, the private sector expects a high rate of devaluation, the government will be more willing to actually allow for a high rate of devaluation. There can thus be situations where there are two equilibria: if the private sector expects a low rate of devaluation (for instance that the exchange rate remains fixed), the government will keep the exchange rate fixed. If, on the other hand, the private sector, for some reason left unexplained, changes beliefs with respect to the rate of devaluation (suddenly expects that the rate of devaluation increases), the government will actually change the rate of devaluation. In this way, the expectations of the private sector are self-fulfilling and multiple equilibria can occur, where the change from one equilibrium to another is caused by a sunspot variable.

The second-generation models have undoubtedly settled some issues. It is important to notice, though, that some implications of the models are still subject to debate. First and foremost, it is somewhat unsatisfactory that the shift from one equilibrium to another is left practically unexplained and occurs when a sunspot variable is realized. Furthermore, where the second-generation models have illuminated the role of the constraints subject to which a government acts, the second-generation models, on the other hand, describe only rather sparsely the role of financial markets in the run-up to crises. The paper will also touch upon those issues.

Finally, it should be pointed out that this survey focuses explicitly on second-generation models and will thus not attempt to survey the literature on the Asian currency crisis (with the exception of the second-generation models that have been used to describe the Asian crisis),[5] the reason being that some of the models on the Asian crisis can actually be viewed as special cases of the models surveyed in this paper.[6] Finally, the fact that when a crisis starts in one country, it often spreads to other countries, a phenomenon now referred to as *contagion*, will not be discussed in any detail.[7]

The organization of the paper is straightforward. In the following section, the first-generation models are briefly presented (so as to make possible a comparison between the first- and second-generation models), but the many extensions of the basic model will not be discussed in any detail. Section 3 contains the main body of the paper. In this section, the second-generation models are introduced and discussed in detail, the still open issues are touched upon, and the empirical evidence is evaluated. A final section concludes with a discussion of some of the policy implications which can be derived from the models.

2. First-generation models of currency crises

Virtually all articles on speculative attacks on fixed but adjustable exchange rates contain a reference to Krugman (1979) which, as mentioned, paved the way for a whole generation of papers. Krugman (1979) focused on a pressure for a rate of growth of the money supply higher than the rate at which money demand grows. It was an implicit assumption in the model that the underlying pressure for the high growth rate of the money supply was due to a deficit on the government budget which was financed by central bank credit to the government. In this section, the central equations and assumptions of a representative first-generation model are presented so as to facilitate a comparison between the implications arising from second-generation models. The presentation will be kept brief, as more detailed discussions are already available in the survey articles mentioned in note 2.

2.1. *The model*

The economic environment in a benchmark first-generation model is simple: perfect foresight prevails, there are no imperfections in the economy, domestic and foreign goods are perfect substitutes, full capital mobility is assumed, and uncovered interest parity prevails. Prices are fully flexible and purchasing power parity prevails at all times. The price index of the foreign country is assumed constant and normalized to one, i.e. the domestic price level equals the nominal exchange rate and the rate of price inflation equals the rate of change in the exchange rate. The money market is described by

$$m_t^d - e_t = L(\dot{e}_t), \quad \text{with} \quad L' < 0 \tag{1}$$

$$m_t^s = \ln(D_t + R_t) \tag{2}$$

where (1) represents the demand for money, m^d, and (2) defines the money supply, m^s. $\dot{e}_t$ is the change in the (log of the) nominal exchange rate, e_t, from time t to $t + \Delta t$. From the simplified balance sheet of a representative central bank it follows that the logarithm of the money supply equals the logarithm of the sum of the central bank's holding of foreign exchange reserves (quoted at its domestic currency value), R, plus the central bank's holdings of domestic credit, D. With a fixed exchange rate $e_t \equiv \bar{e}$, so $\dot{e}_t = 0$, the demand for money turns out to be a constant: $m_t^d = \bar{e} \equiv \bar{m}$.

An important assumption in the model is that D_t grows at the constant exogenous rate μ

$$\frac{\dot{D}_t}{D_t} = \mu \tag{3}$$

because the government finances a deficit on its budget by selling bonds to the central bank, i.e. in practice a monetary financing of the government deficit occurs and there is thus a pressure for the money supply to expand. With a constant money demand $\bar{m}$, though, equilibrium on the money market implies that this growth in the money supply will not be realized. More precisely, the growth in domestic credit, in combination with the constant money supply (and demand), implies that the foreign exchange reserves will shrink at the rate

$$\frac{\dot{R}_t}{R_t} = -\frac{\dot{D}_t}{D_t} = -\mu$$

Because of the fixed exchange rate, the private agents will not demand the domestic money injected into the economy from the increase in D. Instead, the private agents turn immediately to the central bank in order to convert domestic money to foreign money, i.e. no actual increase in m occurs. As the private agents continuously adjust their portfolio holdings in accordance with their preferences (here represented through the constant demand for money), foreign exchange reserves will shrink at exactly the same rate as the domestic credit component of the central bank's balance sheet is increased.

2.1.1. *The speculative attack*

In itself, the constant outflow of foreign exchange reserves will not necessarily lead to a speculative attack. On the other hand, a speculative attack will be launched if the central bank announces that the policy of a fixed exchange rate will be abandoned if the foreign exchange reserves reach some lower level. With this announcement, it is a probability one event that the fixed exchange rate policy will actually be abandoned — which is a first implication of the model. A second implication of the model is that when the agents on the financial markets form expectations rationally, they will try to control the point in time where the fixed exchange rate policy is abandoned (in order to avoid a capital loss on their holdings of assets denominated in domestic currency). In this model, the private agents can control the switch from a fixed to a floating exchange rate only by means of a speculative attack *before* the foreign exchange reserves reach the lower level.

By a simple arbitrage argument, Flood and Garber (1984) showed that the speculative attack will be launched exactly when the shadow exchange rate (the exchange rate that would prevail if the exchange rate was floating) equals the fixed exchange rate. In particular, they provided a closed solution for the point in time where the speculative attack is launched (call this point in time T) and also showed that the attack occurs before the point in time where foreign exchange reserves would be lost had there been no speculative attack (call this point in time $\bar{T}$), i.e. $T < \bar{T}$. Furthermore, at T the speculative attack depletes the remaining stock of foreign exchange reserves. In showing this result, Flood and Garber (1984) relied on the fact that in perfect foresight models, predictable jumps in asset prices can a priori be ruled out as any such event will immediately (as soon as any such jump is predicted to occur) be eliminated.[8]

2.1.2. *Extensions of the basic first-generation model*

In the literature, the basic Krugman (1979)/Flood and Garber (1984) set-up has been subject to numerous changes in the underlying assumptions such as different exchange rate regimes after the speculative attack (Obstfeld, 1984), imperfect substitution between domestic and foreign assets (Willman, 1988), rigidities in prices of goods (Blackburn, 1988), issues of capital controls (Wyplosz, 1986), changes in the growth rate of domestic credit *after* the breakdown of the policy of a fixed exchange rate, which have the implication that multiple equilibria for the rate of devaluation can occur (Obstfeld, 1986a),[9] optimizing behavior of the private agents where money is introduced either through a money-in-the-utility function approach (Claessens, 1988) or a Cash-in-Advance approach (Calvo, 1987), letting the probability of a devaluation depend on the general stance of the economy (Stansfield and Sutherland, 1995), and formulations in discrete time, which have the implication that the collapse will be brought about through two successive speculative attacks (Obstfeld, 1986b).

Turning to empirical analyses using the framework of first-generation models, earlier analyses, such as Blanco and Garber (1986), were positive in their assessment of the ability of first-generation models to explain episodes of speculative attacks, whereas more recent analyses have expressed considerably more scepticism. Especially, where first-generation models imply that the private agents are able to predict the timing of the crises by identifying secular trends (in D and R, as well as obvious policy inconsistencies), the findings of Eichengreen and Wyplosz (1993), Rose and Svensson (1994), Eichengreen *et al.* (1994, 1995, 1996), and Kaminsky *et al.* (1998) cast considerable doubt on this implication. In Section 3.7, these issues will be discussed in considerably more detail.

2.2. *Discussion of the basic first-generation monetary model*

Apart from the lack of empirical support, criticism concerning some of the assumptions underlying the theoretical predictions can also be raised. Primarily, three aspects of the first-generation models have been discussed:[10]

1. The description of respectively private agents and the government is somewhat unbalanced. In particular, private agents are supposed to react in

a rather sophisticated manner by calculating shadow exchange rates and launch speculative attacks so as to eliminate even the smallest arbitrage opportunity, whereas the government is described as a practically non-acting agent. Indeed, it appears puzzling that the government does not change its strategy of a constant growth in D if the government considers a fixed exchange rate to be important.

2. In close accordance with 1., the models do not describe the preferences of the government in a consistent manner. For instance, why does the government pursue a fixed exchange rate policy until the collapse, and more importantly why does the government finance its deficit by selling bonds to the central bank thereby paving the way for the continuous reduction of the foreign exchange reserves?

3. In the models, it is a basic assumption that a change in the exchange rate policy occurs when the foreign exchange reserves reach a lower bound. In a world of free capital movements, though, such an assumption seems to be rather restrictive. First, it will in principle always be possible to raise credit on the international capital markets so that funds can be added to the existing stock of foreign exchange reserves. Second, as already mentioned in the introduction, the central bank can make it expensive for private agents to take short positions in the domestic currency, and thereby reduce the speculative pressure.[11]

   For completeness of this brief discussion, the main empirical 'problem' with the first-generation models is:

4. The first-generation models predict a secular trend in fundamentals (in the basic model, this trend being represented by the outflow of foreign exchange reserves). In a number of recent currency crises, though, it is difficult to find secular trends in fundamentals. In these recent crises, it seems to be the case that agents 'suddenly' changed their assessment of an exchange rate peg being sustainable to the exchange rate peg being unsustainable.

3. Second-generation models of currency crises

Even when the first paper containing a representative second-generation model was circulated in 1991 (Obstfeld, 1991 and later published as Obstfeld, 1997), it was not until after the 1992–1993 ERM crises that the models really became part of the standard vocabulary when explaining currency crises. The reason for the embracement of second-generation models is quite straightforward: the ERM crises came practically unexpected as argued in Rose and Svensson (1994), i.e. no secular trend in fundamentals could be observed and models that could describe why agents' belief (with respect to the duration of an exchange rate peg) changed so suddenly were thus urgently needed.[12]

3.1. *Definition of second-generation models*

Some authors make a distinction between first- and second-generation models by the number of equilibria in a given model (see e.g. De Grauwe, 1997). Others make the distinction between first- and second-generation models by considering whether the government minimizes a loss function or not. Obviously, this is just a matter of definition, but one should be aware of the fact that it is perfectly possible to have multiple equilibria in a model where the government does not optimize, as hinted upon already in Flood and Garber (1984), and explained in detail in Obstfeld (1986a), Dellas and Stockman (1993), and Flood and Marion (1996, 2000).[13] On the other hand, it should also be emphasized that it is equally well possible to have an optimizing policymaker and a well-defined unique equilibrium, as in Drazen and Masson (1994), Masson (1995), and Eichengreen and Jeanne (1998). It follows that the modelling of the incentives of the government and the number of equilibria has *per se* no connection with each other. Therefore, in what follows a second-generation model refers to a model where *the government minimizes a loss-function*.[14]

Following this brief discussion of definitions of second-generation models, it is of no surprise that other authors have used different names for the different generations of models. For instance, Velasco (1996) and Jeanne (1999) use the phrases speculative-attack and cost-benefit models for first- and second-generation models respectively, whereas Buiter *et al.* (1998) use the phrases exogenous- versus endogenous-policy models.

3.2. *The framework of second-generation models*

In general, the benchmark second-generation model can be described by particular specifications of three economic variables (or functions of economic variables): the preferences of the government, the economic fundamentals, and the cost of abandoning the policy of a fixed exchange rate.

Government preferences.   As mentioned, in second-generation models the costs and benefits associated with the maintenance of fixed exchange rate policy are explicitly modelled. It is assumed that the preferences of the government are described by a function which features a trade-off between the goal of a fixed exchange rate and a variable Λ which is affected by a combination of respectively the realized (π), the expected (π^e), and consequently the surprise ($\pi - \pi^e$) rate of devaluation.

In general, π_t is defined by the rate of change in the nominal exchange rate between either the last period and this period or this period and the next, i.e. $\pi_t = e_t - e_{t-1}$ or $\pi_t = e_{t+1} - e_t$ with e_t again being the logarithm to the nominal exchange rate in period t. The exchange rate is defined as the number of units of domestic currency needed to buy one unit of foreign currency, i.e. $\pi_t > 0$ implies a devaluation of the domestic currency. Whether π_t is defined as $e_t - e_{t-1}$ or $\pi_t = e_{t+1} - e_t$ depends on the economic environment within which the government operates, but it is important to recognize that the specification of π is not necessarily a trivial matter, as discussed in Section 3.5.1.

Furthermore, the government is supposed to be concerned with the value of a real variable Λ_t. Λ_t is a stochastic variable (to be described in further detail below) which affects the loss of the government in the following way: if π^e is increased (for given π), the loss of the government is increased and if π is increased (for given π^e), the loss of the government is decreased. In this last situation, the devaluation is a surprise for the private sector. Furthermore, Λ_t is affected by a shock, ε_t, which will also be described in more detail below. Finally, the government has preferences concerning an optimal constant level of Λ_t which is denoted by Λ^*.

The preferences of the government in a typical second-generation model can be formulated in more detail. Actually, this is a relatively straightforward task, as it is generally assumed that the government *minimizes* a loss-function which is quadratic in the squared rate of devaluation and the squared difference between Λ_t and Λ^*, i.e. a typical static loss-function would equal

$$l_t = (\Lambda_t - \Lambda^*)^2 + \omega\pi_t^2$$

with ω as the trade-off parameter. The intertemporal loss-function is given by $\mathcal{L}_t = \sum_{i=0}^{\infty} \beta^i l_{t+i}$ with β as the government's discount factor. As the constraints (subject to which $\mathcal{L}_t$ is minimized) are often formulated such that Λ_t is not correlated with Λ_{t+i}, $i = 1, 2, ...$, the minimization of $\mathcal{L}_t$ often boils down to the minimization of l_t.

The specific functional form of the loss-function is of no great importance. What is important is that the loss-function allows for some trade-off between the goals of the government (π and $(\Lambda_t - \Lambda^*)$), that the loss increases with the realized rate of devaluation, and that the loss increases when the realized value of Λ_t differs from the preferred value Λ^*. The advantage of the linear-quadratic form is that it generates simple solutions.

The real variable. The government is assumed to minimize l_t subject to the specification of Λ_t. The specification of Λ_t thus constitutes the constraint subject to which the government evaluates the costs and benefits of the fixed exchange rate regime. Depending on the issue to be analyzed, Λ_t can represent:

Production: If the government would like a high level of output/production, y_t, together with a fixed exchange rate, i.e. $l_t = (y_t - \bar{y})^2 + \omega\pi_t^2$ with $\bar{y} = \Lambda^*$ as the government's preferred level of production, the determinants of $y_t = \Lambda_t$ could be represented by an expectation-augmented Phillips-curve, $y_t = \bar{y} + \alpha(\pi - \pi^e) - \varepsilon_t^y$, as in Obstfeld (1996b). In such a model, $\bar{y}$ is the natural level of production and $k = \tilde{y} - \bar{y} > 0$, with k representing the distortion in the economy, i.e. there is an incentive for the government to surprise the private agents. The idea underlying this specification is that if the private agents expect a high π, they push up nominal wages. If no change in π occurs, real wages have increased, leading to a reduction in production. If, on the other hand, $(\pi - \pi^e) > 0$, the government has surprised the private agents by increasing inflation more than expected, the result of which is a decrease in real wages and a boom in production.

A practically equivalent formulation is used in Obstfeld (1994), Flood and Marion (1997), and Andersen (1998)[15] where the level of the exchange rate is considered: $y_t = \alpha[e_t - E_{t-1}(e_t) - \varepsilon_t^y]$ with $E_{t-1}(e_t)$ as the expectation formed in the last period concerning the exchange rate prevailing in this period. Output could also be formulated more as an IS-curve-like equation, such as $y_t = -\gamma i_T + \eta e_t - \beta \varepsilon_t^y$, where i_T is the interest rate which could be either a composite interest rate averaging over all maturities (Ozkan and Sutherland, 1995) or, by shifting around the maturity T, one could study term structure implications, as in Ozkan and Sutherland (1998). In this IS-curve formulation, i_T depends on the expected rate of devaluation.

Unemployment: If the government has preferences concerning a low degree of deviation of actual unemployment u around natural unemployment, the constraint would typically be an expectations-augmented Phillips-curve for unemployment, possibly extended to a dynamic specification by assuming some kind of persistence characterizing the dynamics of unemployment, such as $u_t = \rho u_{t-1} - a[e_t - E_{t-1}(e_t) - \varepsilon_t^u]$ as in Masson (1995), Jeanne (1997a, 1997b), and Eichengreen and Jeanne (1998). Alternatively, the model can be specified in terms of **employment**, n, as $n_t = n^* + \alpha[e_t - E_{t-1}e_t - k - \varepsilon_t^n]$, as in Obstfeld (1991, 1997) and Drazen and Masson (1994). In these models, n^* is the level of employment found optimal by the policymaker and k is a distortion in the economy causing n to be lower than n^* in periods of no surprise devaluations.

Taxes: De Koch and Grilli (1993), Velasco (1996), and Sachs et al. (1996) assume that the government dislikes taxes and that one source of government income is due to seigniorage revenues. The constraint subject to which the government operates is of the kind: $\tau_t = \Psi - (\pi_t - \pi_t^e)m + \varepsilon_t$, where τ_t represents tax revenues in period t and Ψ represents some fixed government expenditures which need to be financed either through conventional taxes or through seigniorage revenues, represented by $(\pi_t - \pi_t^e)m$. The idea underlying this specification is that an increase in π^e lowers the demand for money and thus the seigniorage tax base which, for fixed π, implies a need for higher conventional taxes to be raised. On the other hand, for a given expected rate of devaluation, a surprise increase in π will yield higher revenues from seigniorage as the seigniorage tax base is predetermined when setting π. The government has preferences concerning a tax level for instance equal to zero.

Public debt: Obstfeld (1994) and Cole and Kehoe (1996) assume that the real burden of public debt can be lowered through a surprise devaluation. To understand this, consider the realized (i.e. after inflation has been determined) real interest rate $r_{t+1} = \bar{r} + \pi_{t+1}^e - \pi_{t+1}$, with $\bar{r}$ as a constant exogenously given ex ante real interest rate. If the private sector expects a high rate of devaluation this leads to a higher realized real interest rate and consequently higher real interest rate payments on public debt, if no devaluation is realized. These higher interest rate payments affect the government's loss negatively. If, on the other hand, a surprise devaluation occurs, the realized real interest rate is decreased. The lower interest rate then causes lower interest rate payments on public debt in real terms.

'General specifications': Bensaid and Jeanne (1997) keep the model in rather general terms and assume that the government has preferences concerning some 'cost' c_t which the government incurs if it raises the interest rate in order to defend the fixed exchange rate. The cost is represented by some function $\gamma(i)$, $\gamma' > 0$ with i as the nominal interest rate that depends on expected inflation. Jeanne and Masson (1996, 2000) assume that the government derives net benefit $B(\phi_t, \pi_t)$ when pegging the exchange rate with ϕ_t as the exogenous variables which affect the government's decision to keep the exchange rate pegged or not and π_t as the probability of a devaluation, and $B'_1 > 0$ and $B'_2 < 0$. For instance, they suggest that interest rates increase when the probability of a devaluation increases and the higher interest rates lead to higher unemployment, higher payments on government debt, and so forth. Morris and Shin (1998) write the payoff to the government from defending the fixed exchange rate as v and assume that this payoff is reduced by the amount $c(\alpha, \theta)$ if a proportion α of all speculators attacks the currency when the fundamentals of the economy are in state θ. They assume that $c'_1 > 0$ and $c'_2 < 0$, i.e. the more speculators attack the currency the more 'expensive' it is for the government to defend the fixed exchange rate. Obviously, these 'general specifications' are simply the generalizations of the particular well-specified models of e.g. production, taxes, and so forth.

Costs of a devaluation.   One last piece of a representative second-generation model is still missing. In the literature, it is often assumed that the government has to pay a fixed cost if it does not keep the exchange rate fixed. It is assumed that the cost amounts to a given number, C, if the government changes the exchange rate in period t and amounts to zero if the government keeps its promise of a fixed exchange rate in period t. One way to think of C is that it measures the political prestige which would be lost when giving up a declared exchange rate policy. Alternatively, C could measure the loss of credibility in attempts to reduce inflation. Furthermore, in systems of multilateral exchange rate pegging (such as the ERM), other countries in the exchange rate mechanism may reduce their weight on the policy of pegging the exchange rate if the domestic country devalues, i.e. an element of international exchange rate coordination would be lost. Other interpretations of C can be imagined. It is admitted in the literature that the interpretation of this cost is a somewhat delicate matter, as it is not easy to measure quantitatively.

Jeanne (1997a) makes C stochastic in an exogenously specified form (in the empirical implementation in Jeanne, 1997a the cost is assumed to be captured by a linear time trend and the real exchange rate), whereas De Koch and Grilli (1993) make C endogenous by assuming that the private agents 'punish' the government by playing a trigger strategy if the government does not keep its promise of a fixed exchange rate. Especially, in the model of De Koch and Grilli (1993) the private agents punish the government by expecting a high rate of devaluation in (a finite number of) future periods.

3.3. *Solution of the model*

In this section, particular choices of l_t and Λ_t will be used to illustrate the general solution of second-generation models. The specific preferences of the government are assumed to include taxes and the rate of devaluation, i.e. the government minimizes the linear-quadratic loss-function

$$l_t = \tau_t^2 + \omega \pi_t^2 \tag{4}$$

where τ_t measures the tax revenues, π_t is the rate of devaluation defined as $(\varepsilon_{t+1} - \varepsilon_t)/\varepsilon_t$, and ω is a trade-off parameter. In this model $\Lambda^* = 0$, i.e. the government would like to keep taxes as low as possible. The constraint takes the form

$$\tau_t = \Psi - (\pi_t - \pi_t^e)m + \varepsilon_t \tag{5}$$

As is standard, it is assumed that private agents form expectations before the shock has been revealed, whereas the government sets the rate of devaluation after the shock has been revealed. In every period, the government has two possibilities when financing the fixed expenditures Ψ: raising conventional taxes or raising a one time seigniorage revenue from a surprise devaluation of the currency.

Basically, the government can pursue two strategies when it decides on its exchange rate policy: the government can take the private sector's expectations as given or it can try to influence the private sector's expectations. Refer to the first strategy as the discretionary (or no-commitment) policy and to the second as the commitment policy. If the government takes expectations as given, it will minimize (4) subject to (5) which yields the discretionary rate of devaluation

$$\pi_t = \left(\frac{m}{m^2 + \omega}\right)(\Psi + \pi_t^e m + \varepsilon_t) \tag{6}$$

and the tax flow

$$\tau_t = \left(\frac{\omega}{m}\right)\pi_t$$

To ease notation, define $\theta = 1/(m^2 + \omega)$. Under the discretionary policy (the no-commitment policy), the government's actual loss turns out to be

$$l^{NC} = \theta\omega(\Psi + \pi_t^e m + \varepsilon_t)^2 \tag{7}$$

The private agents form expectations rationally and expect a rate of devaluation given by the statistical mean of (6), and the government can thus expect the loss

$$E(l^{NC}) = \theta\omega\left[\left\{\left(\frac{1}{\theta\omega}\right)\Psi\right\}^2 + \sigma^2\right] \tag{8}$$

when $E(\varepsilon_t) = 0$ and $E(\varepsilon^2) = \sigma^2$ as the variance of the shock.

If the government 'promised' credibly never to change the exchange rate, i.e. $\pi_t = 0$, $\forall t$, conventional taxes would need to take account of balancing the government's budget, i.e. $\tau_t = \Psi + \pi_t^e m + \varepsilon_t$. Under this fixed exchange rate regime (the 'commitment-regime'), the loss would be

$$l_t^C = (\Psi + \pi_t^e m + \varepsilon_t)^2 \tag{9}$$

giving an expected loss of

$$E(l_t^C) = \Psi^2 + \sigma^2$$

It is assumed that the commitment policy consists in explicitly committing to a fixed exchange rate, and when entering a period of fixed exchange rates $E(l^{NC}) > E(l^C)$, or

$$\Psi^2 \left(\frac{1}{\theta\omega} \right) > \sigma^2 \tag{10}$$

It is a standard assumption in the literature that (10) is satisfied when the government enters a period with a fixed exchange rate. (10) implies that the variance of the shocks that hit the economy is relatively small compared to the parameters that determine the inflation bias in a discretionary regime.

An escape clause. Assume now that the government initially keeps the exchange rate fixed and has to pay the cost C if it alters this policy. In order to illustrate when the government abandons the policy of a fixed exchange rate, rewrite (7) as

$$l_t^{NC} = \theta\omega\varepsilon_t^2 + 2\theta\omega b\varepsilon_t + \theta\omega c$$

and (9) as

$$l_t^C = \varepsilon_t^2 + 2b\varepsilon_t + c$$

where $b = (\Psi + \pi_t^e m)$ and $c = (\Psi + \pi_t^e m)^2$. l_t^{NC} and l_t^C can now be illustrated as in Figure 1 for *some given value of π_t^e.*

The figure illustrates how the exchange rate policy is determined in this static model. If the government changes the exchange rate, it sets the rate of change as in (6). The distance $l_t^C - l_t^{NC}$ is the extra loss from keeping the exchange rate fixed. This 'extra loss' arises as a consequence of the lost ability to accommodate shocks in an *ex post* optimal way, i.e. *when the exchange rate is fixed*, the loss from pursuing a discretionary policy is lower than the loss from pursuing the fixed exchange rate policy, *for given expectations* concerning the rate of devaluation. Of course, this last insight is basically the general time-inconsistency problem; see Barro and Gordon (1983).

If the government does not keep its promise of a fixed exchange rate, it incurs the cost C, i.e. it will only be an optimal policy for the government to change the exchange rate when $l_t^C - l_t^{NC} \geqslant C$. In total, the government calculates $l^C - (l^{NC} + C) = \Pi$, and if $\Pi < 0$, it clearly pays for the government to break with

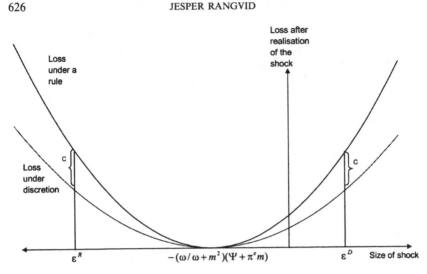

Figure 1. Realized loss when keeping the exchange rate fixed respectively floating. C is the cost to be paid when abandoning the fixed exchange rate regime.

its exchange rate promise. The critical values for determining whether the fixed exchange rate is optimal turn out to be the values that yield $l^C - l^{NC} - C = 0$. Therefore, the size of C implicitly determines the critical values of the shocks, for numerical values larger than these it will be optimal for the government to let $\pi_t \neq 0$. In conclusion; if a shock larger than ε_t^D is realized, the government will devalue; if a shock smaller than ε_t^R is realized, the government will revalue.

It is thus an important implication of the model that the government at the beginning of all periods in time compares the expected loss if it keeps the exchange rate fixed with the expected loss if it changes the exchange rate. This implication of the model can be contrasted with the description of the government in first-generation models. In first-generation models, the government passively monitors the approach of the speculative attack and does not try to change this situation. Neither does the government evaluate whether this abandonment of the policy of a fixed exchange rate is affecting the goals of the government in a positive or a negative way.

It is emphasized that Figure 1 is drawn for a given value of π_t^e. The determination of π_t^e is crucial in the second-generation models of currency crises. Solving the equation $l_t^C - l_t^{NC} = C$ for ε_t, one finds the critical values

$$\varepsilon_t^D = \left(\frac{1}{m}\right)\sqrt{C(m^2 + \omega)} - (\Psi + \pi_t^e m) \tag{11}$$

$$\varepsilon_t^R = -\left(\frac{1}{m}\right)\sqrt{C(m^2 + \omega)} - (\Psi + \pi_t^e m) \tag{12}$$

(11) and (12) show that the critical values of the shocks are contingent upon the expected rate of devaluation; if agents change expectations with respect to the rate of devaluation, the critical values of the shock will be changed. Consequently, it can be that several levels of π_t are realized in equilibrium.

3.3.1. *Multiple equilibria*

It is crucial for the occurrence of multiple equilibria that the critical values of the shock depend on the expectations of the private sector concerning the rate of devaluation. In essence, this dependence implies that a sudden change in π_t^e can lead to an actual change in π_t even when none of the other parameters in the economy have changed. More precisely, when knowing the goals of the government, the private sector will calculate the mean of the rate of devaluation

$$E(\pi_t) = E(\pi_t \mid \varepsilon_t > \varepsilon_t^D) \cdot P(\varepsilon_t > \varepsilon_t^D) + E(\pi_t \mid \varepsilon_t < \varepsilon_t^R) \cdot P(\varepsilon_t < \varepsilon_t^R) \qquad (13)$$

where $P(\cdot)$ is the probability of $(\cdot)$ being realized and $E(\cdot)$ is the statistical mean of $(\cdot)$.

In the following, it is assumed that ε_t is uniformly distributed on the interval $[-\mathcal{U}, \mathcal{U}]$ and ε_t and ε_{t-1} are independent, so the density function of ε_t is

$$f(\varepsilon_t) = \begin{cases} \dfrac{1}{2\mathcal{U}} & \text{for } \varepsilon_t \in [-\mathcal{U}, \mathcal{U}] \\[2mm] 0 & \text{for } \varepsilon_t \notin [-\mathcal{U}, \mathcal{U}] \end{cases}$$

With the uniform distribution, (13) is

$$E(\pi_t) = E(\pi_t \mid \varepsilon_t \in [-\mathcal{U}, \varepsilon_t^R]) \cdot P(\varepsilon_t \in [-\mathcal{U}, \varepsilon_t^R])$$

$$+ E(\pi_t \mid \varepsilon_t \in [\varepsilon_t^D, \mathcal{U}]) \cdot P(\varepsilon_t \in [\varepsilon_t^D, \mathcal{U}]) \qquad (14)$$

As $P(\varepsilon_t \in [-\mathcal{U}, \varepsilon_t^R]) = (\varepsilon_t^R + \mathcal{U})/2\mathcal{U}$, $P(\varepsilon_t \in [\varepsilon_t^D, \mathcal{U}]) = (\mathcal{U} - \varepsilon_t^D)/2\mathcal{U}$, $E(\varepsilon_t \mid \varepsilon_t \in [-\mathcal{U}, \varepsilon_t^R]) = (\varepsilon_t^R - \mathcal{U})/2$, and $E(\varepsilon_t \mid \varepsilon_t \in [\varepsilon_t^D, \mathcal{U}]) = (U + \varepsilon_t^D)/2$, (6) and (14) can be used to obtain

$$E(\pi_t) = \theta m \left[\left(1 - \frac{(\varepsilon_t^D - \varepsilon_t^R)}{2\mathcal{U}} \right)(\Psi + \pi_t^e m) - \frac{(\varepsilon_t^D)^2 - (\varepsilon_t^R)^2}{4\mathcal{U}} \right] \qquad (15)$$

When the private agents take into account the possibility of both a revaluation and a devaluation, they will expect a rate of change in the exchange rate as given by (15). In order to graphically illustrate the equilibria in the economy, though, it is assumed that the private agents assign a positive probability to the event of a devaluation only, i.e. $P(\varepsilon_t \in [-\mathcal{U}, \varepsilon_t^R]) = 0.$[16] With this assumption,

$E(\pi_t) = E(\pi_t \mid \varepsilon_t \in [\varepsilon_t^D, \mathcal{U}]) \cdot P(\varepsilon_t \in [\varepsilon_t^D, \mathcal{U}])$, or

$$E(\pi_t) = \theta m \left(\frac{\mathcal{U} - \varepsilon_t^D}{2\mathcal{U}} \right) \left(\Psi + \frac{\mathcal{U} + \varepsilon_t^D}{2} + \pi_t^e m \right) \tag{16}$$

Imposing the assumption of rational expectations, $E(\pi_t) = \pi_t^e$, both the left-hand and the right-hand side of (16) will be increasing in π_t^e. Depending on the slope of the right-hand side, multiple values for π_t^e can equalize (16) and there can thus be multiple equilibria for the rate of devaluation. In particular, if the slope of the right-hand side exceeds one, a possibility of multiple equilibria arises. On the other hand, if the slope of the right-hand side is everywhere less than one, one unique equilibrium is secured. This is the basic *formal* message in second-generation models of currency crises, if the focus in these models is on the issue of multiple equilibria.

Substituting for $E(\pi_t) = \pi_t^e$ in (16)

$$E(\pi_t) \equiv f[\varepsilon^D] = \theta m \left(\frac{\mathcal{U} - \varepsilon_t^D}{2\mathcal{U}} \right) \left(\Psi + \frac{\mathcal{U} + \varepsilon_t^D}{2} \right) \cdot \left[1 - \theta m^2 \left(\frac{\mathcal{U} - \varepsilon_t^D}{2\mathcal{U}} \right) \right]^{-1} \tag{17}$$

(17) yields the expected rate of devaluation conditioned upon the following: a uniform distribution of the shock, rational expectations, and a zero-probability assigned to the event of a revaluation.

The finding of multiple equilibria is most easily proved by the use of a graphical illustration. Rational equilibria require $\pi^e = E(\pi)$. Illustrating (16) in a $(\pi^e, E(\pi))$-diagram will give equilibria where the right-hand side of (16) crosses the 45° line.

With the uniform distribution, $d\varepsilon^D/d\pi^e \mid_{\varepsilon^D > -\mathcal{U}} = -m$ and $d\varepsilon^D/d\pi^e \mid_{\varepsilon^D = -\mathcal{U}} = 0$, and the slope of the right-hand side of (16) can be calculated as

$$\frac{dE(\pi)}{d\pi^e} = \begin{cases} \theta m^2 \left[\dfrac{1}{2} + \dfrac{1}{2\mathcal{U}} (\Psi + \pi^e m) \right] & \text{for } \varepsilon^D > -\mathcal{U} \\[3mm] \theta m^2 & \text{for } \varepsilon^D = -\mathcal{U} \end{cases} \tag{18}$$

i.e. the slope is linear for $\varepsilon^D = -\mathcal{U}$ and convex for $\varepsilon^D > -\mathcal{U}$, as $d(d\varepsilon^D/d\pi^e \mid_{\varepsilon^D > -\mathcal{U}})/d\pi^e = \theta m^2/2\mathcal{U} > 0$. A typical representation of (18) would thus be as in Figure 2. In this figure, the number of equilibria amounts to three (labelled A, B, and C) which is the maximum number of equilibria with the present setting of the economy, i.e. with a uniform distribution of the shock.

3.3.2. *Implications of multiple equilibria*

In order to understand the economic intuition driving the result of multiple equilibria, consider the seigniorage budget constraint: $\tau_t = \Psi - (\pi - \pi^e)m + \varepsilon_t$.

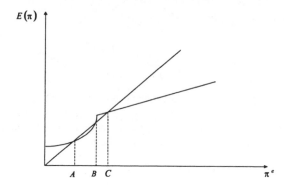

Figure 2. Economy with three different equilibria.

Imagine now a situation where a higher expected rate of devaluation reduces the revenues from seigniorage and therefore, ceteris paribus, higher conventional taxes will be necessary to balance the government budget. If the government does not like the higher taxes, it can instead raise π thereby increasing seigniorage revenues. This implies that the possibility of agents *expecting* a higher rate of devaluation makes the government more willing to actually use the exchange rate instrument.

Alternatively, consider the production constraint: $y_t = \bar{y} + \alpha(\pi - \pi^e) - \varepsilon_t^y$. A higher expected rate of devaluation leads to higher nominal wages being demanded. If the government does not change the exchange rate, the higher *real* wages (resulting from higher nominal wages and unadjusted prices) lead to lower production. If the government devalues, on the other hand, it accommodates the expected higher nominal wages and keeps real wages at their original levels leaving production unaffected.

Multiple equilibria in a second-generation model thus imply that an economy which has an otherwise relatively low rate of devaluation can see its exchange rate suddenly being exposed to a speculative attack even when fundamentals are 'relatively' strong and none of the parameters related to the fundamentals have changed; the only part of the economy which has changed is the expectation held by the private sector concerning the rate of devaluation (from $\pi^e = A$ to $\pi^e = C$ for instance). Alternatively stated: expectations are jump variables and jump variables cannot be controlled by the government — the government can only try to influence expectations.

3.4. *Dependence on 'fundamentals'*

It is important to point out that it is only in certain circumstances that the government will accommodate the expectations of the private sector. Actually, the number of equilibria in a given economy depends crucially on the level of 'fundamentals'. The fundamentals in the above example are represented by Ψ

(higher Ψ implies 'worse' fundamentals as taxes need to be increased in order to balance the government's budget). An increase in Ψ can either decrease or increase the number of equilibria, but will always lead to a higher average rate of devaluation. As

$$\left. \frac{dE(\pi)}{d\Psi} \right|_{\pi^e = 0} = \theta m \left[\frac{1}{2} + \frac{\Psi}{2\mathcal{U}} \right] > 0$$

starting from a situation such as A in Figure 3 (with a unique equilibrium at a low rate of devaluation) and decreasing the 'strength' of the economy, i.e. increase Ψ, one arrives at a situation as depicted in Figure 4 and the number of equilibria changes from one to two, these being given by point A and B. Increasing Ψ, the locus in Figure 4 is shifted upwards and one arrives at a situation such as in

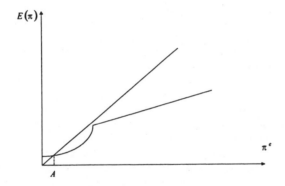

Figure 3. Economy with one uniquely determined low rate of devaluation equilibrium.

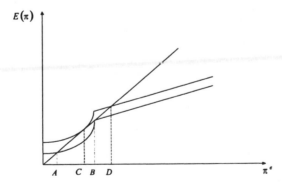

Figure 4. Economies with two equilibria.

Figure 2 (with three equilibria which is the maximum number of equilibria that can be generated in the present model with its uniform distribution of the shock). If the fundamentals in the economy become worse, two new equilibria are realized, point C and D in Figure 4, both with a higher rate of devaluation than point A and B in the figure. Finally, with the 'worst fundamentals', one arrives at a situation such as in Figure 5, at which the agents expect only one equilibrium, A, with a high rate of devaluation. At this equilibrium, the economy behaves as in a floating exchange rate regime, as $\varepsilon^D = -\mathcal{U}$ and all shocks to the economy are consequently transmitted through to the exchange rate and the exchange rate regime provides no stabilization.

Basically, the figures illustrate that when fundamentals are very bad, only one equilibrium will prevail (the floating exchange rate), when 'fundamentals' are very good, only one equilibrium will prevail (the fixed exchange rate or very low π^e), but for intermediate levels of the 'fundamentals' multiple equilibria can result. For this reason, Morris and Shin (1998) call the three situations the *stable* region (Figure 3), the *ripe-for-attack* region (Figures 2 and 4), and the *unstable* region (Figure 5) respectively, whereas Jeanne (1999) is slightly more lyrical and labels the three regions heaven, purgatory, and hell respectively.

Obstfeld (1996a, 1996b) has argued that the tripartite partition of fundamentals is an essential part of the story on multiple equilibria. For instance, consider an economy with very strong fundamentals. In such an economy, a sudden shift in π^e will not necessarily cause the loss under a fixed exchange rate to be higher than the loss that will be realized if a change in the exchange rate occurs. This argument runs: with strong fundamentals, the private sector's expectations will be influenced, as the private sector does not need to fear that the government will devalue, i.e. their expectations will not 'jump' from a low rate of devaluation to a high one. On the other hand, with very bad fundamentals, the government finds it too costly not to accommodate shocks, and a regime of fixed exchange rates cannot be maintained.

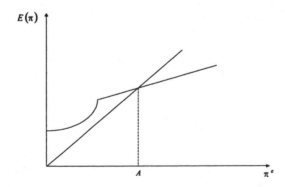

Figure 5. Economy with one uniquely determined high rate of devaluation equilibrium.

632   JESPER RANGVID

3.5. *The relevance of multiple equilibria*

It seems reasonable to claim that the use of alternative economic environments (cost-benefit analyses of economies plagued by unemployment, economies with tax-level considerations, and so forth) is today seen as an improvement of the 'printing money' set-up of first-generation models. On the other hand, the relevance of multiple equilibria when explaining the occurrence of currency crises is still subject to debate. In the following, the consequences for the prediction of multiple equilibria when assuming either a trend in fundamentals or lack of common knowledge will be studied.[17]

3.5.1. *Trend in fundamentals*

Consider first a situation where fundamentals are trending. For instance, this trend in fundamentals could be due to an increasing rate of unemployment, a continuing real exchange rate appreciation etc. Krugman (1996) notices that a trend in fundamentals is the crucial assumption in first-generation models (the shrinking foreign exchange reserves), whereas most second-generation models are formulated without any trend in fundamentals. He then makes the point that if there is a trend in fundamentals in a typical second-generation model, the private agents will attack the currency as soon as they know that they will succeed with their attack — not before and not after — and the timing of the speculative attack will be uniquely determined, i.e. the possibility of multiple equilibria has been eliminated.

The intuition underlying this result is probably best illustrated by referring to the intuition underlying the speculative attach as a unique equilibrium in the first-generation models. Consider the first-generation model of Section 2: if there was no speculative attack before the point in time where foreign exchange reserves reached their critical level (time $\bar{T}$), the private agents were sure to make a profit at $\bar{T}$, the reason being that at $\bar{T}$ the exchange rate would jump to its corresponding shadow exchange rate. Realizing that 'everybody' will have this profit opportunity at $\bar{T}$, some agents will launch a speculative attack immediately before $\bar{T}$ (call this point in time $\bar{T}^-$ for instance) enabling these particular agents to get all the profit. But as there is also a profit opportunity at $\bar{T}^-$, some agents will launch a speculative attack immediately before $\bar{T}^-$ (call this point in time $\bar{T}^{--}$). This process continues until the earliest point in time at which a speculative attack will succeed (labelled T in Section 2), where there is no jump in the exchange rate and all profit opportunities have been eliminated. Furthermore, notice that if no attack has occurred until for instance period $\bar{T}^-$ and neither occurs at $\bar{T}^-$, the fixed exchange rate regime survives this period also, i.e. at $\bar{T}^-$ there are two equilibria: a 'good' (no attack) and a 'bad' (an attack). Actually, in all time periods $t \in [T, \bar{T}]$ there are multiple equilibria (the condition for the multiplicity of equilibria thus being that there has not already been a speculative attack), but these equilibria are all ruled out as a consequence of the backward induction process just described.

Consider now the second-generation model. With a trend in fundamentals there will with certainty be a finite point in time where the government will find it too costly to keep the exchange rate fixed. Subject to the constraint that there has not already been a speculative attack, the government will at this point in time abandon the fixed exchange rate regime with certainty, i.e. in a deterministic second-generation model there will be a unique point in time, $\overline{T}$, at which there will be a jump in the exchange rate. Using the backward induction argument, though, agents will eliminate all profit opportunities, and thus eliminate the multiple equilibria in all time periods $t \in [T, \overline{T}]$ with, again, T as the earliest point in time where a speculative attack will succeed. Trending fundamentals thus pave the way for a unique equilibrium in second-generation models, Krugman (1996) argues.

Two caveats need to be made, though. First, as Kehoe (1996) comments, it is only when the government is concerned with the private sector's expectations concerning the rate of devaluation in *future* periods (for instance, expectations concerning the future rate of devaluation which then influence the current level of interest rates) that the backward induction argument goes through. Kehoe (1996) then relates this insight to the fact that many second-generation models focus on situations where it is expectations concerning the rate of devaluation in the *present* period that matter (for instance, the level of wages determined by the expectations formed in the past concerning the rate of devaluation in the present period). Second, as Krugman himself (Krugman, 1999) admits, multiple equilibria actually do seem important in so far as in a number of recent currency crises, it is simply difficult to argue that a trend in fundamentals was present ('I was wrong; Maury Obstfeld was right', Krugman, 1999, p. 1).[18]

3.5.2. *The role of common knowledge*

Morris and Shin (1998, 1999) attack the second-generation literature from a somewhat different perspective. They argue that the finding of multiple equilibria hinges too strongly on the assumptions that (*i*) private agents have perfect common knowledge concerning the true state of fundamentals and (*ii*) that all agents know what all other agents do for every state of the fundamentals.[19]

Before reviewing the argumentation of Morris and Shin, consider first how shifts between the different equilibria occur in a typical multiple equilibria model. In models of multiple equilibria, a shift between one equilibrium, such as A in Figure 2, to another equilibrium, such as B in Figure 2 (which occurs without any change in the fundamentals) is typically described by a 'sunspot' variable. Basically, a sunspot variable is a variable which is not necessarily related to the state of the fundamentals in the economy, which all agents can observe, and which serves the purpose of coordinating the beliefs of all agents. For instance (referring to Figure 2), all agents know that fundamentals are within the ripe-for-attack region (and all agents know that all other agents also know this). Furthermore, before the realization of the sunspot variable, all agents know that all other agents believe equilibrium A will be realized and, after the realization of the sunspot variable, all agents know that all other agents believe equilibrium B will be realized, i.e. the agents will attack the currency only because they see other agents attack the currency and not because something has happened to the fundamentals. In the literature surveyed in this paper, such sunspot variables are typically interpreted as e.g. the action of one big agent in the foreign exchange market (a George Soros type of agent), statements from governments, and policy actions or policy outcomes not directly related to the state of the fundamentals.[20] Therefore, in second-generation models with multiple equilibria, the shift between the different equilibria, and thus the actual outbreak of a currency crisis, is left to be explained by an extraneous event from outside the economy, and the outbreak of the currency crisis itself is thus not endogenously determined.

The ability of all the agents to figure out with perfection that fundamentals are within the ripe-for-attack region (and the ability of all the agents to observe the sunspot variable) thus plays a crucial role for the determination of which particular equilibrium is realized in models of multiple equilibria. Indeed, Morris and Shin (1998, 1999) show that if the assumption that the agents are able to observe with perfection the true state of fundamentals is relaxed, this has severe implications for the finding of multiple equilibria.

To be more specific, Morris and Shin assume that a single private agent observes a noisy signal concerning the true state of fundamentals only. Basically, if the true state of fundamentals is Ψ, Morris and Shin assume that an agent j observes a noisy signal $s_j = \Psi + \varepsilon_j$ only, with $\varepsilon_j \sim (0, \sigma)$ as the noise to the signal of agent j, i.e. agent j does not observe precisely Ψ. Furthermore, agent j knows that the other agents do not observe Ψ with precision. With unobservable Ψ, agents no longer possess common knowledge with respect to the true state of fundamentals. Instead, agents possess common knowledge with respect to the distribution of the (now stochastic) fundamental Ψ as well as the distribution of ε_j. It follows that when one agent does not know with certainty what level of the fundamentals the other agents observe, the agent does not know either, what the actions of the other agents will be: will the other agents attack the currency or will they refrain from doing so (alternatively stated: agent j does not know whether the other agents have observed some signal $\hat{s}$ suggesting that fundamentals are within the unstable region, in which case the agents would for sure attack the currency if common knowledge of Ψ prevailed, or have the other agents observed some signal $\bar{s}$ suggesting that fundamentals are within the stable region, in which case they would for sure not attack the currency if common knowledge of Ψ prevailed)? It follows that when a particular agent j cannot ascertain what the other agents do in equilibrium, obviously this particular agent j will not and cannot attack the currency only because the other agents do so. Basically, this rules out any possibility of multiple equilibria. Actually, now agent j will attack the currency only when the signal s_j he observes is at a level such that he believes that the true fundamentals Ψ are such that all agents believe that all other agents will attack the currency — and thus agent j attacks the currency himself.[21] Therefore, there will be a unique level of the fundamentals for values worse than this, the exchange rate is attacked because the signal that agent j receives is such that he estimates that all other agents will attack and for values better than this unique level of the fundamentals, the exchange rate is not attacked, i.e. the multiplicity of equilibria has been eliminated.[22]

Intuitively, a multiplicity of equilibria is not realized because each individual agent no longer attacks the currency because the other agents do so, but attacks the currency only because the individual agent *believes* that the other agents attack the currency; and the value of the signal that makes the individual agent believe that the other agents attack the currency is uniquely determined.[23]

The model in Morris and Shin (1998) is static and merely developed to study the implications for the number of equilibria when assuming away the common knowledge of Ψ. In Morris and Shin (1999), they suggest a dynamic framework thereby allowing for an exact determination of the point in time where a currency crisis occurs. In addition, the dynamic set-up allows for a characterization of the dynamics of agents' belief with respect to the vulnerability of a currency peg as fundamentals change. Furthermore, Corsetti *et al.* (1999) use the insights from the Morris and Shin approach to study whether the presence of one large investor (relative to a high number of small investors) in the foreign exchange market makes a country more vulnerable to currency attacks. Basically, Corsetti *et al.* (1999) find that when the large trader is better informed than the small traders, a country becomes more prone to speculative attacks, as the large trader serves the purpose of coordinating the beliefs of the smaller agents.

3.5.3. *Multiple equilibria? Two quotations*

It seems fair to end the discussion on the relevance on multiple equilibria by two citations: 'I hereby capitulate. I cannot see any way to make sense of the contagion of 1997–1998 without supposing the existence of multiple equilibria', Krugman (1999), p. 8–9 and 'the fact that an optimistic view about East Asian economies prevailed for so long (in the face of some reports of banking sector problems), the rapidity of the change in view, and the suddenness and severity of the resulting crises all argue in favor of the multiple equilibrium story', Masson (1998), p. 6. In the end, though, the debate has to be resolved by analyzing the empirical evidence; see Section 3.7.

3.6. *The role of financial markets*

As mentioned, the first- and second-generation models differ with respect to the variables included in the models and the modelling of the government. Furthermore, the models also differ with respect to the description of financial markets. In first-generation models, financial markets play an important role in the sense that the agents on the financial markets (the only agents in the economy that are actually modelled) ensure that no arbitrage possibilities arise by launching the speculative attack as soon as they will succeed with the attack. Furthermore, the agents try to predict the timing of a currency crisis and are perfectly successful in doing so in deterministic models and are rather successful in stochastic models by behaving in such a way that interest rates increase as the probability of a crisis increases. On the other hand, in second-generation models, financial markets are basically unimportant (for given levels of the fundamentals), as the behavior of the agents on the financial markets is not modelled, i.e. they do not behave as in first-generation models by calculating shadow exchange rates, do not rebalance their portfolios, do not behave such that interest rates increase (for given levels of the fundamentals), and so forth. In second-generation models, the agents in financial markets merely join the speculative attack as it is realized.[24]

The reason for this distinct treatment of financial markets in respectively first- and second-generation models is that the models focus on two different aspects of currency crises. Where the first-generation models focus less on the underlying reasons for the speculative attack (e.g. why is the government financing its budget deficit by printing money?) and more on the description of the attack itself, the second-generation models, on the other hand, focus on the description of the underlying reasons for the speculative attack (the cost-benefit analysis of the government), and thus less on the speculative attack itself.

3.7. *Empirical evidence*

The development of new theories to explain currency crises has been followed by the development of new methods to empirically discriminate between the different theories. Furthermore, the determinants of currency crises, the extent to which currency crises can be predicted, and other aspects of the currency crises of the 1990s have been investigated.

Where the first-generation models predicted secular trends in fundamentals and expansionary monetary policy in the periods leading up to currency crises, both of which enable the private agents to predict the timing of currency crises, the second-generation models predict that (*i*) real economic variables are in 'in less favorable conditions in periods leading up to currency crises', (*ii*) currency crises are in fact difficult to predict, and (*iii*) the economies can be in states of multiple equilibria in periods of currency crises.

Notice that the implications of the sentence 'fundamentals were in less favorable conditions in periods leading up to currency crises' are not straightforward to test empirically, but it is obvious from Figures 2 to 5 that whether a currency crisis will occur or not depends on the level of fundamentals — for instance if fundamentals are very good, no currency crisis will occur. Furthermore, the multiple equilibria story suggests that as long as the fundamentals are 'in less favorable conditions', as in Figure 4, periods where no currency crisis occurs can occur, but if in some period a sunspot variable is realized a currency crisis takes place. For these reasons, Eichengreen *et al.* (1994, 1995, 1996) compare the behavior of a considerable number of economic variables around periods of currency turmoils with the behavior of the same variables in periods of tranquility in the foreign exchange markets. The idea is that if real variables are in less favorable conditions in periods leading up to turmoils than in periods of no turmoils, and if monetary or real variables are not trending in

SECOND GENERATION MODELS   637

periods leading up to turmoils, currency crises could be interpreted as the results of shifts between different equilibria. On the other hand, if secular trends can be identified in periods leading up to currency turmoils, currency crises can be interpreted as occurring for the reasons emphasized in first-generation models. Eichengreen *et al.* look at developed countries, but their methodology has been used also by e.g. Moreno (1995) to analyze the experience of the Pacific Basin Economies, and by Kaminsky and Reinhart (1999) to analyze primarily developing countries. In all of these analyses, it is a common finding that monetary variables are indeed trending in periods leading up to currency turmoils as predicted by first-generation models, i.e. foreign exchange reserves are declining, domestic credit is growing at a considerable pace, and nominal interest rates are increasing. With respect to real variables, the typical findings are that output is lower and unemployment higher in periods leading up to currency crises than in periods of tranquility and that there is no clear trend in the development of these real variables. Basically, these findings thus suggest that currency crises could occur both as a consequence of expansionary monetary policy, but also as a consequence of shifts in expectations.[25]

An alternative empirical procedure that can be used to evaluate which variables are more important in empirical descriptions of currency crises, is to investigate which variables predict currency crises. For instance, Kaminsky *et al.* (1998) try to suggest 'leading indicators of currency crises', while Begg and Pattillo (1999) evaluate three different procedures for forecasting currency crises.[26] The variables that Kaminsky *et al.* (1998) and Begg and Pattillo (1999) find to predict currency crises 'best' are monetary variables, such as falling foreign exchange reserves, high growth rates of domestic credit, and so forth, whereas real variables do not normally help when predicting currency crises. It is important to emphasize, though, that the extent to which currency crises can be predicted is not impressive in the analyses, i.e. many actual incidents of currency crises are not predicted by the models and in many periods where the models predicted currency crises to occur, no currency crises actually did occur. Finally, Goldfajn and Valdés (1998) use survey data to test whether market participants have in fact been able to predict currency crises and, basically, find this not to be the case, i.e. market participants have not been able to foresee the coming of currency crises.

Are these findings good or bad news for second-generation models? Obviously, the fact that mainly monetary variables help in explaining and predicting currency crises is not evidence in favor of second-generation models. On the other hand, the fact that currency crises in general seem so difficult to predict is not evidence in favor of first-generation models. It should also be recognized that second-generation models suggest some element of predictability of currency crises (fundamentals have to be in less favorable conditions for multiple equilibria to arise), but the extent to which currency crises are predictable is higher in first-generation models (with trends in fundamentals). Furthermore, it is interesting to notice that some authors have claimed that currency crises can indeed be predicted (Kaminsky *et al.*, 1998), even when only to a minor extent, but the findings of e.g. Goldfajn and Valdés (1998) and Begg and Pattillo (1999) cast some doubt of this.

Obviously, when investigating whether currency crises can be predicted as well as the behavior of macroeconomic variables around times of currency crises, one does not directly *test* whether currency crises are self-fulfilling or whether the parameter restrictions implicitly assumed in the specific settings of second-generation models are fulfilled. Not many analyses have explicitly tested these restrictions, as the non-linearity of the models make them harder to take to data. Actually, to date, only Jeanne (1997a) has explicitly derived a likelihood ratio test for the existence of multiple equilibria in second-generation models of currency crises. He tests his model on data from the French franc crisis during 1992–1993 and finds that the restrictions cannot be rejected. Less formal tests have been proposed by Jeanne and Masson (1996, 2000) who use regime-switching models to search for jumps in the probabilities of being either in a regime of a low rate of devaluation or a high rate of devaluation, i.e. whether jumps between equilibria such a *A* and *B* in Figure 4 have described incidences of currency crises. For instance, Jeanne and Masson (1996, 2000) present estimates of the matrices of transition between different states (equilibria), and find that these estimates support the existence of multiple equilibria for the French franc crisis during 1992–1993. Furthermore, Masson (1999) presents results suggesting that fundamentals were within the region of multiple equilibria for a number of emerging markets recently exposed to speculative attacks.

4. Conclusion and policy implications

Throughout the 1990s a wave of speculative attacks has been realized, all of which have serious financial and economic consequences on the economies of the countries being exposed to the attacks. These events have made economists think about their recommendations of a pegged exchange rate as a goal in the conduct of monetary policy, and the second-generation models of currency crises add a new dimension to this recommendation.

While the problem of speculative attacks has been definitively solved in the eleven European countries which introduced a single currency on January 1, 1999, one common currency is obviously not a realistic option for the world as a whole (at least not within any reasonable time horizon). Therefore, in the following some brief perspectives on the options for small open economies are considered.[27]

Some economists, previously being proponents of pegged exchange rates, now advocate the use of more domestic orientated goals in monetary policy (inflation targets, price level targets, monetary aggregate targets, GDP targets and so forth), see Svensson (1994) and Mishkin (1999a). When relying on a policy of targeting for instance inflation or the price level, the exchange rate is seen more as a residual. In particular, it is argued that if domestic inflation is kept low, the exchange rate will be stable too. It can be argued that the repeated speculative attacks throughout the 1990s have strengthened such policy recommendations *per se*. It should be emphasized, though, that this kind of policy is not a 'free lunch' and such strategies have both advantages and disadvantages in comparison with an explicit exchange rate goal (see e.g. Buiter *et al.*, 1998 and Mishkin, 1999a for a discussion).

Related to the discussion of domestic orientated policy goals, other authors have argued for a return to floating exchange rates as a policy option in times of difficulties with pegged exchange rates, see e.g. Obstfeld (1995), Krugman (1998), and Mishkin (1999b). In the same vein, Obstfeld and Rogoff (1995) discuss the implications of recent empirical experiences and second-generation currency crises models for understanding the difficulty of keeping the exchange rate fixed, Mishkin (1999b) argues that the damages to the real part of the economy following a currency crisis by far outweigh the costs associated with the uncertainty of the future exchange rate in a floating exchange rate regime. In particular, Mishkin (1999b) discusses the implications of the large sudden devaluations often associated with currency crises, as in Asia, for firms' and banks' balance sheets.[28]

Furthermore, recognizing that national currencies are here to stay, some authors have discussed the possibility of throwing sand in the wheels of international finance (Eichengreen, Tobin and Wyplosz, 1995; ul Haq, 1996) by which is meant the imposition of controls on international capital movements. Mishkin (1999b), on the other hand, argues that the problems of sudden reversals of capital flows in times of currency turmoils are more to be seen as a consequence of the turmoils than their cause, and thus argues against capital controls.

Finally, when should a country pursue the goal of pegged exchange rates? To quote Mishkin (1999b), p. 722: 'Indeed, countries with a past history of poor inflation performance may find that only with a very strong commitment mechanism to an exchange rate peg (as in a currency board) can inflation be controlled'.

When considering whether a country should choose a fixed exchange rate, possibly combined with some form of capital controls, or return to floating exchange rates and instead follow a monetary policy strategy of targeting e.g. inflation, it is important to point out that it is difficult on the premises of welfare comparisons to advocate any specific kind of nominal pegging in monetary policy (Buiter *et al.*, 1998).[29] In the end, all models predict that exchange rates can actually be kept fixed if economic fundamentals are good.[30] On the other hand, if the economic fundamentals are not 'good', policies of pegged exchange rates can be quite harmful. The final recommendation turns out to be something along the lines: no matter which particular monetary policy strategy is pursued, it is of utmost importance that the strategy is pursued wholeheartedly, leaving no room for financial markets to misunderstand the commitment to the particular strategy.

Acknowledgements

The paper is based on a chapter of my Ph.D. dissertation. I would like to thank Tom Engsted, Jan Jakobsen, Henrik Jensen, Finn Østrup, and two anonymous referees for comments.

Notes

1. For a survey on historic examples of currency crises, see Bordo and Schwartz (1996).
2. Surveys of papers dealing with extensions of the basic first-generation model are found

in Agénor *et al.* (1992), Blackburn and Sola (1993), Agénor and Flood (1994), Garber and Svensson (1995), Calvo (1998), and Calvo and Végh (1999).

3. Furthermore, in the EMS, the central banks could borrow unlimited (at least in principle) amounts of credit from the other central banks and thus always keep foreign exchange reserves above some given minimum.

4. These high costs could be due to for instance high interest rate payments on public debt, where the high interest rates result from the expectations of the private sector regarding a high future rate of devaluation.

5. An impressive bibliography on the Asian crisis is maintained by Nouriel Roubini on http://www.stern.nyu.edu/~nroubini/asia/AsiaHomepage.html and a second bibliography is maintained on http://www.nber.org/crisis/. Agénor *et al.* (1999) collect a number of papers on the Asian crisis.

6. Eichengreen (1999), p. 140: 'In the end, then, I do not really view the new models developed in response to the Asian crisis as analytically distinct from the first- and second-generation models that preceded them but rather as interesting special cases of those more general frameworks'.

7. For instance, the EMS crises in 1992–1993 started with the Finish markka giving up its peg to the ECU, but was soon thereafter followed by crises in the other Scandinavian countries and in the member countries of the EMS (with the exception of the Netherlands). The crises in South America in the mid-1990s started in Mexico in December 1994, but soon spread to a number of countries in the region and eventually turned into what is now labelled the Tequila crises. Finally, the crisis in Asia started with Thailand giving up the peg of the Baht to the dollar on July 2, 1997, which was soon thereafter followed by crises in other countries in the region, e.g. Indonesia, South Korea, and so forth.

   Eichengreen *et al.* (1996) were first to empirically investigate the issue of contagion, whereas Masson (1998, 1999) discusses different kinds of contagion: 'spill-over effects' (a devaluation in one country has consequences for the competitiveness of a trading partner), 'monsoonal-effect' (crises in several countries being due to common underlying factors), and 'pure contagion' (changes in expectations not related to macroeconomic fundamentals). Masson argues that monsoonal effects and spill-overs could not account for the events in Asia, whereas pure contagion has some explanatory power. Additional perspectives on the theory of contagion can be found in Drazen (1999), Calvo and Mendoza (1999), and Loisel and Martin (1999), and additional perspectives on the empirical aspects of contagion in Glick and Rose (1999).

8. In general, if a (positive) jump in the price of an asset can be predicted to occur with certainty at some time $\bar{t}$, say, all agents will (short) sell the particular asset just before $\bar{t}$ and thereby press downward the price; see also Section 3.5.1. Basically, this eliminates the jump before it actually occurs.

   Note, though, that for instance Blanco and Garber (1986) show that in their stochastic first-generation model, the timing of the speculative attack is not perfectly foreseeable and the exchange rate can therefore jump to its corresponding shadow exchange rate when a realignment occurs. In their modelling of the dynamics of the ERM exchange rates, Rangvid and Sørensen (2001) also let the exchange rate jump to its corresponding shadow exchange rate in case of a realignment.

9. See also the discussion on multiple equilibria in the following sections of this survey.

10. It is important to emphasize, though, that even when the first-generation models are too simplistic to describe the actual economic environments within which governments operate, several of the insights from this generation of models are still of prime

importance when trying to understand currency crises. In particular, the role of investors on the foreign exchange markets and the reason why agents through the elimination of arbitrage possibilities need to launch a speculative attack (in certain situations) and thereby not allow for a smooth transition from a pegged to a floating exchange rate regime.

11. The assumption of a lower bound on the foreign exchange reserves is occasionally seen as a substitute for the assumption of a situation where the growth rate of domestic credit exceeds the international real interest rate. Especially, Obstfeld (1986b) shows that if $\mu > r$, with r as the international real interest rate, the government's intertemporal budget constraint is violated.

12. There are some surveys which discuss the similarities and differences between first- and second-generation models, e.g. Sutherland (1994), Cavallari and Corsetti (1996), Flood and Marion (1997), Calvo (1998), Krugman (1998), and Jeanne (1999). In this survey, second-generation models are more explicitly discussed.

13. Recognizing that Flood and Garber (1984) and Obstfeld (1986a) already mentioned the possibility of multiple equilibria, it seems reasonable to argue that the phrase second-generation models is less adequate if the phrase is meant to imply that a given model can deliver several equilibria.

14. It will be clear in the remaining part of the survey, though, that quite some space will be devoted to the issue of multiple equilibria.

15. Andersen (1998) focuses specifically on terms of trade shocks more than general employment shocks.

16. The same assumption is used in for instance Obstfeld (1994, 1997) and Bensaid and Jeanne (1997). The assumption does not seem especially strong, as casual observations suggest that agents, when considering an exchange rate being ripe for an attack, agree upon the direction of the misalignment. For instance, in the 1992–1993 ERM crises, speculation only concerned devaluations of the currencies (notice that no speculation against the Dutch guilder occurred, as this currency could have been judged to be 'stronger' than the German mark in 1992–1993 as reflected in e.g. differences in interest rates), in December 1994 speculation concerned a devaluation of the Mexican peso (and not a revaluation), and the recent crises in Asia concerned devaluations of the Asian currencies.

17. In addition to the issues discussed in the text, Garber (1996) argues that the EMS crises in 1992–1993 and the Mexico crises in 1994 can actually be understood within the framework of a first-generation model. The reason for the embracement of the second-generation models, he argues, is more political as, 'it is expedient for the official sector to put the blame on destabilizing speculators rather than on destabilizing policies', Garber (1996), p. 404. However, also within the framework of second-generation models there is actually a possibility for 'blaming policymakers' for conducting destabilizing policies in the sense that if policymakers let fundamentals deteriorate to the ripe-for-attack region the exchange rate can be exposed to self-fulfilling currency attacks, whereas if policymakers on the other hand keep fundamentals within the stable region, no attack will occur.

18. Krugman (1999) still claims, though, that if there is a secular trend, multiple equilibria can be ruled out.

19. In Morris and Shin (2000), the implications of assuming away common knowledge for a larger class of models used in macroeconomics and financial economics are surveyed.

20. An example is the Danish referendum on the Maastricht Treaty on June 2, 1992 which is occasionally interpreted as the event that ultimately caused the outbreak of the 1992–1993 ERM problems.

21. It follows that every single agent not only has to be concerned with what he believes to be the true state of fundamentals, but also what he believes that the other agents will do in equilibrium, knowing that they also face uncertainty with respect to the true state of fundamentals and the actions of other agents.

22. It follows that the Morris and Shin (1998) set-up relies on the assumption that the action of one agent attacking the currency is a strategic compliment to other agents attacking the currency (i.e. the more agents attack the currency, the higher is the gain for the individual agents of attacking the currency). Consequently, the result hinges on the assumption that it is not too expensive to participate in the currency attack. Actually, Morris and Shin (1998) show that if the cost of participating in the speculative attack is increased, the agent will refrain from doing so.

23. Especially, the cut-off value for the occurrence of a speculative attack measured in terms of the state of the fundamentals will depend on such items as the accuracy of the signal (the variance of ε), the distribution of ε, and the distribution of the fundamentals.

24. For deteriorating fundamentals, though, the arguments of Krugman (1996) become important; see Section 3.5.1.

25. Note, though that Kaminsky and Reinhart (1999) conclude that their findings of a 'multitude of weak and deteriorating economic fundamentals suggest that it would be difficult to characterize it (the crises they study) as self-fulfilling crises'.

26. Furthermore, Kaminsky *et al.* (1998) present very detailed tables summarizing the empirical literature on the issue with respect to periods, countries, methodology, variables, and so forth.

27. The following comments are not intended to be a complete analysis of the issues considered, but are to be seen more as a summarization of the discussion in the literature. In addition to the issues discussed in the main text, Alogoskoufis (1994) can be consulted for a survey of the traditional literature on the choice of exchange rate regimes.

28. Eichengreen *et al.* (1999) discuss how emerging markets can move from pegged exchange rates to greater exchange rate flexibility in a more smooth fashion than that associated with a currency crisis.

29. An interesting recent short paper that evaluates the benefits of respectively fixed and floating exchange rates by the traditional Poole (1970) approach, is Calvo (1999). He takes the implications of the recent currency crises into account when evaluating the two regimes.

30. Which is supported also by empirical evidence, as some small open economies with traditionally strong economic fundamentals, such as e.g. Austria and the Netherlands, actually have been able to peg their exchange rate over longer periods of time, see Obstfeld and Rogoff (1995).

References

Agénor, P. R., Bhandari, J. S. and Flood, R. P. (1992) Speculative attacks and models of balance of payments crises. *IMF Staff Papers*, 39, 357–394.

Agénor, P. R., Miller, M., Vines, D. and Weber, A. A. (1999) *The Asian Financial Crisis.* Cambridge University Press.

Agénor, P. R. and Flood, R. P. (1994) Macroeconomic policy, speculative attacks and balance of payments crises. In *Handbook of International Macroeconomics*, ed. by F. van der Ploeg, chap. 8, pp. 224–250. Blackwell Publishers.

Alogoskoufis, G. S. (1994) On inflation, unemployment, and the optimal exchange rate regime. In *Handbook of International Macroeconomics*, ed. by F. van der Ploeg, chap. 7, pp. 192–223. Blackwell Publishers.

Andersen, T. M. (1998) Shocks and the viability of a fixed exchange rate commitment. *Open Economies Review*, 9, 139–156.

Barro, R. J. and Gordon, D. B. (1983) Rules, discretion and reputation in a model of monetary policy. *Journal of Monetary Economics*, 12, 101–121.

Begg, A. and Pattillo, C. (1999) Are currency crises predictable? A test. *IMF Staff Papers*, 46, 107–138.

Bensaid, B. and Jeanne, O. (1997) The instability of fixed exchange rate systems when raising the nominal interest rate is costly. *European Economic Review*, 41, 1461–1478.

Blackburn, K. (1988) Collapsing exchange rate regimes and exchange rate dynamics: some further examples. *Journal of International Money and Finance*, 7, 373–385.

Blackburn, K. and Sola, M. (1993) Speculative currency attacks and balance of payments crises. *Journal of Economic Surveys*, 7, 119–144.

Blanco, H. and Garber, P. M. (1986) Recurrent devaluation and speculative attacks on the Mexican peso. *Journal of Political Economy*, 94, 148–166.

Bordo, M. D. and Schwartz, A. J. (1996) Why clashes between internal and external stability goals end in currency crises, 1797–1994. *Open Economies Review*, 7, 437–468.

Buiter, W. H., Corsetti, G. and Pesenti, P. A. (1998) *Financial Markets and European Monetary Coorperation — the lessons of the 1992–1993 Exchange Rate Mechanism crisis*. Cambridge University Press.

Calvo, G. A. (1987) Balance of payments crises in a cash-in-advance economy. *Journal of Money, Credit, and Banking*, 19, 19–32.

—— (1998) Varieties of capital-market crises. In *The Debt Burden and its Consequences for Monetary Policy*, ed. by G. A. Calvo and M. King, chap. 7, pp. 181–202. Macmillan Press.

—— (1999) Fixed versus flexible exchange rates. Preliminaries of a Turn-of-Millennium rematch. *mimeo*.

Calvo, G. A. and Vegh, C. A. (1999) Inflation stabilization and BOP crises in developing countries. *NBER Working Paper*, 6925, Forthcoming in *Handbook of Macroeconomics*.

Calvo, G. A. and Mendoza, E. G. (1999) Rational contagion and the globalization of Securities Markets. Forthcoming in *Journal of International Economics*.

Cavallari, L. and Corsetti, G. (1996) Policy making and speculative attacks in models of exchange rate crises: a synthesis. *Economic Growth Center, DP 752. Yale University*.

Claessens, S. (1988) Balance-of-payments crises in a perfect foresight optimizing model. *Journal of International Money and Finance*, 7, 363–372.

Cole, H. L. and Kehoe, T. J. (1996) A self-fulfilling model of Mexico's 1994–1995 debt crisis. *Journal of International Economics*, 41, 309–330.

Corsetti, G., Morris, S. and Shin, H. S. (1999) Does one Soros make a difference? The role of a large trader in currency crises. *mimeo*.

De Grauwe, P. (1997) Exchange rate arrangements between the Ins and the Outs. *CEPR Discussion Paper*, 1640.

De Koch, G. and Grilli, V. (1993) Fiscal policies and the choice of exchange rate regime. *Economic Journal*, 103, 347–358.

Dellas, H. and Stockman, A. (1993) Self-fulfilling expectations, speculative attacks, and capital controls. *Journal of Money, Credit, and Banking*, 25, 721–730.

Drazen, A. (1999) Political contagion in currency crises. *NBER Working Paper*, 7211.

Drazen, A. and Masson, P. R. (1994) Credibility of policies versus credibility of policy makers. *Quarterly Journal of Economics*, 109, 735–754.

Eichengreen, B., Rose, A. K. and Wyplosz, C. (1994) Speculative attacks on pegged exchange rates: an empirical exploration with special reference to the European Monetary System. *CEPR Discussion Paper*, 1060.

—— (1995) Exchange Market mayhem: the antecedents and aftermath of speculative attacks. *Economic Policy*, 21, 251–296.

—— (1996) Contagious currency crises: firsts tests. *Scandinavian Journal of Economics*, 98, 463–484.

Eichengreen, B. and Wyplosz, C. (1993) The unstable EMS. *Brookings Papers on Economic Activity*, 1, 51–143.

Eichengreen, B., Tobin, J. and Wyplosz, C. (1995) Two cases for sand in the wheels of international finance. *Economic Journal*, 105, 162–172.

Eichengreen, B. and Jeanne, O. (1998) Currency crises and unemployment: Sterling in 1931. *NBER Working Paper*, 6563.

Eichengreen, B., Masson, P., Savastano, M. and Sharma, S. (1999) Transition strategies and nominal anchors on the road to greater exchange-rate flexibility. *Princeton Essays in International Finance*, 213.

Flood, R. P. and Garber, P. M. (1984) Collapsing exchange rate regimes: some linear examples. *Journal of International Economics*, 17, 1–14.

Flood, R. P. and Marion, N. P. (1996) Speculative attacks: fundamentals and self-fulfilling prophecies. *Mimeo, Dartmouth College*.

—— (1997) Perspectives on the recent currency crisis literature. *mimeo, Dartmouth College*.

—— (2000) Self-fulfilling risk predictions: an application to speculative attacks. *Journal of International Economics*, 50, 245–268.

Garber, P. M. (1996) Comment on Krugman (1996). In *NBER Macroeconomics Annual*, ed. by B. S. Bernanke and J. J. Rotemberg, pp. 378–392. The MIT Press.

Garber, P. M. and Svensson, L. E. O. (1995) The operation and collapse of fixed exchange rate regimes. In *Handbook of International Economics*, ed. by G. Grossman and K. Rogoff, vol. III, chap. 36, pp. 1865–1911. Elsevier Science Publishers B.V.

Glick, R. and Rose, A. K. (1999) Contagion and trade: why are currency crises regional. *Journal of International Money and Finance*, 18, 603–618.

Goldfajn, I. and Valdés, R. O. (1998) Are currency crises predictable?. *European Economic Review*, 42, 873–885.

Jeanne, O. (1997a) Are currency crises self-fulfilling? a test. *Journal of International Economics*, 43, 263–286.

—— (1997b) The persistence of unemployment under a fixed exchange rate peg. *Mimeo*.

—— (1999) Currency crises: a perspective on recent theoretical developments. *CEPR Discussion Paper*, 2179.

Jeanne, O. and Masson, P. (1996) Was the French franc crisis a sunspot equilibrium? *Mimeo*.

—— (2000) Currency crises, sunspots, and Markov-switching regimes. *Journal of International Economics*, 50, 327–350.

Kaminsky, G. L. and Reinhart, C. M. (1999) The twin crises: the causes of banking and balance-of-payments problems. *American Economic Review*, 89, 473–500.

Kaminsky, G. L., Lizondo, S. and Reinhart, C. M. (1998) Leading indicators of currency crises. *IMF Staff Papers*, 45, 1–48.

Kehoe, T. J. (1996) Comment on Krugman (1996). In *NBER Macroeconomics Annual*, ed. by B. S. Bernanke and J. J. Rotemberg, pp. 378–392. The MIT Press.

Krugman, P. R. (1979) A model of balance of payments crises. *Journal of Money, Credit, and Banking*, 11, 311–325.

—— (1996) Are currency crises self-fulfilling? In *NBER Macroeconomics Annual*, ed. by B. S. Bernanke and J. J. Rotemberg, pp. 345–407. The MIT Press.

—— (1998) Currency crises. http://web.mit.edu/krugman/www/.

—— (1999) Balance sheets, the transfer problem, and financial crises. http://web.mit.edu/krugman/www/.

Loisel, O. and Martin, P. (1999) Coordination, cooperation, contagion, and currency crises. *CEPR Discussion Paper*, 2075.

Masson, P. R. (1995) Gaining and losing ERM credibility: the case of the United Kingdom. *Economic Journal*, 105, 571–582.

—— (1998) Contagion: monsoonal effects, spillovers, and jumps between multiple equilibria. *IMF Working Paper*. WP/98/142.

—— (1999) Contagion: macroeconomic models with multiple equilibria. *Journal of International Money and Finance*, 18, 587–602.

Mishkin, F. S. (1999a) International experiences with different monetary policy regimes. *Journal of Monetary Economics*, 43, 579–605.

—— (1999b) Lessons from the Asian crisis. *Journal of International Money and Finance*, 18, 709–723.

Moreno, R. (1995) Macroeconomic behavior during periods of speculative pressure or realignment: evidence from Pacific Basin economies. *FRBSF Economic Review*, pp. 3–16.

Morris, S. and Shin, H. Song (1998) Unique equilibrium in a model of self-fulfilling currency attacks. *American Economic Review*, 88, 587–597.

—— (1999) A theory of the onset of currency attacks. In *The Asian Financial Crises*, ed. by A. M. Vines and Weber, chap. 7, pp. 230–255. Cambridge University Press.

Obstfeld, M. (1984) Balance-of-payments crises and devaluation. *Journal of Money, Credit, and Banking*, 16, 208–217.

—— (1986a) Rational and self-fulfilling Balance-of-payments crises. *American Economic Review*, 76, 72–81.

—— (1986b) Speculative attack and the external constraint in a maximizing model of the balance of payments. *Canadian Journal of Economics*, 19, 4–22.

—— (1991) Destabilising effects of exchange rate escape-clauses. *NBER Working Paper*, 4603.

—— (1994) The logic of currency crises. *Banque de France — Cahiers économiques et monétaires*, 43, 189–213.

—— (1996a) Comment on Krugman (1996). In *NBER Macroeconomics Annual*, ed. by B. S. Bernanke and J. J. Rotemberg, pp. 393–403. The MIT Press.

—— (1996b) Models of currency crises with self-fulfilling features. *European Economic Review*, 40, 1037–1047.

—— (1997) Destabilising effects of exchange rate escape-clauses. *Journal of International Economics*, 43, 61–77.

Obstfeld, M. and Rogoff, K. (1995) The mirage of fixed exchange rates. *Journal of Economic Perspectives*, 9, 73–96.

Ozkan, F. G. and Sutherland, A. (1995) Policy measures to avoid a currency crisis. *Economic Journal*, 105, 510–519.

—— (1998) A currency crisis model with an optimising policymaker. *Journal of International Economics*, 44, 339–364.

Poole, W. (1970) Optimal choice of monetary policy instruments in a simple stochastic macro model. *Quarterly Journal of Economics*, 84, 197–216.

Radelet, S. and Sachs, J. (1998) The onset of the East Asian financial crisis. *NBER Working Paper*, 6680.

Rangvid, J. and Sørensen, C. (2001) Determinants of the implied shadow exchange rates from a target zone. 45, 1665–1696.

Rose, A. K. and Svensson, L. E. O. (1994) European exchange rate credibility before the fall. *European Economic Review*, 38, 1185–1216.

Sachs, J., Tornell, A. and Velasco, A. (1996) The Mexican peso crisis: sudden death or death foretold?. *Journal of International Economics*, 41, 265–283.

Stansfield, E. and Sutherland, A. (1995) Exchange rate realignments and realignment expectations. *Oxford Economic Papers*, 47, 211–228.

Sutherland, A. (1994) Currency crisis models: bridging the gap between old and new approaches. In *European Currency Crises and After*, ed. by C. Bordes, E. Girardi and J. Mélitz, chap. 4, pp. 57–82. Manchester University Press.

Svensson, L. E. O. (1994) Fixed exchange rates as a means to stability: what have we learned?. *European Economic Review*, 38, 447–468.

646   JESPER RANGVID

ul Haq, M., Kaul, I. and Grunberg, I. (1996) *The Tobin tax: coping with financial volatility*. Oxford University Press.

Velasco, A. (1996) Fixed exchange rates: Credibility, flexibility, and multiplicity. *European Economic Review*, 40, 1023–1035.

Willman, A. (1988) The Collapse of the fixed exchange rate regime with sticky prices and imperfect substitutability between domestic and foreign bonds. *European Economic Review*, 32, 1817–1838.

Wyplosz, C. (1986) Capital controls and balance of payments crises. *Journal of International Money and Finance*, 5, 167–179.

[18]

Balance Sheets, the Transfer Problem, and Financial Crises

PAUL KRUGMAN   krugman@mit.edu
MIT, Department of Economics, Cambridge, MA 02139

Abstract

In a world of high capital mobility, the threat of speculative attack becomes a central issue of macroeconomic policy. While "first-generation" and "second-generation" models of speculative attacks both have considerable relevance to particular financial crises of the 1990s, a "third-generation" model is needed to make sense of the number and nature of the emerging market crises of 1997–98. Most of the recent attempts to produce such a model have argued that the core of the problem lies in the banking system. This paper sketches another candidate for third-generation crisis modeling—one that emphasizes two facts that have been omitted from formal models to date: the role of companies' balance sheets in determining their ability to invest, and that of capital flows in affecting the real exchange rate.

For the founding fathers of currency-crisis theory—a fraternity among whom Bob Flood holds a place of high honor—the emerging market crises of 1997–8 inspire both a sense of vindication and a sense of humility. On one side, the number and severity of these crises has demonstrated in a devastatingly thorough way the importance of the subject; in a world of high capital mobility, it is now clear, the threat of speculative attack becomes a central issue—indeed, for some countries *the* central issue—of macroeconomic policy. On the other side, even a casual look at recent events reveals the inadequacy of existing crisis models. True, the Asian crisis has settled some disputes—as I will argue below, it decisively resolves the argument between "fundamentalist" and "self-fulfilling" crisis stories. (I was wrong; Maury Obstfeld was right). But it has also raised new questions.

One way to describe the problem is to think in terms of the celebrated (Eichengreen, Rose, and Wyplosz, 1995) distinction between "first-generation" and "second-generation" crisis models. First-generation models, exemplified by Krugman (1979) and the much cleaner paper by Flood and Garber (1984), in effect explain crises as the product of budget deficits: it is the ultimately uncontrollable need of the government for seignorage to cover its deficit that ensures the eventual collapse of a fixed exchange rate, and the efforts of investors to avoid suffering capital losses (or to achieve capital gains) when that collapse occurs provoke a speculative attack when foreign exchange reserves fall below a critical level. Second-generation models, exemplified by Obstfeld (1994), instead explain crises as the result of a conflict between a fixed exchange rate and the desire to pursue a more expansionary monetary policy; when investors begin to suspect that the government will choose to let the parity go, the resulting pressure on interest rates can itself push the government over the edge. Both first- and second-generation models have considerable relevance to particular crises in the 1990s—for example, the Russian crisis of 1998 was evidently driven in the first instance by the (correct) perception that the weak government was about to be forced to finance itself via the printing press, while the sterling crisis of 1992 was equally evidently driven by the perception that the UK government would under pressure choose domestic employment over exchange stability.

In the major crisis countries of Asia, however, neither of these stories seems to have much relevance. By conventional fiscal measures the governments of the afflicted economies were in quite good shape at the beginning of 1997; while growth had slowed and some signs of excess capacity appeared in 1996, none of them faced the kind of clear tradeoff between employment and exchange stability that Britain had faced 5 years earlier (and if depreciation was intended to allow expansionary policies, it rather conspicuously failed!) Clearly something else was at work; we badly need a "third-generation" crisis model both to make sense of the recent crises and to help warn of crises to come.

But what should a third-generation model look like? Most of the recent attempts to produce such a model have argued that the core of the problem lies in the banking system. McKinnon and Pill (1996) and others, myself included (Krugman, 1998), have suggested that moral-hazard-driven lending could have provided a sort of hidden subsidy to investment, which collapsed when visible losses led governments to withdraw their implicit guarantees; this line of thought has been taken to considerable lengths in the influential papers of Corsetti, Pesenti, and Roubini (1998). Meanwhile, an alternative line of work, followed in particular by Chang and Velasco (1998) attempts to explain currency crises as the byproduct of a bank run, modeled a la Diamond and Dybvig (1983) as a self-fulfilling loss of confidence that forces financial intermediaries to liquidate their investments prematurely.

But is a bank-centered view of the crisis really right? Certainly in most cases the financial crisis did involve troubles for banks as well as for currencies. But it also involved other difficulties, most notably an epidemic of financial distress that cannot be resolved simply by fixing the banks. As evidence about the Asian crisis has accumulated, I have found myself increasingly skeptical about whether either a moral-hazard or a Diamond–Dybvig story can really get at the essential nature of what went wrong.

In any case, this paper sketches out yet another candidate for third-generation crisis modeling, one that emphasizes two factors that have been omitted from formal models to date: the role of companies' balance sheets in determining their ability to invest, and that of capital flows in affecting the real exchange rate. The model is at this point quite raw, with several loose ends hanging. However, it seems to me to tell a story with a more realistic "feel" than earlier efforts, my own included. It also sheds some light on the policy dilemmas faced by the IMF and its clients in the last two years.

The remainder of this paper is in five parts. The first discusses in general terms some features of the financial crises of 1997–8, and the failure (in my view) of our models so far to reproduce some key stylized facts. The second part lays out a rough model intended to capture what I now believe to be two essential pieces of the puzzle: the role of balance sheet difficulties in constraining investment by entrepreneurs, and the impact of the real exchange rate on those balance sheets. The third part shows how these effects produce a feedback loop that can cause a potentially healthy economy to experience a self-fulfilling financial crisis. The fourth part offers a crude interpretation of the "IMF strategy" of limiting currency depreciation in order to protect against this balance-sheet effect, and shows how this strategy may simply replace one destructive feedback loop with another. A final section offers some tentative policy conclusions.

1. Recent Crises: Stylized Facts and Models

The Asian crisis arrived with little warning. By normal criteria, government budgets were in good shape; current account deficits were large in Thailand and Malaysia, but relatively moderate in Korea and Indonesia; despite some slowdown in growth in 1996, there was not a strong case that any of the countries needed a devaluation for competitive or macroeconomic reasons. Indeed, right up to the summer of 1997 many observers echoed the conclusion of the now-notorious World Bank report, *The East Asian Miracle* (1993), that good macroeconomic and exchange-rate management was a key ingredient in the Asian recipe for success. And as Stiglitz (1998) has emphasized, even after the fact it is very difficult to come up with any set of conventional indicators that picks out the Asian countries as particularly at risk of financial crisis, or identifies 1997–8 as a time of unusual risk.

So what went wrong? As already suggested, there are two major views in the post-crisis theoretical literature.

The first is that underneath the apparent soundness of macroeconomic policy was a large, hidden subsidy to investment via implicit government guarantees to banks, cronies of politicians, etc. The "over-borrowing syndrome" was modeled in advance of the crisis by McKinnon and Pill (1996), and for a time became the reigning orthodoxy after my own brief exposition (Krugman, 1998); Corsetti, Pesenti, and Roubini (1998a,b) have emphasized that to the extent that implicit guarantees led banks to engage in moral-hazard lending, it represented a hidden government budget deficit, and the unfunded liabilities of these banks represented a hidden government debt. According to this view, then, the apparent soundness of budgetary and macroeconomic policy was an illusion: under the surface, the governments were actually engaged in reckless and unsustainable spending.

The alternative view, strongly expressed by Radelet and Sachs (1998), is that the countries were not doing anything wrong; their investments were basically sound. At most they can be said to have suffered from some kind of "financial fragility" that made them vulnerable to self-fulfilling pessimism on the part of international lenders. Chang and Velasco (1998a,b) have made the most thoroughly worked-out attempt to model this financial fragility, relying on a version of the Diamond–Dybvig (1983) model of bank runs. In this model, investors face a choice between short-term investments with a low rate of return and long-run investments with a higher rate of return; unfortunately, the long-run investments yield relatively little if they must be liquidated prematurely, and investors are assumed to be unsure ex ante about when they will want to consume. Financial intermediaries can resolve this dilemma by pooling the resources of many investors and relying on the law of large numbers to avoid holding more short-term assets than necessary. However, such intermediaries then become vulnerable to self-fulfilling panics, in which fear of losses leads depositors to demand immediate payment, forcing destructive liquidation of long-run assets that validates these fears. In a closed economy the central bank can protect against such panics by acting as a lender of last resort; Chang and Velasco argue that in an open economy with a fixed exchange rate, the limited size of the central bank's reserves may prevent it from playing the same role.

There is no question that both of these views capture some aspects of what happened to Asia. On one side, "crony capitalism" was certainly a reality: the excesses of Thai financial companies, of members of the Suharto family, of megalomaniac *chaebol* are undeniable. On the other side, bank runs played an important role in the unfolding of the crisis, particularly in Indonesia, and a freezing up of the credit system played at least some role in deepening the recession after the crisis hit.

Yet as evidence about the crisis has accumulated, both explanations have come to seem inadequate to the task of explaining the severity of the event.

Consider first the moral hazard argument. If one really takes that argument seriously, it implies not only that there should be over-investment and excessive risk-taking by entrepreneurs with access to guaranteed finance, but also that the availability of implicit guarantees should tend to crowd out "legitimate" investment that bears the full burden of risk. Yet as Radelet and Sachs point out, in the runup to the crisis all forms of investment in the emerging Asian economies were booming, including direct foreign purchases of equity and real estate, investments that clearly were *not* protected by any form of implicit guarantee. One might point to the severity of the problem of non-performing loans after the crisis as evidence that bad banking was a key problem in the crisis economies. But as many observers have noted, and as is documented in the recent World Bank report *The Road to Recovery* (1998), the bulk of the bad loan problem is a *consequence* of the crisis—of the severe recessions and currency depreciations that followed the collapse of capital inflows. Since nobody expected a crisis of anything like this severity, the prevalence of bad loans we observe ex post does not mean that anything like the same amount of bad lending was taking place ex ante.

What about the financial fragility story? Here my main concern is not so much with Chang and Velasco as with Diamond–Dybvig—specifically, with the way that financial fragility and its real effects are modeled. In the Diamond–Dybvig model the costs of premature liquidation are *physical*—a bank run literally leads to investments being cannibalized before completion, with the output cost to the economy the result of a literal destruction of physical capital. There are a few real examples of this process in Asia—half-completed structures left to disintegrate for lack of funding, or dismantled for scrap metal. There are also some more complex stories that can be viewed metaphorically as examples of physical liquidation—for example, potentially profitable export opportunities not taken because working capital has been sold to pay off bank loans. But surely the main channels through which financial panic has turned good assets into bad involve not so much physical liquidation of unfinished projects as macroeconomic crisis: companies that looked solvent before the crisis have gone under because collapsing investment has produced a severe recession, or because capital flight has led to currency depreciation that makes their dollar debts balloon. Or to put it another way, Diamond and Dybvig used a physical metaphor for the costs of premature liquidation as a way to focus on the problem of multiple equilibria on the part of depositors; fair enough. But to make sense of the Asian crisis it is probably important to have a better metaphor, one that comes closer to matching the stylized facts of actual experience.

What are these stylized facts? Let me suggest three facts that a model should probably address—and which some or all of the existing models do not, as far as I can tell, seem to capture.

(i) *Contagion*: The most stunning aspect of the global financial crisis has been the way that events in small economies like Thailand or Russia have led more or less directly to crises in economies thousands of miles distant, with few direct trade or financial links.

From my point of view the power of contagion in the last two years settles a long-running dispute about currency crises in general: the dispute between "fundamentalists" and "self-fulfillers." In the original first-generation models, the suddenness of currency crises did not mean that their timing was arbitrary; on the contrary, such crises emerged when some set of fundamental factors (typically the level of reserves) fell below a critical level. Obstfeld (1994) argued that in second-generation models, by contrast, the timing of crisis was indeed arbitrary; in fact, a currency crisis could occur to a country whose fixed exchange rate might otherwise have survived indefinitely. I argued in reply (Krugman, 1996) that this was a misleading point: the reason that the timing of crisis seemed determinate in first-generation models was not because of the difference in the mechanism of crisis, but because in those models there was assumed to be a secular deterioration in the fundamentals—a deterioration that ensured, through backward induction, that a speculative attack would always occur as soon as it could succeed. This point was, I still think, correct. However, I then went on to argue that we should view a predictable secular deterioration in fundamentals as the normal case, whatever the specifics of the model, and that spontaneous self-fulfilling crises would therefore be rare events.

I hereby capitulate. I cannot see any way to make sense of the contagion of 1997–8 without supposing the existence of multiple equilibria, with countries vulnerable to self-validating collapses in confidence, collapses that could be set off by events in faraway economies that somehow served as a trigger for self-fulfilling pessimism. It follows that any useful model of the crisis must involve some mechanism that produces these multiple equilibria—a criterion met by the financial fragility models, but not by the moral hazard approach.

(ii) *The transfer problem*: If there is a single statistic that captures the violence of the shock to Asia most dramatically, it is the reversal in the current account: in the case of Thailand, for example, the country was forced by the reversal of capital flows to go from a deficit of some 10 percent of GDP in 1996 to a surplus of 8 percent in 1998. The need to effect such a huge change in the current account represents what may be history's most spectacular example of the classic "transfer problem" debated by Keynes and Ohlin in the 1920s. In practice this swing has been achieved partly through massive real depreciation, partly though severe recession that produces a compression of imports.

Yet despite the evident centrality of the transfer problem to what actually happened to Asia, this issue has been remarkably absent from formal models. Perhaps because the modelers have been mainly concerned with the behavior of investors rather than with the real economy per se, all of the major models so far have been one-good models in which domestic goods can be freely converted into foreign and vice versa without any movement in the terms of trade or the real exchange rate.

Is this an acceptable strategic simplification? Perhaps not: in the model I develop below, the difficulty of effecting a transfer, the need to achieve the current account counterpart of a reversal of capital flows either via real depreciation or via recession, turns out to be the heart of the story.

(iii) *Balance sheet problems*: Finally, descriptive accounts both of the problems of the crisis countries and of the policy discussions that led the crisis to be handled in the way it was place extensive emphasis on the problems of firms' balance sheets. On one side, the deterioration of these balance sheets played a key role in the crisis itself—notably, the explosion in the domestic currency value of dollar debt had a disastrous effect on Indonesian firms, and fear of corresponding balance sheet effects was a main reason why the IMF was concerned to avoid massive depreciation of its clients' currencies. On the other side, the prospects for recovery are now, by all accounts, especially difficult because of the weakened financial condition of firms, whose capital has in many cases been wiped out by the combination of declining sales, high interest rates, and a depreciated currency. Notice that while these balance sheet problems are in turn a cause of the problem of non-performing loans at the banks, they are not a banking problem per se; even a recapitalization of the banks would still leave the problem of financially weakened companies untouched.

The role of balance-sheet problems in constraining firms has been the subject of some recent work in the macroeconomics literature, notably Kiyotaki and Moore (1997) and Bernanke, Gertler, and Gilchrist (forthcoming). So far, however, despite the attention given to balance sheets in practical discussions, the issue has been neglected in the currency crisis literature.

What I will do in the remainder of this paper, then, is to try to develop a model informed by these observations. As in the Diamond–Dybvig approach, this is a model potentially characterized by multiple equilibria, in which a loss of confidence can produce a financial collapse that validates investor pessimism. However, the mechanism of that collapse is different: instead of creating losses via the premature liquidation of physical assets, a loss of confidence leads to a transfer problem. That is, in order to achieve the required reversal of its current account, the country must experience a large real depreciation; this depreciation, in turn, worsens the balance sheets of domestic firms, validating the loss of confidence. A policy that attempts to limit the real depreciation implies a decline in output instead—and this, too, can validate the collapse of confidence.

Moreover, once the crisis occurs it can have a sustained impact on the economy, because of that impact on balance sheets; as one Thai economist recently put it, the crisis leads to the "decapitation of the entrepreneurial class," and the economy cannot return to normal until it manages either to repair the balance sheets of its existing entrepreneurs or grows a new set.

It seems to me that this story—in which, incidentally, banks do not necessarily play a key role, although they could presumably also be introduced—comes closer than any of the previous models to having the right "feel" for making sense of recent events. But in any case, let us now proceed to the statement and analysis of the model.

2. The Model

I consider an open economy that produces a single good each period using capital and labor; for simplicity the production function is assumed Cobb–Douglas:

$$y_t = G(K_t, L_t) = K_t^\alpha L_t^{1-\alpha} \tag{1}$$

Capital is created through investment; I will assume, again for simplicity, that capital lasts only one period, so that this period's capital is equal to last period's investment. (This assumption also puts to one side Diamond–Dybvig-type concerns over maturity mismatch).

The residents of this economy are divided into two distinct classes. Workers play a passive role—they lack access to the capital market, and therefore must spend all their income within each period. Capital is both created and owned by a class of entrepreneurs, who are assumed to be single-mindedly engaged in accumulation at this point, saving and investing (either at home or abroad) all their income. Only these entrepreneurs have the ability to undertake domestic investment, which as we will soon see plays a crucial role in the story.

The good produced by this country is *not* a perfect substitute for traded goods produced elsewhere. Indeed, I will assume (yet another simplification) that there is a unitary elasticity of substitution, with a share μ of both consumption and investment spending on imports, $1 - \mu$ on domestic goods. The rest of the world is assumed to be much larger than the domestic economy, and to spend a negligible fraction of its income on domestic goods. (The disparity between the domestic and foreign marginal propensities to spend on domestic goods—$1 - \mu$ in the case of domestic spending, 0 for foreign spending—gives rise to the transfer problem that is crucial to this approach). If the foreign elasticity of substitution is also 1, the value of domestic exports in terms of foreign goods is fixed, say at X, and the value in terms of domestic goods is therefore pX, where p is the relative price of foreign goods (a.k.a real exchange rate).

Bearing in mind that a share $1 - \alpha$ of domestic income accrues to workers who must spend it, and defining I and C as investment and consumption expenditures in terms of domestic goods, we can determine the real exchange rate as follows. Market clearing for domestic goods requires that

$$y = (1 - \mu)I + (1 - \mu)C + pX = (1 - \mu)I + (1 - \alpha)(1 - \mu)y + pX \qquad (2)$$

which implies

$$p_t = \frac{y_t[1 - (1 - \alpha)(1 - \mu)] - (1 - \mu)I_t}{X} \qquad (3)$$

We can immediately notice that the higher is investment, the lower the real exchange rate.

The next step is to describe the determination of investment. The central idea here is that the ability of entrepreneurs to invest may be limited by their wealth. Specifically, following Bernanke et al (forthcoming) I assume that lenders impose a limit on leverage: entrepreneurs can borrow at most λ times their initial wealth.

$$I_t \leq (1 + \lambda)W_t \qquad (4)$$

Underlying this limitation on borrowing, presumably, are some kind of microeconomic motives, probably involving asymmetric information. For the purposes of this paper, however, I simply assume the existence of the constraint and take λ as a given.

This constraint need not be binding; although entrepreneurs are assumed to save all of their income, they may choose not to borrow up to the limit. In particular, they will not borrow beyond the point at which the real return on domestic investment equals that on foreign investment. One way to determine this limit is to compare the foreign real interest rate, r^*, with the return achieved by converting foreign goods into domestic, then converting the next-period return back into foreign goods. Because a share μ of investment falls on foreign goods, the price index for investment relative to that of domestic output is $p^{-\mu}$; the return on investment in terms of domestic goods is therefore

$$1 + r_t = G_k(I_{t-1}p^{-\mu}, L) \tag{5}$$

But a unit of foreign goods can be converted into p_t units of domestic goods this period, the return converted into $1/p_{t+1}$ units next period; so the statement that the return on domestic investment must be at least as large as that on foreign bonds may be written

$$(1 + r_t)(p_t/p_{t+1}) \geq 1 + r^* \tag{6}$$

Finally, investment cannot be negative:

$$I_t \geq 0 \tag{7}$$

As we will see, depending on circumstances (4), (6), or (7) may be the binding constraint.

The last element in the statement of the model is the definition of entrepreneurs' wealth. Domestic entrepreneurs own all domestic capital; they may also own other claims on foreigners, and/or have debts to foreigners. I assume that some claims are denominated in terms of the domestic good, others in terms of the foreign good; meanwhile, since capital lasts only one period, the value of domestic capital is simply the income accruing to capital within the current period. Let D, F be the net debts of domestic entrepreneurs indexed to domestic and foreign goods respectively; I will sloppily refer to these as "domestic currency" and "foreign currency" debt respectively, although they are really denominated in goods rather than moneys. Then the wealth of entrepreneurs in period t is

$$W_t = \alpha y - D - pF \tag{8}$$

Obviously a full model should try to endogenize the "currency composition" (again, actually goods composition, since the model is not explicitly monetary) of debt; again, however, I simply take it as a given.

We now have a rough but workable model that can be used to examine one way in which a financial crisis can occur in an open economy.

3. The Transfer Problem and Financial Crisis

According to our model, the amount that domestic entrepreneurs can borrow from foreigners to finance investment depends on their wealth. At the same time, however, the wealth of each individual entrepreneur itself depends on the level of such borrowing in the economy as a whole, because the volume of capital inflow affects the terms of trade and hence the valuation of foreign-currency-denominated debt. We can therefore immediately see the outlines of a story about financial crisis: a decline in capital inflows can adversely affect the balance sheets of domestic entrepreneurs, reducing their ability to borrow and hence further reducing capital inflows. But we need to be a bit more precise.

Imagine a game in which lenders decide, in random order, how much credit to offer to successive domestic entrepreneurs. The offer of credit depends on what the lenders *think* will be the value of the borrower's collateral. But because some debt is denominated in foreign goods, this value depends on the real exchange rate, and hence on the actual level of borrowing that takes place. A rational-expectations equilibrium of this game will be a set of self-confirming guesses—that is, the expected level of investment implicit in the credit offers must match the actual level of investment that takes place given those offers.

As a first step, let us derive the relationship between investment and the wealth of entrepreneurs. From (8), we know that wealth depends, other things being the same, on the real exchange rate p; from (3) we know that p depends on I. We therefore have that

$$\frac{dW}{dI} = \frac{(1-\mu)F}{X} \tag{9}$$

Let us define I_f as the "financeable" level of investment—that is, the level of investment that would occur if the leverage constraint (4) were binding. Since the ability of entrepreneurs to borrow depends on their wealth, we have

$$\frac{dI_f}{dI} = \frac{(1+\lambda)(1-\mu)F}{X} \tag{10}$$

If dI_f/dI is less than 1, the behavior of this model is relatively uninteresting: an economy with a high rate of return on investment may find that adjustment in its capital stock is delayed by financing constraints, but there will be nothing resembling an Asian-style financial crisis. But suppose that $dI_f/dI > 1$. Then there can indeed be multiple equilibria, with the possibility that a loss of lender confidence will be validated by financial collapse.

The picture would look like Figure 1.[1] On the horizontal axis is the expected level of investment, which determines via its effect on the real exchange rate, and hence on balance sheets, how much credit is extended to domestic firms. On the vertical axis is the actual level of investment that results. (The picture could alternatively be drawn in terms of the expected and actual levels of p). At high levels of expected I the financing constraint (4) is not binding; instead, investment is determined by the rate-of-return constraint (6). At low levels of expected I firms are bankrupt, and cannot invest at all—that is, they are hard against the non-negativity constraint (7). In an intermediate range I is constrained by financing, and the schedule is therefore steeper than the 45-degree line.

There are clearly three equilibria in this picture. The intermediate, internal equilibrium may be dismissed as likely to be unstable under any plausible mechanism of expectation formation. This leaves us with two possible outcomes: a high-level outcome H in which investment takes place up to the point where domestic and foreign rates of return are equal; and a low-level outcome L in which lenders do not believe that domestic entrepreneurs have any collateral, their failure to provide funds means a depreciated real exchange rate, and that unfavorable real exchange rate means that entrepreneurs are in fact bankrupt, validating lenders' poor opinion.

And we therefore now have our extremely stylized version of the Asian financial crisis: something—it does not matter what—caused lenders to become suddenly pessimistic, and

40   KRUGMAN

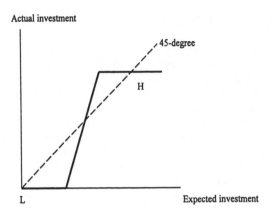

Figure 1.

the result was a collapse from *H* to *L*. The collapse does not indicate that the previous investments were unsound; the problem is instead one of financial fragility.

The difference between this story of financial fragility and that told by Chang and Velasco can be highlighted by considering the conditions under which this fragility can occur—namely, when $dI_f/dI > 1$. By construction here, this criterion has nothing to do with the mismatch between short-term debt and long-term investments; nor does it appear to depend on foreign exchange reserves. Instead, as we see from (10), the factors that can make financial collapse possible are:

(i)   High leverage

(ii) Low marginal propensity to import

(iii) Large foreign-currency debt relative to exports

These factors matter, of course, because they make the circular loop from investment to real exchange rate to balance sheets to investment more powerful.

We can now also offer a possible answer to the great mystery: Why Asia? Why now? If we ask what was special about Asian economies, something that may have made them peculiarly vulnerable to financial crisis, the answer is high leverage: all of the now afflicted countries had unusually high levels of λ. If we ask why now—given that high leverage, "crony capitalism," etc. have been characteristic of Asian economies for decades—the answer is that only after 1990 did these economies begin extensive borrowing denominated in foreign currencies, borrowing that placed them at risk of financial collapse if the real exchange rate depreciated.

4. The Dilemma of Stabilization

Although standard models of currency crisis have not to date taken account of the problems posed by foreign-currency debt, practitioners have been aware of this issue for decades. And the risks of financial trauma because of that debt were a major reason why the IMF advised its Asian clients to follow the much-criticized "IMF strategy" of defending their currencies with high interest rates rather than simply letting them decline.

This model does not allow a direct analysis of monetary policy. We can, however, take a very rough cut at the nature and consequences of the IMF strategy by imagining that the effect of that strategy is to hold the real exchange rate p constant even when the willingness of foreign lenders to finance investment declines. In that case, of course, something else must give; and the natural assumption is that output declines instead.

Indeed, if we hold p constant, output will be determined by a sort of quasi-Keynesian multiplier process; rearranging (2) we have

$$y = \frac{pX + (1 - \mu)I}{1 - (1 - \alpha)(1 - \mu)} \tag{11}$$

But given that a share α of output goes to profits, a decline in investment will reduce entrepreneurs' wealth:

$$\frac{dW}{dI} = \frac{\alpha(1 - \mu)}{1 - (1 - \alpha)(1 - \mu)} \tag{12}$$

and hence once again there will be a feedback from actual to financeable investment:

$$\frac{dI_f}{dI} = \frac{(1 + \lambda)\alpha(1 - \mu)}{1 - (1 - \alpha)(1 - \mu)} \tag{13}$$

It is immediately clear that stabilizing the real exchange rate, while closing one channel for potential financial collapse, opens another: if leverage is high, the economy may stabilize its real exchange rate only at the expense of a self-reinforcing decline in output that produces an equivalent decapitation of the entrepreneurial class.

5. Policy Implications

One would ordinarily be somewhat diffident about drawing policy implications from so rough a framework. However, policy must be and is being made, by and large without any explicit analytical framework at all; so here are some conclusions inspired from the model. They pertain to three rather different questions. First is the question of prophylactic measures: what can we do to prevent such crises in the future? Second is the question of policy in the crisis: how can the crisis be halted or at least limited? Finally there is the question of what to do once the crisis has occurred: how does one rebuild the economy?

Prophylactic measures: In the aftermath of the Asian crisis, a broad consensus has emerged among responsible people that countries need to take much greater care with their banking systems—that they need "transparency," better capital standards, more careful regulation of risk-taking, an end to cronyism, etc. Underlying such recommendations is the belief that the crisis was largely due either to moral hazard, Diamond–Dybvig-type problems, or both. And it is hard to disagree that such measures are a good thing. If I am right about the mechanism of crisis, however, even a very clean and prudent banking system may not be enough to protect open economies from the risk of self-reinforcing financial collapse.

A more controversial proposal is for the widespread imposition of Chilean-type restrictions on short-term borrowing denominated in foreign currencies. The idea here is that by reducing short-term foreign-currency exposure, countries can reduce the risks of being forced into crisis by a loss of confidence.

I have been skeptical about this argument on the general grounds that as long as a country has free convertibility of capital, short-term foreign loans are only one of many different possible sources of capital flight. We cannot deal with the issue of maturity structure in this model, since such issues have been ruled out by assumption. But in the spirit of the model, consider the following situation: domestic firms are financed by a mixture of short-term debt denominated in domestic currency, and long-term debt denominated in foreign currency. Does the fact that the foreign currency debt is long-term protect the country from financial crisis? Surely not: if people expect a financial crisis, the holders of domestic short-term debt will refuse to roll it over, generating an exchange rate depreciation that bankrupts the firms even though the foreign-currency debt itself is long term.

So what is the appropriate prophylactic policy? The answer from this model, at any rate, seems to be to discourage firms from taking on foreign-currency-denominated debt of any maturity. Loosely speaking, there appears to be a sort of external diseconomy to borrowing in foreign currencies: because such borrowing magnifies the real-exchange-rate impact of adverse shocks, and because real depreciation interacts with capital-market imperfections to cause economic distress, the decision by an individual firm to borrow in dollars imposes costs on the rest of the economy.

Dealing with crisis: Much of the vituperative public debate over how to deal with crisis has involved the question of whether to let the exchange rate go or stabilize it. The answer suggested by this model is that this is a real choice, but that both answers may be equally bad. Is there a third way?

One possibility would be the provision of emergency lines of credit. However, in the context of this model it appears that these credit lines would have to do more than provide balance-of-payments financing, or even provide lender-of-last resort facilities to banks: they would have to make up the credit being lost by firms, so as to allow investment to continue. Thus the credit lines would have to be very large indeed, and also be accompanied by a mechanism that funnels the funds to troubled entrepreneurs. (This would be especially difficult politically, since in the midst of crisis there is widespread and often justified vilification of those same entrepreneurs, on the grounds that their excesses brought on the crisis in the first place). Of course if one takes the model seriously, a sufficiently large credit line would never actually have to be used, since its very existence would prevent the crisis from ever getting under way (but one has to be credibly willing to use it in order not to have to).

Another possibility is to rule out the possibility of a downward financial spiral by being ready to impose a curfew on capital flight. Again, there is substantial sympathy even among respectable opinion for standstill agreements on foreign-currency debt; but this may well not be sufficient, if capital-account convertibility means that other forms of capital flight are still possible. All of which raises the possibility that it might be necessary, and even in the interests of investors themselves, to impose emergency capital controls . . . enough said.

After the fall: Finally, what we hope is the current question: once the crisis has happened, how does one get the economy going again? To date most actual efforts have focused on bank restructuring and recapitalization; but if this model is on the right track, this will not be sufficient. The main problem at this point, the model (like many practitioners) suggests, is that the firms and entrepreneurs who drove investment and growth before the crisis are now effectively bankrupt and unable to raise capital.

If this is right, the key to resuming growth is either to rescue those entrepreneurs, through some kind of "private sector Brady Plan," or to grow a new set of entrepreneurs—or both. A likely source of new entrepreneurs is, of course, from abroad: a welcome mat for foreign direct investment might be just what the doctor ordered.

Again, all of this is based on a liberal interpretation of a very rough model. It seems to me, however, that this model does provide at least a different perspective on how to think about these issues.

As I said at the beginning of this paper, the Asian crisis inspires mixed emotions in those of us who, like Bob Flood, have shared a decades-long fascination with the issue of currency crises. Our obsession has been spectacularly and tragically vindicated; but the world seems to keep finding new ways to generate crises. Let us hope that the lessons of this "third-generation" crisis are learned, and that no future crises arise in the same way; but even if that hope is fulfilled, one can be sure that there are many more generations to come.

Notes

1. Strictly speaking, there are two other possibilities even if $dI_f/dI > 1$. If domestic-currency debt is very high, entrepreneurs may be unable to borrow even with a favorable exchange rate; if D is low, even a very unfavorable rate will not cause financial collapse. I neglect these cases for the sake of the main story.

References

Bernanke, Ben, Mark Gertler, and Simon Gilchrist. (forthcoming). "The Financial Accelerator in a Quantitative Business Cycle Framework." In J. Taylor and M. Woodford (eds.), *Handbook of Macroeconomics*.

Chang, Roberto, and Andres Velasco. (1998). "Financial Crises in Emerging Markets: A Canonical Model." NBER Working Paper No. 6606.

Corsetti, Giancarlo, Paolo Pesenti, and Nouriel Roubini. (1998). "Paper Tigers? A Model of the Asian Crisis." Mimeo.

Diamond, Douglas, and Philip Dybvig. (1983). "Bank Runs, Deposit Insurance, and Liquidity." *Journal of Political Economy* 91 401–419.

Eichengreen, Barry, Andrew Rose, and Charles Wyplosz. (1995). "Exchange Market Mayhem: The Antecedents and Aftermath of Speculative Attacks." *Economic Policy*, 251–312.

44

Flood, Robert, and Peter Garber. (1984). "Collapsing Exchange Rate Regimes: Some Linear Examples." *Journal of International Economics* 17, 1–13.
Kiyotaki, Nobuhiro, and John Moore. (1997). "Credit Cycles." *Journal of Political Economy* 105, 211–248.
Krugman, Paul. (1979). "A Model of Balance-of-Payments Crises." *Journal of Money, Credit, and Banking* 11, 311–325.
Krugman, Paul. (1996). "Are Currency Crises Self-Fulfilling?" In B. Bernanke and J. Rotemberg (eds.), *NBER Macroeconomics Annual 1996.* Cambridge: MIT Press.
Krugman, Paul. (1998). "What Happened to Asia?" Mimeo, MIT.
McKinnon, Ronald, and Huw Pill. (1996). "Credible Liberalizations and International Capital Flows: The 'Overborrowing Syndrome.'" In T. Ito and A. Krueger (eds.), *Financial Deregulation and Integration in East Asia.* Chicago: University of Chicago Press.
Obstfeld, Maurice. (1994). "The Logic of Currency Crises." *Cahiers economique et monetaires* 43, 189–212.
Radelet, Steven, and Jeffrey Sachs. (1998). "The Onset of the East Asian Financial Crisis." Mimeo.

Robert P. Flood, Jr. – Bibliography

Birth Date: January 7, 1949

Degrees: B.A., Wake Forest University, 1970
               M.A., University of Rochester, 1975
               Ph.D., University of Rochester, 1977

Experience

   Rochester Graduate Work
      Concentrations in International Economics, Monetary Economics
      Dissertation: supervised by Michael Mussa
      Essays on Real and Monetary Aspects of Various Exchange Rate Systems
   Research Assistant, International Monetary Research Program, London, 1975.
   Assistant Professor, Department of Economics, University of Virginia, 1976–81.
   Economist, Board of Governors of the Federal Reserve System, 1980–82.
   Associate Professor, Department of Economics, University of Virginia, 1981–83.
   Professor, Department of Economics, Northwestern University, 1983–89
   Senior Economist, International Monetary Fund, 1987–present.

Editorial Work

   Co-Editor, *Journal of International Economics*, 1983–87
   Associate Editor, *Journal of Money, Credit and Banking*, 1983–present.
   Associate Editor, *American Economic Review*, 1989–93.
   Associate Editor, *International Journal of Finance and Economics*, 1995–present.
   Associate Editor, *International Journal of Finance and Money*, 1995–present.
   Editor, *IMF Staff Papers*, 1998–present.

Research Associations

   Research Associate, National Bureau of Economic Research 1979-97.
   Research Associate, Georgetown University Center for International Economic Policy.
   Research Professor, Dartmouth College.

Published Papers:

   "Growth, Prices and the Balance of Payments," *Canadian Journal of Economics*, May,1977.

   "Exchange Rate Expectations in Dual Exchange Markets," *Journal of International Economics*, February, 1978.

ROBERT P. FLOOD JR. – BIBLIOGRAPHY

"Backward Looking and Forward Looking Solutions to Monetary Models of Inflation With Rational Expectations," *Economics Letters* 1, 1978 (with P. Garber).

"An Example of Exchange Rate Overshooting," *Southern Economic Journal*, July, 1979.

"An Economic Theory of Monetary Reform," *Journal of Political Economy*, February, 1980 (with P. Garber).

"A Pitfall in Estimation of Models With Rational Expectations," *Journal of Monetary Economics*, July, 1980 (with P. Garber).

"Market Fundamentals Versus Price Level Bubbles: The First Tests," *Journal of Political Economy*, August, 1980 (with P. Garber).

"Perfect Foresight and the Stability of Monetary Models," *Economica*, August, 1981 (with E. Burmeister and S. Turnovsky).

"Explanations of Exchange-Rate Volatility and Other Empirical Regularities in Some Popular Models of the Foreign Exchange Market," Vol. 15 supplement to *Journal of Monetary Economics*, Autumn, 1981.

"The Transmission of Disturbances Under Alternative Exchange-Rate Regimes," *Quarterly Journal of Economics*, February, 1982. (with N. Marion).

"Activist Policy in the Open Economy," A.E.A. Papers and Proceedings, *American Economic Review*, May, 1982.

"Bubbles, Runs and Gold Monetization," in P. Wachtel (ed.), *Crises in the Financial Structure*. Lexington Books, 1982 (with P. Garber).

"A Model of Stochastic Process Switching," *Econometrica*, May, 1983. (with P. Garber).

"Process Consistency and Monetary Reform: Some Further Evidence," *Journal of Monetary Economics*, pp. 279–295, 1983 (with P. Garber).

"On The Equivalence of Solutions in Rational Expectations Models," *Journal of Economic Dynamics and Control*, 1983 (with E. Burmeister and P. Garber)

"Gold Monetization and Gold Discipline," *Journal of Political Economy*, February, 1984 (with P. Garber), reprinted as Chapter 10 in R. Aliber (ed.), *The Reconstruction of International Monetary Arrangements*. MacMillan, 1987.

"Exchange Rate Regimes in Transition: Italy 1974," *Journal of International Money and Finance*, December,1983 (with N. Marion).

"Multi-Country Tests for Price Level Bubbles," *Journal of Monetary Economics* 8, 1984, pp. 329–340 (with P. Garber and L. Scott).

"Collapsing Exchange Rate Regimes: Some Linear Examples," *Journal of International Economics*, August, 1984. (with P. Garber)

"Exchange Rate and Price Dynamics with Asymmetric Information," *International Economic Review*, October, 1984 (with R. Hodrick).

"Central Bank Intervention in a Rational Open Economy: A Model With Asymmetric Information," in J. Bhandari (ed.), *Exchange Rate Management Under Uncertainty*. MIT Press. 1985 (with R. Hodrick).

"Exchange Rate Dynamics, Sticky Prices and the Current Account," *Journal of Money Credit and Banking*, August, 1985 (with C. Engle).

"Optimal Price and Inventory Adjustment in an Open Economy Model of the Business Cycle," *Quarterly Journal of Economics*, 1986 (with R. Hodrick).

"Bubbles, Process Switching and Asset Price Volatility," *Journal of Finance*, July, 1986. (with R. Hodrick)

"Real Aspects of Exchange Rate Regime Choice," *Journal of International Economics*, November, 1986 (with R. Hodrick).

"Risk Neutrality and the Spread in a Two-Tier Foreign Exchange Market," *Economics Letters*, 1987 (with N. Marion).

"Monetary Policy Strategies," *Staff Papers*, International Monetary Fund, Vol. 36, pp.612–32, 1989 (with P. Isard).

"Evolution of Exchange Rate Regimes," *Staff Papers*, International Monetary Fund, Vol. 36, 1989 (with J. Horne and J. Bhandari).

"Testable Implications of Indeterminacies in Models with Rational Expectations," *Economics Perspectives*, Spring 1990, Vol. 4, No. 2 (with R. Hodrick).

"An Empirical Exploration of Exchange Rate Target Zones," Supplement to the *Journal of Monetary Economics*, Autumn 1991,. pp. 7–66 (with D. Mathieson. and A. Rose).

"Speculative Attacks and Models of Balance of Payments Crisis," *Staff Papers*, International Monetary Fund, Vol. 39, June, pp. 357–394 (with Agenor and J. Bhandari).

"Macroeconomic Policy, Speculative Attacks and Balance of Payments Crisis," (revised version of previous paper) in F. Van Der Ploeg (ed.), *The Handbook of International Macroeconomics*, Basil Blackwell, 1994 (with R. Agenor).

"Linkages Between Speculative Attack and Target Zone Models of Exchange Rates," *Quarterly Journal of Economics*, Vol. 106, pp. 1367–1372 (with P. Garber).

"The Linkage Between Speculative Attack and Target Zone Models of Exchange Rates: Further Results," in M. Miller and P. Krugman (eds.), *Exchange Rate Targets and Currency Bands*, Cambridge University Press,1992.

"A Theory of Optimum Currency Areas: Revisited," G. Tavlas, ed., *Greek Economic Review*, 1992 (with J. Aizenman).

"Speculative Attacks and Models of Balance-of-Payments Crisis," *Staff Papers*, International Monetary Fund, Vol. 39, June 1992, pp. 357-94 (with P.R. Agenor and J. Bhandari).

"Macroeconomic Policy, Speculative Attacks and Balance of Payments Crises," in F. Van Der Phol, ed., *The Handbook of International Economics*, Basil: Blackwell Publishers, 1994.

"What is Policy Switching?," *Finance and Development*, September, 1992.

"An Evaluation of Recent Evidence on Stock Market Bubbles" in R. Flood and P. Garber, *Speculative Bubbles, Speculative Attacks and Policy Switching*. MIT Press, 1994, (with R. Hodrick and P. Kaplan).

"Exchange Rate Regime Choice," P. Newman, ed., *The New Palgrave Dictionary of International Finance*, 1994 (with N. Marion).

"Two-Tier Foreign Exchange Markets," in P. Newman, ed., *The New Palgrave Dictionary of International Finance*, 1994 (with N. Marion).

"Issues Concerning Nominal Anchors for Monetary Policy," in T Balino and C. Cottarelli, eds., Frameworks for Monetary Stability, 1994, International Monetary Fund (with M. Mussa).

"Exchange Rate Economics: What's Wrong with the Conventional Approach?," in J. Frankel, G. Galli and A. Giovannini, eds., *The Microstructure of Foreign Exchange Markets*, NBER, University of Chicago Press, 1996 (with M. Taylor).

"Fixing Exchange Rates: A Vitual Quest for Fundamentals," *Journal of Monetary Economics*, Vol. 36, pp. 3-37, 1995 (with A. Rose).

"Fixes of the Forward Discount Puzzle," *Review of Economics and Statistics* 1996 (with A. Rose).

"Mexican Foreign Exchange Market Crises From the Perspective of the Speculative Attack Literature," in *International Capital Markets: Developments, Prospects and Policy Issues*, International Monetary Fund, August 1995 (with C. Kramer).

"Bubbles, Noise and the Trading Process in Speculative Markets," in *International Capital Markets: Developments, Prospects and Policy Issues*, International Monetary Fund, August 1995 (with T. Ito and C. Kramer).

"Collapsing Exchange Rate Regimes: Another Linear Example," *Journal of International Economics*, Vol. 41, No. 3/4, November 1996, pp. 223-234 (with P. Garber and C. Kramer).

"Economic Models of Speculative Attacks and the Drachma Crisis of May 1994, " *Open Economies Review*, Vol. 7, 1996, pp., 591-600 (with C. Kramer).

"The Size and Timing of Devaluations in Capital-Controlled Developing Countries," *Journal of Development Economics*, 1997 (with N. Marion).

"Policy Implications of Second Generation Crisis Models," *IMF Staff Papers*, September 1997, pp. 10-17 (With N. Marion).

"Reserve and Exchange Rate Cycles," *Journal of International Economics*, October 1998 (with W. Perravdin and P. Vitale).

"Self-Fulfilling Risk Predictions: An Application to Speculative Attacks," forthcoming, *Journal of International Economics* (with N. Marion).

"Perspectives on the Recent Currency Crisis Literature," forthcoming R. Dornbusch and M. Obstfeld, eds., *Essays on Honor of Robert Mundell* (with N. Marion).

"Is Launching the Euro Unstable in the Endgame," forthcoming P. Krugman, ed., NBER Conference Volume.

Books:

Speculative Bubbles, Speculative Attacks and Policy Switching, MIT Press, 1994 (with Peter Garber).

Comments and Reviews:

Review of M. Frattiani and K. Tavernier (eds.), "Bank Credit, Money and Inflation in Open Economies," *Journal of Monetary Economics*, August 1978.

Comment on W. Buiter and M. Miller, "Real Exchange-Rate Overshooting and the Output Cost of Bringing Down Inflation," *European Economic Review*, Vol. 18, 1982.

"Stochastic Process Switching and Inflation: A Comment on Real Exchange Rate Overshooting and the Output Cost of Bringing Down Inflation: Some Further Results" in J. Frenkel, ed., *Exchange Rates and International Macroeconomics*, University of Chicago Press, 1984.

Comment on W. McKibbin and J. Sachs, "Coordination of Monetary and Fiscal Policies in Industrial Economics," in J. Frenkel, ed., International Aspects of Fiscal Policy, University of Chicago Press, 1988.

Comment on K. Singleton, "Speculation and the Volatility of Foreign Currency Exchange Rates," Carnegie-Rochester Conference Volume, Vol. 26, 1987.

Comment on J. Frankel and R. Meese, "Are Exchange Rates Excessively Volatile?" NBER Macroeconomics Annual, 1987.

"Comment on Cukierman," Carnegie-Rochester Conference Volume.

Comment on R. Baillie paper, "Commodity Prices and Aggregate Inflation: Would a Commodity Price Rule be Worthwile?" Carnegie-Rochester Conference Series on Public Policy, vol. 31, 1989.

"Monetary Policy Strategies: A Correction," *Staff Papers*, International Monetary Fund (with P. Isard), 1990.

Comment on P. Krugman and M. Miller, "Why Have a Target Zone?" Carnegie-Rochester Conference Series on Public Policy, vol. 38, 1993 (with M. Spencer).

[19]

KYKLOS, Vol. 52 – 1999 – Fasc. 3, 415–439

On Keynes' Animal Spirits

Roberto Marchionatti*

I. INTRODUCTION

In Chapter 12 of *The General Theory,* explaining the formation of entrepreneurial expectations on investment, Keynes emphasises the fact that

'a large proportion of our positive activity depends on spontaneous optimism':

an entrepreneur takes action as a result of what he calls *animal spirits* –

'a spontaneous urge to action rather than inaction, and not as the outcome of a weighted average of quantitative benefits multiplied by quantitative probabilities' (Keynes 1973b, p. 161)[1].

Only if reasonable calculation

'is supplemented and supported by animal spirits',

---

* Professor of Economics, Department of Economics, University of Torino, via Po 53, Torino, 10124 Italy. I gratefully acknowledge useful comments on preliminary versions of the paper from Anna Carabelli, Bill Gerrard, Roger Koppl, Ian Steedman, participants of the Austrian Economics Colloquium at the New York University in the April 1998, and two anonymous referees, as well as the financial support of MURST national funds.

1. According to many authors (see Carabelli 1988, Koppl 1991, Moggridge 1992) Keynes took the notion from Descartes (see Keynes' hand-written 'Notes on Modern Philosophy I. 1903–4', where he quotes approximately from Descartes – 'The body is moved by animal spirits, the fiery particles of the blood distilled by the heat of the heart' – and comments: 'unconscious mental action'). Matthews (1991) notes that Hume also used the phrase in *A Treatise of Human Nature* and reminds that Marshall and the Cambridge school gave 'a significant amount of attention to the psychological springs of economic behaviour'. Actual meaning and properties of the animal spirits were discussed by Descartes in the *Traité de l'Homme* (1633) and in his last work, *Les passions de l'âme* (1644) to which Keynes referred in his remarks: this is a notion dated back to Greek physicians of the third century b. C. probably discovered by Descartes, according to his scholars, in Galen's work and in J. Fernel's *De Naturali Parte Medicinae* (1551). In any case the term was commonly used in the physiology of seventeenth and eighteenth centuries: animal

ROBERTO MARCHIONATTI

Keynes writes, individual initiative will be adequate,

'so that the thought of ultimate loss which often overtakes pioneers is put aside as a healthy man puts aside the expectation of death' (Keynes 1973b, p. 162).

More generally, Keynes asserts that in an uncertain environment the decisions of economic agents about the future depend only in part, if indeed at all, on rational calculation; rather, as he says in a famous letter to Hugh Townshend, they are based on other 'not rational' motives, 'habit, instinct, preference, desire, will, etc.' (Keynes 1979, p. 294), and 'passions', an old-fashioned term used by Keynes in *My early beliefs* (1938) speaking in an Humean mood of

'thin rationalism skipping on the crust of lava' (Keynes 1972, p. 447).

This idea has not had much success among economists after Keynes. The hypothesis of the existence of non-rational motives and animal spirits seems to make long-term expectations exogenous. This solution has been considered unacceptable because the hypothesis of exogeneity of expectations means their influence would be totally arbitrary, giving excessive importance to the irrational behaviour of economic agents[2]. For this reason, animal spirits have for a long time fallen into disfavour and have been substantially excluded from scientific inquiry, also between the majority of Keynesian economists, with the exception

spirits were considered as nervous forces, fluids, circulating through brain and body; the degree of one's vitality depending on the vigour and abundance of these animal spirits. At that time the term was used, not necessary in technical sense, by many writers and scholars in describing and studying human passions, but essentially following two different strands: in order to know human passions Descartes and the rationalist school used a psycho-physical (and metaphysical) conception of passions, on the contrary Hume and others, for example Mandeville, used an experimental and psychological method of studying passions. From an epistemological point of view, I think that it could be said that the sense of the usage of the expression animal spirits by Keynes is essentially Humean.

2. According to the mainstream traditional view, in the face of genuine uncertainty there is no basis on which to form a rational judgement. The idea that, as Lucas says, 'in cases of uncertainty, economic reasoning will be of little value' (Lucas 1981, p. 224) has been dominant in the last decades. Under the 'rational postulate', adopted by the mainstream, the only way to deal satisfactory with expectation formation is to use Muth's rational expectations hypothesis (Muth 1961) which enables the introduction of endogenous expectations. Rational expectation models assume that expectations correctly identify the mean and variance of stochastic variables affecting future contingencies, and thus resolve the problem of the mistaken belief of economic agents with regard to the future. Under this hypothesis expectations can be incorrect but not systematically so. In a rational expectation model animal spirits can be considered, as in Howitt and Mc Afee (1992), as a case of extraneous random variables. Unfortunately for the theoretical strength of rational expectation hypothesis, a variety of criticisms has shown that there would be no reason for all systematic errors of expectations to be eliminated through the market process (for a summary account of this criticism see Pesaran 1987).

ON KEYNES' ANIMAL SPIRITS

of the post-Keynesian work of authors such as Joan Robinson (1962), who considered animal spirits in terms of a function relating the growth rate of capital with the expected level of profit, George Shackle (1967) and, more recently, Paul Davidson (see for example 1991), who stressed the role of animal spirits as evidence of the essential irrationality of the investment decision. Since the mid-eighties, in the context of the neo-Keynesianism and the renaissance of post-Keynesianism and of other non-mainstream traditions, a new interest in Keynes' analysis of economic behaviour under genuine uncertainty and in the concept of animal spirits has emerged. In the neo-Keynesian context Greenwald and Stiglitz (1987) see animal spirits as a 'picturesque' way to describe the motivations of entrepreneurs and express Keynes' 'non-neo-classical vision of how the economy worked' (p. 120). However, they find animal spirits an old-fashioned notion. Woodford (1991) and Farmer (1994) refer to animal spirits, interpreted as sunspots, in their attempt to incorporate the belief structure of agents in modern macroeconomic analysis and, particularly, to give a role in equilibrium models for the Marshall's and Keynes' view that the optimistic or pessimistic belief of investors may influence the level of economic activity. In the post-Keynesian context many contributions (see Dow and Dow 1985, Lawson 1991, and Gerrard 1994 for a synthesis) suggest that animal spirits may be interpreted as the 'rational' response to genuine uncertainty in a non-neo-classical theoretical context of rationality. In an Austrian perspective Koppl (1991, see also Butos and Koppl 1997) states that

'it may be useful to take animal spirits *seriously* by searching for the economic conditions under which the impulsive side of human nature matters and the conditions under which it does not' (p. 207)

but, he concludes, summarising a widely accepted judgement,

'we cannot hope for much from a positive theory of animal spirits' (Butos and Koppl 1997, p. 207, note 2).

In this paper I should like to propose a view which interprets animal spirits not only seriously but also constructively. Animal spirits are of course a phenomenon not entirely analysable in economic terms; what I maintain is that they should not be considered a phenomenon completely unrelated to the economic analysis and I consider it possible, at least in part, to formulate a positive theory of animal spirits. The objective of my paper is threefold: firstly, to offer an interpretation of Keynes on this subject, essentially referring to the rich post-Keynesian literature which recently emerged (Section II); secondly, to connect and compare Keynes' idea of rationality, or, better, reasonableness, with that of 'bounded' rationality (Section III); finally, to suggest a framework of analysis for a positive theory of animal spirits (Section IV).

ROBERTO MARCHIONATTI

II. AN APPROPRIATE CONTEXT FOR ANIMAL SPIRITS: KEYNES' LONG TERM EXPECTATIONS ANALYSIS

Expectations are a major issue in *The General Theory*. Emphasis on expectations and uncertainty is a constant in Keynes' analyses from about 1910: the origins of this lie in the influence of the English neo-classical tradition, particularly Marshall's theory of the credit cycle (see Kregel 1977), and his own studies on the probability theory. In chapter 5 of *The General Theory* Keynes writes that business decisions depend on expectations about

> 'what the consumers will be prepared to pay when he (the entrepreneur) is ready to supply them after the elapse of what may be a lengthy period' (Keynes 1973b, p. 46).

These expectations fall into two groups, short-term and long-term: short-term expectations are concerned with the outlook for sales, whilst long-term expectations deal with investment. In practice, an entrepreneur does not entertain a single undoubting expectation of what the sale-proceeds of a given output will be, but several hypothetical expectations held with varying degrees of probability and definiteness. Keynes tends to ignore differences between short-term expectations of prices and actual prices received for goods produced as a consequence of those expectations: that is to say, he assumes that short-term expectations are fulfilled[3].

Unlike short-term expectations, however,

> 'it is of the nature of long-term expectations that they cannot be checked at short intervals in the light of realised results' (p. 51),

thus

> 'the factor of current long-term expectations cannot be even approximately eliminated or replaced by realised results' (p. 51).

Long-term expectations, Keynes maintains in chapter 12 of *The General Theory*, depend on the most probable forecast that the agents can make *and* on the confidence with which they make that forecast. This distinction reminds us of

---

3. Keynes writes: 'It will often be safe to omit express reference to short-term expectation, in view of the fact that in practice the process of revision of short-term expectation is a gradual and continuous one, carried on largely in the light of realised results; so that expected and realised results run into and overlap one another in their influence' (Keynes 1973b, p. 50). As Carabelli (1989, p. 223) says, here Keynes was probably expressing his disagreement with Hawtrey who emphasised the role of difference between expected and realised magnitudes. But it is important to stress that the quotation does seem to indicate that Keynes accepted the assumption of 'rational expectations' in a short-run context (see Patinkin 1984 and Meltzer 1989).

ON KEYNES' ANIMAL SPIRITS

another one: probability and weight in Keynes' *A Treatise on Probability* (1973a)[4].

The probability-relation represents the rational belief in a proposition on the basis of the available evidence and it is defined by Keynes as $p = a|h$, where p is the probability of the proposition a, given the evidence h. This rational belief 'is capable of degree', according to whether the knowledge of h is certain or probable or incomplete: the latter is the knowledge

> 'we have in ordinary thought by passing from one proposition to another without being able to say what logical relation, if any, we have perceived between them'(Keynes 1973a).

Keynes speaks also of 'vague knowledge' which does not seem

> 'likely that it is susceptible of strict logical treatment' (Keynes 1973a, p. 17).

Speaking of probability as being concerned with degree of rational belief seems to imply, Keynes says, that it is in some sense quantitative and capable of measurement, but

> 'so far from our being able to measure them, it is not even clear that we are always able to place them in an order of magnitude' (Keynes 1973a, p. 29);

besides probability, if it exists, may be unknown, which is implied by the existence of vague knowledge:

> 'The evidence justifies a certain degree of knowledge, but the weakness of our reasoning power prevents our knowing what this degree is' (Keynes 1973a, p. 34).

At the best, in such cases,

> 'we only know *vaguely* with what degree of probability the premises invest the conclusion' (Keynes 1973a, p. 34).

Whereas the probability measures the difference of the favourable and unfavourable evidence, *the weight of an argument* ($V = V(a|h)$) measures its sum[5], i.e., the total evidence of a proposition. The weight of an argument is also a mea-

---

4. Recent developments in Keynesian scholarship (see Carabelli 1988, Davis 1994, Gerrard 1994 and 1995, Lawson 1985 and 1991, Meeks 1991, Runde 1990) have shed light upon Keynes' epistemological position, particularly through the analysis of the role of *A Treatise of Probability* in the context of Keynes' work as an economist. The present analysis is indebted with these works.

5. The weight of an argument is introduced by Keynes in order to re-enforce Bernoulli's second maxim, according to which we must take into account all the information we have: 'should not this be re-enforced by a further maxim, that we ought to make the weight of our arguments as great as possible by getting all the information we can?' (Keynes 1973a, p. 83).

ROBERTO MARCHIONATTI

sure of the completeness of the evidence. Weight and probability vary accord-ing to evidence: as the available evidence increases, so the weight of an argu-ment increases. However, the probability may either increase or decrease, in relation to whether the added knowledge strengthens the favourable or un-favourable evidence:

'new evidence will sometimes decrease the probability of an argument'.

says Keynes,

'but it will always increase its weight' (Keynes 1973a, p. 27).

Low weight means poor informative evidence, which is connected with uncom-pleted or vague knowledge. In this connection the concept of weight of argu-ment is used in chapter 12 of *The General Theory* on long-term expectation which actually represents the crucial link between the 1936 book and *A Treatise on Probability*[6].

The specific form that weight assumes in *The General Theory* is the 'state of confidence'. Confidence is defined in terms of

'how highly we rate the likelihood of our best forecast turning out quite wrong' (Keynes 1973a, p. 148).

Low confidence depends on the fact that our knowledge is unclear –

'our knowledge of the future is fluctuating, vague and uncertain'

writes Keynes in his 1937 article in the *Quarterly Journal of Economics,* a 'summary' of *The General Theory* (Keynes 1973c, p.113). However,

'very uncertain does not mean the same thing as 'very improbable' (Keynes 1973b, p.148, note 1),

---

6. The weight of argument is the only doctrine of *A Treatise on Probability* to which Keynes makes explicit reference in *The General Theory* (see note p. 148). Another explicit reference to *A Trea-tise* around the time of *The General Theory* is in 1938 discussion with Hugh Townshend on liq-uidity preference. The issue of continuity or change in Keynes' philosophical belief after 1921 is controversial. Without doubt there was a change in interest: Keynes in *The General Theory* is interested not in speculative but in practical rationality; and a change of emphasis: the domain of vague knowledge, non-comparability of probabilities and weights, unknown probabilities, ex-panded considerably. The dramatic events in the world economy after 1929 probably influenced this intellectual change.

ON KEYNES' ANIMAL SPIRITS

Keynes notes, referring to a non-probabilistic meaning of uncertainty[7]. According to Keynes, in presence of such an uncertainty

'it is reasonable ... to be guided to a considerable degree by the facts we *feel* somewhat confident about',

because

'it would be foolish, in forming our expectations, to attach great weight to matters which are very uncertain' (Keynes 1973b, p. 148).

Under such circumstances, in which rational calculation is of little use, the state of confidence can inhibit entrepreneurial decisions about investments, whose proceeds are distributed over a large number of periods, even if the marginal efficiency of capital exceeds the rate of market interest, on the basis of the most probable forecast. The question is how to get around the informative and cognitive shortage, so permit investment activity, and avoid being in the position of Buridan's ass – in which agents are indifferent in relation to which alternative to choose. In his answer, based on the observation of markets and business psychology, Keynes considers two phases of capitalism. Under *old-fashioned capitalism* where, Keynes says,

'enterprises were mainly owned by those who undertook them or by their friends or associates' (Keynes 1973b, p. 150)

– that is to say, where there was no separation between the ownership and management of the firm –

'decisions about investment depended on the genuine expectations of the professional entrepreneur, *individuals of sanguine temperament and constructive impulses who embarked on business as a way of life,* not really relying on a precise calculation of prospective profit' (Keynes 1973b, p. 150, my italics).

Entrepreneurial activity thus assumed a peculiarly mixed character, resembling

'a mixed game of skill and chance' (Keynes 1973b, p. 150)

where investment is the result not merely of

'cold calculation'

7. This is explicitly introduced by Keynes in his 1937 article: 'By 'uncertain' knowledge, let me explain. I do not mean merely to distinguish what is known for certain from what is only probable ... The sense in which I am using the term is that in which the prospect of a European war is uncertain, or the price of copper and the rate of interest twenty years hence, or the obsolescence of a new invention, or the position of private wealth owners in the social system in 1970. About this matter *there is no scientific basis on which to form any calculable probability whatever. We simply do not know*' (Keynes 1973c, p. 113, my italics).

421

ROBERTO MARCHIONATTI

but also of

'temptation to take a chance',

and

'satisfaction (profit apart) in constructing a factory, a railway, a mine or a farm' (Keynes 1973b, p.150).

Under *mature capitalism*, with the separation between ownership and management of the firm *and* the development of organised investment markets, decisions about investment depend essentially on the expectations of stock market investors. Investment is governed

'by the average expectation of those who deal on the Stock Exchange as revealed in the price of shares' (Keynes 1973b, p. 151).

The Stock Exchange

'revalues many investments every day' (Keynes 1973b, p. 151),

giving an opportunity to individuals to revise their commitments frequently, hence significantly influencing the rate of current investment. To evaluate the existing investment, stock market investors make reference to convention, the essence of which

'lies in assuming that the existing state of affairs will continue indefinitely, except in so far as we have specific reasons to expect a change' (Keynes 1973b, p. 152)[8].

As Keynes remarks in the 1937 *QJE* article, in organised investment markets investment valuations depend on

'the judgement of the rest of the world',

---

8. In the *General Theory* and after, Keynes emphasised the role of social conventions as a force able to stabilise social life. This represents a major change in Keynes' philosophical view. As he writes in *My early beliefs* criticising his early philosophical position: 'We were not aware that civilisation was a thin and precarious crust erected by the personality and the will of a very few, and only maintained by rules and conventions skilfully put across and guilefully preserved' (Keynes 1972, p. 447). In this sense *My early beliefs* cannot be considered 'a reaffirmation of his early rationalism', as maintained by Butos and Koppl (1997). On the concept of conventions and its importance in Keynes see Lawson (1993) and Davis (1997). As Davis says, the intellectual development at Cambridge in the 1930s – and particularly the influence of Wittgenstein – could be responsible for the positive attention by Keynes to the concept of convention; I think that in the evolution of Keynes' thought on this subject his uninterrupted intellectual dialogue with Hume is also important: as it is well known, according to Hume 'custom is the great guide of human nature'.

422

ON KEYNES' ANIMAL SPIRITS

that is they are the result of the endeavour

'to conform with the behaviour of the majority or the average' (Keynes 1973c, p. 114).

For Keynes this technique is compatible

'with a considerable measure of continuity and stability in our affairs, *so long as we can rely on the maintenance of convention*' (Keynes 1973b, p. 152)[9].

But this type of convention governing investment is fundamentally arbitrary and consequently precarious. Its precariousness is heightened in proportion to the number of people owning equities who are ignorant with respect to the prospects of a particular investment. Note that stock market operators, i.e., professional speculators, who possess judgement and knowledge beyond that of the average private investor, do not counteract these factors of market fragility and precariousness. This is because they are concerned with speculation, the activity of forecasting the psychology of the market, that is they attempt to anticipate the basis of conventional valuation a short while ahead.

Coexistence of the two types of property-management relation, to which Keynes refers to, makes business activity a mix of enterprise, stock market evaluations and speculation. Enterprise is based as far as possible on reasonable calculation, supplemented by a particular 'way of life', 'spontaneous optimism', temptation and satisfaction to take a chance, and animal *spirits*. Investor activity is instead fundamentally guided by conventional judgements. Thus, comprehensively, business behaviour becomes a mix of reasonable calculation, conventional judgement and animal spirits. In order to avoid the position of Buridan's ass, businessmen must therefore refer to motives which are

'not rational in the sense of being concerned with the evaluation of the consequences',

but are rather

'decided by habit, instinct, preference, desire, will, etc.' (Keynes 1979, p. 294).

9. Keynes writes: 'If there exist organised investment markets and if we can rely on the maintenance of the convention, an investor can legitimately encourage himself with the idea that the only risk he runs is that of a genuine change in the news over the near future, as to likelihood of which he can attempt to form his own judgement, and which is unlikely to be very large. For, assuming that the convention holds good, it is only these changes which can affect the value of investment, and he need not to lose his sleep merely because he has not any notion what his investment will be worth ten years hence. Thus investment becomes reasonably 'safe' for the individual investor over short periods however many, if he can fairly rely on there being no breakdown in the convention and on his therefore having an opportunity to revise his judgement and change his investment, before there has been time for much to happen. Investments which are 'fixed' for the community are thus made 'liquid' for the individuals' (Keynes 1973b, p. 152–153).

ROBERTO MARCHIONATTI

All these factors are crucial in strengthening confidence and, subsequently, the magnitude of investment. Conventional judgements and animal spirits together may be interpreted as a determinant of the rate of confidence or as a substitute for reasonable calculation when confidence is low[10]. They act as a mechanism of fulfilling expectations on the basis of successful rules and spontaneous optimism until a record of failure is accumulated which dictates the rejection of that particular belief model.

III. RATIONALITY IN KEYNES' ANALYSIS
AND MODERN MICROECONOMICS

Keynes rejected total irrationality in explaining human behaviour under uncertainty; he stressed that

> 'we should not conclude ... that everything depends on waves of irrational psychology' (Keynes 1973b, p.162).

On the contrary, he wished to remind us of the limited informational and cognitive basis of human decisions:

> 'human decisions affecting the future ... cannot depend on strict mathematical expectation, since the basis for making such calculations does not exist' (Keynes 1973b, p. 162–163)[11].

Under conditions where knowledge is uncertain and vague, Keynes considered it *reasonable* to be guided by

> 'the facts about which we feel somewhat confident' (Keynes 1973b, p. 148).

More generally, when individuals lack the relevant knowledge, it becomes reasonable to act on the basis of conventional rules. Furthermore, when conventions become less credible it is reasonable for agents to be moved by more psychological factors. In the presence of structural uncertainty, factors which are not 'rational'

> 'in the sense of being concerned with the evaluation of consequences',

---

10. The present interpretation of the relation between confidence and animal spirits is different from that of Gerrard (1995). According to the latter, animal spirits 'can be seen, at least in part, as being determined by the state of confidence', confidence itself being based 'on the evaluation of the weight of the available evidence and the risk of error' (Gerrard 1995, p. 191).
11. Keynes' treatment of human behavior in the face of uncertainty shows strong similarities with the David Hume's sceptical view. This resemblance is not accidental, being 'the superb Hume', as he defined him, a philosopher studied and admired by Keynes (see Meeks 1991).

ON KEYNES' ANIMAL SPIRITS

may actually prevail and be determinant. Economic agents do the best they can depending on their varying circumstances: to pretend to act always in accordance with neo-classical rationality in the presence of uncertainty would be to follow, paradoxically, 'a pseudo-rationality', employing

'a mythical system of probable knowledge' (Keynes 1973c, p. 124).

Two points stressed by Keynes – the limited informational and cognitive basis of human behaviour and the reasonableness of acting on the basis of conventional rules in conditions of genuine uncertainty – are at the heart of contemporary microeconomics of bounded rationality, which began with the pioneering works of Herbert Simon between the middle of the Fifties and the Seventies (Simon 1982), then supported by the enormous literature initiated by Daniel Kahneman, Amos Tversky and their collaborators (recently surveyed in Camerer 1994). This microeconomics is founded on the empirical evidence that subjects rarely behave according to the rational postulate, on the contrary they systematically depart from rationality in judgement under uncertainty. Subjects use heuristics or rules of thumb, which imply that they make systematic errors, often referred as biases or anomalies (see the surveys by Tversky and Thaler 1990, Kahneman, Ketsch and Thaler 1991, Conslik 1996). These

'biases are not fragile effects ... but rather substantial and important behavioral regularities' (Conslik 1996, p. 671).

which will not in general be eliminated, although their extent is a matter of degree (see Smith and Walker 1993, and Frey and Eichenberger 1994).

In this article our specific interest lies in the fact that bounded rationality microeconomics has defined a logical connection between uncertainty and behavioural rules and has shown that it is possible to replace the 'rationality postulate' with a 'bounded rationality postulate' without surrendering theoretical and analytical manageability, going beyond the dilemma of the choice between a bounded theory based on the rationality postulate and the supposed substantial absence of theorising. Behavioural rules originate from an attempt to simplify behaviour to less-complex patterns – economising scarce cognitive and computational resources – , in conditions of genuine uncertainty. In the suggestive theory proposed by Heiner (1983 and 1986), uncertainty is due to the existence of a gap between cognitive ability and the difficulty of the decision-problem (C-D gap), which creates indecipherability of the environmental complexity. This gap makes the use of simplified behavioral rules necessary. In the presence of complex decision problems, competence is restricted by the existence of cognitive limitations in processing information or interpreting potential information, vulnerable expectation perceptions and unreliable probability information. Subse-

ROBERTO MARCHIONATTI

quently indecipherability follows, giving rise to possible errors in behavior. Under such conditions, attempts at optimisation are unreliable because the complexity of a decision may preclude the use of all available information[12]. On the contrary it is 'rational' to follow rules of behaviour different from substantive rationality, which depend primarily on experience; these rules give regularity to behaviour, which may make it more systematic than it would be following optimisation rules from an omniscient agent (see Heiner 1983, Kuran 1988, Akerlof 1991, Simon 1991). This regularity permits the analysability of economic behaviour, so rebutting the objection made by rational expectation theorists according to whom not perfectly rational behaviour would not be systematic, and therefore not analysable.

Behavioural rules may act as a world view, essentially based on past experience, determining how information is perceived and the actions it elicits: they may be reduced to a simplified model which delineates events, determines the probability that such events will occur, and evaluates the consequences of alternative courses of action (see Bookstaber and Langsam 1985). In general, simplification and omission imply only small errors, the removal costs of that may be sizeable: this expresses the same idea by Akerlof and Yellen (1985) with their near-rationality theory. Yet there are always some logical possibilities that are beyond any world view, which impose severe costs to following the responses dictated by the model: these are unexpected events, past experience of which does not exist, and which recreate uncertainty[13]. The emergence of substantial losses will subsequently induce change in the behavioural rule: when the environment changes, traditional rules become outdated and there is room for what Day (1984, see also Day and Pingle 1991 and Pingle and Day 1996) calls 'unmotivated search' and 'hunch' to be productive[14].

---

12. Heiner constructs a 'reliability condition' which establishes a rule involving the use of particular decision strategies. The strategy of behaviour adopted is one economising scarce cognitive and computational resources. In a complex environment it is in fact hardly rational to try to maximise, that is, to be 'perfectly rational': for a boundedly rational agent the heuristic often provides an adequate and cheaper solution where more elaborate processes would be unduly expensive.

13. As Arthur (1994) says, in a world of bounded rationality, a belief model 'must cumulate a record of failure before it is worth discarding. In general, there may be a constant slow turnover of hypothesis acted upon. One could speak of this as a system of temporarily fulfilled expectations' (p. 47).

14. According to Day (1984) curiosity and sense of adventure, which he considers typical impulses of creative scientists and business innovators, drive unmotivated search; hunch involves something less and more than conscious thought and requires a special intuitive intellectual faculty, which can be sharpened by experience.

426

ON KEYNES' ANIMAL SPIRITS

On the basis of these theoretical microeconomic developments it is possible to redefine the rationality postulate as a bounded one that includes types of behaviour which, in context, may be treated analytically but which had previously been excluded within the traditional framework of perfect rationality. Such behaviour is the consequence of the existence of genuine uncertainty. The hypothesis of bounded rationality enables us to appreciate the modernity of Keynes' analysis on the issue of economic behaviour under uncertainty. Keynes's reasonability may be interpreted as the economising behaviour of the bounded rationality hypothesis. Hence, it may be said that recent analysis shows that 'non-rational' behaviour is 'reasonable', and what is more, conventional rule behaviour is analytically analysable. But what can we say about 'animal spirits'?

IV. ENTREPRENEURIAL BEHAVIOUR AND ANIMAL SPIRITS: TOWARDS A POSITIVE THEORY

In this section I should like to show that it is possible to formulate a positive theory of animal spirits. In Keynes' analysis, animal spirits are mainly connected with entrepreneurial behaviour. Hence our starting point is the characterisation of entrepreneurship by Keynes and his strong similarity with the analyses of entrepreneurial behaviour by such authors as Marshall and Schumpeter.

1. Animal Spirits and Entrepreneurship in Marshall, Keynes and Schumpeter Tradition

Keynes characterizes entrepreneurial nature and motivations as follows: entrepreneurial activity is traditionally carried out by

'individuals of sanguine temperament and constructive impulses',

who consider business

'a way of life' (Keynes 1973b, p.150)

and, in their activity, play a mixed game of skill and chance. This characterisation of entrepreneurship by Keynes bears strong similarities with those of Marshall and Schumpeter: we may indeed talk of a common view of the role of entrepreneurial activity in market societies. An inquiry into the nature of entrepreneurship within this tradition may help us in an analysis of animal spirits.

ROBERTO MARCHIONATTI

In Marshall's *Principles*, the entrepreneur is one selected by the struggle for survival, an

'able man, assisted perhaps by some strokes of good fortune' (Marshall 1890, p. 315),

who possesses such qualities as

'alertness, inventiveness, ready versatility' (Marshall 1890, p. 305), 'broad faculties of judgement, promptness, resource, carefulness and steadfastness of purpose' (Marshall 1890, p. 312).

In *Industry and Trade*, referring to the Lancashire cotton industry, whose entrepreneurs had that

'free individuality which has made Britain great' (Marshall 1919, p. 578),

Marshall found essential characteristics of

'strong individuality, resolution and directness of purpose' (Marshall 1919, p. 584)

and exceptional energy. And it is these endowments that enable the entrepreneur

'to force the pace'

of those industries in which

'bold and tireless enterprise can reap a quick harvest' (Marshall 1890, p. 603).

It is the entrepreneur

'who by his quick resolutions and dexterous contrivances, and perhaps also a little by his natural recklessness 'forces the pace'' (Marshall 1890, p. 603).

The entrepreneur seizes the

'opportunities for bold but wise and profitable adventure' (Marshall 1890, p. 601).

Actually, the individual entrepreneur has a limited knowledge of the current state of affairs:

'one cannot tell whether the tide is rising or falling' (Marshall 1890, p. 607),

but usually the consensus on conventions between businessmen helps. Forced on by competition, the entrepreneur

'tries every opening, forecasting probable future events' (p. 619).

Thus it is skill and impulses that permit the Marshallian entrepreneur to exploit perceived opportunities for 'adventure'. Fundamentally, then, this person is an innovator. Which brings us to Schumpeter.

428

ON KEYNES' ANIMAL SPIRITS

Where the boundaries of routine end, Schumpeter writes in *The Theory of Economic Development*, the individual is without data for his decisions and rules of conduct. Of course he can foresee and estimate on the basis of experience, but

'many things must remain uncertain, still others are only ascertainable within wide limits, some can perhaps only be guessed' (Schumpeter 1934, p. 85).

In economic life, Schumpeter says,

'action must be taken without working out all the details of what is to be done' (Schumpeter 1934, p. 85).

Under such conditions

'the success of everything depends upon intuition, the capacity of seeing things in a way which afterwards proves to be true, even though it cannot be established at the moment' (Schumpeter 1934, p. 85).

It is here, says Schumpeter, that entrepreneurial behaviour may be termed 'rational' in the particular sense that

'conscious rationality enters much more into the carrying out of new plans, which themselves have to be worked out before they can be acted upon, than into the mere running of an established business which is largely a matter of routine' (Schumpeter 1934, p. 91).

But, he continues, the conduct and motivations of the entrepreneur are not rational in any other sense. Indeed there is very little conscious rationality in entrepreneurial behaviour. Motivations are manifold:

'the dream and the will to found a private kingdom', or also 'a dynasty',

the will to conquer,

'the impulse to fight, to prove oneself superior to others, to succeed for the sake, not for the fruits of success, but of success itself' (Schumpeter 1934, p. 93);

and finally

'the joy of creating, of getting things done' (Schumpeter 1934, p. 93).

Schumpeter emphasises that the fundamental characteristics of the entrepreneur, who represents one who goes beyond accustomed channels, are intuition and the capacity to correctly foresee future trends *without* a sufficient informational basis. Their motivations are not based on 'cold calculation': this is quite similar to Keynes' idea, where the individual feels the temptation

'to take a chance'

429

ROBERTO MARCHIONATTI

and takes satisfaction

'in constructing a factory, a railway, a mine or a farm' (Keynes 1973b, p. 150).

The motivation of entrepreneurs, as presented by Schumpeter, amounts to a specification of Keynes' animal spirits – i.e., 'non-rational' factors that induce entrepreneurial activity toward investment. Industrial performance depends on the existence and persistence of these spirits. The question is what, if anything, determines these animal spirits or the rate of innovative propensity? Is it indeed possible to define an 'animal spirits rule', that is to say, can we analyse this factor which apparently so affects the rate of investment? Like the state of confidence, such an analysis must depend upon the actual observation of markets. If we were able to find economic factors which regularly influence the existence of animal spirits, then we could say that their analysis is, partly at least, within the field of economic theory, and we could subsequently refute the alleged characteristic of total arbitrariness which has induced most economists to ignore them.

2. A Positive Theory of Animal Spirits: A Suggested Framework of Analysis

In the above-mentioned tradition, the factor influencing the entrepreneurial behaviour is a political, social and economic 'atmosphere', a term used by all three authors. Atmosphere is the result of a delicate balance: the amount of political, social and economic change affects atmosphere, hence also animal spirits, level of confidence and investment. Sudden and/or wide variations of atmosphere are viewed as a threat to group survival and so negatively affect entrepreneurial activity. An analysis of the atmosphere factors requires analysing separately the different meanings of the term political and social on the one hand and economic on the other hand.

In chapter 12 of *The General Theory*, Keynes remarks on the political and social atmosphere

'congenial to the average business man'

as a factor positively influencing animal spirits:

'economic prosperity is excessively dependent on a political and social atmosphere, which is congenial to the average businessman. If the fear of a Labour Government or a New Deal depresses enterprise, this need not be the result either of reasonable calculation or of a plot with political intent; it is the mere consequence of upsetting the delicate balance of spontaneous optimism' (p. 162).

ON KEYNES' ANIMAL SPIRITS

In this passage a meaning of atmosphere as institutional atmosphere emerges, where the term institutional refers to the rules of game of a society. They determine the context in which the social game is played, more or less favorable to business ideology. In fact entrepreneurs possess, as a group, a common ideology, that is, referring to the analytical framework offered by Denzau and North (1994), a

'shared mental model'

that

'provide both an interpretation of the environment and a prescription as to how that environment should be structured' (p. 4).

Their common ideology is essentially 'free individuality': an institutional environment supporting it, has to be considered a necessary condition of an effective entrepreneurial behaviour. It was Schumpeter who strongly underlined, some years after Keynes, the crucial importance of a particular institutional atmosphere, favorable to free contracting, for the existence of entrepreneurs in chapters 12 and 13 of *Capitalism, Socialism and Democracy*[15]. In Keynes the role of the institutional atmosphere is connected to the perception by entrepreneurs of political and ideological changes which modify the rules of social game: a change contrary to the entrepreneurial ideology modifies entrepreneurs behaviour inducing emotions[16] which influence animal spirits negatively. This is the sense in which we may interpret Keynes' statement that:

'we must have regards ... to the nerves and hysteria and even the digestions and reactions to the weather of those upon whose spontaneous activity it largely depends' (p. 162).

A fundamental effect of the existence of psychological and emotional factors put in movement by changes in political and social atmosphere is that

'slumps and depressions are exaggerated in degree' (p. 162),

---

15. According to Schumpeter (1942) the institutions of property and free contracting in particular expressed 'the needs and ways of the truly private economic activity' (pp. 141–142), but the capitalist process 'pushes into the background all those institutions' (pp. 141–142), so produces an *atmosphere* of 'almost universal hostility to its own social order' (p. 143), which 'undermines the role and, along with the role, the social position of the capitalist entrepreneur' (p. 133) and eventually prevents the capitalist engine from functioning.
16. The problem of the effects of emotions on economic behaviour is a very recent topic for the economists. For a partial survey see Elster (1998).

ROBERTO MARCHIONATTI

Keynes writes. This can be interpreted, as in Middleton (1996), as a reference to

'a sort of psychological multiplier effect'

in the sense that overreaction to the current situation causes estimated future events and information to get worse[17]. This theme is treated by Keynes in chapter 22 of *The General Theory*, 'Notes on the trade cycle'. Specifically, Keynes tries to explain the fundamental reason for sudden changes in expectations: evidently, it is the nature of organised investment markets, determined by ignorant purchasers and speculators, that determines a sudden downturn

'when disillusion falls upon an over-optimistic and over-bought market'.

Disillusion comes about

'because doubts arise concerning the reliability of the prospective yield',

and doubts

'spread rapidly'.

Furthermore,

'the dismay and uncertainty as to the future which accompanies a collapse in the marginal efficiency of capital precipitates a sharp increase in liquidity preference' (Keynes 1973b, p. 316)[18].

Now, let us turn to the concept of economic atmosphere. The concept of economic atmosphere actually originates from Marshall's analysis of industrial districts. The external economies generated in such districts – such as hereditary skill, growth of subsidiary trades, constant intercommunication of ideas, interaction between suppliers and users – which engender advantageous learning

17. Middleton (1996) introduces an adaptation level-theoretic model of animal spirits as a key to understanding non periodic or chaotic cyclical fluctuations: he proposes that Keynes' reference may be intepreted as a suggestion that a primary determinant of the state of confidence is the amount of social and economic change to which agents are exposed.
18. This phenomenon of over-reaction in investment markets has been studied by behavioural finance: based on Kahneman-Tversky (1982), which showed that people, in violation of Bayes'. rule, have a tendency to overvalue recent information and undervalue long-term tendencies, De Bondt and Thaler (1986) predicted a stock market anomaly from the psychology of decision making, a result taken up by following studies. Kirman (1994), explicitly following Keynes' statement that, in financial markets, agents consider 'what average opinion expects average opinion to be', presents a theoretical explanation of how swings in market opinion may be generated: changes in opinion occur as a result of stochastic interaction between individuals who try to assess what market opinion is and act accordingly. If the majority opinion is known, agents' behaviour is completely rational, and mistaken when the majority is not clear: this gives rise to bubble-like phenomena in which prices rise and fall away from fundamental values for periods of an unpredictable length.

ON KEYNES' ANIMAL SPIRITS

processes, are a fundamental element in the growth of the industries concentrated there and enable the persistence of the so-called 'spontaneous optimism' so abundant in successful districts. More generally, referring to recent developments in the field of economics of innovation, we may speak of positive externalities in the form of learning processes (learning by doing, by using, by interacting and by imitating), network externalities and technological interdependence, all of which shape and facilitate the innovation adoption process (see for example Rosenberg 1976, David and Rosembloom 1990, Malerba 1992, see also Sachwald 1998).

It is important to stress that a condition of exploitation of these externalities is the existence of a particular social atmosphere, that is the existence of those psychological and sociological factors which, creating a favorable atmosphere *between* entrepreneurs, make the existence of economic relations possible. Recently, Casson (1995) discussed the role of business culture – where culture is defined as a collective subjectivity: a shared set of values, norms and beliefs – a concept close to that of shared mental model used by Denzau and North – in determining the quality of entrepreneurship, hence his performance: the most important aspect of business culture is individuated in the extent to which it promotes trust.

'Trust facilitates cooperation between entrepreneurs, which is just as important as competition in achieving efficiency' (p. 79)[19].

Keynes in his analysis of the longevity of an industry, in earlier writings from the middle of the nineteen-twenties about the state of the Lancashire cotton industry, referred to the concept of economic atmosphere in connection with another Marshallian concept, the life cycle of the firm (see Marchionatti 1995). Keynes raises the issue of the failure of the British cotton industry to adjust and change. This is attributed to the age of the firms involved: Keynes maintains that in their old age, firms and industries display an 'acquiescent' behaviour or failure in innovative activity, due to the breakdown of what he calls animal spirits in the *General Theory*. Recent analyses of firm dynamics confirm Marshall and Keynes' theories: Evans (1987) finds that firm growth decreases with firm age; and Antonelli and Marchionatti (1996) find that the traditional successful pat-

19. Casson (1995) stresses the fact that 'one of the characteristics of the industrial revolution in Britain seems to have been the emergence of high-trust cultures amongst regional business elites ... In regions where cooperation between independent businesses was intense, regional economic performance will almost certainly have been better than it would have been had larger-scale business prevailed' (p. 91).

ROBERTO MARCHIONATTI

tern of behaviour and the actual organisational structure of the firms in a mature industry can constitute a barrier to the adoption of new complex technologies. In this sense, animal spirits are connected to the age structure of the industry itself: an industry where old firms prevail probably presents a low rate of innovation and structural change.

The last important factor to be considered is that old-firm industries are generally subjected to aggressive competition from new-firm industries. Under such circumstances, if a (typically consequent) situation of structural excess capacity arises, it may result in excess competition, which fails to provoke proper adjustment within the old-firm industry[20]: this was the case of the English cotton industry analysed by Keynes. The pressure of competition affects adjustment to the point where benefits from investment equal costs; beyond this point it reduces investment. Within the field of 'market structure and innovation', the inverted-U relation between R&D investment and the number of competitors is well known (see Kamien and Schwartz 1982).

From our analysis it emerges that an entrepreneur's choice to follow the 'animal spirits rule of behaviour' is not a completely non-economical (or irrational) decision, but seems rather to be explicable with reference to the political, social and economic atmosphere. The first meanings refer to the rules of game of a society and to the existence of an institutional context favorable to the existence of entrepreneurs: changes in it induce psychological reactions able to explain sudden changes in animal spirits and in expectations. The economic meaning of atmosphere refers to a set of organisational and environmental factors economically analysable with concepts elaborated in the field of the economics of innovation – the existence of Marshallian external economies, the age of the firm and the intensity of competition. When external economies 'dwindle', firms get old and competition becomes 'excessive', then animal spirits and enterprise fade. This fact would explain long-term industrial decay in terms of a failure to solve a problem of dynamic efficiency, based on the persistence of an innovative behaviour.

V. CONCLUDING REMARKS

According to Keynes in an uncertain environment it is reasonable that the decisions of economic agents should depend on conventional judgements and animal spirits, in addition and supporting rational calculation. Mainstream theorists

---

20. The relation between productive excess capacity and incentive to dump has been analysed and formalised into a model by Marchionatti and Usai 1997.

ON KEYNES' ANIMAL SPIRITS

have rejected this statement for quite some time now on the assumption that, in the case of genuine uncertainty, rationality will be of little value because outside the realm of rationality only the savage territory of irrationality exists. The theoretical framework of bounded rationality permits reconsideration and support of Keynes' hypothesis: in an uncertain environment reasonability represents an economising principle manifested in a range of behaviours, while attempts to optimise are often unreliable and expressions of 'pseudo-rationality'. Keynes' analysis of economic behaviour under uncertainty may be considered as a general model able to contain empirical evidence that agents are trying to be rational (reasonable) in their behaviour and particularly in the formation of long-term expectations. In this context animal spirits, a phenomenon traditionally not considered by economic theory, can be analysed referring to the institutional and economic atmosphere, the first being analysed in terms of psychological reactions induced by changes in the institutional context, the latter in terms of motivations of innovative behaviour, as a factor influencing long-term industrial growth.

REFERENCES

Akerlof. George A. (1991). Procrastination and Obedience, *American Economic Review*. 81: 1–19.
Akerlof. George A. and Janet L. Yellen (1985). Can Small Deviations From Rationality Make Significant Differences to Economic Equilibria?, *American Economic Review*. 75: 708–720.
Antonelli. Cristiano and Roberto Marchionatti (1998). Technological and Organisational Change in a Process of Industrial Rejuvenation. The Case of the Italian Cotton Textile Industry, *Cambridge Journal of Economics*. 22: 1–18.
Arestis, Philip and Malcom Sawyer (eds.) (1996). *The Elgar Companion to Radical Political Economy*. London: Edward Elgar.
Arthur, W. Brian. (1994). Inductive Reasoning and Bounded Rationality, *American Economic Review*. 84: 406–411.
Bookstaber, Richard and Joseph Langsam (1985). On the Optimality of Coarse Behavior Rules, *Journal of Theoretical Biology*. 116: 161–193.
Butos, William N. and Roger G. Koppl (1997). The Varieties of Subjectivism: Keynes and Hayek on Expectations, *History of Political Economy*. 29: 327–359.
Camerer, Colin F. (1994). Individual Decision Making, in: J. Kagel and A. Roth (eds.), *Handbook of Experimental Economics*. Princeton, N.J.: Princeton University Press: 587–704.
Carabelli, Anna (1988). *On Keynes's Method*. London: Macmillan.
Casson, Mark (1995). *Entrepreneurship and Business Culture*. Brookfield, Verm.: Aldershot.
Conlisk. John (1996). Why Bounded Rationality?, *Journal of Economic Literature*. 34: 669–700.
David, Paul A. and J. L. Rosembloom (1990). Marshallian Factor Market Externalities and the Dynamics of Industrial Localisation, *Journal of Urban Economics*. 28: 349–370.
Davidson, Paul (1991). Is Probability Theory Relevant for Uncertainty? A Post Keynesian Perspective, *Journal of Economic Perspectives*. Winter: 129–143.
Davis, John B. (1994). *Keynes's Philosophical Development*. Cambridge: Cambridge University Press.

ROBERTO MARCHIONATTI

Davis, John B. (1997). Keynes on History and Convention, in: G.C. Harcourt and P.A. Riach (eds.), *A 'Second Edition' of the General Theory*. London: Routledge: vol. 2, 203–221.

Day, Richard H. (1984). Disequilibrium Economic Dynamic, *Journal of Economic Behavior and Organization*. 5: 57–76.

Day, Richard H. and Mark Pingle (1991). Economizing Economizing, in: R. Franz, H. Singh and J. Gerber (eds.), *Handbook of Behavioral Economics*. Greenwich: JAI Press: 511–524.

De Bondt, Werner F.M. and Richard H. Thaler (1986). Does the Stock Market Overreact?, *Journal of Finance*. 40: 793–805.

Denzau, Arthur T. and Douglass C. North (1994). Shared Mental Models: Ideologies and Institutions, *Kyklos*. 47: 3–31.

Dow, Alexander and Sheila Dow (1985). Animal Spirits and Rationality, in: T. Lawson and H. Pesaran (eds.), *Keynes' Economics. Methodological Issues*. London: Routledge: 46–55.

Dow, Sheila and John Hillard (eds.) (1995). *Keynes, Knowledge and Uncertainty*. London: Edward Elgar.

Elster, Jon (1998). Emotions and Economic Theory, *Journal of Economic Literature*. 36: 47–74.

Evans, Davis S. (1987). The Relationship Between Firm Growth, Size and Age: Estimates for 100 Manufacturing Industries. *Journal of Industrial Economics*. 197–211.

Farmer, Roger (1994). *The Macroeconomics of Self-Fulfilling Prophecies*. Cambridge, MA: MIT Press.

Frey, Bruno S. and Reiner Eichenberger (1994). Economic Incentives Transform Psychological Anomalies, *Journal of Economic Behavior and Organization*. 23: 215–234.

Gerrard, Bill (1994a). Beyond Rational Expectations: A Constructive Interpretation of Keynes's Analysis of Behaviour under Uncertainty, *Economic Journal*. 104: 327–337.

Gerrard, Bill (1994b). Animal Spirits, in: P. Arestis and M. Sawyer (eds.), *The Elgar Companion to Radical Political Economy*. London: Edward Elgar: 15–19.

Gerrard, Bill (1995). Probability, Uncertainty and Behaviour: a Keynesian Perspective, in: S. Dow and J. Hillard (eds.), *Keynes, Knowledge and Uncertainty*. London: Edward Elgar: 119–132.

Greenwald B. and J. Stiglitz (1987). Keynesian, New Keynesian and New Classical Economics, *Oxford Economic Papers*. 39: 119–132.

Harcourt, Geoff C. and P.A. Riach (eds.) (1997). A *'Second Edition' of the General Theory*. London: Routledge.

Heiner, Ronald A. (1983). The Origin of Predictable Behavior, *American Economic Review*. 73: 560–595.

Heiner, Ronald A. (1989). The Origin of Dynamic Predictable Behavior, *Journal of Economic Behavior and Organization*. 12: 233–258.

Howitt, Peter and Preston McAfee (1992). Animal Spirits, *American Economic Review*. 82: 493–507.

Kahneman, Daniel and Amos Tversky (1982). Prospect Theory: An Analysis of Decision Under Risk, *Econometrica*. 24: 178–191.

Kahneman, Daniel, Jack L. Ketsch and Richard D. Thaler (1991). Anomalies: The Endowment Effect, Loss Aversion, and Status Quo Bias, *Journal of Economic Perspectives*. 5: 193–206.

Kamien, Morton I. and Nancy L. Schwartz (1982). *Market Structure and Innovation*. Cambridge: Cambridge University Press.

Keynes, John M. (1972). *The Collected Writings of John Maynard Keynes, vol. X, Essays in Biography* (D. Moggridge editor). London: Macmillan for the Royal Economic Society.

Keynes, John M. (1973a). *The Collected Writings of John Maynard Keynes, vol. VIII, A Treatise on Probability* (D. Moggridge editor). London: Macmillan for the Royal Economic Society.

Keynes, John M. (1973b). *The Collected Writings of John Maynard Keynes, vol. VII, The General Theory of Employment, Interest and Money* (D. Moggridge editor). London: Macmillan for the Royal Economic Society.

Keynes, John M. (1973c). *The Collected Writings of John Maynard Keynes, vol. XIV, The General Theory and after. Part II. Defence and Development* (D. Moggridge editor). London: Macmillan for the Royal Economic Society.

ON KEYNES' ANIMAL SPIRITS

Keynes, John M. (1979). *The Collected Writings of John Maynard Keynes,* vol. XXIX, *The General Theory and after. A Supplement* (D. Moggridge editor). London: Macmillan for the Royal Economic Society.

Keynes, John M. (1981). *The Collected Writings of John Maynard Keynes,* vol. XIX, *Activities 1922–1929. The return to Gold and Industrial Policy. Part II* (D. Moggridge editor). London: Macmillan for the Royal Economic Society.

Kirman, Alan (1994). Epidemic of Opinion and Speculative Bubbles in Financial Markets, in: M.P. Taylor, *Money and Financial Markets.* Oxford: Blackwell: 354–368.

Koppl, Roger (1991). Animal Spirits, *Journal of Economic Perspectives.* 5: 203–210.

Kregel, Jan (1977). On the Existence of Expectations in English Neoclassical Economics, *Journal of Economic Literature.* 14: 495–499.

Kuran, Timur (1988). The Tenacious Past: Theories of Personal and Collective Conservatism, *Journal of Economic Behavior and Organization.* 10: 143–171.

Lawson, Tony (1985). Uncertainty and Economic Analysis, *Economic Journal.* 95: 909–927.

Lawson, Tony (1991). Keynes and the Analysis of Rational Behaviour, in: R. O'Donnell (ed.), *Keynes as Philosopher-Economist.* London: Macmillan.

Lawson, Tony (1993). Keynes and Convention, *Review of Social Economy.* 51: 174–200.

Lawson, Tony and Hashem Pesaran (eds.) (1985). *Keynes' Economics. Methodological Issues.* London: Routledge.

Lucas, Robert E. (1981). *Studies in Business-Cycles Theory.* Cambridge: MIT Press.

Malerba, Franco (1992). Learning by firms and incremental technical change, *Economic Journal.* 102: 845–859.

Mankiw, N. Gregory and David Romer (eds.) (1991). *New Keynesian Economics.* Cambridge, MA: MIT Press.

Marchionatti, Roberto (1995). Keynes and the Collapse of the British Cotton Industry in the 1920s: a Microeconomic Case Against Laissez-Faire, *Journal of Post-Keynesian Economics.* 17: 427–445.

Marchionatti, Roberto and Stefano Usai (1997). Voluntary Export Restraints, Dumping and Excess Capacity, *The Manchester School.* 65: 499–512.

Marshall, Alfred (1920/1890). *Principles of Economics.* London: Macmillan.

Marshall, Alfred (1919). *Industry and Trade.* London: Macmillan.

Matthews, Robin (1991). Animal Spirits, in: G. Meeks (ed.). *Thoughtful Economic Man.* Cambridge: Cambridge University Press.

Meeks, Gay (1991). Keynes on the Rationality of Decision Procedures under Uncertainty: the Investment Decision, in: G. Meeks (ed.). *Thoughtful economic man.* Cambridge: Cambridge University Press.

Meltzer, Allan H. (1989). *Keynes's Monetary Theory: A Different Interpretation.* Cambridge: Cambridge University Press.

Middleton, Elliott (1996). Adaptation Level and Animal Spirits, *Journal of Economic Psychology.* 17: 479–498.

Moggridge, Donald E. (1992). The Source of Animal Spirits, *Journal of Economic Perspectives.* 6: 207–212.

Muth, John F. (1961). Rational Expectations and the Theory of Price Movements, *Econometrica.* 26: 384–405.

O'Donnell, Rod (1989). *Keynes: Philosophy, Economics and Politics.* London: Macmillan.

O'Donnell, Rod (1991). Keynes on Probability, Expectations and Uncertainty, in: R. O'Donnell (ed.), *Keynes as Philosopher-Economist.* London: Macmillan.

Patinkin, Dom (1984). Keynes and Economics Today, *American Economic Review.* 74: 97–102.

Pesaran, Hashem (1987). *The Limits of Rational Expectations.* Cambridge and Oxford: Basil Blackwell.

Robinson, Joan (1962). *Essays in the Theory of Economic Growth.* London. Macmillan:

Pingle, Mark and Richard H. Day (1996). Models of Economizing Behavior: Experimental Evidence, *Journal of Economic Behavior and Organization.* 29: 191–209.

437

ROBERTO MARCHIONATTI

Rosenberg, Nathan (1976). *Perspectives on Technology.* Cambridge: Cambridge University Press.

Runde, Jochen (1990). Keynesian uncertainty and the weight of arguments, *Economics and Philosophy.* 6: 275–292.

Sachwald, Frédérique (1998). Cooperative Agreement and the Theory of the Firm: Focusing on Barriers to Change, *Journal of Economic Behavior and Organization.* 35: 203–228.

Schumpeter, Joseph A. (1934). *Theory of Economic Development.* Cambridge, Mass.: Harvard University Press.

Schumpeter, Joseph A. (1942). *Capitalism, Socialism and Democracy.* London: George Allen and Unwin.

Shakle, G.L.S. (1967). *The Years of High Theory.* Cambridge: Cambridge University Press.

Simon, Herbert A. (1955). A behavioral model of rational choice, *Quarterly Journal of Economics.* 69: 174–183.

Simon, Herbert A. (1982). *Models of bounded rationality,* volume 2. Cambridge, Mass.: MIT Press.

Simon, Herbert A. (1991). *Models of my life.* New York: Basic Books.

Smith, Vernon and James M. Walker (1993). Monetary Rewards and Decision Cost in Experimental Economics, *Economic Inquiry.* 31: 245–261.

Tversky, Amos and Richard H. Thaler (1990). Anomalies: Preference Reversals, *Journal of Economic Perspectives.* 4: 201–211.

Woodford M. (1991). Self-fulfilling expectations and fluctuations in aggregate demand, in: N.G. Mankiw and D. Romer (eds.), *New Keynesian economics.* Cambridge, MA: MIT Press.

SUMMARY

According to Keynes the formation of entrepreneurial expectations on investment in an uncertain environment depends on conventional judgements and animal spirits, in addition to and supporting rational calculation. Conventions and animal spirits have no room in the mainstream theoretical framework, because their existence makes long-term expectations exogenous and their influence totally arbitrary. For this reason in particular animal spirits have been excluded from scientific enquiry. This paper argues that: a) the theoretical framework of bounded rationality permits reconsidering and supporting Keynes' hypothesis that in an uncertain environment it is reasonable that the decisions of economic agents should depend on non rational motives, b) in this context, animal spirits can be considered as a typical entrepreneurial impulse, depending on political, social and economic atmosphere: the latter being analysed in terms of motivations of innovative behaviour.

[20]

KYKLOS, Vol. 50 – 1997 – Fasc. 4, 561–574

On George Soros and Economic Analysis

Rod Cross and Douglas Strachan*

'Economic theory needs to be fundamentally reconsidered. There is an element of uncertainty in economic processes that has been largely left unaccounted for. None of the social sciences can be expected to yield firm results comparable to the natural sciences, and economics is no exception. We must take a radically different view of the role that thinking plays in shaping events'

George Soros (1995, p. 67)

There is more than a touch of Renaissance Man about George Soros. Whilst completing an undergraduate degree in economics at LSE he came under the influence of Karl Popper. After a spell working as an analyst specialising in arbitrage opportunities between US and European financial markets, he produced a Popperian treatise on philosophy, 'The Burden of Consciousness' (1961/2). The *Quantum Fund* operated by Soros came to be possibly the most prominent investment fund on the world stage. Operating on the basis of leverage, the Quantum Fund earned an average annual yield of 35%, if profits had been reinvested, over the twenty-five years from 1969 (Soros 1995). Soros himself became a major media figure in Europe after the Fund made $1 billion from taking a short position on sterling before the exit of the £ sterling from the ERM on 15 September 1992. Not content with just making money, Soros regarded the operations of the Quantum Fund as a series of tests for his theories of how the players in financial markets interact with the economic systems in

* University of Strathclyde and ICMM. Correspondence: Department of Economics, University of Strathclyde, Curran Building, 100 Cathedral Street, Glasgow G4 0LN, Scotland, UK, Tel: 0141-548-3855/3856/3840, Fax: 0141-552-5589, E-Mail: economics@strath.ac.uk.

ROD CROSS AND DOUGLAS STRACHAN

which they participate, publishing the results of his 'real-time' experiments in *The Alchemy of Finance* (1987, 1994). In recent years Soros has become one of the world's leading philanthropists by way of the funds provided by the Soros Foundation to promote reconstruction in his native Hungary and elsewhere in Central and Eastern Europe (see Soros 1995 and Slater 1996 for autobiographical and biographical details).

I. WHY SOROS?

The focus in the present essay is on the Soros view of economic analysis. This is interesting for several reasons. Practitioners often upbraid economic theorists with the jibe, 'if you're so smart, why aren't you so rich?'. Soros, despite some spectacular losses, has managed to sustain high returns on his investment strategies over too many years for the possibility that he was just plain lucky to loom large. Thus there is a *prima facie* case for taking seriously the Soros account of how economic actors interact with the economic systems in which they participate. Here there is maybe a parallel with John Maynard Keynes, whose investment strategies, albeit on a much smaller scale, were, a few disasters apart, successful enough to convince practitioners that his economic analysis was worth taking seriously.

It is also intriguing that Soros was not only trained in economic analysis but has also published, during his working life as an investment practitioner, a major treatise on economic analysis (Soros 1987, 1994). Although his formal economics education took place in the early 1950s, Soros has clearly kept up with developments in areas such as the theory of efficient markets. Practitioners often dismiss economic analysis as being 'okay in theory but not in practice' without bothering to articulate a theory that would be 'okay in both theory and practice'. Soros has done both.

Finally, Soros is unusual in having a sophisticated understanding of the philosophy of science. Many criticisms of economic theory are based on false epistemological premises. A popular one is that economic theories are fundamentally flawed because they have not been, and could not be, demonstrated to be true. Exposed to Popper early on, Soros understands that no theory can be demonstrated to be true, be it in the physical, natural or social sciences. Instead theories can only be assessed indirectly via attempts to falsify them. Thus the Soros assessment of standard economic analysis avoids false epistemological premises and raises issues that are possibly valid.

A telling criticism of some alternative schools of thought in economics is that they are more 'attitudes of mind' than fecund in the sense of producing

ON GEORGE SOROS AND ECONOMIC ANALYSIS

substantive bodies of analysis. In the rest of this essay we will argue that Soros, suitably reconstructed, is immune from this criticism.

II. THE SOROS CRITIQUE

The starting point for Soros is the fallibility of knowledge about the external world. As Popper pointed out, the logic of *modus ponens* cannot be applied to scientific hypotheses, which leaves the logic of *modus tollens*. Thus scientific hypotheses are conjectures that can be demonstrated to be false, but cannot be demonstrated to be true. The fallibility of human knowledge about the external world provides the cornerstone for the Soros philosophy of life:

> ' ... we cannot live without a set of reasoned beliefs ... the question is, can we have a set of beliefs based on the recognition that our beliefs are inherently flawed? ...I believe we can and, in my own life, I have been guided by my own fallibility' (Soros 1995, p. 212).

According to Soros, the central problem with standard economic theory is that it assumes that economic agents have perfect, in the non-reflexive sense to be defined later, knowledge about their economic world. This is inconsistent with the inherently fallible nature of human knowledge, and hence standard economic theory is based on false premises about what it is possible for economic agents to know.

The Soros alternative account of the behaviour of economic agents was derived from his analysis of the logical problem of self-reference. This can be illustrated by the liar's paradox. Consider the claim: 'all short statements in economics are false'. If this claim is true it must also be false, because of the self-reference to the present economics essay. This type of self-referential problem provided the background to the Soros articulation of why knowledge of economic and social systems is different to that of physical systems. The problem is that the agents who are trying to acquire knowledge of economic and social systems are themselves participants whose behaviour affects the economic or social environment they are trying to understand. This gives rise to the Soros notion of reflexivity in economic behaviour:

> ' ... on the one hand, reality is reflected in people's thinking – I call this the cognitive function; on the other hand reality is affected by people's decisions – I call this the participating function – these events have a different structure from the events studied by natural science – they need to be thought about differently ... I call these events reflexive' (Soros 1995, p. 214).

A basic problem with this argument is that observations in the natural sciences are also theory dependent: observations of, say, sub-atomic particles are gener-

563

ROD CROSS AND DOUGLAS STRACHAN

ated by theories speculating that such particles exist. The Soros response is that theories in economics can *change* the behaviour of the reality observed in a sense that, say, Heisenberg's uncertainty principle does not *change* the behaviour of quantum phenomena.

Thus emerges a trichotomy between true, false and reflexive statements. Economics can generate true statements, but only in the context of purely axiomatic models. Economic propositions about empirical phenomena can be expressed as the implications of hypothetico-deductive models, as with the Popper characterisation. Such propositions are refutable, but, according to Soros, they are inconsistent with the evidence. The problem is to model how thinking *and* participating agents interact with historical events. If economic agents cannot do other than act on the basis of reflexive beliefs or statements about the world, the truth value of such statements is inherently uncertain. And so, therefore, is economic knowledge.

At first pass this position appears nihilistic about the possibility of economic knowledge. Non-reflexive economic theories are going to be falsified in situations where reflexivity 'plays an important role'. This is taken to be the case in financial markets:

> ' ... the theory of rational expectations and efficient markets is highly misleading ... I believe that the performance of the Quantum Fund alone falsifies the random walk theory' (Soros 1995, p. 219).

This leaves reflexive statements, which can be considered as similar to the incantations involved in alchemy:

> ' ... the alchemists made a big mistake trying to turn base metals into gold by incantation ... with chemical elements alchemy doesn't work ... but it does work in the financial markets, because incantations can influence the decisions of the people who shape the course of events' (Soros 1995, p. 221).

Thus neo-classical economists, rather than drawing their metaphors about the workings of economic systems from Newtonian mechanics (see Mirowski 1989), would have found more appropriate metaphors from Newton's writings on alchemy. Hence the title of the major Soros treatise on economics, *The Alchemy of Finance* (1987, 1994).

The apparent nihilism of *The Alchemy of Finance*, however, is partly dispelled by the subsequent clarification in Soros (1995). Here the distinction drawn between *near-equilibrium* and *far-from-equilibrium* conditions is given greater significance. In *near-equilibrium* conditions, which might be considered to be 'the normal situation',

564

ON GEORGE SOROS AND ECONOMIC ANALYSIS

> ' ... the discrepancy between thinking and reality is not very large and there are forces at play that tend to bring them close together, partly because people can learn from experience, and partly because people can actually change and shape social conditions according to their desires' (Soros 1995, p. 69).

In such situations economic theories that ignore reflexivity might not be too wide of the mark. In *far-from-equilibrium* conditions, however, which might be thought of as circumstances in which major changes in the economic environment take place,

> ' ... the prevailing bias and the prevailing trend reinforce each other until the gap between them becomes so wide that it brings a catastrophic collapse' (Soros 1995, p. 70).

An example of a bias that can generate far-from-equilibrium conditions is provided by errors in valuation. So, in the international lending boom beginning in the late 1970s, for example, banks judged the borrowing capacity of debtor countries by looking at debt-GDP or debt service-export ratios. The problem is that such ratios are reflexive, in that they reflect the lending activities of the participant banks as well as any 'fundamentals' affecting borrowing capacity. Thus trends of increased lending were established on the basis of reflexive valuations. Eventually the gap between beliefs about borrowing capacity and the reality of actual borrowing capacity became so large that the bias underlying the beliefs came to be realised, and lending collapsed.

Thus reflexivity in economic behaviour is capable of bringing about far-from-equilibrium situations and regime changes. This, far from being nihilistic, is an intriguing account of endogenously-generated regime changes. In terms of economic analysis the suggestion is that the behaviour of economic agents using rules of thumb such as valuation ratios, and of economic modellers themselves, need to be introduced into economic models in order to capture the interaction between thinking and reality. The way forward, then, is to eschew the reductionist search for finer-grain microfoundations and instead study how complex economic systems can emerge from the interactions between agents operating both as thinkers and actors (Soros 1995, p. 220).

III. RATIONAL EXPECTATIONS AND EFFICIENT MARKETS

From the foregoing discussion it is clear that Soros views the postulates of rational expectations and market efficiency that have dominated the economics literature on financial markets in recent years as implausible descriptions of behaviour.

ROD CROSS AND DOUGLAS STRACHAN

The rational expectations hypothesis has two components: each agent maximises an objective function subject to some perceived constraints; and the constraints perceived by the agents in the system are mutually consistent. Thus

' ... the decisions of one person form parts of the constraints upon others, so that consistency, at least implicitly. requires people to be forming beliefs about others' decisions, about their decision processes, and even about their beliefs' (Sargent 1993, p. 6).

If agents were not behaving in such a way there would be unexploited opportunities for profit, which would be inconsistent with the neo-classical conception of market equilibrium. Rational expectations in this sense are clearly inconsistent with the Soros first principle that human knowledge is fallible. If the rational expectations hypothesis were true, agents would be able to know the equilibrium probability distributions for the events about which they form expectations. Economists themselves do not know what such probability distributions are, and are obliged to use econometric techniques to attempt to estimate probability distributions and 'laws' of motion. Such inferences are inevitably fragile and fallible, as is apparent from the disagreements amongst economists and econometricians. Thus the rational expectations hypothesis is implausible both because it attributes knowledge to economic agents that even economists and econometricians do not have, and in that it ignores the inevitably fallible and conjectural nature of any body of scientific knowledge.

The implication of efficient markets drawn from the rational expectations hypothesis is also inconsistent with the Soros view. In its *weak* form the efficient markets hypothesis says that market prices reflect any 'laws' of motion evident in prices, so that any correlation between the present price and past prices is eliminated; in *semi-strong* form the hypothesis says that market prices also reflect any publicly available information about the processes determining market prices; in *strong* form the hypothesis has market prices reflecting or discounting insider information as well (see Shiller 1996). In a world of efficient markets, changes in market prices should be random in the sense of being uncorrelated with past prices and publicly or privately available information. This would leave no room for the investment strategies pursued by Soros and the Quantum Fund to be consistently more successful than the rest of the market. The Quantum Fund could have been amazingly lucky, but it is more plausible to agree with Soros that

' ... the performance of the Quantum Fund alone falsifies the random walk theory' (Soros 1995, p. 219).

566

IV. KEYNES AND SOROS

In rejecting the idea that the uncertainties surrounding economic behaviour can be tamed by assuming that agents have perfect knowledge of some objective equilibrium probability distributions, Soros is in the same camp as John Maynard Keynes. The untractable nature of the uncertainty surrounding economic decision-taking was stressed in the *General Theory* (Keynes 1936, ch.12) and in Keynes' response to his reviewers (Keynes 1937):

> ' ... the outstanding fact is the extreme precariousness of the basis of knowledge on which our estimates of prospective yield have to be made ... our knowledge of the factors which will govern the yield of an investment some years hence is usually very slight and often negligible ... if we speak frankly, we have to admit that our basis of knowledge for estimating the yield ten years hence of a railway, a copper mine, a textile factory, the goodwill of a patent medicine, an Atlantic liner, a building in the City of London amounts to little and sometimes to nothing ... in fact, those who seriously attempt to make any such estimate are often so much in the minority that their behaviour does not govern the market' (Keynes 1936, pp. 149–150).

Keynes then proceeds to point out that the existence of securities markets means that the underlying physical investments

> ' ... are governed by the average expectation of those who deal in the Stock Exchange as revealed in the price of shares, rather than by the genuine expectations of the professional entrepreneur' (1936, p. 151).

How, then, are the expectations of those dealing in securities determined?

Here there are several similarities between Soros and Keynes. A first is that, in both Soros and Keynes, investors follow conventions or rules of thumb. In Soros this is the trend-following behaviour pursued by investors, particularly prevalent in funds whose performance is measured relative to the rest of the market, rather than in absolute terms. The expectation implicit in such an investment strategy is that the present trend will continue. In Keynes the trend is called a *convention*, whose essential feature is the assumption

> ' ... that the existing state of affairs will continue indefinitely' (1936, p. 152).

Such conventions can survive in what Soros would call near-equilibrium conditions, and are compatible with

> ' ... a considerable measure of continuity and stability in our affairs' (Keynes 1936, p. 152).

Such conventions, however, as in Soros, rely on expectations for which there is no secure epistemological foundation:

ROD CROSS AND DOUGLAS STRACHAN

' ... we are assuming, in effect, that the existing market valuation, however arrived at, is uniquely *correct* in relation to our existing knowledge of the facts which will influence the yield of the investment, and that it will only change in proportion to changes in this knowledge; though, philosophically speaking, it cannot be uniquely correct, since our existing knowledge does not provide a sufficient basis for a mathematical calculation' (Keynes 1937, p. 152).

A second area of similarity concerns what happens in what Soros calls far-from-equilibrium conditions. In such circumstances trends are broken, and conventions regarding the correctness of existing market valuations are no longer tenable. In Keynes such circumstances arise inevitably in systems where valuations are established as

'the outcome of the mass psychology of a large number of ignorant individuals'

because there are

' ... no strong roots of conviction to hold it steady'.

Keynes' 'abnormal times' correspond to Soros' 'far-from-equilibrium conditions' in which perceptions and reality are far from being synchronised. For Keynes such changes occur

' ... when the hypothesis of an indefinite continuance of the existing state of affairs is less plausible than usual even though there are no express grounds to anticipate a definite change'.

The implication is that

' ... the market will be subject to waves of optimistic and pessimistic sentiment, which are unreasoning and yet in a sense legitimate where no solid basis exists for a reasonable calculation' (Keynes 1936, p. 154).

A third area where Soros and Keynes are close is in relation to reflexivity. In Soros the theories which economic agents use to attempt to understand their environment also change the environment when used as a basis for decision-taking. In Keynes this sort of self-referential behaviour arises because investors are inevitably involved in a game requiring each participant to guess what the basis of conventional valuation will be in the future. The conventional valuation that emerges will depend on a particular participant's own guess about what other participants will be guessing, who in turn will be guessing about the particular participant's guess. Thus the market valuation will be reflexive. This is the basis for Keynes' striking beauty contest metaphor:

'professional investment may be likened to those newspaper competitions in which the competitors have to pick out the six prettiest faces from a hundred photographs, the prize being

ON GEORGE SOROS AND ECONOMIC ANALYSIS

awarded to the competitor whose choice most nearly corresponds to the average preferences of the competitors as a whole; so that each competitor has to pick, not those faces which he himself finds prettiest, but those which he thinks likeliest to catch the fancy of the other competitors, all of whom are looking at the problem from the same point of view ... it is not a case of choosing those which, to the best of one's judgement, are really the prettiest, nor even those which average opinion genuinely thinks the prettiest ... we have reached the third degree where we devote our intelligence's to anticipating what average opinion expects the average opinion to be ... and there are some, I believe, who practice the fourth, fifth and higher degrees' (Keynes 1936, p. 156).

V. HOW TO DO ECONOMIC ANALYSIS

Keynes' remarks about the untractable uncertainty surrounding at least some economic decisions led some of his followers to a form of analytical nihilism:

'... since certainty is not attainable, neither is knowledge ...' (Coddington 1983, p. 58).

Keynes, however, did construct frameworks with which to analyse economic systems, and

'... even the most cursory acquaintance with the facts of his life shows that he was not reduced to the state of puzzled indecision that a wholehearted adoption of ... unattainable standards for beliefs to qualify as knowledge ... would entail' (Coddington 1983, pp. 58–59).

The Soros point of departure is the fallible, conjectural nature of any form of scientific knowledge, so unattainable standards for knowledge are not used as yardsticks. Instead, for Soros the key distinction is that economic knowledge is necessarily reflexive, with economic agents being both thinkers and actors in relation to their economic environment. This then raises the question of the appropriate form for economic analysis to take in such circumstances. The following avenues of inquiry look promising in this respect.

1. Bounded Rationality

An obvious first step is to drop the strong rationality assumptions employed in the rational expectations hypothesis, and use Herbert Simon's notion of bounded rationality instead. Rational expectations models focus on outcomes, not on the behavioural context of decisions, which if the rational expectations hypothesis were true would be characterised not just by individual optimisation but also by the mutual consistency of agents' perceptions about the world. Boundedly rational models drop this restrictive characterisation and focus

ROD CROSS AND DOUGLAS STRACHAN

instead on the heuristic devices agents use as decision rules, and how these decision rules are updated or revised in the light of experience. The task of modelling economic systems is then one of populating models with agents who are boundedly rational in the sense that they do not know what any aggregate probability distributions or equilibria are. Thus instead of assuming that agents have worked out how the complex system in which they participate behaves, the way the system itself behaves is constructed from the heuristic devices used by the agents.

This approach is pursued in Sargent (1993). The starting point is that

'... when implemented numerically or econometrically, rational expectations models impute *more* knowledge to the agents within the model (who use the *equilibrium* probability distributions in evaluating their Euler equations) than is possessed by an econometrician, who faces estimation and inference problems that the agents in the model have somehow solved' (p. 3).

Instead the boundedly rational models

'... expel rational agents from our model environments and replace them with 'artificially intelligent' agents who behave like econometricians ... these 'econometricians' theorise, estimate and adapt in attempting to learn about probability distributions which, under rational expectations, they already know' (p. 3).

Taking economic agents to behave like econometricians might appear absurd until it is realised that

'... in economics, procedures for revising theories in light of data are typically informal, diverse and implicit' (p. 22).

Thus the distinction between economic agents and economists/econometricians is blurred and the Soros self-referential notion of reflexivity is introduced:

'... such a system can contain intriguing self-referential loops, especially from the standpoint of macroeconomic advisers, who confront the prospect that they are participants in the system that they are modelling, at least if they believe that their advice is likely to be convincing' (p. 23).

2. Complexity

In many sciences the traditional emphasis has been on searching for finer grain explanations of phenomena. Thus in 20th century physics there has been an emphasis on attempting to understand the nature and structure of sub-atomic particles. In economics, albeit a form of alchemy according to Soros, this trait has been evident in the insistence on micro foundations for macro models.

ON GEORGE SOROS AND ECONOMIC ANALYSIS

During the last decade this emphasis has been countered by an increase in interest in models of complexity, wherein the problem is to work out how complex systems can be constructed or emerge from basic elements that are taken as in some sense irreducible (see Anderson, Arrow and Pines 1988 for discussion of this approach to economic systems).

Soros clearly sees this as the way for economic analysis to go:

> '... it is high time to liberate social phenomena from the straitjacket of natural science, especially as natural science itself is undergoing a radical change ... analytical science is superseded in certain fields by the study of complexity ... the science of complexity studies open, evolutionary systems ... all it seeks to do is build models or run simulations ... but even here I find that the difference between social and natural phenomena is not sufficiently recognised ... most computer programmes deal with the evolution of populations ... to study the interaction between thinking and reality, we need a model of model-builders whose models, in turn, must contain model-builders *ad infinitum* ... the infinite nesting of models must be brought to closure somewhere if the models are to serve any practical use ... as a result, the models cannot reflect reality in its full complexity' (Soros 1995, p. 220).

Thus although models of complexity are proposed, there is inevitably a degree of arbitrariness surrounding the way such models avoid the infinite regress of self-reference.

Models of complexity have come to be seen as promising ways to resolve some of the anomalies surrounding the rational expectations-efficient markets paradigm regarding financial markets. Simple technical trading rules of the type stressed by Keynes and Soros have been shown to out-perform investment strategies based on the standard paradigm (Brock, Lakonishok and Le Baron 1992, for example). And the standard paradigm implies that no trade should take place in rational expectations equilibria (Tirole 1982), whereas trading volumes remain significant even in quiescent financial markets. In models of complexity these anomalies are resolved by specifying agents who are heterogeneous in the sense of using different trading rules. Thus some traders may extrapolate trends, others make buck trends thinking that what goes up must come down, some agents may believe that market prices are determined by 'fundamental' economic forces, and yet others may see market prices as reflecting the weights of the different belief systems of other traders (Brock and Hommes 1996). The heterogeneous agents in such a system are then endowed with a form of artificial intelligence which allows them to change their beliefs in light of how their initial hunches fare in terms of generating trading profits (Arthur, Holland, Le Baron, Palmer and Taylor 1994). Thus trading profits act as a 'fitness' function, and beliefs, and therefore market prices, evolve according as to whether particular belief systems allow the traders adopting them to

ROD CROSS AND DOUGLAS STRACHAN

survive in the market place. Thus the Soros view of reflexivity in financial markets is at least partially reflected in this active research area.

3. Heterostasis

Standard economic analysis assumes that economic systems are *homeostatic* or self-adjusting, in the sense that shocks that move economic systems away from equilibria are followed by a return to the initial equilibria once the shocks abate (see Arrow 1988). This assumption is broadly consistent with the Soros account of what happens in near-equilibrium conditions, but not with his account of what happens in far-from-equilibrium conditions. In the Soros examples of the latter conditions (1994, 1995) it is reasonably clear that the reflexive processes brought into play in far-from-equilibrium conditions change economic equilibria rather than being accompanied by a return to the *status quo ante* once the shocks abate.

The *heterostasis* involved in the alternative postulate that out-of-equilibrium behaviour can change the equilibrium attractor, however, has been recognised by some of the leading proponents of economic analysis. Marshall, for example, recognised that temporary shocks to demand or supply could be accompanied by changes in demand or supply conditions that would remain once the shocks abated, so changing market equilibria (Marshall 1890, pp. 425–426). And Keynes answered his own question

'are economics systems self-adjusting?'

in the negative (Keynes 1934).

One way of capturing the way economic equilibria are shaped by out-of-equilibrium conditions is to allow for self-organising behaviour (Bak, Chen, Scheinkman and Woodford 1993, for example). Another approach is to allow economic systems to be hysteretic. Hysteresis models are populated by heterogeneous agents with heterogeneous beliefs who respond discontinuously or in a non-linear manner to shocks. The outcome is that economic systems display *remanence*, in that they do not return to the *status quo ante* if a shock is applied and then removed. This means that each new extremum value of the shock variable creates a new equilibrium, and that economic equilibria evolve according to the sequence of non-dominated extremum values of the shocks experienced (see Cross 1993, 1995 and Amable, Henry, Lordon and Topol 1995). It does not require too great a leap of the imagination to connect this notion of

ON GEORGE SOROS AND ECONOMIC ANALYSIS

hysteretic or heterostatic equilibria with the Soros account of the power of reflexivity in far-from-equilibrium conditions.

VI. SOME CONCLUDING REMARKS

A not uncommon criticism of economic theories is that they are out of touch with practice, by which is presumably meant reality. George Soros, unlike many of the other critics, has made a constructive contribution by articulating a method of analysis which could put economic theory into closer contact with reality. In this essay we have argued that, although approaching the issues from a Popperian background, the Soros approach is resonant with Keynes on economic behaviour in the face of uncertainty. This line of thought is sometimes depicted as being nihilistic about the possibility of economic knowledge. We have argued, on the contrary, that foundations of the Keynes-Soros type are analytically fecund, as can be seen in recent work on bounded rationality, complex economic systems and heterostatic equilibria selected by self-organisation or hysteresis.

REFERENCES

Amable, B., J. Henry, F. Lordon and R. Topol (1995). Hysteresis Revisited: a Methodological Approach, in: R. Cross (ed.), *The Natural Rate of Unemployment: Reflections on 25 Years of the Hypothesis*. Cambridge: Cambridge U.P.

Anderson, P.W, K.J. Arrow and D. Pines (eds.) (1988). *The Economy as an Evolving Complex System*. Massachusetts: Addison-Wesley.

Arrow, K.J. (1988). Workshop on the Economy as an Evolving Complex System: Summary, in: P.W. Anderson, K.J. Arrow and D. Pines (eds.), *The Economy as an Evolving Complex System*. Massachusetts: Addison-Wesley.

Arthur, W.B, J.H. Holland, B. Le Baron, R. Palmer and P. Taylor (1994). An Artificial Stock Market, mimeo, Santa Fe Institute.

Bak, P., K. Chen, J. Scheinkman and M. Woodford (1993). Aggregate Fluctuations from Independent Sectoral Shocks: Self-Organised Criticality in a Model of Production and Inventory Dynamics, *Richerche Economiche*. 47: 3–30.

Brock, W.A., J. Lakonishok and B. Le Baron (1992). Simple Technical Trading Rules and the Stochastic Properties of Stock Returns, *Journal of Finance*. 47: 1731–1764.

Brock, W.A. and C.H. Hommes (1996). Models of Complexity in Economics and Finance, mimeo, University of Wisconsin.

Coddington, A. (1983). *Keynesian Economics: the Search for First Principles*. London: Allen & Unwin.

Cross, R. (1993). On the Foundations of Hysteresis in Economic Systems, *Economics and Philosophy*. 9: 53–74.

Cross, R. (1995). Is the Natural Rate Hypothesis Consistent with Hysteresis?, in: R. Cross (ed.), *The Natural Rate of Unemployment: Reflections on 25 Years of the Hypothesis*. Cambridge: Cambridge U.P.

ROD CROSS AND DOUGLAS STRACHAN

Keynes, J.M. (1934). Poverty in Plenty: Is the Economic System Self-Adjusting?, *The Listener*, 21 November.

Keynes, J.M. (1936). *The General Theory of Employment, Interest and Money.* London: Macmillan.

Keynes, J.M. (1937). The General Theory of Employment, *Quarterly Journal of Economics.* 5: 209–223.

Marshall, A. (1890). *The Principles of Economics.* London: Macmillan.

Mirowski, P. (1989). *More Heat than Light.* Cambridge: Cambridge U.P.

Sargent, T.J. (1993). *Bounded Rationality in Macroeconomics.* Oxford: Oxford U.P.

Shiller, R.J. (1996). *Rational Expectations*, 2nd ed. Cambridge: Cambridge U.P.

Slater, R. (1996). *Soros: the Life, Times and Trading Secrets of the World's Greatest Investor.* Chicago: Richard D. Irwin.

Soros, G. (1987, 1994). *The Alchemy of Finance.* New York: John Wiley and Sons.

Soros, G. (1995). *Soros on Soros: Staying Ahead of the Curve.* New York: John Wiley and Sons.

Tirole, J. (1982). On the Possibility of Speculation under Rational Expectations, *Econometrica.* 91: 1163–1181.

SUMMARY

This essay considers the Soros critique of the epistemological and analytical foundations underlying theories of rational expectations equilibria and efficient markets. Similarities between Soros and Keynes are found. It is pointed out that Soros is guarded rather than nihilistic about the possibilities of economic knowledge, and developments in economic analysis that resonate with the Soros view are discussed.

[21]

Banks, Financial Liberalisation and Financial Crises in Emerging Markets

Graham Bird and Ramkishen S. Rajan

1. INTRODUCTION

𝕿 HE East Asian financial crisis has raised a series of important issues. Amongst them is the question of the role of the banking sector and financial liberalisation in contributing to financial crises. How do weaknesses in the domestic banking sector, when combined with both domestic and international financial liberalisation, engender currency crises?

That these connections exist has been established by the empirical literature. The co-existence of banking and currency crises has been found to be the norm during the late 1980s and early 1990s. Most frequently banking crises appear to have taken the lead (Kaminsky and Reinhart, 1999), and these twin crises seem to be far more pervasive in developing economies than developed ones (Glick and Hutchison, 1999). Banking crises themselves seem to be more likely following financial liberalisation, with sharp increases in domestic (bank) lending acting as significant predictors of currency crises.[1] The IMF (1998) has suggested that the greater frequency of banking crises worldwide since the 1980s is 'possibly related to the financial sector liberalisation that occurred in many countries during this period' (p. 115).

These 'twin crises' have inspired a number of recent theoretical contributions to the literature on financial crises in emerging economies.[2] What is however

GRAHAM BIRD is from the Surrey Centre for International Economic Studies, University of Surrey, UK. RAMKISHEN S. RAJAN is from the School of Economics, University of Adelaide, Australia and the Institute of Southeast Asian Studies, Singapore. Comments by two anonymous referees of this journal are gratefully acknowledged. The usual disclaimer applies.

[1] Eichengreen and Arteta (2000, Table 1) succinctly summarise the principal empirical studies on banking crises. Their comprehensive empirical investigation finds rapid domestic credit growth to be one of the few robust causes of banking crises.

[2] The pioneering work in this area is Velasco (1987), who introduced a banking sector within a conventional Krugman (1979) framework. There are a number of closely related insolvency models

© Blackwell Publishers Ltd 2001, 108 Cowley Road, Oxford OX4 1JF, UK
and 350 Main Street, Malden, MA 02148, USA.

890   GRAHAM BIRD AND RAMKISHEN S. RAJAN

lacking in the literature is a simple conceptual framework within which these connections can be conceptualised and drawn out and in which the role of banks is explicitly discussed. This paper seeks to provide just such a framework to explore the role of banks, bank inefficiencies and financial liberalisation in explaining the sustained interest rate premium offered in a number of emerging economies in East Asia despite evidence of fairly credible *ex ante* pegged exchange rates. Within this framework, international financial liberalisation can be seen as fuelling a boom in domestic credit, which leads to acute balance sheet problems for domestic banks, and exposes the country concerned to a currency crisis in the event of a sudden reversal of capital inflows, which banking weakness may itself trigger.

The layout of the paper is as follows. Section 2 identifies empirically certain features of the East Asian financial crisis that any theory needs to be capable of explaining. Section 3 provides a simple analytical framework that is consistent with the observed facts. Section 4 extends this analysis, while Section 5 examines how a banking crisis may translate into a currency crisis. Section 6 goes on to discuss, in some detail, selected policy issues that emerge. Section 7 offers a few concluding remarks.

2. BOOM, BUST AND BANKS IN EAST ASIA: KEY EMPIRICAL FEATURES

In order to provide an empirical background for the analysis which follows, it is helpful to divide the boom-bust story in East Asia into three episodes covering the 'boom' period (1990–1996), the transitional period of increasing economic and financial weakness (1996 to mid 1997) and the 'bust' period (mid 1997 onwards).

a. The 'Boom' Period (1990–1996)

During the early 1990s, and partly as a consequence of their own economic growth, East Asian economies experienced persistent current account deficits which balance of payments accounting tells us have to be financed either by

that have been recently developed, including Burnside et al. (1998), Chinn and Kletzer (2000), Corsetti et al. (1999b) and Dooley (2000) (also see Chinn et al., 1999). These models have been motivated by the notion of contingent liabilities most clearly elucidated by Diaz-Alejandro (1985). Related models (of moral hazard driven lending) include Krugman (1999) and McKinnon and Pill (1998 and 1999). In contrast to these insolvency models, the suddenness and ferocity of capital reversals in East Asia have spurred the development of 'illiquidity' models. Prominent examples include Chang and Velasco (1998) and Goldfajn and Valdes (1997), which are essentially open economy extensions of the Diamond and Dybvig (1983) bank panic model. Rajan (2000) emphasises the distinction between the *insolvency* versus *illiquidity based* bank models and considers their relevance to the Thai crisis.

BANKS, LIBERALISATION AND EMERGING MARKETS　　891

inflows of foreign capital or by running down international reserves. It was also during this period that many East Asian countries took steps to liberalise both the domestic financial sector and the capital account of the balance of payments. In Thailand, for example, the Bangkok International Banking Facility (BIBF) was established, which allowed domestic financial institutions to accept loans and deposits from abroad in foreign currency and to lend them both domestically and abroad.[3]

For all countries in the region, net private capital inflows were positive and generally exceeded current account deficits; international reserves therefore increased (Table 1).[4] This accumulation was particularly high in the cases of Malaysia and Thailand, which, along with Indonesia, were among the ten largest emerging market recipients of net private capital flows during the period under consideration (Lopez-Mejia, 1999).

The 'other investment' component constituted about 70 per cent of the private capital inflows on average in the case of Thailand. This was also the largest single component of capital flows in the cases of Indonesia and the Philippines. Malaysia was the only exception, with direct investment constituting some 70 per cent of total capital flows on average. This 'other investment' category includes short and long term credits (including use of IMF credit) as well as currency and deposits and other accounts receivable and payable.[5] Table 2 illustrates these trends and also shows the importance of real bank credit in the case of Thailand; while Table 3 provides a snapshot of the broad macroeconomic consequences of these inflows.

Although the capital inflows financed a sharp increase in monetary growth, with the ratio of broad money to international reserves rising rapidly throughout the region, the premium on East Asian interest rates over global rates was not eliminated (Table 4). It is difficult to explain this in a conventional manner by interpreting it as representing the extent to which markets expected exchange rates to depreciate, since currency values were stable over this period. For instance, the coefficient of variation, averaged over 1990–1996, was zero in the case of both the Thai baht and the Malaysian ringgit (based on IMF data).[6] Nor does the rapid monetary growth suggest that the effects of capital inflows were being fully sterilised.

---

[3] As an anonymous referee correctly noted, approaches to financial sector and capital account deregulation were not uniform across East Asia. The World Bank (2000) provides a succinct summary of the external liberalisation strategies and policies undertaken by the crisis-hit regional economies.

[4] Official flows were significant only in the Philippines. Without them there would have been a drain on reserves as private capital inflows were, on average, insufficient to offset current account deficits.

[5] This component of capital flows has been found to be the most volatile, while direct investment is the most stable (Bird and Rajan, 2000b; and World Bank, 1999).

[6] While the coefficients of variation were positive in the case of the Philippines and Indonesia, these reflected the crawling pegs of those currencies *vis-à-vis* the US dollar.

TABLE 1
Asia-5: Net Capital Flows, 1990–1997
(percentage of GDP)

	1991	*1992*	*1993*	*1994*	*1995*	*1996*	*Simple Average*[b]	*1997*[c]
Indonesia:								
Private Capital Flows	4.6	2.5	3.1	3.9	6.2	6.3	5.1	1.6
Direct Investment	1.2	1.2	1.2	1.4	2.3	2.8	1.7	2.0
Portfolio Investment	0.0	0.0	1.1	0.6	0.7	0.8	0.5	−0.4
Other Investment	3.5	1.4	0.7	1.9	3.1	2.7	3.0	0.1
Official Flows	1.1	1.1	0.9	0.1	−0.2	−0.7	0.7	1.0
Change in Reserves[a]	−2.4	−3.0	−1.3	0.4	−0.7	−2.3	−1.7	1.8
Malaysia:								
Private Capital Flows	11.2	15.1	17.4	1.5	8.8	9.6	10.2	4.7
Direct Investment	8.3	8.9	7.8	5.7	4.8	5.1	7.2	5.3
Portfolio Investment	0.0	0.0	0.0	0.0	0.0	0.0	0.0	0.0
Other Investment	2.9	6.2	9.7	−4.2	4.1	4.5	2.9	−0.6
Official Flows	0.4	−0.1	−0.6	0.2	−0.1	−0.1	0.0	−0.1
Change in Reserves[a]	−2.6	−11.3	−17.7	4.3	2.0	−2.5	−5.1	3.6
Philippines:								
Private Capital Flows	1.6	2.0	2.6	5.0	4.6	9.8	4.1	0.5
Direct Investment	2.0	1.3	1.6	2.0	1.8	1.6	1.8	1.4
Portfolio Investment	0.3	0.1	−0.1	0.4	0.3	−0.2	0.2	−5.3
Other Investment	0.2	0.6	1.1	2.5	2.4	8.5	2.1	4.5
Official Flows	3.3	1.9	2.3	0.8	1.4	0.2	2.0	0.8
Change in Reserves[a]	−2.3	−1.5	−1.1	−1.9	−0.9	−4.8	−1.8	2.1
Thailand:								
Private Capital Flows	10.7	8.7	8.4	8.6	12.7	9.3	11.5	−10.9
Direct Investment	1.5	1.4	1.1	0.7	0.7	0.9	1.6	1.3
Portfolio Investment	0.0	0.5	3.2	0.9	1.9	0.6	1.4	0.4
Other Investment	9.2	6.8	4.1	7.0	10.0	7.7	8.5	−12.6
Official Flows	1.1	0.1	0.2	0.1	0.7	0.7	0.1	4.9
Change in Reserves[a]	−4.3	−2.8	−3.2	−3.0	−4.4	−1.2	−4.3	9.7
Korea:								
Private Capital Flows	10.7	8.7	8.4	8.6	12.7	9.3	11.5	−10.9
Direct Investment	1.5	1.4	1.1	0.7	0.7	0.9	1.6	1.3
Portfolio Investment	0.0	0.5	3.2	0.9	1.9	0.6	1.4	0.4
Other Investment	9.2	6.8	4.1	7.0	10.0	7.7	8.5	−12.6
Official Flows	1.1	0.1	0.2	0.1	0.7	0.7	0.1	4.9
Change in Reserves[a]	−4.3	−2.8	−3.2	−3.0	−4.4	−1.2	−4.3	9.7

Notes:
[a] Minus sign denotes a rise and vice versa.
[b] 1989 to 1996.
[c] Estimates.

Source: IMF.

BANKS, LIBERALISATION AND EMERGING MARKETS   893

TABLE 2
Real Bank Credit to the Private Sector (%), 1990–1997[a]

	Growth Rate (%), 1990–95[b]	Growth Rate (%), 1996	Growth Rate (%), 1997	Bank Credit to Private Sector[b,c] (% of GDP), 1991	Bank Credit to Private Sector[b,c] (% of GDP), 1996	Bank Credit to Private Sector[b,c] (% of GDP), 1997
Indonesia	18.8	11.5	19.2	45.8	55.4	61.0
Malaysia	13.5	24.5	23.3	75.3	89.8	100.4
Philippines	12.7	39.9	27.7	18.9	50.0	57.6
Thailand	20.2	11.6	8.6	67.7	100.0	116.3

Notes:
[a] Deflated by consumer prices.
[b] Annual average.
[c] Credit other than to central bank.

Source: Bisignano (1998) and IMF.

TABLE 3
'Effects' of Capital Inflows (%), 1989–1995

	Inflow Episode	Cumulative Inflows/GDP at End of Period	Mean Ratio	GDP Growth[a]	Inflation Rate[a,b]	Current Account Deficit[a,b]	Change in Investment[a,b]	Change in Consumption[a,b]
Indonesia	1990–95	8.3	1.8	2.2	1.3	0.2	5.7	−5.2
Malaysia	1989–95	45.8	9.4	4.0	1.4	2.9	4.8	−1.8
Philippines	1989–95	23.1	4.3	2.2	−3.1	0.7	1.7	6.1
Thailand	1988–95	51.5	9.9	3.9	−1.1	2.3	13.4	−11.2
South Korea	1991–95	9.3	2.3	−2.5	0.8	5.0	4.7	1.1
Memo Item								
Mexico	1989–94	27.1	5.3	2.9	−74.4	7.1	2.4	6.7

Notes:
[a] Change from immediately preceding period of equal length.
[b] As per cent of GDP.

Source: Lopez-Mejia (1999).

Whatever accounted for it, the persistence of the interest rate differential in favour of the East Asian economies throughout 1990–1996 encouraged 'carry trade'; financial operators borrowed foreign exchange in the US and Japan and, having converted it into local currency, lent in local markets. In large measure the rapid credit expansion was intermediated through the banking sector. Short term debt inflows often took the form of interbank lending, and bank lending to the private sector increased sharply across the region (Table 5). East Asian banks were therefore major players in the accumulation of foreign exchange denominated short term debt (Table 6). According to BIS data, in Thailand, banks accounted for 86 per cent of net foreign liabilities by 1996.[7]

---

[7] This was not the case in all countries in the region. In Indonesia the major government-linked conglomerates undertook most of the borrowing (78 per cent in 1996).

894   GRAHAM BIRD AND RAMKISHEN S. RAJAN

TABLE 4

Macroeconomic Conditions Leading to Unhedged External Borrowing in East Asia, January 1991–
June 1997 (%)

Country	Interest Rate Spread[a] (%)	Annual Average Appreciation v/s $[b]	Exchange Rate Variability[c]
Indonesia	11.5	−3.8	0.7
Malaysia	1.6	1.2	2.6
Philippines	6.5	0.9	3.8
Thailand	4.0	−0.3	1.2
South Korea	4.1	−3.2	3.4

Notes:
[a] Local deposit rate less LIBOR ($) for East Asian economies, period average.
[b] + implies an appreciation; − implies a depreciation.
[c] Standard deviation of percentage deviation of exchange rate from regression time trend.

Source: World Bank (1998).

TABLE 5

International Bank and Bond Finance for the East Asian Economies[a]
($ billions), 1990–1997

	1990–94	Q1: 1996 – Q3: 1996	Q4: 1996 – Q3: 1997
Net interbank lending	14	43	11
Bank lending to non-banks	2	15	11
Net bond issuance	3	17	32
Total	19	75	54

Note:
[a] Aggregate for Indonesia, Malaysia, Philippines, South Korea and Thailand.

Source: BIS.

TABLE 6

Asia-5: External Debt, 1994–1999
(percentage of GDP)

Country	1994	1995	1996	1997	1998	1999
Indonesia[a]	57.0	56.3	53.4	63.9	149.4	95.5
Malaysia	38.6	37.6	38.4	44.0	58.8	55.3
Philippines	60.4	53.1	50.5	55.3	73.3	68.0
Thailand	44.9	49.1	49.8	62.0	76.8	61.5
South Korea	24.1	26.0	31.6	33.4	46.9	33.0
of which: Short Term Debt						
Indonesia[a]	6.5	8.7	7.5	27.5	76.4	45.1
Malaysia	7.5	7.2	9.9	11.1	11.7	9.4
Philippines	8.1	7.1	8.7	10.3	11.0	3.6
Thailand	20.2	24.5	25.1	24.6	27.0	21.1
South Korea	13.3	14.6	17.9	13.4	9.6	10.9

Note:
[a] The data for Indonesia exclude trade credits.

Source: IMF.

b. Increasing Financial Weakness (1996–mid 1997)

A number of factors combined to weaken Thailand's economic performance, as well as that of other East Asian economies (Ito, 2000; and Rajan, 2000). Pegged *de facto* to the US dollar, the Thai baht rose in value against the yen and other key currencies; the US dollar appreciated by nearly 50 per cent against the yen between June 1995 and April 1997. Not unconnected to this, but also as a consequence of adverse movements in the income terms of trade, Thailand's current account balance of payments weakened significantly and exports actually fell by 1.3 per cent in 1996. Concerns about the size and maturity of its external debt, particularly in the light of faltering export performance, also began to worry foreign creditors.

Combined with this, as well as with political uncertainties and a continuing fall in asset prices, there were emerging signs of economic downturn and financial sector weakness. As financial institutions began to threaten to fail, the authorities intervened to bail them out and claims by the monetary authorities over domestic financial institutions rose sharply from the second quarter of 1996. Indeed, central bank credit to financial institutions in Thailand rose from 2 per cent of GDP in 1996 to 15 per cent by the end of 1997 (World Bank, 1999). This brought with it a massive infusion of liquidity into the banking system.

c. The 'Bust' Period (Mid 1997 Onwards)

With Japanese interest rates expected to rise and Thailand being downgraded by major credit agencies, external creditors became unwilling to roll over existing debts (BIS, 1998; Ito, 2000; and Rajan, 2000). With an effectively pegged exchange rate, a current account deficit, and falling capital inflows, Thailand's international reserves began to decline from about mid 1996 onwards. The authorities remained keen to protect the exchange rate and attempted to support the value of the baht by buying it forward, committing as much as $25 billion in the forward market in November–December 1996.[8] When these commitments came due in mid 1997, selling pressures on the baht intensified and on 2 July, 1997 the authorities acquiesced to the pressure and allowed the currency to float. Fuelled by doubts about the country's reserve position, by dollar purchases involving corporations anxious to cover their unhedged dollar liabilities, as well, no doubt, as by fear of further capital outflows and exchange rate depreciation, the baht's value fell almost immediately by about 20 per cent. By December 1997 its value had fallen by about 45 per cent, which according to most judgments about its equilibrium value represented significant overshooting (Bird and Milne,

---

[8] Despite the drop in reserves, Thailand's monetary base rose sharply because of an increase in domestic credit creation, largely associated with the assistance that was being provided to troubled financial institutions (Rajan, 2000).

896   GRAHAM BIRD AND RAMKISHEN S. RAJAN

1999).[9] Meanwhile contagion spread and the currencies of neighbouring currencies also depreciated.[10]

Fears about the weakness of the banking system constrained the authorities from raising interest rates in an earlier attempt to stabilise the currency. The worry was that this would result in further bankruptcies and bank failures. Instead, up until mid 1997, the policy preference was for intervention in both spot and forward foreign exchange markets. It was only when the crisis hit that interest rates were increased in a sustained attempt to stem capital outflows.

Is there a simple analytical framework that can be used to accommodate the events described above and which captures the interplay between the banking sector, financial liberalisation and currency crisis?

3. A SIMPLE ANALYTICAL FRAMEWORK

A reasonable place to start is with a traditional model of the effects of financial liberalisation against the background of financial repression, with an added assumption that financial intermediation occurs largely through the banking sector, with households placing their savings with the banks and the banks lending to firms for purposes of investment.[11] This is illustrated by Figure 1 where the authorities fix an interest rate at a level (i_c) below the equilibrium one. As a consequence there is excess demand and credit rationing.[12]

---

[9] More generally, Willett (2000) discusses how financial markets have a tendency to react 'too late' and when they do, they tend to 'over react'. Corbett and Vines (1999) and Rajan (2000) make a clear distinction between the initial currency devaluation and the outright financial and economic collapse thereafter.

[10] The regionwide contagion in East Asia may be broadly divided into four sub-periods. The devaluation of the Thai baht was the first period (July 1997). The second period was when the contagion spread to the other Southeast Asian countries (Indonesia, Malaysia and the Philippines specifically) between July and mid October 1997. The third period was when the crisis engulfed the larger East Asian region (Hong Kong, Singapore, South Korea and Taiwan) following the pre-emptive devaluation of the New Taiwan dollar in October 1997. Once the South Korean won was devalued in November 1997, this then reverberated back to Southeast Asia and eventually emerging economies in general. This was the fourth period (Berg, 1999). The crisis did intensify in mid 1998, but this was due to a pronounced liquidity crunch in emerging markets as a whole following the Russian debt moratorium.

[11] This assumption is not unreasonable in view of the empirical evidence in the previous section. Indeed, Rojas-Suarez and Weisbrod (1995, p. 4) have noted that in developing economies, 'bank deposits constitute the most important form of household savings, and bank loans are the most important source of external finance for firms'. Survey data of firms in East Asia for the period 1996–98 reveal that bank lending constituted some 35 per cent of total working capital in Thai firms and about 20 per cent in the case of Indonesia and Malaysia (Hallward-Driemeier et al., 1999). Rajan (1999) develops the microfoundations of this model, partly inspired by an earlier model of costly banking by Edwards and Vegh (1997).

[12] If the ceiling is applied only to the deposit rate (savers), with lenders being able to charge the market rate then the banks will earn a risk-free spread. However, ceilings usually apply to both loans and deposits. In the case of Thailand, ceilings were abolished on deposits in 1990 and on lending in 1992.

BANKS, LIBERALISATION AND EMERGING MARKETS   897

FIGURE 1
Loan Market Equilibrium with Financial Repression and in Autarky

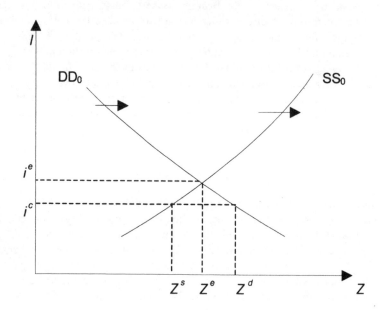

Financial liberalisation allows a (higher) equilibrium rate (i^e) to be established. This causes both the supply of loanable funds to increase, as saving is encouraged, and the demand for them to fall, as fewer investment projects appear profitable. But advocates of liberalisation claim that the marginal efficiency of capital will rise and that there will therefore be beneficial effects for economic growth.[13] Since the market is cleared at the equilibrium interest rate, there is no reason to ration credit by other means.

However, the model so far relates to a closed economy and needs to be modified to allow for a liberalised capital account and access to international capital. International financial liberalisation may also include trade in financial services.

Here the key questions are: how does the domestic rate of interest compare with interest rates abroad; what is expected to happen to the exchange rate, is currency depreciation anticipated; and does the country carry a risk premium because of concerns about default and the small probability of a large negative exogenous shock. Making allowance for these factors, foreign capital will flow in

---

[13] Some commentators have claimed that financial repression prevents lenders from charging risk premia and that this in turn eliminates potentially high yielding investments, which may therefore be facilitated by financial liberalisation (Fry, 1982).

FIGURE 2
International Finance Liberalisation and Capital Account Deregulation

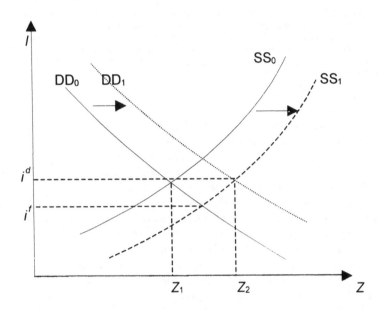

for as long as the domestic rate of interest exceeds the foreign rate. In terms of Figure 2 the supply curve of loans will shift to the right, with $Z^2 - Z^1$ reflecting capital inflows.[14] Of course, this increase in the supply of credit will tend to push down the domestic rate of interest until it is equal to the foreign rate (i^f), after allowing for expected currency depreciation and risk premia. Thus in equilibrium in a country with both a liberalised domestic financial system and international financial liberalisation, the following equality will tend to hold:

$$i^d = i^f + \hat{e} + rp$$

where i^d is the domestic interest rate, i^f is the foreign interest rate, $\hat{e}$ is the expected exchange rate depreciation, and rp is the risk premium.

But will it automatically follow that, with $\hat{e}$ and rp both equal to zero, $i^d = i^f$? Certainly, any interest rate differentials could partly reflect imperfect international capital mobility in developing economies (for instance, see Willett and Ahn, 1998), though even here the evidence of imperfect capital mobility is not airtight (Huang and Li, 1999). Nonetheless, the sustained interest differential in East Asia despite years of significant capital influx is a puzzle. In fact, in their

---

[14] The shift may not be parallel (Rajan, 1999).

BANKS, LIBERALISATION AND EMERGING MARKETS   899

review of capital flows and the domestic financial sectors in developing East
Asian economies, Folkerts-Landau and Associates (1995) concluded that:

> (t)he ability of banks to accumulate foreign liabilities or domestic liabilities denominated in
> foreign currency was improved as part of the early deregulation process. Capital inflows were
> ... encouraged by the relatively high interest rates that prevailed in the region. Although specific
> causes differed among countries, high interest rates were the result of such factors as ... interest
> rate deregulation, the encouragement of competition among financial institutions, and the
> relatively high costs of intermediation (p. 41).

In other words, the rapid convergence of interest rates may be prevented if the
domestic banking sector is relatively inefficient and if capital inflows are
intermediated only via the domestic banking sector. In these circumstances i^d
may continue to exceed i^f. However, with fuller international financial
liberalisation and increasing foreign competition, which may involve the
establishment of foreign subsidiaries in the domestic banking sector, the costs
of the domestic banks may be expected to fall. This will shift the supply curve of
bank lending down and to the right. Thus, as modelled here, bank inefficiencies
are assumed to be directly proportional to quantity of lending made by the banks.

The rationale for the fall in the cost structure of the financial system could
either be due to reduced costs of foreign funds (growth in foreign liabilities of
domestic banks) or pro-competitive gains due to foreign competition, as foreign
institutions gradually establish subsidiaries domestically. Entry into the domestic
market of foreign banks could drive the cost structure of the banking sector down,
as state of the art technology and best practices are introduced into the country
(Levine, 1996). To the extent that trade in financial services requires the right of
establishment of foreign enterprises, this conclusion is not dissimilar to that of the
conventional trade literature, which argues that international trade could act as a
disciplining device.

There is a growing body of literature which emphasises a direct relationship
between the extent of international financial liberalisation (loosely proxied by
measures of foreign participation in the banking sector) and various measures of
efficiency (Claessens and Glaessner, 1998). For instance, using bank-level data for
80 countries during the period 1988–1995, Claessens et al. (1998) found that the
greater the degree of foreign bank penetration, the lower the domestic bank
profitability and overall expenses. Similarly, using aggregate accounting 1976 data
for 14 developed countries, Terrell (1986) found that domestic banks in countries
that allowed the entry of foreign banks had lower profits and greater efficiency.

Up to now this simple model captures many of the features identified in East
Asia in general, and in Thailand in particular. Domestic financial liberalisation
combined with capital account liberalisation resulted in an increase in short term
capital inflows that were largely intermediated through the banking system. Much
of what happened in the boom period is therefore explained satisfactorily by this
model.

900   GRAHAM BIRD AND RAMKISHEN S. RAJAN

However, while the model predicts that liberalised capital flows will tend to equalise domestic and foreign interest rates, with the inefficiency of domestic banks preventing this from happening immediately, the data in the previous section showed that in Thailand the spread over LIBOR was essentially unaffected by capital inflows. What was going on? Thailand did not carry a high risk premium, and there was little expectation, if any, of a proximate devaluation. Moreover, even if the foreign exchange market intervention that took place to prevent a rise in the value of the baht was sterilised, this failed to stop the growth of monetary aggregates.

The model does, of course, provide a clue. Where a rightward movement (and pivot) in supply schedule of bank loans (SS) has no discernible effect on the domestic rate of interest, in spite of the fact that it is higher than foreign interest rates, it may be because the demand schedule for bank loans (DD) has also moved right as shown in Figure 2.[15] Since in Thailand (and in some other East Asian economies), household saving rates were high and fiscal deficits were relatively low, it is reasonable to conjecture that it was firms that increased their demand for bank loans. Given the broader agenda of economic liberalisation, it may be surmised that firms believed that the economy would grow still faster and therefore increased investment and their demand for finance. The net effect of international financial liberalisation on domestic interest rates depends on the relative magnitudes of the rightward shifts in the demand and supply schedules. If the former exceeds the latter, interest rates will *rise* relative to the pre-liberalisation situation; something that has been observed in some of the available empirical evidence (Honohan, 1998).

For the domestic banks, international financial intermediation seemed to be profitable business. They could borrow short term at relatively low foreign interest rates and lend long term at higher domestic rates. Although their debt was denominated in foreign currency, the exchange risks seemed small (almost non-existent) given the authorities' credible commitment to a pegged exchange rate. And there was also the belief that an implicit safety net was in place if things went wrong (which created a moral hazard). With high profits and low perceived risks, and prudential regulations and supervision that did not prevent them from doing it, international financial intermediation was an entirely rational thing for the banks to do. But, of course, *ex post* risks did exist. These were associated with the vulnerability of the banks arising from their exposure to exchange rate devaluation and a mismatch in the maturity of their assets and liabilities, as well as the diminishing marginal productivity of capital and the sensitivity of firm performance to the performance of a faltering national economy. The banks *ex post* overborrowed and overlent (McKinnon and Pill, 1998 and 1999).

Claessens and Glaessner (1998, p. 5) have noted:

---

[15] The caveat in footnote 14 holds here too.

BANKS, LIBERALISATION AND EMERGING MARKETS 901

(m)any financial markets in Asia are quite closed to international competition in financial services, even though these same economies have substantially relaxed their controls on capital movements in recent years (p. 5).

A key characteristic of the East Asian economies was then that international financial liberalisation increased the demand for bank credit (due to capital account deregulation) at least as much as its supply (financial sector internationalisation). Relatively high domestic rates did not therefore fall as interest rate parity theory suggests, and capital inflows were perpetuated.

4. EXTENSIONS OF THE ANALYSIS

Other aspects of the analysis are less transparent from the simple model outlined in the previous section. First, with a segmented market for deposits, and domestic depositors being paid a higher rate of interest than foreign depositors, the domestic banks had an incentive to bias themselves towards foreign deposits: an incentive that was exacerbated by offshore institutions – finance houses in Thailand and merchant banks in Korea – being given tax breaks and exemptions from reserve requirements for foreign borrowing. Since large firms could, to some extent, take advantage of low foreign interest rates by borrowing abroad directly rather than via the intermediation of the domestic banking sector, it tended to be the smaller and perhaps less efficient firms that increased their demand for loans from the private banking sector.[16]

If this is so, then, as far as the domestic banks are concerned, there is an adverse selection problem in terms of the nature of their assets, which further weakens their balance sheets.[17] The proportion of non-performing loans (NPLs) burdening the banks may therefore be expected to rise over time. Following Peek and Rosengren (1995), one could incorporate NPLs by directly subtracting them from the total amount of loan supply curve. This in turn implies that a rise in NPLs leads to a leftward shift of the loan supply curve, i.e. a *de facto* increase in bank cost structure, leading to a reduction of domestic credit and a rise in the domestic equilibrium interest rate.

In fact, if there is asymmetric information such that foreign investors are not aware of the increased NPLs and if consequently country/currency risk premia remain unchanged, we have the paradoxical result that increased domestic financial fragility could induce additional capital inflows in the short to medium term. This is consistent with the experience of a number of emerging economies in East Asia where capital inflows increased despite some evidence of domestic

---

[16] Rajan (1992) has argued that borrowers who expect relatively high profits in the future will prefer arm's-length or direct financing to bank finance.
[17] Evidence of a two-tier loan market has been found in Latin America (Reinhart and Reinhart, 1999).

902   GRAHAM BIRD AND RAMKISHEN S. RAJAN

financial weaknesses in the form of growing NPLs (World Bank, 1998). It is revealing therefore that there was a sharp rise in the bank and bond lending to the East Asian region between the first quarter of 1995 and third quarter of 1996 just prior to the crisis (Table 6).

5. BANKING AND CURRENCY CRISES

What could disturb the short run equilibrium described in the previous sections? Consider the following scenario. A rise in foreign interest rates combined with a perceived increase in country risk makes foreign creditors less willing to rollover existing debts.[18] Other things being even, and consistent with uncovered interest rate parity, this should lead to capital reversal and an increase in the domestic rate of interest. But what if the authorities, aware of the balance sheet weaknesses of domestic banks are concerned that an increase in the rate of interest will lead to defaults and bankruptcies? They may, in these circumstances, relax monetary policy and allow the domestic money supply to increase to replace foreign capital inflows: effectively shifting the domestic component of supply schedule to the right to compensate for the decline in capital inflows or capital outflows. They may also bail out those institutions that do fail. However, by preventing the rise in domestic interest rates that would otherwise occur, this strategy perpetuates the capital outflows.

This is a reasonable approximation to what happened in Thailand during the period of increasing financial weakness from 1996 to mid 1997. Moreover, the sterilisation of falling international revenues designed to ensure the smooth growth of the money supply during a period of crisis also helps explain why the monetary base in Thailand rose in spite of the fall in reserves (Rajan, 2000).

Why was this a precursor to a currency crisis? With an increasing current account deficit and falling capital inflows, the authorities had a stark choice: either to abandon the exchange rate peg or to run down international reserves. The danger in devaluation is that it creates panic and the very crisis that the authorities are seeking to avoid. The danger with running down reserves is that it

---

[18] By emphasising both 'push' and 'pull' factors (internal and external factors) as possible triggers to the crisis, we take no position here on reason for the crisis in Thailand and rest of East Asia. To be sure, Ito (2000), Rajan (2000) and others underscore 'fundamental' weaknesses in Thailand leading to a rise in risk premium as a reason for the crisis. In contrast, Eichengreen (1999) has emphasised the anticipated rise in Japanese short term interest rates in the Spring of 1997 as being the trigger to a fall in capital flows while McKibbin (1998) has stressed the role of the US interest rate hike in late March 1997 and subsequent drop in the US stock market. The analytical framework developed above does not require a position to be taken on the trigger of the crisis. All that is required is that the risk-adjusted 'world interest rate' rises. This could be due to a hike in foreign interest rates, rise in expected depreciation or increase in risk premium. We thank an anonymous referee for urging a clarification of this point.

is a non-credible long term option and therefore engenders expectations of devaluation which are, in effect, self-fulfilling. The authorities find themselves uncomfortably situated between a rock and a hard place. There is an inevitable internal dynamic that drives the country towards a currency crisis, and this is where Thailand arrived in July 1997. So what we find is that a simple analytical model provides us with a useful framework within which we can reasonably well explain the important linkages between domestic and international financial liberalisation, banking crises and currency crises.

Although this has not been our principal focus, the analysis is also capable of explaining how a currency crisis might cause a banking crisis. Following devaluation, the domestic currency value of unhedged foreign liabilities rises relative to domestic assets. In any case, the risk-adjusted value of assets falls, since there are increased risks of firm bankruptcy and default as interest rates rise and the economy moves into recession. This turns a currency crisis into a banking crisis, and risks outright currency and banking collapse (Corbett and Vines, 1999).

6. POLICY IMPLICATIONS

As with any crisis, there are plenty of suggestions in the literature after the event about what needs to be done to minimise the risks of another one. In the case of East Asia these include the need to encourage the growth of bond and other capital markets in order to reduce dependence on bank intermediation, the need for strong prudential and supervisory arrangements in the financial sector, particularly with respect to banks, to avoid severe maturity mismatches and excessive foreign exchange exposure, and the need to circumvent the moral hazard problems associated with financial safety nets. These issues are discussed at some length by Eichengreen (1999), Goldstein and Turner (1996) and elsewhere and will not be pursued here, even though they make sense in the context of the foregoing analysis.

Instead, we focus on four other policy issues which are of particular relevance in the context of financial crises in emerging markets.

a. Bank Internationalisation and Sequencing

To a certain extent the failure of interest rates to converge following capital account liberalisation may be due to relatively inefficient and uncompetitive domestic banking structures in the East Asian economies. Where liberalisation leads to bigger demand-side effects (due to domestic economic boom) than supply-side effects (due to efficiency gains) there is a reason for encouraging the internationalisation of banks in advance of capital account liberalisation.

Studying trade flows in banking services involving more than 3,600 banks among 141 countries, Wengel (1995) has found that the relaxation of exchange and capital controls reduces the incentives for banks to set up subsidiaries. Given this possible 'substitution effect' between capital flows and bank development, allowing bank internationalisation to occur prior to capital account liberalisation might mitigate against 'excessive' capital inflows following financial liberalisation.

In terms of the model outlined in the previous section, bank internationalisation will shift the supply curve of the domestic banking system to the right by making it more competitive and efficient, and this should then reduce capital inflows, other things being constant. Moreover, if the banking system has a more internationally diversified asset base, it should be less prone to instability and crises (Claessens and Glaessner, 1998; and Eichengreen, 1999). Bank internationalisation may also encourage domestic regulatory and supervisory procedures to be raised to international standards (Levine, 1996).

Care must still be taken, however, to ensure that foreign competition is introduced gradually, in order to avoid disrupting the domestic financial system by enticing domestic banks to opt for increasingly risky investments (i.e. 'gambling for redemption'). An increase in bad loans due to risky investments will partially offset the efficiency gains associated with greater international competition.

b. Restraints on Capital Inflows

In the context of the GATS, the WTO has emphasised that countries could maintain selective controls on the capital account while moving towards the internationalisation of the banking sector (Claessens and Glaessner, 1998; Kono and Schuknecht, 1999; and Kono and Associates, 1997). Our analysis provides strong grounds for such sequencing. In fact, it is possible that the failure to appreciate the distinction between bank internationalisation and capital account decontrol was a root cause of the Thai crisis. For instance, Bank of Thailand official, Tivakul (1995, p. 39) noted that international financial liberalisation was undertaken in Thailand (with the creation and expansion of the BIBF facilities) as part of the country's acceptance of the GATS. Certainly capital restraints may be a useful tourniquet, while other measures associated with prudential standards and supervision and bank internationalisation are put in place.[19]

---

[19] Bird (1998) provides a brief review of the arguments both for and against capital restraints. Calmoris (1998) estimates that even under the most optimistic scenario it may take at least five years to put in place the necessary supervisory procedures and other arrangements to strengthen the banking system (also see Eichengreen, 1999).

BANKS, LIBERALISATION AND EMERGING MARKETS   905

As in Chile, capital levies should be aimed at preventing crises and should therefore be imposed in a countercyclical manner, being tightened when there is an upsurge in capital inflows and relaxed when inflows subside. There is a growing body of evidence (reviewed in Bird and Rajan, 2000a and 2000b) suggesting that while controls do not affect the level of inflows (and therefore the extent of real exchange rate appreciation) they do extend their duration (lengthening their overall maturity structure).

Controls do of course have disadvantages. There are, for example, potential problems of evasion on the one hand, or distortion and trade reduction on the other.[20] There are significant administrative costs, and the possibility of rent-seeking activities that carry related resource costs. But even so, capital restraints may still remain a useful interim policy instrument, tiding over the period between domestic financial liberalisation, the introduction of adequate prudential supervision and bank internationalisation, and the liberalisation of the capital account. It is informative to note that Chile, while fairly open to foreign banks, has maintained restraints on capital inflows (Claessens and Glaessner, 1998).

c. Deposit Insurance and the Lender of Last Resort Facility

While deposit insurance and a lender of last resort facility may mitigate against crises of confidence by reducing the chances of bank collapse, they could also give rise to moral hazard problems by encouraging the underpricing of risks. Moreover, there is the danger that once in the throes of a financial crisis a lender of last resort can hasten a currency collapse since, in effect, all the economy's broad money becomes a liability of the central bank.[21] The trick is to retain what is good about deposit insurance and the lender of last resort function while avoiding the worst excesses of moral hazard, which in turn surely depends on the coverage and level at which it is set. But what does the empirical evidence reveal?

In a cross-country study of 97 countries over 1975–1997 Hutchison and McDill (1999) find that explicit deposit insurance and a liberalised financial system increase the likelihood of banking crises, putting this down to the moral hazard effect.[22] However, in another cross-country study, Cull (1998) finds that the impact of deposit insurance is situation dependent. If adopted as part of an

---

[20] Tamirisa (1998) has empirically confirmed the adverse impact of capital restraints on international trade in a cross-section of countries.

[21] Chinn et al. (1999) and Dooley (2000) make similar observations and further suggest that the bunching together of crises across countries (i.e. contagion) may occur because of revisions in expectations regarding the expected values of official lines of credit to the financial systems.

[22] Hutchison and McDill (1999) further find that the more 'independent' the central bank (from the government authorities) the lower the probability of a banking crisis. This may provide an added rationale for advocating the independence of central banks beyond the more 'conventional' rationale discussed in Willett (1988).

906   GRAHAM BIRD AND RAMKISHEN S. RAJAN

overall reform of the financial sector, particularly in the context of a strong legal framework, it seems to have a positive effect on financial depth and development. But it has the opposite effects when adopted during a period of financial volatility. Confirming these ambiguous effects of deposit insurance, Eichengreen and Arteta (2000) rightly conclude that:

> there is at least as much evidence that deposit insurance reduces crisis risk by solving the depositor run problem than there is of it encouraging crises by weakening market discipline ... (T)hese are questions deserving of additional research (p. 31).

d. Exchange Rate Regime

Pegged rates become misaligned, and if held on to for too long often lead to a currency crisis. Some have suggested that the East Asian economies should have abandoned their pegs as capital flowed in, since exchange risk would then have created a disincentive against a buildup of unhedged positions. Furthermore, protecting a pegged exchange rate by interest rate policy may not be viable where the domestic financial system is fragile. The worry here is that the medicine may be worse than the disease. Accordingly, a case may be made that the greater the degree of financial fragility the less 'fixed' ought to be the country's exchange rate. The analysis here suggests that East Asian economies needed a greater degree of exchange rate flexibility.

Still, empirical evidence fails to unearth any particular nexus between exchange rate regimes and banking crises (Eichengreen and Arteta, 2000). Flexible exchange rates also encounter a range of well known difficulties. In the context of developing countries, their variability due to the thinness of foreign exchange markets, and relatively poor access to hedging, may make them particularly unsuitable. Extreme variability implies that currency misalignment still occurs, and this is likely to lead to resource misallocation, reduced investment and foreign trade, and a lower rate of economic growth, especially where there is impeded access to forward cover (Bird and Rajan, 2000b and 2000c).[23] Accordingly, exchange rate policy is another area where there is no straightforward answer. The theoretical basis for rejecting outright intermediate regimes in favour of corner solutions, as has been the current fad, remains dubious [24] Frankel (2000) appropriately notes that:

> (n)o single currency regime is right for all countries or at all times. The choice of exchange rate arrangement should depend on the particular circumstances facing the country in question. This proposition may sound obvious. But it needs to be stated. Recent experience has many lessons to

---

[23] Of course, such exchange rate variability ought to facilitate the natural development of hedging instruments and capital markets. However, in the short term, the welfare costs could be significant.
[24] In search of a theoretical basis for this preference for corner exchange rate options (of credibly fixed or flexible arrangements), Frankel et al. (2000) have recently suggested that the major disadvantage of intermediate or middle of the road exchange rate options is their lack of transparency/verifiability, unlike a simple peg or a simple float.

offer. There is a danger of over-generalising, however – of applying a given lesson to all countries regardless of circumstances.

7. CONCLUDING REMARKS

The East Asian crisis has drawn into sharp relief the connections between weaknesses in the domestic banking sector, financial liberalisation and currency crises. This paper has shown how a simple analytical model provides a useful and realistic framework within which to discuss these connections. The model is particularly relevant in the context of East Asian economies where the domestic banking sector has been very important, both as an outlet for domestic savers and as a source of finance for firms.

We have suggested that a key characteristic of the East Asian economies was that economic liberalisation did as much to increase the demand for bank credit as it did to increase the supply, and that domestic banks acted as a friction preventing 'complete' international financial integration despite open capital accounts. Relatively high domestic rates did not therefore fall as interest rate parity theory suggests, and capital inflows were perpetuated. It was only when global interest rates rose and/or perceived risks increased that capital reversal occurred. Expansionary domestic monetary policy aimed at avoiding the effects of rising interest rates then perpetuated the capital outflows.

The analysis also carries with it some messages for policy. How do the policy lessons tally with what is happening? While improving prudential supervision and standards is clearly relevant, it is only part of the story. A graduated and sequenced internationalisation of the domestic banking system is also a relevant part of financial sector reform aimed at raising efficiency. Moreover, there are policy pitfalls to be avoided. Amongst the most important of these is 'premature' capital account liberalisation. Emerging economies need to retain the option of using capital restraints in order to manage capital inflows, at least until other reforms to the domestic financial sector have been completed.

REFERENCES

Bank of International Settlements (BIS) (1998), *68th Annual Report* (Basle: BIS).
Berg, A. (1999), 'The Asia Crisis: Causes, Policy Responses, and Outcomes', IMF Working Paper No. 99/138 (October).
Bird, G. (1998), 'The Pros and Cons of Liberalising the Capital Account', *Economic Notes*, **27**, 141–56.
Bird, G. and A. Milne (1999), 'Miracle to Meltdown: A Pathology of the East Asian Financial Crisis', *Third World Quarterly*, **20**, 421–37.
Bird, G. and R. Rajan (2000a), 'Restraining International Capital Flows: What Does it Mean?', *Global Economic Quarterly* (forthcoming).

908   GRAHAM BIRD AND RAMKISHEN S. RAJAN

Bird, G. and R. Rajan (2000b), 'International Currency Taxation and Currency Stabilisation in Developing Countries', *Journal of International Development* (forthcoming).

Bird, G. and R. Rajan (2000c), 'International Currency Taxation and Currency Stabilisation in Developing Countries', *Journal of Development Studies* (forthcoming).

Bisignano, J. (1998), 'Precarious Credit Equilibria: Reflections on the Asian Financial Crisis', BIS Working Paper No. 64 (BIS, March).

Burnside, C., M. Eichenbaum and S. Rebelo (1998), 'Prospective Deficits and the Asian Currency Crisis', NBER Working Paper No. 6758 (October).

Calmoris, C. (1998), 'Blueprints for a New Global Financial Architecture', mimeo (undated).

Chang, R. and A. Velasco (1998), 'The Asian Liquidity Crisis', NBER Working Paper No. 6796 (November).

Chinn, M., M. Dooley and S. Shrestha (1999), 'Latin America and East Asia in the Context of an Insurance Model of Currency Crises', *Journal of International Money and Finance*, **18**, 659–81.

Chinn, M. and K. Kletzer (2000), 'International Capital Inflows, Domestic Financial Intermediation and Financial Crises Under Imperfect Information', Santa Cruz Center for International Economics Working Paper No. 7 (January).

Claessens, S. and T. Glaessner (1998), 'Internationalisation of Financial Services in Asia', World Bank Policy Research Working Paper No. 1911 (April).

Claessens, S., A. Demirgüç-Kunt and H. Huisinga (1998), 'How Does Foreign Entry Affect the Domestic Banking Market?', World Bank Policy Research Working Paper No. 1918 (June).

Corbett, J. and D. Vines (1999), 'The Asian Currency and Financial Crises: Lessons from Vulnerability, Crisis, and Collapse', *World Economy*, **22**, 155–77.

Corsetti, G., P. Pesenti and N. Roubini (1999b), 'Paper Tigers?: A Model of the Asian Crisis', *European Economic Review*, **43**, 1211–36.

Diamond, P. and P. Dybvig (1983), 'Bank Runs, Deposit Insurance, and Liquidity', *Journal of Political Economy*, **91**, 401–19.

Diaz-Alejandro, C. (1985), 'Good-Bye Financial Repression, Hello Financial Crash', *Journal of Development Economics*, **19**, 1–24.

Dooley, M. (2000), 'A Model of Crises in Emerging Markets', *Economic Journal*, **110**, 256–72.

Edwards, S. and C. Vegh (1997), 'Banks and Macroeconomic Disturbances Under Predetermined Exchange Rates', *Journal of Monetary Economics*, **40**, 239–78.

Eichengreen, B. (1999), *Toward a New International Financial Architecture: A Practical Post-Asia Agenda* (Washington, DC: Institute for International Economics).

Eichengreen, B. and C. Arteta (2000), 'Banking Crises in Emerging Markets: Presumptions and Evidence', mimeo (August).

Folkerts-Landau, D. and Associates (1995), 'Effects of Capital Flows on the Domestic Financial Sectors in APEC Developing Countries', in M. Khan and C. Reinhart (eds.), *Capital Flows in the APEC Region*, IMF Occasional Paper 122.

Frankel, J. (2000), 'No Single Currency Regime is Right for All Countries or at All Times', *Princeton Essays in International Finance No. 215* (International Finance Section, Princeton University, August).

Frankel, J., S. Schmukler and L. Servén (2000), 'Verifying Exchange Rate Regimes', World Bank Policy Research Working Paper No. 2397 (July).

Fry, M. (1982), 'Models of Financially Repressed Developing Economics', *World Development*, **10**, 317–27.

Glick, R. and M. Hutchison (1999), 'Banking and Currency Crises: How Common Are Twins?', Center for Pacific Basin Monetary and Economic Studies Working Paper No. PB99–07 (Federal Reserve Bank of San Francisco, December).

Goldfajn, I. and R. Valdes (1997), 'Capital Flows and the Twin Crises: The Role of Liquidity', IMF Working Paper No. 97/87 (July).

Goldstein, M. and P. Turner (1996), 'Banking Crisis in Emerging Economies: Origins and Policy Options', BIS Economic Papers 46 (October).

Hallward-Driemeier, M., D. Dwor-Frecaut and F. Colaco (1999), 'Asian Corporate Recovery: A Firm Level Analysis', mimeo (undated).

BANKS, LIBERALISATION AND EMERGING MARKETS   909

Honohan, P. (1998), 'How Interest Rates Changed Under Financial Liberalization: A Cross-Country Review', World Bank Policy Research Working Paper No. 2313 (April).

Huang, G. and Y. Li (1999), 'Capital Mobility Before and During the Currency Crisis: Experience of Four Asian Countries', mimeo (undated).

Hutchison, M. and K. McDill (1999), 'Are all Banking Crises Alike?: The Japanese Experience in International Experience', NBER Working Paper No. 7253 (July).

International Monetary Fund (IMF) (1998), *World Economic Outlook 1998* (Washington, DC: IMF).

Ito, T. (2000), 'Capital Flows in Asia', in S. Edwards (ed.), *Capital Flows and the Emerging Economies: Theory, Evidence and Controversies* (Chicago: University of Chicago Press, forthcoming).

Kaminsky, G. and C. Reinhart (1999), 'The Twin Crises: The Causes of Banking and Balance-of-Payments Problems', *American Economic Review*, **89**, 473–500.

Kono, M. and L. Schuknecht (1999), 'Financial Services Trade, Capital Flows, and Financial Services', WTO Staff Working Paper ERAD-98-12.

Kono, S. and Associates (1997), 'Opening Markets in Financial Services and the Role of the GATS', *WTO Special Studies* (Geneva).

Krugman, P. (1979), 'A Model of Balance of Payments Crises', *Journal of Money, Credit and Banking*, **11**, 311–28.

Krugman, P. (1999), 'What Happened to Asia?', in R. Sato, R. Ramachandran and K. Mino (eds.), *Global Competition and Integration* (Boston: Kluwer Academic Publishers).

Levine, R. (1996), 'Foreign Banks, Financial Development, and Economic Growth', in C. Barfield (ed.), *International Financial Markets: Harmonisation Versus Competition* (Washington, DC: AEI Press).

Lopez-Mejia, A. (1999), 'Large Capital Flows: A Survey of the Causes, Consequences, and Policy Responses', IMF Working Paper 99/17 (February).

McKibbin, W. (1998), 'The Crisis in Asia: An Empirical Assessment', Brookings Discussion Papers in International Economics No. 136 (Brookings Institution).

McKinnon, R. and H. Pill (1998), 'The Overborrowing Syndrome: Are East Asian Economies Different?', in R. Glick (ed.), *Managing Capital Flows and Exchange Rates: Perspectives from the Pacific Basin* (New York: Cambridge University Press).

McKinnon, R. and H. Pill (1999), 'International Overborrowing: A Decomposition of Credit and Currency Risks', *World Development*, **26**, 1267–82.

Peek, J. and E. Rosengren (1995), 'Bank Lending and the Transmission of Monetary Policy', in J. Peek and E. Rosengren (eds.), *Is Bank Lending Important for the Transmission of Monetary Policy?* (Federal Reserve Bank of Boston).

Rajan, R. (1992), 'Insiders and Outsiders: The Choice Between Informed and Arm's-Length Debt', *Journal of Finance*, **47**, 1367–40.

Rajan, R. (1999), 'Banks, Financial Liberalisation and the "Interest Rate Premium Puzzle" in East Asia', CIES Discussion Paper No. 99/12 (Centre for International Economic Studies, Adelaide, August).

Rajan, R. (2000), '(Ir)relevance of Currency Crisis Theory to the Devaluation and Collapse of the Thai Baht', *Princeton Study in International Economics* (International Economics Section (formerly International Finance Section), Princeton University, forthcoming).

Reinhart, C. and V. Reinhart (1999), 'On the Use of Reserve Requirements in Dealing with Capital Flows Problems', *International Journal of Finance and Economics*, **4**, 27–54.

Rojas-Suarez, L. and S. Weisbrod (1995), 'Financial Fragilities in Latin America: The 1980s and 1990s', IMF Occasional Paper 132.

Tamirisa, N. (1998), 'Exchange and Capital Controls as Barriers to Trade', IMF Working Paper 98/81 (July).

Tivakul, A. (1995), 'Globalisation of Financial Markets in Thailand and Their Implications for Monetary Stability', *Quarterly Bulletin* (Bank of Thailand, June), 37–44.

Velasco, A. (1987), 'Financial Crises and Balance of Payments Crises: A Simple Model of the Southern Cone Experience', *Journal of Development Economics*, **27** (October), 263–83.

910   GRAHAM BIRD AND RAMKISHEN S. RAJAN

Wengel, J. (1995), 'International Trade in Banking Services', *Journal of International Money and Finance*, **14**, 47–64.

Willett, T. (2000), 'International Financial Markets as Sources of Crises or Discipline: The Too Much Too Late Hypothesis', *Princeton Essays in International Finance No. 218* (International Finance Section, Princeton University, May).

Willett, T. (ed.) (1988), *Political Business Cycles: The Political Economy of Money, Inflation, and Unemployment* (Durham, NC: Duke University Press).

Willett, T. and Y. Ahn (1998), 'Upward Biases in Estimates of Capital Mobility for Developing Countries', mimeo (May).

World Bank (1998), *Global Development Finance 1998* (New York: Oxford University Press).

World Bank (1999), *Global Economic Prospects and the Developing Countries* (New York: Oxford University Press).

World Bank (2000), *East Asia: Recovery and Beyond* (New York: Oxford University Press).

[22]

Cambridge Journal of Economics 2002, **26**, 237–260

Financial crisis in Southeast Asia: dispelling illusion the Minskyan way

Philip Arestis and Murray Glickman*

This paper extends Minsky's financial instability hypothesis to the case of the open, 'liberalised', economy, making it possible to put forward a specifically Minskyan account of the road to the financial crisis in Southeast Asia (1997/1998). The analysis suggests that the threats to growth and employment emanating from the financial sector which Minsky identified in the closed economy setting are much intensified in open, liberalised, developing economies. Financial liberalisation is an important key factor in this process. Rival explanations of the crisis are examined and rejected in favour of the extended Minskyan explanation. The policy implications are derived and discussed.

Key words: Crisis, Open economy, Southeast Asia; Financial liberalisation, Financial instability
JEL classifications: E12, G15, G32, 053.

Only an economics critical of capitalism can be a guide to successful policy for capitalism. (Minsky, 1986)

1. Introduction

Hyman Minsky's *Financial Instability Hypothesis* would seem to have obvious application to the recent experience of financial crisis in Asia. It is therefore a matter of surprise that, while many commentators may have been influenced by his ideas, so few have attempted to use them explicitly as a basis for analysing the crisis.[1] The whole of the November 1998 issue of the *Cambridge Journal of Economics*, for example, was devoted to the crisis in Asia. Yet it contained just one direct reference to Minsky (1986). In an attempt to fill the analytical gap, this paper seeks to build on Minsky's work to show that it does indeed offer the basis for a convincing interpretation of the crisis in Asia and one which has important implications for policy.

Manuscript received 29 March 1999; final version received 3 February 2000.
Address for correspondence: Philip Arestis, South Bank Business School, South Bank University London, 103 Borough Road, London SE1 0AA, UK; email: p.arestis@sbu.ac.uk

*South Bank University London and University of East London. Participants at a seminar held at Queens' College Cambridge on 9 March 1999 offered many insightful comments on, and a host of lively and helpful criticisms of, an earlier version of this paper. The authors are grateful to them. They also wish to thank Gary Dymski, Malcolm Sawyer and two anonymous referees for pointing them in the direction of some significant revisions to the argument contained in the paper, which, the authors hope, have helped to clarify and tighten it considerably.

[1] See, though, Arestis (1998) and Kregel (1998) for two exceptions.

238   P. Arestis and M. Glickman

One factor which may have contributed to the neglect of so rich a potential source of understanding is that, in contrast to the patently open nature of the Asian crisis, Minsky's model is developed within a closed economy framework.[1] Another is that his work pre-dates the current era of financial 'liberalisation'. In the next section of this paper, we argue that his *Financial Instability Hypothesis* can in fact be extended readily to the open-economy, 'liberalised', case. On this theoretical basis, the paper's third section proceeds to put forward a specifically Minskyan account of the road to financial crisis in Southeast Asia, whilst the fourth section considers and rejects a number of rival explanations in favour of this Minskyan account. Major policy implications of the discussion are then developed, before, finally, some conclusions are offered.

Minsky's vision was that 'the *normal* functioning of our economy leads to financial trauma and crises . . . [I]n short, . . . financially complex capitalism is inherently flawed' (Minsky, 1986, p. 287, italics in original). In contrast, the conventional wisdom of today is that markets 'work'. On this latter view, the proposition that the source of financial crisis must be exogenous to the financial system and located either in government failure or 'shocks' (or both) is taken as more or less axiomatic truth. Equally, the fact that financial crisis and the spread of financial 'liberalisation' have coincided in Asia can only be regarded as a matter of chance.

The contention of this paper is that such judgements are based on a failure to under-stand (or a refusal to recognise) the endemic instability of financial markets. We are sure our extension of Hyman Minsky's ideas (essentially, 1957, 1975, 1982, 1986) to dispel these *illusions of the age* would have been warmly applauded by the man himself, had he been alive today.

2. Minsky in a closed, an open and a 'liberalised' economy

In this part of the paper, we set out and attempt to justify our extension of Minsky's theory to the open economy (Section 2.2) and the financially 'liberalised' economy (Section 2.3). First, however, in Section 2.1, we point to various features of his closed-economy analysis that are of relevance to our extension of it and elaborate on them to the brief extent necessary to support our later argument.

2.1 Minsky's closed-economy analysis

The essence of Minsky's originality is to be found in the central *motif* of his work, the thesis that forces capable of producing financial fragility are built into the system itself. The following passage succinctly expresses his view:

[I]n a world of uncertainty, given capital assets with a long gestation period, . . . the successful functioning of an economy within an initially robust financial structure will lead to a structure that becomes more fragile as time elapses. Endogenous forces make a situation dominated by hedge finance unstable . . . . (Minsky, 1986, p. 213)

Certain elements of the analysis Minsky developed to support this thesis are key for the purposes of the present discussion. These are identified under the series of sub-headings that follow.

[1] Minsky (1992, p. 356) does, however, recognise the importance of open-economy analysis to the issues with which he is concerned.

2.1.1 The drive towards financial innovation. For Minsky, the 'drive to innovate financing practices by profit-seeking households, businesses, and bankers' (*ibid.,* p. 197) is at the root of the financial instability inherent in capitalism. For, as he argues: 'Profits are available to innovators in financial structures and institutions as well as to innovators in products, production techniques, and marketing' (p. 298) and '[a]s capitalism abhors un-exploited profit opportunities, market instruments and usages develop to exploit interest rate gaps' (p. 213).

In all this, financial intermediaries play a central role. 'Because bankers live in the same expectational climate as businessmen',[1] Minsky writes, 'profit-seeking bankers will find ways of accommodating their customers' (p. 228). Specifically, '[t]hey actively solicit borrowing customers, undertake financing commitments, . . . build connections with business and other bankers, and seek out funds' (pp. 229–30). It is noteworthy here that Minsky does not simply cite bankers' innovating activities as lenders but stresses the fact that their compulsion to innovate extends to their own borrowing activities too.

2.1.2 Hedge, speculative and Ponzi finance. It is not necessary to elaborate in a general way on this celebrated conceptual trinity in this paper.[2] However, critical to the discussion below is the fact that Minsky characterises the *speculative-financing unit* in two closely related but not entirely overlapping ways. On the one hand, he offers a definition in terms of such a unit's own cash flow prospects. Thus he writes that 'the balance sheet cash flows from a unit can be larger than the expected income receipts so that the only way they can be met is by rolling over . . . debt; units that roll over debt are engaged in speculative finance' (1986, p. 203). At the same time, he also refers to the speculative-financing unit in terms of the impact on it of changes in financial market conditions. For example, he states: 'speculative . . . finance units are vulnerable to . . . financial-market developments . . . as well as to product and factor market events: increases in interest rates will raise cash-flow commitments without increasing prospective receipts. Furthermore, as they must continuously refinance their positions, they are vulnerable to financial market disruptions' (*ibid.*, p. 209).

For Minsky, the 'prototypical speculative financial organization' (*ibid.*, p. 207) is the commercial bank. In the case of banks, his two characterisations are clearly coincident: they have continually to engage in refinancing their liability structures *and* they are vulnerable to adverse developments in financial markets. However, even in the closed economy, other cases are not so clear cut. Consider a firm that has issued variable-rate, long-dated debt on terms that it expects to be able to meet comfortably at the time of issue. At that point in time the firm is, on the first of Minsky's criteria, a hedge-financing unit,[3] for it does not foresee having to roll its debt over. On the other hand, it is, from the moment the debt is issued, in a speculative financing position in the sense that it is vulnerable to adverse changes in financial market conditions. We draw attention to this ambiguity here since it takes on some significance when Minsky's theory is extended to the open economy.[4]

---

[1] *Pace* Gertler (1988), for example, it is this feature that is fundamental in Minsky's analysis and not what Minsky called (1995, p. 207) 'peculiar asymmetries in information' that may exist between banks and their clients.

[2] Extended discussions of the concepts of hedge-, speculative and Ponzi-financing can be found, for example, in Minsky (1978, 1982, 1995).

[3] A hedge-financing unit is defined as one whose 'realized and expected income cash flows are sufficient to meeet all . . . payment commitments on outstanding liabilities' (Minsky, 1986, p. 203).

[4] See Section 2.2 below.

240   P. Arestis and M. Glickman

The speculative financing state is also critical in that it exposes the unit to the risk of 'being forced into Ponzi-financing arrangements[1] by income shortfalls or interest cost escalations', this involuntary shift constituting 'a systemic part of the process that leads to widespread bankruptcy' (*ibid.*, p. 209).

2.1.3 'Making on the carry'.   In Minsky's theory, not only is the drive to innovate endogenous but the prospective gains which fuel it also arise endogenously in the form of arbitrage opportunities generated by an (initially) healthy financial state. 'In a world dominated by hedge finance and in which little value is placed on liquidity . . . the interest rate structure', he argues, 'yields profit opportunities in financing positions in capital assets' (Minsky, 1986, pp. 210–11). These arise in three ways:

(a) 'in an economy with a robust financial structure, short-term interest rates . . . will be significantly lower than the yield from owning capital' (p. 211);

(b) 'interest and principal payments on longer-term private debts, which are synchronized to their pay-outs on quasi-rents that capital assets are expected to yield, will be low relative to these quasi-rents' (*ibid.*); and

(c) 'the interest rate on short-term money-like liabilities of firms and financial institutions will be lower than on the longer-term liabilities used in hedge-financing positions in capital assets' (*ibid.*).

These are the factors that 'induce units to engage in speculative finance' (*ibid.*). The use of the generic term *unit* is significant here, reflecting Minsky's insight that these inducements alter the portfolio choices not only of firms but of households and financial institutions too.

It is pertinent to note that a firm which switches from equity to long-term debt as a source of finance may or may not, by so doing, become a speculative-financing unit in either of the two senses distinguished above. However, a unit that borrows short to finance the acquisition of longer-term assets is speculatively financed in both senses, and, throughout his writings, Minsky emphasises that this seeking to 'make on the carry' (*ibid.*) between a short-term liability structure and a long-term asset profile is the prime factor that injects fragility into the financial structure as 'an endogenous phenomenon' (p. 210).

2.1.4 Lowering the orthodox barrier: success breeds success.   The drive to innovate in the direction of speculative financing, Minsky recognises, meets with resistance. 'Bankers', he notes, 'are always seeking to innovate in financial usages. But orthodoxy and conservatism can form a barrier to the assimilation of innovation' (Minsky, 1986, p. 212). However, he notes that legislative and administrative intervention by governments and central bankers may be one operative force conducive to change (p. 197). Another that certainly will be operative is the fact that a 'period of success of the economy . . . will lead to a lowering of the financial innovation barrier, whereas a period of bankruptcies . . . has the potential for raising (it)' (p. 212, note).

As Minsky points out, it is significant that even the effect of success in driving financial innovation forward is an endogenous outcome. 'The intrusion of speculative relations into a system of mainly hedge financing', he observes, 'increases the demand for assets and therefore . . . leads to capital gains.' And, conversely, '[a] regime in which capital

---

[1] In which the unit has to 'increase debt to pay debt' (Minsky, 1986, p. 203)

gains are being earned and are expected is a favorable environment for engaging in speculative . . . finance' (*ibid.*, p. 210).

Furthermore, he notes, 'the governor mechanism . . . is often dominated by positive, disequilibrating feedbacks. An increase in the demand prices for capital assets relative to the supply prices of investment output increases investment, which increases not only profits but also the ratio of profits to payment commitments on outstanding debts, the amount of financing available from banks and financial markets at any set of terms, and businessmen's willingness to invest' (*ibid.*, p. 228).

2.1.5 The transition from robustness to fragility. Eventually 'success breeds a disregard of the possibility of failure: the absence of serious financial difficulties over a substantial period leads to the development of a euphoric economy in which increasing short-term financing of long positions becomes a normal way of life' (Minsky, 1986, p. 213). In such an atmosphere, even hedge financing can become 'based upon unrealistic euphoric expectations with respect to . . . product and factor markets' (p. 209). Thus, for Minsky, waves of bullish sentiment that sweep financial systems are not episodes dissociated from what has gone before but are themselves part of a multi-faceted endogenous process.

The effect is to undermine an initially robust financial structure, in which hedge financing predominates (*ibid.*, p. 305). For 'a marked increase in the fragility of an economy occurs as . . . financing relations assure that an investment boom will lead to an environment with increased speculative financing of positions, which in turn will lead to conditions conducive to a crisis' (pp. 217–18). For Minsky, crisis is characterised by the inability of units to refinance their positions 'through normal channels' (Minsky, 1977, p. 140).

2.1.6 The triggers of crisis. '[I]n a fragile financial system continued normal functioning can be disrupted by some not unusual event', Minsky writes (*ibid.* p. 139). Indications as to what these events might be are given in the following passage:

A break in the boom occurs whenever . . . reversals in present-value relations take place. Often this occurs after the increase in demand financed by speculative finance has raised interest rates, wages of labor, and prices of material so that profit margins and thus the ability to validate the past are eroded. (Minsky, 1986, p. 220)

The disruptive events cited here are of course themselves entirely endogenous to the process. At the same time, it is important for present purposes to note that Minsky's theory allows for the possibility that the catalyst of crisis may also be some other, 'external' event.[1] However, such an event would be far removed from the *exogenous shock* that is the staple of neo-classical theory. For Minsky insists that 'financial fragility . . . is not due to either accidents or policy errors . . . [O]ur economy endogenously develops fragile or crisis-prone financial structures' (1977, pp.139–40). The crucial point here is that, for Minsky, the reasons why a 'shocking' event actually has the power to shock are emphatically endogenous.

Minsky, as we have already noted, stresses the fact that banks themselves frequently engage in speculative financing. He sees this as a key factor leading to the generalisation of crisis conditions, observing that speculative financing activity on their part means that the

---

[1] *Vide* the use of the word *often* in the passage just cited.

242   P. Arestis and M. Glickman

pressures of disruptive events 'are often acutely felt by financial intermediaries, and a deterioration in their ability to make position will adversely affect the balance sheets of their liability holders'. As a result a 'potential for contagion exists', although, he adds, '[i]ntervention by central banks . . . serves to abort such contagious developments' (1986, p. 219).

2.2 The Minskyan open economy
Some further comment on Minsky's hedge- and speculative-financing concepts is necessary at this stage as a preliminary to applying his theoretical framework to the open-economy case.

If the commercial bank is Minsky's prototypical speculative unit, the corresponding prototypical hedge-financing unit, *in a closed economy*, might be a firm which financed itself by means of equity (Minsky, 1986, p. 305) or, perhaps, long-dated fixed-interest debt. In an open economy, however, categorisation is not so straightforward, since the dividends and capital gains expected from, or the debt servicing payable by, such an organisation might be due in foreign currency. The unit would then be in an analogous position to an organisation with long-dated *variable-rate* debt in a closed economy: it could be characterised as a hedge-financing unit in so far as it appears able to meet its financial obligations given the existing climate of expectations; but it could, on the other hand, be viewed as a speculative financing unit in the sense that it was vulnerable to adverse changes in financial conditions, specifically, movements in the exchange rate.

Of course a unit which borrowed *short*-term in foreign currency to finance domestic long-term assets would also be speculatively financing itself under both of Minsky's criteria: as well as needing continually to roll debts over, it would also be vulnerable to changes in interest rates. Additionally, however, it would be vulnerable to exchange-rate movements. It would seem appropriate to extend Minsky's typology to reflect this open-economy phenomenon by dubbing such an organisation a *super-speculative*-financing unit.

On the basis of these observations, we can begin to develop a Minskyan open-economy analysis. Assume that a domestic upswing is in progress in an economy in which hedge-financing predominates. Profitability increases absolutely and relative to the cost of capital, and risk assessments become less guarded and more upbeat. As confidence grows symmetrically, a more venturesome mood sweeps the financial as well as the real sector. In a globalised system, this mood will spread rapidly beyond the confines of the country concerned. In the absence of capital controls, international portfolio investors will turn their attentions to the domestic economy: especially if short-term rates are low in the major financial centres, liquid funds will switch into the domestic currency; local banks will experience an upsurge in deposits and will be able to expand their own international borrowing; and prices of local stock market securities of all kinds will also tend to rise. Capital inflows will tend to offset any tendency for the domestic upswing to push interest rates higher. The authorities will have no difficulty pegging the country's currency against the US dollar if that is their policy. If they choose not to do so, the exchange rate will tend to rise. Either way, the external position will be interpreted as evidence of economic 'health', fuelling the optimistic mood further and establishing a lively interest in foreign currency arbitrage.

Minsky's theory can be readily extended to provide an illuminating explanatory framework for this arguably not over-stylised account of the course of events as an economy opens itself up to global financial markets. The primary impact of openness is to import the drive towards financial innovation into the economy in question, as foreign wealth-holders seek out investment opportunities and local households, firms and banks begin to look abroad for finance.

This era of innovation creates new possibilities for local hedge-financed units to become speculatively financed, once we allow for this concept to be extended in the way suggested above. Even a unit that raises finance from foreign sources in ways that leave asset and liability maturities matched becomes vulnerable to foreign exchange market movements. And, of course, those units that are attracted by currently low-cost opportunities to borrow short term in foreign currency become, in our terms, super-speculative. Openness thus internationalises the drive to 'make on the carry'.

Furthermore, the insertion of international financial practices into the domestic arena represents an extremely potent tool for breaking down the domestic orthodoxy barrier. Rising asset prices, investment and profits validate the initial waves of foreign borrowing and thereby fuel the appetite for more. Hence the disequilibrating positive feedbacks Minsky identifies are fully operative as factors reducing domestic financial conservatism. However, openness expands their range: the strength of the exchange rate as it rides on capital inflows serves to encourage still further the taking of positions, and especially short-term positions, in foreign currency. For Minsky, success is an endogenous factor driving financial innovation forward. Openness extends significantly the scope and therefore the endogenous impact of achievable success.

The upshot is that, sooner or later, the economy falls into a state of internationalised financial fragility. It then becomes prone (i) to crisis that is domestic in origin but impacts on its external situation (what we term below a *d to e* crisis), (ii) to crisis that is external in origin but impacts on its domestic situation (*e to d*) and (iii) to crisis-intensifying interactions between (i) and (ii).

A *d to e* crisis would have its origins in classic Minskyan factors (see Minsky, 1986, p. 217), such as the advent of rising costs in the domestic capital goods industries. As Minsky argues (*ibid*), the result will be present-value reversal and a decline in asset prices, which will mean that speculatively and super-speculatively financed units will find refinancing increasingly difficult to come by and its terms increasingly onerous. As they default in increasing numbers and commercial failure spreads, a flight towards liquidity will break out. Some investors will seek to diversify the now larger liquid element in their portfolios by shifting into other currencies. Others will act in anticipation of behaviour of this kind. The domestic currency will be sold heavily, triggering an exchange rate crisis. Even units that are hedged in the sense that their asset and liability maturities are matched will now become vulnerable to the fact that they are speculatively financed in the other sense that their debts are denominated in foreign currency whereas their cash inflows are not. Furthermore, the potential for contagion will have a global reach.

The possibility of an *e to d* crisis can be analysed on Minskyan terms on the basis that, once an economy is open to global financial markets, its state entity can regarded as a financing unit in relation to the external value of its currency. On the one hand, its residents will accumulate debts to the rest of the world denominated in foreign currencies. On the other, its central bank may accumulate assets—foreign currency reserves. So long as reserves are substantial in relation to debts, the country remains in the equivalent of a hedge-financed position: the payments necessary to maintain the external value of its currency can always be made. However, as endogenous processes drive up the foreign liabilities, and especially the short-term liabilities, of residents of our putative open economy, its debt-to-reserves ratio rises and it becomes increasingly doubtful that its

244   P. Arestis and M. Glickman

authorities will continue to be able to finance the transactions they may be called upon to undertake to protect the exchange rate. The state will then become, in effect, a speculative- and, ultimately, a Ponzi-financing unit in relation to the wider world.

Under these conditions, the exchange rate becomes a source of uncertainty in relation to which expectations can wax and wane with destabilising consequences (see, also, Dymski, 1998). Even in the absence of actual evidence of deterioration in domestic financial conditions, speculators may begin to doubt the ability of the state to support its currency and, if it were not already in a Ponzi state in this regard, it will become such now as they may move, possibly on a massive scale, against the currency concerned.

This external crisis will feed into the domestic situation, first because super-speculatively-financed units, especially, will be hit, and secondly since, if speculators are to act on their fears of rising debt/reserves ratios, they will first have to liquidate holdings of domestic assets. As they do so, domestic asset prices will fall and the balance sheet positions of domestic borrowers and lenders alike will deteriorate. Even domestic units that have remained hedge-financed in the sense that they have resisted the lure of foreign borrowing may well find themselves dragged down into speculative and Ponzi positions, which may be difficult to refinance.

The financial instability of the open economy can in this way be understood in characteristically Minskyan terms. Openness vastly expands the drive towards financial innovation and extends opportunities for 'making on the carry'. As a result, it decidedly broadens the routes by which units, including the state itself, can shift from hedged to speculative and Ponzi conditions. The economy is thus driven endogenously into a fragile condition in which it becomes increasingly exposed to disruptive events which, if domestic in origin, will amplify themselves via their external consequences and, if initially external, will bring adverse domestic repercussions in their train.[1]

The fact that, in the way just outlined, the state can be regarded as a financing unit in an open economy has a further consequence. Once it has shifted from a hedged into a speculative and, *a fortiori*, into a Ponzi condition, the authorities will tend to hold back from expanding domestic liquidity in the face of collapsing domestic asset prices and instead raise interest rates to bolster the exchange rate, bowing to pressures emanating from the international financial system. As we noted earlier, Minsky stresses the capacity of the monetary authorities to constrain the contagious potential of fragility in a closed-economy setting. However, in an open setting, in which the state becomes a financing unit in relation to the external value of its currency, this capacity is, as we have now shown, much blunted. As result, the deflationary dynamics of financial fragility become very much more threatening.

2.3 Minsky and financial 'liberalisation'

The open economy just described possesses 'liberated' features in that its capital movements are unregulated. However, financial 'liberation' starts in, and focuses on, the domestic economy, and it is primarily through its domestic effects that liberalisation intensifies the instability of the financial system.

The first of these needs little explanation in Minskyan terms. Financial liberalisation produces an upward step-change in the intensity of the domestic drive towards financial innovation, as it sweeps away the rules and conventions which previously governed the

---

[1] This duality is reminiscent of Kaminsky and Reinhart (1999), but our analysis differs substantially from theirs, as made clear in Section 4 below.

way banks related to one another and their customers. It thereby speeds up the process by which debt ratios of commercial concerns and financial institutions rise, escalating financial fragility, and it hastens the day when banking and financial crises loom (see, also, Coggins, 1998).

The second effect is on attitudes—market sentiment. Proponents of financial liberalisation seem increasingly to favour the view that it may be necessary to prepare the ground for liberation[1] with 'sequenced' programmes of 'free' market reforms (Williamson and Mahar, 1998). Our position, however, is that such reforms,[2] only serve to weaken the barrier of financial conservatism which, in Minsky's view,[3] acts to contain pressures leading to fragility in the financial system. For, suppose a policy package of the kind just described is in place and that its deflationary bias does not altogether stop a Minskyan upswing in its tracks. If it is widely believed that the policy mix is a sufficient condition for macroeconomic 'stability', it will in effect surround the already buoyant economy with an aura of safety. What could go wrong? All known dragons have been slain beforehand for, according to the theory that inspires such reforms, the threat to prosperity comes from irresponsible government, and this threat evaporates in a suitably prudent policy climate. And, since the theory is part of the conventional wisdom of our age, it is likely to be embedded in the belief systems of decision makers in the private sector. In the current ideological state of the world, these policies will achieve 'credibility'.

The effect could well be to raise to still higher and more dangerously unrealistic levels the feelings of invulnerability that, on a Minskyan analysis, conditions of economic buoyancy induce. For if he is right that the true sources of instability are in fact endogenous to the private sector and if we now superimpose a state of liberationist policy 'credibility' on the economy, the result will be that private-sector decision makers will not so much disregard danger as look totally in the wrong direction for it. Seeing none, they will lower their commercial guard even further.[4] *Credulity* would seem to be a rather better word than credibility to describe what the policy achieves.

Extending Minsky's analysis, it therefore seems reasonable to argue that a sequencing of reforms, such as some liberationists recommend, looks likely to spread a layer of illusion over business attitudes, weakening inhibitions against speculation still further and reinforcing the tendency towards euphoria that Minsky postulated as the source of financial fragility. As he observed in parallel circumstances:

Legislation . . . reflect(s) the views about . . . the economy . . . held by our rulers and their court intellectuals . . . Legislated changes, such as . . . the deregulation mania of the later 1970s and 1980s reflect some theory. If the theory is at variance with the way the economy behaves, the reforms will do little good and may do great harm. (Minsky, 1986, p. 198)[5]

---

[1] A liberalised financial system seems to be a tender plant indeed. Perhaps economic 'botanists' should be seeking to propagate an altogether hardier variety, one that can survive and flourish in a much wider range of policy climates and real sector soils.

[2] The shopping list of reforms might include: (i) 'sound' public finances, i.e. budgetary balance or surplus, (ii) fiscal and monetary policies aimed exclusively at price stability, (iii) tying the exchange rate to one of the major currencies, (iv) greater transparency in the behaviour of the monetary authorities.

[3] See Section 2.1.4 above.

[4] For example, 'credibility' will contribute to a 'neglect . . . of old text book rules for the prudent operation of banks and businesses that were universally accepted . . . in earlier days' such as Minsky held to be partly responsible for the financial instability in the US evident in the 1970s and 1980s (Minsky, 1986, p. 199).

[5] In this vein, 'sequenced' programmes should be judged on the basis of the mounting evidence that is emerging from countries in which they have been implemented. On this score, such sequencing would seem to have been a clear failure (see, for example, Arestis and Demetriades, 1997).

246   P. Arestis and M. Glickman

3. A Minskyan account of the road to financial crisis in Asia

In this section, we argue that Minsky's analytical framework, extended along the lines just proposed, provides a solid and coherent basis for theorising about the course of events that led to financial crisis in Southeast Asia in 1997.

3.1 Timing

In our review of Minsky's theory in the preceding section, we drew attention to his stress on the barriers presented by established financial usage, which he viewed as bulwarks against the emergence of financial fragility. Our extension of his theory suggests that one major consequence of the financial liberalisation of an economy will be that many of these barriers will be swept away in short order. On this analysis, one would expect liberalisation to lead rapidly to crisis. That is indeed what seems to have occurred in Southeast Asia in the 1980s and 1990s. The most telling example is, perhaps, Thailand, where a haemorrhage of foreign capital in early July 1997 brought the economy to a state of near collapse, a development which sparked the whole Asian crisis (on which see, for example, Jomo, 1998). Thailand[1] had barely completed the liberalisation of its financial system at the point in time when crisis erupted (see Table 1).

Critical to our argument, however, is the fact that Thailand is by no means an isolated case. On the contrary, in all the five most affected countries,[2] the savage banking and financial crisis that marked the second half of 1997 followed close on the heels of programmes of far-reaching financial liberalisation (see, for example, Chang, 1998; Jomo, 1998; Wade, 1998, for relevant details). As Table 1 makes plain, the liberalisation process began in the late 1970s to mid-1980s in each of these countries but was only completed in the early to mid-1990s. As an indicator of the extent of 'progress' towards liberalisation, the share of state-owned banks in total sectoral assets in the year prior to liberalisation and in the most recent year for which information is available is given in the table. Controls on the flow of capital had been removed in all these countries with the exception of South Korea, which still retained significant controls in 1996 [although these have since been dismantled under the terms of the International Monetary Fund (IMF) rescue package].[3]

3.2 Short-term liability structures and speculative financing

The Minskyan account is also confirmed by the way that liberalisation in Southeast Asia prompted dramatic shifts towards speculative and super-speculative financing in the strict and extended Minskyan senses discussed in the preceding section of this paper. Liberalisation opened the way for local banks to become heavily involved in risky domestic lending activities and to extend their foreign operations dramatically. Local firms were set free to borrow abroad. The promotion of stock markets[4] together with external liberal-

---

[1] Banks in Thailand lacked any expertise in collateral evaluation, and committed themselves heavily to lending to property developers to support the purchase of vastly over-priced office blocks (see Jomo, 1998, ch. 6).

[2] South Korea, Indonesia, the Philippines and Malaysia as well as Thailand.

[3] Malaysia has, subsequently to the crisis, reimposed controls (see note b to Table 1).

[4] Arestis *et al.* (2001) and Singh (1997) emphasise the liquidity of stock market assets as the key factor making them vehicles for speculation and thus a source of macroeconomic instability. As the stock market grows in importance, short-termism is encouraged and the financial system consequently becomes more fragile (see, also, Arestis and Demetriades, 1996, 1997). Financial liberalisation is, therefore, unlikely to enhance long-term growth prospects, least of all in developing countries, which are particularly susceptible to the problems stock market speculation creates.

Table 1. *The timing of liberalisation and its impact on state-owned banks*

Country	Start of liberalisation	Largely liberalised financial sector	Total asset share of state-owned banks (%)	
			Single year before liberalisation	Most recent year
Indonesia	1983	1989–96	76	40
South Korea	1983	1996–98	81	32[a]
Malaysia	1978	1992–96[b]	n a	8
Philippines	1981	1994–96	28	22
Thailand	mid-1980s	1992–96[c]	n a	19

[a]Share of total deposits.
[b]Malaysia reimposed wide-ranging capital controls on the 1st September 1998.
[c]Currency controls were introduced in May and June of 1997 to deter currency speculators.
Source: Reproduced from Williamson and Mahar (1998, Tables 3 and 4).

Table 2. *Growth of bank credit*

	Bank credit growth *less* real GDP growth (%)			Share of property sector in bank lending (%) (end-1997)
	1990–94	1995	1996	
Thailand	10·0	11·1	5·8	30–40
Indonesia	10·4	4·4	5·7	25–30
Malaysia	3·1	10·5	13·1	30–40
Philippines	10·7	27·4	31·5	15–20
South Korea	2·6	2·2	−0·6	15–25

Source: Goldstein (1998).

isation in conditions which offered large arbitrage margins on liquid and short-term capital helped create an investment climate characterised by buoyant expectations of capital gain and muted risk perceptions.

In such a climate, gearing ratios mounted. Table 2 shows how substantial the expansion of bank credit was in relation to GDP in the 1990s in four of the five countries. The exception was South Korea, where the growth rate of bank credit was significantly lower than elsewhere and, indeed, was negative in 1996. This exception is instructive: in South Korea the process of liberalisation was still incomplete in 1996 (see Table 1).

Most of the inflow of funds was directed towards speculative activities. Between 1996 and 1997, this inflow was of the order of $109bn, 11% of the pre-crisis aggregate GDP of the five most affected countries (Arestis, 1998; Kregel, 1998). The credit boom it fuelled was directed towards the property sector to a remarkable extent and, from a Minskyan point of view, in a totally predictable fashion: banks and their clients at home and abroad followed the classic Minskyan pattern of zealously seeking out opportunities to 'make on the carry' as the wave of optimism unleashed by liberalisation gathered strength. According to the United Nations Conference on Trade and Development (UNCTAD) (1998) '[r]eal estate loans are estimated to have accounted for 25–40% of bank lending in Thailand, Malaysia and Philippines in 1998, funded to an important extent by short-term

248   P. Arestis and M. Glickman

foreign borrowing' (p. 63). The value of the collateral on bank loans was heavily dependent on increases in asset prices. This was fragility in the making, with property companies
and banks who lent to them extremely vulnerable to a downturn in prices, a rise in interest
rates or currency appreciation.

3.3 External balance

This property boom can be regarded as super-speculative (in the sense defined earlier) in
view of the fact that it was dependent on continuous capital inflows to provide the
necessary funds to keep the process going. When the crisis emerged, the property sector
suffered substantially, as did others where similar super-speculative risk-taking was
evidenced by the growth in foreign currency exposures that developed as governments in
the five countries removed or loosened controls on companies' foreign borrowing,
abandoned direction of borrowing and investments and resisted calls to strengthen bank
supervision.

Firms discovered that they could borrow abroad half as cheaply as at home. As a result,
large capital flows took place, which swelled domestic banks' reserves and promoted a
local credit boom. The willingness of Asian firms and banks to borrow was matched by the
willingness to lend exhibited by overseas wealth holders, who perceived inferior prospective returns elsewhere as a result of slow growth in the industrialised countries and the
economic problems of Latin America. International investors readily exploited the high
growth and interest rates found in these Asian countries, transferring vast amounts of
capital to Asia.

Table 3 gives some indication of the scale of the international private credit flow in the
peak years of the boom, 1995 and 1996 (row 2), of the dominant role played by commercial banks in this flow (rows 4 and 5) and of the size of this credit flow in relation to the
total external financing requirement of the countries concerned (row 1).

With these net capital inflows on this scale, foreign debt inevitably escalated, most of it
private and short-term (maturing in 12 months or less). Indeed, World Bank (1997)
estimates show that, in 1996, Indonesia received the world's third largest private foreign
capital flow ($17.96bn), Malaysia the fourth ($16bn) and Thailand the sixth largest
($13bn). Simultaneously, net inflows of long-term debt, foreign direct investment and
equity purchases, which stood at only $25bn in 1990, soared to more than $110bn in
1996 (reported in Greenspan, 1997).

Table 3. *Five Asian economies: external financing^a ($bn)*

		1995	1996	1997	1998e
(1)	External financing, net	83·0	99·0	28·3	−4·2
(2)	Private flows, net	80·4	102·3	0·2	−27·6
(3)	Private creditors, net	65·1	83·7	−4·2	−41·3
(4)	Commercial banks, net	53·2	62·7	−21·2	−36·1
(5)	Non-banks, net	12·0	21·0	17·1	−5·3
(6)	Official flows, net	2·6	−3·3	28·1	23·4
(7)	International financial institutions	−0·3	−2·0	22·4	19·3
(8)	Reserves excl. gold (− = increase)	−14·1	−16·9	31·5	−42·1

e = estimate.
^aIndonesia, Malaysia, South Korea, Thailand, Philippines.
Source: Institute of International Finance (IIF) (1999, p. 3).

Table 4. *Short-term external debt*

Country	Short-term debt owed to banks reporting to BIS June 1997 ($bn)	Reserves (IMF data) ($bn)	Short-term debt to reserves ratio (%)
South Korea	70·2	31·3	224
Indonesia	34·7	18·9	184
Thailand	45·6	37·7	121
Philippines	8·3	9·4	88
Malaysia	16·3	26·6	61

Source: IIF (1998).

Foreign lending on this scale was often at interest rates which reflected only a very modest risk premium relative to safe returns on investment in the lender country, a state of affairs which, Minsky's theory suggests, is evidence of financial robustness in the initial stages of the process. However, once perceived risk levels began to rise, what Minsky called the normal functioning of the financial system was always likely to be disturbed. In an open, liberalised situation, this disturbance would be likely to express itself in substantial capital outflows.

Table 4 shows how substantial the accumulation of short-term external debt became: by 1997 each of the five Asian countries most affected by the crisis faced, to a greater or lesser degree, a major external debt problem as measured by its short-term debt to foreign currency reserves ratios. Furthermore, the shift in net external private finance in these countries between 1996 and 1997 was around 11% of their combined GDP (reported in the *Financial Times*, 25 March 1998).

We argued above that, as speculative financing activity by firms, households and banks drives up the ratio of private sector debt to national foreign currency reserves, the state, on our extended Minskyan analysis, is turned into a speculative- and ultimately a Ponzi-financing unit in relation to the exchange rate. The applicability of this conceptual framework to the Asian crisis seems evident from the data presented in this section.

3.4 The scale of the crisis and differential impacts

Consciousness of the scale of the Asian financial crisis seems to have been transitory, at least among commentators outside the region. This is perhaps because predictions of global spread did not materalise. However, it is important not to lose sight of the ferocity of the impact of the crisis on the economies most affected by it.

Row 2 of Table 3 shows that the massive private net lending flows to the five economies of 1995 and 1996 went into reverse in 1997 and substantially so in 1998 according to the estimate for that year.[1] Net official flows (row 6), which had previously been negative, became significantly positive in 1997 and 1998, boosted by support from international financial institutions such as the IMF and the World Bank (row 7). These flows, of course, reflect the scale of the foreign exchange crisis, as does the substantial fall in the official reserves of the five countries recorded for 1997 (row 8).

Table 5 shows the impact of the crisis in three further key dimensions. Between July

---

[1] The decline of over $100bn in net overall private flows between 1996 and 1997 (row 2) is roughly equivalent to 10% of the pre-crisis GDP of these countries (Wolf, 1998).

250   P. Arestis and M. Glickman

Table 5. *Southeast Asian crisis: impact on currencies, share prices and interest rates (July 1, 1997–February 16, 1998)*

Country	Depreciation of the currency *vis-à-vis* the dollar (%)	Changes in the share price index (%)	Changes in interest rates (basis prints)
Indonesia	231·00	−81·74	2,398
SouthKorea	83·04	−63·06	965
Malaysia	55·43	−58·41	373
Philippines	51·37	−49·17	0
Thailand	87·09	−48·37	−25

Source: Martinez (1998, p. 8).

Table 6. *Emerging markets: real GDP growth (percentage change on previous year)*

	1995	1996	1997	1998e
Average real GDP growth	4·5	5·0	5·1	1·3
Five Asian economies[a]	8·3	7·0	4·4	−7·2

e = estimate; f = forecast.
[a]Indonesia, Malaysia, South Korea, Thailand, Philippines.
Source: IIF (1999, Table 6, p. 8).

1997 and February 1998, currency depreciations on a dramatic scale were recorded in all five countries and, as the table shows, these collapses occurred in Indonesia, South Korea and Malaysia against a backdrop of large and, in two cases, spectacular upward movements in interest rates. Table 5 also charts the scale of the fall of Asian stock markets in the wake of the crisis. It is estimated that, between June 1997 and January 1998, equity losses exceeded \$700bn, \$430bn of which were lost by US investors (Greenspan, 1998). By early February 1998, equity markets in the five countries examined here had declined (in local currency terms) by 53% to 76% from their 1996 or 1997 peaks (Chote, 1998, p. 2).

Another indication of the severity of the crisis emerges from estimates of the bail-out costs of support for the banking sectors in the affected countries, which range from 7% of GDP in the case of the Philippines to over 20% in Thailand (Kaminsky and Reinhart, 1998, p. 447; see, also, Bhattacharya *et al.*, 1997). Finally, Table 6, which contrasts real GDP growth in the five most affected countries with that in the 'emerging markets' group of countries as a whole, indicates the size of the real sector effects of the credit boom years of 1995 and 1996 as well as of the consequent crisis.

At the same time, the crisis did not affect the five countries equally. Demirguc-Kunt and Detragiache (1998) in a study of 53 countries (for the period 1985–95) have shown that, although financial liberalisation increases the probability that banking crises will occur, their severity can be substantially lower in countries where the regulatory environment is strong, where '[s]uch institutions include effective prudential regulation and supervision of financial intermediaries and of organised security exchanges, and a well-functioning mechanism to enforce contracts and regulations' (p. 2). Their findings point to a Minskyan element in the differential impact of the crisis among the five countries:

where the state is willing or able to act to strengthen the barriers of financial orthodoxy, it may go some way towards mitigating the fragility-inducing effects of liberalisation.

The contention of this paper is that a crisis of the proportions witnessed in Southeast Asia could not have arisen from trivial causes and that a theory which identifies deep-seated malfunctions as a source of crisis is therefore *ipso facto* more credible than ones that do not. The Minskyan account is able to present a disparate set of phenomena as an integral whole, part of a clearly articulated endogenous process. Whether there exist any competing accounts that can stand up to scrutiny against it is a question to which we turn in the next section.

4. Rival explanations of the Asian financial crisis

In distinguishing between various theories put forward to explain the crisis in Southeast Asia, Neely (1999) contrasts 'fundamentalist' with 'panic' views. In this section, we use these labels to categorise a number of orthodox 'explanations' of the crisis, which we examine and reject in Sections 4.1 and 4.2. We then go on to consider and criticise three equally unconvincing further propositions, namely that the crisis was attributable to 'bail-out' (Section 4.3), to supposed defects of the Asian model (Section 4.4) and to cronyism (Section 4.5). Finally, in Section 4.6, we present some general observations on the differences between our Minskyan analysis of the Asian crisis and these rival explanations.

4.1 The 'fundamentalist' view

According to this view, associated with the work of Krugman (1979), the roots of the crisis and its contagious qualities lie in the governmental quasi-guarantee implicit in the exchange-rate pegging policy widely followed in Asia (see, for example, Krugman, 1998B, 1998C). Thus a recent official comment runs: 'The 10-year experience of currency pegs, more or less guaranteeing that fluctuations relative to the dollar would be less than 10 per cent, was another significant contributory factor' (UNCTAD, 1998).

More specifically, the competitiveness of the Asian economies whose exchange rates were tied to the US dollar declined as the latter appreciated against the yen and other major currencies. Furthermore, pegged exchange rates encouraged local banks to undertake predominantly short-term borrowing in foreign currencies and to lend the converted proceeds domestically. Implicitly, the exchange rate risk inherent in such activities was transferred to the governments of these countries, and these lacked systems to monitor, let alone to challenge, such behaviour. A combination of higher US interest rates in early 1997, and the decline in the world prices of Southeast Asian countries' major exports over the same period (Krugman, 1997), then caused this particular bubble to burst. The prices of assets which had been used as collateral fell, and domestic lending declined. Under these circumstances, capital began to flee the region, putting pressure on the exchange rate pegs, which were eventually abandoned. As a result of the level of foreign-currency indebtedness, currency depreciations led to widespread bankruptcies and a slowdown in economic growth.

The crucial first link in this posited causal chain looks distinctly weak, in our judgement. A pegged exchange-rate does, admittedly, offer an agent engaging in a foreign currency transaction a measure of security and, as a result, encourages such transactions to take place. After all, that is its purpose. However, whether exchange-rate pegging, in the absence of any other changes, would have been sufficient to produce the crisis conditions witnessed in Asia so recently seems extremely doubtful.

252   P. Arestis and M. Glickman

The Miskyan account, on the other hand, places exchange-rate pegging in the setting of the much broader policy shift implied by financial liberalisation. As we argued earlier, it is the wholesale sweeping away of established financial practice intentionally brought about by financial liberalisation that is the instrumental factor breaking down bankers' natural risk aversion in a liberalised economy. Furthermore, as also noted earlier (see sub-section 2.3 above), exchange-rate pegging actually figures in the sequenced programme of reform advocated in some quarters as an underpinning for liberalisation. It is therefore not a policy whose effects are to be considered in isolation, as the fundamentalist view does. Rather, it should be examined in the context of the whole liberationist philosophy which gives it its significance.

4.2 The 'panic' view

Turning now to the 'panic' view, as propounded by, for example, Radelet and Sachs (1998A, 1998B), the essential argument maintains that, although economic fundamentals were sound in Southeast Asia, sudden and swift changes in expectations produced the impetus for the massive capital outflows that occurred. The thesis draws on literature focusing on self-fulfilling expectations and hedging behaviour in international capital markets (for example Obstfeld, 1996). According to this view, capital outflows were the result of international investors' irrational behaviour in the face of unreasonably harsh fiscal and monetary policies prescribed by the IMF. Perhaps the bluntest statement of the irrationality thesis is Dean's (2001) remark that 'Asian currency and equity markets seemed simply to collapse of their own accord' (p. 267).

When the arguments that supporters of the lender-panic thesis put forward to defend their position are examined closely, it is clear that they amount to no more than loose, *a priori*, speculations. One line of 'reasoning' runs as follows: the crisis was unanticipated; there were no warning signals such as, for example, downgrading by debt rating agencies; *ergo*, it must all have been due to irrationality on the part of lenders. A related argument refers specifically to the crisis period itself: banks had, until the crisis broke, been prepared to lend without any sort of government guarantee or insurance[1] (see, for example, Neely, 1999). Once it was under way, however, the affected countries experienced widespread credit crunches, such that even viable domestic exporters, with confirmed sales, could not obtain credit. *Ergo* lenders must have worked themselves into a state of irrationality. A final suggestion is that the trigger of the crisis was the sudden withdrawal of funds from the region, preceding any deflation of asset values. This, of course, could only be due to irrational behaviour on the part of lenders.

It is not clear how seriously one should take theorists who normally identify totally with a methodology that posits the individual as the unit of analysis but now invoke collective insanity as an explanatory variable. Also, this 'explanation' ends where it should begin: why did lenders, as a group, suddenly fall victim to irrationality at this precise point in human history? Furthermore, it ill becomes orthodox economists, whose other great touchstone is the so-called axiom of rationality, to have any truck at all with this kind of argument.

The postulation of an abnormal episode of lender-irrationality implies a normal state of affairs in which, as Harvey (1996) puts it, ' "fundamentals" are assumed to determine rates, while market participants second-guess the fundamentals'. But, as he goes on to argue, the weakness of this view is that 'Exchange rate forecasting is then analogous to guessing a

---

[1] Note the contrast here with the moral hazard story reviewed in the immediately following section.

dice roll or predicting the weather; the expectations have no effect on the actual outcome' (p. 574). In fact, as Glickman (1994) argues, prices in financial markets are *always* determined by short-run expectations and systemic irrationality is, as a result, consistent with the most clear-headed rationality on the part of individual participants. On this point it is pertinent to note Minsky's own view as reported in the Introduction to Fazzari and Papadimitriou (1992):

> In day-to-day conversations, it is clear that Minsky has little patience with interpretations . . . that tie predictions of endogenous instability to 'irrational' behavior . . . [B]ehavior at the micro level may be quite rational, even essential to survival. Banks . . . may be quite aware of increasing systemic fragility, but this problem is a financial externality over which individuals agents have no control. (p. 8)

The 'panic', like the 'fundamentalist', view is intended to account for the connection between banking and financial crises, on the one hand, and currency crises, on the other, noted by Kaminsky and Reinhart (1998, 1999). Financial crises happen as economies enter a recession after a prolonged expansion in economic activity fuelled by credit creation and capital flows. In the Kaminsky and Reinhart approach, it is recognised that financial liberalisation takes place before banking sector crises, which in turn precede currency crises, the latter worsening the former in 'a vicious spiral' (1999, p. 473). Their explanation, with its emphasis on the normal behaviour of the economic cycle, seems at first glance similar to our extended Minsky model. The differences, however, are critical, the most important being that euphoric expansion is explained within our theoretical model and not merely assumed as it is in theirs.

4.3 Bail-out

The 'bail-out' thesis contends that implicit or explicit deposit guarantees offered to, coupled with poor supervision of, the banking system, produce a moral hazard problem of overlending (see, for example, Krugman, 1998A). At the international level the interaction between capital flows and financial liberalisation, leads to what McKinnon and Pill (1997) have labelled 'The Overborrowing Syndrome'.

According to this view, the willingness of the authorities to support failing financial institutions is a key factor encouraging the latter to indulge in excessive risk-taking and speculative behaviour. This phenomenon, it is suggested, is a prime source of the financial fragility and euphoria that in turn leads foreign currency markets to lose touch with fundamentals. Prevent it and all will be right with the (financial) world.

The bail-out theory may employ Minsky-like terminology, but it confuses the cause-and-effect relationship he identifies and, we would argue, thoroughly misinterprets reality as a result. It is a matter of historical fact that intervention by the state, in whatever sphere, has been prompted by prior perceived failure in the unregulated environment. In the financial domain, this has certainly been the case: instability has always pre-dated intervention. To imagine therefore that ending intervention would be sufficient to bring about an end to instability would be like imagining that one could completely cure a recurrently ill patient who happened also to be suffering side-effects from certain prescribed drugs, simply by taking him off all medication.

Since the *raison d'être* of 'bail-out' is as a policy response to *prior* perceived fragility within the banking system, it is a matter of logic, therefore, that fragility cannot be regarded as simply a product of government-induced imperfections. That said, it is important to note that Minsky was fully alert to the issues raised by official support given

254   P. Arestis and M. Glickman

to ailing financial institutions (see, for example, Minsky, 1986, p. 199). However, the conclusions he reached were very different from those of the modern bail-out theorists: the support the authorities were on occasion obliged to offer to giant banks, he remarked (*ibid.*) 'implies that (they) are too big for a non-interventionist, free-market economy'.

4.4 'Defects' of the Asian model

A further argument holds the supposed problematic nature of the Asian Model, the core of which is industrial policy, as squarely responsible for the Southeast Asian crisis. This view was stated emphatically by the *Economist*: 'Most of the financial mess is of Asia's own making, and nowhere is this clearer than in South Korea. For years, the government has treated the banks as tools of state industrial policy, ordering them to make loans to uncreditworthy companies and industries' (15 November 1997; see also Brittan, 1997). Various responses can be made to this argument. The first is to point out that not all five countries discussed in this paper pursued activist industrial policies with the same vigour (for details, see Jomo and Rock, 1998). Consequently, the contention that 'industrial policy could not have been a major factor in causing crisis in the Southeast Asian economies, because there was, simply, little of it around' (Chang, 2000, p. 9), seems eminently justified. Furthermore, the argument can be turned on its head: the Southeast Asian problems can be explained in part by the way the countries concerned backed away from the Asian Model.

That the Asian Model worked well is widely acknowledged internationally. For example, the World Bank (1993) stated that, in the case of these economies, 'government interventions (have) resulted in higher and more equal growth than otherwise would have occurred' (p. 6). Ever since the early 1990s, however, the model has been in retreat. Financial liberalisation has itself been partly responsible. But other aspects of the model were independently being eclipsed. In the case of South Korea, for example, it has been argued that 'it was the demise of industrial policy rather than its perpetuation which drove the Korean economy into crisis' (Chang *et al.*, 1998, p. 739). Indeed, 'It was, for example, the end to the policy of investment coordination that allowed the proliferation of duplicative investments in the key industries that fuelled the massive foreign borrowing between 1993 and 1997 . . . In addition, the demise of industrial policy, as well as the official end in 1993 to the three-decade-old five-year-planning practice, led to the disappearance of the "rational" criteria according to which government supports had been previously allocated' (Chang, 2000, p. 11). It thus becomes empirically difficult to justify the argument that industrial policy, in the form of the Asian Model, was responsible for the crisis. It is altogether more plausible to make the reverse argument, that pressures to back away from Model played their part in the crisis which ensued.

4.5 Cronyism

A view articulated in this journal and elsewhere by Wade (1998) and Wade and Veneroso (1998) is that the source of the crisis in Southeast Asia was the extraordinarily high household savings (encouraged by government policies), which led to unacceptably high debt–equity ratios. The latter could only persist through 'mutually supportive and symbiotic relationships between government, banking and industry—what neo-conventional commentators now call "crony capitalism"' (Dean, 2001, p. 268). Their conclusion is that unrestricted inflows of foreign capital upset that symbiosis and resulted in the crisis. The trouble with the cronyism thesis is that it leaves critical questions of timing unanswered, as Chang (1998) has suggested: viz. (i) why did cronyism produce catastrophe so suddenly in 1997, and (ii) why did it not undermine the region's high growth rates long before? It is also pertinent to ask why hard-headed foreign investors, supposedly so acutely conscious of information asymmetries, committed such vast quantities of funds to the economies of the region so contentedly and for so long a time.

The nature and scope of cronyism must have changed before the crisis. As mentioned above, under the discussion of the Asian Model, the dismantling of industrial policy, financial regulation and five-year planning after the late 1980s reduced significantly the influence of the state in resource allocation. The inference is that, following the dismantling of controls and financial liberalisation, the ensuing financial euphoria must have been associated with increased corrupt behaviour in both the private and public sectors (Kindleberger, 1996, ch. 5). But despite this expectation, in reality the situation was very different. As reported in Table 7, the 'corruption perception index' (CPI), compiled by Transparency International, improved substantially in the period leading up to the crisis: on a scale of 0 (very corrupt) to 10 (very clean), all five countries in our sample experienced diminishing cronyism. We may conclude, agreeing with Chang (2000) and Radelet and Sachs (1998A), that the credit ratings of all the economies that were about to be overtaken by the crisis were actually improving over the period of the 1990s until its very eve.

4.6 Some general comments

As Krugman (1997) has acknowledged, 'the . . . recent theoretical literature on self-sustaining currency crisis does not do the job' (Dean, 2001, p. 267). It is the main thesis of this paper that our extension of Minsky's closed economy model can do so comfortably. A comparison between these rival views and ours suggests that, whilst there may be some common ground, the differences are crucial. The most striking of these relates to the question of whether the source of the Asian crisis was endogenous or exogenous and the related issue of the coincidence or otherwise of financial liberalisation and financial crisis. A further crucial difference is that whilst at least some of the two views just reviewed hold one group of actors or another, lenders, borrowers or the authorities, responsible for the crisis, our Minskyan thesis incorporates all of them into an endogenous interpretation of the crisis. We may conclude therefore that ours is more general approach.

Table 7. *Corruption perception index (scale: 0 = very corrupt; 10 = very clean)*

Country	Period	
	1988–92	1996
Malaysia	5·10	5·32
South Korea	3·50	5·02
Thailand	1·85	3·33
Indonesia	0·57	2·65
Philippines	1·96	2·69

Source: Transparency International (1997); see also Chang (2000, pp. 786–7, note 12).

256   P. Arestis and M. Glickman

5. Policy implications

In his closed-economy analysis, Minsky emphasises the stabilising capabilities of 'big government' (a fiscal authority involved with large spending and tax programmes) and a 'big bank' (a lender-of-last-resort) (see, for example, Minsky, 1986, ch. 13). The key role of big government is to influence investment via business profits. Thus, in a downturn deficits are necessary to boost profits and the 'big bank' acts to prevent debt deflation. A further implication is explicit in the conclusion reached by the World Bank (1993) that 'A policy of moderate financial repression at positive interest rates may have boosted aggregate investment and growth in the HPAE's [High Performing Asian Economies] by transferring income from depositors, primarily households, to borrowers, primarily firms' (pp. 238–9).

These policy tools can only be effective, however, if accompanied by increased central bank supervision of bank balance sheets. As Minsky (1988) puts it, 'rather than assuming a hands-off position on the oversight of activities, the Federal Reserve will have to increase its role in guiding financial behaviour along lines that contribute to stability' (p. 28). Specific policies to enhance central bank supervision include higher reserve requirements and extensive use of discount window facilities in ways that encourage hedge financing. 'Reforms that tilt the credit arrangements of industrial and commercial firms toward hedge rather than speculative or Ponzi finance are desirable' (Minsky, 1988, p. 28). For example, central bank provision of discount facilities may be predicated upon bank purchases of less risky assets and lower asset-to-equity ratios.

This analysis, however, is *only* applicable in the case of a closed economy. In the open economy of a financially globalised world, there is currently no counterpart to 'big government' or 'the big bank', but the implication of our analysis is that we must build in this direction. A revamped IMF/World Bank may be a relevant suggestion. This could well take the form of Keynes's (1980) suggestion of an international clearing union. Davidson's (1992/93) and Arestis's (1999) proposals, the first concerning the international scene and the second the European stage, are firmly based on Keynes' proposal. But such action could validate risky bank behaviour, and would need to be supplemented by the open-economy counterpart of Minsky's proposals to encourage hedge financing. Under current conditions of a globalised drive towards financial innovation, the most readily available tool for achieving this goal would seem to be capital controls.

This suggestion may be particularly relevant to the countries under scrutiny in this paper as well as other developing economies. As we have argued above, relaxation of capital controls has contributed substantially to the fragility of the financial system. The experience of countries such as China and India, where capital controls remain much in evidence and which were little affected by the crisis, is very telling.

We should also note that Malaysia reimposed wide-ranging capital controls on 1 September 1998, allowing interest rates to fall and financial markets to recover, and that even IMF officials now argue that capital controls may be the least damaging way out of this crisis. Mainstream economists, too, argue in favour of capital controls (for example, Krugman, 1998C). UNCTAD (1998) summarises the argument by suggesting that 'In the absence of global mechanisms for stabilising capital flows, controls will remain an indispensable part of developing countries' armory of measures for the purpose of protection against international financial instability' (1998, p. XI). Wittingly or not, policy makers are coming round to an acceptance of the following prescription put forward by Minsky (1977): 'Once a fragile financial structure exists, . . . policy should try to induce behaviour that tends to diminish the weight of speculative finance in the economy. This may very well require some control over the liability structures and asset/equity ratios of giant corporations and banks' (p. 152).

Not all official responses to the crisis have been inspired by such insight into its nature, however. For example, in November 1997 the Indonesian government, on IMF advice, closed 16 'unsound' banks, whilst the Thai authorities responded to the crisis by closing 50 finance companies, and it is expected that five of the country's 15 commercial banks will be allowed to fail. The Indonesian government's bank closures, far from resolving the crisis, worsened the financial panic. Depositors and investors responded by removing a further $2bn in a flight to safety. In a leaked internal report, *Indonesia Standby Agreement: Review Under Emergency Financing Procedures* (reported in the *Guardian*'s Notebook, 15 January 1998), the IMF acknowledged this worsening, recognising that two-thirds of deposits were actually shifted, and admitted that the authorities had had to pump in resources equivalent to 5% of GDP to prevent systemic collapse.

These arguments are reinforced by the fact that the Asian financial crisis emerged shortly after the financial sectors of the countries affected had been deregulated. This experience suggests that any benefits of financial liberalisation would have to be weighed against the cost of increased financial fragility. In fact, a number of contributors have taken the view that some degree of financial regulation is preferable to liberalisation in developing countries (see, for example, Caprio and Summers, 1993; Stiglitz, 1994; Hellman *et al.*, 1996). In Asian countries liberalisation has produced particularly high costs and low benefits because they have in any case achieved consistently high levels of saving which are then re-cycled as loans to corporations and, furthermore, the latter are closely linked with governments (Wade and Venoroso, 1998, p. 5).

A major policy implication of orthodox analysis is that even more extensive liberalisation of finance, international trade and the labour market, as well as more privatisation, is called for. However, the conflict between the principles underlying such free market prescriptions and the interventionist practice inherent in, for example, the IMF-inspired $110bn aid package for Asia seems to have gone unnoticed. There is a strong case for suggesting that financial liberalisation is *never* a good policy prescription, even in principle, because it necessarily makes the financial system more fragile. Liberalisation has both a domestic aspect (removing interest rate and credit allocation controls) and an external aspect (removal of capital controls). The absence of such controls inevitably removes safeguards that might contribute towards preserving the stability of the financial system. Sound supervision and other conventional prudential measures may help to alleviate fragility but can never eliminate it. Thus, some form of 'financial repression' may be necessary, as Arestis and Demetriades (1997) and Hellman *et al.* (1996) have argued, especially in the case of developing countries.

6. Summary and conclusions

The Southeast Asian crisis began in early July 1997. Serious contagion of financial disturbance across countries ensued, fuelled by the fact that the region's currencies were on the whole pegged to the US dollar. Rigid in the face of changes in domestic conditions, these currencies became prime targets for speculators once the latter took the view that they were overvalued. The *currency* crisis in Thailand in the summer of 1997 (when the baht was devalued) spread almost overnight to Malaysia, Indonesia and the Philippines. In November 1997, South Korea's currency also came under heavy pressure from specu-

258   P. Arestis and M. Glickman

lators. The won was devalued but the IMF had to be called in to help finance its short-term debts. Several major firms in South Korea were declared insolvent and by mid-December smaller firms were failing at the rate of 50 per day. Short-term interest rates soared to just over 30%.

Minsky argued that high growth rates and low unemployment were threatened by the instability of the financial system. The lesson to be drawn from recent financial crises in Southeast Asia, and elsewhere, is that liberalisation intensifies this threat by adding further major stresses to the financial infrastructure. Our thesis is that we have witnessed in Southeast Asia a financial crisis explicable in classically Minskyan terms, in which financial liberalisation has acted as the key euphoria-inducing factor. The timing and features of liberalisation in the five countries are exactly right to account for the state of fragility which evidently existed when the crisis broke and for the form that the crisis took. Grabel (1995) has argued that, under financial liberalisation, economies are forced to bear a greater degree of 'ambient' risk than they would otherwise face. A Minskyan analysis gives us a clear insight into how that comes about.

Whilst orthodox accounts of the Asian crisis are essentially *a priori*, a close examination of the course of events which led to the crisis points to the very different conclusion that the fundamental problem was not over- but under-regulation, as we have argued (see also Singh, 1998; Chang, 1998). Our extension of Minsky's work shows how dangerous an illusion it is to imagine that a governmental retreat from involvement in the functioning of the financial system will do anything to enhance stability. Our contention is that the Minskyan approach, by providing us with the tools to dispel such illusions, offers original and general insights into the financial crises that have been so grave a feature of the world economy in the last twenty years.

Bibliography

Arestis, P. 1998. Recent banking crises: Minsky versus the financial liberalisationists, presented at the International Conference on The Legacy of Hyman Minsky, University of Bergamo (Department of Economics), Bergamo, Italy, 10–12 December

Arestis, P. 1999. The independent European Central Bank: Keynesian alternatives, *Arche Interdisciplinar*, vol. VIII, no. 23, 145–77

Arestis, P. and Demetriades, O. P. 1996. Finance and growth: institutional considerations and causality, *Zagreb International Review of Economics and Business*, vol. 2, no. 1, 37–62

Arestis, P. and Demetriades, O. P. 1997. Financial development and economic growth: assessing the evidence, *Economic Journal*, vol. 107, no. 442, 783–99

Arestis, P., Demetriades, O. P. and Luintel, K. 2001. Financial development and economic growth: the role of stock markets, *Journal of Money, Credit and Banking*, vol. 33, no. 1, 16–41

Bhattacharya, A., Claessens, S. and Hermandez, L. 1997. 'Recent Financial Market Turbulence in Southeast Asia', mimeo, The World Bank, Washington, DC

Brittan, S. 1997. Asian model R.I.P., *Financial Times*, 4 December

Caprio, G. and Summers, L. 1993. 'Finance and its Reform: Beyond Laissez-Faire, Policy Research', Working Paper No. 1171, The World Bank, Washington DC

Chang, H-J. 1998. Korea: the misunderstood crisis, *World Development*, vol. 26, no. 8, 1555–61

Chang, H-J. 2000. The hazard of moral hazard—untangling the Asian crisis, *World Development*, vol. 28, no. 4, 775–88

Chang, H-J., Park, H-J. and Yoo, C. G. 1998. Interpreting the Korean crisis: financial liberalisation, industrial policy and corporate governance, *Cambridge Journal of Economics*, vol. 22, 735–46

Chote, R. 1998. Financial crises: the lessons of Asia, in *Financial Crises and Asia*, Centre for Economic Policy Research Conference Report, no. 6, London, Centre for Economic Policy Research

Coggins, B. 1998. *Does Financial Deregulation Work? A Critique of Free Market Approaches*, Cheltenham, Edward Elgar

Davidson, P. 1992–93. Reforming the world's money, *Journal of Post Keynesian Economics*, vol. 15, no. 2, 153–79

Dean, J. (2001), East Asia through a glass darkly: disparate lenses on the road to Damascus, pp. 267–92, in Lim, H., Park, K. and Harcourt, G. C. (eds), *Editing Economics: Essays in Honour of Mark Perlman*, London, Routledge

Demirguc-Kunt, A. and Detragiache, E. 1998. 'Financial Liberalisation and Financial Fragility', Working Paper of the International Monetary Fund, 98/83, June, Research Department, International Monetary Fund, Washington, DC

Dymski, G. A. 1998. 'Bubble Economy and Financial Crisis in East Asia and California: A Spatialized Minsky Perspective', mimeo, University of California, Riverside

Fazzari, S. and Papadimitriou, D. B. (eds) 1992. *Financial Conditions and Macroeconomic Performance: Essays in Honour of Hyman P. Minsky*, Armonk, M. E. Sharpe

Gertler, M. 1988. Financial structure and aggregate economic activity, *Journal of Money, Credit and Banking*, Part 2, 559–88

Glickman, M. 1994. The concept of information, intractable uncertainty and the current state of the efficient markets theory, *Journal of Post Keynesian Economics*, vol.16, no. 3, 325–49

Goldstein, M. 1998. *The Asian Financial Crisis: Causes, Cures, and Systemic Implications*, Policy Analyses in International Economics, no. 55, Washington, Institute for International Economics

Grabel, I. 1995. Speculation-led economic development: a post-Keynesian interpretation of financial liberalization programs, *International Review of Applied Economics*, vol. 9, no. 2, 127–49

Greenspan, A. 1997. *Testimony Before the Committee on Banking and Financial Services*, 13 November, Washington, DC, House of Representatives

Greenspan, A. 1998. *Testimony Before the Committee on Banking and Financial Services*, 30 January, Washington, DC, House of Representatives

Harvey, J. T. 1996. Orthodox approaches to exchange rate determination, *Journal of Post Keynesian Economics*, vol.18, no. 4, 567–83

Hellman, T., Murdock, K. and Stiglitz, J. E. 1996. Deposit mobilisation through financial restraint, in Hermes, N. and Lensink, R. (eds), *Financial Development and Economic Growth*, London, Routledge

Institute of International Finance 1998. *Capital Flows to Emerging Market Economies*, September, 29, Washington, DC, Institute of International Finance

Institute of International Finance 1999. *Capital Flows to Emerging Market Economies*, April, 25, Washington, DC, Institute of International Finance

Jomo, S. K. 1998. *Tigers in Trouble*, London: Zed Press

Jomo, S. K. and Rock, M. 1998. ''Economic Diversification and Primary Commodity Processing in the Second-tier South-East Asian Newly Industrialising Countries', UNCTAD Discussion Paper No. 136, Geneva, United Nations conference on Trade and Development

Kaminsky, G. L. and Reinhart, C. M. 1998. Financial crises in Asia and Latin America: then and now, *American Economic Review*, vol. 88, no. 2, 444–8

Kaminsky, G. L. and Reinhart, C. M. 1999. The twin crises: the causes of banking and balance-of-payments problems, *American Economic Review*, vol. 89, no. 3, 473–500

Keynes, J. M. 1980. Activities 1940–4: Shaping the post-war world: the clearing union, in Robinson, A. and Moggridge, D. (eds), *The Collected Writings of John Maynard Keynes*, vol. XXV, London: Macmillan

Kindleberger, C. 1996. *Manias, Panics, and Crashes: A History of Financial Crises*, 3rd edn, London, Macmillan

Kregel, J. 1998. Minsky and Asia: 'It' Did Happen Again, paper presented at the International Conference on The Legacy of Hyman Minsky, University of Bergamo (Department of Economics), Bergamo, Italy, 10–12 December

Krugman, P. 1979. A model of balance-of-payments crises, *Journal of Money, Credit, and Banking*, vol. 11, no. 3, 311–25

Krugman, P. 1997. The currency crisis, http://www.mit.edu/Krugman (October)

Krugman, P. 1998A. What happened in Asia?, http: //www.mit.edu/Krugman (January)

Krugman, P. 1998B. Bubble, boom, crash: theoretical notes on Asias crisis, http: //www.mit.edu/Krugman (January)

260   P. Arestis and M. Glickman

Krugman, P. 1998C. Saving Asia: it's time to get radical, *Fortune Investor*, 7 September

Martinez, G. O. 1998. What lessons does the Mexican crisis hold for recovery in Asia?, *Finance and Development*, vol. 35, no. 2, 6–9

McKinnon, R. and Pill, H. 1997. Credible economic liberalisation and overborrowing, *American Economic Review*, vol. 87, Papers and Proceedings, 189–93

Minsky, H. P. 1957. Central banking and money market changes, *Quarterly Journal of Economics*, vol. 71, 171–87

Minsky, H. P. 1975. *John Maynard Keynes*, New York, Columbia University Press

Minsky, H. P. 1977. A theory of systemic fragility, in E. I. Altman and A. W. Sametz (eds), *Financial Crises: Institutions and Markets in a Fragile Environment*, New York, John Wiley

Minsky, H. P. 1978. The financial instability hypothesis: a restatement, *Thames Papers in Political Economy*, Autumn

Minsky, H. P. 1982. *Can 'It' Happen Again?: Essays in Instability and Finance*, Armonk, M. E. Sharpe

Minsky, H. P. 1986. *Stabilizing an Unstable Economy*, New Haven, Yale University Press

Minsky, H. P. 1988. Back from the brink, *Challenge*, no. 31, 22–8

Minsky, H. P. 1992. Hyman P. Minsky, in Arestis, P. and Sawyer, M. (eds), *A Biographical Dictionary of Dissenting Economists*, Aldershot, Edward Elgar

Minsky, H. P. 1995. Financial factors in the economics of capitalism, *Journal of Financial Services Research*, no. 9, 197–208

Neely, M. C. 1999. Paper tigers? How the Asian economies lost their bite, *The Regional Economist*, January, 5–9

Obstfeld, M. 1996. Models of currency crises with self-fulfilling features, *European Economic Review*, vol. 40, no. 1, 1037–47

Radelet, S. and Sachs, J. 1998A. The East Asian financial crisis: diagnosis, remedies and prospects, *Brookings Papers on Economic Activity*, no. 1, 1–90

Radelet, S. and Sachs, J. 1998B. 'The Onset of the East Asian Financial Crisis', NBER Working Paper, no. 6680, August

Singh, A. 1997. Stock markets, financial liberalisation and economic development, *Economic Journal*, vol. 107, no. 442, 771–82

Singh, A. 1998. '"Asian Capitalism" and the Financial Crisis', mimeo, University of Cambridge

Stiglitz, J. E. 1994. The role of the state in financial markets, pp. 19–52 in Bruno, M. and Pleskovic, B. (eds), *Proceedings of the World Bank Annual Conference on Development Economics, 1993*, Washington, DC, World Bank

Transparency International 1997. *Corruption Perception Index*, www.transparency.de/documents/source-book/c/cvA/a6.html

United Nations Conference on Trade and Development 1998. *Trade and Development Report, 1998*, New York and Geneva, United Nations

Wade, R. 1998. From 'miracle' to 'cronyism' in the Asian crisis, *Cambridge Journal of Economics*, vol. 22, no. 6, 693–706

Wade, R. and Venoroso, F. 1998. The Asian crisis: the high debt model versus the Wall Street–Treasury–IMF complex, *New Left Review*, March/April, no. 228, 3–23

Williamson, J. and Mahar, M. 1998. *A Survey of Financial Liberalisation*, Princeton Essays in International Finance, no. 211, Princeton NJ, Princeton University, International Finance Section, November

Wolf, M. 1998. Flows and blows, *Financial Times*, 3 March

World Bank 1993. *The East Asian Miracle: Economic Growth and Public Policy*, Oxford, Oxford University Press

World Bank 1997. *World Development Report 1997: The State in a Changing World*, Oxford, Oxford University Press

[23]

Cambridge Journal of Economics 1998, **22**, 663–676

Capital market crises: liberalisation, fixed exchange rates and market-driven destabilisation

Lance Taylor*

External financial crises are not caused by an alert private sector taking advantage of the public sector's foolish actions such as running an unsustainable fiscal deficit or creating moral hazards. They are better described as private sectors (both domestic and foreign) acting to make destabilising short-term profits when policy and circumstances provide the preconditions and the regulatory authorities acquiesce. Policy alternatives are discussed in the present global macroeconomic environment, in particular the counter-productive interventions of the International Monetary Fund in East Asia.

1. Tolstoy was wrong (about international capital markets, at least)

Everyone knows the epigraph to *Anna Karenina*, 'Happy families are all alike; every unhappy family is unhappy in its own way'. Tolstoy may well have been right about families, but the extension of his judgement to economies hit by capital market crises distinctly fails. Their causes and unhappy consequences in Latin America and Asia over the past 20 years have many elements in common.

These boom and bust episodes were *not* caused by excessive fiscal expansion or the creation of wholesale moral hazards by market-distorting state interventions. Rather, they pivoted around the government's withdrawal from regulating the real side of the economy, the financial sector, and especially the international capital market. This pre-meditated laxity created strong incentives for destabilising private sector financial behaviour, on the part of both domestic and external players. Feedbacks of their actions to the macroeconomic level upset the system.

To think about how markets can be rebuilt in more stable fashion, we have to under-stand why the crises happened in the first place. That is not an easy task. A plausible place to begin is with the models that economists have designed to explain events such as Latin America's 'Southern Cone' crisis around 1980, European problems with the ERM in 1992, Mexico and the 'tequila' crisis in 1994, and events in East Asia in 1997–98. We begin in Section 2 with a review of mainstream work—accounting conventions, crisis

Manuscript received 11 August 1998.

* New School for Social Research. This paper draws heavily on the results of a project on International Capital Markets and the Future of Economic Policy, Center for Economic Policy Analysis, New School for Social Research, with support from the Ford Foundation. Comments by Alice Amsden, Jane D'Arista, Thorsten Block, Sandy Darity, Roberto Frenkel, Gerry Helleiner, and the referees are gratefully acknowledged. An expanded version of this paper will be published by the United Nations Conference on Trade and Development.

models, 'moral hazards', and other abstract niceties. We then go on to a narrative pro-posed by people who operate close to macro policy choices and micro financial decisions. Experience shows that the overlap between mainstream models and the reality they are supposed to describe is slight; the practitioners' framework fits history better. In Section 3, it is used as a basis for suggestions about reasonable policy lines to follow in wake of the recent disasters.

2. Existing theory

This section comprises a review of existing crisis theories. It begins with relatively innocuous but important accounting conventions, and goes on to present mainstream models and a more plausible alternative.

Accounting preliminaries

Table 1 presents a simplified but realistic set of accounts for an economy with five institutional sectors—households, business, government, a financial sector, and the rest of the world.

How each sector's saving originates from its incomes and outlays is illustrated in the top panel. Households in the first line receive labour income W, transfers from business J_b (that is, dividends, rents, etc.) and from government J_g, and interest payments ξ_h on their assets held with the financial system. They use income for consumption C_h, to pay taxes T_h, and to pay interest Z_h to the financial system. What is left over is their saving S_h. To keep the number of symbols in Table 1 within reason, households are assumed to hold liabilities of the financial system only. That is, their holdings of business equity are 'small' and/or do not change, and they neither borrow nor hold assets abroad. The last two assumptions reflect a major problem with the data—it is far easier to register funds flowing

Table 1. *Macroeconomic accounting relationships*

Generation of savings	
Household:	$S_h = W + J_b + J_g + \xi_h - C_h - T_h - Z_h$
Business:	$S_b = \Pi - J_b - T_b - Z_b - eZ_b^*$
Government:	$S_g = T_h + T_b - C_g - J_g - Z_g - eZ_g^*$
Financial system:	$0 = Z_h + Z_b + Z_g - \xi_h$
Foreign:	$S_f = e[M + Z_b^* + Z_g^* - E]$
Resource balance	
	$S_h + S_b + S_g + S_f = W + \Pi - (C_h + C_g) + e(M - E)$
Investment–saving balance	
	$(I_h - S_h) + (I_b - S_b) + (I_g - S_g) = S_f$
Accumulation	
Household:	$(I_h - S_h) = \Delta D_h - \Delta H_h$
Business:	$(I_b - S_b) = \Delta D_b + e\Delta D_b^*$
Government:	$(I_g - S_g) = \Delta D_g + e\Delta D_g^*$
Financial system:	$0 = \Delta H_h - (\Delta D_h + \Delta D_b + \Delta D_g - e\Delta R^*)$
Foreign:	$0 = S_f - e(\Delta D_b^* + \Delta D_g^*) + e\Delta R^*$
Spreads	
Interest rate:	$\Sigma_i = i - [i^* + (\Delta e / e)^E] = i - (i^* + e^E)$
Capital gains:	$\Sigma_Q = (\Delta Q / Q)^E - [i^* + (\Delta e / e)^E = \hat{Q}^E - (i^* + e^E)$

into a country via the capital market than to observe money going out as capital flight by numerous less than fully legal channels. Repatriation of such household assets is implicitly treated as foreign lending to business or government in the discussion that follows.

Similar accounting statements apply to the other sectors. Business gets gross profit income Π, and has outlays for transfers to households, taxes T_b, and interest payments to the local financial system (Z_b) and the rest of the world. The latter payment, eZ_b^*, amounts to Z_b^* in foreign currency terms converted to local currency at the exchange rate e. Business saving S_b is profits net of these expenditures. It will be lower insofar as interest payments Z_b and eZ_b^* are high. Firms in Asia are often said to suffer from constricted saving possibilities because their debt/equity ratios are high. Standard stabilisation programmes that drive up interest rates and currency values and thereby Z_b and eZ_b^* can easily lead to heavy business losses (negative values of S_b), culminating in waves of bankruptcy.

Government saving S_g is total tax revenue net of public consumption C_g, transfers to households, and interest payments at home (Z_g) and abroad (eZ_g^*). For simplicity, the financial system is assumed to have zero saving, so that its interest income flows from households, business, and government just cover its payments to households. Finally, 'foreign saving', S_f, in local currency terms is the exchange rate times the foreign currency values of imports (M) and interest payments less exports (E). The implication is that the rest of the world applies part of its overall saving to cover 'our' excess of spending over income.

This interpretation shows up clearly in the 'resource balance' equation or the sum of all the savings definitions. It shows that total saving results from the excesses of income from production $(W + \Pi)$ over private and public consumption $(C_h + C_g)$, and of imports over exports. Or in other words S_f equals total income minus total outlays and the sum of domestic saving supplies.

Likewise, the 'investment–saving balance' shows that the sum over sectors of investment less saving must equal zero. Much of the macroeconomic drama in recent crises results from large shifts in these 'financial deficits'. They show up in each sector's accumulation of assets and liabilities in the penultimate panel of the table.

Households, for example, are assumed to finance their deficit $(I_h - S_h)$ by running up new debt ΔD_h with the financial system, partially offset by their greater holdings of the system's liabilities or the increase ΔH_h in the 'money' supply.[1] Business and government both cover their deficits by new domestic (the ΔD terms) and foreign (the ΔD^* terms) borrowing.

The accounts for the financial system and the rest of the world are slightly less transparent, but essential to the following discussion. The former's flow balances show that new money creation ΔHh is backed by increases in domestic debt owed by households, business, and government, as well as by increases in the system's foreign reserves $e\Delta R^*$. In the foreign balance, reserve increments and foreign saving are 'financed' by increases in the foreign debts of business and government $e(\Delta D_b^* + \Delta D_g^*)$.

How the 'spreads' in Table 1's last panel enter the analysis is taken up below. What we can do now is say something about how the public sector was supposed to be the prime culprit for 'old' financial upheavals, for example, the debt crisis of the 1980s. This assertion is far from the truth, but it is so widely accepted that we must discuss it on its own terms.

---

[1] The 'Δ' term signifies a change over time, e.g., $\Delta H_h = H_h(t) - H_h(t-1)$ where $H_h(t)$ and $H_h(t-1)$ are money stocks at the ends of periods t and $t-1$ respectively.

666   L. Taylor

Mainstream crisis models

The first post-Second World War wave of developing economy crises in which private external financial flows played a significant role took place around 1980. The countries affected included Turkey in the late 1970s, the Southern Cone in 1980–81, Mexico and many others in 1982, and South Africa in 1985. The Southern Cone collapses attracted great attention. They teach significant lessons about how market deregulation by the public sector and private responses to it can be extremely destabilising.

The academic models underlying the belief that the public sector fiscal expansion 'caused' the early crises are built around a regime shift (or 'transcritical bifurcation' in the jargon of elementary catastrophe theory). They emphasise how gradually evolving 'fundamentals' can alter financial returns in such a way as to provoke an abrupt change of conditions or crisis—a ball rolls smoothly over the surface of a table until it falls off.

The regime change is triggered when the profit from liquidating a 'distortion' created by the state intervention becomes large enough—investors choose their moment to punish the government for interfering in the market. Such sentiments underlie balance-of-payments crisis models of the sort proposed by Krugman (1979) and pursued by many others. They assert that expansionary policy when the economy is subject to a foreign exchange constraint can provoke a flight from the local currency.[1]

In a typical scenario, the nominal exchange rate is implicitly assumed to be fixed or have a predetermined percentage rate of devaluation $\hat{e} = \Delta e / e$. Moreover, the local interest rate i exceeds the foreign rate i^*. Under a 'credible' fixed-rate regime, the expected rate of devaluation $\hat{e}^E = (\Delta e / e)^E$ will equal zero. From the last panel of Table 1, the interest rate 'spread' $\Sigma_i > 0$ will favour investing in the home country.

Now suppose that the government pursues expansionary fiscal policy, increasing the fiscal deficit $I_g - S_g$. If the household and business sectors do not alter their behaviour, the investment–saving balance in Table 1 shows that foreign saving S_f or the external current-account deficit has to rise. A perceived 'twin deficit' problem of this sort lies at the heart of traditional IMF stabilisation packages that have thrown many countries (now including those in East Asia) into recession.[2] The external imbalance can lead to crisis via several channels. We describe two.

The first is based on the recognition that the government has to issue more debt, i.e., in the 'Accumulation' panel of Table 1, ΔD_g or ΔD_g^* must rise when $I_g - S_g$ is increased. Assume that the government is credit-constrained in external markets so that ΔD_g expands. To maintain its own balances, the financial system can 'monetise' this new debt so that ΔH_h goes up as well. If the domestic price level P is driven up by money creation (which does not always happen), then the real value of the currency eP^* / P (where P^* is the foreign price level) will appreciate or decline in absolute value. Imports are likely to rise and exports to fall, leading to greater external imbalance. With more borrowing ruled out by assumption, foreign reserves will begin to erode.

Falling reserves suggest that the trade deficit cannot be maintained indefinitely. When

---

[1] The following discussion concentrates on 'first generation' speculative attack models because they have had the major impact on the policy debate. 'Second generation' models make the fundamentals sensitive to shifts in private expectations, thereby allowing extrinsic, random 'sunspot' shocks to generate multiple equilibria. The mathematical complications are intriguing to the academic mind but add little to attempts to understand historical crises. There are numerous surveys of these models. Nouriel Roubini's useful website, www.stern.nyu.edu/~nroubini/asia/AsiaHomepage, contains an ample selection.

[2] Pieper and Taylor (1998) present a fairly up-to-date review. In various numbers of its *World Economic Outlook*, the IMF is 'up front' about attributing crisis in both Latin America and Asia to 'incompatibilities;' between macro policies and the exchange rate regime as well as 'excessive regulation' and 'too little competition' in the financial sector.

they are exhausted, presumably there will have to be a discrete 'maxi'-devaluation, a regime shift which will inflict a capital loss on external investors holding liabilities of the home country denominated in local currency. At some point, it becomes rational to expect the devaluation to occur, making $\hat{e}^E$ strongly positive and reversing the spread. A currency attack follows. The economically untenable fiscal expansion is instantly erased.

A second version of this tale is based on the assumption that the local monetary authorities raise 'deposit' interest rates to induce households to hold financial system liabilities created in response to greater public borrowing. In the financial system balance in the first panel of Table 1, ξ_h will increase so that interest rates on outstanding domestic debts have to go up as well.

The spread Σ_t immediately widens. Foreign players begin to shift portfolios toward home assets, so that from the foreign accumulation balance in Table 1 reserves begin to grow. If the monetary authorities allow the reserve increase to feed into faster growth of the money supply, we are back to the previous story. If they 'sterilise' a higher ΔR^* by cutting the growth of household (ΔD_h) or business (ΔD_b) debt, then interest rates will go up even further, drawing more foreign investment into the system. From the foreign accumulation balance, pressures will mount for the current account deficit S_f to increase, say via exchange appreciation induced by inflation or else a downward drift of the nominal rate as the authorities allow the currency to gain strength. A foreign crisis looms again.

Moral hazards

The notion of moral hazard comes from the economic theory of insurance. The basic idea is that insurance reduces incentives for prudence—the more fire insurance I hold on my house, the more arson becomes an intriguing thought. Insurance companies frustrate such temptation by allowing homeowners to insure their properties for no more than 75% or so of their market valuations.

In the finance literature, moral hazard has been picked up in diverse lines of argument. Writing in an American context, the unconventional macroeconomist Hyman Minsky (1986) saw it as arising after the 1930s as a consequence of counter-cyclical policy aimed at moderating real/financial business cycles. As is always the case, such economic engineering had unexpected consequences.

One was a move of corporations toward more financially 'fragile' positions, leading them to seek higher short-term profitability. With no fears of price and sales downswings, high-risk/high-return projects became more attractive. This shift was exemplified by increased 'short-termism' of investment activities, and the push toward merger and acquisition (M&A) activity in the 1970s and 1980s.

Second, the intermediaries financing such initiatives gained more explicit protection against risky actions by their borrowers through 'lender of last resort' (or LLR) interventions on the part of the Federal Reserve. The resulting moral hazard induced both banks and firms to seek more risky placements of resources. Banks, in particular, pursued financial innovations. Among them were the elimination of interest-rate ceilings on deposits and the consequent creation of money market funds which effectively jacked up interest rates in the 1970s, a push towards high risk/high return loans that led to the Savings and Loan (S&L) crisis of the 1980s, the appearance of investment funds and 'asset securitisation' at about the same time, and the later emergence of widespread derivatives markets and hedge funds.

To an extent all these changes were driven by a gradual relaxation of restrictions on external capital movements (D'Arista, 1998). When Eurocurrency markets began to

668   **L. Taylor**

boom in the 1970s, the higher deposit rates they paid put pressure on US regulators to lift interest-rate ceilings. Meanwhile, without reserve requirements offshore banks (and offshore branches of American banks) could lend more cheaply in the domestic market, leading to further deregulation. The US took the lead in pushing for new regulatory mechanisms, e.g., the 'Basle' standards for capital adequacy adopted in 1988.

Unfortunately, these changes introduced a strong pro-cyclical bias into regulation, just the opposite of the sort of system that should be in place. In an upswing, banks typically have no problem in building up equity to satisfy adequacy requirements. In a downswing, however, unless they already have the capital they can easily be wiped out. As will be seen, such regulatory structures helped exacerbate developing-country financial crises.

So far, moral hazard looks sensible; it can be used to underpin plausible historical narratives. Extensions out of context begin to stretch verisimilitude. Deposit insurance, for example, certainly played a role in the S&L crisis in the US. In the Garn St. Germain Act of 1982, depositors were allowed to have any number of fully insured $100,000 accounts with an S&L. With their prudential responsibilities removed by the Act, S&L managers were free to engage in any high-risk, high-return projects they saw fit—which they immediately proceeded to do.

However, a frequently stated extension of this observation to developing country markets makes less sense. For example, deposit guarantees have been accused of worsening the Southern Cone crises, but in Chile they had been abolished precisely to avoid moral hazard! Similarly, for (South) Korea, Krugman's (1998) assertion that the government provided implicit guarantees for banks and industrial corporations holds no water. He argues that Korean conglomerates or *chaebol* engaged in reckless investment and had low efficiency, as proven by their low profitability. But as Chang, Park, and Yoo (1998) point out, profitability was low only *after* interest payments, not before. Moreover, over the 1980s and 1990s the government did *not* bail out any *chaebol*; in the period 1990–97 three of the 30 biggest ones went bankrupt. The government did have a history of stepping in to restructive enterprises in trouble, but that left little room for moral hazard—managers knew they would lose control over their companies if they failed to perform.

Despite such shaky empirical antecedents, moral hazard is given a central role in mainstream crisis models. In a typical example, Dooley (1997) argues that developing country governments self-insure by accumulating international reserves to back up poorly regulated financial markets. National players feel justified in offering high returns to foreign investors, setting up a spread. Domestic liabilities are acquired by outsiders (or perhaps nationals resident in more pleasant climes or just engaging in offshore manipulations) until such point as the stock of insured claims exceeds the government's reserves. A speculative attack follows.

The leitmotif of an alert private sector chastising an inept government recurs. This time the state encourages reckless investment behaviour. All a sensible private sector can be expected to do is to make money out of such misguided public action.

A more plausible theory
A more realistic perspective is that the public and private sectors generate positive financial feedbacks between themselves first at the micro and then at the macro level, ultimately destabilising the system. This line of analysis is pursued by Salih Neftci (1998), a market practitioner, and Roberto Frenkel (1983), a macroeconomist. Both focus on an initial situation in which the nominal exchange rate is 'credibly' fixed (setting the $\hat{e}^E$ terms

equal to zero in Table 1's equations for spreads), and show how an unstable dynamic process can arise. A Frenkel–Neftci (or FN) cycle begins in financial markets which generate capital inflows. They spill over to the macroeconomy via the financial system and the balance of payments as the upswing gains momentum. At the peak, before a (more or less rapid) downswing, the economy-wide consequences can be overwhelming.

To trace through an example, suppose that a spread Σ_i (e.g., on Mexican government peso-denominated bonds with a high interest rate but carrying an implicit exchange risk) or Σ_Q (e.g., capital gains from booming Bangkok real estate, where $\hat{Q}$ is the growth rate of the relevant asset price) opens. A few local players take positions in the relevant assets, borrowing abroad to do so. Their exposure is risky but *small*. It may well go unnoticed by regulators; indeed for the system as a whole the risk is negligible.

Destabilising market competition enters in a second stage. The pioneering institutions are exploiting a spread of (say) 10%, while others are earning (say) 5% on traditional placements. Even if the risks are recognised, it is difficult for other players not to jump in. A trader or loan officer holding 5% paper will reason that the probability of losing his or her job is close to 100% *now* if he or she does not take the high-risk/high-return position. Such potentially explosive behaviour is standard market practice, as interview studies by Rude (1998) and Sharma (1998) make clear. In the former's words, 'the speculative excesses of the international investors in the Asian financial crisis were not an exception, . . . but instead the result of normal business practices and thus to a certain degree inevitable.'

After some months or years of this process, the balance sheet of the local financial system will be risky overall, short on foreign currency and long on local assets.[1] Potential losses from the long position are finite—they at most amount to what the assets cost in the first place. Losses from short-selling foreign exchange are in principle unbounded—who knows how high the local currency-to-dollar exchange rate may finally have to rise?

In a typical macroeconomic paradox, individual players' risks have now been shifted to the aggregate. Any policy move that threatens the overall position—for example, cutting interest rates or pricking the property bubble—could cause a collapse of the currency and local asset prices. The authorities will use reserves and/or regulations to prevent a crash, consciously ratifying the private sector's market decisions. Unfortunately, macro-economic factors will ultimately force their hand.

In a familiar scenario, suppose that the initial capital inflows have boosted domestic output growth. The current-account deficit S_f will widen, leading at some point to a fall in reserves as capital inflows level off and total interest payments on outstanding obligations rise. Higher interest rates will be needed to equilibrate portfolios and attract foreign capital. In turn, S_b will fall or turn negative as illiquidity and insolvency spread à la Minsky, threatening a systemic crisis. Bankruptcies of banks and firms may further contribute to reducing the credibility of the exchange rate.

A downturn becomes inevitable, since finally no local interest rate will be high enough to induce more external lending in support of what is recognised as a short foreign exchange position at the economy-wide level. Shrewd players will unwind their positions

---

[1] For analysis in the Asian context, see Islam (1998). There may also be problems with maturity structures of claims, especially if local players borrow from abroad short term. Nervous foreign lenders may then compare a country's total external payment obligations over the next year (say) with its international reserves. Such ratios proved disastrous for Mexico in 1995 and several Asian countries in 1997. A maturity mismatch in which local players borrow short term abroad and lend long term at home may be less significant—a property developer will default on his or her loan if the property market crashes, regardless of whether it is formally of short or long duration.

670   L. Taylor

before the downswing begins (as Mexican nationals were said to have done before the December 1994 devaluation); they can even retain positive earnings over the cycle by getting out while the currency weakens visibly. But others—typically including the macro-economic policy team—are likely to go under.

The dynamics of this narrative differ from that of standard crisis models—it does *not* involve a regime shift when a spread Σ_I or Σ_Q switches sign from positive to negative. Rather, movements in the spread itself feed back into cyclical changes within the economy that finally lead to massive instability. Reverting to catastrophe theory jargon, the standard models invoke a 'static' instability such as a buckling beam. More relevant to history are 'dynamic' or cyclical instabilities that appear when effective damping of the dynamic system vanishes. A classic engineering example is the Tacoma Narrows suspension bridge. Opened in July 1940, it soon became known as 'Galloping Gertie' because of its antics in the wind. Its canter became strong enough to make it disintegrate in a 41-mile-per-hour windstorm in November of that year. Despite their best efforts, economists have yet to design a system that fails so fast.

Finally, a *soupçon* of moral hazard enters an FN crisis, but more by way of pro-cyclical regulation than through 'promised' LLR interventions or government provision of 'insurance' in the form of international reserves. After a downswing, some players will be bailed out and others will not, but such eventualities will be subject to high discount rates while the cycle is on the way up. In that phase, traders and treasurers of finance houses are far more interested in their spreads and regulatory acquiescence in exploiting them than in what sort of safety net they may or may not fall into some time down the road.

3. Policy alternatives

A companion paper (Taylor, 1998) reviews experiences in the Southern Cone around 1980, Mexico in 1994–95, and Asia in 1997–98. Its principal conclusion is that financial crises are not made by an alert private sector taking advantage of the public sector's fiscal or moral hazard foolishness. They are better described as private sectors (both domestic and foreign) acting to make high short-term profits when policy and history provide the preconditions and the public sector acquiesces. Mutual feedbacks between the financial sector and the real side of the economy then lead to a crisis. By global standards, the financial flows involved in a Frenkel–Neftci conflagration are not large—$10–20 billion of capital flows annually (around 10% of the inflow the US routinely absorbs) for a few years are more than enough to destabilise a middle income economy. The outcomes are now visible worldwide.

A number of policy issues are posed by these episodes. It is convenient to discuss them under three headings: steps which can be taken at the country level to reduce the likelihood of future conflagrations; actions both an afflicted country and the international community can take to cope with a future crisis, when and if it happens; and how the international regulatory system might be modified to enhance global economic comity and stability.

Avoiding Frenkel–Neftci cycles

Rather than a formal model, Neftci and Frenkel provide a framework which can be used to analyse crisis dynamics. There are five essential elements: (1) the nominal exchange rate is fixed or close to being predetermined; (2) there are few barriers to external capital inflows and outflows; (3) historical factors and current circumstances act together to create wide spreads of the form Σ_I and Σ_Q in Table 1—these in turn generate capital movements which push the domestic financial system in the direction of being long on domestic assets and short on foreign holdings; (4) regulation of the system is lax and probably pro-cyclical; (5) macroeconomic repercussions via the balance of payments and the financial systems' flows of funds and balance sheets set off a dynamic process that is unstable.

To a greater or lesser extent, national policy-makers can prevent these components from coming together explosively.

(1) There are often good reasons to have a pegged nominal exchange rate. It is anti-inflationary, which was crucially important to Latin American stabilisation packages, beginning with Mexico's in the late 1980s. It can also enhance export competitiveness, as happened when countries in South-east Asia pegged to the falling dollar after the Plaza Accord. Problems with a pegged rate arise when it contributes to big spreads and (especially) when it is over-valued. These are good arguments for a thoughtfully designed crawling nominal depreciation or (harder for developing economies with thin foreign exchange markets to manage) a 'dirty' float. An even better argument is that such an exchange rate regime can help avoid real appreciation, which in turn can widen the trade deficit, bring in capital inflows or induce reserve losses, and kick off an unstable macro cycle.

(2) Without international assistance it is virtually impossible to prevent capital from fleeing the country in a crisis; it is much more feasible to construct obstacles to slow it down (at least) as it comes in. In the recent period, Chile and Colombia have had some success with prior deposits and taxes on inflows, especially when they are short term. In a not much more distant past, Asian economies had fairly effective restrictions on how much and how easily households and firms could borrow abroad. In non-crisis times, acquisition of foreign assets can also be monitored.

The key task is to prevent a locational mismatch in the macro balance sheet, with a pre-ponderance of foreign liabilities (especially short term) and national assets. Local regulatory systems can certainly be configured toward this end. If imbalances are detected, the relevant authorities can direct or encourage players to unwind their positions.

(3) Under a fixed exchange rate regime, it is easy to spot a 10% differential between local and foreign short-term interest rates or a similarly sized gap between the growth rate of the local stock-market index or property prices and a foreign borrowing rate. Such yields are an open invitation to capital inflows that can be extremely destabilising. Whether policy-makers feel they are able to reduce interest rates or deflate an asset market boom is another question, one that merits real concern.

Another source of potential spreads is through off-balance-sheet and derivative operations. Here, local regulators can be at a major disadvantage—they do not necessarily know the latest devices. Staying up to date as far as possible and inculcating a culture of probity in the local financial system are the best defences here.

(4) There is of course a serious question as to whether many developing-country regulatory systems can meet such goals, especially in the wake of liberalisation episodes. Another difficulty arises with timing. It is very difficult to put a stop to capital flows *after* the financial system has a locationally unbalanced position; at such a point, interest rate increases or a discrete devaluation can easily provoke a crash. The authorities have to stifle a destabilising cycle early in its upswing; otherwise, they may be powerless to act.

(5) Each balance-of-payments crisis is *sui generis*; to produce a set of formal descriptions one would have to write a separate model for each episode in each country. Many of the

672   L. Taylor

components, however, would be the same. The simplest classification is in terms of disequilibria between stocks and flows, along with microeconomic correlates. Here are some examples:

Flow–flow. One key issue here is identifying the internal 'twin(s)' of an external deficit. In the country examples discussed in Taylor (1998), the financial deficits were in the hands of the private sector—business or households. The follow-up question is how they are being paid for. Are rising interest obligations likely to cut into savings and investment flows? Are flows cumulating to produce locational or maturity mismatches in balance sheets? Another precursor of crisis is the relationship between the volume of capital inflows and the current-account deficit. If the former exceeds the latter, reserves will be rising, perhaps lulling the authorities into a false sense of security. As in the Southern Cone crises, it will rudely vanish when interest payments on accumulating foreign debt begin to exceed the amount of capital flowing in.

Stock–flow. Have some asset or liability stocks become 'large' in relation to local flows? East Asia's short-term debt exceeding 10% of GDP in 1996 was a typical example; it was a stock with a level that could change rapidly, with sharply destabilising repercussions. Rapid expansion of bank credit to the private sector as a share of GDP while booms were underway in the Southern Cone, Mexico, and Thailand might have served as an early warning indicator, had the authorities been looking. The causes included monetisation of reserve increases and growth of loans against collateral assets such as securities and property with rapidly inflating values.

Stock–stock. Besides lop-sided balance sheets in the financial sector, indicators such as debt/equity ratios and the currency composition of portfolios (including their 'dollarisation' in Latin America recently) become relevant here. They can signal future problems with financing investment–saving differentials of the sort presented in Table 1. For example, producers of non-traded goods may borrow in dollar terms from the local banking system. In the event of a devaluation, their real incomes would fall and some might not be able to service their debts. A crisis could follow, even if banks had held their 'dollar' liabilities and assets generally in balance. It could be avoided if the central bank had ample reserves to back an LLR operation in dollars, but many countries are not so lucky.

Microeconomics. Micro-level developments go along with these macro changes. Investment coordination across firms may be breaking down, leading to 'excess competition'; property speculation and luxury consumption may be on the rise.

The problem with all such indicators is that they lag an unstable dynamic process. By the time they are visibly out of line it may be too late to attempt to prevent a crisis; its management becomes the urgent task of the day.

Moral hazard abroad?

Within countries, moral hazard did not play a central role in generating crises. On the side of the lenders, it also did not seem to be important. In the East Asian crisis, international banks were the big offenders. In 1996 there had been a net flow of capital into the five most affected economies of $93 billion. There was a net outflow of $12 billion in 1997, with the most volatile item being commercial bank credit, which shifted from an inflow of over $50 billion in 1996 to an outflow of $21 billion the following year. The overall turnaround of $105 billion was close to the five countries' total reserves of $127 billion and exceeded 10% of their combined GDP (about two percentage points higher than the impact of the 1982 debt crisis on the GDP of Latin America). It was a supply shock with sharp contractionary effects on the macroeconomy. Taking advantage of the short-term nature of their credits, the banks ran from their borrowers before they had a chance to default, making default itself, or a massive international bail-out, a self-fulfilling prophecy.

Did the banks enter heavily into Asian lending because of moral hazards from home, or did they just like the spreads? One will never know for certain. Perhaps the Americans were emboldened by the Mexican 'rescue' of 1995, which pumped tens of billions of dollars through that economy back to its creditors on Wall Street (the Mexicans themselves are now trying to cope with bad internal debt to the tune of 15% of GDP that the rescue left behind). But the same cannot be said about the Europeans and Japanese. The fact that all international players left so fast suggests that they did not place much faith in the 'implicit guarantees' that the Asian governments allegedly had offered.

Rescue attempts

Once a country enters into a payments crisis, it cannot cope on its own. International assistance has to be called in. Each situation follows its own rules, but there are a few obvious 'dos' and 'don'ts' for the actions of the rescue team. We begin with the former.

The contrast between Mexico's and Asia's 'rescues' is striking. At least for the creditors, the rescue did happen in 1995; in 1998 it did not. Very slow disbursement of funds by the International Monetary Fund may well be crippling the Asian effort permanently, pushing fundamentally healthy economies from illiquidity into insolvency. Against the $105 billion external shock that the region received in 1997, international financial institutions may disburse around $45 billion in 1998.

The first and most obvious 'do' that emerges is to disburse rescue money fast. In Helleiner's (1998) words, '[f]inance that is supplied only on the basis of negotiated conditions and which is released only the basis of compliance with them . . . is *not* liquidity'. East Asian economies became highly illiquid in 1997. By mid-1998, their position had not significantly improved, despite more than six months of Fund psychotherapy accompanied by liquidity transfusions on a homeopathic scale.

In fact, the transfusions might not even have been required if the rescuers had 'bailed-in' the countries' creditors instead of bailing *them* out. By appealing to G7 regulatory authorities if need be, the IMF presumably has enough clout to prevent international creditors—especially large international banks—from closing out Asian borrowers overnight. This is a sort of 'do' that should be built into rescue protocols before the next crisis strikes.

After a crisis, countries often also have an ample load of 'bad debt', typically non-performing assets of the banking sector. Domestic re-financing via a bond issue to the non-bank private sector, an administratively enforced credit roll-over, and price inflation are three ways of dealing with the problem. The latter two would almost certainly require re-imposition of tight controls on outward capital movements, which the international community would have to abet.

Distributional questions also come to the fore. As nations, the Asians are big and visible. But what about small, poor, raw material or assembled goods exporters in sub-Saharan Africa, Central America, the Pacific, and the Caribbean? Several have been hit by rapid reversals of private capital inflows. Presumably they merit international help as much as Korea or Thailand. They are not now receiving it.

Within all afflicted countries, income generation and employment problems are critical. The authorities can repress their peoples, up to a point, but ultimately they will have to

674   L. Taylor

offer them a degree of social and economic support. Such an effort goes diametrically against the emphasis of Fund-type packages. As Singh (1998) puts it

To provide such assistance effectively and on an adequate scale will require not only considerable imagination but also a large expansion in government activity and often direct intervention in the market processes. Such emergency safety net programs may include wider subsidies, food for work schemes, and public works projects. How to pay for these measures within the limits of fiscal prudence, let alone within IMF fiscal austerity programs, will be a major issue of political economy for these countries.

The most obvious 'don't' is *not* to liberalise the capital accounts of affected countries further. If the single most apparent cause of crisis was a door three-quarters open, the last thing one wants to do is move it the rest of the way. A similar observation applies to attempts to restructure economic institutions in depth in crisis-afflicted economies. This strategy is now being pursued by the IMF in Asia, Russia, and elsewhere, using conditionality-laden credit disbursements as bait. This effort runs directly against well-entrenched social and economic structures. It will undoubtedly fail, leaving a big store of political resentment to be paid for in the future.

Changing the global regulatory system
The foregoing observations lead naturally to five suggestions for restructuring international financial arrangements.

First, recent experiences demonstrate that the global macroeconomic/financial system is not well understood. 'Miracle economies' one month turn into incompetent bastions of 'crony capitalism' the next, and the commentators do not skip a beat. Under such circumstances, an immediate recommendation is for humility on the part of the major institutional players (Eatwell and Taylor, 1998). There is *no* reason to force all countries into the same regulatory mould; international institutions should wholeheartedly support whatever capital market, trade, and investment regimes that any nation, after due consultation, chooses to put into place.

Second, international agencies should support national regulatory initiatives. There was a lot of information available from the BIS and other sources about the gathering storm in Asia; it was not factored into either the private or public sectors' calculations. If national regulators are made more aware of what is happening in their countries, perhaps they can take prudent steps to avoid a pro-cyclical bias in their decisions.

Third, the IMF seems unlikely to receive large additional sums of money to allow it to serve as a (conditional) lender of last resort. It will therefore have to become more of a signaller to other sources of finance, for example, central banks and the BIS. That opens room for new forms of regional cooperation such as Japan's summer 1997 proposal for an Asian bail-out fund, which died after being opposed vigorously by the US government and the IMF. Such institutional innovations should be thought through seriously, and very possibly put into place.

Fourth, specific changes in international regulatory practices may make sense. One obvious modification to the Basle capital adequacy provisions is to permit 20% as opposed to 100% backing on loans to non-OECD countries for maturities of (say) only three months or less, as opposed to one year at present. Such an adjustment should substantially reduce incentives for banks to concentrate their lending to developing countries in the short term.

Finally, there is no independent external body with power to assess the IMF's actions.

More transparency (especially regarding relationships between the American government and the Fund) and independent evaluations of the IMF are sorely needed in light of its largely unsuccessful economy-building enterprises in post-socialist nations and now in East Asia.

Postcript

It will take the economic historians many years to sort out the tumultous changes in Russia during the 1990s, and certainly the currency crisis of summer 1998 is not yet fully understood. Nevertheless, its key features were consistent with the framework sketched in this paper. The capital market had been open since the 'global shock' of 1992, facilitating capital flight (permitted by the trade surplus and foreign lending) to the tune of $20–30 billion per year. The exchange rate was strong, with real ruble purchasing power at least doubling between 1993 and 1996, when the nominal rate was stabilised as an anti-inflation 'anchor'. Finally, there was virtually no domestic financial regulation.

Money emission had been cut back sharply (indeed the money/GDP ratio was very low by international standards), and the government was paying high interest rates on short-term liabilities. Equity prices rose sharply, beginning in 1996. Both interest rate and capital gains spreads were large and foreign investors poured in. As the relevant intermediaries, Russian financial institutions assumed a locationally unbalanced position (long in rubles, short in dollars); in particular, banks borrowed heavily abroad to speculate on the government's short-term liabilities. They were effectively bankrupted by the devaluation in August.

The main contrast with Mexico and East Asia was that, owing to a collapse in tax collection, there was a large fiscal deficit which supported the government bill market. The other side of that coin was strict monetary policy in a Muscovite re-run of early Reagonomics. The resulting high interest rates and strong ruble were part and parcel of the débâcle.

Bibliography

Chang, H.-J. Park, H. J. and Yoo, C. G. 1998. Interpreting the Korean crisis: financial liberal-isation, industrial policy, and corporate governance, *Cambridge Journal of Economics*, this issue
D'Arista, J. 1998. 'Financial Regulation in a Liberalized Global Environment', Center for Economic Policy Analysis, New School for Social Research, mimeo
Dooley, M. P. 1997. 'A Model of Crises in Emerging Markets', Department of Economics, University of California at Santa Cruz, mimeo
Eatwell, J. and Taylor, L. 1998. 'International Capital Markets and the Future of Economic Policy', Center for Economic Policy Analysis, New School for Social Research, mimeo
Frenkel, R. 1983. Mercado financiero, expectativas cambiales, y movimientos de captal, *El Trimestre Economica*, vol. 50, 2041–76.
Helleiner, G. K. 1998. *The East Asian and Other Financial Crises: Causes, Responses, and Prevention*, Geneva, United Nations Conference on Trade and Development
Islam, A. 1998. *Dynamics of Asian Economic Crisis and Selected Policy Implications*, Bangkok, Economic and Social Commission for Asia and the Pacific
Krugman, P. 1979. A model of balance-of-payments crises, *Journal of Money, Credit, and Banking*, vol. 11, 311–25.
Krugman, P. 1998. 'What Happened to Asia?' Department of Economics, Massachusetts Institute of Technology, mimeo
Minsky, H. P. 1986. *Stabilizing an Unstable Economy*, New Haven, CT, Yale University Press

676   L. Taylor

Neftci, S. N. 1998. 'FX Short Positions, Balance Sheets, and Financial Turbulence: An Interpretation of the Asian Financial Crisis, Center for Economic Policy Analysis, New School for Social Research, mimeo

Pieper, U., and Taylor, L. 1998. The revival of the liberal creed: the IMF, the World Bank, and inequality in a globalized economy, in Baker, D. Epstein, G. and Pollin, R. (eds) *Globalization and Progressive Economic Policy: What are the Real Constraints and Options?* New York, Cambridge University Press

Rude, C. 1998. 'The 1997–98 East Asian Financial Crisis: A New York Market-informed View', New York, Department of Economic and Social Affairs, United Nations, mimeo

Sharma, K. 1998. 'Understanding the Dynamics behind Excess Capital Inflows and Excess Capital Outflows in East Asia', New York, Department of Economic and Social Affairs, United Nations, mimeo

Singh, A. 1998. ' "Asian Capitalism" and the Financial Crisis', Center for Economic Policy Analysis, New School for Social Research, mimeo

Taylor, L. 1998. Lax public sector, destabilizing private sector: origins of capital market crises, in United Nations Conference on Trade and Development, *International Monetary and Financial Issues for the 1990s*, vol. 10, forthcoming

[24]

Review of International Economics, 10(1), 92–112, 2002

Monetary Policy in the Aftermath of Currency Crises: The Case of Asia

Taimur Baig and Ilan Goldfajn*

Abstract

The paper evaluates monetary policy and its relationship with the exchange rate in the five Asian crisis coun-tries. The findings are compared with previous currency crises in recent history. It is found that there is no evidence of overly tight monetary policy in the Asian crisis countries in 1997 and early 1998. There is also no evidence that high interest rates led to weaker exchange rates. The usual tradeoff between inflation and output when raising interest rates suggested the need for a softer monetary policy in the crisis countries to combat recession. However, in some countries, corporate balance sheet considerations suggested the need to reverse overly depreciated currencies through firmer monetary policy.

1. Introduction

What is the appropriate monetary policy in the aftermath of a currency crisis? Should interest rates be raised to appreciate the currency? The Asian crisis has put these ques-tions at the center of economic policymaking. This paper attempts to shed light on this question by analyzing a few episodes of large currency depreciation in the aftermath of currency crises during the Asian crisis.

The analysis of the appropriate monetary policy in the aftermath of currency crises has four building blocks. The first is to evaluate whether the exchange rate has over-shot during the crisis; or in other words, whether the real exchange rate (RER) has become undervalued and needs to be brought back to equilibrium. The second block is to identify the mechanisms through which the RER could be corrected in case it is undervalued (or maintained in case the new level is deemed appropriate). Under-valuation can be reversed through either nominal currency appreciation or higher inflation at home than abroad (or a combination of the two). If avoiding an inflation buildup is an important concern and/or nominal appreciation is desirable for the benefit of domestic corporate and bank balance sheets, the extent to which the rever-sal occurs through nominal appreciations is fundamental. A key factor in evaluating the likelihood of this reversal is to estimate the exchange rate passthrough in the economy—the extent to which the correction is expected to occur through inflation in the economy, in the absence of major changes in policies. The third block is to iden-tify through which policies and under what circumstances the reversal occurs through nominal appreciation. In particular, it is important to evaluate whether nominal appre-ciations occur mainly in cases where interest rates are kept high. In addition, it is also important to evaluate whether other economic conditions, for example the state of the banking system and corporate sector, influence the relationship between interest and

_____

*Baig: International Monetary Fund, Room 3-314D, 700 19th Street, NW, Washington, DC 20008, USA. Tel: (202) 623-8790; Fax: (202) 589-8790; E-mail: tbaig@imf.org. Goldfajn: Pontificia Universidade Catolica, Departamento de Economia, Marques de Sao Vicente, 225 Rio de Janeiro, Brazil. Tel: (5521) 274-2797; Fax: (5521) 294-2095; E-mail: goldfajn@econ.puc-rio.br. We wish to thank Bijan Aghevli, Andrew Berg, Debra Glassman, David Goldsbrough, Prakash Loungani, Kanitta Meesook, Jonathan Ostry, Mark Stone, Wanda Tseng, Jeromin Zettelmeyer, and seminar participants and reviewers at the International Monetary Fund, the World Bank, and the University of Washington at Seattle.

exchange rates. Finally, the fourth block is to evaluate the desirability of raising interest rates. Even if one identifies a set of policies and conditions that maximizes the effect of interest rates on the exchange rate, the costs of raising interest rates in terms of output loss, unemployment, and financial system fragility could outweigh the benefits of a more appreciated nominal exchange rate.

There is considerable debate on each of the four building blocks in general, and for the case of Asia in particular. The debate on the right measure of undervaluation (or overvaluation) has always been controversial, with some even doubting the notion that a currency could be fundamentally out of line. In the case of Asia, there is doubt whether the currencies were overvalued before the crisis and whether, despite the large real depreciation that followed the crisis, the currencies became undervalued (some argue that the extent of the shock justifies a much lower real exchange rate). With respect to the extent of exchange rate passthrough, initial estimates suggest that the Asian economies have a much lower passthrough than typical developing countries, which implies that the real depreciation has persisted for longer than in other crisis cases, but also implies that the correction of the RER would likely occur through nominal appreciations (unless the current passthrough estimates reflect longer lags in Asia).

In this context, the relationship between interest rates and exchange rates has come under renewed focus. The traditional approach stresses that tight monetary policy is necessary to support the exchange rate and curb inflationary pressures. In the short run, higher interest rates make speculation more expensive by increasing the cost of shorting the domestic currency. Also, higher interest rates increase the return that an investor obtains from investing in the country. In the long run, higher interest rates may affect the exchange rate by reducing absorption and improving the current account. However, in the discussion of the role of monetary policy in the Asian crisis; several economists have raised the possibility that an increase in interest rates would have a negative effect on the exchange rate.

The other big debate on the role of monetary policy is on the *desirability* of increasing interest rates to support the exchange rate. Some doubt the optimality of tight policies. This line of argument takes as given that high interest rates may eventually stabilize the exchange rate, but argues that the costs of doing so are very high and that letting the exchange rate float freely (and possibly become more undervalued for a while) is the least costly option. The costs of a tight monetary policy are usually identified with a large recession, unemployment, financial system bankruptcies, credit crunch, and corporate failures. Of course, there are also costs in letting the exchange rate depreciate further, as argued by Goldstein (1998):

> When market participants lose confidence in a currency and attach a high probability to further falls, it is difficult to induce them to hold the currency without higher interest rates. . . . Moreover, halting a free fall of the currency takes on added importance when banks or corporations in the crisis country have large foreign currency obligations coming due in the short term.

Section 2 explores the issue of the extent of undervaluation in Asia and some other cases. It goes on to analyze the exchange rate passthrough in the Asian crisis case and compares it with other cases in history. Section 3 explores the link between exchange rates and interest rates in the aftermath of the Asian crisis. In section 4, the tradeoffs involved in the decision to raise interest rates are analyzed.

2. Overshooting and Reversals

The effectiveness and desirability of implementing tight monetary policies to stabilize a currency crisis depends to a certain extent on the underlying causes of the crisis. A fair amount of attention has been dedicated to the question of what caused the Asian crisis. There are three broad explanations:

1. *BOP crisis driven by traditional fundamentals* (Krugman, 1978; Flood and Garber, 1984). Overvaluation of the RER coupled with too much credit expansion results in excess demand and a growing balance of payments deficit that culminates in crisis and the adjustment of the RER.
2. *Crisis as a result of panic by investors* (Radelet and Sachs, 1998). The Asian currency crisis must be understood as a run on international reserves; i.e., as the international equivalent of commercial bank runs. Countries were vulnerable to runs because of high ratios of short-term debt to reserves.
3. *Crisis driven by more sophisticated fundamentals* (Krugman, 1998). The Asian financial crisis was caused by overlending to risky and unproductive projects fueled by explicit and implicit guarantees. The crisis occurred as the boom ended.

There is also the possibility of a combination of the explanations above. For example, one may advance the argument that fundamental reasons made the countries vulnerable to speculative attacks and that panic was an element of the crises but not their ultimate cause.

Tight monetary policy is less controversial if one believes the underlying cause for the crises is point (1) above. Increases in domestic interest rates serve simultaneously to increase the interest rate differential with respect to the rest of the world and reduce the level of activity in the economy. In contrast, the panic and financial crisis explanations are not an overheating story and, therefore, there is a *possible* tradeoff for policymakers between recession (or the health of the banking system) and currency stabilization.

In general, it would be futile to try to appreciate the currency if one believed the currency has not overshot. Therefore, the following section evaluates the equilibrium real exchange rates for both the Asian and some other currency crises cases.

Was There Overshooting?

Table 1 shows available estimates of RER overvaluation prior to the Asian crises (Indonesia, Korea, Malaysia, Philippines and Thailand) and to five other crisis cases (Mexico, 1982; Chile, 1982; Mexico, 1994; Sweden, 1992; and UK, 1992). The overvaluation estimates for the five Asian countries are taken from the literature. Goldman Sachs uses the Dynamic Equilibrium Emerging Markets Exchange Rates model to calculate the equilibrium value for a large set of countries. For each country, a cointegrating relationship between the multilateral real exchange rate and a set of fundamentals (using leads and lags) is calculated using quarterly data since 1980. The relationship between the real exchange rate and the fundamentals is interpreted as a long-term relationship and its predicted value the equilibrium exchange rate. The fundamentals include a large set of variables that are known to influence the equilibrium real exchange rate—including terms of trade, openness, government size, and capital flows. The exact set of fundamentals varies per country. The difference between the equilibrium value and the actual exchange rate is defined as a misalignment measure (overvaluation/undervaluation). Chinn (1998) uses the purchasing power

Table 1. REER Overvaluation Measures and Real Depreciations for Selected Crisis Cases (Percentages + Overvaluation)

	Overvaluation Chinn (1998) May 1997[a]	Overvaluation Goldman Sachs (1998) June 1997[b]	Goldfajn and Valdés (1996) Month prior to crisis	Real depreciation 12 months after crisis[c]
Thailand	7.0	3.9		26.0
Malaysia	7.9	4.4		25.2
Philippines	19.1	5.5		22.1
Indonesia	−5.5	1.2		68.2
Korea	−9.1	3.3		26.5
Chile (82)			17.7	19.9
Mexico (82)			25.6	43.8
Mexico (94)			22.6	27.8
Sweden (92)			9.7	20.1
UK (92)			4.6	11.1

[a] PPI-based calculation.
[b] Based on J. P. Morgan database.
[c] Based on REER from June 97 to June 98 in Asian cases.

parity concept to evaluate whether seven East Asian currencies were overvalued before the crisis. He uses a simple model that uses deviations from PPP and a trend in the real exchange rate to define misalignment. For the other crisis cases, the overvaluation measures were derived in Goldfajn and Valdés (1996) using a methodology similar to Goldman Sachs' methodology (1997, 1998).

The existence of large overvaluations would imply that one should expect large corrections of the RER in the aftermath of the crisis and would not necessarily call for policy action. The Latin American crisis cases had clear misalignment in their RER of the order of 20–25% prior to the crisis. In contrast, the European cases had only mild overvaluations. Few observers indicated at the time of the ERM crises that overvaluation was at the root of the problem. In fact, several papers, including Eichengreen et al. (1994), advanced the hypothesis that the 1992 European crises were of the self-fulfilling nature (the so-called second-generation models).

In Asia, the different estimates indicate that Malaysia, the Philippines, and Thailand systematically appear to have had the most overvalued currencies, while Korea and Indonesia had the least overvalued (Chinn's estimate indicates that the won was actually undervalued). The magnitude of the subsequent real devaluations were not correlated with the initial overvaluation measures. In fact, besides Thailand, the larger depreciations occurred precisely in Indonesia and Korea. In all the Asian cases the extent of the real devaluation was larger than the initial overvaluation. One could argue that the previous overvaluation estimates are not reliable or, alternatively, that the crisis altered significantly the equilibrium RERs such that a larger depreciation of the RER is justified. In fact, some argue that the large terms-of-trade decline in Korea justified a large equilibrium depreciation after the crisis. However, the results suggest that there was scope to believe that the currencies had overshot or, at least, that further declines in the exchange rate were not desirable.

Table 2. *Inflation, Depreciation, and Passthrough Coefficients for Selected Crisis Cases*

	CPI inflation[a]	Depreciation[a,b]	Passthrough coefficient[c] (after 1 year)	Passthrough coefficient[c] (after 2 years)
Thailand	10.8	47.7	0.23	
Malaysia	6.3	39.3	0.16	
Philippines	9.9	38.8	0.26	
Indonesia	59.6	394.4	0.15	
Korea	6.7	35.3	0.19	
Chile (82)	31.2	92.6	0.34	0.43
Mexico (82)	108.3	269.6	0.40	0.58
Mexico (94)	48.5	122.5	0.40	0.69
Sweden (92)	4.8	52.3	0.09	0.16
UK (92)	1.7	32.4	0.05	0.14

[a] First 12 months of the crisis. For Korea based on September 97 to July 98.
[b] Based on NEER for Asian countries and bilateral rates with respect to the dollar in the other cases.
[c] CPI inflation divided by depreciation.

RER Reversion and Exchange Rate Passthrough

There are two ways to reverse an undervaluation—through nominal currency appreciation or through higher inflation at home than abroad (or a combination of the two). If avoiding an inflation build-up is an important concern and/or nominal appreciation is desirable for the benefit of domestic corporate and bank balance sheets, the extent to which the reversals occur through nominal appreciations is fundamental. A key factor in evaluating the likelihood of this reversion is to estimate the exchange rate passthrough in the economy.

Table 2 shows nominal depreciations, inflation and exchange rate passthrough coefficients for the 10 episodes. It is evident that the Latin American cases are different. They had larger depreciations, higher inflations, and larger passthrough coefficients (in the order of 0.4) than the European and Asian cases. The European cases had depreciation rates of about 30–50% but only single-digit inflations in the first 12 months after the crisis, implying very low passthrough coefficients. Thus Asia is an intermediate case compared to these two cases, both in terms of inflation and passthrough coefficients.

It is interesting to note that the reversal of the real exchange rate occurred more slowly in the European cases. Inflation rates were higher in the second year after the crisis; the passthrough coefficients doubled or tripled when looking instead over the first 24 months. This suggests that, if the Asian crisis cases follow the European pattern of slower but longer adjustment of RER, there is a potential role for policies to avoid inflationary reversals. (Of course, what determines the extent of the passthrough is not only the effectiveness of short-run policies but also the inflationary history and labor market institutions of the country in question.)

In a more systematic way, Golfajn and Gupta (1999) analyze all the episodes of currency collapses that resulted in undervaluations greater than 15% from a sample of 80 countries between 1980 and 1998. The undervaluation series is defined as deviations of the actual exchange rate from a Hodrick–Prescott filtered series. The filtered series captures stochastic trends in the series. The series represents the predicted equilibrium RER and captures the permanent changes in the relative prices between countries, and the estimated undervaluation series represents the cyclical component of the RER movements since, as a misalignment, it must eventually correct itself. The approach also nets out from the undervaluation measure trends in the equilibrium RER, as for example the Balassa–Samuelson effect.

Table 3 shows the number of cases found for different degrees of undervaluations. Since 1980, there are 116 cases with undervaluations of more than 10% but only 28 with more than 30%. We calculated the probability of reversing an undervaluation through appreciation of the nominal exchange rate rather than higher inflation. We defined that a reversal is through nominal appreciation if the exchange rate is responsible for more than 50% of the reversal. The results show that the probability of a reversal through nominal appreciation is less than 40%.

Table 4 shows that the average duration of the episodes is 30 months with the overshooting reversing slowly over a period of about 20 months. This suggests that the reversal of undervaluation in Asia may be drawn out. This is an important consideration since there may be a role for policies to reduce the duration of the process even if the reversal occurs through nominal appreciation.

Table 3. Number of Undervaluation Cases

Depreciation cutoff (%)	Number of cases	Proportion of cases	
		Tight policy[a]	Banking crises[b]
10	99	32.3	41.4
15	77	29.2	45.4
20	49	22.5	46.9
25	36	17.2	50.0
30	28	13.6	57.1

[a] Tight policy is defined as real rates higher in the period than average rates.
[b] Banking crises dummies are obtained from several sources. See source.
Source: Goldfajn and Gupta (1998).

Table 4. Duration of Undervaluation Cases

Months	Build-up	Reversal	Total
1–3	0.49	0.13	0.03
4–6	0.14	0.09	0.12
7–12	0.16	0.17	0.13
13–18	0.04	0.21	0.18
19–24	0.05	0.12	0.10
25–36	0.05	0.10	0.13
37–48	0.03	0.04	0.06
48+	0.04	0.14	0.25

3. Relationship Between Interest Rates and Exchange Rates

Theoretical Considerations

The conventional wisdom is that monetary policy tightens liquidity and stabilizes the exchange rate. In the short run, higher interest rates make speculation more expensive. Also, higher interest rates increase the return that an investor obtains from investing in the country. In the long run, higher interest rates may affect the exchange rate by reducing absorption and improving the current account. In the midst of an exchange rate crisis, interest rates are raised to make speculation against the currency more costly. If borrowing (shorting) the domestic currency to invest in the foreign currency is allowed, raising interest rates directly increases the costs of speculation. Even if shorting the domestic currency is not allowed, the increase in interest rates affects the opportunity cost of an investor deciding whether to invest in the domestic economy.

The expected return in investing in the country depends on the promised interest rate and the expected depreciation. The interest differential with respect to the rest of the world should allow for both an exchange rate risk premium and a probability of default, defined as including partial payment, delay of payments, or introduction of exchange controls:

$$E[i] = i^* + E[\Delta e] + R,$$

where $E[\Delta e]$ is the expected depreciation, $E[i]$ is the expected return of an investment in the domestic economy, i^* is the safe return on an equivalent international asset, and R is the risk premium that is demanded by risk-averse foreign investors faced with exchange rate volatility. The risk premium must include also a portion for the uncertainty induced by default probability. In principle, increases in interest rates should increase the expected return, turning investing in the domestic economy more attractive relative to abroad (i.e., making the right-hand side of the equation above larger than the left-hand side) and inducing capital inflows, which would increase the supply of dollars and immediately appreciate the exchange rate up to the point where the equation holds again. (In the Dornbusch (1976) model the exchange rate should actually overshoot its target such that agents expect a future depreciation.)

However, interest increases may reduce the expected return by increasing the probability of default. Interest rates may affect the probability of default by increasing the borrowing costs of corporations, by depressing the economy and reducing profits, by altering the net worth of corporations adversely exposed to interest rate changes, or, by affecting the health of the banking system that tends to be naturally exposed to interest rate changes. The latter have a compounding effect on the economy since problems in the banking system may lead to credit crunches, disintermediation, and bad allocation of credit.

Formally, the expected return on the domestic asset, $E[i]$, can be written as the product of the domestic interest rate, i, times the probability of repayment, ρ; so $E[i] = \rho(i)i$. The equation can be rewritten in the following way:

$$\rho(i)i = i^* + E[\Delta e] + R,$$

where $r' < 0$ and $r'' < 0$.

Therefore, even though one should expect increases in interest rates to attract capital, there may be cases where additional increases in interest rates reduce the expected return and generate capital outflows. In such cases, raising interest rates paradoxically depreciates the currency.

The level of interest rates needed to defend (or appreciate) a currency may be substantial. For example, as shown by Stiglitz (1998), in order to defend an *expectation* of a 1% fall in the exchange rate the next day, the overnight interest rate must be at least 1% per day (which is 3678% per annum). If agents are risk-averse (and there is a positive risk premium, R) and the default probability is large, the required interest rate would be larger.

Proponents of tighter monetary policy argue that higher interest rates need only be temporary. Once the exchange rate has been stabilized interest rates could be allowed to decline. This argument is important given that the costs of persistently high interest rates could be substantial.

However, the question then is why should a *temporary* increase in interest rates lead to *permanent* effects on the exchange rate? One answer is that temporarily tight policies may signal the determination of the monetary authority to pursue exchange rate stability and low inflation. Temporary policies may then change the beliefs of investors. Even when the tight policies are withdrawn, the exchange rate would stabilize at a higher level.

Tight monetary policies do not always serve as a credible signaling device. Drazen and Masson (1994) have shown that, if the costs of implementing the tight policies are too high, the temporary policy would actually reduce credibility because investors know that the policy could not be sustained. Under this theory, the relationship between interest rates and the exchange rate could be negative. When there are doubts about the determination of the authorities and temporary increases in interest rates lead to important reputational gains to the authorities, the effect of raising interest rates should be positive. However, when the reputational arguments are not essential and there are important structural problems, raising interest rates may have the opposite effect.

Interest Rate Policy in the Asian Crises Episodes: 1997–98

This section analyzes interest rate policy in the aftermath of the five Asian crises (Indonesia, Korea, Malaysia, the Philippines, and Thailand). The first issue is what measure of the nominal interest rate better represents the tightness of monetary policy and its effect on the exchange rate. Figure 1 shows the "policy rates" for each of the crisis countries in 1996–98. The "policy rates" are the 1-month repo rate for Thailand, the 91-day T-bill rate for the Philippines, the 3-month Klibor for Malaysia, the 30-day JIBOR rate for Indonesia, and the overnight interbank rate for Korea. The figure suggests that, for most of the countries, the major movements of monetary policy can be captured by any of the interest rates since they tend to move together. In what follows we use the "policy rates" as our representative nominal interest rate. The figure also shows the sharp increases in nominal interest rates in the aftermath of the crisis. Most of the countries, however, seem to have waited to raise interest rates until late in 1997 or early 1998.

Indonesia initially raised interest rates substantially in July/August 1997 but reduced them subsequently, only raising them to higher levels in March/April 1998. Korea raised interest rates significantly at the end of the year, after the crisis. Thailand increased nominal rates continuously from May 1997 to March 1998.

The second issue is the appropriate expected inflation rate to be used in calculating real interest rates. The approach taken here is to calculate several measures of real interest rates based on different assumptions regarding expected inflation. Figure 2 shows five measures of real interest rates for each country. The measures are based on

© Blackwell Publishers 2002

100 *Taimur Baig and Ilan Goldfajn*

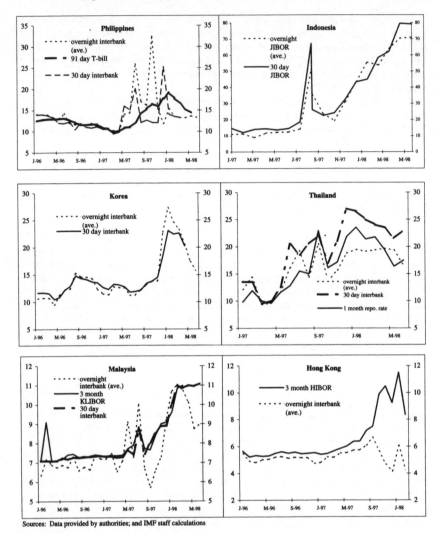

Sources: Data provided by authorities; and IMF staff calculations

Figure 1. Nominal Interest Rates (percent per annum)

expected inflation, which in turn is proxied by: (i) the following month's inflation, $\pi(t+1)$, annualized, (ii) survey forecasts from the Consensus Forecasts, (iii) the quarterly moving-average inflation centered at t, (iv) the previous month's inflation, $\pi(t-1)$, annualized, and (v) the previous 12-month inflation. The measures (iv)–(v) are based on an adaptive expectations assumption; (i)–(ii) are based on rational expectations assumptions (theoretically, the survey forecasts should be based on all the information available); and measure (iii) is a combination of the two assumptions. The main result is that, for each country, there are two distinct groups of real interest rates with similar paths within the group but differing substantially across them.

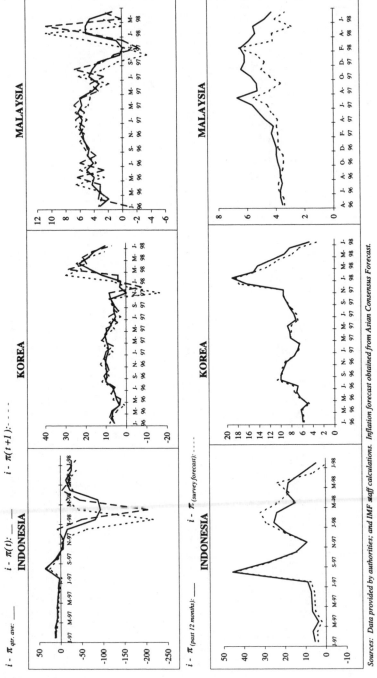

Sources: Data provided by authorities; and IMF staff calculations. Inflation forecast obtained from Asian Consensus Forecast.

Figure 2. Real Interest Rates (various measures)

102   *Taimur Baig and Ilan Goldfajn*

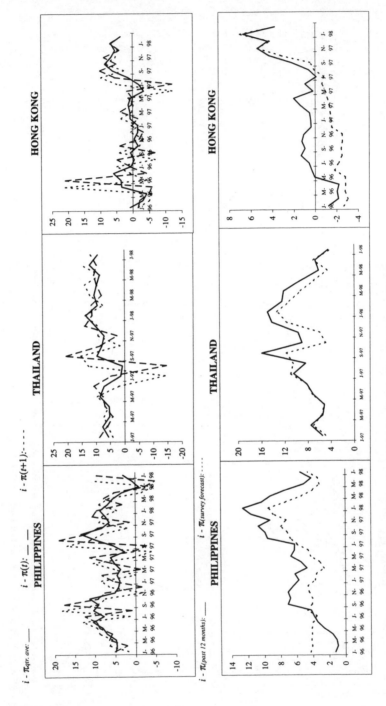

Sources: Data provided by authorities; and IMF staff calculations. Inflation forecast obtained from Asian Consensus Forecast.

Figure 2. Continued

One group, shown in the lower panel of Figure 2 for each country, is composed by the real interest rates constructed using the past-12-month-inflation rates and the one based on survey data, which, surprisingly, implies that the forecasters in the survey probably based their forecast mainly on past information. These rates are always positive throughout the crisis and its aftermath. Korea has the highest real rates of the five Asian countries in a range of 10–20% during the period, followed by Thailand at around 10%. The rest of the countries exhibit relatively moderate rates, such as Malaysia (2–6%) or Philippines (4–12%).

The other group of real interest rates uses some combination of previous, current, or future inflation as the measure of inflationary expectations. This group shows that Indonesia, Korea, and Malaysia had negative real interest rates in early 1998 and Thailand had the same in the third quarter of 1997. This is probably the consequence of the fact that inflation picked up very strongly and nominal interest rates lagged behind. For Indonesia and the Philippines, real interest rates did not reach their pre-crisis levels even a year later. The main conclusion is that there is little evidence of tight monetary policies in the Asian crisis countries in 1997 and early 1998, based on real interest rates using forward-looking measures of expected inflation.

The third issue is whether real rates are an appropriate measure to evaluate the tightness of monetary policy. One of the arguments raised in the theoretical section is that high interest rates stabilize currencies by increasing the attractiveness of the economy to (foreign) investors. This means that one could look instead at uncovered interest rate differentials to evaluate the tightness of policies. Again the procedure was to calculate several measures of uncovered interest rate differentials based on different estimates of expected depreciation. Figure 3 shows the results using expected depreciation calculated from the *Financial Times* Currency Forecaster. Similar to the real interest rate results, negative interest rate differentials are found for Malaysia, the Philippines, Korea, and Indonesia at the beginning of 1998 and for Thailand in July 1997. Also, very high interest differentials (larger than 20% per annum) emerge from March 1998 in all the countries. The results from the uncovered interest rate differentials confirm that there is little evidence of overly tight monetary policies in Asia at the beginning of the crisis through early 1998.

The relationship between real interest rates and real exchange rates for the five countries considered is shown in Figure 4. As explained in the theory section, the traditional approach stresses that one should expect a positive correlation between exogenous interest rate shocks and the exchange rate. We have no independent data on monetary policy shocks, but it is still interesting to look at the simple correlations. The evidence is mixed. In the period of the crisis July 1997 to July 1998, a fairly positive correlation exists for Hong Kong (0.55), Indonesia (0.57), Malaysia (0.42), and the Philippines (0.13). In contrast, we observe negative correlations in Korea (–0.46) and Thailand (–0.46).

One could analyze econometrically the relationship between real exchange rates and real interest rates by looking at historical data to increase the number of data points available. However, in this paper, we are restricting our attention to the correlation between these variables in crisis episodes. There are two alternative approaches. One is to extend the sample of crisis episodes and run a panel dataset regression. This approach is followed in Goldfajn and Gupta (1999). Another approach is to use higher-frequency (daily) data. In this case, we will need to focus our attention on the relationship between nominal exchange rates (national currency per unit of dollar) and nominal interest rates. Figure 5 shows the impulse responses of a vector autoregression of the changes in nominal interest rates on the changes in nominal exchange rates.

104 _Taimur Baig and Ilan Goldfajn_

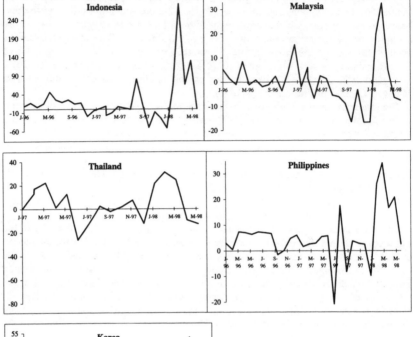

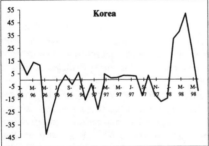

Sources: Interest rate data provided by authorities; Currency forecast obtained from Financial Times Currency Forecaster

a/ Interest Rate Differential calculated by subtracting short term US treasury Bill yield and currency depreciation forecast from representative nominal rates. All numbers have been annualized.

Figure 3. Uncovered Interest Rate Differential[a]

The results show that the effect of a shock in interest rates on the exchange rate is insignificant in all the five cases (perhaps, the only exception is the Philippines). This confirms previous results obtained by Ghosh and Phillips (1998) and Kaminsky and Schmukler (1998).

It is interesting to observe how the correlation of interest rates and exchange rates has evolved over time. Table 5 shows rolling regressions for the five Asian crisis cases plus a panel regression. The exchange rates are defined at local currency unit per dollar.

Real Effective Exchange Rates ——————
Real Interest Rates a/ — — — —

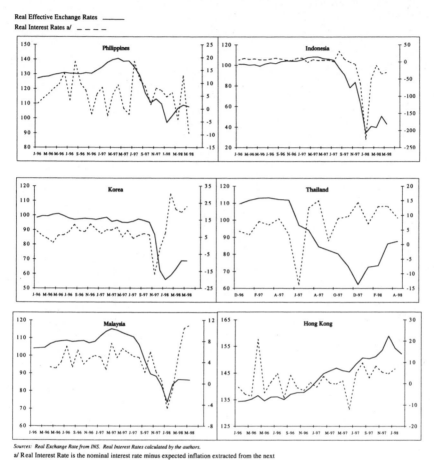

Sources: Real Exchange Rate from INS. Real Interest Rates calculated by the authors.
a/ Real Interest Rate is the nominal interest rate minus expected inflation extracted from the next
month's inflation.

Figure 4. Real Exchange and Interest Rates

As expected, when running the panel regression for the whole sample one does not
obtain a negative correlation. However, there are periods where there was a negative
correlation between the variables. In particular, one obtains a significant negative
correlation in the period from the Thailand crisis to October 1997 and from January
to April 1998. Looking at particular countries, the strongest negative correlations are
seen in Indonesia and Korea in 1997 and in the Philippines in 1998. The only positive
correlation is found for Malaysia, in the last four months of 1997.

In summary, this section has two main results. First, we find little evidence that monetary policy was overly tight in the immediate aftermath of the crises. Second, there is
no clear evidence that higher interest rates led to weaker exchange rates. If anything,
we find that there are periods where higher rates led to stronger exchange rates.

106   *Taimur Baig and Ilan Goldfajn*

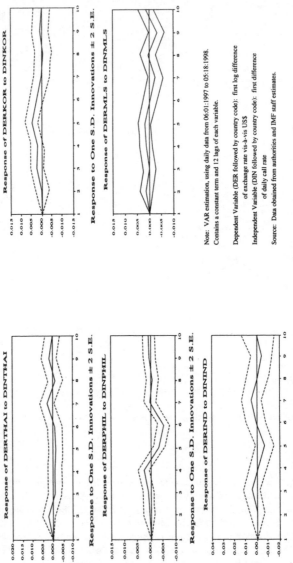

Figure 5. Impulse Response of Exchange Rate Changes due to Innovations in Interest Rate Changes

Table 5. Individual and Panel Data Regression of Nominal Exchange Rates on Nominal Interest Rates: Daily Data

	97:6–97:9	97:7–97:10	97:8–97:11	97:9–97:12	97:10–98:1	97:11–98:2	97:12–98:3	98:1–98:4	Whole sample
Fixed-effects panel (with one lag of independent variable)									
Coefficient estimate	-0.0003	-0.0002	-0.0001	-0.00006	-0.00002	-0.0001	-0.002	-0.002	-0.00009
t-statistic	-2.49**	-1.66*	-1.21	-0.29	-0.11	-0.38	-1.61*	-1.76*	-0.52
Country by country regression (with one lag of independent variable)									
Indonesia									
Coefficient estimate	-0.0006	-0.0005	-0.0006	-0.0003	0.0008	0.0005	0.0003	0.0004	-0.0004
t-statistic	-2.95**	-2.27**	-2.04**	-0.258	0.31	0.14	0.63	0.66	-0.71
Malaysia									
Coefficient estimate	0.0001	0.00008	0.002	0.005	0.001	0.002	0.001	-0.002	0.0001
t-statistic	0.28	0.16	1.00	2.21**	0.4	0.37	0.20	-0.33	0.19
Philippines									
Coefficient estimate	-0.0002	0.00003	0.000006	-0.000004	-0.000007	-0.0003	-0.0007	-0.006	-0.00004
t-statistic	-0.41	0.14	0.02	-0.01	-0.02	-0.65	-3.51**	-3.63**	-0.19
Korea									
Coefficient estimate	0.0002	-0.002	-0.01	-0.003	0.002	-0.001	0.002	0.003	-0.0009
t-statistic	0.39	-2.32**	-3.16**	-0.78	-0.45	-0.32	0.55	0.83	-0.38
Thailand									
Coefficient estimate	0.001	0.001	0.0006	0.001	0.001	-0.001	0.0009	-0.0008	0.0008
t-statistic	1.11	1.33	0.54	0.67	0.55	-0.56	0.33	-0.36	0.82

Significance at 10% and 5% levels are denoted by * and **, respectively.

4. Optimality and Tradeoffs in Raising Interest Rates

The previous section considered the question whether interest rates were very high during the Asian crises. While we do not find evidence of excessively tight monetary policy at the beginning of the crisis, our analysis so far has precluded any discussion on whether, in the context of the Asian crises, there was a case to be made in favor of high interest rates. Even if one accepts the hypothesis that a temporary rise in interest rates can stabilize exchange rates, the costs of using monetary policy may be too large to justify high rates. This section evaluates the benefits of raising interest rates to defend the currency with the alternative of letting the exchange rate overshoot.

The alternative to raising interest rates is not necessarily a free fall in the exchange rate, although the risk of a spiral inflation–depreciation exists. It is possible that large declines in the exchange rate could prompt the operation of automatic stabilizers. In the medium term, the real depreciation of the currency could induce a reversal of the current account and would generate capital inflows that would appreciate the currency. In the short run, the expectations of future recovery could bring stabilizing speculators back to the market.

The question of raising the interest rate to cause nominal appreciation, or at least stabilize the currency, is traditionally reconciled with the output–inflation tradeoff. Sustaining tight monetary policy can have negative effects on output, unemployment, and investment, the latter with important repercussions in the long run. On the other hand, allowing the exchange rate to overshoot has a negative effect on inflation. In addition, too large an exchange rate misalignment for too long may also cause recession and layoffs in the nontradable sector.

The proponents of using higher interest rates to stabilize the currency argue that the increase in interest rates need only be temporary and, therefore, the effect on output is limited. Few will dispute that a prolonged period of very high interest rates may produce such a decline in output that may tilt the tradeoff in favor of letting the exchange rate overshoot. In fact it is well known, from the experiences during the great depression and subsequent stock market crashes, that the optimal response of a first round of corporate failures is to increase liquidity (or, equivalently, reduce interest rates) rather than sustain a tight monetary policy.

It is important to consider the issue of raising rates along with factors that are not part of the conventional tradeoff. Furman and Stiglitz (1998) carry out a broad-based analysis of this issue. The relative effect of interest and exchange rates on the balance sheets of corporations (in the banking system, in particular) warrants equal attention. In this framework, the key is to evaluate the relative exposure of companies to changes in interest rates and exchange rates. The increases in interest rates raise the cost of borrowing to highly leveraged companies and, in the banking system, increases in interest rates may significantly reduce profits owing to the existence of maturity mismatches. In addition, failures in the nonbank corporate sector may induce failures in the banking system through increases in nonperforming loans. On the other hand, in the same manner that increases in interest rates may induce problems in the corporate sector, an overdepreciated currency increases the funding costs of corporations exposed to foreign currency. In particular, in developing countries with fixed exchange regimes, banks and companies tend to have a currency mismatch in their portfolio and are vulnerable to large changes in the exchange rate. One of the reasons foreign investors become skeptical about the outlook of an economy undergoing rapid currency devaluation stems from the fact that the domestic corporate sector becomes extremely fragile as the devaluation increases the foreign debt burden in domestic currency denomination. An economy's exposure to foreign debt is a crucial consideration in the policy tradeoff.

The evidence on the relative cost of interest rate versus exchange rate changes on the corporate sector is scarce. For the banking system, the study by Demirguc-Kunt and Detragiache (1997) for 30 developing and industrial countries shows that high interest rates substantially increase the probability of a financial crisis, while depreciation of currencies has little, if any, effect. Goldfajn and Gupta (1999) find that, for countries experiencing simultaneous banking and currency crises, countries with tight monetary policy have a significantly lower probability of success.

So how can policymakers distinguish between countries that will suffer more from interest rates and the ones that will be more vulnerable to currency depreciation? In Table 6, we show, for the Asian crisis cases, a few indicators that hint at the relative cost of interest rate versus exchange rate changes. Table 7 shows the same indicators for other cases of currency crises. Corporate debt/equity and credit of private sector/GDP ratios indicate how extended the private sector is, as well as its vulnerability to interest rate hikes. External debt, short-term debt in particular, indicate the extent of foreign currency exposure. From the perspective of the traditional tradeoff (output versus inflation), the overall low rates of inflation and large declines in output in the five Asian crisis cases suggest that the relative cost of an additional increase in interest rates may have been higher than an additional decline in the exchange rates. This is particularly true if a comparison with the previous Latin American currency crises is made, where inflation rates tended to be higher and output declines smaller. The only caveat is if the lags in Asia were to imply a larger passthrough in the future, as suggested in section 2, and, therefore, a higher inflation.

A different perspective emerges if one considers the relative exposures to exchange rates versus interest rates. Indonesia had the highest external debts and the largest real depreciation compared with Asia and with other currency crises cases. This suggests a large exposure to exchange rate change, and the importance of stabilizing the currency. Korea, with a relatively low external debt (compared with both Asian and other crises)

Table 6. Asia 5: Selected Indicators for Policy Tradeoff, 1998

	Thailand	Malaysia	Philippines	Indonesia	Korea
Traditional tradeoff (growth versus inflation)					
CPI inflation[a]	9.9	6.1	10.4	55.4	7.3
Growth rate, 1998	−8.0	−7.5	−0.5	−13.7	5.9
Real exchange rate (July 1997 = 100)[a]	86.0	76.0	80.9	32.6	73.3
Balance sheet tradeoff					
Corporate debt/equity ratio (%)	419.0	200.0	63.0	950.0	518.0
Credit to private sector/GDP ratio, end-1997 (%)	145.0	162.0	56.0	61.0	74.0
External debt (% of GDP)	59.6	43.6	62.1	78.0	51.2
of which: short-term debt	19.4	10.4	15.7	15.0	14.3
Monetary policy					
Nominal interest rates on July 1998	16.1	11.0	14.9	79.2	13.0
Real interest rates[b]	7.9	3.5	9.1	26.2	7.0

[a] One year after onset of the crisis.
[b] Real interest rate calculated using the exact formula $(1 + i)/(1 + \text{inf}) - 1$.

110   *Taimur Baig and Ilan Goldfajn*

Table 7. Selected Indicators for Policy Tradeoff, Other Currency Cases

	Chile (82)	Mexico (82)	Mexico (94)	Sweden (92)	UK (92)
Traditional tradeoff (growth versus inflation)					
CPI inflation[a]	30.1	208.7	52.0	4.4	1.02
Growth rate[b]	−2.3	−4.1	−7.5	−1.2	1.0
Real exchange rate (crisis period = 100)	76.7	55.5	75.4	76.3	98.1
Balance sheet tradeoff					
Credit to private sector/ GDP, devaluation year (%)	68.2	7.0	40.0	54.0	127.0
External debt (as percent of GDP)	67.3	52.1	37.3	NA	NA
of which: short-term debt	12.3	15.2	7.0	NA	NA
Monetary policy					
Nominal interest rates in the month of the crisis	34.8	34.2	26.4	82.4	8.8
Real interest rates[c]	8.1	−24.6	7.3	78.5	5.56

[a] 12-month inflation from onset of the crisis. The same holds for REER.
[b] Annual GDP growth rate from the quarter of the crisis.
[c] Real interest rate calculated as the nominal interest minus CPI inflation, both defined above.

and high debt/equity ratio of domestic corporates suggests a high exposure to interest rate increases. In the case of Thailand, both the high debt to equity ratio and the large ratio of credit to the private sector as a percentage of GDP suggests a large exposure to high interest rates as well. This assessment, in conjunction with the traditional trade-off (large drop in output and relatively low inflation), suggests that a trend towards lower rates was beneficial for Korea and Thailand. The Philippines had a relatively high real rate if one considers that its debt to equity and private credit to GDP ratios are relatively low and the expected decline in output is moderate. In contrast, Malaysia had a relatively low rate considering the low debt to equity ratio (although the credit to the private sector was substantial).

The choice of policy stance during a financial crisis is crucial, given the high stakes involved. Overly tight monetary policy might exacerbate the crisis, while an overly depreciated currency can cause serious problems as well. The above discussion high-lights the importance of reconciling the traditional tradeoff with corporate balance sheet considerations. In light of the evidence, an across-the-board tightening of monetary policy for the Asia five is difficult to defend. Thailand and Korea were, according to the selected indicators, more susceptible to high rates than currency devaluation, thus requiring an easing of the monetary policy. It is difficult to make the same case for Indonesia and the Philippines though. Finally, Malaysia is the clearest candidate for a relatively soft stance.

5. Conclusions

By evaluating the monetary policy and its relationship with exchange rate in the five Asian crisis countries, this paper argues that there is room to believe that the exchange rates had overshot during the crisis and that further declines were not desirable, naturally raising the question of the appropriate policies to revert this overshooting.

We find that there is no evidence of overly tight monetary policy in the Asian crisis countries in 1997 and early 1998. Negative real rates were seen in Indonesia, Korea, and Malaysia in early 1998 and in Thailand in the third quarter of 1997. No evidence of large uncovered interest rate differentials is found in 1997 and early 1998. There is also no evidence that high interest rates led to weaker exchange rates. Simple correlations using monthly data provide mixed results; VAR estimations with daily data imply, if anything, that higher interest rates are associated with stronger exchange rates.

There are a couple of issues one should consider regarding this result. First, the Asian crisis generated an increase in the risk premium demanded for holding the crisis countries' assets. This increase is associated with both a higher interest rate and a more depreciated exchange rate that would tend to bias the result in favor of finding a perverse effect of interest rates on the exchange rate. However, the perverse effect is not found despite this natural bias. Second, we recognize that the relationship between interest rate and exchange rates is more complex and is affected by other macroeconomic policies and the political support and credibility they enjoy. In absence of this credibility, even large increases in interest rates would not stem exchange rate depreciation.

The paper highlights the need to reconcile the traditional interest rate–exchange rate tradeoff with a corporate balance sheet approach. The cost associated with high interest rates to stabilize the currency can be overwhelming if the banking sector is fragile. On the other hand, if the corporate sector is heavily exposed to foreign debt, then increasing interest rates may be the appropriate policy. Monetary policy in the aftermath of a currency crisis requires close attention to these issues.

References

Baig, Taimur and Ilan Goldfajn, "Financial Market Contagion in the Asian Crisis," *IMF Staff Papers* 46 (1999):167–95.

Chinn, Menzie, "Before the Fall: Were East Asian Currencies Overvalued?" NBER working paper 6491 (1997).

Demirguc-Kunt, Asli and Enrica Detragiache, "The Determinants of Banking Crises: Evidence from Industrial and Developing Countries," IMF working paper WP/97/106 (1997).

Drazen, Alan and Paul Masson, "Credibility of Policies versus Credibility of Policymakers," *Quarterly Journal of Economics* 109 (1994):735–54.

Dornbusch, Rudiger, "Expectations and Exchange Rate Dynamics," *Journal of Political Economy* 84 (1976):1161–76.

Eichengreen, Barry, Andrew Rose, and Charles Wyplosz, "Speculative Attacks on Pegged Exchange Rates: An Empirical Exploration with Special Reference to the European Monetary System," NBER working paper 4898 (1994).

Flood, Robert and Peter Garber, "Collapsing Exchange Rate Regimes: Some Linear Examples," *Journal of International Economics* 17 (1984).

Furman, Jason and Joseph Stiglitz, "Economic Crises: Evidence and Insights from East Asia," *Brookings Papers on Economic Activity* 2 (1998):1–135.

Ghosh, Atish and Steven Phillips, "Interest Rates, Stock Markets Prices and Exchange Rates in East Asia," IMF working paper WP/98/68 (1998).

Goldfajn, Ilan and Poonam Gupta, "Does Monetary Policy Stabilize the Exchange Rate?" IMF working paper WP/99/42 (1999).

Goldfajn, Ilan and Rodrigo Valdés, "The Aftermath of Appreciations," NBER working paper 5650 (1996).

112 *Taimur Baig and Ilan Goldfajn*

Goldstein, Morris, *The Asian Financial Crisis: Causes, Cures, and Systemic Implications*, Washington: Institute for International Economics (1998).

Goldman Sachs, *New Tools for Forecasting Exchange Rates in Emerging Markets: Goldman Sachs Dynamic Equilibrium Emerging Markets Exchange Rates*, New York (1997).

———, *Emerging Market Currency Analysis*, New York (1998).

Kaminsky, Graciela and Sergio Schmukler, "The Relationship Between Interest Rates and Exchange Rates in Six Asian Countries," unpublished (1998).

Krugman, Paul, "A Model of Balance of Payment Crises," *Journal of Money, Credit and Banking* 11 (1978):311–25.

———, "What Happened to Asia?" web.mit.edu (1998).

Radelet, Steven and Jeffrey Sachs, "The East Asian Financial Crisis: Diagnosis, Remedies, Prospects," *Brookings Papers on Economic Activity* 1 (1998):1–90.

Stiglitz, Joseph, "Knowledge for Development: Economic Science, Economic Policy and Economic Advice," Annual Bank Conference on Development Economics, Washington: World Bank (1998).

[25]

THE WORLD BANK ECONOMIC REVIEW, VOL. 15, NO. 2 289-314

Crisis Transmission: Evidence from the Debt, Tequila, and Asian Flu Crises

José De Gregorio and Rodrigo O. Valdés

This article analyzes how external crises spread across countries. The authors analyze the behavior of four alternative crisis indicators in a sample of 20 countries during three well-known crises: the 1982 debt crisis, the 1994 Mexican crisis, and the 1997 Asian crisis. The objective is twofold: to revisit the transmission channels of crises, and to analyze whether capital controls, exchange rate flexibility, and debt maturity structure affect the extent of contagion. The results indicate that there is a strong neighborhood effect. Trade links and similarity in precrisis growth also explain (to a lesser extent) which countries suffer more contagion. Both debt composition and exchange rate flexibility to some extent limit contagion, whereas capital controls do not appear to curb it.

The increasing globalization of the economy has put the issue of transmission of crises across countries in the front line. Although the word contagion is a rather new concept in international finance, it has been the focus of a large number of policy-oriented seminars and debates. Both regional and time clustering of currency crises are at the heart of the discussion. There are several important questions that need to be answered. In this article, we focus on two of them. First, what are the propagation channels of international crises across countries (other than common shocks)? Second, are there useful policy instruments for shielding countries from contagion? In particular, do capital controls, exchange rate flexibility and the external debt maturity structure affect contagion? We seek to answer these questions using evidence from three key events: the 1982 debt crisis, the 1994 Mexican devaluation, and the 1997 Asian crisis.

There is an ongoing discussion about the proper definition of contagion (see, for example, Kaminsky and Reinhart 1998; Forbes and Rigobón 1999). Here we simply refer to it as the co-movement suffered by countries during crisis periods and that is unexplained by initial conditions or common shocks. It is a characteristic of crises because it is precisely during these periods in which the

José De Gregorio is with the Ministry of Economics, Mining and Energy in Chile, and the Department of Industrial Engineering at the Universidad de Chile (*jdegregorio@minecon.cl*). Rodrigo O. Valdés is with the Ministry of Finance in Chile (*rvaldes@minhda.cl*). This article is part of the WIDER/World Bank research project "Contagion: How It Spreads and How It Can Be Stopped." Rodrigo O. Valdés acknowledges partial financial support from FONDECYT grant 1990338. The authors thank Ilan Goldfajn, Leonardo Hernández, Guillermo Perry, Carmen Reinhart, Roberto Rigobón, and two anonymous referees for helpful suggestions, and Pamela Mellado for excellent research assistance.

290   THE WORLD BANK ECONOMIC REVIEW, VOL. 15, NO. 2

issue is important from a policy perspective. Nevertheless, as Rigobón (1999) emphasizes, contagion could be confused with the presence of a large common shock. In our empirical investigation, we attempt to separate the effects of contagion from other large common shocks. However, because we select crisis periods, we cannot strictly compare whether they are essentially of a different nature than tranquil times. This issue has led many to question the view that contagion is a particular phenomenon during crisis and is different from simple interdependence. We do not solve this problem, although we compare different transmission mechanisms through which interdependence across countries occurs.[1]

This article is closely related to other studies of contagion, particularly those that analyze the existence of contagion and the likelihood of alternative propagation channels by examining a number of currency crises. According to Eichengreen, Rose, and Wyplosz (1997) and Glick and Rose (1998), trade links are the key transmission channel of crises across countries. While the first study focuses on Organisation for Economic Co-operation and Development (OECD) countries, the second studies five international crises using a narrower form of contagion than the one we use, namely, contagion originating from "ground zero." Kaminsky and Reinhart (1998) claim that financial links are potentially an important transmission mechanism. However, they argue that because of the high correlation between trade and financial links, it is difficult to distinguish between both channels. We revisit the existence of contagion as well as the most likely transmission channels.

Instead of focusing on transmission from ground-zero countries to the rest of the world, we look at the impact of crises elsewhere on the likelihood that a country will suffer a crisis. This allows us to study the fact that many times contagion happens from country A to country B, but what may cause problems in country C is not a crisis in A, but the problems in B. A typical case we have in mind is that a crisis in Mexico may affect Chile more through its impact on Argentina and Brazil than through the crisis in Mexico itself. For this reason, focusing on ground-zero countries could give an incomplete picture of the evidence.

Section I discusses our basic empirical approach. Section II provides evidence of the existence of contagion and investigates the transmission channels behind this phenomenon. Section III investigates the extent to which capital controls, exchange rate flexibility, and debt structure shield countries against contagion effects. Section IV presents concluding remarks.

I. EMPIRICAL APPROACH

This section describes our empirical methodology. To measure contagion or transmission of crises across countries, we follow an approach that combines previous work by Sachs, Tornell, and Velasco (1996); Eichengreen, Rose, and Wyplosz

---

1. We use indistinctly the expressions contagion, interdependence, and co-movements.

(1997); and Glick and Rose (1998). In particular, we try to explain the cross-sectional variation in alternative crisis indicators during particular events using (i) a set of initial macroeconomic conditions, and (ii) a weighted average of the evolution of the crisis indicator in other countries. With (i), we seek to control for country-specific characteristics that may directly explain the extent of crises as well as common factors that affect countries differently depending on macroeconomic characteristics (for example, an international interest rate shock). With (ii), we seek to measure and characterize contagion. Because alternative weighting schemes can be associated a priori with different transmission channels, we are able to study what may drive contagion.

We focus the analysis on three important events of the past 25 years from the perspective of developing countries: crisis 1, the 1982 debt crisis; crisis 2, the 1994 Mexican devaluation; and crisis 3, the 1997 Asian crisis. In the spirit of Glick and Rose (1998), we identify a ground-zero country for each crisis and date the episode accordingly. This is used just to date the beginning of the crisis, not to define how it spreads to other countries. We assume that when the crisis begins, all countries are subject to contagion. We use a dummy to control only for the ground-zero country, which captures the fact that this country by definition cannot suffer from contagion.

In the case of the debt crisis, we use Mexico as the ground-zero country and date the initial period of the crisis in August 1982, when Mexico announced a moratorium on its external debt. In the case of the tequila crisis, the ground-zero country is naturally Mexico and the initial date is December 1994. Finally, we consider that the Asian crisis started in Thailand in July 1997.

We analyze the performance of four alternative crisis indicators in 20 countries, 8 from Latin America, 6 from Asia, and 6 controls (small, open OECD countries). Appendix table A-1 lists the countries as well as their neighborhood codes.

Measuring Contagion

To measure contagion, we explain the performance of crisis indicators in the countries, using particular averages of what happens in other countries. More formally, indexing countries by i ($i = 1, 2, \ldots, 20$) and crises by j ($j = 1, 2, 3$), we estimate cross-section models of the following form:

$$(1) \qquad \Delta CI_{i,t,j} = \beta_0 + \beta_1 X_{i,j} + \beta_2 \sum_{k \neq i} M_{i,k,j} \Delta CI_{k,t,j} + \beta_3 \sum_{k \neq i} M_{1,1} \Delta CI_{k,t,j} + \epsilon_{i,t,j},$$

where $\Delta CI_{i,t,j}$ denotes the change in crisis indicator CI in country i, during crisis j, between one month before that crisis and month t; $X_{i,j}$ is a vector of initial macroeconomic conditions in country i prior to crisis j; $M_{i,k,j}$ is a fixed number that weights ex ante the importance of country k in explaining the performance of country i; $M_{1,1}$ is a fixed number that weights equally all countries different from i; and $\epsilon_{i,t,j}$ is a random shock.

We construct a series of matrixes with weights $M_{i,k,j}$ to calculate particular linear combinations of other countries' returns. Each linear combination represents a particular theory of contagion.

292   THE WORLD BANK ECONOMIC REVIEW, VOL. 15, NO. 2

The $M_{1,1}$ allows us to control for the effect of the size of each crisis. In other words, it controls for the effect of the common shock that occurs elsewhere. After normalizing the weights, this is equivalent to adding for each country the average crisis in all other countries. If we had a very large sample, this could be approximated by the average across countries, and solved by including a dummy variable for each crisis. However, in our sample, this could lead to biases as long as countries subject to large shocks—that is, large changes in the crisis indicator—also have a large weight in the average change in the crisis indicator. There would be an obvious and strong upward bias because the country with a large weight would be included in both the left- and right-side variables. For this reason, we exclude the country when computing the average external shock for each observation.

When the true β_2 is positive (that is, there is contagion) and the $M_{i,k,j}$ weights are nonnegative, the ordinary least squares (OLS) estimation of equation 1 has a positive bias.[2] A shock in $\epsilon_{i,t,j}$ that triggers a crisis in a country will affect, through contagion, the performance of other countries; the other countries, in turn, will affect country i's performance, introducing a positive correlation between the error term ($\epsilon_{i,t,j}$) and one of the regressors ($\Sigma_{k \neq i} M_{i,k,j} \Delta CI_{k,t,j}$). However, because this bias is monotonic in β_2 and hence there is no bias when β_2 is zero (and there is negative bias when $\beta_2 < 0$), the issue is not a serious problem for our particular purposes. As long as we focus on comparing alternative models, it is valid to compare different OLS estimates of β_2. The same is true when we compare alternative measures for curbing contagion. In a very large sample, this effect would not exist because the feedback from a single country to others would be small. Here we presume this is also small; as long as there are about 20 countries per episode, the effect of a particular $\varepsilon_{i,t,j}$ should be small.

We consider the following four crisis indicators:

- A foreign exchange market pressure index at a three-month horizon after the crisis, denoted by PI-3.
- A foreign exchange market pressure index at a 12-month horizon after the crisis, denoted by PI-12.
- The level of the real exchange rate 12 months after the crisis, denoted by RER.
- A credit rating indicator, denoted by CR.

When using indicators with the same time horizon in different crises, we are implicitly assuming that the three crises have similar contagion patterns in the time dimension. This does not need to be the case. The credit rating measure partially takes into account this issue.

In constructing PI-3 and PI-12, we follow the standard procedure of calculating a weighted average of changes in the real exchange rate and the stock of international reserves in each country/observation. In the case of crises 2 and 3, we also include (minus) the change in the real interest rate with respect to the 12-

---

2. We consider only nonnegative $M_{i,k,j}$ weights.

month average level observed prior to the crisis. As in Kaminsky and Reinhart (1999), we weight each component of the index such that each one has equal (crisis-specific) volatility. A negative change in PI shows an increase in market pressure that may arise from any of the three components.[3] We use data from International Monetary Fund (IMF; various years) for international reserves, interest rates (short-run deposits), and inflation. We use the JP Morgan database for real exchange rates, in which a downward movement in RER means depreciation.[4]

For credit rating, we use the credit risk indicator compiled by *Institutional Investor*. Because it is published only in March and September of each year, we are not able to have a perfect dating for each crisis. However, this allows us to select the horizon we consider more appropriate in each crisis. For crisis 1, we use the 1-year change in the index published in March 1983; for crisis 2, we use the 6-month change published in September 1995 (which seems to better capture the Mexican downgrade); and for crisis 3, we use the 12-month change published in March 1998.

The 60×60 matrix with weights $M_{i,t,j}$ can take several forms. However, because cross-crisis contagion makes little economic sense, we restrict it to a block diagonal with three 20×20 submatrixes. Moreover, because we are not interested in explaining contagion suffered by ground-zero countries, the matrixes have zeros in the respective row. Furthermore, to avoid running regressions in which an independent variable is a function of that same dependent variable, we restrict the main diagonal to be zero. We follow the same procedure when constructing the $M_{1,1}$ matrix of equal weights. In any case, the concept of own contagion does not make sense.

Depending on the exact definition of contagion, there are two alternative classes of weighting matrixes. If contagion is defined as occurring exclusively from the ground-zero country to other countries, then the matrix has to have nonzero elements only in the columns corresponding to the ground-zero country. This is the approach taken by Glick and Rose (1998). Alternatively, if contagion is defined more broadly as transmission of crises from a particular set of countries to others, then the nonzero elements could appear anywhere in the 20×20 matrixes, except in the row of the ground-zero country. This is the approach followed by Eichengreen, Rose, and Wyplosz (1997) in trying to explain the probability of crisis (a binary variable) in a group of OECD countries. They consider that there is contagion as long as a weighted "crises elsewhere" variable affects the probability of crisis in an individual country.[5] We focus our analysis on the second type of contagion, although we also analyze the first type.

3. None of the results change in any important way if we exclude from PI interest rates for crises 2 and 3.

4. Because of dramatic jumps unrelated to the crises, we excluded international reserves from the indicators for South Africa in crises 2 and 3 and the real interest rate for Brazil in crisis 2.

5. The approach taken by Kaminsky and Reinhart (1998) is conceptually similar although formally different. They estimate the incidence of crises as a function of fundamentals and the number of crises in alternative clusters of countries. This is equivalent to having matrixes with ones in particular entries.

294 THE WORLD BANK ECONOMIC REVIEW, VOL. 15, NO. 2

To test for the presence of contagion, we check whether β_2 in equation 1 is significantly different from zero. To compare the strength of contagion across different weighting matrixes (of the second type), we rescale them such that each row adds up to one. Thus, β_2 shows the impact of a particular weighted average of crisis indicators elsewhere in the crisis indicators of the average (not ground-zero) country. Then different weighting matrixes allow us to identify the most important transmission channels.

Macroeconomic Fundamentals

The vector $X_{i,j}$ of initial macroeconomic conditions includes country-specific characteristics that may explain the extent of the crises in each country. Specifically, we consider a set of variables that are typically related to currency attacks and balance of payments crises according to standard models (first, second, and later generations) and the existing empirical evidence.[6] The list of variables is the following:

1. *Credit boom 1*. Total credit to the private sector (as a percentage of gross domestic product, GDP) in excess of the long-run trend of the ratio credit/GDP calculated using a Hodrik-Prescott filter (see Gourinchas, Landerretche, and Valdés 2001). We consider 1981, 1994, and 1996 as the initial conditions for crises 1, 2, and 3, respectively.
2. *Credit boom 2*. Total credit (as a percentage of GDP) in excess of the long-run trend of the ratio credit/ GDP, for the same years as for credit boom 1.
3. RER *overvaluation*. Twelve-month average of RER misalignment prior to each crisis calculated using as equilibrium RER an HP filter with information up to the month before each crisis (therefore the filter is one-sided).
4. *Fiscal balance/GDP*. Fiscal balance as a percentage of GDP, for the same years as for credit booms.
5. *Current account/GDP*. Current account balance as a percentage of GDP, for the same years as for credit booms.
6. *GDP growth*. GDP annual growth rate, for the same years as for credit booms.
7. *Debt/GDP*. Debt to GDP ratio. For OECD countries, we estimate the stock of debt by adding up current account deficits since 1950. This is for the same years as for credit booms.
8. *Inflation*. Consumer price index 12-month inflation measured in the month before each crisis (measured as $p/(1 + p)$, where p is the rate of inflation).

Before analyzing the presence of contagion, it is interesting to evaluate whether these macroeconomic fundamentals matter in explaining which countries suffer stronger crises (or a crisis at all) during an international crisis. Sachs, Tornell, and Velasco (1996) address this issue, although they focus only on the Tequila crisis. Their main result is that excess credit creation and RER misalignment are

---

6. See Eichengreen, Rose, and Wyplosz (1997); Kaminsky, Lizondo, and Reinhart (1998); and the comprehensive study by Berg and Pattillo (1998) for details.

the most important variables in explaining the extent of crises across countries. They do not find any relevant role for the current account deficit. Berg and Pattillo (1998) find similar results using several alternative methodologies. They find that the most important indicators of vulnerabilities are the rate of growth of domestic credit, a measure of real exchange rate overvaluation, and the ratio of reserves to the M2 money supply. They find that the current account deficit, the budget deficit, and the composition of external liabilities are good predictors of external fragilities only in some cases (estimations).

Table 1 presents the results of estimating equation 1 without contagion effects. In the equation, we include ground-zero countries, so we estimate a standard crisis-prediction equation. In our estimations, the current account balance appears as a highly significant explanatory variable in *PI-3*, *PI-12*, and *RER* (the "objective" indicators). Credit boom (private credit), RER overvaluation, fiscal balance, and GDP growth are significant in some of the crisis indicators. In the case of the RER depreciation indicator, it is interesting to note that the signs of the current account balance and the fiscal balance are opposite. This indicates that an increase in the current account increases the real depreciation 12 months later, but the converse occurs with the fiscal balance. The interpretation is not straightforward. By accounting, we can decompose the current account deficit into private and public components, the latter being the budget balance. An in-

TABLE 1. Crisis Indicators and Initial Conditions

	Crisis indicator			
Variable	Change in *PI-3*[a]	Change in *PI-12*[b]	Change in credit rating	Change in *RER*[c]
Constant	−0.08	−4.62	−1.92	−1.25
	(−0.04)	(−2.94)	(−2.41)	(−0.68)
Credit boom	−30.82	—	−15.92	−44.35
	(−1.64)		(−1.75)	(−2.27)
RER overvaluation	−0.24	−0.45	—	—
	(−1.43)	(−2.63)		
Fiscal budget/GDP	—	—	—	−0.77
				(−2.14)
Current account/GDP	0.44	0.67	—	1.04
	(1.70)	(2.54)		(3.49)
GDP growth	—	1.50	—	—
		(3.22)		
R^2	0.17	0.31	0.05	0.29
F-statistic *p*-value	0.02	0.00	0.09	0.00
Observations	60	60	60	60

Note: Data are for 20 countries for three crisis periods. See table A-1 for countries and text for crisis periods. Values are from OLS regressions with constants (not reported). White's robust *t*-tests are in parentheses. We report variables with at least 80 percent significance.
[a]Foreign exchange market pressure index three months after the crisis.
[b]Foreign exchange market pressure index 12 months after the crisis.
[c]Level of the real exchange rate 12 months after the crisis.
Source: Authors' calculations.

296   THE WORLD BANK ECONOMIC REVIEW, VOL. 15, NO. 2

crease in the budget deficit would raise the current account deficit, deteriorating the RER indicator, but there is a direct effect partially offsetting the current account effect.

An interesting result is that, other than credit boom, macro-variables do not explain changes in credit rating. Credit rating is a "subjective" crisis indicator because it is based on the assessment of vulnerabilities assigned by the market.

Neither the debt/GDP ratio nor inflation has significant effects in explaining any of the crisis indicators. As shown by the R^2 statistics, the macroeconomic fundamentals we consider have a limited capability for explaining the cross-country experience during crisis periods, a result consistent with the already large literature on crisis forecasting.

II. Contagion and Transmission Channels

This section investigates the presence of contagion in the three crises we study and analyzes the likelihood of alternative transmission channels. It discusses the construction of alternative weighting matrixes and presents some empirical results.

Weighting Matrixes

There are several potential channels for the propagation of contagion. The most important are direct trade links, trade competition in third markets, macroeconomic similarities, and financial links. Eichengreen, Rose, and Wyplosz (1997) and Glick and Rose (1998) find evidence that trade links are the most important channel of propagation. Kaminsky and Reinhart (1998) also find strong evidence of regional contagion. They conclude that this pattern could be associated with trade links as well as with financial links. A key problem is that the two are correlated. An additional problem is that measures to control for financial links are limited.

Controlling for the average shock elsewhere is a form of controlling for the international environment. In addition, we may capture the channels through which interdependence or contagion occurs by weighting the shocks elsewhere by some characteristics of the relationship among countries. Thus, different weighting matrixes $M_{i,k,j}$ allow us to investigate the importance of alternative transmission channels of contagion (from country i to country k). We consider the following matrixes:

1. Equal weights for all countries k, allowing us to control for differences across crises.
2. Direct trade links measured by the ratio of bilateral trade between countries i and k to total trade of country i. This set of weights is motivated by trade-based contagion theories, such as competitive devaluation.
3. Trade competition in third markets measured through a similarity index of the trade pattern based on the relative importance in total exports of

six sectors (agriculture, food, fuel, ores, high-tech manufacturing, and low-tech manufacturing). This matrix has the same motivation as in point 2.
4. Neighborhood (regional) dummies for Latin American, Asian, and industrial countries (see appendix table A-1 for details). This matrix is motivated by the presumption that contagion is regional (explained primarily by financial links after controlling for trade links).
5. An overall macroeconomic similarity index that combines RER misalignment, current account balance, credit boom, fiscal balance, and GDP growth. Macroeconomic similarities may explain contagion if, for instance, investors learn and update their priors during a crisis (that is, there is a "wake-up call" during crisis).
6. Specific macroeconomic similarity indexes, including external similarity (encompassing RER and current account), credit boom, and GDP growth.
7. All of the above measures, but with respect to only neighboring countries. This allows us to evaluate the alternative contagion channels at the regional level.

Both trade-pattern similarity, because of data availability, and neighbor dummy matrixes, by definition, are constant across crises. The rest of the matrixes are crisis-specific. All the matrixes are symmetric, except the one with direct trade links. The reason for the lack of symmetry of the trade-link matrix is that trade is measured with respect to total trade of the country; thus, bilateral trade is symmetric, not its importance with respect to each country.

To construct a similarity index between countries i and k when considering a single variable (for example, GDP growth or credit boom), we calculate:[7]

$$(2) \qquad \theta_{i,k,j} = \exp(-|x_{i,j} - x_{k,j}|),$$

where x_i is the standardized variable under analysis in country i. The standardization is based on cross-country, crisis-specific observations.[8]

When constructing similarity indexes that combine multiple variables (for example, trade pattern, external conditions, and overall macroeconomic similarity), we calculate:

$$(3) \qquad \theta_{i,k,j} = \exp(-\sum_s |x_{s,i,j} - x_{s,k,j}|),$$

where s indexes the different variables entering the index and $x_{s,i,j}$ is the standardized variable s in country i and crisis j.

To facilitate comparability across different matrixes, we rescale the $\theta_{i,k,j}$'s so that maximum similarity takes the value 1 and minimum similarity takes the value 0. Thus, we calculate the weight $M_{i,k,j}$ as follows:

---

7. The procedure for constructing similarity indexes is somewhat ad hoc because it introduces some nonlinear transformations in the data; however, it allows us to reduce the effect of outliers.

8. By standardized variable, we refer to a variable in a given crisis minus its mean divided by its standard deviation.

298   THE WORLD BANK ECONOMIC REVIEW, VOL. 15, NO. 2

(4)
$$M_{i,k,j} = \frac{\theta_{i,k,j} - \min(\theta_{i',k',j})}{\max(\theta_{i',k',j}) - \min(\theta_{i',k',j})}$$

where i', k', and j represent all possible country combinations in crisis j. Furthermore, for a straightforward interpretation of the results, we rescale $M_{i,k,j}$ again so that $\Sigma_i \, M_{i,k,j} = 1$. Thus, β_2 reflects the impact of a weighted average of what is happening elsewhere on the average country.

Empirical Results

Tables 2 to 5 present the estimation of equation 1 using PI-3, PI-12, RER, and CR, respectively, and with alternative weighting matrixes for each crisis indicator. The variable "contagion index" corresponds to β_2, while "equal weight" corresponds to β_3. All regressions include a constant and dummies for the ground-zero countries (not reported).

The results for the PI-3 indicator show that contagion is strongly and almost exclusively driven by neighborhood and direct trade effects. None of the "wider" matrixes (those considering not only neighbors) yields a significant coefficient that could indicate the presence contagion. Indeed, when constraining weighting matrixes to neighboring countries, most of the results are significant. The point estimate of direct trade links is smaller than that of the neighbor dummies, and, because we are constraining weights to be one, we can conclude that the neighbor effect is quantitatively stronger than that of direct trade. This probably reflects the close trade links that exist between neighbors rather than a proper propagation channel. In fact, when we consider direct trade with neighboring countries only, the estimate is highly significant, but the point estimate is still smaller than what the neighbor dummy matrix yields. Interestingly, neither macroeconomic similarities nor the common shock proxy plays any role in explaining the cross-country propagation of contagion at this three-month horizon.

None of the parameters corresponding to the variables measuring macroeconomic initial conditions, except for credit boom, changes in any important way when we incorporate the contagion index. In fact, credit boom ceases to be significant in all specifications. Consequently, once the effects of interdependence across crises are included, the R^2 increases from 0.17 in table 1 to values around 0.5. This reveals the importance that contagion and transmission of crisis across countries have on the vulnerability to external crisis.[9]

The results for PI-12 show a different picture (table 3). For this indicator, we observe that a real exchange rate overvaluation, a current account deficit, and low growth increase the (absolute) value of the crisis indicator, that is, increase the incidence of crisis. After controlling for the equal-weight matrix, the R^2s increase with respect to the value reported in table 1, but the marginal explanatory power of this variable is not as large as that of the three-month exchange

---

9. It is also worth mentioning that, aside from the PI-12 indicator, results do not change if we exclude the $M_{1,1}\Delta CI_{k,t,j}$ term in the regressions.

TABLE 2. Three-Month Change in Foreign Exchange Market Pressure Index and Total Contagion

	Weighting matrix								
Variable	Direct trade	Trade pattern	Neighbor dummy	Macro similarity	External similarity	Credit similarity	Growth similarity	Trade with neighbors	Trade pattern with neighbors
Credit boom	-5.32	-13.22	0.68	-13.07	-15.45	-21.92	-12.55	-2.09	-3.34
	(-0.33)	(-0.78)	(0.05)	(-0.68)	(-0.91)	(-0.96)	(-0.74)	(-0.14)	(-0.21)
RER overvaluation[a]	-0.24	-0.26	-0.21	-0.25	-0.25	-0.26	-0.25	-0.21	-0.21
	(-1.73)	(-1.78)	(-1.75)	(-1.71)	(-1.74)	(-1.79)	(-1.72)	(-1.63)	(-1.61)
Current account/GDP	0.45	0.24	0.41	0.28	0.27	0.26	0.27	0.49	0.40
	(1.98)	(1.00)	(2.05)	(1.18)	(1.18)	(1.15)	(1.20)	(2.30)	(1.87)
Contagion index	0.63	-0.54	0.71	-0.18	-3.40	-1.24	-0.73	0.61	0.47
	(2.37)	(-0.52)	(4.29)	(-0.12)	(-1.14)	(-0.65)	(-0.38)	(3.50)	(2.91)
Equal weight	-0.06	1.05	-0.08	0.71	3.80	1.91	1.21	-0.02	0.10
	(-0.14)	(1.01)	(-0.26)	(0.45)	(1.31)	(0.89)	(0.67)	(-0.07)	(0.31)
R^2	0.51	0.46	0.60	0.46	0.47	0.46	0.46	0.56	0.53
F-statistic p-value	0.00	0.00	0.00	0.00	0.00	0.00	0.00	0.00	0.00
Observations	60	60	60	60	60	60	60	60	60

Note: Data are for 20 countries for three crisis periods. See table A-1 for countries and text for crisis periods. Values are from OLS regressions with constants and dummy variables in the three ground-zero countries (not reported). White's robust *t*-tests are in parentheses. External similarity combines current account and RER overvaluation similarity.

[a]See text for definition.

Source: Authors' calculations.

TABLE 3. Twelve-Month Change in Foreign Exchange Market Pressure Index and Total Contagion

Variable	Weighting matrix								
	Direct trade	Trade pattern	Neighbor dummy	Macro similarity	External similarity	Credit similarity	Growth similarity	External similarity of neighbors	Growth of neighbors
RER overvaluation[a]	-0.46	-0.42	-0.45	-0.51	-0.44	-0.46	-0.46	-0.52	-0.43
	(-2.66)	(-2.60)	(-2.98)	(-2.96)	(-2.32)	(-2.68)	(-2.64)	(-3.17)	(-2.79)
Current account/GDP	0.45	0.48	0.39	0.53	0.47	0.48	0.47	0.39	0.41
	(1.56)	(1.87)	(1.59)	(1.94)	(1.73)	(1.75)	(1.68)	(1.50)	(1.63)
GDP growth	1.31	1.18	1.53	1.49	1.26	1.26	1.12	1.36	1.84
	(2.62)	(2.59)	(3.51)	(2.97)	(2.63)	(2.64)	(1.46)	(2.98)	(3.94)
Contagion index	-0.13	-2.80	-1.72	-3.03	0.15	-0.49	0.42	-1.08	-1.41
	(-0.34)	(-2.46)	(-3.50)	(-1.33)	(0.06)	(-0.33)	(0.22)	(-2.42)	(-3.37)
Equal weight	0.72	3.31	2.28	3.51	0.45	1.10	0.18	1.60	2.00
	(1.63)	(2.93)	(4.26)	(1.59)	(0.18)	(0.72)	(0.10)	(3.31)	(4.18)
R²	0.40	0.46	0.52	0.42	0.40	0.40	0.40	0.46	0.50
F-statistic p-value	0.00	0.00	0.00	0.00	0.00	0.00	0.00	0.00	0.00
Observations	60	60	60	60	60	60	60	60	60

Note: Data are for 20 countries for three crisis periods. See table A-1 for countries and text for crisis periods. Values are from OLS regressions with constants and dummy variables in the three ground-zero countries (not reported). White's robust t-tests are in parentheses. External similarity combines current account and RER overvaluation similarity.

[a]See text for definition.

Source: Authors' calculations.

market pressures indicator. We find that for this indicator, co-movement is almost exclusively driven by the common shock (proxied by the equal-weight matrix, that is, crisis elsewhere). Transmission through trade, neighbor effects, and similarities do not appear to play an important additional role. In fact, none of the weighting matrixes yields significantly positive parameters. If we do not control for the equal-weight matrix, the results change dramatically, with several weighting matrixes having significantly positive results. However, this follows from the fact that the equal weight and other matrixes are collinear across crises. In what follows, we no longer consider *PI-12* in the analysis and conclude that there is no particular form of contagion in this indicator beyond the existence of common shocks (although there is a high degree of co-movement across countries).[10]

In the case of the indicator based on 12-month RER depreciation (table 4), we find that contagion indexes are significantly positive when we consider direct trade links, neighbors, and growth similarity. The strong negative sign for trade pattern similarity indicates that there is evidence against third-market competition being an important transmission mechanism of crises.

Conventional wisdom indicates that when a country has a currency crisis, a real depreciation will hurt competitors in those markets, leading to competitive devaluations. However, because a crisis in a country is usually coupled with an output collapse, it may create opportunities for the country's main competitors. This may be what is happening with the reverse sign we find, at least at the one-year horizon. It might also be that trade pattern similarity is not appropriately measuring third-market competition, and perhaps third-market competition could be better proxied by some regional effect. We still find that initial conditions measured by the current account deficit and budget deficit help to explain 12-month RER depreciation. Credit boom is the only initial macroeconomic variable that looses significance in the RER equation when we include contagion.

Finally, in the case of change in credit rating (table 5), we find that the direct trade links, neighbors, overall macro similarity, and growth similarity matrixes yield significant contagion coefficients. When considering only similarities with neighboring countries, we find that both trade and external macroeconomic similarity appear to be very important channels of contagion. As in the previous case, initial conditions measured by credit boom looses significance when we include contagion. With the CR index, we find no initial condition to be significant when we include contagion.

The evidence presented so far is not able to discriminate completely among (statistically significant) competing weighting matrixes. Following Eichengreen, Rose, and Wyplosz (1997), table 6 presents the results of estimating equation 1

---

10. We look again at *PI-12* only when examining contagion from ground-zero countries because the specification and the implication of the results are different. In addition, in the remaining results, we exclude the equal-weight matrix from the analysis because it is not significant for indicators other than *PI-12*.

TABLE 4. Real Exchange Rate Depreciation and Total Contagion

Variable	Weighting matrix								
	Direct trade	Trade pattern	Neighbor dummy	Macro similarity	External similarity	Credit similarity	Growth similarity	External similarity of neighbors	Growth of neighbors
Credit boom	-14.77	-23.81	-9.55	-10.78	-20.24	-13.95	-11.33	-7.25	-9.34
	(-0.77)	(-1.23)	(-0.49)	(-0.51)	(-1.02)	(-0.60)	(-0.61)	(-0.37)	(-0.48)
Fiscal budget/GDP	-0.65	-0.96	-0.68	-0.77	-0.90	-0.86	-0.52	-0.63	-0.68
	(-1.95)	(-2.90)	(-2.06)	(-2.26)	(-2.60)	(-2.54)	(-1.57)	(-1.92)	(-2.05)
Current account/GDP	1.08	0.94	1.09	1.07	1.03	1.02	1.14	1.08	1.09
	(4.02)	(3.47)	(4.12)	(3.84)	(3.72)	(3.69)	(4.34)	(4.11)	(4.07)
Contagion index	0.65	-2.39	0.60	1.52	-1.57	0.67	4.14	0.64	0.56
	(2.17)	(-1.99)	(2.36)	(1.14)	(-0.68)	(0.48)	(2.81)	(2.53)	(2.13)
Equal weight	0.10	3.09	0.26	-0.76	2.37	0.06	-3.08	0.21	0.33
	(0.26)	(2.58)	(0.72)	(-0.55)	(1.01)	(0.04)	(-2.21)	(0.60)	(0.95)
R^2	0.49	0.48	0.49	0.45	0.44	0.44	0.51	0.50	0.48
F-statistic p-value	0.00	0.00	0.00	0.00	0.00	0.00	0.00	0.00	0.00
Observations	60	60	60	60	60	60	60	60	60

Note: Data are for 20 countries for three crisis periods. See table A-1 for countries and text for crisis periods. Values are from OLS regressions with constants and dummy variables in the three ground-zero countries (not reported). White's robust t-tests are in parentheses. External similarity combines current account and RER overvaluation similarity.

Source: Authors' calculations.

TABLE 5. Change in Credit Rating and Total Contagion

Variable	Weighting matrix								
	Direct trade	Trade pattern	Neighbor dummy	Macro similarity	External similarity	Credit similarity	Growth similarity	Trade with neighbors	External similarity of neighbors
Credit boom	-0.95	-8.21	1.28	0.41	-7.10	-24.71	-3.80	1.58	3.63
	(-0.12)	(-1.06)	(0.19)	(0.05)	(-0.86)	(-2.41)	(-0.49)	(0.24)	(0.58)
Contagion index	0.75	-2.09	0.74	2.15	-0.38	-6.63	2.33	0.82	0.83
	(2.70)	(-2.01)	(5.34)	(1.82)	(-0.20)	(-2.59)	(2.16)	(5.11)	(6.10)
Equal weight	0.10	2.59	0.04	-1.23	0.99	7.46	-1.51	0.09	0.02
	(0.33)	(2.59)	(0.16)	(-1.16)	(0.58)	(2.82)	(-1.47)	(0.39)	(0.10)
R^2	0.48	0.45	0.62	0.45	0.41	0.48	0.46	0.61	0.65
F-statistic p-value	0.00	0.00	0.00	0.00	0.00	0.00	0.00	0.00	0.00
Observations	60	60	60	60	60	60	60	60	60

Note: Data are for 20 countries for three crisis periods. See table A-1 for countries and text for crisis periods. Values are from OLS regressions with constants and dummy variables in the three ground-zero countries (not reported). White's robust t-tests are in parentheses. External similarity combines current account and RER overvaluation similarity.

Source: Authors' calculations.

304 THE WORLD BANK ECONOMIC REVIEW, VOL. 15, NO. 2

TABLE 6. Contagion and Competing Weighting Matrixes

Variable	Change in PI-3[a] (1)	(2)	Change in RER[b] (1)	(2)	(3)	Change in credit rating (1)	(2)	(3)	(4)
Credit boom	0.00	0.01	−0.13	−0.10	−0.08	0.01	0.02	0.07	0.04
	(0.02)	(0.05)	(−0.69)	(−0.54)	(−0.44)	(0.12)	(0.26)	(1.2)	(0.59)
RER overvaluation[b]	−0.21	−0.22	—	—	—	—	—	—	—
	(−1.74)	(−1.78)							
Fiscal budget/GDP	—	—	−0.68	−0.62	−0.68	—	—	—	—
			(−2.07)	(−1.92)	(−2.10)				
Current account/GDP	0.37	0.38	1.08	1.10	1.10	—	—	—	—
	(1.95)	(1.92)	(4.06)	(4.19)	(4.17)				
Direct trade matrix	−0.22	—	0.50	0.37	—	−0.12	—	—	—
	(−0.74)		(1.47)	(1.12)		(−0.42)			
Neighbor dummy matrix	0.82	0.76	—	0.41	0.50	0.81	0.71	−2.00	—
	(3.48)	(2.22)		(1.26)	(1.91)	(4.36)	(5.09)	(−2.62)	
Macro similarity matrix	—	—	—	—	—	—	0.13	—	—
							(0.48)		
Growth similarity matrix	—	—	0.40	—	0.47	—	—	—	—
			(0.89)		(1.22)				
Trade with neighbors	—	−0.08	—	—	—	—	—	—	1.04
		(−0.24)							(2.83)
External similarity with neighbors matrix	—	—	—	—	—	—	—	2.90	−0.25
								(3.64)	(−0.61)
R^2	0.60	0.60	0.49	0.50	0.50	0.58	0.62	0.69	0.66
F-statistic p-value	0.00	0.00	0.00	0.00	0.00	0.00	0.00	0.00	0.00
Observations	60	60	60	60	60	60	60	60	60

Note: Data are for 20 countries for three crisis periods. See table A-1 for countries and text for crisis periods. Values are from OLS regressions with constants and dummy variables in the three ground-zero countries (not reported). White's robust t-tests are in parentheses. External similarity combines current account and RER overvaluation similarity.

[a]Foreign exchange market pressure index three months after the crisis.
[b]Level of the real exchange rate 12 months after the crisis.
Source: Authors' calculations.

simultaneously including competing relevant contagion indexes. We consider some of the matrixes that appeared as more relevant in tables 2–5 in pairs, using the same initial macroeconomic conditions as before.

The results show that in the cases of indicators based on PI-3 and country CR, the identification is straightforward. In both cases, the neighborhood effect appears as the most relevant propagation mechanism for contagion. In the second case, we also observe that external similarities with respect to neighbors appears to be a strong mechanism (which is a particular form of a neighborhood effect). Trade links no longer appear important in these two cases when we control for the effect of neighbors. Although trade links and neighbor effects are highly correlated, our results suggest that the prime candidate for contagion is not trade, as documented in other papers, but geographical proximity.[11] The results are less clear-cut in the case of the indicators based on RER. Because of strong collinearity, some times we observe that a pair of matrixes is highly significant when considered individually, but is no longer significant (individually) when considered together. Despite this issue, it is possible to exclude some explanations and rank others informally according to point estimates. Direct trade links and neighbors appear as the two most relevant matrixes.[12]

Contagion from Ground-Zero Countries

An alternative way of defining contagion is to limit it to propagating from ground-zero countries only. In this case, we try to explain the cross-country variation of our crisis indicators using different weights of ground zero for each country. This definition of contagion is obviously more restrictive than the previous approach. Moreover, it is potentially misleading if the ground-zero country is not correctly identified. However, this exercise is useful for testing the robustness of our results.

Because the temporal evolution of the ground-zero country can be very different from what actually happened in other countries, we modify our strategy slightly. In particular, we analyze whether a weighted change in PI-3 at ground zero is able to explain changes in PI-12, RER, and CR. The weighting matrixes are similar to those we used in the previous subsection, although we no longer have the straightforward intuition for the estimated parameter we had before (a weighted average of what is happening elsewhere). Therefore, we use standardized parameters.

Table 7 presents the results for the cases in which we find statistically significant contagion. It shows that with the PI-12 indicator, contagion marginally arises only when we consider the equal-weight matrix. This result is proof of comovement, perhaps caused by a large shock, which is different across crises, but it is not necessarily evidence of contagion. With the indicator based on the RER, direct trade ties between countries and the ground-zero country appear to generate contagion. Finally, changes in credit rating can be explained for countries that are neighbors of the ground-zero country (especially if they have similar initial external macroeconomic conditions) or have direct trade links with it.

---

11. We cannot avoid making references to the case of Chile, which suffered contagion from Asia due to high trade links, but is also dependent on movements in Latin America, a region with weak trade links. Chile's trade with Argentina and Brazil, its main trade partners in the region, is well below 10 percent.

12. One can further analyze this issue of collinearity by estimating a model of the following form:

$$\Delta CI_{i,t,j} = \beta_0 + \beta_1 X_{i,j} + \beta_2 \times \left(\gamma \sum_{k \neq i} M_{i,k,j} \Delta CI_{k,t,j} + (1 - \gamma) \sum_{k \neq i} M'_{i,k,j} \Delta CI_{k,t,j} \right) + \epsilon_{i,t,j}$$

where γ measures the relative importance of $M_{i,k,j}$ vis-à-vis $M'_{i,k,j}$. The results for RER (not reported) show a significant β_2 but very imprecise estimates of γ, showing that any combination of the two matrixes would be valid.

TABLE 7. Contagion from a Ground-Zero Country

Variable	Pressure indicator and weighting matrix					
	Change in PI-12/equal weights[a]	Change in RER/direct trade[b]	Change in credit rating/direct trade	Change in credit rating/neighbor dummy	Change in credit rating/external similarity of neighbors	Change in credit rating/trade with neighbors
Credit boom	—	-0.23 (-1.12)	-0.06 (-0.80)	-0.04 (-0.62)	-0.02 (-0.46)	-0.05 (-0.69)
RER overvaluation[b]	-0.48 (-2.79)	—	—	—	—	—
Fiscal budget/GDP	—	-0.57 (-1.58)	—	—	—	—
Current account/GDP	0.50 (1.77)	1.04 (3.67)	—	—	—	—
GDP growth	1.44 (3.03)	—	—	—	—	—
Contagion index	0.24 (1.69)	1.78 (2.04)	0.27 (2.53)	0.43 (4.38)	0.45 (4.72)	0.29 (2.76)
R^2	0.37	0.41	0.41	0.52	0.54	0.43
F-statistic p-value	0.00	0.00	0.00	0.00	0.00	0.00
Observations	60	60	60	60	60	60

Note: Data are for 20 countries for three crisis periods. See table A-1 for countries and text for crisis periods. Values are OLS regressions with constants and dummy variables in the three ground-zero countries (not reported). White's robust t-tests are in parentheses. Contagion index corresponds to the standardized parameter of a weighted average of change in PI-3 according to a particular matrix M. External similarity combines current account and RER overvaluation similarity.
[a]Foreign exchange market pressure index three months after the crisis.
[b]Level of the real exchange rate 12 months after the crisis.
Source: Authors' calculations.

III. Policies to Curb Contagion

One key policy question is how countries can curb (or even stop) contagion. A leading prescription is to limit financial integration. Other policy prescriptions to limit the extent of contagion are exchange rate flexibility and avoiding short-term debt. The issue of contagion and alternative policies is an empirical one. This section evaluates the usefulness of these three policy measures in curbing contagion.

Capital Controls and Contagion

Capital controls could curb contagion if financial links are an important propagation channel. However, the usefulness of limiting financial integration is less clear if contagion arises due to trade links, or if initial similarity in macroeconomic conditions and crises are the consequence of real shocks. Nevertheless, it could be argued that capital controls might help an orderly adjustment, avoiding typical problems that an unregulated financial sector often produces, such as overshooting the exchange rate. Of course, capital controls have costs in tranquil times because the country does not take full advantage of capital movements. However, defenders of capital controls point to contagion as one of the reasons for having capital controls as a preventive measure.

Edwards (1999) evaluates whether capital controls in Chile were a useful device for avoiding contagion. He measures contagion as the correlation between domestic and Asian interest rates (specifically, interest rates in Hong Kong), controlling for domestic devaluation and exchange rates in the United States. He concludes that controls on capital inflows may have been able to protect Chile from relatively small shocks, but were not able to prevent contagion stemming from large external shocks.

It should be mentioned that the objective of capital control measures goes beyond avoiding contagion. Among other objectives, capital controls have been used to avoid excess real exchange rate appreciation, to curb capital inflows, and to modify the foreign debt term structure.[13]

To evaluate whether financial integration facilitates contagion, we use a standard capital control index and analyze whether contagion is weaker in countries with a higher index. In particular, we estimate models of the following form:

$$(5) \qquad \Delta CI_{i,t,j} = \beta_0 + \beta_1 X_{i,j} + [\beta_2 + \beta_3 CC_{i,j}]\sum_{k \neq i} M_{i,k,j}\Delta CI_{k,t,j} + \in_{i,t,j},$$

where $CC_{i,j}$ is a capital control index of country i during crisis j. If capital controls were effective in curbing contagion, the estimation should yield a negative and significant β_3.

To construct the capital control index, we use the standard dummy variables that appear in IMF (various years). For restrictions on payments on capital transactions and the surrender requirement of export proceeds, we assign values of

---

13. See De Gregorio, Edwards, and Valdés (2000) for an evaluation of the Chilean experience.

0, 1, or 2, depending on whether neither, one, or both of the restrictions apply. We consider the status as of December in 1981, 1994, and 1996 for the corresponding crises.

Table 8 presents the results of the estimation of equation 5 for our three crisis indicators that show contagion and for the same weighting matrixes used in last section. The results show that capital controls do not have any relevant effect in limiting contagion. Indeed, the associated parameter is generally not significantly different from zero. It has to be noted, however, that we use a broad definition of capital controls, and the most commonly used and specific forms of controls or regulations cannot be captured with these 0, 1, 2 indicators. However, the results indicate that countries that had more pervasive forms of control did not avoid contagion more than countries with looser controls.

Exchange Rate Flexibility and Contagion

Exchange rate flexibility is expected to reduce contagion by avoiding some of the overvaluation episodes to begin with and limiting the scope of speculation. To evaluate the effect of exchange rate flexibility on contagion, we use the same approach as with capital controls. In particular, we estimate an equation similar to equation 5, but with an indicator of exchange rate flexibility for country i in crisis j instead of $cc_{i,j}$. We use a 0, 1, 2 indicator (2 is maximum flexibility) based on data gathered by Goldfajn and Valdés (1999). The data were constructed using IMF (various years). That report groups exchange rate regimes into three categories: fixed (including narrow bands), flexible, and floating.

Table 9 presents the results. They show that flexibility has a significant effect in limiting contagion only when we measure contagion using changes in credit ratings. Point estimates show a large effect: Moving from a fixed exchange rate regime to a floating one reduces contagion by two-thirds. This result is robust to alternative weighting matrixes. It is interesting because it indicates that the market evaluates better and is less vulnerable to economies with flexible exchange rate regimes.

When measuring contagion with real depreciation, we find that flexibility *increases* contagion, although this result is marginally significant under only two weighting matrixes. This latter result is not surprising because the exchange rate is the variable that adjusts when external shocks hit the economy. Moreover, part of the adjustment may be an overshooting of the real exchange rate. We do not find significant effects of flexibility in the case of PI-3.

Overall, we can conclude only for the CR indicator that having a flexible exchange rate may reduce contagion.

Debt Maturity Structure and Contagion

Having debt maturity tilted toward the long run would limit the scope of financial runs against a particular country. To evaluate whether the debt maturity structure has any impact on the extent of contagion, we run an equation similar to equation 5, but with the ratio of short-term debt to total debt for country i in

TABLE 8. Capital Controls and Contagion

	Pressure indicator and weighting matrix								
Variable	Change in PF-3/direct trade[a]	Change in PF-3/ neighbors[a]	Change in PF-3/trade with neighbors[a]	Change in RER/direct trade[b]	Change in RER/ neighbors[b]	Change in RER/ growth similarity[b]	Change in credit rating/ direct trade	Change in credit rating/ trade with neighbors	Change in credit rating/ external similarity of neighbors
Credit boom	-0.04 (-0.23)	0.01 (0.07)	-0.02 (-0.12)	-0.16 (-0.86)	-0.13 (-0.70)	-0.17 (-0.84)	-0.01 (-0.11)	0.02 (0.26)	0.04 (0.58)
RER overvaluation[b]	-0.26 (-1.86)	-0.23 (-1.76)	-0.22 (-1.65)	—	—	—	—	—	—
Fiscal budget/GDP	—	—	—	-0.57 (-1.69)	-0.56 (-1.75)	-0.76 (-2.26)	—	—	—
Current account/GDP	0.38 (1.67)	0.37 (1.79)	0.46 (2.15)	1.09 (4.10)	1.18 (4.42)	1.05 (3.87)	—	—	—
Contagion index	0.48 (1.65)	0.64 (2.77)	0.56 (2.36)	0.82 (3.19)	0.94 (3.71)	1.00 (2.71)	0.84 (2.64)	1.12 (4.95)	0.92 (4.69)
Contagion × capital controls	0.14 (0.64)	0.04 (0.23)	0.04 (0.23)	-0.15 (-0.69)	-0.35 (-1.45)	-0.06 (-0.20)	-0.03 (-0.15)	-0.23 (-1.53)	-0.08 (-0.56)
R^2	0.51	0.60	0.56	0.49	0.51	0.47	0.48	0.62	0.66
F-statistic p-value	0.00	0.00	0.00	0.00	0.00	0.00	0.00	0.00	0.00
Observations	60	60	60	60	60	60	60	60	60

Note: Data are for 20 countries for three crisis periods. See table A-1 for countries and text for crisis periods. Values are from OLS regressions with constants and dummy variables in the three ground-zero countries (not reported). White's robust t-tests are in parentheses. External similarity combines current account and RER overvaluation similarity.
[a]Foreign exchange market pressure index three months after the crisis.
[b]Level of the real exchange rate 12 months after the crisis.
Source: Authors' calculations.

309

TABLE 9. Exchange Rate Flexibility and Contagion

	Pressure indicator and weighting matrix								
Variable	Change in PI-3/direct trade[a]	Change in PI-3/ neighbors[a]	Change in PI-3/trade with neighbors[a]	Change in RER/direct trade[b]	Change in RER/ neighbors[b]	Change in RER/ growth similarity[b]	Change in credit rating/ direct trade	Change in credit rating/ trade with neighbors	Change in credit rating/ external similarity of neighbors
Credit boom	-0.05 (-0.30)	0.02 (0.14)	-0.01 (-0.07)	-0.18 (-0.92)	-0.11 (-0.60)	-0.23 (-1.19)	-0.21 (-0.28)	-0.05 (-0.67)	-0.02 (-0.26)
RER overvaluation[b]	-0.22 (-1.58)	-0.22 (-1.79)	-0.23 (-1.75)	—	—	—	—	—	—
Fiscal budget/GDP	—	—	—	-0.60 (-1.85)	-0.62 (-1.96)	-0.72 (-2.27)	—	—	—
Current account/GDP	0.43 (2.06)	0.40 (2.09)	0.50 (2.50)	1.04 (3.90)	1.10 (4.23)	1.00 (3.78)	—	—	—
Contagion index	0.74 (1.97)	0.62 (2.42)	0.44 (1.62)	0.40 (1.03)	0.18 (0.50)	0.35 (0.79)	1.54 (4.50)	1.36 (4.92)	1.23 (5.87)
Contagion × exchange rate flexibility	-0.12 (-0.42)	0.07 (0.31)	0.17 (0.71)	0.23 (0.94)	0.46 (1.74)	0.52 (1.81)	-0.68 (-2.67)	-0.54 (-2.12)	-0.43 (-2.27)
R^2	0.51	0.60	0.57	0.49	0.52	0.50	0.54	0.64	0.69
F-statistic p-value	0.00	0.00	0.00	0.00	0.00	0.00	0.00	0.00	0.00
Observations	60	60	60	60	60	60	60	60	60

Note: Data are for 20 countries for three crisis periods. See table A-1 for countries and text for crisis periods. Values are from OLS regressions with constants and dummy variables in the three ground-zero countries (not reported). White's robust t-tests are in parentheses. External similarity combines current account and RER overvaluation similarity.

[a]Foreign exchange market pressure index three months after the crisis.

[b]Level of the real exchange rate 12 months after the crisis.

Source: Authors' calculations.

crisis j instead of $CC_{i,j}$. We use data from the Bank of International Settlements (BIS) (various years) and consider the short term to be less than a year. Two of the countries in our sample (Sweden and Finland) have positive net external assets and report to the BIS from "within," and one country (Singapore) is considered a banking center and thus is highly leveraged. For these countries, we consider a zero in the ratio short debt/total debt and include a special dummy variable in the equation multiplying the contagion index.

Table 10 shows that a tilt toward short-term financing increases contagion when we measure it using changes in credit rating. The effects are economically relevant, highly significant, and robust to alternative weighting matrixes. With 12-month real depreciation and direct trade, there is a marginally significant positive effect.

IV. Concluding Remarks

This article has examined the channels through which crises spread across countries. For this purpose, we examined the behavior of crisis indicators as a function of initial conditions and the average of crisis indicators elsewhere. The latter variable attempts to capture interdependence or co-movements. This relationship could be simply the result of common shocks hitting a number of countries. To understand how these external common shocks and shocks originating in other countries spread to other places, we constructed a weighted average of crisis indicators elsewhere. The weighting schemes attempt to capture different transmission mechanisms. We used the importance of bilateral (also called direct) trade, competition in third markets, regional relationship, and indexes of similarities.

We found that the channel of propagation of crises depends on both indicators and horizons. Three months after a crisis, there are strong neighborhood effects. Rather than trade links and/or macroeconomic similarities, what seems to better explain cross-country correlation is the proximity of countries or regional effects. The same happens when we analyze changes in country credit ratings at longer horizons (6 to 12 months).

Thus the regional weighting scheme is the strongest quantitatively and is statistically the most robust. This implies that crisis spread mainly, but not uniquely, as the Russian crisis in 1998 witnessed, through regions. No wonder the debt crisis was centered in Latin America and the 1997 crisis in Asia. Part of this could be explained by direct trade links, because regions tend to have important trade relationships. But the effect of trade links, although important, cannot account for the whole regional effect. Another candidate for explaining this regional effect is financial links, through cross-border ownership of assets, stock market links, and others. At this stage, we do not have good indicators for constructing weighting matrixes to control for financial links. This is clearly an area that deserves further research.

A question that arises in most of the literature on currency crisis and contagion is whether crises are triggered by bad sentiments or by self-fulfilling prophecies. In

TABLE 10. Composition of Capital Inflows and Contagion

Variable	Pressure indicator and weighting matrix								
	Change in PI-3/direct trade[a]	Change in PI-3/ neighbors[a]	Change in PI-3/trade with neighbors[a]	Change in RER/direct trade[b]	Change in RER/ neighbors[b]	Change in RER/ growth similarity[b]	Change in credit rating/ direct trade	Change in credit rating/ trade with neighbors	Change in credit rating/ external similarity of neighbors
Credit boom	-0.05 (-0.28)	-0.01 (-0.04)	-0.03 (-0.16)	-0.09 (-0.45)	-0.07 (-0.34)	-0.17 (-0.78)	0.04 (0.60)	0.01 (0.21)	0.03 (0.51)
RER overvaluation	-0.23 (-1.72)	-0.22 (-1.76)	-0.21 (-1.65)	—	—	—	—	—	—
Fiscal budget/GDP	—	—	—	-0.60 (-1.83)	-0.55 (-1.69)	-0.74 (-2.22)	—	—	—
Current account/GDP	0.47 (2.04)	0.34 (1.61)	0.45 (2.07)	1.08 (3.99)	1.11 (4.10)	1.05 (3.77)			
Contagion index	0.70 (1.79)	0.53 (1.32)	0.50 (1.50)	0.75 (1.96)	3.86 (1.74)	1.17 (2.02)	0.35 (0.84)	0.35 (1.20)	0.34 (1.15)
Contagion × Short-term debt	0.57 (0.27)	-0.58 (-0.40)	-0.51 (-0.33)	3.60 (1.71)	-2.26 (-1.68)	1.73 (0.79)	4.38 (2.91)	3.95 (4.14)	2.47 (2.32)
R^2	0.51	0.60	0.56	0.51	0.52	0.48	0.57	0.72	0.70
F-statistic p-value	0.00	0.00	0.00	0.00	0.00	0.00	0.00	0.00	0.00
Observations	60	60	60	60	60	60	60	60	60

Note: Data are for 20 countries for three crisis periods. See table A-1 for countries and text for crisis periods. Values are from OLS regressions with constants and dummy variables in the three ground-zero countries (not reported). White's robust *t*-tests are in parentheses. External similarity combines current account and RER overvaluation similarity.

Source: Authors' calculations.

TABLE A-1. Country List

Country	Neighborhood code
Argentina	1
Brazil	1
Chile	1
Colombia	1
Ecuador	1
Mexico	1
Peru	1
Venezuela	1
Indonesia	2
Korea	2
Malaysia	2
Philippines	2
Singapore	2
Thailand	2
Sweden	3
Finland	3
Portugal	3
Australia	3
New Zealand	3
South Africa	3

the context of contagion, this implies that a crisis could occur just because of contagion. In this article, we show that, although the crisis indicators are affected by contagion, fundamentals explain a large fraction of the crises. In particular, the current account deficit, exchange rate overvaluation, and credit boom affect our market pressure indicators. Given the sample size, the results change in some specifications and some caveats could be added, but we can conclude that fundamentals matter and it is not just what is going on elsewhere that causes crisis to happen.

At a 12-month horizon, fundamentals matter and both trade links and initial macroeconomic conditions explain which countries suffer stronger contagion. We find that the cross-country variation of a 12-month real exchange rate depreciation depends on growth and external similarities (overvaluation and current account deficit) and direct trade links. At this horizon, neighborhood (regional) effects are still important. Common shocks seem to explain cross-country correlation of a 12-month change in a foreign exchange market pressure index. For the other indicators of crisis we use—the 3-month change in foreign exchange market pressure index, the 12-month real exchange rate depreciation, and the change in the credit rating—we find that co-movements explained by specific forms of contagion are more important. To this end, we conclude that although crises may be triggered by common shocks, transmission across countries depends on regional, trade, and macroeconomic characteristics of the countries.

A policy issue that has been in the middle of the discussion on contagion is the way in which links across countries could be limited during crisis periods. The issue of the optimality of contagion should be addressed first, but at this stage we have taken a practical view in analyzing whether there may be policies that could curb contagion. To this end, we analyze the impact of capital controls, exchange rate flexibility, and debt composition. We find that capital controls do not affect contagion. Exchange rate flexibility and the structure of external debt have effects on some of our crisis indicators, affecting the country credit rating. Exchange rate flexibility also affects the real depreciation after 12 months.

REFERENCES

Berg, Andrew, and Catherine Pattillo. 1998. "Are Currency Crises Predictable? A Test." IMF Working Paper WP/98/154.

Bank of International Settlements (BIS). Various years. *The Maturity, Sectorial and Nationality Distribution of International Bank Lending*. Basle: BIS.

De Gregorio, José, Sebastian Edwards, and Rodrigo O. Valdés. 2000. "Capital Controls: Do They Work?" *Journal of Development Economics* 63(1):59–83.

Edwards, Sebastian. 1999. "How Effective Are Capital Controls?" *Journal of Economic Perspectives* 14(4):65–84.

Eichengreen, Barry, Andrew K. Rose, and Charles Wyplosz. 1997. "Contagious Currency Crises." Mimeo, University of California, Berkeley, July. Available online at http://haas.berkeley.edu/~arose.

Forbes, Kristin, and Roberto Rigobón. 1999. "Measuring Contagion: Conceptual and Empirical Issues." Mimeo, MIT.

Glick, Reuven, and Andrew K. Rose. 1998. "Contagion and Trade: Why Are Currency Crises Regional?" Mimeo, University of California, Berkeley, August. Available online at http://haas.berkeley.edu/~arose.

Gourinchas, Pierre Olivier, Oscar Landerretche, and Rodrigo O. Valdés. 2001. "Credit Booms: Is Latin America Different?" *Economía* 1(2):47–99.

Goldfajn, Ilan, and Rodrigo O. Valdés. 1999. "The Aftermath of Appreciations." *Quarterly Journal of Economics* 114(1):229–62.

International Monetary Fund (IMF). Various years. *Exchange Arrangements and Exchange Restrictions*. Washington, D.C.: IMF.

———. Various years. International Financial Statistics. Washington, D.C.: IMF.

Kaminsky, Graciela L., and Carmen M. Reinhart. 1999. "The Twin Crises: The Causes of Banking and Balance of Payments Problems." *American Economic Review* 89(3):473–500.

———. 1998. "On Crises, Contagion, and Confusion." Mimeo, University of Maryland, November.

Kaminsky, Graciela L., Saul Lizondo, and Carmen M. Reinhart. 1998. "Leading Indicators of Currency Crises." IMF *Staff Papers*, March.

Rigobón, Roberto. 1999. "On the Measurement of the International Propagation of Shocks." Mimeo, MIT.

Sachs, Jeffrey, Aaron Tornell, and Andres Velasco. 1996. "Financial Crises in Emerging Markets: The Lessons from 1995." *Brookings Papers on Economic Activity* 1.

Name Index